Dictionary of Computer Vision and Image Processing

Dictionary of Computer Vision and Image Processing

Second Edition

R. B. Fisher

University of Edinburgh, UK

T. P. Breckon

Durham University, UK

K. Dawson-Howe

Trinity College Dublin, Ireland

A. Fitzgibbon

Microsoft Research, UK

C. Robertson

Epipole Ltd., UK

E. Trucco

University of Dundee, UK

C. K. I. Williams

University of Edinburgh, UK

WILEY

This edition first published 2014
© 2014 John Wiley & Sons Ltd

Registered office
John Wiley & Sons Ltd, The Atrium, Southern Gate, Chichester, West Sussex, PO19 8SQ, United Kingdom

For details of our global editorial offices, for customer services and for information about how to apply for permission to reuse the copyright material in this book please see our website at www.wiley.com.

Library of Congress Cataloging-in-Publication Data

Dictionary of computer vision and image processing / R. B. Fisher, T. P. Breckon, K. Dawson-Howe, A. Fitzgibbon, C. Robertson, E. Trucco, C. K. I. Williams. – 2nd edition.
    pages cm
  Includes bibliographical references.
  ISBN 978-1-119-94186-6 (pbk.)
  1. Computer vision–Dictionaries.   2. Image processing–Dictionaries.   I. Fisher, R. B.
  TA1634.I45 2014
  006.3'703–dc23

                                                                    2013022869

A catalogue record for this book is available from the British Library.

ISBN: 9781119941866

Set in 9/10pt Garamond by Aptara Inc., New Delhi, India
Printed and bound in Singapore by Markono Print Media Pte Ltd

1   2014

Contents

Preface

This dictionary arose out of a continuing interest in the resources needed by students and researchers in the fields of image processing, computer vision and machine vision (however you choose to define these overlapping fields). As instructors and mentors, we often found confusion about what various terms and concepts mean for the beginner. To support these learners, we have tried to define the key concepts that a competent generalist should know about these fields.

This second edition adds approximately 1000 new terms to the more than 2500 terms in the original dictionary. We have chosen new terms that have entered reasonably common usage (e.g., those which have appeared in the index of influential books) and terms that were not included originally. We are pleased to welcome Toby Breckon and Chris Williams into the authorial team and to thank Andrew Fitzgibbon and Manuel Trucco for all their help with the first edition.

One innovation in the second edition is the addition of reference links for a majority of the old and new terms. Unlike more traditional dictionaries, which provide references to establish the origin or meaning of the word, our goal here was instead to provide further information about the term.

Another innovation is to include a few videos for the electronic version of the dictionary.

This is a dictionary, not an encyclopedia, so the definitions are necessarily brief and are not intended to replace a proper textbook explanation of the term. We have tried to capture the essentials of the terms, with short examples or mathematical precision where feasible or necessary for clarity.

Further information about many of the terms can be found in the references. Many of the references are to general textbooks, each providing a broad view of a portion of the field. Some of the concepts are quite recent; although commonly used in research publications, they may not yet have appeared in mainstream textbooks. Subsequently, this book is also a useful source for recent terminology and concepts. Some concepts are still missing from the dictionary, but we have scanned textbooks and the research literature to find the central and commonly used terms.

The dictionary was intended for beginning and intermediate students and researchers, but as we developed the dictionary it was clear that we also had some confusions and vague understandings of the concepts. It surprised us that some terms had multiple usages. To improve quality and coverage, each definition was reviewed during development by at least two people besides its author. We hope that this has caught any errors and vagueness, as well as providing alternative meanings. Each of the co-authors is quite experienced in the topics covered here, but it was still educational to learn more about our field in the process of compiling the dictionary. We hope that you find using the dictionary equally valuable.

To help the reader, terms appearing elsewhere in the dictionary are underlined in the definitions. We have tried to be reasonably thorough about this, but some terms, such as 2D, 3D, light, camera, image, pixel, and color were so commonly used that we decided not to cross-reference all of them.

We have tried to be consistent with the mathematical notation: italics for scalars (s), arrowed italics for points and vectors ($\vec{v}$), and bold for matrices ($\mathbf{M}$).

The authors would like to thank Xiang (Lily) Li, Georgios Papadimitriou, and Aris Valtazanos for their help with finding citations for the content from the first edition. We also greatly appreciate all the support from the John Wiley & Sons editorial and production team!

Numbers

1D: One dimensional, usually in reference to some structure. Examples include: a signal $x(t)$ that is a function of time t; the dimensionality of a single property value; and one degree of freedom in shape variation or motion. [Hec87:2.1]

1D projection: The projection of data from a higher dimension to a single dimensional representation (line).

1-norm: A specific case of the p-norm, the sum of the absolute values of the entries of a given vector $\vec{x}$, $\|\vec{x}\|_1 = \sum_{i=0}^{n-1} |\vec{x}_i|$, of length n. Also known as the taxicab (Manhattan) norm or the L1 norm. [Sho07]

2D: Two dimensional. A space describable using any pair of orthogonal basis vectors consisting of two elements. [WP:Two-dimensional_space]

2D coordinate system: A system uniquely associating two real numbers to any point of a plane. First, two intersecting lines (axes) are chosen on the plane, usually perpendicular to each other. The point of intersection is the origin of the system. Second, metric units are established on each axis (often the same for both axes) to associate numbers to points. The coordinates P_x and P_y of a point, P, are obtained by projecting P onto each axis in a direction parallel to the other axis and reading the numbers at the intersections: [JKS95:1.4]

2D Fourier transform: A special case of the general Fourier transform often used to find structures in images. [FP03:7.3.1]

2D image: A matrix of data representing samples taken at discrete intervals. The data may be from a variety of sources and sampled in a variety of ways. In computer vision applications, the image values are often encoded color or monochrome intensity samples taken by digital cameras but may also be range data. Some typical intensity values are: [SQ04:4.1.1]

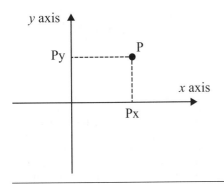

Image values

2D input device: A device for sampling light intensity from the real world into a 2D matrix of measurements. The most popular two-dimensional imaging device is the charge-coupled device (CCD) camera. Other common devices

Dictionary of Computer Vision and Image Processing, Second Edition.
R. B. Fisher, T. P. Breckon, K. Dawson-Howe, A. Fitzgibbon, C. Robertson, E. Trucco and C. K. I. Williams.
© 2014 John Wiley & Sons, Ltd. Published 2014 by John Wiley & Sons, Ltd.

are flatbed scanners and X-ray scanners. [SQ04:4.2.1]

2D point: A point in a 2D space, i.e., characterized by two coordinates; most often, a point on a plane, e.g., an image point in pixel coordinates. Notice, however, that two coordinates do not necessarily imply a plane: a point on a 3D surface can be expressed either in 3D coordinates or by two coordinates given a surface parameterization (see surface patch). [JKS95:1.4]

2D point feature: Localized structures in a 2D image, such as interest points, corners and line meeting points (e.g., X, Y and T shaped). One detector for these features is the SUSAN corner finder. [TV98:4.1]

2D pose estimation: A special case of 3D pose estimation. A fundamental open problem in computer vision where the correspondence between two sets of 2D points is found. The problem is defined as follows: Given two sets of points $\{\vec{x}_j\}$ and $\{\vec{y}_k\}$, find the Euclidean transformation $\{\mathbf{R}, \vec{t}\}$ (the pose) and the match matrix $\{\mathbf{M}_{jk}\}$ (the correspondences) that best relates them. A large number of techniques has been used to address this problem, e.g., tree-pruning methods, the Hough transform and geometric hashing. [HJL+89]

2D projection: A transformation mapping higher dimensional space onto two-dimensional space. The simplest method is to simply discard higher dimensional coordinates, although generally a viewing position is used and the projection is performed.

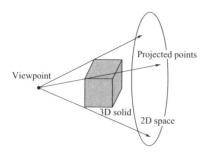

For example, the main steps for a computer graphics projection are as

follows: apply normalizing transform to 3D point world coordinates; clip against canonical view volume; project onto projection plane; transform into viewport in 2D device coordinates for display. Commonly used projection functions are parallel projection and perspective projection. [JKS95:1.4]

2D shape descriptor (local): A compact summary representation of object shape over a localized region of an image. See shape descriptor. [Blu67]

2D shape representation (global): A compact summary representation of image shape features over the entire image. See shape representation. [FP03:28.3]

2D view: Planar aspect view or planar projected view (such as an image under perspective projection) such that positions within its spatial representation can be indexed in two dimensions. [SB11:2.3.1]

2.1D sketch: A lesser variant of the established 2.5D sketch, which captures the relative depth ordering of (possibly self-occluding) scene regions in terms of their front-to-back relationship within the scene. By contrast, the 2.5D sketch captures the relative scene depth of regions, rather than merely depth ordering: [NM90]

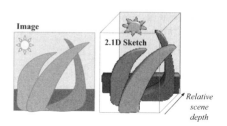

2.5D image: A range image obtained by scanning from a single viewpoint. It allows the data to be represented in a single image array, where each pixel value encodes the distance to the observed scene. The reason this is not called a 3D image is to make explicit the fact that the back sides of the scene objects are not represented. [SQ04:4.1.1]

2.5D model: A geometric model representation corresponding to the 2.5D image representation used in the model to (image) data matching problem of model-based recognition: [Mar82] An example model is:

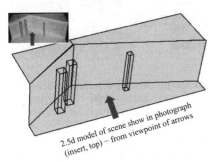

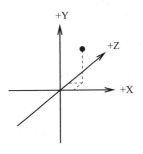

2.5d model of scene show in photograph (insert, top) – from viewpoint of arrows

2.5D sketch: Central structure of Marr's Theory of vision. An intermediate description of a scene indicating the visible surfaces and their arrangement with respect to the viewer. It is built from several different elements: the contour, texture and shading information coming from the primal sketch, stereo information and motion. The description is theorized to be a kind of buffer where partial resolution of the objects takes place. The name 2.5D sketch stems from the fact that, although local changes in depth and discontinuities are well resolved, the absolute distance to all scene points may remain unknown. [FP03:11.3.2]

3D: Three dimensional. A space describable using any triple of mutually orthogonal basis vectors consisting of three elements. [WP:Three-dimensional_space]

3D coordinate system: Same as 2D coordinate system but in three dimensions: [JKS95:1.4]

+Y
+Z
+X

3D data: Data described in all three spatial dimensions. See also range data, CAT and NMR. [WP: 3D_data_acquisition_and_object_ reconstruction] An example of a 3D data set is:

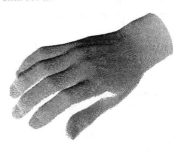

3D data acquisition: Sampling data in all three spatial dimensions. There is a variety of ways to perform this sampling, e.g., using structured light triangulation. [FP03:21.1]

3D image: See range image.

3D imaging: Any of a class of techniques that obtain three-dimensional information using imaging equipment. Active vision techniques generally include a source of structured light (or other electromagnetic or sonar radiation) and a sensor, such as a camera or a microphone. Triangulation and time-of-flight computations allow the distance from the sensor system to be computed. Common technologies include laser scanning, texture projection systems and moiré fringe methods. Passive sensing in 3D depends only on external (and hence unstructured) illumination sources. Examples of such systems are stereo reconstruction and shape from focus techniques. See also 3D surface imaging and 3D volumetric imaging. [FMN+91]

3D interpretation: A 3D model, e.g., a solid object that explains an image or a set of image data. For instance, a certain configuration of image lines can be explained as the perspective projection of a polyhedron; in simpler words, the image lines are the images of some of the polyhedron's lines. See also image interpretation. [BB82:9.1]

3D model: A description of a 3D object that primarily describes its

3

shape. Models of this sort are regularly used as exemplars in model-based recognition and 3D computer graphics. [TV98:10.6]

3D model-based tracking: An extension of model-based tracking using a 3D model of the tracked object. [GX11:5.1.4]

3D moments: A special case of moment where the data comes from a set of 3D points. [GC93]

3D motion estimation: An extension of motion estimation whereby the motion is estimated as a displacement vector $\vec{d}$ in $\mathbb{R}^3$. [LRF93]

3D motion segmentation: An extension to motion segmentation whereby motion is segmented within an $\mathbb{R}^3$ dataset. [TV07]

3D object: A subset of $\mathbb{R}^3$. In computer vision, often taken to mean a volume in $\mathbb{R}^3$ that is bounded by a surface. Any solid object around you is an example: table, chairs, books, cups; even yourself. [BB82:9.1]

3D point: An infinitesimal volume of 3D space. [JKS95:1.4]

3D point feature: A point feature on a 3D object or in a 3D environment. For instance, a corner in 3D space. [RBB09]

3D pose estimation: The process of determining the transformation (translation and rotation) of an object in one coordinate frame with respect to another coordinate frame. Generally, only rigid objects are considered; models of those objects exist *a priori* and we wish to determine the position of the object in an image on the basis of matched features. This is a fundamental open problem in computer vision where the correspondence between two sets of 3D points is found. The problem is defined as follows: Given two sets of points $\{\vec{x}_j\}$ and $\{\vec{y}_k\}$, find the parameters of a Euclidean transformation $\{\mathbf{R}, \vec{t}\}$ (the pose) and the match matrix $\{\mathbf{M}_{jk}\}$ (the correspondences) that best relates them. Assuming the points correspond, they should match exactly under this transformation. [TV98:11.2]

3D reconstruction: The recovery of 3D scene information and organization into a 3D shape via e.g., multi-view geometry. [HZ00:Ch. 10]

....

3D shape descriptor: An extension to regular shape descriptor approaches to consider object shape in $\mathbb{R}^3$. [Pri12: Ch. 17]

3D shape representation: A compact summary representation of shape extending shape representation to consider object shape in R^3. [Pri12:Ch. 17]

3D SIFT: A 3D extension of the SIFT operator defined for use over voxel data. [FBM10]

3D skeleton: A 3D extension of an image skeleton defining a tree-like structure of the medial axes of a 3D object (akin to the form of a human stick figure in the case of considering a person as a 3D object). See also medial axis skeletonization. [Sze10:12.6] See example below:

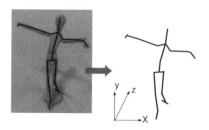

3D stratigraphy: A modeling and visualization tool used to display different underground layers. Often used for visualizations of archaeological sites or for detecting rock and soil structures in geological surveying. [PKVG00]

3D structure recovery: See 3D reconstruction.

3D SURF: A 3D extension to the SURF descriptor that considers the characterization of local image regions in $\mathbb{R}^3$ via either a volumetric voxel-based or a surface-based representation. [KPW+10]

3D surface imaging: Obtaining surface information embedded in a 3D space. See also 3D imaging and 3D volumetric imaging.

3D texture: The appearance of texture on a 3D surface when imaged, e.g., the fact that the density of texels varies with distance because of perspective effects. 3D surface properties (e.g., shape, distances and orientation) can be estimated from such effects. See also shape from texture and texture orientation. [DN99]

3D vision: A branch of computer vision dealing with characterizing data composed of 3D measurements. This may involve segmentation of the data into individual surfaces that are then used to identify the data as one of several models. Reverse engineering is a specialism in 3D vision. [Dav90:16.2]

3D volumetric imaging: Obtaining measurements of scene properties at all points in a 3D space, including the insides of objects. This is used for inspection but more commonly for medical imaging. Techniques include nuclear magnetic resonance, computerized tomography, positron emission tomography and single photon emission computed tomography. See also 3D imaging and 3D surface imaging.

4 connectedness: A type of image connectedness in which each rectangular pixel is considered to be connected to the four neighboring pixels that share a common crack edge. See also 8 connectedness: [SQ04:4.5] Four pixels connected to a central pixel (*):

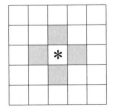

Four groups of pixels joined by 4 connectedness:

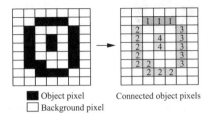

■ Object pixel Connected object pixels
□ Background pixel

4D approach: An approach or solution to a given problem that utilizes both 3D-spatial and temporal information. See 4D representation (3D-spatial + time).

4D representation (3D-spatial + time): A 3D times series data representation whereby 3D scene information is available over a temporal sequence. An example would be a video sequence obtained from stereo vision or some other form of depth sensing: [RG08:Ch. 2]

8 connectedness: A type of image connectedness in which each rectangular pixel is considered to be connected to all eight neighboring pixels. See also 4 connectedness: [SQ04:4.5] Eight pixels connected to a central pixel (*):

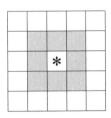

Two groups of pixels joined by 8 connectedness:

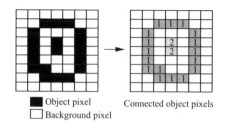

■ Object pixel Connected object pixels
□ Background pixel

8-point algorithm: An approach for the recovery of the fundamental matrix using a set of eight feature point correspondences for stereo camera calibration. [HZ00:11.2]

A*: A search technique that performs best-first searching based on an evaluation function that combines the cost so far and the estimated cost to the goal. [WP:A*_search_algorithm]

a posteriori **probability**: Literally, "after" probability. It is the probability $p(s|e)$ that some situation s holds after some evidence e has been observed. This contrasts with the *a priori* probability, $p(s)$, the probability of s before any evidence is observed. Bayes' rule is often used to compute the *a posteriori* probability from the *a priori* probability and the evidence. See also posterior distribution. [JKS95:15.5]

a priori **probability**: A probability distribution that encodes an agent's beliefs about some uncertain quantity before some evidence or data is taken into account. See also prior distribution. [Bis06:1.2.3]

aberration: Problem exhibited by a lens or a mirror whereby unexpected results are obtained. Two types of aberration are commonly encountered: chromatic aberration, where different frequencies of light focus at different positions:

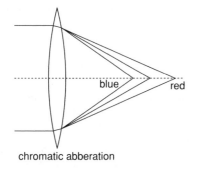

chromatic abberation

and spherical aberration, where light passing through the edges of a lens (or mirror) focuses at slightly different positions. [FP03:1.2.3]

absolute conic: The conic in 3D projective space that is the intersection of the unit (or any) sphere with the plane at infinity. It consists only of complex points. Its importance in computer vision is because of its role in the problem of autocalibration: the image of the absolute conic (IAC), a 2D conic, is represented by a 3×3 matrix ω that is the inverse of the matrix $\mathbf{K}\mathbf{K}^\top$, where $\mathbf{K}$ is the matrix of the internal parameters for camera calibration. Subsequently, identifying ω allows the camera calibration to be computed. [FP03:13.6]

absolute coordinates: Generally used in contrast to *local* or *relative* coordinates. A coordinate system that is referenced to some external datum. For example, a pixel in a satellite image might be at (100,200) in image coordinates, but at (51:48:05N, 8:17:54W) in georeferenced absolute coordinates. [JKS95:1.4.2]

absolute orientation: In photogrammetry, the problem of registration of two corresponding sets of 3D points. Used to register a photogrammetric reconstruction to some absolute coordinate system. Often expressed as the problem of determining the rotation $\mathbf{R}$, translation $\vec{t}$ and scale s that best transforms a set of *model* points $\{\vec{m}_1, \ldots, \vec{m}_n\}$ to corresponding data points $\{\vec{d}_1, \ldots, \vec{d}_n\}$ by minimizing the least-squares error

$$\epsilon(R, \vec{t}, s) = \sum_{i=1}^{n} \|\vec{d}_i - s(\mathbf{R}\vec{m}_i + \vec{t})\|^2$$

Dictionary of Computer Vision and Image Processing, Second Edition.
R. B. Fisher, T. P. Breckon, K. Dawson-Howe, A. Fitzgibbon, C. Robertson, E. Trucco and C. K. I. Williams.
© 2014 John Wiley & Sons, Ltd. Published 2014 by John Wiley & Sons, Ltd.

to which a solution may be found by using singular value decomposition. [JKS95:1.4.2]

absolute point: A 3D point defining the origin of a coordinate system. [WP:Cartesian_coordinate_system]

absolute quadric: The symmetric 4×4 rank 3 matrix $\Omega = \begin{pmatrix} \mathbf{I}_3 & \vec{0}_3 \\ \vec{0}_3^\top & 0 \end{pmatrix}$. Like the absolute conic, it is defined to be invariant under Euclidean transformations, is rescaled under similarities, takes the form $\Omega = \begin{pmatrix} \mathbf{A}^\top \mathbf{A} & \vec{0}_3 \\ \vec{0}_3^\top & 0 \end{pmatrix}$ under affine transforms and becomes an arbitrary 4×4 rank 3 matrix under projective transforms. [FP03:13.6]

absorption: Attenuation of light caused by passing through an optical system or being incident on an object surface. [Hec87:3.5]

accumulation method: A method of accumulating evidence in histogram form, then searching for peaks, which correspond to hypotheses. See also Hough transform and generalized Hough transform. [Low91:9.3]

accumulative difference: A means of detecting motion in image sequences. Each frame in the sequence is compared to a reference frame (after registration if necessary) to produce a difference image. Thresholding the difference image gives a binary motion mask. A counter for each pixel location in the accumulative image is incremented every time the difference between the reference image and the current image exceeds some threshold. Used for change detection. [JKS95:14.1.1]

accuracy: The error of a value away from the true value. Contrast this with precision. [WP:Accuracy_and_precision]

acoustic sonar: Sound Navigation And Ranging. A device that is used primarily for the detection and location of objects (e.g., underwater or in air, as in mobile robotics, or internal to a human body, as in medical ultrasound) by reflecting and intercepting acoustic waves. It operates with acoustic waves in a way analogous to that of radar, using both the time of flight and Doppler effects, giving the radial component of relative position and velocity. [WP:Sonar]

ACRONYM: A vision system developed by Brooks that attempted to recognize three-dimensional objects from two-dimensional images, using generalized cylinder primitives to represent both stored model and objects extracted from the image. [Nev82:10.2]

action cuboid: The 3D spatio-temporal space in which an action detection may be localized in a video sequence:

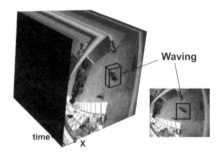

Analogous to a window (or region of interest) in which an object detection may be localized within a 2D image. [GX11:6.4]

action detection: An approach to the automated detection of a given human, vehicle or animal activity (action) from imagery. Most commonly carried out as a video analysis task due to the temporal nature of actions. [Sze10:12.6.4]

action localization: An approach to in-image or in-scene positional localization of a given human, vehicle or animal activity. See also action detection. [Sze10:12.6.4]

action model: A pre-defined or learned model of a given human action which is matched against a given unseen action instance to perform action recognition or action detection. Akin to the use of models in model-based object recognition. [NWF08]

action recognition: Similar to action detection but further considering the classification of actions (e.g., walking, running, kicking, lifting, stretching). See also activity recognition and behavior classification, of which action recognition is often a sub-task, i.e., an activity or behavior is considered as a series of actions:

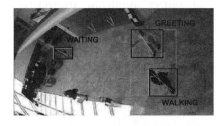

Commonly the terms action, activity and behavior are used inter-changeably in the literature. [Sze10:12.6.4]

action representation: A model-based approach whereby an action is represented as a spatio-temporal feature vector over a given video sequence. [GX11:Ch. 6]

action unit: The smallest atom or measurement of action within an action sequence or action representation removed from the raw measurement of pixel movement itself (e.g., optical flow). [LJ11:18.2.2]

active appearance model: A generalization of the widely used active shape model approach that includes all of the information in the image region covered by the target object, rather than just that near modeled edges. The active appearance model has a statistical model of the shape and gray-level appearance of the object of interest. This statistical model generalizes to cover most valid examples. Matching to an image involves finding model parameters that minimize the difference between the image and a synthesized model example, projected into the image. [NA05:6.5]

active blob: A region-based approach to the tracking of non-rigid motion in which an active shape model is used. The model is based on an initial region that is divided using Delaunay

triangulation and then each patch is tracked from frame to frame (note that the patches can deform). [SI98]

active calibration: An approach to camera calibration that uses naturally occurring features within the scene with active motion of the camera to perform calibration. By contrast, traditional approaches assume a static camera and a predefined calibration object with fixed features. [Bas95]

active contour model: A technique used in model-based vision where object boundaries are detected using a deformable curve representation such as a snake. The term "active" refers to the ability of the snake to deform shape to better match the image data. See also active shape model. [SQ04:8.5]

active contour tracking: A technique used in model-based vision for tracking object boundaries in a video sequence using active contour models. [LL93]

active illumination: A system of lighting where intensity, orientation or pattern may be continuously controlled and altered. This kind of system may be used to generate structured light. [CS09:1.2]

active learning: A machine-learning approach in which the learning agent can actively query the environment for data examples. For example, a classification approach may recognize that it is less reliable over a certain sub-region of the input example space and thus request more training examples that characterize inputs for that sub-region. Considered to be a supervised learning approach. [Bar12:13.1.5]

active net: An active shape model that parameterizes a triangulated mesh. [TY89]

active recognition: An approach to object recognition or scene classification in which the recognition agent or algorithm collects further evidence samples (e.g., more images after moving) until a sufficient level of confidence is obtained to make a decision on identification. See also active learning. [RSB04]

active sensing: 1) A sensing activity carried out in an active or purposive way, e.g., where a camera is moved in space to acquire multiple or optimal views of an object (see also active vision, purposive vision and sensor planning). 2) A sensing activity implying the projection of a pattern of energy, e.g., a laser line, onto the scene (see also laser stripe triangulation and structured light triangulation). [FP03:21.1]

active shape model: Statistical model of the shape of an object that can deform to fit a new example of the object. The shapes are constrained by a statistical shape model so that they may vary only in ways seen in a training set. The models are usually formed using principal component analysis to identify the dominant modes of shape variation in observed examples of the shape. Model shapes are formed by linear combinations of the dominant modes. [WP:Active_shape_model]

active stereo: An alternative approach to traditional binocular stereo. One of the cameras is replaced with a structured light projector, which projects light onto the object of interest. If the camera calibration is known, the triangulation for computing the 3D coordinates of object points simply involves finding the intersection of a ray and known structures in the light field. [CS09:1.2]

active structure from X: The recovery of scene depth (i.e., 3D structure) via an active sensing technique, such as shape from X techniques plus motion.

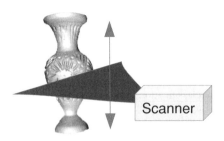

[Sze10:12.2] The figure shows the shape from structured light method, with the light plane being swept along the object:

active surface: 1) A surface determined using a range sensor; 2) an active shape model that deforms to fit a surface. [WP:Active_surface]

active triangulation: Determination of surface depth by triangulation between a light source at a known position and a camera that observes the effects of the illuminant on the scene. Light stripe ranging is one form of active triangulation. A variant is to use a single scanning laser beam to illuminate the scene and a stereo pair of cameras to compute depth. [WP: 3D_scanner#Triangulation]

active vision: An approach to computer vision in which the camera or sensor is moved in a controlled manner, so as to simplify the nature of a problem. For example, rotating a camera with constant angular velocity while maintaining fixation at a point allows absolute calculation of scene point depth, instead of relative depth that depends on the camera speed. See also kinetic depth. [Nal93:10]

active volume: The volume of interest in a machine vision application. [SZH+10:Ch. 1]

activity: A temporal sequence of actions performed by an entity (e.g., a person, animal or vehicle) indicative of a given task, behavior or intended goal. See activity classification. [Sze10:12.6.4]

activity analysis: Analyzing the behavior of people or objects in a video sequence, for the purpose of identifying the immediate actions occurring or the long-term sequence of actions, e.g., detecting potential intruders in a restricted area. [WP:Occupational_ therapy#Activity_analysis]

activity classification: The classification of a given temporal sequence of actions forming a given activity into a discrete set of labels. [Sze10:12.6.4]

activity graph: A graph encoding the activity transition matrix where each node in the graph corresponds to an activity (or stage of an activity) and the arcs among nodes represent the allowable next activities (or stages): [GX11:7.3.2]

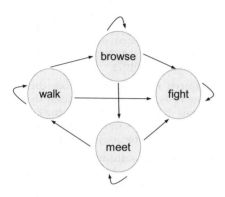

activity model: A representation of a given activity used for activity classification via an approach akin to that of model-based object recognition.

activity recognition: See activity classification.

activity representation: See activity model.

activity segmentation: The task of segmenting a video sequence into a series of sub-sequences based on variations in activity performed along that sequence. [GX11:7.2]

activity transition matrix: An $N \times N$ matrix, for a set of N different activities, where each entry corresponds to the transition probability between two states and each state is itself an activity being performed within the scene. See also state transition probability: [GX11:7.2]

Activity	Walk	Browse	Meet	Fight
Walk	0.9	0.84	0.63	0.4
Browse	0.3	0.78	0.73	0.2
Meet	0.74	0.79	0.68	0.28
Fight	0.32	0.45	0.23	0.60

acuity: The ability of a vision system to discriminate (or resolve) between closely arranged visual stimuli. This can be measure using a grating, i.e.,

a pattern of parallel black and white stripes of equal widths. Once the bars become too close, the grating becomes indistinguishable from a uniform image of the same average intensity as the bars. Under optimal lighting, the minimum spacing that a person can resolve is 0.5 min of arc. [Umb98:7.6]

AdaBoost: An Adaptive Boosting approach for ensemble learning whereby the (weak) classifiers are trained in sequence such that the nth classifier is trained over a training set re-weighted to give greater emphasis to training examples upon which the previous $(n - 1)$ classifiers performed poorly. See boosting. [Bis06:14.3]

adaptation: See adaptive.

adaptive: The property of an algorithm to adjust its parameters to the data at hand in order to optimize performance. Examples include adaptive contrast enhancement, adaptive filtering and adaptive smoothing. [WP: Adaptive_algorithm]

adaptive behavior model: A behavior model exhibiting adaptive properties that facilitate the online updating of the model used for behavior analysis. Generally follows a three-stage process: model initialization, online anomalous behavior detection and online model updating via unsupervised learning. See also unsupervised behavior modeling. [GX11:8.3]

adaptive bilateral filter: A variant on bilateral filtering used as an image-sharpening operator with simultaneous noise removal. Performs image sharpening by increasing the overall "slope" (i.e., the gradient range) of the edges without producing overshoot or undershoot associated with the unsharp operator. [ZA08]

adaptive coding: A scheme for the transmission of signals over unreliable channels, e.g., wireless links. Adaptive coding varies the parameters of the encoding to respond to changes in the channel, e.g., "fading", where the signal-to-noise ratio degrades. [WP: Adaptive_coding]

adaptive contrast enhancement: An image processing operation that applies histogram equalization locally across an image. [WP: Adaptive_histogram_equalization]

adaptive edge detection: Edge detection with adaptive thresholding of the gradient magnitude image. [Nal93:3.1.2]

adaptive filtering: In signal processing, any filtering process in which the parameters of the filter change over time or where the parameters are different at different parts of the signal or image. [WP:Adaptive_filter]

adaptive histogram equalization: A localized method of improving image contrast. A histogram is constructed of the gray levels present. These gray levels are re-mapped so that the histogram is approximately flat. It can be made perfectly flat by dithering: [WP: Adaptive_histogram_equalization]

original — after adaptive histogram equalization

adaptive Hough transform: A Hough transform method that iteratively increases the resolution of the parameter space quantization. It is particularly useful for dealing with high-dimensional parameter spaces. Its disadvantage is that sharp peaks in the histogram can be missed. [NA05:5.6]

adaptive meshing: Methods for creating simplified meshes where elements are made smaller in regions of high detail (rapid changes in surface orientation) and larger in regions of low

detail, such as planes. [WP:Adaptive_mesh_refinement]

adaptive pyramid: A method of multiscale processing where small areas of image having some feature in common (e.g., color) are first extracted into a graph representation. This graph is then manipulated, e.g., by pruning or merging, until the level of desired scale is reached. [JM92]

adaptive reconstruction: Data-driven methods for creating statistically significant data in areas of a 3D data cloud where data may be missing because of sampling problems. [YGK95]

adaptive smoothing: An iterative smoothing algorithm that avoids smoothing over edges. Given an image $I(x, y)$, one iteration of adaptive smoothing proceeds as follows:

1. Compute gradient magnitude image $G(x, y) = |\nabla I(x, y)|$.
2. Make weights image $W(x, y) = e^{-\lambda G(x,y)}$.
3. Smooth the image: $S(x, y) = \dfrac{\sum_{i=-1}^{1} \sum_{j=-1}^{1} A_{xyij}}{\sum_{i=-1}^{1} \sum_{j=-1}^{1} B_{xyij}}$

where
$A_{xyij} = I(x + i, y + j)W(x + i, y + j)$
$B_{xyij} = W(x + i, y + j)$
[WP:Additive_smoothing]

adaptive thresholding: An improved image thresholding technique where the threshold value varies at each pixel. A common technique is to use the average intensity in a neighbourhood to set the threshold: [Dav90:4.4]

Image, I — Smoothed, S — Thresholded I > S–6

adaptive triangulation: See adaptive meshing.

adaptive visual servoing: See visual servoing. [WP:Visual_Servoing]

adaptive weighting: A scheme for weighting elements in a summation, voting or other formulation such that the relative influence of each element is representative (i.e., adapted to some underlying structure). For example this may be the similarity of pixels within a neighborhood (e.g., an adaptive bilateral filter) or a property changing over time. See also adaptive. [YK06]

additive color: The way in which multiple wavelengths of light can be combined to allow other colors to be perceived (e.g., if equal amounts of green and red light are shone onto a sheet of white paper, the paper will appear to be illuminated with a yellow light source (see below). Contrast this with subtractive color: [Gal90:3.7]

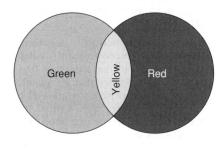

additive noise: Generally, image-independent noise that is added to it by some external process. The recorded image I at pixel (i, j) is then the sum of the true signal S and the noise N.

$$I_{i,j} = S_{i,j} + N_{i,j}$$

The noise added at each pixel (i, j) could be different. [Umb98:3.2]

adjacency: See adjacent.

adjacency graph: A graph that shows the adjacency between structures, such as segmented image regions. The nodes of the graph are the structures and an arc implies adjacency of the two structures connected by the arc. The figure shows the graph associated with the segmented image on the left: [AFF85]

 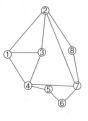

Regions   Adjacency graph

adjacent: Commonly meaning "next to each other", whether in a physical sense of pixel connectivity in an image, image regions sharing some common boundary, nodes in a graph connected by an arc or components in a geometric model sharing some common bounding component. Formally defining "adjacent" can be somewhat heuristic because you may need a way to specify closeness (e.g., on a quantized grid of pixels) or to consider how much shared "boundary" is required before two structures are adjacent. [Nev82:2.1.1]

affective body gesture: See affective gesture.

affective gesture: A gesture made by the body (human or animal) which is indicative of emotional feeling or response. Used in gesture analysis to indicate social interaction. [GX11:5.4]

affective state: The emotional state on an entity (human or animal) relating to emotional feeling or response. Often measured via gesture analysis or facial expression analysis. See affective gesture.

affine: A term first used by Euler. Affine geometry is a study of properties of geometric objects that remain invariant under affine transformations (mappings), including parallelness, cross ratio and adjacency. [WP:Affine_geometry]

affine arc length: For a parametric equation of a curve $\vec{f}(u) = (x(u), y(u))$, arc

13

length is not preserved under an affine transformation. The affine length

$$\tau(u) = \int_0^u (\dot{x}\ddot{y} - \ddot{x}\dot{y})^{\frac{1}{3}}$$

is invariant under affine transformations. [SQ04:8.4]

affine camera: A special case of the projective camera that is obtained by constraining the 3×4 camera parameter matrix $\mathbf{T}$ such that $T_{3,1} = T_{3,2} = T_{3,3} = 0$ and reducing the camera parameter vector from 11 degrees of freedom to 8. [FP03:2.3.1]

affine curvature: A measure of curvature based on the affine arc length, τ. For a parametric equation of a curve $\vec{f}(u) = (x(u), y(u))$, its affine curvature, μ, is

$$\mu(\tau) = x''(\tau)y'''(\tau) - x'''(\tau)y''(\tau)$$

[WP:Affine_curvature]

affine flow: A method of finding the movement of a surface patch by estimating the affine transformation parameters required to transform the patch from its position in one view to another. [Cal05]

affine fundamental matrix: The fundamental matrix which is obtained from a pair of cameras under affine viewing conditions. It is a 3×3 matrix whose upper left 2×2 submatrix is all zero. [HZ00:13.2.1]

affine invariant: An object or shape property that is not changed by (i.e., is invariant under) the application of an affine transformation. [FP03:18.4.1]

affine length: See affine arc length. [WP: Affine_curvature]

affine moment: Four shape measures derived from second and third order moments that remain invariant under affine transformations. They are given by the following equations, where each μ is the associated central moment: [NA05:7.3]

$$I_1 = \frac{\mu_{20}\mu_{02} - \mu_{11}^2}{\mu_{00}^4}$$

$$I_2 = (\mu_{30}^2\mu_{03}^2 - 6\mu_{30}\mu_{21}\mu_{12}\mu_{03}$$

$$+ 4\mu_{30}\mu_{12}^3 + 4\mu_{21}^3\mu_{03}$$
$$- 3\mu_{21}^2\mu_{12}^2)/\mu_{00}^{10}$$
$$I_3 = (\mu_{20}(\mu_{21}\mu_{03} - \mu_{12}^2)$$
$$- \mu_{11}(\mu_{30}\mu_{03} - \mu_{21}\mu_{12})$$
$$+ \mu_{02}(\mu_{30}\mu_{12} - \mu_{21}^2))/\mu_{00}^7$$
$$I_4 = (\mu_{20}^3\mu_{03}^2 - 6\mu_{20}^2\mu_{11}\mu_{12}\mu_{03}$$
$$- 6\mu_{20}^2\mu_{02}\mu_{21}\mu_{03} + 9\mu_{20}^2\mu_{02}\mu_{12}^2$$
$$+ 12\mu_{20}\mu_{11}^2\mu_{21}\mu_{03}$$
$$+ 6\mu_{20}\mu_{11}\mu_{02}\mu_{30}\mu_{03}$$
$$- 18\mu_{20}\mu_{11}\mu_{02}\mu_{21}\mu_{12}$$
$$- 8\mu_{11}^3\mu_{30}\mu_{03} - 6\mu_{20}\mu_{02}^2\mu_{30}\mu_{12}$$
$$+ 9\mu_{20}\mu_{02}^2\mu_{21}^2 + 12\mu_{11}^2\mu_{02}\mu_{30}\mu_{12}$$
$$- 6\mu_{11}\mu_{02}^2\mu_{30}\mu_{21} + \mu_{02}^3\mu_{30}^2)/\mu_{00}^{11}$$

affine quadrifocal tensor: The form taken by the quadrifocal tensor when specialized to the viewing conditions modeled by the affine camera. [HTM99]

affine reconstruction: A three-dimensional reconstruction where the ambiguity in the choice of basis is affine only. Planes that are parallel in the Euclidean basis are parallel in the affine reconstruction. A projective reconstruction can be upgraded to an affine reconstruction by identification of the plane at infinity, often by locating the absolute conic in the reconstruction. [HZ00:9.4.1]

affine registration: The registration of two or more images, surface meshes or point clouds using an affine transformation. [JV05]

affine stereo: A method of scene reconstruction using two calibrated views of a scene from known viewpoints. It is a simple but very robust approximation to the geometry of stereo vision, to estimate positions, shapes and surface orientations. It can be calibrated very easily by observing just four reference points. Any two views of the same planar surface will be related by an affine transformation that maps one image to the other. This consists of a translation and a tensor, known as the disparity gradient tensor, representing the distortion in image shape. If the standard unit vectors X and Y in one image are the projections of some vectors on the object surface and the linear mapping between images is represented by a 2×3 matrix **A**, then the first two columns of **A** will be the corresponding vectors in the other image. Since the centroid of the plane will map to both image centroids, it can be used to find the surface orientation. [Qua93]

affine transformation: A special set of transformations in Euclidean geometry that preserve some properties of the construct being transformed:

- Points remain collinear: if three points belong to the same straight line, their images under affine transformations also belong to the same line and the middle point remains between the other two points.
- Parallel lines remain parallel and concurrent lines remain concurrent (images of intersecting lines intersect).
- The ratio of lengths of the segments of a given line remains constant.
- The ratio of areas of two triangles remains constant.
- Ellipses remain ellipses; parabolas remain parabolas and hyperbolas remain hyperbolas.
- Barycenters of triangles (and other shapes) map into the corresponding barycenters.

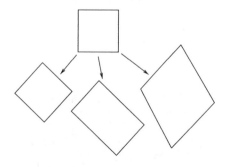

Analytically, affine transformations are represented in the matrix form

$$f(x) = \mathbf{A}x + b$$

where the determinant det(**A**) of the square matrix **A** is not 0. In 2D, the matrix is 2×2; in 3D it is 3×3. [FP03:2.2]

affine trifocal tensor: The form taken by the trifocal tensor when specialized to the viewing conditions modeled by the affine camera. [HTM99]

affinely invariant region: Image patches that automatically deform with changing viewpoint in such a way that they cover identical physical parts of a scene. Since such regions are describable by a set of invariant features they are relatively easy to match between views under changing illumination. [TG00]

affinity matrix: A matrix capturing the similarity of two entities or their relative attraction in a force- or flow-based model. Often referred to in graph cut formulations. See affinity metric. [Sze10:5.4]

affinity metric: A measurement of the similarity between two entities (e.g., features, nodes or images). See similarity metric.

affordance and action recognition: An affordance is an opportunity for an entity to take an action. The recognition of such occurrences thus identifies such action opportunities. See action recognition. [Gib86]

age progression: Refers to work considering the change in visual appearance because of the human aging process. Generally considered in tasks such as face recognition, face detection and face modeling. Recent work considers artificial aging of a sample facial image to produce an aged interpretation of the same: [GZSM07]

agglomerative clustering: A class of iterative clustering algorithms that begin with a large number of clusters and, at each iteration, merge pairs (or tuples) of clusters. Stopping the process at a certain number of iterations gives the final set of clusters. The process can be run until only one cluster remains and the progress of the algorithm can be represented as a dendrogram. [WP: Hierarchical_clustering]

AIC: See Akaike Information Criterion (AIC).

Akaike Information Criterion (AIC): A method for statistical model selection where the best-fit log-likelihood is penalized by the number of adjustable parameters in the model, so as to counter over-fitting. Compare with Bayesian information criterion. [Bis06:1.3]

albedo: Whiteness. Originally a term used in astronomy to describe reflecting power.

Albedo values

1.0   0.75   0.5   0.25   0.0

If a body reflects 50% of the light falling on it, it is said to have albedo of 0.5. [FP03:4.3.3]

algebraic curve: A simple parameterized curve representation using Euclidean geometry for an object that cannot be represented by linear properties (see figure). Parameterized in $\mathbb{R}^n$ Euclidean space, in the form of $\{\vec{x} : f(\vec{x}) = 0\}$: [Gib98:Ch. 1]

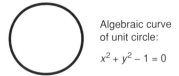

Algebraic curve of unit circle:

$x^2 + y^2 - 1 = 0$

algebraic distance: A linear distance metric commonly used in computer vision applications because of its simple form and standard matrix-based least mean square estimation operations. If a curve or surface is defined implicitly by $f(\vec{x}, \vec{a}) = 0$ (e.g., $\vec{x} \cdot \vec{a} =$

0 for a hyperplane), the algebraic distance of a point $\vec{x}_i$ to the surface is simply $f(\vec{x}_i, \vec{a})$. [FP03:10.1.5]

algebraic point set surfaces: A smooth surface model defined from a point cloud representation using localized moving least squares fitting of an algebraic surface (namely an algebraic sphere). [GG07]

algebraic surface: A parameterized surface representation using Euclidean geometry defined in $\mathbb{R}^n$ Euclidean space. Regular 3D surfaces such as planes, spheres, tori and generalized cylinders occur in $\mathbb{R}^3$, in the form of $\{\vec{x} : f(\vec{x}) = 0\}$. [Zar71]

aliasing: The erroneous replacement of high spatial frequency (HF) components by low-frequency ones when a signal is sampled. The affected HF components are those that are higher than the Nyquist frequency, or half the sampling frequency. Examples include the slowing of periodic signals by strobe lighting and corruption of areas of detail in image resizing. If the source signal has no HF components, the effects of aliasing are avoided, so the low-pass filtering of a signal to remove HF components prior to sampling is one form of anti-aliasing. Consider the perspective projection of a checkerboard. The image is obtained by sampling the scene at a set of integer locations. The spatial frequency increases as the plane recedes, producing aliasing artifacts (jagged lines in the foreground, moiré patterns in the background):

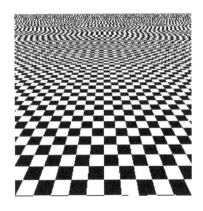

Removing high-frequency components (i.e., smoothing) before downsampling mitigates the effect: [FP03:7.4]

alignment: An approach to geometric model matching by registration of a geometric model to the image data. [FP03:18.2]

ALVINN: Autonomous Land Vehicle In a Neural Network; an early attempt, at Carnegie Mellon University, to learn a complex behavior (maneuvering a vehicle) by observing humans. [Pom89]

ambient light: Illumination by diffuse reflections from all surfaces within a scene (including the sky, which acts as an external distant surface). In other words, light that comes from all directions, such as the sky on a cloudy day. Ambient light ensures that all surfaces are illuminated, including those not directly facing light sources. [FP03:5.3.3]

ambient space: Refers to the dimensional space surrounding a given mathematical object in general terms. For example, a line can be studied in isolation or within a 2D space – in which case, the ambient space is a plane. Similarly a sphere may be studied in 3D ambient space. This is of particular relevance if the ambient space is nonlinear or skewed (e.g., a magnetic field). [SMC05]

AMBLER: An autonomous active vision system using both structured light and sonar, developed by NASA and Carnegie Mellon University. It is supported by a 12-legged robot and is intended for planetary exploration. [BHK+89]

amplifier noise: Spurious additive noise signal generated by the electronics in a sampling device. The standard model for this type of noise is Gaussian. It is independent of the signal. In color cameras, where more amplification is used in the blue color channel than in the green or red channels, there tends to be more noise in the blue channel. In well-designed electronics, amplifier noise is generally negligible. [WP: Image_noise#Amplifier_noise_.28 Gaussian_noise.29]

analog/mixed analog–digital image processing: The processing of images as analog signals (e.g., by optical image processing) prior to or without any form of image digitization. Largely superseded by digital image processing. [RK82]

analytic curve finding: A method of detecting parametric curves by transforming data into a feature space that is then searched for the hypothesized curve parameters. An example is line finding using the Hough transform. [XOK90]

anamorphic lens: A lens having one or more cylindrical surfaces. Anamorphic lenses are used in photography to produce images that are compressed in one dimension. Images can later be restored to true form using a reversing anamorphic lens set. This form of lens is used in wide-screen movie photography. [WP:Anamorphic_lens]

anatomical map: A biological model usable for alignment with, or region labeling of, a corresponding image dataset. For example, one could use a model of the brain's functional regions to assist in the identification of brain structures in an NMR dataset. [GHC+00]

AND operator: A Boolean logic operator that combines two input binary images:

p	q	$p\&q$
0	0	0
0	1	0
1	0	0
1	1	1

This approach is used to select image regions by applying the AND logic at each pair of corresponding pixels. The rightmost image below is the result of ANDing the two leftmost images: [SB11:3.2.2]

angiography: A method for imaging blood vessels by introducing a dye that is opaque when photographed by X-ray. Also the study of images obtained in this way. [WP:Angiography]

angularity ratio: Given two figures, X and Y, $\alpha_i(X)$ and $\beta_j(Y)$ are angles subtending convex parts of the contour of the figure X and $\gamma_k(X)$ are angles subtending plane parts of the contour of figure X; the angularity ratios are:

$$\sum_i \frac{\alpha_i(X)}{360°}$$

and

$$\frac{\sum_i \beta_j(X)}{\sum_k \gamma_k(X)}$$

[Lee64]

anisotropic diffusion: An edge-preserving smoothing filter commonly used for noise removal. Also called Perona-Malik diffusion. See also bilateral filtering. [Sze10:3.3]

anisotropic filtering: Any filtering technique where the filter parameters vary over the image or signal being filtered. [WP:Anisotropic_filtering]

anisotropic structure tensor: A matrix representing non-uniform, second-order (i.e., gradient/edge) information of an image or function neighborhood. Commonly used in corner detection and anisotropic filtering approaches. [Sze10:3.3]

annotation: A general term referring to the labeling of imagery either with regard to manual ground truth labeling or automatic image labeling of the output of a scene understanding, semantic scene segmentation or augmented reality approach: [Sze10:14.6, 13.1.2]

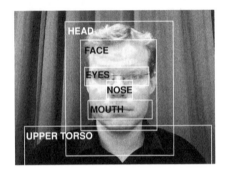

anomalous behavior detection: Special case of surveillance where human movement is analyzed. Used in particular to detect intruders or behavior likely to precede or indicate crime. [WP:Anomaly_detection]

anomaly detection: The automated detection of an unexpected event, behavior or object within a given environment based on comparison with a model of what is normally expected within the same. Often considered as an unsupervised learning task and commonly applied in visual industrial inspection and automated visual surveillance. [Bar12:13.1.3]

antimode: The minimum between two maxima. One method of threshold selection is done by determining the antimode in a bimodal histogram. [WP: Bimodal_distribution#Terminology]

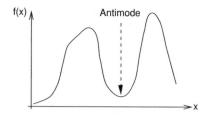

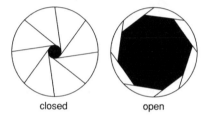

closed   open

aperture: Opening in the lens diaphragm of a camera through which light is admitted. This device is often arranged so that the amount of light can be controlled accurately. A small aperture reduces the amount of light available, but increases the depth of field. The figure shows nearly closed (left) and nearly open (right) aperture positions: [TV98:2.2.2]

aperture control: Mechanism for varying the size of a camera's aperture. [WP:Aperture#Aperture_control]

aperture problem: If a motion sensor has a finite receptive field, it perceives the world through something resembling an aperture, making the motion of a homogeneous contour seem locally ambiguous. Within that aperture, different physical motions are therefore indistinguishable. For example, the two motions of the square below are identical in the circled receptive fields: [Nal93:8.1.1]

BEFORE   AFTER

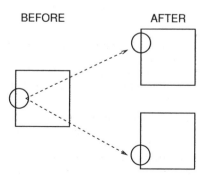

apparent contour: The apparent contour of a surface S in 3D is the set of critical values of the projection of S onto a plane, in other words, the silhouette. If the surface is transparent, the apparent contour can be decomposed into a collection of closed curves with double points and cusps. The convex envelope of an apparent contour is also the boundary of its convex hull. [Nal93:Ch. 4]

apparent motion: The 3D motion suggested by the image motion field, but not necessarily matching the real 3D motion. The reason for this mismatch is that motion fields may be ambiguous; that is, they may be generated by different 3D motions or light source movement. Mathematically, there may be multiple solutions to the problem of reconstructing 3D motion from the image motion field. See also visual illusion and motion estimation. [WP: Apparent_motion]

appearance: The way an object looks from a particular viewpoint under particular lighting conditions. [FP03:25.1.3]

appearance-based recognition: Object recognition where the object model encodes the possible appearances of the object (as contrasted with a geometric model that encodes the shape, in model-based recognition). In principle, it is impossible to encode all appearances when occlusions are considered; however, small numbers of appearances can often be adequate, especially if there are not many models in the model base. There are many approaches to appearance-based recognition, such as using a principal component model to encode all appearances in a compressed framework, using color histograms to summarize the appearance or a set of local appearance descriptors such as Gabor filters extracted at interest points. A common feature of these approaches is learning the models from examples. [TV98:10.4]

appearance-based tracking: Methods for object or target recognition in real

19

time, based on image pixel values in each frame rather than derived features. Temporal filtering, such as the Kalman filter, is often used. [BJ98]

appearance change: Changes in an image that are not easily accounted for by motion, such as an object actually changing form. [BFY98]

appearance enhancement transform: Generic term for operations applied to images to change, or enhance, some aspect of them, such as brightness adjustment, contrast adjustment, edge sharpening, histogram equalization, saturation adjustment or magnification. [Hum77]

appearance feature: An object or scene feature relating to visual appearance, as opposed to features derived from shape, motion or behavior analysis. [HFR06]

appearance flow: Robust methods for real-time object recognition from a sequence of images depicting a moving object. Changes in the images are used rather than in the images themselves. It is analogous to processing using optical flow. [DTS06]

appearance model: A representation used for interpreting images that is based on the appearance of the object. These models are usually learned by using multiple views of the objects. See also active appearance model and appearance-based recognition. [WP: Active_appearance_model]

appearance prediction: Part of the science of appearance engineering, where an object texture is changed so that the viewer experience is predictable. [Kan97]

appearance singularity: An image position where a small change in viewer position can cause a dramatic change in the appearance of the observed scene, such as the appearance or disappearance of image features. This is contrasted with changes occurring when in a generic viewpoint. For example, when viewing the corner of a cube from a distance, a small change in viewpoint still leaves the three surfaces at the corner visible. However, when the

viewpoint moves into the infinite plane containing one of the cube faces (a singularity), one or more of the planes disappears. [MR98]

arc length: If f is a function such that its derivative f' is continuous on some closed interval $[a, b]$ then the arc length of f from $x = a$ to $x = b$ is the integral: [FP03:19.1]

$$\int_a^b \sqrt{1 + [f'(x)]^2}\,dx$$

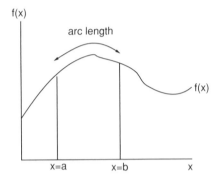

arc of graph: Two nodes in a graph can be connected by an arc (also called an edge). The edges can be either directed or undirected. The dashed lines here are the arcs: [WP: Graph_(mathematics)]

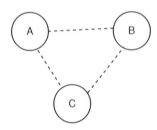

architectural model reconstruction: A generic term for reverse engineering buildings based on collected 3D data as well as libraries of building constraints. [WZ02]

area: The measure of a region or surface's extension in some given units. The units could be image units, such as square pixels, or scene units, such as square centimeters. [JKS95:2.2.1]

20

area-based: Operation applied to a region of an image; as opposed to pixel-based. [CS09:6.6]

ARMA: See autoregressive moving average model.

array processor: A group of time-synchronized processing elements that perform computations on data distributed across them. Some array processors have elements that communicate only with their immediate neighbors, as in the topology shown below. See also single instruction multiple data. [WP:Vector_processor]

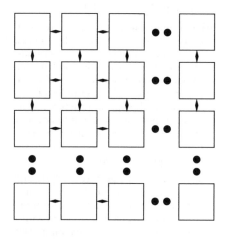

arterial tree segmentation: Generic term for methods used in finding internal pipe-like structures in medical images, such as NMR images, angiograms and X-rays. Example trees include bronchial systems and veins. [BWB+05]

articulated object: An object composed of a number of (usually) rigid subparts or components connected by joints, which can be arranged in a number of different configurations. The human body is a typical example. [BM02:1.9]

articulated object model: A representation of an articulated object that includes its separate parts and their range of movement (typically joint angles) relative to each other. [RK95]

articulated object segmentation: Methods for acquiring an articulated object from 2D or 3D data. [YP06]

articulated object tracking: Tracking an articulated object in an image sequence. This includes both the pose of the object and also its shape parameters, such as joint angles. [WP: Finger_tracking]

aspect graph: A graph of the set of views (aspects) of an object, where the arcs of the graph are transitions between two neighboring views (the nodes) and a change between aspects is called a visual event. See also characteristic view. This graph shows some of the aspects of a hippopotamus: [FP03:20]

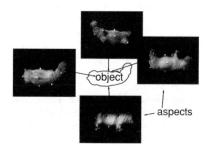

aspect ratio: 1) The ratio of the sides of the bounding box of an object, where the orientation of the box is chosen to maximize this ratio. Since this measure is scale invariant, it is a useful metric for object recognition.
2) In a camera, the ratio of the horizontal to vertical pixel sizes.
3) In an image, the ratio of the image width to height – an image of 640 by 480 pixels has an aspect ratio of 4:3. [Low91:2.2]

aspect: See characteristic view and aspect graph.

asperity scattering: A light scattering effect, common to the modeling or photography of human skin, caused by sparsely distributed point scatters over the surface. In the case of human skin, these point scatters are vellus (short, fine, light-colored and barely noticeable) hairs present on the surface. [INN07:3.3]

association graph: A graph used in structure matching, such as matching a geometric model to a data description. In this graph, each node corresponds to a pairing between a model and a data feature (with the implicit assumption that they are compatible). Arcs in the graph mean that the two connected nodes are pairwise compatible. Finding maximal cliques is one technique for finding good matches. The graph below shows a set of pairings of model features A, B and C with image features a, b, c and d. The maximal clique consisting of A:a, B:b and C:c is one match hypothesis: [BB82:11.2.1]

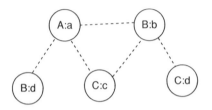

astigmatism: A refractive error with where the light is focused within an optical system. It occurs when a lens has irregular curvature causing light rays to focus at an area, rather than at a point:

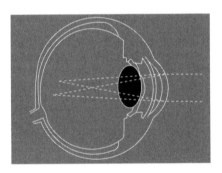

It may be corrected with a toric lens, which has a greater refractive index on one axis than the others. In human eyes, astigmatism often occurs with nearsightedness and farsightedness. [FP03:1.2.3]

asymmetric SVM: A variant on traditional support vector machine classification where the false positives are modeled in the training objective of finding a maximal margin of classification. An asymmetric SVM maximizes the margin between the negative class and the core (i.e., high confidence subset) of the positive class by introducing a secondary core margin in addition to the traditional inter-class margin. They are jointly optimized within the training optimization cycle. [WLCC08]

atlas-based segmentation: A segmentation technique used in medical image processing, especially with brain images. Automatic tissue segmentation is achieved using a model of the brain structure and imagery (see atlas registration) compiled with the assistance of human experts. See also image segmentation. [VYCL03]

atlas registration: An image registration technique used in medical image processing, especially to register brain images. An atlas is a model (perhaps statistical) of the characteristics of multiple brains, providing examples of normal and pathological structures. This makes it possible to take into account anomalies that single-image registration could not. See also medical image registration. [HSS+08]

atomic action: In gesture analysis and action recognition, a short sequence of basic limb movements that form the pattern of movement associated with a higher level action. For example, "lift right leg in front of left leg" for a running action or "swing right hand" and "rotate upper body" for taking a badminton shot. [GX11:Ch. 1]

ATR: See automatic target recognition. [WP:Automatic_target_recognition]

attached shadow: A shadow caused by an object on itself by self-occlusion. See also cast shadow. [FP03:5.3.1]

attention: See visual attention. [WP: Attention]

attenuation: The reduction of a particular phenomenon, e.g., noise attenuation is the reduction of image noise. [WP:Attenuation]

attributed graph: A graph useful for representing different properties of an image. Its nodes are attributed pairs of image segments, their color or shape e.g. The relations between them, such as relative texture or brightness are encoded as arcs. [BM02:4.5.2]

atypical co-occurrence: An unusual joint occurrence of two or more events or observations against *a priori* expectation. [GX11:Ch. 9]

augmented reality: Primarily a projection method that adds, e.g., graphics or sound as an overlay to original image or audio. For example, a fire-fighter's helmet display could show exit routes registered to his or her view of the building. [WP:Augmented_reality]

autocalibration: The recovery of a camera's calibration using only point (or other feature) correspondences from multiple uncalibrated images and geometric consistency constraints (e.g., that the camera settings are the same for all images in a sequence). [Low91:13.7]

autocorrelation: The extent to which a signal is similar to shifted copies of itself. For an infinitely long 1D signal $f(t) : \mathbb{R} \mapsto \mathbb{R}$, the autocorrelation at a shift Δt is

$$R_f(\Delta t) = \int_{-\infty}^{\infty} f(t)f(t + \Delta t)\mathrm{d}t$$

The autocorrelation function R_f always has a maximum at 0. A *peaked* autocorrelation function decays quickly away from $\Delta t = 0$. The sample autocorrelation function of a finite set of values $f_{1..n}$ is $\{r_f(d)|d = 1, \ldots, n - 1\}$ where

$$r_f(d) = \frac{\sum_{i=1}^{n-d}(f_i - \bar{f})(f_{i+d} - \bar{f})}{\sum_{i=1}^{n}(f_i - \bar{f})^2}$$

and $\bar{f} = \frac{1}{n}\sum_{i=1}^{n} f_i$ is the sample mean. [WP:Autocorrelation]

autofocus: Automatic determination and control of image sharpness in an optical or vision system. There are two major variations in this control system: active focusing and passive focusing. Active autofocus is performed using a sonar or infrared signal to determine the object distance. Passive autofocus is performed by analyzing the image itself to optimize differences between adjacent pixels in the CCD array. [WP:Autofocus]

automated visual surveillance: The generalized use of automatic scene understanding approaches commonly including object detection, tracking and, more recently, behavior classification: [Dav90:Ch. 22]

automatic: Performed by a machine without human intervention. The opposite of "manual". [WP: Automation]

automatic target recognition (ATR): The detection of hostile objects in a scene using sensors and algorithms. Sensors are of many different types, sampling in infrared and visible light and using acoustic sonar and radar. [WP:Automatic_target_recognition]

autonomous vehicle: A mobile robot controlled by computer, with human input operating only at a very high level, e.g., stating the ultimate destination or task. Autonomous navigation requires the visual tasks of route detection, self-localization, landmark location and obstacle detection, as well as robotic tasks such as route planning and motor control. [WP:Autonomous car]

autoregressive model: A model that uses statistical properties of the past behavior of some variable to predict future behavior of that variable. For example, a signal x_t at time t satisfies an autoregressive model of order p if $x_t = \sum_{n=1}^{p} \alpha_n x_{t-n} + \omega_t$, where ω_t is noise. The model could also be nonlinear. [WP:Autoregressive_model]

autoregressive moving average (ARMA) model: Combines an autoregressive model with a moving average for the statistical analysis and future value prediction of time series information. [BJ71]

autostereogram: An image similar to a random dot stereogram in which the corresponding features are combined into a single image. Stereo fusion allows the perception of a 3D shape in the 2D image. [WP:Autostereogram]

average smoothing: See mean smoothing.

AVI: Microsoft format for audio and video files ("audio video interleaved"). Unlike MPEG, it is not a standard, so that compatibility of AVI video files and AVI players is not always guaranteed. [WP:Audio_Video_Interleave]

axial representation: A region representation that uses a curve to describe the image region. The axis may be a skeleton derived from the region by a thinning process. [RM91]

axiomatic computer vision: Approaches relating to the core principles (or axioms) of computer vision. Commonly associated with the interpretation of Marr's theory for the basic building blocks of how visual interpretation scene understanding should ideally be performed. Most recently associated with low-level feature detection (e.g., edge detection and corner detection). [KZM05]

axis of elongation: 1) The line that minimizes the second moment of the data points. If $\{\vec{x}_i\}$ are the data points, and $d(\vec{x}, L)$ is the distance from point $\vec{x}$ to line L, then the axis of elongation A minimizes $\sum_i d(\vec{x}_i, A)^2$.

Let $\vec{\mu}$ be the mean of $\{\vec{x}_i\}$. Define the scatter matrix $\mathbf{S} = \sum_i (\vec{x}_i - \vec{\mu})(\vec{x}_i - \vec{\mu})^T$. Then the axis of elongation is the eigenvector of $\mathbf{S}$ with the largest eigenvalue. See also principal component analysis. The figure shows a possible axis of elongation for a set of points:

2) The longer midline of the bounding box with largest length-to-width ratio. [JKS95:2.2.3]

axis of rotation: A line about which a rotation is performed. Equivalently, the line whose points are fixed under the action of a rotation. Given a 3D rotation matrix $\mathbf{R}$, the axis is the eigenvector of $\mathbf{R}$ corresponding to the eigenvalue 1. [JKS95:12.2.2]

axis–angle curve representation: A rotation representation based on the amount of twist θ about the axis of rotation, here a unit vector $\vec{a}$. The quaternion rotation representation is similar. [WP:Axis-angle_representation]

B-rep: See surface boundary representation.

b-spline: A curve approximation spline represented as a combination of basis functions:

$$\vec{c}(t) = \sum_{i=0}^{m} \vec{a}_i B_i(x)$$

where B_i are the basis functions and $\vec{a}_i$ are the control points. B-splines do not necessarily pass through any of the control points; however, if b-splines are calculated for adjacent sets of control points the curve segments will join up and produce a continuous curve. [JKS95:13.7.1]

b-spline fitting: Fitting a b-spline to a set of data points. This is useful for noise reduction or for producing a more compact model of the observed curve. [JKS95:13.7.1]

b-spline snake: A snake made from b-splines. [BHU00]

back projection: 1) A form of display where a translucent screen is illuminated from the side facing away from the viewer.
2) The computation of a 3D quantity from its 2D projection. For example, a 2D homogeneous point $\vec{x}$ is the projection of a 3D point $\vec{X}$ by a perspective projection matrix **P**, so $\vec{x} = \mathbf{P}\vec{X}$. The backprojection of $\vec{x}$ is the 3D line $\{\text{null}(\mathbf{P}) + \lambda \mathbf{P}^+\vec{x}\}$ where $\mathbf{P}^+$ is the pseudoinverse of **P**.
3) Sometimes used interchangeably with triangulation.
4) Technique to compute the attenuation coefficients from intensity profiles covering a total cross section under various angles. It is used in CT and MRI to recover 3D from essentially 2D images.
5) Projection of the estimated 3D position of a shape back into the 2D image from which the shape's pose was estimated. [Jai89:10.3]

background: In computer vision, generally used in the context of object recognition. The background is either the area of the scene behind the objects of interest or the part of the image whose pixels sample from the background in the scene. As opposed to foreground. See also figure–ground separation. [JKS95:2.5]

background labeling: Methods for differentiating objects in the foreground of an image or objects of interest from those in the background. [Low91:10.4]

background modeling: Segmentation or change detection method where the scene behind the objects of interest is modeled as a fixed or slowly changing background, with possible foreground occlusions. Each pixel is modeled as a distribution which is then used to decide if a given observation belongs to the background or an occluding object. [NA05:3.5.2]

background normalization: Removal of the background by some image-processing technique to estimate the background image and then dividing or subtracting the background from an original image. The technique is useful for non-uniform backgrounds. [JKS95:3.2.1] The following figures show the input image:

Dictionary of Computer Vision and Image Processing, Second Edition.
R. B. Fisher, T. P. Breckon, K. Dawson-Howe, A. Fitzgibbon, C. Robertson, E. Trucco and C. K. I. Williams.
© 2014 John Wiley & Sons, Ltd. Published 2014 by John Wiley & Sons, Ltd.

background subtraction: The separation of image foreground components achieved by subtracting pixel values belonging to the image background obtained by a background modeling technique: [MC11:3.5.1]

Background Model | Foreground Objects

the background estimate obtained by the dilate operator with ball(9, 9) structuring element:

and the (normalized) division of the input image by the background image:

back lighting: A method of illuminating a scene where the background receives more illumination than the foreground. Commonly this is used to produce a silhouette of an opaque object against a lit background, for easier object detection. [Gal90:2.1.1]

back-propagation: One of the best-studied neural network training algorithms for supervised learning. The name arises from using the propagation of the discrepancies between the computed and desired responses at the network output back to the network inputs. The discrepancies are one of the inputs into the network weight recomputation process. [WP: Backpropagation]

back-tracking: A basic technique for graph searching: if a terminal but non-solution node is reached, the search does not terminate with failure, but continues with still unexplored children of a previously visited non-terminal node. Classic back-tracking algorithms are breadth-first, depth-first, and A*. See also graph, graph searching, search tree. [BB82:11.3.2]

bag of detectors: An object detection approach driven by ensemble learning using a set of independently trained detection concepts (detectors), possibly of the same type (*e.g.*, random forest). Results from the set are combined using bagging or boosting to produce detection results. [HBS09]

bag of features: A generalized feature representation approach whereby a set of high-dimensional feature descriptors (e.g., SIFT or SURF) are encoded via quantization to a set of identified unordered code-words in the same dimensional space. This quantization set is denoted as the codebook (or dictionary) containing visual words or visual codewords. The frequency of occurrence of these quantized features within a given sample image, represented as a histogram, is commonly used as an input to a classifier in generalized object recognition, object detection and scene classification approaches. See object recognition for additional terminology. [Sze10:14.4.1]

bag of words: See bag of features.

bagging: An ensemble learning approach where the overall result of the ensemble set is formed as either a majority vote, in the case of classification, or a mean value, in regression cases. [Bis06:14.2]

balanced filter: A phrase in general usage to refer to a filtering approach that gives equivalent weights to samples spatially, spectrally or temporally in any direction (e.g., Gaussian smoothing, mean filtering or low-pass filtering). By contrast, an unbalanced filter, such as bilateral filtering, could be considered an adaptive approach.

bandpass filter: A signal processing filtering technique that allows signals between two specified frequencies to pass but cuts out signals at all other frequencies. [FP03:9.2.2]

bar: A raw primal sketch primitive that represents a dark line segment against a lighter background (or its inverse).

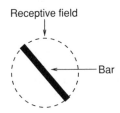

Receptive field

Bar

Bars are also one of the primitives in Marr's theory of vision. The following small dark bar is observed inside a receptive field: [MH80]

bar-code reading: Methods and algorithms used for the detection, imaging and interpretation of parallel black lines of different widths, arranged to give details on products or other objects. Bar codes themselves have many different coding standards and arrangements. An example bar code is: [Gal90:Ch. 7]

bar detector: 1) Method or algorithm that produces maximum excitation when a bar is in its receptive field; 2) device used by thirsty undergraduates. [WP:Feature_detection_(nervous_system)#History]

barrel distortion: Geometric lens distortion in an optical system that causes the outlines of an object to curve outward, forming a barrel shape. See also pincushion distortion. [Hec87:6.3.1]

Barycentric coordinates: A scheme for position-invariant geometry, where point positions are expressed as a weighted sum of a set of control points. For example, in a triangular mesh, points on the surface of the mesh can be expressed as a weighted sum of the containing triangle's vertices. [FP03:12.1.1]. Here, the Barycentric coordinates of point $\vec{X}$ are (a, b, c) because $\vec{X} = a\vec{A} + b\vec{B} + c\vec{C}$:

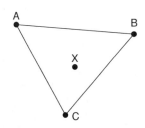

barycentrum: See center of mass.

bas-relief ambiguity: The ambiguity in reconstructing a 3D object with Lambertian surface reflectance using shading from an image under orthographic projection. If the true surface is $z(x, y)$, then the family of surfaces $az(x, y) + bx + cy$ generate identical images under these viewing conditions, so any reconstruction for any values of a, b, c is equally valid. The ambiguity is thus up to a three-parameter family. [BKY99]

baseline: Distance between two cameras in a binocular stereo system: [DH73:10.6]

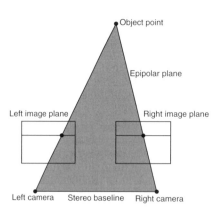

basis function representation: A method of representing a function as a sum of simple (usually orthonormal) functions. For example, the Fourier transform represents functions as a weighted sum of sines and cosines. [Jai89:1.2]

batch learning: A machine learning training approach whereby all of the training set is processed together as a batch set before any update to the learning concept is made. This contrasts with incremental learning or online learning, where an update is made after individually processing each instance of the training set. Batch vs. incremental learning is commonly a trade-off in back-propagation training for neural networks and gradient descent approaches in general. [Bis06:2.5.4]

Bayer pattern: A distribution pattern of cells on a CCD digital camera for sensing RGB color such that half the cells sense green light whilst the remaining

cells are equally split between sensing red or blue light. This is because of the luminance component of the image being largely determined by the sensed green light values the human visual system is more sensitive to high-frequency detail. A color image is created via demosaicing of the Bayer pattern: [Sze10:2.3]

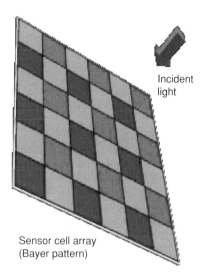

Sensor cell array (Bayer pattern)

Bayes' rule: The relationship between the conditional probability of event A given B and the conditional probability of event B given event A. This is expressed as

$$P(A|B) = \frac{P(B|A)P(A)}{P(B)}$$

providing that $P(B) \neq 0$. [SQ04:14.2.1]

Bayes' theorem: See Bayes' rule.

Bayesian adaptation: An adaptive training approach for Bayesian learning whereby a Bayesian classifier that has been pre-trained on a large ubiquitous training set is adapted to a specific deployment or usage environment by adjustment (re-weighting) using a smaller adaptation set drawn from that environment. [Tos11:8.3.2]

Bayesian classifier: A mathematical approach to classifying a datapoint by selecting the class most likely to have generated it. If $\vec{x}$ is the data and c is a class, then the posterior probability of that class is $p(c|\vec{x})$. This probability can be computed using Bayes' rule, which says that $p(c|\vec{x}) = \frac{p(\vec{x}|c)p(c)}{p(\vec{x})}$. Subsequently, we can compute $p(c|\vec{x})$ in terms of the probability $p(\vec{x}|c)$ of having observed the given data $\vec{x}$ under class c, $p(c)$ the prior probability of class c, and $p(\vec{x})$, which is computed as $p(\vec{x}) = \sum_{c'} p(\vec{x}|c')p(c')$ summing over all classes. The Bayesian classifier is the most common statistical classifier currently used in computer vision processes. Note that the Bayesian classifier is so called not because it is a Bayesian statistical model, but because of the use of Bayes' rule. [DH73:2.2]

Bayesian data association: The use of probability following Bayes' rule to tackle the data association problem of multiple target tracking based on association by maximum *a posteriori* probability given the image features present. [GX11:5.1.3]

Bayesian filtering: A probabilistic data fusion technique. It uses a formulation of probabilities to represent the system state and likelihood functions to represent their relationships. In this form, Bayes' rule can be applied and further related probabilities deduced. [WP:Bayesian_filtering]

Bayesian graph: A graph model used to illustrate a joint probability distribution. Nodes in the graph represent variables (states) and edges represent the influence of one variable (denoted states) upon another. A generalization of a Bayesian network. [MYA95]

Bayesian information criterion: A model selection approach, following Bayes' rule, based on the likelihood of a given model, with a given parameterization, considering the evidence of the data, the prior probability of model occurrence for a given parameterization and a model complexity penalization term (following the principle of Occam's razor). Related to Akaike Information Criterion (AIC). [Bis06:4.4.1]

Bayesian learning: A machine learning approach based on conditional probability following the principle of Bayes' rule. For example, see Bayesian classifier. [Bar12:Ch. 9]

Bayesian model learning: See probabilistic model learning.

Bayesian model selection: See Bayesian information criterion.

Bayesian network: Another name for a directed graphical model. [WP: Bayesian_network]

Bayesian Occam's razor: An extension to the principle of Occam's razor, following Bayes' rule, stating that the model (or hypothesis) with the greatest likelihood given the data will dominate the posterior probability, hence it is the best model choice. See also Bayesian information criterion. [Mac92]

Bayesian parameter inference: A conditional probability parameter estimation approach following the principle of Bayes' rule. Also known as Bayesian parameter estimation. [KS88]

Bayesian saliency: A saliency map generation approach, within an image or another space, where saliency is defined by the likelihood of a given observation (e.g., value) in relation to all the others in the set. [GX11:Ch. 9]

Bayesian statistical model: Consider a statistical model M with a parameter vector θ. A common approach to statistical modeling is to estimate the parameters of the model given data D, e.g., by maximum likelihood estimation. The Bayesian approach instead uses probability to quantify the uncertainty about θ. We start with a prior distribution $p(\theta|M)$. This is combined with the likelihood function $p(D|\theta, M)$ to yield the posterior distribution $p(\theta|D, M)$, i.e., $p(\theta|D, M) = \frac{p(D|\theta, M)p(\theta|M)}{p(D|M)}$. The normalizer $p(D|M)$ is called the marginal likelihood. In words this equation can be written as $posterior = \frac{likelihood \times prior}{marginal\ likelihood}$. The model can be used to make predictions by averaging over the posterior; e.g., for a supervised learning task with input x and output y, we have $p(y|x, D, M) = \int p(y|x, \theta, M)p(\theta|D, M)\, d\theta$. [Bis06:1.2.3]

Bayesian temporal model: An extension of the Bayesian model to the temporal domain to consider tightly correlated temporal data, such as in facial expression analysis where the next state is predicted at time t given the state at time $t - 1$ together with the observation at time t. [GX11:4.2.2]

BDRF: See bidirectional reflectance distribution function.

beam splitter: An optical system that divides unpolarized light into two orthogonally polarized beams, at 90° to each other, as in this figure: [Hec87:4.3.4]

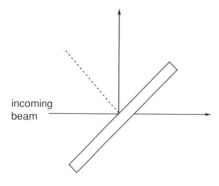

incoming
beam

behavior affinity matrix: An affinity matrix capturing the similarity of behaviors for behavior classification and similar tasks.

behavior analysis: Model based vision techniques for identifying and tracking behavior in humans. Often used for threat analysis. [WP: Applied_behavior_analysis]

behavior class distribution: 1) The global prior distribution of multiple classes within a behavior classification task.
2) The within class distribution of a given class when used in a behavior classification task. See also within-class scatter matrix and distribution overlap.

behavior classification: The classification of a given activity

sequence to one of a discrete set of labels corresponding to an *a priori* behavior model. [WM00]

behavior correlation: The use of techniques generally derived from cross-correlation matching to the spatio-temporal analysis of video sequences for behavior analysis and behavior detection. [SI05]

behavior detection: The detection of specific behavior patterns within video sequences. See also behavior analysis and anomalous behavior detection. [GX11:Ch. 8]

behavior footprint: A temporal statistical distribution of behavior patterns occurring at a given pixel or region of interest within an image. Records behavior occurrence at that point in the image. Commonly represented as a histogram: [GX11:10.1]

behavior hierarchy: A hierarchical behavior representation consisting of three layers: atomic actions (i.e., basic limb movement sequences); actions as a sequence of atomic actions (e.g., running and walking); and activities (or events) composed of a sequence of actions over space and time (e.g., a person walking to the car to fetch their bag). [GX11:1.1]

behavior interpretation: A general term referring to the extraction of high-level semantic descriptions of behavior patterns occurring in video sequences. See also behavior analysis and general image interpretation. [GX11:Ch. 3]

behavior learning: Generation of goal-driven behavior models by some learning algorithm, e.g., reinforcement learning. [SB98:1.1]

behavior localization: The localization of a given behavior occurrence or behavior pattern within a single image (i.e., object localization), within a scene context (i.e., 3D localization) or within a video sequence (i.e., temporal localization). The figure shows temporal localization: [GX11:6.4]

walking across
road to car park

behavior model: A pre-defined or learned model of a given behavior used for the tasks of behavior detection, behavior classification and general behavior analysis. Akin to the use of models in model-based object recognition, whereby the model is matched against a given unseen behavior instance to aid semantic understanding. [GX11:Ch. 11]

behavior pattern: A temporal sequence of actions (or events) forming an activity that conforms to a given human (or animal) behavior. Generally represented as a temporal feature vector. The tasks of behavior analysis, behavior detection and behavior classification thus form a specialization of generalized pattern recognition within this context. See also behavior hierarchy and behavior model. [GX11:8.1.1]

behavior posterior: The posterior probability, $P(Z_t|e_t)$, at time t of the occurrence of a given behavior, Z_t, in a behavior pattern of events, e_t. See also behavior hierarchy. [GX11:9.1]

behavior prediction: The prediction of a given behavior pattern, generally at a given location in a multi-camera system, based on current knowledge of behavior patterns until the current point in time. In addition, for the multi-camera case, implicit (or explicit) knowledge of the multi-camera topology. See also multi-camera behavior correlation. [GX11:Ch. 15]

behavior profile: A semantic labeling of a given behavior model to correspond to an *a priori* behavior pattern. Commonly used in anomalous behavior detection. Often used synonymously with behavior model. [GX11: Ch. 8]

behavior profiling: The use of a behavior profile in a given behavior analysis task. [GX11:Ch. 8]

behavior representation: See behavior model

behavioral context: 1) The context in which a computer vision system operates with regards to the actions of agents in its environment. 2) Contextual information used to aid in behavior interpretation. [GX11:Ch. 2]

behavioral saliency: The consideration of the notion of salience with regard to behavior analysis. The identification of behavior patterns which deviate from that considered normal. See anomalous behavior detection. [BI05]

belief network: Another name for a directed graphical model or Bayesian network. [Mur12:6.2]

belief propagation: Assume a joint probability distribution over a set of random variables defined by a probabilistic graphical model. With knowledge of the values of some set of variables e (the evidence), it is desired to carry out probabilistic inference to obtain the conditional distribution for (a subset of) the remaining variables x, i.e., $p(x|e)$. In belief propagation, the posterior marginal distribution of each variable in x is obtained via a message-passing process. The algorithm is exact for graphs without loops; more generally the *junction tree algorithm* can be used to compute posterior marginals for any probabilistic graphical model. The forward–backward algorithm is a special case of belief propagation applied to the hidden Markov model (HMM). [Bis06:8.4.4]

Beltrami flow: A noise suppression technique where images are treated as surfaces and the surface area is minimized in such a way as to preserve edges. See also diffusion smoothing. [SKM98]

bending energy: 1) A metaphor borrowed from the mechanics of thin metal plates. If a set of landmarks is distributed on two infinite flat metal plates and the differences in the coordinates between the two sets are vertical displacements of the plate, one Cartesian coordinate at a time, then the bending energy is the energy required to bend the metal plate so that the landmarks are coincident. When applied to images, the sets of landmarks may be sets of features.
2) Denotes the amount of energy that is stored because of an object's shape. [DLSZ91]

Bernoulli distribution: The distribution of a binary discrete random variable which takes on value 1 with probability p and value 0 with probability $1 - p$. [Bis06:2.1]

best next view: See next view planning.

between-class scatter matrix: Given some vector data grouped into a number of classes, with $\vec{m}_i$ being the mean of class i, and $\vec{m}$ being the overall mean of the data, the between-class scatter matrix is defined as $\mathbf{S}_B = \sum_i n_i (\vec{m}_i - \vec{m})(\vec{m}_i - \vec{m})^\top$, where n_i is the number of data points in class i. It is used in the computation of the Fisher linear discriminant (FLD). See also within-class scatter matrix. [Bis06:4.1]

Bhattacharyya distance: A measure of the (dis)similarity of two probability distributions. Given two arbitrary distributions $p_i(\mathbf{x})_{i=1,2}$ the Bhattacharyya distance between them is: [PS06:4.5]

$$d^2 = -\log \int \sqrt{(p_1(\mathbf{x})p_2(\mathbf{x})}.d\mathbf{x}$$

bias field estimation: A process used in magnetic resonance imaging (MRI) to estimate the intensity inhomogeneities present in the measured imagery because of properties of the imaging device itself. Bias is corrected via filtering prior to viewing or image analysis. [LXAG09]

BIC: See Bayesian information criterion.

bicubic spline interpolation: A special case of surface interpolation that uses cubic spline functions in two dimensions. This is like bilinear surface interpolation except that the interpolating surface is curved, instead of flat. [WP:Bicubic_interpolation#Bicubic_convolution_algorithm]

bidirectional reflectance distribution function (BRDF): If the energy arriving at a surface patch, denoted $E(\theta_i, \phi_i)$, and the energy radiated in a particular direction is denoted $L(\theta_e, \phi_e)$ in polar coordinates, then BRDF is defined as the ratio of the energy radiated from a patch of a surface in some direction to the amount of energy arriving there. The radiance is determined from the irradiance by

$$L(\theta_e, \phi_e) = f(\theta_i, \phi_i, \theta_e, \phi_e)E(\theta_e, \phi_e)$$

where the function f is the bidirectional reflectance distribution function. This function often only depends on the difference between the incident angle ϕ_i of the ray falling on the surface and the angle ϕ_e of the reflected ray: [FP03:4.2.2]

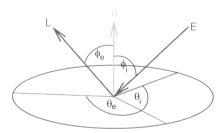

bidirectional texture function (BTF): A general solution for texture modeling in computer graphics (notably in texture synthesis) for textures that change appearance with illumination and viewing angle. Modeled in a similar way to a bidirectional reflectance distribution function (BRDF) such that the texture output is indexed by incident illumination and viewing angle. Unlike the BRDF where the response value is simply reflectance, response values of the BTF are whole image patches. [TFCS11:8.4.2]

bilateral filtering: A non-iterative alternative to anisotropic filtering where images can be subject to smoothing but edges present in the images are preserved. [WP:Bilateral_filter]

bilateral smoothing: See bilateral filtering.

bilateral symmetry: A constrained property of symmetry such that a given object (or 2D shape) is divisible into symmetrical halves on either side of a single unique line or plane. A common property of many biological organisms, mammals and plants: [Tyl96]

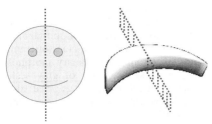

Axes of bilateral symmetry

bilinear surface interpolation: To determine the value of a function $f(x, y)$ at an arbitrary location (x, y), of which only discrete samples $f_{ij} = \{f(x_i, y_j)\}_{i=1\,j=1}^{n\;\;\;m}$ are available. The samples are arranged on a 2D grid, so the value at point (x, y) is interpolated from the values at the four surrounding points. In the diagram below, $f_{\text{bilinear}}(x, y) =$

$$\frac{A + B}{(d_1 + \bar{d}_1)(d_2 + \bar{d}_2)}$$

where

$$A = d_1 d_2 f_{11} + \bar{d}_1 d_2 f_{21}$$

$$B = d_1 \bar{d}_2 f_{12} + \bar{d}_1 \bar{d}_2 f_{22}$$

The gray lines offer an easy *aide memoire*: each function value f_{ij} is multiplied by the two closest d values: [TV98:8.4.2]

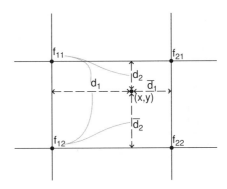

bilinear transform: In image geometry, a spatial non-affine transformation characterized by a pixel-wise mapping where the transformed pixel coordinate, (x', y'), is a multiplication of two linear functions of the original pixel coordinate, (x, y). For example, $x' = a_0 + a_1 x + a_2 y + a_3 xy$, $y' = a_4 + a_5 x + a_6 y + a_7 xy$ for parameter coefficients a_0 to a_7. In general, transforms facilitate translation, rotation and warping in the pixel-wise mapping, $(x, y) \longrightarrow (x', y')$: [SB11:7.11]

bilinearity: A function of two variables x and y is bilinear if it is linear in y for fixed x and linear in x for fixed y. For example, if $\vec{x}$ and $\vec{y}$ are vectors and $\mathbf{A}$ is a matrix such that $\vec{x}^\top \mathbf{A} \vec{y}$ is defined, then the function $f(\vec{x}, \vec{y}) = \vec{x}^\top \mathbf{A} \vec{y} + \vec{x} + \vec{y}$ is bilinear in $\vec{x}$ and $\vec{y}$. [WP:Bilinear_form]

bimodal histogram: A histogram with two pronounced peaks, or modes. This is a convenient intensity histogram for determining a binarizing threshold: [RYS95]

33

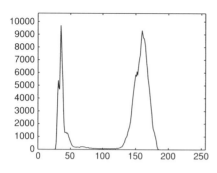

bin-picking: The problem of getting a robot manipulator equipped with vision sensors to pick parts, e.g., screws, bolts or components of a given assembly, from a random pile. A classic challenge for hand–eye robotic systems, involving at least segmentation, object recognition in clutter and pose estimation. [RK96]

binarization: See thresholding.

binary classifier: A two-class classification approach often used in explicit two-class problems or for detection problems, indicating the presence, *true*, or absence, *false* in a two-state decision. [Bar12:19.5.1]

binary decision: A two-state decision, {0, 1} or {*false*, *true*}, generally output from a binary classifier. [Bar12:19.5.1]

binary graph cut optimization: Partitioning into two discrete sets via the graph cut optimization algorithm. (See graph cut).

binary image: An image whose pixels can be in either an "on" or an "off" state, represented by the integers 1 and 0 respectively: [DH73:7.4]

binary mathematical morphology: A group of shape-based operations that can be applied to binary images, based around a few simple mathematical concepts from set theory. Common usages include noise reduction, image enhancement and image segmentation. The most basic operators, the dilate operator and the erode operator, take two pieces of data as input: the input binary image and a structuring element (also known as a kernel). Virtually all other mathematical morphology operators can be defined in terms of combinations of erosion and dilation along with set operators such as intersection and union. Some of the more important are the open operator, the close operator and skeletonization. Binary morphology is a special case of gray scale mathematical morphology. See also mathematical morphology operation. [SQ04:7.1]

binary moment: Given a binary image $B(i, j)$, there is an infinite family of moments indexed by the integer values p and q. The pqth moment is given by $m_{pq} = \sum_i \sum_j i^p j^q B(i, j)$. [KH90]

binary noise reduction: A method of removing salt-and-pepper noise from binary images. For example, a point could have its value set to the median value of its eight neighbors. [Pet95]

binary object recognition: Model-based techniques and algorithms used in object recognition from binary images. [RHBL07]

binary operation: An operation, such as the pixel subtraction operator, that takes two images as inputs. [SOS00:2.3]

binary region skeleton: See skeleton.

binocular: A system that has two cameras looking at the same scene simultaneously usually from a similar viewpoint. See also stereo vision. [TV98:7.1]

binocular stereo: A method of deriving depth information from a pair of calibrated cameras set at some distance apart and pointing in approximately the same direction. Depth information comes from the parallax between the two images and relies on being able to derive the same feature in both images. [JKS95:12.6]

binocular tracking: A method of tracking objects or features in 3D using binocular stereo. [BS99]

biometric feature: A feature with properties that can be used for identity verification of individuals. e.g., features used in gait analysis, face recognition and fingerprint identification [NA05:3.5.5]

biometrics: The science of discriminating individuals from accurate measurement of their physical features, such as retinal lines, finger lengths, fingerprints, voice characteristics and facial features. [WP:Biometrics]

bipartite matching: Graph matching technique often applied in model-based vision to match observations with models or stereo matching to solve the correspondence problem. Assume a set V of nodes partitioned into two non-intersecting subsets V^1 and V^2. In other words, $V = V^1 \cup V^2$ and $V^1 \cap V^2 = 0$. The only arcs E in the graph lie between the two subsets, i.e., $E \subset \{V^1 \times V^2\} \cup \{V^2 \times V^1\}$. This is the bipartite graph. The bipartite matching problem is to find a maximal set of nodes from the two subsets connected by arcs such that each node is connected by exactly one arc to a node in the other subset. One maximal matching in the graph below, with sets $V^1 = \{A, B, C\}$ and $V^2 = \{X, Y\}$, is pairs (A, Y) and (C, X). The selected arcs are solid and other arcs are dashed: [WP:Matching_(graph_theory)#Maximum_matchings_in_bipartite_graphs]

V^1 V^2

bit map: An image with one bit per pixel. [JKS95:3.3.1]

bit-plane encoding: An image compression technique where the image is broken into bit planes and run length coding is applied to each plane. To get the bit planes of an eight-bit gray scale image, the picture has a Boolean AND operator applied with the binary value corresponding to the desired plane. For example, ANDing the image with 00010000 gives the fifth bit plane. [Jai89:11.2]

bitangent: See curve bitangent. [WP: Bitangent]

bitshift operator: The bitshift operator shifts the binary representation of each pixel to the left or right by a set number of bit positions. Shifting 01010110 right by two bits gives 00010101. The bitshift operator is a computationally cheap method of dividing or multiplying an image by a power of two. A shift of n positions is a multiplication or division by 2^n. [WP:Bitwise_operation#Bit_shifts]

bivariate time-series: A data set with two variables varying temporally (i.e., over time) sampled in unison.

black body radiation: The electromagnetic radiation emitted by a black body object (an opaque, non-reflective material object) held at constant, uniform temperature (e.g., a bulb filament or coating in an artificial light source). The spectrum of the radiation emitted (i.e., the color of the light) is dependent only on the temperature of the body and increases in intensity over the color range from dull red to brilliant blue-white (through the visible portion of the electromagnetic spectrum) as temperature increases. The name black body refers to the visual appearance of such objects at room temperature. [FP03:6.1.2]

blade edge: A surface orientation discontinuity where a fold edge is seen against the background with the other side of the fold: [BB82:Ch. 9]

Blade Edges **Fold Edges**

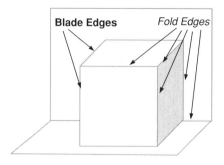

blanking: Clearing a CRT or video device. The vertical blanking interval (VBI) in television transmission is used to carry data other than audio and video. [WP:Blanking_(video)]

blending operator: An image processing operator that creates a third image C by a weighted combination of the input images A and B. In other words, $C(i, j) = \alpha A(i, j) + \beta B(i, j)$ for two scalar weights α and β. Usually, $\alpha + \beta = 1$. The results of some process can be illustrated by blending the original and result images. In this figure, the blending adds a detected boundary to the original image: [WGG99]

blind deconvolution: Performing image deconvolution without prior knowledge of the convolution operator that has been applied to the image (or the optical transfer function or point spread function characteristics of the camera sensor at the time of image capture). Associated with image deblur ring. [SB11:6.9]

blind image forensics: Performing digital image forensic techniques on a digital image without prior knowledge of whether the image has been manipulated (e.g., there is no underlying file security checksum or access to the original image). [NCLS06]

blob analysis: A process used in medical image analysis. There are four steps:
1. Derive optimum foreground/background threshold to segment objects from their background.
2. Binarize the images by applying a thresholding operation.
3. Perform region growing and assign a label to each discrete group (blob) of connected pixels.
4. Extract physical measurements from the blobs.
[WP:Blob_detection]

blob extraction: Part of blob analysis. See connected component labeling. [WP:Connected-component_labeling]

block coding: A class of signal coding techniques. The input signal is partitioned into fixed-size blocks, and each block is transmitted after translation to a smaller (for image-compression) or larger (for error-correction) block size. [Jai89:11.1]

blocking artifact: An artifact resulting from the use of a block coding compression scheme caused by information loss resulting either from the use of lossy compression or from an error in data transmission (data transmission errors are more common in video compression for streaming video). See also compression noise: [Lan12:Compression]

Original | Blocking Artefacts (compression)

blocks world: The simplified problem domain in which much early research into artificial intelligence and computer vision was carried out. The essential feature of the blocks world is the restriction of analysis to simplified geometric objects such as polyhedra and the assumption that geometric descriptions, such as image edges, can easily be recovered from the image: [Nal93:Ch. 4]

blooming: Too much light entering a digital optical system causes saturation of the CCD pixels so that charge over-spills into surrounding elements giving vertical or horizontal streaking in the image (depending on the orientation of the CCD). [CS09:3.3.5]

Blum's medial axis: See medial axis transform.

blur: A measure of sharpness in an image. Blurring can arise from a variety of causes including: the sensor being defocus ed; noise in the environment or image capture process; motion of the target or sensor; an image-processing operation: [WP: Blur]

blur estimation: Estimation of the point spread function or optical transfer function for the process of image deblur ring by deconvolution. See also image restoration. [SB11:6.9]

body part tracking: The tracking of human body parts in a video sequence, often used for human pose estimation. [PA06]

boosting: An ensemble learning approach for the combination of multiple weak learners (classifiers) where each classifier has a weight proportional to its performance on the training set. The base (weak) classifiers are trained in sequence such that the nth classifier is trained over a training set re-weighted to give greater emphasis to training examples upon which the previous $(n-1)$ classifiers performed poorly (i.e., AdaBoost). Contrasts with bagging, in which all weak learners have equal weight in the ensemble and are trained independently. [Bis06:14.3]

border detection: See boundary detection.

border tracing: Given a pre-labeled (or segmented) image, the border is the inner layer of each region's connected pixel set. It can be traced using a simple 8-connective or 4-connective stepping procedure in a 3×3 neighborhood. [Nev82:8.1.4]

bottom-up: An approach that starts from the smallest entities within a given topology (e.g., image pixels, mesh vertexes or low-level features) and performs agglomerative clustering, general global structure extraction or feature detection by successive merging of scene information in a hierarchical methodology targeting general image understanding. Opposite of top-down. In computer vision, describes algorithms that use the data to generate hypotheses at a low level, that are refined as the algorithm proceeds. [Sch89:Ch. 6]

bottom-up event detection: An event detection approach that follows a bottom-up methodology. Within this context one could use motion features, action units or atomic actions as the lowest level in the hierarchy. See also behavior hierarchy.

bottom-up segmentation: A segmentation approach that involves agglomerative clustering. See bottom-up. [BU08]

boundary: A general term for the lower dimensional structure that separates two objects, such as the curve between neighboring surfaces or the surface between neighboring volumes. [JKS95:2.5.1]

boundary description: Functional, geometry-based or set-theoretic description of a region boundary. For an example, see chain code. [Dav90:7.8]

boundary detection: An image-processing algorithm that finds and labels the edge pixels between two neighboring image segments after segmentation. The boundary represents physical discontinuities in the scene, e.g., changes in color, depth, shape or texture. [Nev82:7.1]

boundary grouping: An image-processing algorithm that attempts to complete a fully connected image-segment boundary from many broken pieces. A boundary might be broken because it is commonplace for sharp transitions in property values to appear in the image as slow transitions; it might sometimes disappear for reasons including: noise, blur, digitization artifacts, poor lighting and surface irregularities. [LP90]

boundary length: The length of the boundary of an object. See also perimeter. [WP:Perimeter]

boundary matching: See curve matching.

boundary property: Characteristic of a boundary, such as arc length or curvature. [KR88]

boundary representation: See boundary description and B-rep.

boundary-region fusion: A region growing segmentation approach where two adjacent regions are merged when their characteristics are close enough to pass some similarity test. The candidate neighborhood for testing similarity can be the pixels lying near the shared region boundary. [WP:Region_growing]

boundary segmentation: See curve segmentation.

bounding box: The smallest rectangular prism that completely encloses an object or a set of points. The ratio of the lengths of the box sides is often used as a classification metric

in model-based recognition. [WP: Minimum_bounding_box]

box filter: An alternative name for the mean filter. The name "box" derives from the use of a local neighborhood in which all of the pixels have equal weight (i.e., $\frac{1}{n^2}$ for an $n \times n$ neighborhood). [Dav90:Ch. 3]

BRDF: See bidirectional reflectance distribution function. [WP: Bidirectional_reflectance_distribution_function]

breakpoint detection: See curve segmentation.

breast scan analysis: See mammogram analysis.

Brewster's angle: When light reflects from a dielectric surface it is polarized perpendicularly to the surface normal. The degree of polarization depends on the incident angle and the refractive indices of the air and reflective medium. The angle of maximum polarization is called Brewster's angle and is given by

$$\theta_B = tan^{-1}\left(\frac{n_1}{n_2}\right)$$

where n_1 and n_2 are the refractive indices of the two materials. [Hec87:8.6]

brightness: The quantity of radiation reaching a detector after incidence on a surface. Often measured in lux or ANSI lumens. When translated into an image, the values are scaled to fit the bit patterns available. For example, if an eight-bit byte is used, the maximum value is 255. See also luminance. [DH73:7.2]

brightness adjustment: Increase or decrease in the luminance of an image. To decrease, one can linearly interpolate between the image and a pure black image. To increase, one can linearly extrapolate between a black image and the target. The extrapolation function is

$$v = (1 - \alpha) * i_0 + \alpha * i_1$$

where α is the blending factor (often between 0 and 1), v is the output pixel value and i_0 and i_1 are the corresponding image and black pixels. See also gamma correction and contrast enhancement. [WP:Gamma_correction]

brightness constancy: 1) The mechanism of the human visual system that stabilizes relative shifts in object brightness caused by constantly varying illumination in the environment such that objects always appear with the same lightness. 2) The assumption made in a computer vision approach that object brightness is constant despite varying illumination in the environment. See also color constancy, illumination constancy. In this figure, the illumination varies in intensity: [Gol10]

Varying illumination Intensity

broadcast video: Refers to video of a content type, image quality and encoding format (see video transmission format) targeted at either analog or digital transmission to a mass audience. Often uses video deinterlacing, lossy compression and MPEG encoding. [Sze10:8.4.3]

Brodatz texture: A well-known set of texture images often used for testing texture-related algorithms. [NA05:8.2]

building detection: A general term for a specific, model-based set of algorithms for finding buildings in data. The range of data used is large, encompassing stereo images, range images, and aerial and ground-level photographs. [LN98]

bundle adjustment: An algorithm used to optimally determine the three-dimensional coordinates of points and camera positions from two-dimensional image measurements. This is done by minimizing some cost function that includes the model fitting error and the camera variations. The *bundles* are the light rays between detected 3D features and each camera center. The bundles are iteratively adjusted (with respect to both camera centers and feature positions). [FP03:13.4.2]

burn-in: 1) A phenomenon of early tube-based cameras and monitors where, if the same image was presented for long periods of time, it became permanently burnt into the phosphorescent layer. Since the advent of modern monitors in the 1980s, this no longer happens. 2) The practice of shipping only electronic components that have been tested for long periods, in the hope that any defects will manifest themselves early in the component's life (e.g., 72 hours of typical use). 3) The practice of discarding the first several samples of a Markov chain Monte Carlo process in the hope that a very low-probability starting point will converge to a high-probability point before beginning to output samples. [NA05:1.4.1]

butterfly filter: A linear filter designed to respond to "butterfly" patterns in images. A small butterfly filter convolution kernel is

$$\begin{array}{ccc} 0 & -2 & 0 \\ 1 & 2 & 1 \\ 0 & -2 & 0 \end{array}$$

It is often used in conjunction with the Hough transform for finding peaks in the Hough feature space, particularly when searching for lines. The line parameter values of (p, θ) will generally give a butterfly shape with a peak at the approximate correct values. [LB87]

C

CAD: See computer-aided design. [WP: Computer-aided_design]

calculus of variations: See variational approach.

calibration object: An object or small scene with easily locatable features used for camera calibration: [HZ00:7.5.2]

camera: 1) The physical device used to acquire images.
2) The mathematical representation of the physical device and its characteristics, such as position and calibration.
3) A class of mathematical models of the projection from 3D to 2D, such as affine-, orthographic- or pinhole camera. [NA05:1.4.1]

camera calibration: Methods for determining the position and orientation of cameras and range sensors in a scene and relating them to scene coordinates. There are essentially four problems in calibration:

- *interior orientation*: determining the internal camera geometry, including its principal point, focal length and lens distortion;
- *exterior orientation*: determining the orientation and position of the camera with respect to some absolute coordinate system;
- *absolute orientation*: determining the transformation between two coordinate systems, and the position and orientation of the sensor in the absolute coordinate system from the calibration points;
- *relative orientation*: determining the relative position and orientation between two cameras from projections of calibration points in the scene.

These are classic problems in the field of photogrammetry. [FP03:Ch. 3]

camera connectivity matrix: An $n \times n$ matrix modeling relative camera view connectivity over a multi-camera topology based on the strength of multi-camera behavior correlation (or activity correlation) between any two cameras in the set. See also camera topology inference. [GX11:13.3]

camera coordinates: 1) A viewer-centered representation relative to the camera. The camera coordinate system is positioned and oriented relative to the scene coordinate system and this relationship is determined by camera calibration.
2) An image coordinate system that places the camera's principal point at the origin (0, 0), with unit aspect ratio and zero skew. The focal length in camera coordinates may or may not equal 1. If image coordinates are such that

---

Dictionary of Computer Vision and Image Processing, Second Edition.
R. B. Fisher, T. P. Breckon, K. Dawson-Howe, A. Fitzgibbon, C. Robertson, E. Trucco and C. K. I. Williams.
© 2014 John Wiley & Sons, Ltd. Published 2014 by John Wiley & Sons, Ltd.

the 3×4 projection matrix is of the form

$$\begin{bmatrix} f & 0 & 0 \\ 0 & f & 0 \\ 0 & 0 & 1 \end{bmatrix} [\mathbf{R} \mid \vec{t}]$$

then the image and camera coordinate systems are identical. [HZ00:5.1]

camera geometry: The physical geometry of a camera system. See also camera model. [Sch89:Ch. 2]

camera lucida: A (passive) optical projection device used by artists (or scientific illustrators) that projects a view of the scene onto the page, under a perspective projection, such that it can be traced. Pre-dates modern photography and is still used in some photogrammetry contexts: [HA87]

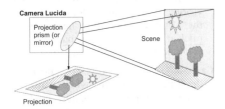

camera model: A mathematical model of the projection from 3D (real-world) space to the camera image plane. For example see pinhole camera model. [Sch89:Ch. 2]

camera motion compensation: See sensor motion compensation.

camera motion estimation: See sensor motion estimation. [WP:Egomotion]

camera pose: The location and orientation of the camera in a given frame of reference. See pose. [Sze10:Ch. 7]

camera position estimation: Estimation of the optical position of the camera relative to the scene or observed structure. This generally consists of six degrees of freedom (three for rotation and three for translation). It is often a component of camera calibration. Camera position is sometimes called the extrinsic parameters of the camera. Multiple camera positions may

be estimated simultaneously with the reconstruction of 3D scene structure in structure and motion recovery algorithms. [SD03]

camera topology inference: The automatic topology inference of the relative positions and field of view overlap (if any) of a set of cameras in a multi-camera system based on temporal evaluation of scene features, target tracking information or higher level multi-camera behavior correlation from each camera view. [GX11:Ch. 13]

Canny edge detector: The first of the modern edge detectors. It took account of the trade-off between sensitivity of edge detection and accuracy of edge localization. The edge detector consists of four stages:

1. Gaussian smoothing to reduce noise and remove small details;
2. gradient magnitude and direction calculation;
3. non-maximal suppression of smaller gradients by larger ones to focus edge localization;
4. gradient magnitude thresholding and linking that uses hysteresis to start linking at strong edge positions and also to track weaker edges.

The figure shows an example of the edge detection results: [JKS95:5.6.1]

canonical configuration: A stereo camera configuration in which the optical axes of the cameras are parallel, the baselines are parallel to the image planes and the horizontal axes of the image planes are parallel. This results in epipolar lines that are parallel to the horizontal axes, hence simplifying the search for correspondences: [Che90]

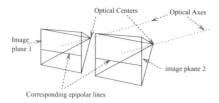

Optical Centers   Optical Axes

Image plane 1

image pkane 2

Corresponding epipolar lines

canonical correlation analysis (CCA): With two vector-valued random variables $\vec{x}$ and $\vec{y}$, the goal of CCA is to get an insight into the (linear) relationships between the two sets of variables. This is achieved by finding linear combinations $u = \vec{a}^\top \vec{x}$ and $v = \vec{b}^\top \vec{y}$ so that the cross correlation between u and v is maximized. The variables u and v are the first pair of canonical variables. The second pair of canonical variables is obtained by maximizing the same correlation, subject to the constraint that they are uncorrelated with the first pair of canonical variables; this process may be continued up to the minimum dimensionality of $\vec{x}$ and $\vec{y}$. In practice, the canonical correlation vectors are obtained via eigenvector computations. See also kernel canonical correlation analysis [MKB79:Ch. 10]

canonical direction: The simplest, most obvious, normal (given prior environment or domain knowledge) or shortest magnitude direction within the context used. For example, the canonical direction of travel, implied from the motion field, is forward. [BPNG99:Ch. 3]

canonical factor: The base vectors identified in canonical correlation analysis, such that the correlation between the projection of the two multidimensional variables upon which CCA is being performed onto these canonical factors (vectors) are mutually maximised. [GX11:5.4.2]

canonical variate: The magnitude of the maximized projection onto the canonical factor in canonical correlation analysis. [GX11:5.4.2]

capsule endoscopy: An endoscope technique, for examination of the human digestive tract for medical diagnosis, that uses a small un-tethered camera that is the size and shape of a pharmaceutical pill. The capsule is swallowed by the patient and records images of the gastrointestinal tract including the small intestine which is difficult to image via traditional tethered endoscopy approaches. Images are transmitted from the capsule via wireless data transmission and the capsule is recovered naturally when passed by the patient. [SSM06]

cardiac gated dynamic SPECT: A single photon emission computed tomography (SPECT) technique for facilitating cardiac image analysis whereby the timing of a sequence of image acquisition is dictated (i.e., gated) from an electrocardiogram (heart monitor) such that the SPECT images show the heart over a full contraction cycle. [JYW05]

cardiac image analysis: Techniques involving the development of 3D vision algorithms for tracking the motion of the heart from nuclear magnetic resonance and echocardiograph images. [Par02]

Cartesian coordinates: A position description system where an n-dimensional point, $\vec{P}$, is described by exactly n coordinates with respect to n linearly independent and often orthonormal vectors, known as axes: [WP:Cartesian_coordinate_system]

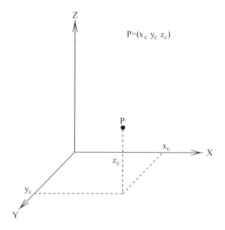

cartography: The study of maps and map-building. Automated cartography is the development of algorithms that reduce the manual effort in map building. [WP:Cartography]

cascaded Hough transform: An application of several successive Hough transforms, with the output of one transform used as input to the next. [TGPM98]

cascaded learning: A supervised learning technique whereby a binary classifier is formed by successive selection of the best performing weak classifier (weak learner) from a large set. This is initially performed using a variant of boosting over the training set and then over the examples that the previously selected classifiers mis-classified. This selected set of weak learners is then ordered (by order of training performance) in a pass-through cascade to classify unseen examples. Commonly used for object detection (e.g., faces): [Sze10:14.1] For example:

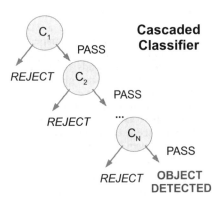

cascading Gaussians: A term referring to the fact that the convolution of a Gaussian with itself is another Gaussian. [JKS95:4.5.4]

cast shadow: A shadow thrown by an object on another object. See also attached shadow. [FP03:5.3.1]

CAT: See X-ray CAT.

catadioptric optics: The general approach of using mirrors in combination with conventional imaging systems to get wide viewing angles (180°). It is desirable that a catadioptric system has a single viewpoint because it permits the generation

of geometrically correct perspective images from the captured images. [WP:Catadioptric_system]

categorization: The subdivision of a set of elements into clearly distinct groups, or categories, defined by specific properties. Also the assignment of an element to a category or recognition of its category. [WP:Categorization]

category: A group or class used in a classification system. For example, in mean and Gaussian curvature shape classification, the local shape of a surface is classified into four main categories: planar, ellipsoidal, hyperbolic and cylindrical. Another example is the classification of observed grazing animals into one of {sheep, cow or horse}. See also categorization. [WP: Categorization]

caustic: The surface enveloping the set of camera rays, i.e., it is tangent to all rays. Often seen in reflective light models as the projection of that envelope onto another surface: [SRT11:3.4.6]

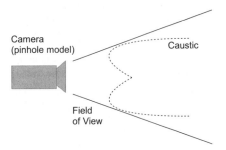

CAVE: A recursive acronym for Cave Audio-Visual Experience – an immersive audio-visual environment comprising of several screens surrounding the viewer (forming a complete 3D surround "cave" environment) with integrated head tracking to adapt content display to the viewer's head movements. [AGTL09:6.1]

CBIR: See content-based image retrieval. [WP:Content-based_image_retrieval# Query_techniques]

CCD: Charge-coupled device. A solid state device that can record the number of photons falling on it.

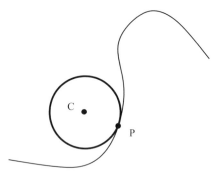

A 2D matrix of CCD elements are used, together with a lens system, in digital cameras where each pixel value in the final image corresponds to the output of one or more of the elements. [FP03:1.4.1]

CCIR camera: Camera fulfilling color conversion and pixel formation criteria laid out by the *Comité Consultatif International pour la Radio*. [Umb98:1.7.3]

cell microscopic analysis: Automated image-processing procedures for finding and analyzing different cell types from images taken by a microscope vision system. Common examples are the analysis of pre-cancerous cells or blood cells. [WP:Live_blood_analysis]

cellular array: A massively parallel computing architecture, composed of a high number of processing elements. Particularly useful in machine vision applications when a simple 1:N mapping is possible between image pixels and processing elements. See also systolic array and single instruction multiple data. [WP:Systolic_array]

center line: See medial line.

center of curvature: The center of the circle of curvature (or osculating circle) at a point $\vec{P}$ of a plane curve at which the curvature is nonzero. The circle of curvature is tangent to the curve at $\vec{P}$, has the same curvature as the curve at $\vec{P}$, and lies towards the concave (inner) side of the curve. The figure shows the circle and center of curvature, $\vec{C}$, of a curve at point $\vec{P}$: [FP03:19.1.1]

center of mass: The point within an object at which the force of gravity appears to act. If the object can be described by a multidimensional point set $\{\vec{x}_i\}$ containing N points, the center of mass is $\frac{1}{N} \sum_{i=0}^{N} \vec{x}_i f(\vec{x}_i)$, where $f(\vec{x}_i)$ is the value of the image (e.g., binary image or gray scale) at point $\vec{x}_i$. [JKS95:2.2.2]

center of projection: The position of the observer or camera in a 3D to 2D planar projection (e.g., perspective projection). Within a pinhole camera model this corresponds to the camera position within the global frame of reference with the center of projection occurring behind the imaging plane where all of the projection lines from the scene converge. Also known as the camera center or the optical center. [HZ00:6.1]

center-surround operator: An operator that is particularly sensitive to spot-like image features, which have higher (or lower) pixel values in the center than in the surrounding areas. The following simple convolution mask can be used for orientation-independent spot detection:

$$
\begin{array}{ccc}
-\frac{1}{8} & -\frac{1}{8} & -\frac{1}{8} \\
-\frac{1}{8} & 1 & -\frac{1}{8} \\
-\frac{1}{8} & -\frac{1}{8} & -\frac{1}{8}
\end{array}
$$

[JRW97]

central moment: An image moment that is translation invariant because the center of mass has been subtracted during the calculation. If $f(c, r)$ is the input image pixel value (binary image or gray scale) at row r and column c then the pqth central moment is $\sum_c \sum_r (c - \hat{c})^p (r - \hat{r})^q f(c, r)$ where $(\hat{c}, \hat{r})$ is the center of mass of the image. [Sch89:Ch. 6]

central projection: Defined by projection of an image on the surface of a sphere onto a tangential plane by rays from the center of the sphere. The intersection of a plane with the sphere is a "great circle". The image of the great circle under central projection is a line. Also known as the "gnomonic" projection. [Sch89:Ch. 2]

CENTRIST bag of words descriptor: A feature descriptor, akin to the seminal SIFT descriptor, specifically targeted at scene classification tasks via a bag of words classification framework. It primarily encodes the structural properties of a scene, suppressing detailed textural information, resulting in superior scene classification performance compared to contemporary feature descriptors within the same framework. [WR11]

centroid: See center of mass.

certainty representation: Any of a set of techniques for encoding the belief in a hypothesis, conclusion, calculation etc. Example representation methods are probability and fuzzy logic. [Mor88]

chain code: An efficient method for boundary representation where an arbitrary curve is represented by a sequence of small vectors of unit length in a limited set of possible directions. Depending on whether the grid has 4 connectedness or 8 connectedness, the chain code is defined as the digits from 0 to 3 or 0 to 7, assigned to the four or eight neighboring grid points counter-clockwise. For example, the string 222233000011 describes the small curve in the figure using a 4-connected coding scheme, starting from the upper right pixel: [JKS95:6.2.1]

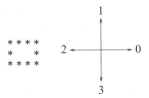

chamfer matching: A matching technique based on the comparison of contours and on the concept of chamfer distance assessing the similarity of two sets of points. It can be used for matching edge images using the distance transform. See also Hausdorff distance. To find the parameters that register a library image and a test image, the binary edge map of the test image is compared to the distance transform. Edges are detected on image 1 and the distance transform of the edge pixels is computed. The edges from image 2 are then matched. In the figure, translation and scale parameters are used: [ZRH03:2.3]

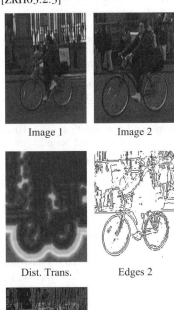

Image 1   Image 2

Dist. Trans.   Edges 2

Best Match

chamfering: See distance transform.

change detection: See motion detection.

character recognition: See optical character recognition.

character verification: A process that confirms that printed or displayed characters are within some tolerance that guarantees that they are readable by humans. Used in applications such as labeling. [PP03]

characteristic view: An approach to object representation in which an object is encoded by a set of views of the object. The views are chosen so that small changes in viewpoint do not cause large changes in appearance (e.g., a singularity event). Real objects have an unrealistic number of singularities, so practical approaches to creating characteristic views require approximations, such as only using views on a tessellated viewsphere, or only representing the viewpoints that are reasonably stable over large ranges on the viewsphere. See also aspect graph and appearance-based recognition. [WF90]

chess-board distance metric: See Manhattan distance. [WP:Chebyshev_distance]

chi-squared distribution (χ^2): The distribution of squared lengths of vectors drawn from a normal distribution. Specifically let the cumulative distribution function of the χ^2 distribution with d degrees of freedom be denoted $\chi^2(d, u)$. Then the probability that a point $\vec{x}$ drawn from a d-dimensional Gaussian distribution will have squared norm $|\vec{x}|^2$ less than a value τ is given by $\chi^2(d, \tau)$. This figure shows empirical and theoretical plots of the χ^2 probability density function with five degrees of freedom: [WP:Chi-squared_distribution]

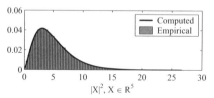

chi-squared test: A statistical test of the hypothesis that a set of sampled values has been drawn from a given distribution. See also chi-squared distribution. [WP:Chi-squared_test]

chip sensor: A CCD or other semiconductor-based, light-sensitive imaging device. [ABD+91]

chord distribution: A 2D shape description technique based on all chords in the shape (that is all pairwise segments between points on the boundary). Histograms of their lengths and orientations are computed. The values in the length histogram are invariant to rotation and scale linearly with the size of object. The orientation histogram values are invariant to scale and shifts. [YJ84]

chroma: The color portion of a video signal that includes hue and saturation, requiring luminance to make it visible. It is also referred to as chrominance. [WP:Chroma]

chroma keying: The separation of a given object or background color-based on its chrominance value alone. Often used in media production to separate a motion silhouette from a controlled studio background to allow the insertion of an artificial background: [MNTT12:2.2.6]

chromatic aberration: A focusing problem where light of different wavelengths (color) is refracted by different amounts and consequently images at different places. As blue light is refracted more than red light, objects may be imaged with color fringes at places where there are strong changes in lightness. [FP03:1.2.3]

chromaticity diagram: A 2D slice of a 3D color space. The CIE 1931 chromaticity diagram is the slice

46

through the *xyz* color space of the CIE L*A*B* model where $x + y + z = 1$. This slice is shown in the figure. The color gamut of standard 0-1 RGB values in this model is the bright triangle in the center of the horseshoe-like shape. Points outside the triangle have had their saturations truncated. See also CIE chromaticity coordinates. [WP:CIE_xyY#CIE_xy_chromaticity_ diagram_and_the_CIE_xyY_color_ space]

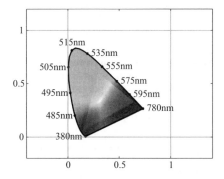

chrominance: 1) The part of a video signal that carries color.
2) One or both of the color axes in a 3D color space that distinguishes intensity and color. See also chroma. [WP: Chrominance]

chromosome analysis: Vision technique used for the diagnosis of some genetic disorders from microscope images. This usually includes sorting the chromosomes into the 23 pairs and displaying them in a standard chart. [PRS+95]

CID: Charge injection device. A type of semiconductor imaging device with a matrix of light-sensitive cells. Every pixel in a CID array can be individually addressed via electrical indexing of row and column electrodes. It is unlike a CCD because it transfers collected charge out of the pixel during readout, thus erasing the image. [BM76]

CIE chromaticity coordinates: Coordinates in the CIE color representation system with reference to three ideal standard colors X, Y and Z. Any visible color can be expressed as a weighted sum of these three ideal colors, e.g.,

$p = w_1 X + w_2 Y + w_3 Z$. The normalized values are given by

$$x = \frac{w_1}{w_1 + w_2 + w_3}$$

$$y = \frac{w_2}{w_1 + w_2 + w_3}$$

$$z = \frac{w_3}{w_1 + w_2 + w_3}$$

Since $x + y + z = 1$, we only need to know two of these values, say (x, y). These are the chromaticity coordinates. [JKS95:10.3]

CIE L*A*B* model: A color representation system based on that proposed by the *Commission Internationale de l'Eclairage* (CIE) as an international standard for color measurement. It is designed to be device-independent and perceptually uniform (i.e., the separation between two points in this space corresponds to the perceptual difference between the colors). L*A*B* color consists of a luminance, L*, and two chromatic components: A* from green to red and B* from blue to yellow. See also CIE L*U*V* model. [JKS95:10.3]

CIE L*U*V* model: A color representation system where colors are represented by luminance (L*) and two chrominance components (U*V*). A given change in value in any component corresponds approximately to the same perceptual difference. See also CIE L*A*B* model. [JKS95:10.3]

circle: A curve consisting of all points on a plane lying a fixed radius *r* from the *center* point C:

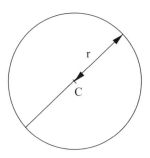

The arc defining the entire circle is known as the *circumference* and is of length $2\pi r$. The area contained inside the curve is given by $A = \pi r^2$. A circle centered at the point (h, k) has equation $(x - h)^2 + (y - k)^2 = r^2$. The circle is a special case of the ellipse. [NA05:5.4.3]

circle detection: A class of algorithms, e.g., the Hough transform, that locate the centers and radii of circles in digital images. In general images, scene circles usually appear as ellipses: [Dav90:Ch. 9]

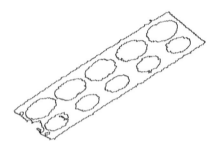

circle fitting: Deriving circle parameters from either 2D or 3D observations. As with all fitting problems, one can search the parameter space using a good metric (e.g., a Hough transform) or can solve a well-posed least-squares problem. [JKS95:6.8.4]

circular convolution: The circular convolution (c_k) of two vectors $\{x_i\}$ and $\{y_i\}$ that are of length n is defined as $c_k = \sum_{i=0}^{n-1} x_i y_j$ where $0 \le k < n$ and $j = (i - k) \bmod n$. [WP:Circular_convolution]

circularity: One measure C of the degree to which a 2D shape is similar to a circle is given by

$$C = 4\pi \left(\frac{A}{P^2} \right)$$

where C varies from 0 (non-circular) to 1 (perfectly circular). A is the object area and P is the object perimeter. [WP: Circular_definition]

city block distance: See Manhattan distance.

class separability: A measure of the separability of two or more classes based on their class conditional distributions, e.g., on the between-class scatter matrix and within-class scatter matrix (as for the Fisher linear discriminant) or on the Bhattacharyya distance. [Fuk90:Ch. 10]

classification: A general term for the assignment of a label (or class) to a structure (e.g., pixels, regions, lines etc.). Example classification problems include: labeling pixels as road, vegetation or sky; deciding whether cells are cancerous based on shape; deciding whether the observed face belongs to an allowed system user. [Dav90:1.2.1]

classifier: An algorithm assigning a class to an input pattern or data. See also classification, unsupervised learning, clustering, supervised classification and rule-based classification. [FP03:Ch. 22]

clipping: Removal or non-rendering of objects that do not coincide with the display area. [NA05:3.3.1]

clique: A fully connected subgraph of a graph, G. In a fully connected graph, every vertex is a neighbor of all others. The figure shows a clique with five nodes:

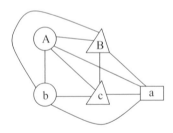

(There are other cliques in the graph with fewer nodes, e.g., ABac with four nodes etc.) [WP: Clique_(graph_theory)]

close operator: The application of two binary morphology operators (the dilate operator followed by the erode operator), which has the effect of filling small holes in an image. The figure shows the result of closing with a mask 22 pixels in diameter: [JKS95:2.6]

closed-circuit television (CCTV): A video capture system installed in a specific environment, with limited viewer access, for the purposes of visual surveillance. [GS05]

closed set recognition: Performing recognition over a closed set of entities such that the query object must be in the *a priori* set. Commonly used in biometrics where, e.g., an individual is recognized from a known set in a face recognition database. [Wec06:7.7]

closed world: The assumption that a complete taxonomy of scene objects is known and that each pixel should be explained as belonging to one of the scene objects. A specialization of the general artificial intelligence closed-world assumption, i.e., that everything that is not known to be true is false. Here interpreted as every pixel not explained as belonging to a known scene object is thus not part of a (relevant) scene object. [IB95]

clump splitting: In some classes of images a clump of objects may be detected or isolated, e.g., clumps of cells in biological images. Clump splitting seeks segmentation of the multiple objects from the clump.

clustering: 1) Identifying the subsets of a set of data points $\{\vec{x}_i\}$ based on some property, such as proximity.
2) Grouping together image regions or pixels into larger, homogeneous regions sharing some property. See also: agglomerative clustering, divisive clustering, graph theoretic clustering, hierarchical clustering, k-means clustering, non-parametric clustering, spectral clustering and squared error clustering. [FP03:14.1.2]

clutter: A generic term for unmodeled or uninteresting elements in an image. For example, a face detector generally has a model for faces and other objects are regarded as clutter. The background of an image is often expected to include clutter. Loosely speaking, clutter is more structured than noise. [FP03:18.2.1]

CMOS: Complementary metal-oxide semiconductor. A technology used in making image sensors and other computer chips. [NA05:1.4.1]

CMY: See CMYK.

CMYB: See CMYK.

CMYK: Cyan, magenta, yellow and black color model. It is a subtractive model where colors are absorbed by a medium, e.g., pigments in paints. Where the RGB color model adds hues to black to generate a particular color, the CMYK model subtracts from white. Red, green and blue are secondary colors in this model: [Gal90:3.7]

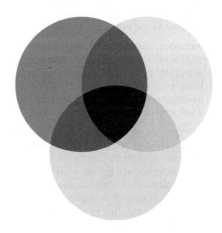

coarse-to-fine processing: Multi-scale algorithm application that begins by processing at a large, or coarse, level and then, iteratively, processes to a small, or fine, level. Importantly, results from each level must be propagated to ensure a good final result. It is used for computing, e.g., optical flow. [FP03:7.7.2]

coaxial illumination: Front lighting with the illumination path running along the imaging optical axis. An advantage of this technique is that there are no visible shadows or direct

49

specularities from the camera's viewpoint: [ZS93]

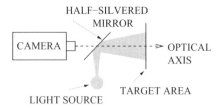

HALF–SILVERED MIRROR

CAMERA

OPTICAL AXIS

LIGHT SOURCE

TARGET AREA

codebook: The set of identified code-words resulting from feature descriptor clustering when using a bag of words classification approach. [Sze10:14.4.3]

codeword: See codebook and bag of features.

cognitive vision: A part of computer vision focusing techniques for recognition and categorization of objects, structures and events, learning and knowledge representation, control and visual attention. [CN06:Ch. 4]

coherence detection: Stereo vision technique where two images are searched for maximal patch correlations to generate features. It relies on having a good correlation measure and a suitably chosen patch size. [Hen97]

coherence scale/volume: In 2D or 3D confocal microscopy, the region or area in which the light waves are in coherence (e.g., in synchronization). Beyond a certain distance or time synchronization differences arise. The coherence time is the time interval during which light waves traveling over a certain distance (the coherence length) maintains a phase difference of less than π. The coherence surface is the spatial region over which the phase difference of the optical field is less than π. It follows that the coherence volume is the product of the coherence length and the coherence surface. Interference between superimposed coherent waves are only visible in this volume. [Paw06:Ch. 5]

coherent fiber optics: Many fiber-optic elements bound into a single cable component with the individual fiber

spatial positions aligned, so that it can be used to transmit images. [Oko82]

coherent light: Light, e.g., generated by a laser, in which the emitted light waves have the same wavelength and are in phase. Such light waves can remain focused over long distances. [WP:Collimated_light]

coincidental alignment: When two structures seem to be related, but in fact the structures are independent or the alignment is just a consequence of being in some special viewpoint. Examples are the collinearity of random edges or coplanarity of surfaces, or object corners being nearby. See also non-accidentalness. [HN00]

collimate: To align the optics of a vision system, especially those in a telescopic system. [WP:Collimated_light]

collimated lighting: A special form of structured light (e.g., directional back lighting). A collimator produces light in which all the rays are parallel:

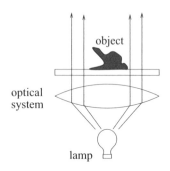

camera

object

optical system

lamp

It is used to produce well-defined shadows that can be cast directly onto a sensor or an object. [KKK03]

collinearity: The property of lying along the same straight line. [HZ00:1.3]

collineation: See projective transformation.

color: Color is both a physical and a psychological phenomenon. Physically, color refers to the nature of an object texture that allows it to reflect or absorb particular parts of the light incident on it. See also reflectance. The psychological aspect is characterized by the visual sensation experienced when light of a particular frequency or wavelength is incident on the retina. The key paradox here concerns why light of slightly different wavelengths should be be so perceptually different (e.g., red and blue). [Hec87:4.4]

color-based database indexing: See color-based image retrieval. [WP:Content-based_image_retrieval# Color]

color-based image retrieval: An example of the more general image database indexing process, where one of the main indices into the image database comes from color samples, the color distribution from a sample image, or a set of text color terms (e.g., "red"). [WP:Content-based_image_retrieval# Color]

color clustering: See color image segmentation.

color constancy: The ability of a vision system to assign a color description to an object that is independent of the lighting environment. This allows the system to recognize objects under many different lighting conditions. The human vision system does this automatically, but most machine vision systems cannot. For example, humans observing a red object in a cluttered scene under a blue light will still see the object as red. A machine vision system might see it as a very dark blue. [WP:Color_constancy]

color co-occurrence matrix: A matrix (actually a histogram) whose elements represent the sum of color values existing in a given image in a sequence, at a certain pixel position relative to another color existing at a different position in the image. See also co-occurrence matrix. [WP:Co-occurrence_matrix]

color correction: 1) Adjustment of colors to achieve color constancy. 2) Any change to the colors of an image. See also gamma correction. [WP:Color_correction]

color differential invariant: A type of differential invariant based on color information, such as $\frac{\nabla R \cdot \nabla G}{||\nabla R|| ||\nabla G||}$, which has the same value invariant to translation, rotation and variations in uniform illumination. [MGD98]

color doppler: A method for noninvasively imaging blood flow through the heart or other body parts by displaying flow data on a two-dimensional echocardiographic image. Blood flow in different directions is displayed in different colors. [HNH+87]

color edge detection: The process of edge detection in color images. A simple approach combines (e.g., by addition) the edge strengths of the individual RGB color planes. [Kos95]

color efficiency: A trade-off that is made with lighting systems, where conflicting design constraints require energy-efficient production of light while simultaneously producing a sufficiently broad spectrum illumination that the colors look natural. An obvious example of a skewed trade-off is with low pressure sodium street lighting. This is energy efficient but has poor color appearance. [Sel07]

color feature: A feature that incorporates color information within its description of the image or local region of interest. [GGWG12:Ch. 14]

color gamut: The subset of all possible colors that a particular display device (CRT, LCD, printer) can display. Physical differences in how various devices produce colors mean each scanner, display and printer has a different gamut, or range, of colors that it can represent. The RGB color gamut can only display approximately 70% of the colors that can be perceived. The CMYK color gamut is much smaller, reproducing about 20% of perceivable colors. The color gamut achieved with premixed inks (such as the Pantone

Matching System) is also smaller than the RGB gamut. [WP:Gamut]

color grading: The process of altering or enhancing color in video or image content. Commonly applied to older video content, pre-dating modern color quality techniques, recorded to analog media prior to re-broadcast or re-release for viewing on contemporary hardware. See also color correction, image enhancement. [Hur10:Introduction]

color halftoning: See dithering. [WP: Halftone#Multiple_screens_and_color_halftoning]

color histogram matching: Used in color indexing where the similarity measure is the distance between color histograms of two images, e.g., by using the Kullback–Leibler divergence or Bhattacharyya distance. [HSE+95]

color HOG: A color extension to the histogram of oriented gradients descriptor calculating gradients in a given color space (based on color similarity) in place of the original gray scale gradient approach.

color image: An image where each element (pixel) is a tuple of values from a set of color bases. [Umb98:1.7.3]

color image restoration: See image restoration.

color image segmentation: Segmenting a color image into homogeneous regions based on some similarity criteria. The figure shows boundaries around typical regions: [DMS99]

color indexing: Using color information, e.g., color histograms, for image database indexing. A key issue is varying illumination. It is possible to use ratios of colors from neighboring locations to obtain illumination invariance. [WP:Color_index]

color layout descriptor: Part of the compact set of MPEG-7 descriptors designed to capture the global, spatial color distribution of an image. This descriptor is produced by spatially dividing the image into 64 blocks (8 × 8), regardless of size, from which a representative color (e.g., the mean color) is extracted. This set of 64 colors, transformed to YCrCb color space, is then represented using the discrete cosine transform coefficients of each of the YCrCb color channels. [ISO02]

color matching: The phenomenon of trichromacy means any color stimulus can be matched by a mixture of the three primary stimuli. Color matching is expressed as :

$$C = R\mathbf{R} + G\mathbf{G} + B\mathbf{B}$$

where a color stimulus C is matched by R units of primary stimulus $\mathbf{R}$ mixed with G units of primary stimulus $\mathbf{G}$ and B units of primary stimulus $\mathbf{B}$. [Win05:2.5.1]

color mixture model: A mixture model based on distributions in some color representation system that specifies both the color groups in a model as well as their relationships to each other. The conditional probability of an observed pixel $\vec{x}_i$ belonging to an object O is modeled as a mixture with K components. [JR99]

color models: See color representation system. [WP:Color_model]

color moment: A color image description based on histogram moments of each color channel, e.g., the mean, variance and skewness of the histograms. [MMG99]

color normalization: Techniques for normalizing the distribution of color values in a color image, so that the image description is invariant to illumination. One simple method for producing invariance to lightness is to use vectors of unit length for color entries, rather than coordinates in the color representation system. [WP: Color_normalization]

color quantization: The quantization (i.e., discretization) of the image signal into a number of bins each representing a specific level of intensity (i.e., pixel values). Occurs at image capture, at the CCD or CMOS sensor level, within the camera. For RGB color image capture this is facilitated using the Bayer pattern on the sensor itself. Also performed as a secondary process, re-quantization for color reduction or color re-mapping:

256 gray (color) quantisation levels   16 gray (color) quantisation levels

Coarser quantization allows image compression with fewer bits. [SB11:2.3.2]

color re-mapping: An image transformation where each original color is replaced by another color from a colormap. If the image has indexed colors, this can be a very fast operation and can provide special graphical effects for very low processing overhead: [WAF+98]

Original   Color remapped

color representation system: A 2D or 3D space used to represent a set of absolute color coordinates. RGB and CIE L*U*V* model are examples of such spaces. [WP: List_of_color_spaces_and_their_uses]

color similarity: The relative difference between two color values in a given color space representation. See also similarity metric. Within perceptual psychology, the perceived color difference by human subjects under natural or controlled conditions. See also brightness constancy. [BWKW98:Ch. 2]

color space: See color representation system. [WP:Color_space]

color structure descriptor: Part of the compact set of MPEG-7 descriptors designed to capture the structure of the image color content. Uses an extension to the concept of a color histogram: a structuring element is used to produce a histogram based on local color occurrence within the local neighborhood (under the structuring element) instead of just at each individual pixel. See also color layout descriptor. [ISO02]

color temperature: A scalar measure of colour. 1) The temperature of a given colour C is the temperature in kelvins at which a heated black body would emit light that is dominated by colour C. It is relevant to computer vision in that the illumination color changes the appearance of observed objects. The color temperature of incandescent lights is about 3200 kelvins and sunlight is about 5500 kelvins. 2) Photographic color temperature is the ratio of blue to red intensity. [WP: Color_temperature]

color texture: Variations (texture) in the appearance of a surface (or region, illumination etc.) arising from spatial variations in the color, reflectance or lightness of a surface. [JH98]

colorimetry: The measurement of color intensity relative to some standard. [WP:Colorimetry]

colorization: The process of adding color to a gray scale image or video content. Performed manually or via an automatic process. [Sze10:10.3.2]

combinatorial explosion: Correctly, how the computational requirements of an algorithm increase very quickly relative to the increase in the number of elements to be processed, as a consequence of having to consider all combinations of elements. For example, consider matching M model features to D data features with $D \geq M$ where each data feature can be used at most once and all model features must be matched. Then the number of possible matchings that need to be considered is $D \times (D - 1) \times (D - 2) \ldots \times (D - M + 1)$. Here, if M increases by only one, approximately D times as much matching effort is needed. Combinatorial explosion is used loosely to refer to non-combination algorithms whose effort grows rapidly with even small increases in input data sizes. [WP: Combinatorial_explosion]

compactness: A descriptor that is scale invariant, translation invariant and rotation invariant, based on the ratio $\frac{perimeter^2}{area}$. [JKS95:2.5.7]

compass edge detector: A class of edge detector based on combining the response of separate edge operators applied at several orientations. The edge response at a pixel is commonly the maximum of the responses over the several orientations. [RT99]

composite filter: Hardware or software image processing method based on a mixture of components such as noise reduction, feature detection and grouping. [WP:Composite_image_filter]

composite video: A television video transmission method created as a backward-compatible solution for the transition from black-and-white to color television. Black-and-white TV sets ignore the color component while color TV sets separate out the color information and display it with black-and-white intensity. [WP:Composite_video]

compression: See image compression.

compression noise: Noise artifacts introduced by lossy compression techniques in image storage or transmission. See also blocking artifact. [SB11:1.3.2]

compressive sensing: An efficient signal representation technique that uses a sparse representation to allow the signal to be stored and reconstructed using relatively few measurement samples. Achieved by solving an underdetermined system of linear equations in conjunction with the sparseness constraint on the original signal. Used in registration and image compression. Also denoted as "compressed sensing" "compressed sampling" or "sparse sampling". [Ela10:Ch. 9]

compressive video: 1) The use of standard video compression for video transmission or storage. 2) The use of compressive sensing techniques for video transmission or storage. [SSC08]

computational camera: A digital camera that uses controllable optics and computational decoding built into the device itself to produce new types of image, e.g., wide-field-of-view images, high-dynamic-range images, multi-spectral images and depth images. [Nay06]

computational complexity: A bound on the theoretical number of basic computational operations required to perform a given algorithm or process independent of the hardware upon which it is implemented. For example an algorithm that iterates over every pixel in a $w \times h$ dimension image (e.g., a mean filter) has computational complexity, denoted $O()$, bounded by $O(wh)$. [Mit97:7.1]

computational imaging: See computational photography and computational cameras.

computational photography: The use of image analysis and image processing techniques applied to one or more photographs to create novel images beyond the capabilities of traditional digital camera photography. See also computational cameras. [Sze10:Ch. 10]

computational symmetry: General term referring to algorithmic treatment of symmetries. See symmetry detection, bilateral symmetry, symmetric axis transform (SAT).. [LHKG10]

computational theory: An approach to computer vision algorithm description promoted by Marr. A process can be described at three levels: implementation (e.g., as a program), algorithm (e.g., as a sequence of activities) and computational theory. This third level is characterized by the assumptions behind the process, the mathematical relationship between the input and output processes and the description of the properties of the input data (e.g., assumptions of statistical distributions). The advantage claimed for this approach is that it makes explicit the essentials of the process, which can then be compared to the essentials of other processes solving the same problem. By this method, the implementation details that can confuse comparisons can be ignored. [MP79]

computational tractability: Within computational complexity theory, whether or not a given process or algorithm is feasible within a given finite number of computational operations (relating to time-scale) and resources (relating to memory or storage). Those which are not feasible are referred to as computationally intractable. [GJ79]

computational vision: See computer vision.

computed axial tomography: Also known as CAT. An X-ray procedure used in conjunction with vision techniques to build a 3D volumetric image from multiple X-ray images taken from different viewpoints. The procedure can be used to produce a series of cross sections of a selected part of the human body, that can be used for medical diagnosis. [WP:X-ray computed tomography]

computer-aided design (CAD): 1) A general term for design processes in which a computer assists the designer, e.g., in the specification and layout of components. For example, most mechanical parts are now designed by a CAD process.

2) A term used to distinguish objects designed with the assistance of a computer. [WP:Computer-aided_design]

computer vision: A broad term for the processing of image data. Every professional will have a different definition that distinguishes computer vision from machine vision, image processing or pattern recognition. The boundary is not clear, but the main issues that lead to this term being used are an emphasis on the underlying theories of optics, light and surfaces; underlying statistical, property and shape models; theory-based algorithms (in contrast to commercially exploitable algorithms); and issues related to what humans broadly relate to "understanding" as contrasted with "automation". [JKS95:1.1]

concave mirror: The type of mirror used for imaging, in which a concave surface is used to reflect light to a focus. The reflecting surface is usually rotationally symmetric about the optical or principal axis and the mirror surface can be part of a sphere, paraboloid, ellipsoid, hyperboloid or other surfaces. It is also known as a "converging mirror" because it brings light to a focus. In the case of a spherical mirror, the mirror focal point, F, is half way between the vertex and the sphere center, C: [WP: Curved_mirror#Concave_mirrors]

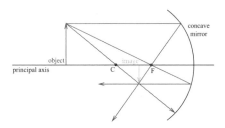

concave residue: The set difference between a shape and its convex hull. For a convex shape, the concave residue is empty. The figure shows some shapes (in black) and their concave residues (in gray): [RPLK08]

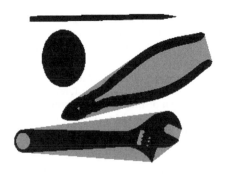

concavity: Loosely, a depression, dent, hollow or hole in a shape or surface. More precisely, a connected component of a shape's concave residue. [WP:Concave]

concavity tree: A hierarchical description of an object in the form of a tree. The concavity tree of a shape has the convex hull of its shape as the parent node and the concavity trees of its concavities as the child nodes. These are subtracted from the parent shape to give the original object. The concavity tree of a convex shape is the shape itself. The figure shows a gray shape and its concavity tree: [Dav90:6.6]

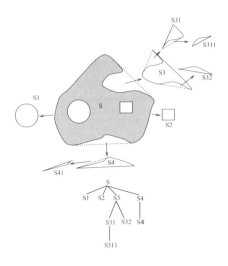

concurrence matrix: See co-occurrence matrix.

condensation tracking: Conditional density propagation tracking. The particle filter technique applied by Blake and Isard to edge tracking. A framework for object tracking with multiple simultaneous hypotheses that switches between multiple continuous autoregressive process motion models according to a discrete transition matrix. Using importance sampling it is possible to keep only the N strongest hypotheses. [IB98]

condenser lens: An optical device used to collect light over a wide angle and produce a collimated output beam. [WP:Condenser_(microscope)]

conditional density propagation: The term "condensation" (as used in condensation tracking) is a loose acronym of conditional density propagation. See also particle filter. [IB98]

conditional dilation: A binary image operation that is a combination of the dilate operator and a logical AND operator with a mask that only allows dilation into pixels that belong to the mask. This process can be described by the formula: dilate$(X, J) \cap M$, where X is the original image, M is the mask and J is the structuring element. [HHR01]

conditional distribution: A distribution of one variable given the values of one or more other variables. See also conditional probability. [WP: Conditional_probability_distribution]

conditional independence: Given three disjoint sets of variables X, Y and Z, if $p(X, Y|Z) = p(X|Z)p(Y|Z)$ then X and Y are conditionally independent given Z. A special case is if Z is the empty set: if $p(X, Y) = p(X)p(Y)$ then X and Y are independent. [Bis06:p. 372]

conditional probability: Given two disjoint sets of random variables X and Y, the conditional probability $p(X|Y)$ is defined as $p(X|Y) = \dfrac{p(X, Y)}{p(Y)}$ if $p(Y) > 0$, and is read as the distribution of X given the value of Y. [Bis06:1.2]

conditional random field (CRF): An undirected graphical model (UGM) defines a joint probability distribution over a set of <u>random variables</u>. A conditional random field defines a conditional joint distribution over one set of variables y given another set of variables x. The form of this distribution is similar to a UGM, involving a product of clique potentials. The CRF addresses the <u>supervised learning</u> task of predicting y given x. In computer vision, CRF is used in <u>dense stereo matching</u>, where the task is to estimate the <u>depth</u> of each pixel on the image grid given a pair of input images. [Mur12:Ch. 17]

conditional replenishment: A method for coding video signals, where only the portion of a video image that has changed since the previous frame is transmitted. Effective for sequences with largely stationary backgrounds, but more complex sequences require more sophisticated algorithms that perform motion compensation. [WP: MPEG-1#Motion_vectors]

cones (eye): Photoreceptive cells occurring on the <u>fovea</u> of the human eye and responsible for color vision. Perform best in bright light. Significantly fewer in number than the co-existent, dim-light performing <u>rods</u>. [Oys99]

confocal: In optics, two lens that share the same <u>focal plane</u> or <u>focal point</u> (i.e., *co*-incident *focal*). In common usage in referring to confocal <u>microscopy</u> imaging. [Pea88:Ch. 1]

conformal mapping: A function from the complex plane to itself, $f : \mathbb{C} \mapsto \mathbb{C}$, that preserves local angles. For example, the complex function $y = \sin(z) = -\frac{1}{2}i(e^{iz} - e^{-iz})$ is conformal. [WP:Conformal_map]

conic: Curves arising from the intersection of a cone with a plane (also called conic sections). This is a family of curves including the circle, ellipse, parabola and hyperbola:

circle   ellipse   parabola   hyperbola

The general form for a conic in 2D is $ax^2 + bxy + cy^2 + dx + ey + f = 0$. [JKS95:6.6]

conic fitting: The fitting of a geometric model of a <u>conic section</u> $ax^2 + bxy + cy^2 + dx + ey + f = 0$ to a set of data points $\{(x_i, y_i)\}$. Special cases include fitting circles and ellipses. [JKS95:6.6]

conic invariant: An <u>invariant</u> of a <u>conic section</u>. If the conic is in canonical form

$$ax^2 + bxy + cy^2 + dx + ey + f = 0$$

with $a^2 + b^2 + c^2 + d^2 + e^2 + f^2 = 1$, then the two invariants to <u>rotation</u> and <u>translation</u> are functions of the eigenvalues of the leading quadratic form matrix $\mathbf{A} = \begin{bmatrix} a & b \\ b & c \end{bmatrix}$. For example, the trace and determinant are invariants that are convenient to compute. For an ellipse, the eigenvalues are functions of the radii. The only invariant to affine transformation is the *class* of the conic (hyperbola, ellipse, parabola etc.). The invariant to <u>projective transformation</u> is the set of signs of the eigenvalues of the 3×3 matrix representing the conic in <u>homogeneous coordinates</u>. [Wei88]

conical mirror: A mirror in the shape of (possibly part of) a cone. It is particularly useful for robot navigation since a camera placed facing the apex of the cone aligning the cone's axis and oriented towards its base can have a full $360°$ view. Conical mirrors were used in antiquity to produce cipher images known as anamorphoses. [PM96]

conjugate direction: Optimization scheme where a set of independent directions are identified on the search space. A pair of vectors $\vec{u}$ and $\vec{v}$ are conjugate with respect to matrix $\mathbf{A}$ if $\vec{u}^\top \mathbf{A} \vec{v} = 0$. A conjugate direction optimization method is one in which a series of optimization directions are devised that are conjugate with respect to the normal matrix but do not require the normal matrix in order for them to be determined. [Has78]

conjugate gradient: A basic technique of numerical optimization in which the minimum of a numerical target function is found by iteratively descending along non-interfering conjugate directions. The conjugate gradient method does not require second derivatives and can find the optima of an N-dimensional quadric form in N iterations. By comparison, a Newton optimization method requires one iteration and gradient descent can require an arbitrarily large number of iterations. [WP: Conjugate_gradient_method]

connected component labeling: 1) A standard graph problem. Given a graph consisting of nodes and arcs, the problem is to identify nodes forming a connected set. A node is in a set if it has an arc connecting it to another node in the set.
2) Used in binary image and gray scale image processing to join together neighboring pixels into regions. There are several efficient sequential algorithms for this procedure. In this figure, the pixels in each connected component have a different color: [JKS95:2.5.2]

connectivity: See pixel connectivity.

conservative smoothing: A noise-filtering technique whose name derives from the fact that it employs a fast filtering algorithm that sacrifices noise suppression power to preserve the image detail. A simple form of conservative smoothing replaces a

pixel that is larger (or smaller) than its 8 connected neighbors by the largest (or smallest) value amongst those neighbors. This process works well with impulse noise but is not as effective with Gaussian noise. [ST99]

constrained least squares: It is sometimes useful to minimize $||A\vec{x} - \vec{b}||_2$ over some subset of possible solutions $\vec{x}$ that are predetermined. For example, one may already know the function values at certain points on the parameterized curve. This leads to an equality constrained version of the least squares problem, stated as: minimize $||A\vec{x} - \vec{b}||_2$ subject to $B\vec{x} = \vec{c}$. There are several approaches to the solution of this problem such as QR factorization and singular value decomposition. As an example, this regression technique can be useful in least squares fitting, where the plane described by $\vec{x}$ is constrained to be perpendicular to some other plane. [Hun73]

constrained matching: A generic term for recognition approaches where two objects are compared under a constraint on either or both. One example of this would be a search for moving vehicles under 20 feet in length. [CR02]

constrained optimization: Optimization of a function f subject to constraints on the parameters of the function. The general problem is to find the x that minimizes (or maximizes) $f(x)$ subject to $g(x) = 0$ and $h(x) >= 0$, where the functions f, g, h may all take vector-valued arguments and g and h may also be vector-valued, encoding multiple constraints to be satisfied. Optimization subject to equality constraints is achieved by the method of Lagrange multipliers. Optimization of a quadratic form subject to equality constraints results in a generalized eigensystem. Optimization of a general f subject to general g and h may be achieved by iterative methods, most notably sequential quadratic programming. [WP:Constraint_optimization]

constraint satisfaction: An approach to problem solving that consists of three components:

- a list of what "variables" need values;
- a set of allowable values for each "variable";
- a set of relationships that must hold between the values for each "variable" (i.e., the constraints).

In computer vision, this approach has been used for structure labeling (e.g., line labeling and region labeling) and geometric model recovery tasks (e.g., reverse engineering of 3D parts or buildings from range data). [WP: Constraint_satisfaction]

constructive solid geometry (CSG): A method for defining 3D shapes in terms of a mathematically defined set of primitive shapes. Boolean set theoretic operations of intersection, union and difference are used to combine shapes to make more complex shapes. For example: [JKS95:15.3.2]

content-based image retrieval: Image database indexing methods that produce matches based on the contents of the images in the database, as contrasted with using text descriptors to do the indexing. For example, one can use descriptors based on color moments to select images with similar invariants. [WP:Content-based_image_retrieval]

context: In vision, the elements, information or knowledge that occur with or accompany some data, contributing to the data's full meaning. For example, in a video sequence one can speak of the spatial context of a pixel, indicating the intensities at surrounding locations in a given frame (image), or of the temporal context, indicating the intensities at that pixel location (same coordinates) but in previous and following frames. Information deprived of appropriate context can be ambiguous: e.g.,

differential optical flow methods can only estimate the normal flow; the full flow can be estimated considering the spatial context of each pixel. At the level of scene understanding, knowing that the image data comes from a theater performance provides context information that can help distinguish between a real fight and a stage act. [DH73:2.11]

context-aware algorithm: A range of techniques spanning tracking, visual salience, object recognition and object detection that use contextual information in addition to the specific subject of the task in maximizing the efficacy of the approach, e.g., traversable scene region awareness in pedestrian detection. More generally the use of additional sensor information providing context (e.g., a global positioning system providing location cues for mobile devices). [YMH09]

context dependent: A process result or outcome achieved using a context-aware algorithm. [YMH09]

contextual event: Significant changes in a scene that are independent of the objects of interest (e.g., people) and location specific in a visual environment. For example, an item may be left in the scene, a vehicle may enter or park, or the street lights may turn on. [GX11:7.1]

contextual image classification: Algorithms that take into account the source or setting of images in their search for features and relationships in the image. Often this context is composed of region identifiers, color, topology and spatial relationships as well as task-specific knowledge. [MS03]

contextual information: Additional information about the image, video or scene being analyzed that aids in the evaluation of the outcome. Obtained from secondary sensing, prior annotation of the content or the scene background excluding the primary target objects of interest. See also context-aware algorithm. [GX11:2.5]

contextual knowledge: *A priori* contextual information about a given image or video (e.g., camera viewing angle or distance to object of interest). See contextual information [GX11:5.1.3]

contextual method: Algorithms that take into account the spatial arrangement of found features in their search for new ones. [CG84]

contextually incoherent: An anomalous occurrence that cannot be readily explained using contextual information or the *a priori* model in use (e.g., behavior model or prior distribution of occurrence). See anomaly detection. [GX11:Ch. 10]

continuous convolution: The convolution of two continuous signals. When processing 2D images, the convolution of two images f and b is: $g(x, y) = f(x, y) \otimes b(x, y) = \int_{-\infty}^{\infty} \int_{-\infty}^{\infty} f(\tau_u, \tau_v)b(x - \tau_u, y - \tau_v)d\tau_u d\tau_v$. [LWL00]

continuous Fourier transform: See Fourier transform.

continuous learning: A general term describing how a system continually updates its model of a process based on current data. For example, background modeling (for change detection) as the illumination changes during the day. [Doy00]

continuous random variable: If the cumulative distribution function of a random variable X is a continuous function, then X is said to be a continuous random variable. In this case the cumulative distribution function can be expressed as the integral of the corresponding probability density function. Contrast with a discrete random variable. Examples of continuous random variables include Gaussian distribution, the multi-variate normal distribution and the gamma distribution. [GS92:2.3]

contour: See object contour.

contour analysis: Analysis of outlines of image regions. [MBLS01]

contour following: See contour linking.

contour grouping: See contour linking.

contour length: The length of a contour in appropriate units of measurement. For instance, the length of an image contour in pixels. See also arc length. [WP:Arc_length]

contour linking: Edge detection or boundary detection processes typically identify pixels on the boundary of a region. Connecting these pixels to form a curve is the goal of contour linking. [GPSG01]

contour matching: See curve matching.

contour partitioning: See curve segmentation.

contour relaxation: A relaxation approach to contour linking for scene segmentation. [SHK03]

contour representation: See boundary representation.

contour tracing: See contour linking.

contour tracking: See contour linking.

contourlets: A contour representation approach using a multi-resolution and multidirectional multifilter bank technique. [DV05]

contrast: 1) The difference in brightness values between two structures, such as regions or pixels.
2) A texture measure. In a gray scale image, contrast, C, is defined as

$$C = \sum_i \sum_j (i - j)^2 P[i, j]$$

where P is the gray-level co-occurrence matrix. [JKS95:7.2]

contrast enhancement: Also known as "contrast stretching". Expands the distribution of intensity values in an image so that a larger range of sensitivity in the output device can be used. This can make subtle changes in an image more obvious by increasing the displayed contrast between image brightness levels:

input image

after contrast enhancement

Histogram equalization is one method of contrast enhancement. [Kim97]

contrast stretching: See contrast enhancement.

control point: Used in a parametric smooth curve representation system to specify the shape of the curve to a given order of complexity (e.g., linear, quadratic or cubic). The curve is defined as an algebraic relationship between all of the specified control points in the space but not necessarily intersecting them:

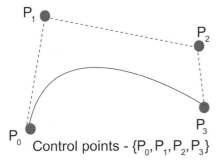

Control points - $\{P_0, P_1, P_2, P_3\}$

A point-based variant on algebraic curves. Can also be extended to surface representation. [FDFH96:11.2]

control strategy: The guidelines behind the sequence of processes performed by an automatic image analysis or scene understanding system. For instance, control can be top-down (searching for image data that verifies an expected target) or bottom-up (progressively acting on image data or results to derive hypotheses). The control strategy may allow selection of alternative hypotheses, processes, parameter values etc. [SHB08:8.1]

convex hull: Given a set of points, S, the convex hull is the smallest convex set that contains S. The figure shows a 2D example: [Dav90:6.6]

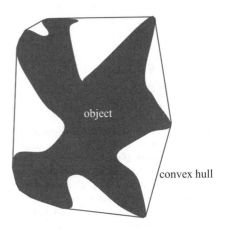

convexity: A property of shape associated with being convex (i.e., a shape outline curving outwards, such as the exterior of a circle or sphere having interior angles measuring less than $180°$. Mathematically it is defined as $\frac{convex\ hull\ perimeter\ length}{perimeter\ length}$. See convex hull. Antonym of non-convexity. [SB11:9.1]

convexity ratio: Also known as "solidity". A measure that characterizes deviations from convexity. The ratio for shape X is defined as $\frac{area(X)}{area(C_X)}$, where C_X is the convex hull of X. A convex figure has convexity factor 1, while all other figures have convexity less than 1. [MK00]

convolution operator: A widely used general image processing and signal processing operator that computes the weighted sum $y(j) = \sum_i w(i)x(j-i)$ where $w(i)$ are the weights, $x(i)$ is the input signal and $y(j)$ is the result. Similarly, convolutions of image data take the form $y(r,c) = \sum_{i,j} w(i,j)x(r-i, c-j)$. Similar forms using integrals exist for continuous signals and images. With appropriate choice of the weight values, convolution can compute low pass/smoothing, high pass/differentiation filtering or template matching/matched filtering, as well as many other linear functions. The image on the right of the figure is the result of convolving (and then inverting) the left image with a $|+1|-1|$ mask: [FP03:7.1.1]

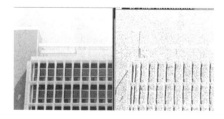

co-occurrence matrix: A representation commonly used in texture analysis algorithms. It records the likelihood (usually empirical) of two features or properties being at a given position relative to each other. For example, if the center of the matrix **M** is position (a, b) then the likelihood that the given property is observed at an offset (i, j) from the current pixel is given by matrix value $\mathbf{M}(a+i, b+j)$. [WP: Co-occurrence_matrix]

Cook–Torrance model: A computer graphics shading model for surface reflectance in 3D rendering. An alternative to the common Phong reflectance model incorporating the physical properties of reflectance and offering superior reflectance rendering for rough and metallic surfaces. [BR03:III.2]

cooperative algorithm: An algorithm that solves a problem by a series of local interactions between adjacent structures, rather than some global process that has access to all data. The value at a structure changes iteratively in response to changing values at the adjacent structures, such as pixels, lines, regions etc. The expectation is that the process will converge to a good solution. The algorithms are well suited for massive local parallelism (e.g., single instruction multiple data) and are sometimes proposed as models for human image processing. An early algorithm to solve the stereo correspondence problem used cooperative processing between elements representing the disparity at a given picture element. See also belief propagation. [ZK00]

coordinate system: A spanning set of linearly independent vectors defining a vector space. One example is the set generally referred to as the X, Y and Z axes. There are, of course, an infinite number of sets of three linearly independent vectors describing 3D space. The right-handed version of this is shown in the figure: [FP03:2.1.1]

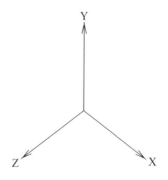

coordinate system transformation: A geometric transformation that maps points, vectors or other structures from one coordinate system to another. It is also used to express the relationship between two coordinate systems. Typical transformations include translation and rotation. See also Euclidean transformation. [WP: Coordinate_system#Transformations]

coplanarity: The property of lying in the same plane. For example, three vectors $\vec{a}, \vec{b}$ and $\vec{c}$ are coplanar if their scalar triple product $(\vec{a} \times \vec{b}) \cdot \vec{c} = 0$ is zero. [WP:Coplanarity]

coplanarity invariant: A projective invariant that allows the determination of when five corresponding points observed in two (or more) views are coplanar in the 3D space. The five points allow the construction of a set of four collinear points whose cross ratio value can be computed. If the five points are coplanar, then the cross ratio value must be the same in the two views. In the figure, point A is selected and the lines AB, AC, AD and AE are used to define an invariant cross ratio for any line L that intersects them: [Gro94]

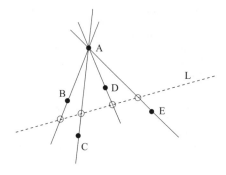

copy detection: A digital image forensics technique for the automatic detection of in-image content duplication ("copy and paste" tampering) and cross-media image duplication in the presence of changes to scale, compression and encoding characteristics: [Kim03]

core line: See medial line.

corner detection: See curve segmentation.

corner feature detector: See interest point feature detectors and curve segmentation.

coronary angiography: A class of image-processing techniques (usually based on X-ray data) for visualizing and inspecting the blood vessels surrounding the heart (coronaries). See also angiography. [WP:Coronary_catheterization]

correlation: The correlation between two numerical random variables X and Y is defined as

$$\text{corr}(X, Y) = \frac{\text{cov}(X, Y)}{\sqrt{\text{var}(X)\text{var}(Y)}}$$

where cov denotes the covariance and var denotes the variance. It is a normalized form of the covariance. [MKB79:2.2.2]

correlation-based optical flow estimation: Optical flow estimated by correlating local image texture at each point in two or more images and noting their relative movement. [CT98]

correlation-based stereo: Dense reconstruction (i.e., at every pixel) computed by the cross correlation of local image neighborhoods in the two images to find corresponding points from which depth can be computed by stereo triangulation. [FHM+93]

correlogram: 1) In general statistical analysis, a plot of the autocorrelation values against either distance or time. 2) In image processing, an extension to the color image histogram recording the statistical co-occurrence of two colors i and j at a given distance, d, in the image for a given distance range, $d = \{0...n\}$. Elements in the correlogram are thus indexed (i, j, d) for the co-occurrence of color pair (i, j) at separation d. See also color co-occurrence matrix. [CM04:15.5.1]

correspondence-based morphing: An approach to mesh model (model to model) morphing based on point correspondences. [FBH+01]

correspondence constraint: See stereo correspondence problem.

correspondence problem: See stereo correspondence problem.

cosine diffuser: Optical correction mechanism for correcting spatial responsivity to light. Since off-angle light is treated with the same response as normal light, a cosine transfer is used to decrease the relative responsivity. [FSS06]

cosine integral images: An extension to the concept of integral images targeting non-uniform filters such as, Gaussian smoothing, Gabor filtering and bilateral filtering. [EW11]

cosine transform: Representation of a signal in terms of a basis of cosine functions. For a 1D even function $f(x)$, the cosine transform is

$$F(u) = 2 \int_0^\infty f(x) \cos(2\pi ux) dx.$$

For a sampled signal $f_{0..(n-1)}$, the discrete cosine transform is the vector $b_{0..(n-1)}$ where, for $k \geq 1$:

$$b_0 = \sqrt{\frac{1}{n}} \sum_{i=0}^{n-1} f_i$$

$$b_k = \sqrt{\frac{2}{n}} \sum_{i=0}^{n-1} f_i \cos\left(\frac{\pi}{2n}(2i+1)k\right)$$

For a 2D signal, $f(x, y)$ the cosine transform $F(u, v)$ is

$$4 \int_0^\infty \int_0^\infty f(x, y) \cos(2\pi ux)$$

$$\cos(2\pi vy) dx dy$$

[Umb98:2.5.2]

cost function: The function or metric quantifying the cost of a certain action, move or configuration, that is to be minimized over a given parameter space. A key concept of optimization. See also Newton optimization method and functional optimization. [HZ00:3.2]

coupled hidden Markov model: An extension to the hidden Markov model (HMM) approach for modeling the interaction of temporal processes, e.g., human interactions in behavior analysis, each itself modeled by an HMM. [GX11:3.3.1]

covariance: The covariance between two numerical random variables X and Y is defined as $\text{cov}(X, Y) = E[(X - E[X])(Y - E[Y])]$ where $E[\cdot]$ denotes expectation. Note that $\text{cov}(X, X)$ is the variance of X. [MKB79:2.2.2]

covariance matrix: In a d-dimensional random vector of $\vec{X}$, the covariance between components X_i and X_j is defined as $\Sigma_{ij} = \text{cov}(X_i, X_j) = E[(X_i - E[X_i])(X_j - E[X_j])]$ where $E[X]$ is the expectation value of X. These entries can be assembled into a $d \times d$ symmetric covariance matrix Σ where the diagonal elements hold the variances of each component. See also sample covariance. [MKB79:2.2.2]

covariance propagation: A method of statistical error analysis, in which the covariance of a derived variable can be estimated from the covariances of the variables from which it is derived. For example, assume that independent variables $\vec{x}$ and $\vec{y}$ are sampled from multi-variate normal distributions with associated covariance matrices $\mathbf{C}_x$ and $\mathbf{C}_y$. The covariance of the derived variable $\vec{z} = a\vec{x} + b\vec{y}$ is $\mathbf{C}_z = a^2\mathbf{C}_x + b^2\mathbf{C}_y$. [HZ00:4.2]

crack code: A contour description method that codes not the pixels themselves but the cracks between them. This is done as a four-directional scheme:

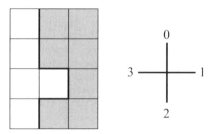

crack code = { 2, 2, 1, 2, 3, 2 }

It can be viewed as a chain code with four directions rather than eight. [WP: Chain_code]

crack detection: A visual industrial inspection for the detection of crack faults in manufactured articles. Also commonly applied to in-situ inspection of load bearing engineering structures or leak detection in pipework. [Dav90:4.4.2]

crack edge: A type of edge used in line-labeling research to represent where two aligned blocks meet. In the figure, neither a step edge nor a fold edge is seen: [Yak76]

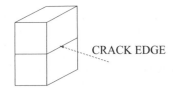

CRACK EDGE

crack following: Edge tracking on the dual lattice or "cracks" between pixels based on the continuous segments of line from a crack code. [MB99]

Crimmins smoothing operator: An iterative algorithm for speckle (salt-and-pepper noise) reduction. It uses a nonlinear noise reduction technique that compares the intensity of each image pixel with its eight neighbors and either increments or decrements the value to try and make it more representative of its surroundings. The algorithm raises the intensity of pixels that are darker than their neighbors and lowers pixels that are relatively brighter. More iterations produce more reduction in noise but at the cost of increased blurring of detail. [Cri85]

critical motion: In the problem of self-calibration of a moving camera, there are certain motions for which calibration algorithms fail to give unique solutions. Sequences for which self-calibration is not possible are known as "critical motion" sequences. [Stu97]

cross correlation: Standard method of estimating the degree to which two series are correlated. Given two series $\{x_i\}$ and $\{y_i\}$, where $i = 0, 1, 2, \ldots, (N - 1)$, the cross correlation, r_d, at a delay d is defined as

$$\frac{\sum_i (x_i - m_x).(y_{i-d} - m_y)}{\sqrt{\sum_i((x_i - m_x)^2}\sqrt{\sum_i(y_{i-d} - m_y)^2}}$$

where m_x and m_y are the means of the corresponding sequences. [Hec87:11.3.4]

cross-correlation matching: Matching based on the cross correlation of two sets. The closer the correlation is to 1, the better the match is. For example, in correlation-based stereo, for each pixel in the first image, the corresponding pixel in the second image is the one with the highest correlation score, where the sets being matched are the local neighborhoods of each pixel. [NA05:5.3.1]

cross ratio: The simplest projective invariant. It generates a scalar from four points of any 1D projective space (e.g., a projective line). The cross ratio for the points ABCD in the figure is:

$$\frac{(r + s)(s + t)}{s(r + s + t)}$$

[FP03:13.1]

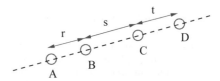

cross-section function: Part of the generalized cylinder representation that gives a volumetric representation of an object. The representation defines the volume by a curved axis, a cross section and a cross-section function at each point on that axis. The cross-section function defines how the size or shape of the cross section varies as a function of its position along the axis. See also generalized cone. The figure shows how the size of the square cross section varies along a straight line to create a truncated pyramid: [PCM89]

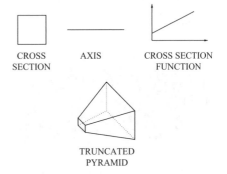

CROSS SECTION   AXIS   CROSS SECTION FUNCTION

TRUNCATED PYRAMID

cross-validation: When comparing different models, one cannot simply compare their performance on the training set, because of the danger of over-fitting. This can be guarded against using a validation set, but if the data available for training and validation is limited, it can be more efficient to use cross-validation. In this scheme the data is divided into k folds, and for each fold $i = 1, \ldots, k$ training is carried out on all folds except the ith and validation is carried out on the ith. The validation results from each fold are then averaged to obtain an overall performance estimate. A leave-one-out test is a special case when k is equal to the number of training examples. [HTF08:7.10]

crossing number: The crossing number of a graph is the minimum number of arc of graph intersections in any drawing of that graph. A planar graph has a crossing number of zero. The figure shows a graph with a crossing number of one: [Dav90:6.8.1]

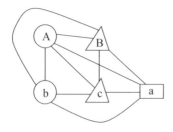

crowd flow analysis: Using motion properties, (e.g., the optical flow field) computed from (human) crowd video sequences for behavior analysis tasks, such as anomalous behavior detection: [ABF06]

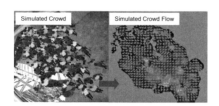

Simulated Crowd   Simulated Crowd Flow

CSG: See constructive solid geometry

CT: See X-ray CAT. [WP:X-ray_computed_tomography]

cubic spline: A spline where the weight functions are third-order polynomials. [PTVF92:Ch. 3]

cuboid descriptor: A localized 3D spatio-temporal space feature descriptor describing a region within a video sequence, akin to the use of region descriptors for 2D images. May also be applied to an object in an explicit 3D voxel space. [GX11:5.4.1]

cumulative abnormality score: A measurement of abnormality used in behavior analysis, given an *a priori* behavior model, that alleviates the effect of noise by accumulating the temporal history of the likelihood of behavioral anomaly occurrences in each region over time. Implemented with a threshold to control anomalous behavior detection alerts in the presence of noise (with additional temporal decay for occurrences below that threshold). [GX11:15.2.4]

cumulative anomaly score: See cumulative abnormality score.

cumulative distribution function: The cumulative distribution function of a random variable X is defined as $F(x) = \Pr(X \leq x)$, i.e., the probability that X does not exceed the value x. The range of F is $[0, 1]$. This definition also applies to vector-valued random variables. [MKB79:2.1]

cumulative histogram: A histogram where the bin contains not only the count of all instances having that value but also the count of all bins having a lower index value. This is the discrete equivalent of the cumulative probability distribution. The figure on the right is the cumulative histogram corresponding to the normal histogram on the left: [WP: Histogram#Cumulative_histogram]

NORMAL HISTOGRAM   CUMULATIVE HISTOGRAM

cumulative scene vector: A vector representation of temporally accumulated activity classification output for a given scene (one activity class per vector dimension). Used to overcome the problem that small periods of scene inactivity cause semantic breakdown in the analysis of per video frame scene vector measurements for behavior analysis. [GX11:7.2.1]

currency verification: Algorithms for checking that printed money and coinage are genuine. A specialist field involving optical character recognition. [FGP96]

curse of dimensionality: The exponential growth of possibilities as a function of dimensionality. This might manifest several effects as the dimensionality increases:

- an increased amount of computational effort required;
- an exponentially increasing amount of data required to populate the data space in order that training works;
- all data points tending to become equidistant from each other.

This causes problems for clustering and machine learning algorithms. [WP: Curse_of_dimensionality]

cursive script recognition: Methods of optical character recognition whereby hand-written cursive (also called joined-up) characters are automatically classified. [BM02:5.2]

curvature: Usually meant to refer to the change in shape of a curve or surface. Mathematically, the curvature κ of a curve is the length of the second derivative $|\frac{\partial^2 \vec{x}(s)}{\partial s^2}|$ of the curve $\vec{x}(s)$ parameterized as a function of arc length s. A related definition holds for surfaces, only here there are two distinct principal curvatures at each point on a sufficiently smooth surface. [NA05:4.6]

curvature primal sketch: A multi-scale representation of the significant changes in curvature along a planar curve. [NA05:4.8]

curvature scale space: A multi-scale representation of the curvature zero-crossing points of a planar object contour as it evolves during smoothing. It is found by parameterizing the contour using arc length, which is then convolved with a Gaussian smoothing of increasing standard deviation. Curvature zero-crossing points are then recovered and mapped to the scale-space representation of the image with the horizontal axis representing the arc length parameter on the original contour and the vertical axis representing the standard deviation of the Gaussian filter. [WP:Curvature_Scale_Space]

curvature sign patch classification: A method of local surface classification based on its mean curvature and Gaussian curvature signs, or principal curvature sign class. See also mean and Gaussian curvature shape classification. [HJ87]

curve: A set of connected points in two or three dimensions, where each point has at most two neighbors. The curve could be defined by a set of connected points, by an implicit function (e.g., $y + x^2 = 0$), by an explicit form (e.g., $(t, -t^2)$ for all t) or by the intersection of two surfaces (e.g., by intersecting the planes $X = 0$ and $Y = 0$). [NA05:4.6.2]

curve binormal: The vector perpendicular to both the curve tangent vector and curve normal vector at any given point: [Mor95]

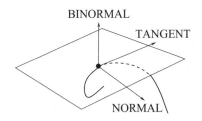

curve bitangent: A line tangent to a curve or surface at two different points: [WP:Bitangent]

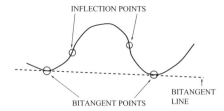

INFLECTION POINTS

BITANGENT LINE

BITANGENT POINTS

curve evolution: An abstraction method whereby a curve can be iteratively simplified, as in this figure:

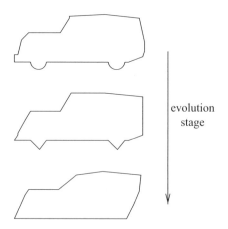

evolution stage

For example, a relevance measure is assigned to every vertex in the curve. The least important can be removed at each iteration by directly connecting its neighbors. This elimination is repeated until the desired stage of abstraction is reached. Another method of curve evolution is progressive curve smoothing with Gaussian smoothing of increasing standard deviation. [TYW01]

curve fitting: Methods for finding the parameters of a best-fit curve through a set of 2D (or 3D) data points. This is often posed as a minimization of the least-squares error between some hypothesized curve and the data points. If the curve, $y(x)$, can be thought of as the sum of a set of m arbitrary basis functions, X_k and written

$$y(x) = \sum_{k=1}^{k=m} a_k X_k(x)$$

then the unknown parameters are the weights a_k. The curve-fitting process can then be considered as the minimization of some log-likelihood function giving the best fit to N points whose Gaussian error has standard deviation σ_i. This function may be defined as

$$\chi^2 = \sum_{i=1}^{i=N} \left[\frac{y_i - y(x_i)}{\sigma_i} \right]^2$$

The weights that minimize this can be found from the design matrix D

$$D_{i,j} = \frac{X_j(x_i)}{\sigma_i}$$

by finding the solution to the linear equation

$$\mathbf{Da} = \mathbf{r}$$

where the vector $r_i = \frac{y_i}{\sigma_i}$. [NA05:4.6.2]

curve inflection: A point on a curve where the curvature is zero as it changes sign from positive to negative: [FP03:19.1.1]

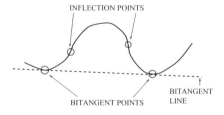

INFLECTION POINTS

BITANGENT LINE

BITANGENT POINTS

curve invariant: Measures taken over a curve that remain invariant under certain transformations, e.g., arc length and curvature are invariant under Euclidean transformations. [HC96]

curve invariant point: A point on a curve that has a geometric property that is invariant to changes in projective transformation. Subsequently, the point can be identified and used for correspondence in multiple views of the same scene. Two well-known planar curve invariant points are curvature inflection points and bitangent points: [LSW88]

68

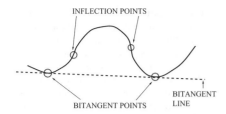

INFLECTION POINTS

BITANGENT POINTS   BITANGENT LINE

curve matching: The comparison of data sets to previously modeled curves or other curve data sets. If a modeled curve closely corresponds to a data set then an interpretation of similarity can be made. Curve matching differs from curve fitting in that curve fitting involves minimizing the parameters of theoretical models rather than actual examples. [Wol90]

curve normal: The vector perpendicular to the tangent vector to a curve at any given point, which also lies in the plane that locally contains the curve at that point: [PH03]

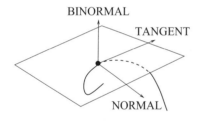

BINORMAL

TANGENT

NORMAL

curve representation system: Methods of representing or modeling curves parametrically. Examples include: b-splines, crack codes, cross-section functions, Fourier shape descriptors, intrinsic equations, polycurves, polygonal approximations, radius vector functions, snakes and splines. [JKS95:6.1]

curve saliency: A voting method for the detection of curves in a 2D or 3D image. Each pixel is convolved with a curve mask to build a saliency map. This map will hold high values for locations in space where likely candidates for curves exist. [JT03]

curve segmentation: Methods of identifying and splitting curves into primitive types. The location of changes between one primitive type and

another is particularly important. For example, a good curve segmentation algorithm should detect the four lines that make up a square. Methods include corner detection, Lowe's curve segmentation and recursive splitting. [KLP94]

curve smoothing: Methods for rounding polygon approximations or vertex-based approximations of surface boundaries. Examples include b-spline in 2D and NURBS in 3D. See also curve evolution. The figure shows a polygonal data curve smoothed by a Bezier curve: [Oli93]

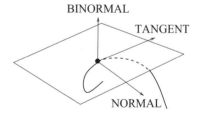

data curve - - - - -
smoothed curve ————
(Bezier)

curve tangent vector: The vector that is instantaneously parallel to a curve at any given point: [WP:Tangent_vector]

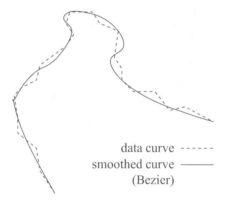

BINORMAL

TANGENT

NORMAL

curvelet: An extension of the wavelet concept commonly known as the "curvelet transform", forming a non-adaptive technique for multi-scale object representation specifically targeted at the shortcomings of wavelet approaches in representing continuous curves and contours. [SCD02]

cut detection: The identification of the frames in film or video where the camera viewpoint suddenly changes, either to a new viewpoint within the current scene or to a new scene. [WP: Shot_transition_detection]

cutset sampling: A variant on the sampling methodology for Bayesian networks that samples only a subset of variables in the network and applies exact inference to the rest. [BD07]

Cyclopean view: A term used in binocular stereo image analysis, based on the mythical one-eyed Cyclops. When stereo triangulation of a scene occurs based on two cameras, one has to consider on which coordinate system to base the reconstructed 3D coordinates or which viewpoint to use when presenting the reconstruction. The Cyclopean viewpoint is located at the midpoint of the baseline between the two cameras. [CSBT03]

cylinder extraction: Methods of identifying the cylinders and the constituent data points from 2.5D and 3D images that are samples from 3D cylinders. [MDN97]

cylinder patch extraction: Given a range image or a set of 3D data points, cylinder patch extraction finds sets of points (usually connected) that lie on the surface of a cylinder and usually also the equation of that cylinder. This process is useful for detecting and modeling pipework in range images of industrial scenes. [FFE97]

cylindrical mosaic: A mosaicing approach where individual 2D images are projected onto a cylinder. This is possible only when the camera rotates about a single axis or the camera center of projection remains approximately fixed with respect to the distance to the nearest scene points. [SKG+98]

cylindrical surface region: A region of a surface that is locally cylindrical. A region in which all points have zero Gaussian curvature and nonzero mean curvature. [WB94]

D

darkfield illumination: A specialized technique that uses oblique illumination to enhance contrast in subjects that are not imaged well under normal illumination conditions. [Gal90: 2.1.1]

data association: In a tracking problem, the task of determining which observations are informative and which are not. [FP03:17.4]

data augmentation: The introduction of unobserved data (or latent or auxiliary variables) to the original data. This strategy is used in the expectation maximization (EM) algorithm for maximizing a likelihood function and in the Markov chain Monte Carlo methods. [HTF08:8.5.2]

data fusion: See sensor fusion. [WP: Data_fusion]

data integration: See sensor fusion. [WP:Data_integration]

data mining: The process of extracting useful information from large data sets. This information may be descriptive (providing understanding of the structure or patterns in the data) or predictive (prediction of one or more variables based on others). The emphasis is on enabling humans to learn underlying structural patterns or behaviors from the data rather than on autonomous machine performance. [Mur12:1.1.1]

data parallelism: Reference to the parallel structuring of the input to programs, the organization of programs or the programming language used. Data parallelism is a useful model for much image processing

because the same operation can be applied independently and in parallel at all pixels in the image. [Sch89: Ch. 8]

data reduction: A general term for processes that reduce the number of data points (e.g., by subsampling, using a cluster center of mass as a representative point or decimation) or the number of dimensions in each data point (e.g., by projection or principal component analysis). [WP: Data_reduction]

data structure: A fundamental concept in programming: a collection of computer data organized in a precise structure, e.g., a tree (see quadtree), a queue or a stack. Data structures are accompanied by sets of procedures or libraries that implement various types of data manipulation, e.g., storage and indexing. [WP:Data_structure]

DCT: See discrete cosine transform.

deblocking filter: A filter applied in compressive video decoding when block coding has been used to act as an appearance enhancement transform removing any macro-scale blocking artifacts. Used in decoding a number of compressive video encoding schemes including H.263 and the H.264 streaming video formats. [LJL+03]

deblur: To remove the effect of a known blurring function on an image. If an observed image I is the convolution of an unknown image I' and a known blurring kernel B, so that $I = I' * B$, then deblurring is the process of estimating I' given I and B. See

Dictionary of Computer Vision and Image Processing, Second Edition.
R. B. Fisher, T. P. Breckon, K. Dawson-Howe, A. Fitzgibbon, C. Robertson, E. Trucco and C. K. I. Williams.
© 2014 John Wiley & Sons, Ltd. Published 2014 by John Wiley & Sons, Ltd.

deconvolution, image restoration and Wiener filtering. [BLM90]

decay factor: The rate of decrease in a variable. This rate may decrease as a function with respect to another variable, e.g., varying exponentially with time. In a discrete system with parameter x, $x_{t+1} = \alpha x_t$, $\alpha < 1$ is the decay factor over timestep, t. [HS98]

decentering distortion (lens): A common cause of tangential distortion. It arises when the lens elements are not perfectly aligned and creates an asymmetric component to the distortion. [WP:Distortion_(optics)#Software_correction]

decimation: 1) In digital signal processing, a filter that keeps one sample out of every N, where N is a fixed number. See also subsampling. 2) "Mesh" decimation: merging of similar adjacent surface patches or surface mesh vertices in order to reduce the size of a model. Often used as a processing step when deriving a surface model from a range image. [WP: Downsampling]

decision boundary: A classifier taking as input a vector $\vec{x}$ in $\mathbb{R}^d$ divides this space into a number of regions and all points in a given (decision) region are assigned to a particular class. The boundaries between these regions are known as decision boundaries. [Bis06:1.5.1]

decision forest: A generalized term encompassing variations on the random forest ensemble learning concept. [Cri11]

decision tree: A tool for helping to choose between several courses of action. An effective structure within which an agent can search options and investigate possible outcomes. It also helps to balance the risks and rewards associated with each possible course of action. A specific example is a tree classifier, where the result of a sequence of decisions is the assignment of an input $\vec{x}$ to a label residing at the attained leaf: [HTF08:9.2]

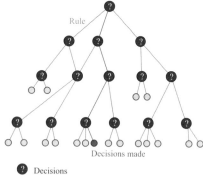

Rule

Decisions made

- ● Decisions
- ○ Results

decoding: Converting a signal that has been encoded back into its original form (lossless coding) or into a form close to the original (lossy coding). See also image compression. [WP: Decoding]

decomposable filter: A complex filter that can be applied as a number of simpler filters applied one after the other. For example the 2D Laplacian of Gaussian filter can be decomposed into four simpler filters. [PY01]

deconvolution: The inverse process of convolution. Deconvolution is used to remove certain signals (e.g., blurring) from images by inverse filtering (see deblur). For a convolution producing image $h = f * g + \eta$ given f and g (the image and convolution mask), where η is the noise and $*$ is the convolution, deconvolution attempts to estimate f. Deconvolution is often an ill-posed problem and may not have a unique solution. See also image restoration. [Low91:14.5]

defocus: Blurring of an image, either accidental or deliberate, by incorrect use or estimation of focus or viewpoint parameters. See also depth from defocus and shape from defocus. [Hor86:6.10]

defocus blur: Deformation of an image because of the predictable behavior of optics when incorrectly adjusted. The blurring is the result of light rays that, after entering the optical system, misconverge on the imaging plane. If the camera parameters are known in advance, the blurring can be partially corrected. [Hor86:6.10]

defogging: Physics-based image restoration techniques which seek to remove the optical effects of light transmission through air (atmosphere) that is heavily saturated with water droplets (i.e., fog) by some form of contrast enhancement. Areas of the image are generally found to be degraded as a function of depth. [NN02]

deformable model: Object descriptors that model a specific class of deformable objects (e.g., eyes and hands) where the shapes vary according to the values of the parameters. If the general, but not specific, characteristics of an object type are known, a deformable model can be constructed and used as a matching template for new data. The degree of deformation needed to match the shape can be used as a matching score. See also modal deformable model and geometric deformable model. [WP: Active_contour_model]

deformable shape: See deformable model.

deformable shape registration: A form of registration between two object shape boundaries that allows a relaxed constraint that those boundaries may be deformed via a non-affine transformation, from one boundary to the other to achieve alignment. Commonly used between sequential video frames to perform deformable object tracking. See also non-rigid registration and elastic registration. Contrasts with affine registration.

deformable superquadric: A type of superquadric volumetric model that can be deformed by bending, twisting etc. in order to fit to the data being modeled. [TM90]

deformable template model: See deformable model.

deformation energy: The metric that must be minimized when determining an active shape model. Composed of terms for both internal energy (or force), arising from the model shape deformation, and

external energy (or force), arising from the discrepancy between the model shape and the data. [WP:Internal_ energy#Description_and_definition]

degradation: A loss of quality suffered by an image, the content of which is corrupted by unwanted processes. For instance, MPEG compression-decompression can alter some intensities, so that the image is degraded. See also JPEG image compression and image noise. [WP:Degradation_ (telecommunications)]

degree of freedom: A free variable in a given function. For instance, rotations in 3D space depend on three angles, so that a rotation matrix has nine entries but only three degrees of freedom. [Nal93:3.1.3]

dehazing: Image restoration techniques that seek to remove various optical effects that have reduced the sharpness of detail in an image. See also defogging. [NN02]

Delaunay triangulation: The Delaunay graph of the point set can be constructed from its Voronoi diagram by connecting the points in adjacent polygons. The connections form the Delaunay triangulation, which has the property that the circumcircle of every triangle contains no other points. The approach can be used to construct a polyhedral surface approximation from a set of 3D sample points. In the figure, the solid lines connecting the points are the Delaunay triangulation and the dashed lines are the boundaries of the Voronoi diagram: [Fau93:10.4.4]

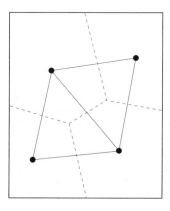

demon: A program that runs in the background, e.g., performing checks or guaranteeing the correct functioning of a module of a complex system. [WP:Daemon_(computing)]

demosaicing: The process of converting a one-color-per-pixel image (as captured by most digital cameras) into a three-color-per-pixel image. [WP: Demosaicing]

Dempster–Shafer: A belief-modeling approach for testing a hypothesis that allows information, in the form of beliefs, to be combined into a plausibility measure for that hypothesis. [WP: Dempster-Shafer_theory]

dendrogram: A hierarchical visual representation of relationships, e.g., feature correlation or similarity, as a tree structure with the leaf nodes all at the same depth: [EKSX96]

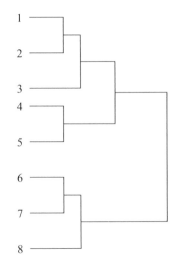

denoising: The removal of either structured (coherent) or random noise from a signal. In image processing, denoising approaches are generally based on intensity domain convolution or time-frequency domain. See image denoising. [SB11:4.4]

dense reconstruction: A class of techniques estimating depth at each pixel of an input image or sequence, thus generating a dense sampling of the 3D surfaces imaged. This can be achieved, e.g., by a range sensor or stereo vision. [ND10]

dense stereo matching: A class of methods establishing the correspondence (see stereo correspondence problem) between all pixels in a stereo pair of images. The generated disparity map can then be used for depth estimation. [KLCL05]

densitometry: A class of techniques that estimate the density of a material from images, e.g., bone density in the medical domain (bone densitometry). [WP: Densitometry]

depth: Distance of scene points from the camera center or the camera imaging plane. In a range image, the intensity value in the image is a measure of depth. [JKS95:13.1]

depth distortion: Systematically incorrect distance estimates, and consequently object shape characteristics, that arise from errors primarily in the intrinsic parameters. [WHR99]

depth estimation: The process of estimating the distance between a sensor (e.g., a stereo pair) and a part of the scene being imaged. Stereo vision and range sensing are two well-known ways to estimate depth. [TO02]

depth from defocus: A method of deriving the depth from parameters that can be directly measured, using the direct relationships among the depth, camera parameters and the amount of blurring in images. [SS94]

depth from focus: A method of determining distance to a point by taking many images in better and better focus. This is also called "autofocus" or "software focus". [WP:Depth_of_focus]

depth gradient image: An image $(d_i(i, j), d_j(i, j))$ which is the gradient of a depth image $d(i, j)$.

depth image: See range image.

depth image edge detector: See range image edge detector.

depth map: See range image.

depth of field: The distance between the nearest and the farthest points in focus for a given camera: [JKS95:8.3]

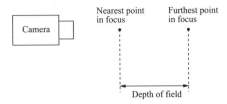

depth of focus: The distance between the nearest and farthest objects in an image that appear to be in focus. Depth of focus is affected by the lens aperture, specified by *f-number*. See also depth of field. [Sze10:2.2.3].

depth perception: The ability to perceive distances from visual stimuli, e.g., motion or stereo vision: [WP: Depth_perception]

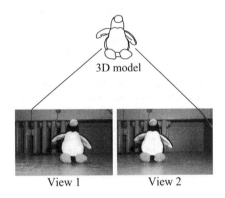

View 1   View 2

depth sensor: See range sensor.

Deriche edge detector: Convolution filter for edge finding, similar to the Canny edge detector. Deriche uses a different optimal operator where the filter is assumed to have infinite extent. The resulting convolution filter is sharper than the derivative of the Gaussian that Canny uses:

$$f(x) = Axe^{-\frac{|x|}{\sigma}}$$

See also edge detection. [Der87]

derivative-based search: Numerical optimization methods assuming that the gradient can be estimated. An example is the quasi-Newton approach, which attempts to generate an estimate of the inverse Hessian matrix. This is then used to determine the next iteration point: [DM77]

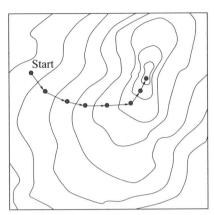

Conjugate gradient search

descattering: Algorithmic approaches to the removal of image attenuation from back-scattering often caused by imaging through media such as fog or water. Such algorithms often use light polarization as a first step and scene reconstruction afterwards. [CLFS07]

description coding: Coding technique that splits media into several streams which are broadcast simultaneously and reconstructed in parallel at the receiver end. [Goy01]

descriptor: See image descriptor and shape descriptor.

detection: 1) Identifying the presence of a signal from noise using a system of detectors either in software or hardware.
2) Identifying the presence of an object or features in an image. See also object detection and feature detection. [Dav90:Ch. 11–12]

detection rate: 1) The speed of detection, measured in hertz.
2) The success rate of detection as a statistic in object detection and feature detection as it relates to the true positive rate of detection for a given instance. [Sze10:Ch. 4; 14.1]

DFT: See discrete Fourier transform.

diagram analysis: Syntactic analysis of images of line drawings, possibly with text in a report or other document. This field is closely related to the analysis of visual languages. [Nag00]

dichroic filter: A filter that selectively transmits light of a given wavelength. [WP:Dichroic_filter]

dichromatic model: A model that states that the light reflected from a surface is the sum of two components: body and interface reflectance. Body reflectance follows Lambert's law; interface reflectance models highlights. The model has been applied to several computer vision tasks including color constancy, shape recovery and color image segmentation. See also color. [NN99]

diffeomorphism: A differentiable one-to-one map between manifolds. The map has a differentiable inverse. [WP: Diffeomorphism]

difference image: An image computed as the pixelwise difference of two images; each pixel in the difference image is the difference between the pixels at the same location in the two input images. In the figure, the image on the right is the difference of the left and middle images (after adding 128 for display purposes): [Sch89:Ch. 5]

difference-of-Gaussians operator: A convolution operator used to locate edges in a gray-scale image using an approximation to the Laplacian of Gaussian operator. In 2D, the convolution mask is:

$$c_1 e^{\left(-\frac{(x^2+y^2)}{\sigma_1^2}\right)} - c_2 e^{\left(-\frac{(x^2+y^2)}{\sigma_2^2}\right)}$$

where the constants c_1 and c_2 control the height of the individual Gaussians and σ_1, σ_2 are the standard deviations. [CS09:4.5.4]

differential geometry: A field of mathematics that studies the local derivative-based properties of curves

and surfaces, e.g., tangent plane and curvature. [TV98:A.5]

differential invariant: Image descriptors that are invariant under geometric transformations. Invariant descriptors are generally classified as global invariants (corresponding to object primitives) and local invariants (typically based on derivatives of the image function). The image function is always assumed to be continuous and differentiable. [WP:Differential_invariant]

differential pulse code modulation: A technique for converting an analog signal to binary by sampling it, expressing the value of the sampled data modulation in binary and then reducing the bit rate by taking account of the fact that consecutive samples do not change much. [Jai89:11.3]

differentiation filtering: See gradient filter.

diffraction: The bending of light rays at the edge of an object or through a transparent medium. The amount by which a ray is bent is dependent on wavelength. [Nal93:2.1.4]

diffraction grating: An array of diffracting elements that has the effect of producing periodic alterations in a wave's phase, amplitude or both. The simplest arrangement is an array of slits (see moiré interferometry): [WP: Diffraction_grating]

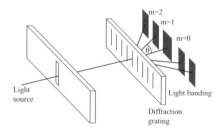

diffraction limit: The fundamental maximum image resolution of an imaging or optical system. This limit is affected by the size of the objective lens and the observed wavelength. [Hec87:p. 148]

diffuse illumination: Light energy that comes from a multitude of directions, hence not causing significant shading or shadow effects. The opposite of diffuse illumination is directed illumination. [CF90]

diffuse reflection: Scattering of light by a surface in many directions:

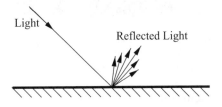

Ideal Lambertian surface diffusion results in the same energy being reflected in every direction regardless of the direction of the incoming light energy. [WP:Diffuse_reflection]

diffusion filtering: Image denoising approach based on nonlinear evolution partial differential equations which seeks to improve images qualitatively by removing noise while preserving details and even enhancing edges. See also anisotropic filtering. [PM90]

diffusion MRI tractography: *In vivo* magnetic resonance imaging that analyzes the diffusion tensor of the return signal to infer the connectivity in the brain neural tracts. [Jon11]

diffusion smoothing: A technique achieving Gaussian smoothing as the solution of a diffusion equation with the image to be filtered as the initial boundary condition. The advantage is that, unlike repeated averaging, diffusion smoothing allows the construction of a continuous scale space. [CLMC92]

diffusion tensor imaging: Magnetic resonance imaging resolution enhancement regime that extracts the return signal anisotropic diffusion tensor and uses it to infer information about tissue direction and connectivity. See also diffusion MRI tractography [Jon11]

digital camera: A camera in which the image sensing surface is made up of individual semiconductor sampling elements (typically one per pixel of

the image); quantized versions of the sensed values are recorded when an image is captured. [WP:Digital_camera]

digital elevation map: A sampled and quantized map where every point represents a height above a reference ground plane (i.e., the elevation): [OM84]

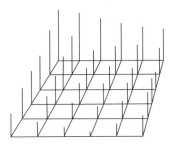

digital geometry: Geometry (points, lines, angles, surfaces etc.) in a sampled and quantized domain. [WP:Digital_geometry]

digital image: Any sampled and quantized image: [Umb98:1.7]

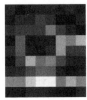

digital image forensics: 1) Methods of detecting specific forms of tampering or unauthorized changes to digital images for content verification. See digital image watermarking.
2) Image analysis methods used in the collection of evidence for criminal investigation. [SM12]

digital image processing: Image processing restricted to the domain of digital images. [WP:Digital_image_processing]

digital image watermarking: Embedding a code (the watermark) into the data of an image. The watermark acts as a digital signature, identifying the image's ownership or authenticity. It may be visible or invisible (hidden watermarking) to the viewer. See also image steganography. [WP:Digital_watermarking]

original image   image with digital image watermark applied

digital panoramic radiography: Dental wraparound digital X-ray imaging system which can image the upper and lower jaws, sinuses and nasal cavity. See also digital radiography. [WP: Panoramic_radiograph]

digital radiography: X-ray imaging where digital sensors replace photographic film or plates. [WP:Digital_radiography]

digital signal processor: A class of coprocessors designed to execute processing operations on digitized signals efficiently. A common characteristic is the provision of a fast multiply and accumulate function, e.g., $a \leftarrow a + b \times c$. [WP:Digital_signal_processor]

digital subtraction angiography: A basic technique used in medical image processing to detect, visualize and inspect blood vessels, based on the subtraction of a background image from the target image, usually where the blood vessels are made more visible by using an X-ray contrast medium. See also medical image registration. [WP: Digital_subtraction_angiography]

digital terrain map: See digital elevation map.

digital topology: Topology (i.e., how things are connected or arranged) in a digital domain (e.g., in a digital image). See also connectivity. [WP:Digital_topology]

digital watermarking: The process of embedding a signature (a watermark) into digital data. In the domain of digital images this is most normally

done for copyright protection. The digital watermark may be invisible or visible: [WP:Digital_watermarking]

digitally reconstructed radiograph (DDR): The approximation of an X-ray image from the equivalent CT data. [MBG+00]

digitization: The process of making a sampled digital version of some analog signal (such as an image). [WP:Digitizing]

dihedral edge: The edge made by two planar surfaces. A "fold" in a surface: [HH89]

dilate operator: The operation of expanding a binary or gray-scale object with respect to the background. This has the effect of filling in any small holes in the object and joining any object regions that are close together:

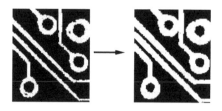

Most frequently described as a morphological transformation. The dual of the erode operator. [Umb98:2.4.6]

dimensionality: The number of dimensions that need to be considered. For example, 3D object location is often considered as a seven-dimensional problem (three dimensions for position, three for orientation and one for the object scale). See also intrinsic dimensionality. [SQ04:18.3.2]

dimensionality reduction: If high-dimensional data has manifold structure, then it can be approximated in a lower-dimensional space. Principal component analysis (PCA) is the standard linear method for this task, but there are also many non-linear methods including Gaussian process latent variable model, isomap, kernel principal component analysis, Kohonen networks, and locally linear embedding. [Mur12:1.4.2]

direct least square fitting: Direct fitting of a model to some data by a method that has a closed form or globally convergent solution. [FPF99]

directed acyclic graph (DAG): A graph containing only *directed* edges. If there is an edge between a pair of vertices u and v it must be either $u \to v$ or $v \to u$, but not both. Also there are no closed paths (hence "acyclic"):

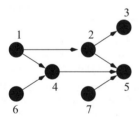

DAGs are used in the definition of directed graphical models. [Bis06:8.1]

directed graph: A graph in which the arcs go in only one direction, in contrast to an undirected graph. OnTopOf(A,B), meaning A is on top of B, is a property that could be used in a directed graph. On the other hand, adjacency is a property that could be used in an undirected graph, adj(A,B), meaning region A is adjacent to region B also implies adj(B,A), i.e., region B is adjacent to region A. [Wei12:Directed Graph]

directed graphical model (DGM): A joint probability distribution over a set of random variables. The graphical

structure is a directed acyclic graph (DAG), with each node in the graph representing a random variable. The joint distribution for a set of variables $\vec{x}$ is given by $p(\vec{x}) = \prod_i p(x_i | Pa_i)$, where Pa_i denotes the parents of node i in the graph. Missing edges in the graph imply conditional independence relationships. For example, in the figure, the factorization is $p(x_1, \ldots, x_7) = p(x_1)p(x_6)p(x_7)p(x_4|x_1, x_6)p(x_2|x_1) \times p(x_3|x_2)p(x_5|x_2, x_4, x_7)$:

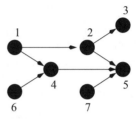

Sometimes the directed arrows can be interpreted as representing causal relationships (see probabilistic causal model), although there is nothing inherently causal about DGMs. The DGM is sometimes referred to as a Bayesian network or belief network. [Mur12:6.2]

directed illumination: Light energy that comes from a particular direction hence causing relatively sharp shadows. The opposite is diffuse illumination. [RBV06]

direction: A vector that describes the relative position of one point with respect to another.

directional derivative: A derivative taken in a specific direction, e.g., the component of the gradient along one coordinate axis. In the figure, the images on the right are the vertical and horizontal directional derivatives of the image on the left: [WP: Directional_derivative]

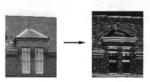

Dirichlet distribution: Let $\vec{x}$ denote a d-dimensional probability vector, i.e., a vector with all elements non-negative and summing to 1. The Dirichlet distribution is a probability distribution over probability vectors given by

$$p(\vec{x}) = \frac{\Gamma(\alpha_1 + \cdots + \alpha_d)}{\Gamma(\alpha_1) \ldots \Gamma(\alpha_d)} \prod_{i=1}^{d} x_i^{\alpha_i - 1},$$

where $\vec{\alpha} = (\alpha_1, \ldots, \alpha_d)$ is a parameter vector with positive entries. [Bis06:2.2.1]

Dirichlet prior: In Bayesian statistics, the Dirichlet distribution is a conjugate prior distribution to the multinomial distribution. [Bis06:2.2.1]

Dirichlet process mixture model: A non-parametric method based on a mixture model with a potentially infinite number of components. A Dirichlet process is a generalization of the Dirichlet distribution. [Mur12:23.2]

discontinuity detection: See edge detection.

discontinuity preserving regularization: A method of preserving edges (discontinuities) from being blurred as a result of some regularization operation (such as the recovery of a dense disparity map from a sparse set of disparities computed at matching feature points). [SSD94]

discontinuous event tracking: Tracking of events (such as a moving person) through a sequence of images. The discontinuous nature of the tracking is caused by the distance that a person (or a hand, arm etc.) can travel between frames and also by the possibility of occlusion (or self-occlusion): [LCST06]

discrete cosine transform (DCT): A transformation that converts digital images into the frequency domain in terms of the coefficients of discrete cosine functions. Used within JPEG image compression. [Umb98:2.5.2]

discrete curve evolution: A method of automatic stepwise simplification of polygonal curves which can neglect minor distortions while preserving the perceptual appearance. See curve evolution.

discrete Fourier transform (DFT): A version of the Fourier transform for sampled data. [Umb98:2.5.1]

discrete random variable: A random variable X is discrete if it only takes on values in some countable subset $\{x_1, x_2, \ldots\}$ of $\mathbb{R}$. Contrast with a continuous random variable. Examples of discrete random variables include the Bernoulli distribution and the Poisson distribution. [GS92:2.3]

discrete relaxation: A technique for labeling objects in which the possible type of each object is iteratively constrained based on relationships with other objects in the scene. The aim is to obtain a globally consistent interpretation (if possible) from locally consistent relationships. [WH97]

discrimination function: A binary function separating data into two classes. See classifier. [DH73:2.5.1]

discrimination-generating Hough transform: A hierarchical algorithm to discriminate among objects and to detect object rotation and translation using projections and slices through a constructed Hough space. See generalized Hough transform.

discriminative graphical model: A probabilistic modeling framework for specifying a collection of statistical, relational models. May be applied to image data to derive probabilistic inferences. Also see discriminative model and graphical model. [ZBR+01]

discriminative model: A machine learning representation that models the dependence of an unobserved variable on an observed one. This is in contrast to a generative model which can be used to predict the unobserved using only knowledge about the observed provided the joint distribution relationship between them is known. [Bar12:23.3]

discriminative random field: A framework for the classification of image regions which incorporates neighborhood interactions in the labels as well as the observed data. [KH03]

disjoint view: When images are captured from different camera (or sensor) viewpoints with non-overlapping fields of view. [AC09]

disparity: The image distance shifted between corresponding points in stereo image pairs: [JKS95:11.1]

Left image features   Right image features   Disparity

disparity gradient: The gradient of a disparity map for a stereo pair, that estimates the surface slope at each image point. See also binocular stereo. [Fau93:6.2.5]

disparity gradient limit: The maximum allowed disparity gradient in a potential stereo feature match. [PMF85]

disparity limit: The maximum allowed disparity in a potential stereo feature match. The notion of a disparity limit is supported by evidence from the human visual system. [San88]

dispersion: Scattering of light by the medium through which it is traveling. [WP:Dispersion_(optics)]

displacement vector: The shortest path between the endpoints of a motion, irrespective of the path taken. See also translation: [Ros09]

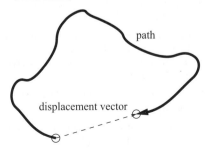

path

displacement vector

dissimilarity metric: A measure of the degree to which two objects or structures are different. Often framed as a Euclidean distance between two feature values. [GL86]

distance function: See distance metric.

distance map: See range image.

distance metric: A measure of how far apart two things are in terms of physical distance or similarity. A metric can be other functions besides the standard Euclidean distance, such as the algebraic distance or Mahalanobis distance. A true metric must satisfy:

- $d(x, y) + d(y, z) \geq d(x, z)$
- $d(x, y) = d(y, x)$
- $d(x, x) = 0$
- $d(x, y) = 0$ implies $x = y$

but computer vision processes often use functions that do not satisfy all of these criteria. [JKS95:2.5.8]

distance transform: An image-processing operation normally applied to binary images in which every object point is transformed into a value representing the distance from the point to the nearest object boundary. This operation is also referred to as chamfering (see chamfer matching): [JKS95:2.5.9]

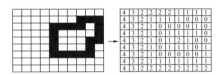

distortion coefficient: A coefficient in a given image distortion model, e.g., k_1, k_2 in the distortion polynomial. See also pincushion distortion, barrel distortion. [NSNI92]

distortion polynomial: A polynomial model of radial lens distortion. A common example is $x = x_d(1 + k_1 r^2 + k_2 r^4)$, $y = y_d(1 + k_1 r^2 + k_2 r^4)$. Here, x and y are the undistorted image coordinates, x_d and y_d are the distorted image coordinates, $r^2 = x_d^2 + y_d^2$, and k_1 and k_2 are the distortion coefficients. Usually k_2 is significantly smaller than k_1; it can be set to 0 in cases where high accuracy is not required. [NSNI92]

distortion suppression: Correction of image distortions (such as nonlinearities introduced by a lens). See geometric distortion and geometric transformation. [DV95]

distributed behavior: Agent-based approach to e.g., optimization where there is a direct analogy between points visited in the search space and independent behaviorally motivated agents. [WB02b]

distributed camera network: A collection of loosely coupled cameras and processing nodes, spread over a wide geographical area with no centralized processor, often with limited ability to communicate. See also disjoint views. [AC09]

distribution overlap: The ambiguous region of classification between two datasets where points may reasonably belong to either distribution: [VFJZ01]

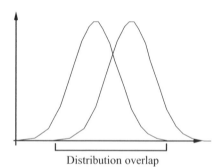

Distribution overlap

dithering: A technique simulating the appearance of different shades or colors by varying the pattern of black and white (or different color) dots. This is a common task for inkjet printers: [Low91:4.3.5]

divide and conquer: A technique for solving problems efficiently by subdividing the problem into smaller subproblems, and then recursively solving these subproblems in the expectation that the smaller problems will be easier to solve. An example is an algorithm for deriving a polygonal approximation of a contour in which a straight line estimate is recursively split in the middle (into two segments with the midpoint exactly on the contour) until the distance between the polygonal representation and the actual contour is below some tolerance: [WP:Divide_and_conquer_algorithm]

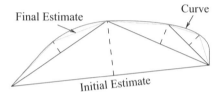

divisive clustering: Clustering or cluster analysis in which all items are initially considered as a single set (a cluster) and are divided into component subsets (clusters). [DMK03]

DIVX: An MPEG-4 video compression technology aiming to achieve sufficiently high compression to enable transfer of digital video contents over the Internet, while maintaining high visual quality. [WP:DivX]

document analysis: A general term describing operations that attempt to derive information from images of documents (including e.g., character recognition and document mosaicing). [DLL03]

document mosaicing: Image mosaicing of documents. [ZGT99]

document retrieval: Identification of a document in a database of scanned documents based on some criteria. [WP:Document_retrieval]

DoG: See difference-of-Gaussians operator.

dominant color descriptor (DCD): A basic color descriptor used in the

MPEG-7 coding standard widely used for image retrieval. It is most suitable for representing local features where a small number of colors are enough to characterize the color information in the region of interest. [Mar03:3.2.2.3]

dominant motion direction: 1) In sensor motion compensation, the motion parameters which describe the greatest change in the image geometry (see also image stabilization).
2) The most probable direction of travel of a large number of freely-moving objects, such as a crowd. [SAG95]

dominant plane: A degenerate case encountered in uncalibrated structure and motion recovery where most or all of the tracked image features are coplanar in the scene. [OI06]

Doppler: A physics phenomenon whereby an instrument receiving acoustic or electromagnetic waves from a source in relative motion measures an increasing frequency if the source is approaching and a decreasing frequency if it is receding. The acoustic Doppler effect is employed in sonar sensors to estimate target velocity as well as position. [WP:Doppler_effect]

downsampling: A reduction in the sampling rate of a signal or image, usually to reduce the amount of data transported. Also known as subsampling. In images, this often means using fewer pixels to represent the same underlying data: [SB11:Ch. 2]

original   downsampled equivalent

downhill simplex: A method for finding a local minimum using a simplex (a geometrical figure specified by $N + 1$ vertices) to bound the optimal position in an N-dimensional space. See also optimization. [WP:Nelder-Mead_method]

DSP: See digital signal processor. [WP: Digital_signal_processing]

dual of the image of the absolute conic (DIAC): If ω is the matrix representing the image of the absolute conic, then ω^{-1} represents its dual (DIAC). Calibration constraints are sometimes more readily expressed in terms of the DIAC than the IAC. [HZ00:7.5]

dual quaternion: A dual quaternion is an ordered pair of quaternions which can be used to represent spatial rigid body displacements in 3D. [WP: Dual_quaternion]

dual-tree wavelet: Also dual-tree complex wavelet transform (DTCWT. An almost shift-invariant wavelet transform that still allows for perfect signal reconstruction. It calculates the dual wavelet transform (DWT) in two decompositions (known as tree-a and tree-b), one of which may be real and one imaginary. [SBK05]

duality: The property of two concepts or theories having similar properties that can be applied to the one or to the other. For instance, several relations linking points in a projective space are formally the same as those linking lines in a projective space; such relations are dual. [Fau93:2.4.1]

duplicate image retrieval: The process of detecting images with the same, or approximately the same content, irrespective of geometry, compression or image encoding used in storage. The degree of similarity may be computed on pixels or features or a combination of both. This is a specific case of image retrieval. [KSH05]

dust filtering: The process of applying operators for the detection or removal of primarily salt-and-pepper noise. The defining noise characteristic of dust is that the intensity value of noisy pixels bears no relation to the surrounding pixel neighborhood. In the figure, (a) the original image has a dust artifact which (b) shows up clearly when analyzing entropy in the high frequency DCT components:

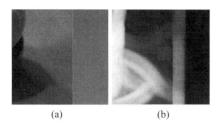

(a)   (b)

dynamic appearance model: A model describing the changing appearance of an object or scene over time. [KL09]

dynamic Bayesian network (DBN): A directed graphical model or Bayesian network to represent a process evolving in time. A DBN is typically specified by an initial state distribution and a transition model, specifying the evolution of the system from the present time into the future, e.g., from time step t to $t + 1$ for a discrete-time system. A hidden Markov model (HMM) is a simple example of a DBN. [KF09:6.2]

dynamic correlation: A Monte Carlo stochastic modeling and identification framework, often used in financial modeling to identify trends. [MB73]

dynamic event: An event that is extended over time, rather than being instantaneous. [VSK05]

dynamic occlusion: In object tracking, the phenomenon of objects becoming partially or fully hidden from view (i.e., occlusion) either by moving out of frame or by moving behind other objects, causing them to appear to split or merge within the scene. In a distributed camera network, this problem can be mitigated by polling images from many views simultaneously. [TMB85]

dynamic programming: An approach to numerical optimization in which an optimal solution is searched for by keeping several competing partial paths throughout and pruning alternative paths that reach the same point with a suboptimal value. [Nal93:7.2.2]

dynamic range: The ratio of the brightest and darkest values in an image. Most digital images have a dynamic range of around 100:1 but humans can perceive detail in dark regions when the range

is even 10,000:1. To allow for this we can create high-dynamic-range images: [SQ04:4.2.1]

dynamic scene: A scene in which some objects move, in contrast to the common assumption in shape from motion that the scene is rigid and only the camera is moving. [BF93]

dynamic stereo: Stereo vision for a moving observer. This allows shape from motion techniques to be used in addition to stereo techniques. [GT95]

dynamic texture: Moving sequences of images whose temporal characteristics exhibit certain statistically similar properties or stationarity of a recognizable texture pattern. Example sequences include fire, waves, smoke and moving foliage. Simulation of dynamic textures is often done by approximating a model of maximum likelihood and using it to extrapolate. [Sze10:13.5.1]

dynamic time warping: A technique for matching a sequence of observations (usually one per time sample) to a model sequence of features, where the hope is for a one-to-one match of observations to features. Because of variations in the rate at which observations are produced, some features may get skipped or others may match to more than one observation. The usual goal is to minimize the amount of skipping or multiple samples matched (time warping). Efficient algorithms to solve this problem are based on the linear ordering of the sequences. See also hidden Markov model (HMM). [WP: Dynamic_time_warping]

dynamic topic model: In large document (or article) collections, a family of probabilistic time series models that help to analyze the time evolution of different topics. Also used as an adaptive behavior model in behavior analysis. [GX11:Ch. 9]

E

early vision: A general term referring to the initial stages of computer vision (i.e., image capture and image processing). Also known as low-level vision. [Hor86:1.4]

earth mover's distance: A metric for comparing two distributions by evaluating the minimum cost of transforming one distribution into the other (e.g., can be applied to color histogram matching): [FP03:25.2.2]

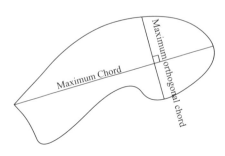

Distribution 1   Distribution 2   Transformation

eccentricity: A shape representation that measures how non-circular a shape is. One way of computing this is to take the ratio of the maximum chord length of the shape to the maximum length of any orthogonal chord: [WP:Eccentricity_(mathematics)]

eccentricity transform: Used to compute multi-scale invariant feature descriptors for shapes. Descriptors are defined as histograms of the eccentricity transform of a scale-space representation of the shape. Originally from the domain of graph-theory, it is computed per-pixel as a geodesic inner distance between the pixel and some other point of importance. [IAP+08]

echocardiography: Cardiac ultrasonic imaging (ultrasonography), a non-invasive technique for imaging the heart and surrounding structures. Generally used to evaluate cardiac chamber size, wall thickness, wall motion, valve configuration and motion, and the proximal great vessels. [WP: Echocardiography]

edge: A sharp variation of the intensity function, represented by its position, the magnitude of the intensity gradient and the direction of the maximum intensity variation. [FP03:Ch. 8]

edge-based segmentation: Segmentation of an image based on edge detection. [BS00b]

edge-based stereo: A type of feature-based stereo where the features used are edges. [Nal93:7.2.2]

edge detection: An image-processing operation that computes edge vectors (gradient and orientation) for every point in an image. The first stage of edge-based segmentation:

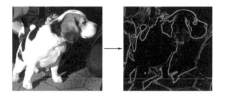

Examples include the Canny edge detector and the Sobel edge detector. [FP03:8.3]

Dictionary of Computer Vision and Image Processing, Second Edition.
R. B. Fisher, T. P. Breckon, K. Dawson-Howe, A. Fitzgibbon, C. Robertson, E. Trucco and C. K. I. Williams.
© 2014 John Wiley & Sons, Ltd. Published 2014 by John Wiley & Sons, Ltd.

edge direction: The direction perpendicular to the normal to an edge, that is, the direction along the edge, parallel to the lines of constant intensity. Alternatively, the normal direction to the edge, i.e., the direction of maximum intensity change (gradient). See also edge detection and edge point. [TV98:4.2.2]

edge enhancement: An image enhancement operation that makes the gradient of edges steeper. This can be achieved, e.g., by adding some multiple of a Laplacian convolved version of the image $L(i, j)$ to the image $g(i, j)$. $f(i, j) = g(i, j) + \lambda L(i, j)$ where $f(i, j)$ is the enhanced image and λ is some constant: [Sch89:Ch. 4]

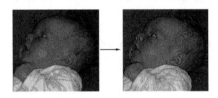

edge finding: See edge detection.

edge following: See edge tracking.

edge gradient image: See edge image. [WP:Image_gradient]

edge grouping: See edge tracking.

edge histogram descriptor (EHD): Part of the compact set of MPEG-7 descriptors designed to capture localized image texture via a histogram of edge orientation. The image is divided into 4×4 sub-regions each generating a five-bin histogram of that region (recording vertical, horizontal, diagonal ($45°$ and $135°$) and non-directional edges) which are concatenated to form an 80-bin descriptor for the entire image (i.e., $4 \times 4 \times 5$). [ISO02]

edge image: An image where every pixel represents an edge or the edge magnitude. [Bor88]

edge linking: See edge tracking.

edge magnitude: A measure of the contrast at an edge, typically the magnitude of the intensity gradient at the edge point. See also edge detection and edge point. [JKS95:5.1]

edge matching: See curve matching.

edge motion: The motion of edges through a sequence of images. See also shape from motion and the aperture problem. [JKS95:14.2.1]

edge orientation: See edge direction.

edge point: 1) A location in an image where some quantity (e.g., intensity) changes rapidly.
2) A location where the gradient is greater than some threshold. [FP03:Ch. 8]

edge-preserving smoothing: A smoothing filter that is designed to preserve the edges in the image while reducing image noise. For example see median filter: [WP:Edge-preserving_smoothing]

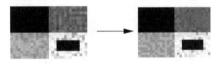

edge sharpening: See edge enhancement.

edge tracking: 1) The grouping of edges into chains of significant edges. The second stage of edge-based segmentation. Also known as edge following, edge grouping and edge linking.
2) Tracking how the edge moves in a video sequence. [Dav90:Ch. 4]

edge type labeling: Classification of edge points or edges into a limited number of types (e.g., fold edge, shadow edge or occluding edge). [Dav90:6.11]

edgel: Small pixel regions or sets of pixels that exhibit edge-like characteristics:

Original image   Corresponding edgels

Can also refer to the pixel which is closest to that edge. More recently used as an abbreviation of "edge pixel". [NP87]

EGI: See extended Gaussian image.

egomotion: The motion of the observer with respect to the observed scene. [FP03:17.5.1]

egomotion estimation: Determination of the motion of a camera. Generally based on image features corresponding to static objects in the scene. See also structure and motion recovery. The figure shows a typical image pair where the camera position is to be estimated: [WP:Egomotion]

Image from Position A   Image from Position B

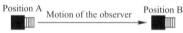

Position A   Motion of the observer   Position B

eigen-decomposition: Let A be a square $d \times d$ matrix with eigenvalues λ_i and eigenvectors $\vec{x}_i$ for $i = 1, \ldots, d$. We assume that the eigenvectors are linearly independent. Subsequently A can be expressed as $A = X\Lambda X^{-1}$, where X is the $d \times d$ matrix whose ith column is $\vec{x}_i$, and Λ is a $d \times d$ diagonal matrix whose diagonal entries are the corresponding eigenvalues, i.e., $\Lambda_{ii} = \lambda_i$. Note that for symmetric matrices we have $A = X\Lambda X^\top$, as the eigenvectors can be chosen such that they are orthogonal to each other and have norm one, so that X is an orthonormal matrix. The eigen-decomposition is a special case of singular value decomposition (SVD). [GL89:Chs 7, 8]

eigenface: Let X be a matrix whose columns are images of faces. An eigenface is an eigenvector obtained from the sample covariance matrix of X. These vectors can be used for face recognition. [FP03:p. 510]

eigenspace-based recognition: Object recognition based on an eigenspace representation. [TV98:10.4]

eigenspace representation: The approximation of an image region by a linear combination of basis vectors that can be thought of as matching between the eigenspace and the image. See also principal component analysis. [TV98:10.4.2]

eigentracking: An approach to tracking rigid and articulated objects that uses a view-based representation. The approach builds on an eigenspace representation, robust estimation techniques and parameterized optical flow estimation. [BJ98]

eigenvalue: A scalar λ that for a matrix A satisfies $Ax = \lambda x$ where x is a nonzero vector (an eigenvector). [SQ04:2.2.3]

eigenvector: A nonzero vector x that for a matrix A satisfies $Ax = \lambda x$ where λ is a scalar (the eigenvalue). [SQ04:2.2.3]

eigenvector projection: Projection onto the principal component analysis (PCA) basis vectors. [SQ04:13.1.4]

elastic matching: Optimization technique that minimizes the warp-deformation cost between locally variable data and the corresponding features or pixels in a given model. Often used in model-based object recognition. [WP:Elastic_matching]

elastic registration: A higher order version of elastic matching where corresponding surfaces or points are matched or merged by minimizing some warp-deformation cost. [SD02]

electromagnetic spectrum: The entire range of frequencies of electromagnetic waves including X-rays, ultraviolet, visible light, infrared, microwave and radio waves: [Hec87:3.6]

Wavelength (in meters)

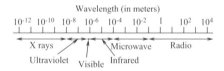

ellipse detection: Algorithms for finding either geometrically skewed circles or actual ellipses. Ellipse detection is one of the key problems in image processing as it can be particularly useful in retrieving the parameters of projective geometry:

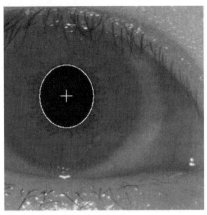

Ellipse detected in pupil tracker

There are five major parameters: (x_0, y_0) for the center, α for the orientation, (a, b) for the major and minor axes. Many approaches (e.g., the Hough transform or RANSAC) use the edge pixels in an image as constraints in searching this space. [HF98]

ellipse fitting: Fitting of an ellipse model to the boundary of some shape or data points: [TV98:5.3]

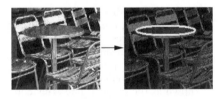

ellipsoid: A 3D volume in which all plane cross sections are ellipses or circles. An ellipsoid is the set of points (x, y, z) satisfying $\frac{x^2}{a^2} + \frac{y^2}{b^2} + \frac{z^2}{c^2} = 1$. In computer vision, an ellipsoid is basic shape primitive that can be combined with other primitives in order to describe a complex shape. [SQ04:9.9]

elliptic snake: An active contour model of an ellipse whose parameters are estimated through energy minimization from an initial position. [SKB+01]

elongatedness: A shape representation that measures how long a shape is with respect to its width (i.e., the ratio of the length of the bounding box to its width):

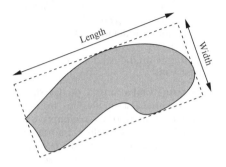

See also eccentricity. [WP:Elongatedness]

EM: See expectation maximization.

emotional state recognition: Automated analysis and classification of the external signs of mood or mental well-being of an individual using a mix of machine vision and sensors. [PVJ01]

empirical color representation: User-centered formulations of the return spectral frequency of light reflections. They fall into two categories: statistical representations, based on ignoring the intensity component of light and modeling with chromaticity [AB01]; basis function representations that are generated by modeling the data in terms of various bases. [JF99]

empirical evaluation: Evaluation of computer vision algorithms in order to characterize their performance by comparing the results of several algorithms on standardized test problems. Careful evaluation is a difficult research problem in its own right. [BP98:Ch. 1]

empirical mode decomposition: A method for analyzing natural signals, which are most often nonlinear and non-stationary, by decomposition without leaving the time domain. It can be compared to methods of analysis such as 2D Fourier transforms and wavelet decomposition although the basis function representations are empirically derived. The technique is defined by an algorithm rather than theory. For a signal $x(t)$:
1. Identify all extrema of $x(t)$.

2. Interpolate between minima (resp. maxima), ending up with some envelope $e_{min}(t)$ (resp. $e_{max}(t)$).
3. Compute the mean $m(t) = (e_{min}(t) + e_{max}(t))/2$.
4. Extract the detail $x(t + 1) = x(t) - m(t)$.
5. Iterate on the residual $x(t + 1)$.
[HSL+98]

encoding: Converting a digital signal, represented as a set of values, from one form to another, often to compress the signal. In *lossy* encoding, information is lost in the process and the <u>decoding</u> algorithm cannot recover it. See also <u>MPEG</u> and <u>JPEG image compression</u>. [WP:Code]

endoscope: An instrument for visually examining the interior of various bodily organs. See also <u>fiberscope</u>. [WP: Endoscopy]

energy minimization: The problem of determining the absolute minimum of a multi-variate function representing (by a potential energy-like penalty) the distance of a potential solution from the optimal solution. It is a specialization of the <u>optimization</u> problem. Two popular minimization algorithms in computer vision are the <u>Levenberg–Marquardt optimization</u> and <u>Newton optimization</u> methods. [WP:Energy_minimization]

ensemble learning: The combination of multiple learning models to try to yield better predictive performance than the individual models. Techniques include <u>bagging</u>, <u>boosting</u> and <u>Bayesian statistical model</u> combinations. [Mur12:14.1]

entropy: 1) Colloquially, the amount of disorder in a system.
2) A measure of the information content of a <u>random variable</u> X. Given that X has a set of possible values or outcomes $\mathbb{X}$, with probabilities $\{P(x), x \in \mathbb{X}\}$, the entropy $H(X)$ of X is defined as

$$\sum_{x \in \mathbb{X}} [-P(x) \log P(x)]$$

with the understanding that $0 \log 0 := 0$. For a multi-variate distribution, the joint entropy $H(X, Y)$ of X, Y is

$$\sum_{(x,y) \in \mathbb{X} \times \mathbb{Y}} [-P(x, y) \log P(x, y)]$$

For a set of values represented as a <u>histogram</u>, the entropy of the set may be defined as the entropy of the probability distribution function represented by the histogram. The figure shows $-p \log p$ as a function of p (left) - probabilities near 0 and 1 signal low entropy, probabilities between those values are less entropic; the entropy of the gray scale histograms in some windows on an image (right): [CT91: Ch. 2]

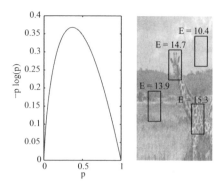

epipolar constraint: A geometric constraint reducing the dimensionality of the <u>stereo correspondence problem</u>. For any point in one image, the possible matching points in the other image are constrained to lie on a line known as the <u>epipolar line</u>. This constraint may be described mathematically using the <u>fundamental matrix</u>. See also <u>epipolar geometry</u>. [FP03:10.1.1]

epipolar correspondence matching: <u>Stereo matching</u> using the <u>epipolar constraint</u>. [ZDFL95]

epipolar geometry: The geometric relationship between two <u>perspective cameras</u>: [FP03:10.1.1]

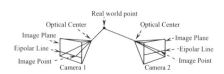

epipolar line: The intersection of the epipolar plane with the image plane. See also epipolar constraint. [FP03:10.1.1]

epipolar plane: The plane defined by any real-world scene point and the optical centers of two cameras. [FP03:10.1.1] [BBM87]

epipolar plane image (EPI): An image that shows how a particular line from a camera changes as the camera position is changed such that the image line remains on the same epipolar plane. Each line in the EPI is a copy of the relevant line from the camera at a different time. Features that are distant from the camera remain in the same position in each line; features that are close to the camera move from line to line (the closer the feature the further it moves): [Low91:17.3.4]

Image 1   Image 8

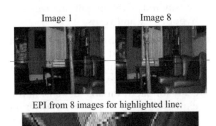

EPI from 8 images for highlighted line:

epipolar plane image analysis: An approach to determining shape from motion in which epipolar plane images (EPIs) are analyzed. The slope of lines in an EPI is proportional to the distance of the object from the camera, where vertical lines correspond to features at infinity. [Low91:17.3.4]

epipolar plane motion: See epipolar plane image analysis.

epipolar rectification: The image rectification of stereo images so that the epipolar lines are aligned with the image rows (or columns). [AF05]

epipolar transfer: The transfer of corresponding epipolar lines in a stereo pair of images, defined by a homography. See also stereo and stereo vision. [FP03:10.1.4]

epipole: The point through which all epipolar lines from a camera appear

to pass. See also epipolar geometry: [FP03:10.1.1]

Image   Epipolar Lines

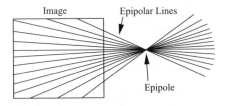

Epipole

epipole location: The operation of locating the epipoles. [Fau93:6.2.1.2]

equalization: See histogram equalization.

erode operator: The operation of reducing a binary or gray scale object with respect to the background. This has the effect of removing any isolated object regions and separating any object regions that are only connected by a thin section:

Most frequently described as a morphological transformation. The dual of the dilate operator. [Low91:8.2]

error propagation: 1) The propagation of errors resulting from one computation to the next computation. 2) The estimation of the error (e.g., variance) of a process based on the estimates of the error in the input data and intermediate computations. [WP: Propagation_of_uncertainty]

essential matrix: In binocular stereo, a matrix E expressing a bilinear constraint between corresponding image points u, u' in camera coordinates: $u'Eu = 0$. This constraint is the basis for several reconstruction algorithms. E is a function of the translation and rotation of the camera in the world reference frame. See also fundamental matrix. [FP03:10.1.2]

Euclidean distance: The geometric distance between two points (x_1, y_1) and (x_2, y_2), i.e., $\sqrt{(x_1 - x_2)^2 + (y_1 - y_2)^2}$.

For n-dimensional vectors $\vec{x}_1$ and $\vec{x}_2$, the distance is $(\sum_{i=1}^{n}(x_{1,i} - x_{2,i})^2)^{\frac{1}{2}}$. [SQ04:9.1]

Euclidean geometry: A system of geometry based on Euclid's five axioms. Negation of the parallel postulate gives rise to non-Euclidean geometries. [WP: Euclidean_geometry]

Euclidean reconstruction: 3D reconstruction of a scene using a Euclidean frame of reference, as opposed to an affine reconstruction or projective reconstruction. The most complete reconstruction achievable, for example, using stereo vision. [Har94]

Euclidean space: A representation of the space of all n-tuples (where n is the dimensionality). For example the three-dimensional Euclidean space (X, Y, Z) is typically used to describe the real world. Also known as Cartesian space (see Cartesian coordinates). [WP:Euclidean_space]

Euclidean transformation: A transformation that operates in Euclidean space (i.e., maintaining the Euclidean spatial arrangements). Examples include rotation and translation. Often applied to homogeneous coordinates. [FP03:2.1.2] [SQ04:7.3]

Euler angle: A set of angles (α, β, γ) describing rotations in three-dimensional space. [JKS95:12.2.1]

Euler–Lagrange equations: The basic equations in the calculus of variations, a branch of calculus concerned with maxima and minima of definite integrals. They occur, e.g., in Lagrangian mechanics and have been used in computer vision for a variety of optimizations, including for surface interpolation. See also variational approach and variational problem. [TV98:9.4.2]

Euler number: The number of contiguous parts (regions) less the number of holes. Also known as the genus. [Jai89:9.10]

even field: The first of the two fields in an interlaced video signal. [Jai89:11.1]

even function: A function where $f(x) = f(-x)$ for all x. [WP:Even_and_odd_functions#Even_functions]

event analysis: See event understanding. [WP:Event_study]

event detection: Analysis of a sequence of images to detect activities in the scene: [MCB+01]

Image from a sequence of images	Movement detected in the image
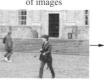	

event understanding: Recognition of an event (such as a person walking) in a sequence of images. Based on the data provided by event detection. [WP: Event_study]

exhaustive matching: Matching method in which all possibilities are considered. As an alternative see hypothesize and verify. [FPZ05]

expectation maximization (EM): An iterative method of carrying out maximum likelihood estimation for models that have missing data, especially for latent variable models. In the expectation (E) step, the expectation values of the latent variables are computed. In the maximization (M) step, the complete data log likelihood is maximized with respect to the parameters of the model. The iteration is guaranteed to converge to a local maximum of the log likelihood. EM is the standard method for fitting mixture models. [Bis06:9.3–9.4]

expectation value: Consider a random variable x and a function $f(x)$. The expectation value of $f(x)$ is defined as $E[f(x)] = \int f(x)p(x)dx$. For $f(x) = x$ the result is the mean. [Bis06:1.2.2]

expert system: A system that uses available knowledge and heuristics to solve problems. See also knowledge-based vision. [Low91:11.2]

exponential smoothing: A method for predicting a data value (P_{t+1}) based on the previous observed value (D_t) and the previous prediction (P_t). $P_{t+1} = \alpha D_t + (1 - \alpha)P_t$ where α is a weighting value

92

between 0 and 1: [WP:Exponential_ smoothing]

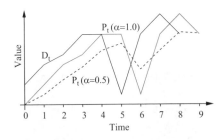

exponential transformation: See pixel exponential operator.

exposure time: The length of time the CCD or CMOS sensor digital camera is exposed to light for the capture of a single image frame. In conjunction with the size of the lens aperture this controls the amount of light reaching the image-forming sensor. [Sze10:2.3]

expression understanding: See facial expression analysis.

extended Gaussian image (EGI): Use of a Gaussian sphere for histogramming surface normals. Each surface normal is considered from the center of the sphere; the value associated with the surface patch with which it intersects is incremented: [FP03:20.3]

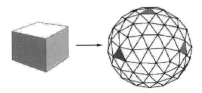

extended light source: A light source that has a significant size relative to the

scene, i.e., is not approximated well by a point light source. This type of light source has a diameter and hence can produce fuzzy shadows: [Hor86:10.5]

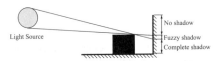

exterior orientation: The position of a camera in a global coordinate system, which is determined by an absolute orientation calculation. [FP03:3.4]

external energy (or force): A measure of fit between the image data and an active shape model that is part of the model's deformation energy. This measure is used to deform the model to the image data. [SQ04:8.5.1]

extremal point: Points that lie on the boundary of the smallest convex region enclosing a set of points (i.e., that lie on the convex hull). [SOS00:4.6.1]

extrinsic parameters: See exterior orientation.

eye location: The task of finding eyes in images of faces. Approaches include blink detection and face feature detection. [MDWW04]

eye tracking: Tracking the position of the eyes in a face image sequence; also gaze direction tracking: [WP: Eye_tracking]

F

f-number: In an optical system, the ratio between the focal length of a lens and its diameter. [FP03:1.2]

face analysis: A general term covering the analysis of face images and models. Often used to refer to facial expression analysis. [KCT00]

face authentication: Verification that (the image of) a face corresponds to a particular individual. This differs from face recognition in that here only the model of a single person is considered: [WP:Facial_recognition_system]

face detection: Identification of faces within an image or a series of images. This often involves a combination of human motion analysis and skin color analysis: [WP:Face_detection]

face feature detection: The location of features (such as eyes, nose and mouth) from a human face. Normally performed after face detection although it can be used as part of face detection: [WP:Face_detection]

face identification: See face recognition. [WP:Facial_recognition_system]

face indexing: Indexing from a database of known faces as a precursor to face recognition. [LW00b]

face liveness detection: Methods of avoiding the problem of spoofing facial recognition biometrics by using a photograph, 3D model or video of a face rather than a real face. These methods include detecting various facial movements as well as features that are hard to fake, such as vasculature. [PWS08]

face modeling: Representing a face using some type of model typically derived from an image (or images). These models are used in face authentication, face recognition etc. [HJ01]

face recognition: The task of recognizing a face from an image as an instance of a person recorded in a database of faces: [WP:Facial_recognition_system]

face tracking: Tracking of a face in a sequence of images. Often used as part of a human–computer interface. [HC00]

face verification: See face authentication. [WP:Facial_recognition_system]

facet-model extraction: The extraction from range data of a model based on facets (small simple surfaces). See also planar patch extraction and planar facet model. [Har84]

facial action coding system (FACS): An attempt to categorize the entire range of facial motion primarily through mapping the physical changes that accompany emotions. The system was originally developed by the psychologists Ekman and Friesen [EF78]. It comprises so-called "action units" (AUs), which are the fundamental actions of individual muscles or groups, and action descriptors (ADs) which are unitary movements that may involve several groups in succession.

facial animation: Computer graphics methods of simulating the human head and face. See also facial action coding system. [WP:Computer_facial_animation]

facial expression analysis: Study or identification of the facial expressions (i.e., quantitative measurement of movements of the human head and face) of a person from an image or sequence of images:

Happy	Perplexed	Surprised

See also facial action coding system. [TKC05]

factor analysis: A latent variable model. The latent variables $\vec{z}$ have independent Gaussian distributions and there is a linear relationship between the latent and visible variables $\vec{x}$, i.e., $\vec{x} = \mathbf{W}\vec{z} + \vec{n}$, where $\vec{n}$ is independent Gaussian noise. Probabilistic principal component analysis is a special case of factor analysis where the noise variables all have the same variance. [Bis06:12.2.4]

factorization: See motion factorization.

false alarm: See false positive.

false negative: A binary classifier $c(x)$ returns + or - for examples x. A *false negative* occurs when the classifier returns - for an example that is in reality +. [Mur12:8.3.4]

false positive: A binary classifier $c(x)$ returns + or - for examples x. A *false positive* occurs when the classifier returns + for an example that is in reality -. [Mur12:8.3.4]

fan-beam reconstruction: An reconstruction method for building images taken by projecting radiation at different angles from a single point and then measuring the resultant return from various sensors. A real-world application is X-ray absorption tomography, where projections are formed by measuring the attenuation of radiation that passes through a physical specimen at different angles: [Par82]

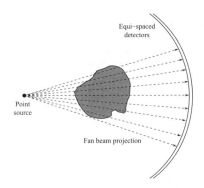

far light source: A light source far from the illuminated object such that the rays of light are effectively parallel:

See also near light source.

FAST interest point detector: A spatio-temporal interest point detector. A corner feature detector which employs a machine learning algorithm to yield large speed increases by learning discriminative properties. Often used with non-maximal suppression to improve noise resilience. The figure shows the detected feature points in the image: [RD06]

fast Fourier transform (FFT): A version of the Fourier transform for discrete samples that is significantly more efficient (order $N\log_2 N$) than the standard discrete Fourier transform (which is order N^2) on data sets with N points. [Low91:13.5]

fast marching method: A type of level set method in which the search can move in only one direction (hence it being faster). [WP: Fast_marching_method]

feature: 1) A distinctive part of something (e.g., the nose and eyes are distinctive features of the face) or an attribute derived from an object or shape (e.g., circularity). See also image feature.
2) A numerical property (possibly combined with others to form a feature vector) and generally used in a classifier. [TV98:4.1]

feature-based optical flow estimation: Calculation of optical flow in a sequence of images from image features. [HB93]

feature-based stereo: A solution to the stereo correspondence problem in which image features from two images

are compared. The main alternative approach is correlation-based stereo. [Gri85]

feature-based tracking: Tracking the motion of image features through a sequence. [TV98:8.4.2]

feature contrast: The difference between two features. This can be measured in many domains (e.g., intensity, orientation etc.). [Umb98:2.6.1]

feature descriptor: See SIFT descriptor and SURF.

feature detection: Identification of given features in an image (or model). For example, see corner detection. [Umb98:2.6]

feature extraction: See feature detection.

feature fusion: Methods to improve the robustness of recognition by simultaneously using different feature filters while examining the co-occurrence probability of the extracted joint features. [SZL+05]

feature location: See feature detection.

feature matching: Matching of image features in several images of the same object (e.g., feature-based stereo) or of features from an unknown object with features from known objects (feature-based object recognition). [TV98:8.4.2]

feature motion: The degree to which objects in the image plane move.

feature orientation: The orientation of an image feature with respect to the image frame of reference. [RCJ95]

feature point: The image location at which a particular feature is found. [KLT05]

feature point correspondence: Matching feature points in two or more images. The assumption is that the feature points are the image of the same scene point. Having the correspondence allows estimation of the depth from binocular stereo, fundamental matrix, homography or trifocal tensor in the case of 3D scene structure recovery or of the 3D target motion in the case of target tracking. [TV98:8.4.2]

feature point tracking: Tracking of individual image features in a sequence of images. [SK05]

feature representation: The way in which parameters of various metrics are stored for interest points in 2D or 3D images. These feature representations are generally stored as vectors with one entry per parameter. A good example of this is the SIFT descriptor, where each entry in the feature vector relates to a feature which is translation invariant, scaling invariant and rotation invariant, or partially invariant to illumination changes and robust to local geometric distortions. [Sze10:Ch. 4]

feature selection: Selection of suitable features (properties) for a specific task, e.g., classification. Typically features should be independent, detectable, discriminatory and reliable. [FP03:22.3]

feature similarity: How much two features resemble each other. Measures of feature similarity are required for feature-based stereo, feature-based tracking, feature matching etc. [Umb98:2.6.1]

feature space: The dimensions of a feature space are the feature (property) values of a given problem. An object or shape is mapped to feature space by computing the values of the set of features defining the space, typically for recognition and classification. In the figure, shapes are mapped to a 2D feature space defined by area and rectangularity: [Umb98:2.6.1]

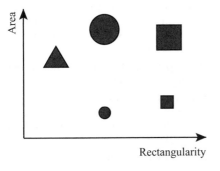

Rectangularity

feature stabilization: A technique for stabilizing the position of an image feature in an image sequence so that it remains in a particular position on a display (allowing or causing the rest of the image to move relative to that feature): [MC96]

Original sequence

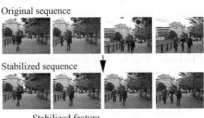

Stabilized sequence

Stabilized feature

feature tracking: See feature-based tracking.

feature vector: A vector formed by the values of a number of image features (properties), typically all associated with the same object or image. [Umb98:2.6.1]

feedback: The use of outputs from a system to control the system's actions. [WP:Feedback]

FERET: A standard database of face images with a defined experimental protocol for the testing and comparison of face recognition algorithms. [WP:FERET_database]

Feret's diameter: The distance between two parallel lines at the extremities of some shape that are tangential to the boundary of the shape. Maximum, minimum and mean values of Feret's diameter are often used (where every possible pair of parallel tangent lines is considered): [WP:Feret_diameter]

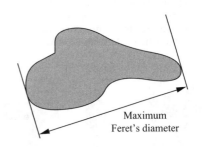

Maximum
Feret's diameter

FFT: See fast Fourier transform.

fiber optics: A medium for transmitting light that consists of very thin glass or plastic fibers. It can be used to provide much higher bandwidth for signals encoded as patterns of light pulses. Alternately, it can be used to transmit images directly through rigidly connected bundles of fibers, so as to see around corners, past obstacles etc. [Hec87:5.6]

fiberscope: A flexible fiber-optic instrument allowing parts of an object to be viewed that would normally be inaccessible. Most often used in medical examinations. [WP:Fiberscope]

fiducial point: A reference point for a given algorithm, e.g., a fixed, known, easily detectable pattern for a calibration algorithm. [WP:Fiducial_marker]

field of view (FOV): The linear or angular limit, θ that may be imaged in a given imaging system because of the lens (optics) or sensor in use:

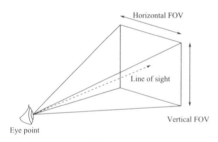

Horizontal FOV

Line of sight

Vertical FOV

Eye point

The field of view depends on the ratio between the sensor width W and the focal length, f, of the lens such that $tan\frac{\theta}{2} = \frac{W}{2f}$. [Sze10:2.2]

figure–ground separation: The segmentation of the area of the image representing the object of interest (the figure) from the remainder of the image (the background): [GW91]

Image   Figure   Ground

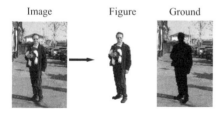

figure of merit: Any scalar that is used to characterize the performance of an algorithm. [WP:Figure_of_merit]

filter: In general, any algorithm that transforms a signal into another. For instance, bandpass filters remove or reduce the parts of an input signal outside a given frequency interval; gradient filters allow only image gradients to pass through; smoothing filters attenuate high frequencies. [Dav90:Ch. 3]

filter ringing: A type of distortion caused by the application of a steep recursive filter. Normally this term applies to electronic filters in which certain components (e.g., capacitors and inductors) can store and later release energy, but there are also digital equivalents of this effect. [WP: Ringing_artifacts]

filtering: Application of a filter. [BB82:3.1]

filtering threshold: Filtering systems generally generate a numeric score indicating how well a feature matches a given profile. Filtered features with scores above the specific filtering threshold are then selected. e.g., cross-correlation matching.

fingerprint database indexing: Indexing into a database of fingerprints using a number of features derived from the fingerprints. This allows a smaller number of fingerprints to be considered when attempting fingerprint identification. [RKCJ96]

fingerprint identification: Identification of an individual through comparison of an unknown fingerprint (or fingerprints) with known fingerprints. [WP:Automated_fingerprint_identification]

fingerprint indexing: See fingerprint database indexing.

fingerprint minutiae: In fingerprint identification, the major features of a fingerprint, such as a loop or whorl. [MMJP09]

finite element model: A class of numerical methods for solving differential problems. Another relevant class is finite difference methods. [WP: Finite_element_method]

finite impulse response filter (FIR): A filter that produces an output value (y_n) based on the current and past input values (x_i). $y_n = \sum_{i=0}^{p} a_i x_{n-i}$ where a_i are weights. See also infinite impulse response filters. [Jai89:2.3]

FIR: See finite impulse response filter.

Firewire (IEEE 1394): A serial digital bus system supporting 400 Mbits per second. Power, control and data signals are carried in a single cable. The bus system makes it possible to address up to 64 cameras from a single interface card and multiple computers can acquire images from the same camera simultaneously. [WP:IEEE_1394]

first derivative filter: See gradient filter.

first fundamental form: See surface curvature.

Fisher linear discriminant (FLD): A classification method that maps high-dimensional K class data into $K - 1$ dimensions in such a way as to maximize class separability. [DH73:4.10]

Fisher–Rao metric: The Rao distance provides a measure of difference between two probability distributions. Given two probability densities p and q which are members of a parameterized family with the parameter a, suppose that $p(x) = p(x|a)$, $q(x) = p(x|a + \delta a)$ where δa is a small change in a. To a first approximation, $D(p, q)$ is a squared distance, in that $D(pf(.|a), p(.|a + \delta a)) = \frac{1}{2}\delta a.J(a).\delta a +$(higher-order terms), where $J(a)$ is the matrix defining a Riemannian metric on the subset from which a takes its values. This metric is known as the Fisher–Rao metric. [May05]

fisheye lens: See wide angle lens. [WP: Fisheye_lens]

fitness function: The name given in the genetic algorithms literature for the objective function which is to be optimized. The fitness function evaluates a given member of the genetic algorithm population returning a value proportional to its optimality. [Mit97:9.2]

fixation: The physiological consequence of fixing visual attention on a single location with the eyes or sensors pointing fixedly at that location. [Dod07]

flat field: 1) An object of uniform color, used for photometric calibration of optical systems.
2) A camera system is *flat-field correct* if the gray scale output at each pixel is the same for a given light input. [Jai89:4.4]

flexible template: A model of a shape in which the relative position of points is not fixed (e.g., defined in probabilistic form). This approach allows for variations in the appearance of the shape. [HTC92]

FLIR: Forward-looking infrared. An infrared system mounted on a vehicle looking along the direction of travel: [WP:Forward_looking_infrared]

Infrared Sensor

flow field: See optical flow field.

flow histogram: A histogram of the optical flow in an image sequence. This can be used, e.g., to provide a qualitative description of the motion of the observer. [DTS06]

flow vector field: Optical flow is described by a vector (magnitude and orientation) for each image point. Hence a flow vector field is the same as an optical flow field. [Fau93:9.2]

fluorescence: The emission of visible light by a substance caused by the absorption of some other (possibly invisible) electromagnetic wavelength. This property is sometimes used in industrial machine vision. [FP03:4.2]

fluorescence microscopy: A technique of close examination used to study specimens which can themselves be made to fluoresce. It is based on exploiting the phenomenon that certain materials emit energy detectable as visible light when irradiated with light at a specific wavelength. The sample may either fluoresce itself or be treated with chemicals which do. [HP98]

fluorescent lighting: A light source where the central mechanism of photon release is electrical excitation of an inert gas containing mercury. Electrons traveling through the gas collide with the mercury atoms releasing photons which collide with a phosphor coating creating light. Manufacturers can vary the color of the light produced by using different combinations of phosphors in the coatings. [WP:Fluorescent_lamp]

fMRI: Functional magnetic resonance imaging (fMRI) is a technique for identifying which parts of the brain are activated by different types of physical stimulation, e.g., visual or acoustic stimuli. An MRI scanner is set up to register the increased blood flow to the activated areas of the brain on an fMRI scan. See also nuclear magnetic resonance. [WP: Functional_magnetic_resonance_imaging]

FOA: See focus of attention. [WP: Attention#Visual_attention]

FOC: See focus of contraction.

focal length: 1) The distance between the camera lens and the focal plane. 2) The distance from a lens at which an object viewed at infinity would be in focus: [FP03:1.2.2]

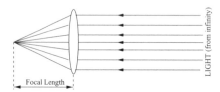

focal plane: The plane on which an image is focused by a lens system. Generally this consists of an array of photosensitive elements. See also image plane. [Hec87:5.2.3]

focal point: The point on the optical axis of a lens where light rays from an object at infinity (also placed on the optical axis) converge: [FP03:1.2.2]

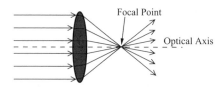

focal surface: A term most frequently used when a concave mirror is used to focus an image (e.g., in a reflector telescope). The focal surface in this case is the surface of the mirror: [WP: Focal_surface]

focus: Arranging for the focal points of various image features to converge on the focal plane. An image is considered to be "in focus" if the main subject of interest is in focus:

In focus   Out of focus

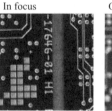

Note that focus (or lack of focus) can be used to derive useful information (e.g., see depth from focus). [TV98:2.2.2]

focus control: The control of the focus of a lens system usually by moving the lens along the optical axis or by adjusting the focal length. See also autofocus. [CGLL84]

focus following: A technique for slowly changing the focus of a camera as an object of interest moves. See also depth from focus. [WP:Follow_focus]

focus-invariant imaging: An imaging system that is designed to be invariant to focus. Such systems have a large depth of field. [BCD97]

focus of attention (FOA): The feature, object or area to which the attention of a visual system is directed. [WP: Attention#Visual_attention]

focus of contraction (FOC): The point of convergence of the optical flow vectors for a translating camera. The component of the translation along the optical axis must be nonzero. Compare focus of expansion. [JKS95:14.5.2]

focus of expansion (FOE): The point from which all optical flow vectors appear to emanate in a static scene where the observer is moving. For example, if a camera system is moving directly forwards along the optical axis then the optical flow vectors all emanate from the principal point (usually near the center of the image): [FP03:10.1.3]

Two images from a moving observer. Blended Image FOE

FOE: See focus of expansion.

fold edge: A surface orientation discontinuity. An edge where two locally planar surfaces meet. The figure shows a fold edge: [WB94]

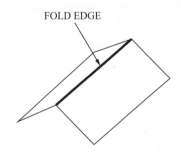

FOLD EDGE

foreground: In computer vision, generally used in the context of object recognition. The area of the scene or image in which the object of interest lies. See figure–ground separation. [JKS95:2.5.1]

foreshortening: A typical perspective effect whereby distant objects appear smaller than closer ones. [FP03:4.1.1]

form factor: The physical size or arrangement of an object. This term is frequently used with reference to computer boards. [FP03:5.5.2]

Förstner operator: A feature detection operator used for corner detection as well as other edge features. [WP: Corner_detection#The_F.C3.B6rstner_corner_detector]

forward–backward algorithm: A special case of belief propagation used to carry out probabilistic inference in a hidden Markov model (HMM) by passing messages forwards and backwards in the hidden Markov chain. [Bis06:13.2.2]

forward-looking radar: A radar system mounted on a vehicle looking along the direction of travel. See also side-looking radar. [KK01]

Fourier–Bessel transform: See Hankel transform. [WP:Hankel_transform]

Fourier domain convolution: Convolution in Fourier space involves simply multiplication of the Fourier transformed image by the Fourier transform filter. For very large filters this operation is much more efficient than using the convolution operator in the original domain. [BB82:2.2.4]

Fourier domain inspection: Identification of defects based on features in the Fourier transform of an image. [TH99]

Fourier image processing: Image processing in Fourier space (i.e., processing images that have been transformed using the Fourier transform). [Umb98:2.5.4]

Fourier matched-filter object recognition: Object recognition in which correlation is determined using a matched filter that is the conjugate of the Fourier transform of the object being located. [CDD94]

Fourier shape descriptor: A boundary representation of a shape in terms of the coefficients of a Fourier transformation. [BB82:8.2.4]

Fourier slice theorem: A slice at an angle θ of a 2D Fourier transform of an object is equal to a 1D Fourier transform of a parallel projection of the object taken at the same angle. See also slice-based reconstruction. [WP: Projection-slice_theorem]

Fourier space: The frequency domain space in which an image (or other signal) is represented after application of the Fourier transform. [WP:Frequency domain]

Fourier space smoothing: Application of a smoothing filter (e.g., to remove high-frequency noise) in a Fourier transformed image. [Umb98:2.5.4]

Fourier transform: A transformation that allows a signal to be considered in the frequency domain as a sum of sine and cosine waves or equivalently as a sum of exponentials. For a two-dimensional image, $F(u, v) = \int_{-\infty}^{\infty} \int_{-\infty}^{\infty} f(x, y)e^{-2\pi i(xu+yv)}dxdy$. See also fast Fourier transform, discrete Fourier transform and inverse Fourier transform. [FP03:7.3.1]

fovea: The high-resolution central region of the human retina. The analogous region in an artificial sensor emulates the retinal arrangement of photoreceptors, e.g., a log-polar sensor. [FP03:1.3]

foveal image: An image in which the sampled pattern is inspired by the arrangement of the human fovea, i.e., sampling is most dense in the image center and gets progressively sparser towards the periphery of the image. [WP:Foveal_imaging#Example_images]

foveation: 1) The process of creating a foveal image.
2) Directing the camera optical axis to a given direction. [WP: Foveated_imaging]

fractal image compression: An image compression method based on exploiting self-similarity at different scales. [WP:Fractal_compression]

fractal measure/dimension: A measure of the roughness of a shape. Consider a curve whose length (L_1 and L_2) is measured at two scales (S_1 and S_2). If the curve is rough, the length grows as the scale increases. The fractal dimension is $D = \frac{log(L_1-L_2)}{log(S_2-S_1)}$. [JKS95:7.4]

fractal representation: A representation based on self-similarity. For example a fractal representation of an image could be based on the similarity of blocks of pixels. [KMK95]

fractal surface: A surface model that is defined progressively using fractals (i.e., the surface displays self-similarity at different scales). [Pen84]

fractal texture: A texture representation based on self-similarity between scales. [JKS95:7.4]

frame: 1) A complete standard television video image consisting of the even fields and the odd fields.
2) A knowledge representation technique suitable for recording a related set of facts, rules of inference, preconditions etc. [TV98:8.1]

frame buffer: A device that stores a video frame for access, display and processing by a computer. For example, such devices are used to store the frame from which a video display is refreshed. See also frame store. [TV98:2.3.1]

frame differencing: A technique for detecting changes in a scene by subtracting (usually) consecutive frames from a video and also possibly taking the absolute value of the resulting difference image. Regions of the difference image with high amplitude are assumed to be in the salient region. [MMN06]

frame grabber: See frame store.

frame of reference: A <u>coordinate system</u> defined with respect to some object, the camera or the real world: [WP:Frame_of_reference]

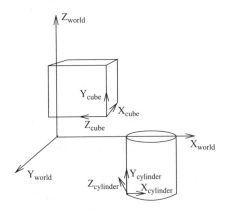

frame rate: The number of images taken, broadcast or digitally processed by a system per second. Frequently quoted in units of frames per second (fps) and used as a performance metric in relation to computational efficiency of a given implementation. [SB11:Ch. 1]

frame store: An electronic device for recording a <u>frame</u> from an imaging system. Typically such devices are used as the interface between a <u>CCIR camera</u> and a computer. [Dav90:2.2]

freeform surface: A surface that does not follow any particular mathematical form; e.g., the folds of a piece of fabric: [BM02:4.1]

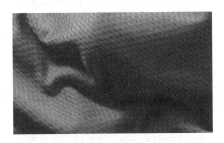

Freeman code: A type of <u>chain code</u> in which a contour is represented by coordinates for the first point followed by a series of direction codes (typically 0 through 7). The figure shows (left)

the Freeman codes relative to the center point and (right) an example of the codes derived from a chain of points: [Jai89:9.6]

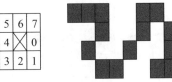

0, 0, 2, 3, 1, 0, 7, 7, 6, 0, 1, 2, 2, 4

Frenet frame: A triplet of mutually orthogonal unit vectors (the <u>curve normal</u>, the <u>curve tangent</u> and the <u>curve binormal</u> or <u>curve bitangent</u>) describing a point on a curve: [BB82:9.3.1]

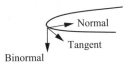

frequency domain filter: A <u>filter</u> defined by its action in <u>Fourier space</u>. See <u>high-pass filter</u> and <u>low-pass filter</u>. [Umb98:3.4]

frequency spectrum: The range of (electromagnetic) frequencies. [Hec87:7.8]

Fresnel diffraction: The apparent bending and fringed structuring of light which appears to occur close to an <u>aperture</u>. [Sha06:p. 357)]

Fresnel equations: The equations that govern the changes in light when moving across an interface between two materials of different refractive indices. The particular equations corresponding to ratios of electric field amplitudes are also known as the Fresnel equations. [Hec87:pp. 433–499]

Fresnel lens: A lens created from many small prisms of varying <u>index of refraction</u> often used in lighthouse illuminators. A Fresnel lens has a much lower bulk than a conventional plano-convex lens of equivalent power. To make the lens, the non-refractive parts of a conventional lens (dark in the figure) are removed:

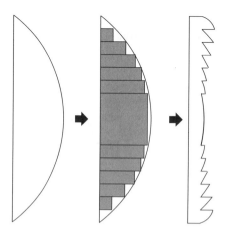

front lighting: A general term covering methods of lighting a scene where the lights are on the same side of the object as the camera: [WP:Frontlight] As an alternative consider back lighting.

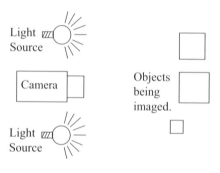

front porch: In analog signals, the prelude to the horizontal synchronization signal. The figure shows it in the context of the anatomy of a typical analog video signal: [Car01]

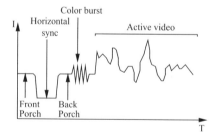

frontal presentation: A planar surface parallel to the image plane. [TSK01]

frontier point: Point on an object surface where the surface normal is known. This can be exploited to infer the surface reflectance and the light distribution in various circumstances. Frontier points may also be used to recover surface shape in stereo applications. [VFC05]

full primal sketch: A representation described as part of Marr's theory of vision, that is made up of the raw primal sketch primitives together with grouping information. The sketch contains described image structures that could correspond with scene structures (e.g., image regions with scene surfaces). [MH80]

function-based model: An object representation based on functionality (e.g., the object's purpose or the way in which it moves and interacts with other objects) rather than its geometric properties. [SB94]

function-based recognition: Object recognition based on object functionality rather than geometric properties. See also function-based model. [RDR94]

functional optimization: An analytical technique for optimizing (maximizing or minimizing) complex functions of continuous variables. [Hor86:6.13]

functional representation: See function-based model. [WP:Function_representation]

fundamental form: A metric useful in determining local properties of surfaces. See also surface curvature. [Fau93:C.3]

fundamental matrix: A bilinear relationship between corresponding points (u, u') in binocular stereo images. The fundamental matrix, $\mathbf{F}$, incorporates the two sets of camera parameters ($\mathbf{K}$, $\mathbf{K}'$) and the relative position ($\vec{t}$) and orientation ($\mathbf{R}$) of the cameras. Matching points $\vec{u}$ from one image and $\vec{u}'$ from the other image satisfy $\vec{u}'^T \mathbf{F} \vec{u}' = 0$ where $\mathbf{S}(\vec{t})$ is the skew symmetric matrix of $\vec{t}$ and $\mathbf{F} = (\mathbf{K}^{-1})^T \mathbf{S}(\vec{t}) \mathbf{R}^{-1} (\mathbf{K}')^{-1}$. See also the essential matrix. [TV98:7.3.4]

fusion: Integration of data from multiple sources into a single representation. [SQ04:18.5]

fuzzy logic: A form of logic that allows a range of possibilities between true and false (i.e., a degree of truth). [WP: Fuzzy_logic]

fuzzy morphology: A type of mathematical morphology operation that is based on fuzzy logic rather than the more conventional Boolean logic. [KN00:1.1]

fuzzy reasoning: See fuzzy logic.

fuzzy set: A grouping of data where each item in the group has an associated grade or likelihood of membership in the set. [WP:Fuzzy_set]

fuzzy similarity measure: A non-finite analog to a similarity measure when evaluating pairs of fuzzy features. The most obvious way of calculating the similarity is based on the inter-feature distances using the fuzzy equivalent of the most usually employed finite distance measures. Several have been proposed as follows: If d is the distance measure between two fuzzy sets A and B on a universe X, then:

- Koczy: $S(A, B) = \frac{1}{1+d(A,B)}$;
- Williams and Steele: $S(A, B) = e^{-\alpha d(A,B)}$ where α is the steepness measure;
- Santini: $S(A, B) = 1 - \beta d(A, B)$ where $\beta = 1, 2, \infty$.

[JK05]

G

Gabor filter: A filter formed by multiplying a complex oscillation by an elliptical Gaussian distribution (specified by two standard deviations and an orientation). This creates filters that are local, selective for orientation, have different scales and are tuned for intensity patterns (e.g., edges, bars and other patterns observed to trigger responses in the simple cells of the mammalian visual cortex) according to the frequency chosen for the complex oscillation. The filter can be applied in the frequency domain as well as the spatial domain. [FP03:9.2.2]

Gabor transform: A transformation that allows a 1D or 2D signal (such as an image) to be represented as a weighted sum of Gabor functions. [NA05:2.7.3]

Gabor wavelets: A type of wavelet formed by a sinusoidal function that is restricted by a Gaussian envelope function. [NA05:2.7.3] [WP: Gabor_wavelet#Wavelet_space]

gait analysis: Analysis of the way in which human subjects move. Frequently used for biometric or medical purposes: [WP:Gait_analysis]

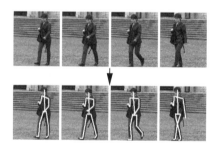

gait classification: 1) Classification of different types of human motion (such as walking or running). 2) Biometric identification of people based on their gait parameters. [WP: Gait#Energy-based_gait_classification]

Galerkin approximation: A method for determining the coefficients of a power series solution for a differential equation. [Whe73]

gallery image: Exemplar image used to test the image retrieval or object recognition abilities of image search algorithms.

gamma: Devices such as cameras and displays that convert between analog (denoted a) and digital (d) images generally have a nonlinear relationship between a and d. A common model for this nonlinearity is that the signals are related by a *gamma curve* of the form $a = c \times d^{\gamma}$, for some constant c. For CRT displays, common values of γ are in the range 1.0–2.5. [BB82:2.3.1]

gamma correction: The correction of brightness and color ratios so that an image has the correct dynamic range when displayed on a monitor. [WP: Gamma_correction]

gamma distribution: A probability density function of a random variable X defined on $[0, \infty)$ obeying a $\Gamma(\alpha, \beta)$ distribution is $p(x) = \frac{\beta^{\alpha}}{\Gamma(\alpha)}x^{\alpha-1}e^{-\beta x}$, where α is a shape parameter and β is an inverse scale parameter. The chi-squared distribution with ν degrees of freedom is a special case of the

Dictionary of Computer Vision and Image Processing, Second Edition.
R. B. Fisher, T. P. Breckon, K. Dawson-Howe, A. Fitzgibbon, C. Robertson, E. Trucco and C. K. I. Williams.
© 2014 John Wiley & Sons, Ltd. Published 2014 by John Wiley & Sons, Ltd.

gamma distribution with $\alpha = \nu/2$, $\beta = 1/2$. [Bis06:p. 688]

gamut mapping: Functional mapping of the color-space coordinates of a source image to color-space coordinates of a reproduction in order to compensate for differences in the source and output medium color gamut capability. [ISO04]

gauge coordinates: A coordinate system local to the image surface itself. Gauge coordinates provide a convenient frame of reference for operators such as the gradient operator. [FRKV92]

gauging: Measuring or testing. A standard requirement of industrial machine vision systems. [WP: Gauge_(instrument)]

Gauss map: In three dimensions, a mapping of an object's surface normals onto the unit sphere. In higher dimensions, it is a mapping of hyper-surfaces in R^n onto the unit sphere $S^{n-1} \in R^n$. Also known as the extended Gaussian image (EGI). [WP:Gauss_map]

Gaussian convolution: See Gaussian smoothing.

Gaussian curvature: A measure of the surface curvature at a point. It is the product of the maximum and minimum of the normal curvatures in all directions through the point. See also mean curvature. [FP03:19.1.2]

Gaussian derivative: The combination of Gaussian smoothing and a gradient filter. This results in a gradient filter that is less sensitive to noise: [FP03:8.2.1]

Original Image	Normal first derivative	Gaussian first derivative

Gaussian distribution: A probability density function with this distribution:

$$p(x) = \frac{1}{\sqrt{2\pi\sigma^2}} \exp\left\{-\frac{(x-\mu)^2}{2\sigma^2}\right\},$$

where μ is the mean and σ is the standard deviation. The Gaussian is also known as the normal distribution. See also the multi-variate normal distribution. [Bis06:2.3]

Gaussian–Hermite moment: Let $f(x,y)$ denote the intensity function of the image defined in ζ. Subsequently the (p,q) order Gaussian–Hermite moment of the image is: $M_{pq} = \int\int_\zeta f(x,y)\hat{H}_p(x:\sigma)\hat{H}_q(y:\sigma)\mathrm{d}x\mathrm{d}y$ where $\hat{H}_p(x:\sigma)$ and $\hat{H}_q(y:\sigma)$ are the corresponding Gaussian–Hermite polynomial functions with scale parameter σ. [YP11]

Gaussian mixture model: A mixture model where each of the components is a Gaussian distribution. For instance, used to represent color histograms with multiple peaks. See also expectation maximization. [Bis06:9.2]

Gaussian noise: Noise whose distribution is Gaussian in nature. Gaussian noise is specified by its standard deviation about a zero mean, and is often modeled as a form of additive noise: [TV98:3.1.1]

Gaussian process: A collection of random variables (i.e., a stochastic process), any number of which have a joint Gaussian distribution. A Gaussian process is completely defined by its mean and covariance functions. [RW06:2.2]

Gaussian process classification: A nonlinear generalization of the logistic regression model for two-class classification, with $p(C_1|\vec{x}) = \sigma(f(x))$, where σ denotes the logistic sigmoid function $\sigma(z) = (1 + e^{-z})^{-1}$ and $f(x)$ is a Gaussian process prior over functions. The model can also be generalized to multiclass classification problems. [RW06:Ch. 3]

Gaussian process latent variable model (GP-LVM): A latent variable model for dimensionality reduction. The nonlinear mapping between the low-dimensional latent space and the data space is modeled using Gaussian process regression. [Mur12:13.5]

Gaussian process regression: A Bayesian approach to regression where a Gaussian process (GP) prior is placed directly over functions. Assuming that the observations are corrupted by Gaussian noise, the posterior over functions is also a Gaussian process. With any given test input this gives rise to a predicted mean and variance. The figure shows a one-dimensional input space with function values observed at four locations (+):

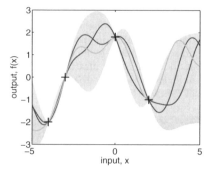

The colored lines show three random samples drawn from the posterior GP and the grey shading denotes the two standard deviation error bars around the mean. The mean prediction of a GP has the same form as in kernel ridge regression, but the latter method does not produce a predictive variance. [RW06:Ch. 2]

Gaussian pyramid: A multi-resolution representation of an image formed by several images, each one a subsampling and Gaussian smoothed version of the original one at increasing standard deviation: [WP:Gaussian_pyramid]

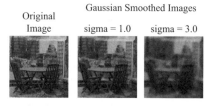

Original Image   Gaussian Smoothed Images   sigma = 1.0   sigma = 3.0

Gaussian smoothing: An image-processing operation aimed at attenuating image noise computed by a convolution operator with a mask sampling a Gaussian distribution: [TV98:3.2.2]

Gaussian speckle: Speckle that has a Gaussian distribution. [LWW83]

Gaussian sphere: A sampled representation of a unit sphere where the surface of the sphere is defined by a number of triangular patches (often computed by dividing a dodecahedron). See also extended Gaussian image: [Nal93:9.2.5]

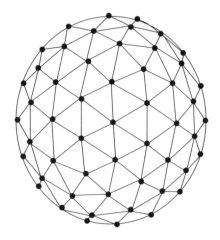

gaze control: The ability of a human subject or a robot head to control the direction of gaze. [Hen03]

gaze direction estimation: Estimation of the direction in which a human subject is looking. Used for human-computer interaction: [NMRZ00]

gaze direction tracking: Continuous gaze direction estimation (e.g., in a video sequence or a live camera feed). [MZ00]

gaze location: See gaze direction estimation.

generalized cone: A generalized cylinder in which the swept curve changes along the axis. [Nal93:9.2.3]

generalized curve finding: A general term referring to methods that locate arbitrary curves. For example, see generalized Hough transform. [Dav90:10]

generalized cylinder: A volumetric representation where the volume is defined by sweeping a closed curve along an axis. The axis does not need to be straight and the closed curve may vary in shape as it is moved along the axis. For example a cylinder may be defined by moving a circle along a straight axis, and a cone may be defined by moving a circle of changing diameter along a straight axis: [FP03:24.2.1]

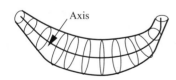

Axis

generalized eigenvalue: See generalized eigenvalue problem.

generalized eigenvalue problem: Let $\mathbf{A} = [a_{j,k}]$ be an $n \times n$ matrix and consider the vector equation $\mathbf{A}x = \lambda x$ where λ is a number. A non-trivial value for λ is called an eigenvalue of the matrix $\mathbf{A}$ and the corresponding solutions (by substitution of λ) are called the eigenvectors of $\mathbf{A}$. The set of all eigenvalues is called the spectrum of $\mathbf{A}$ and the largest among them is known as the spectral radius of $\mathbf{A}$. The problem of finding the eigenvectors and eigenvalues of $\mathbf{A}$ is known as the generalized eigenvalue problem. [Kre83:pp. 345–346]

generalized Hough transform: A version of the Hough transform capable of detecting the presence of arbitrary shapes. [Dav90:10]

generalized mosaic: A simple and effective method for extracting additional information at each scene point. As the camera moves, it senses each scene point multiple times. Fusing the data from multiple images yields an image mosaic that includes additional information about the scene, such as extended dynamic range, higher spectral quality, polarization, focus and distance sensing. [SN01a]

generalized order statistics filter: A filter in which the values within the filter mask are considered in increasing order and then combined in some fashion. The most common such filter is the median filter, which selects the middle value. [CY92]

generate and test: See hypothesize and verify. [WP:Trial_and_error]

generative model: A model representation that, explicitly or implicitly, models the distribution of inputs and outputs such that sampling from them facilitates the generation of a synthetic example in the input space. [Bis06:1.5.4]

generic viewpoint: A viewpoint such that small motions may cause small changes in the size or relative positions of features, but no features appear or disappear. This contrasts with a privileged viewpoint. [WP:Neuroesthetics#The_Generic_Viewpoint]

genetic algorithm: An optimization algorithm seeking solutions by refining iteratively a small set of candidates with a process mimicking genetic evolution. The suitability (fitness) of a set of possible solutions (a population) is used to generate a new population until conditions are satisfied (e.g., the best solution has not changed for a given number of iterations). [WP:Genetic_algorithm]

genetic programming: Application of genetic algorithms to evolve programs that satisfy some evaluation criteria. [WP:Genetic_programming]

genus: In the study of topology, the number of "holes" in a surface. In computer vision, sometimes used as a discriminating feature for simple object recognition. [WP:Genus]

Gestalt: German for "shape". The Gestalt school of psychology, led by Wertheimer, Köhler and Koffka in the first half of the 20th century, had a profound influence on perception theories and, subsequently, on computer vision. Its basic tenet was that a perceptual pattern has properties as a whole, which cannot be explained in terms of its individual components. In other words, the whole is more than the sum of its parts. This concept was captured in some basic laws (proximity, similarity, closure, "common destiny" or good form and saliency) that would apply to all mental phenomena, not just perception. Much work on low-level computer vision, most notably on perceptual grouping and perceptual organization, has exploited these ideas. See also visual illusion. [FP03:14.2]

geodesic: The shortest line between two points (on a mathematically defined surface). [Jai89:3.10]

geodesic active contour: An active contour model similar to the snake model in that it attempts to minimize an energy function between the model and the data, but which also incorporates a geometrical model: [CKS97]

Initial Contour   Final Contour

geodesic active region: A technique for region-based segmentation that builds on geodesic active contours by adding a force that takes into account information within regions. Typically a geodesic active region will be bounded by a single geodesic active contour. [PD02]

geodesic distance: The length of the shortest path between two points along some surface. This is different from the Euclidean distance, which takes no account of the surface. The figure shows the geodesic distance between Calgary and London (following the curvature of the earth): [WP: Distance_(graph_theory)]

geodesic transform: Assigns to each point the geodesic distance to some feature or class of feature. [SHB08:11.5.6]

geographic information system (GIS): A computer system that stores and manipulates geographically referenced data (such as images of portions of the earth taken by satellite). [WP: Geographic_information_system]

geometric algebra: A mathematical language whose function is to unify diverse mathematical formalisms in order to more easily express physical ideas. The geometric algebra of 3D space, e.g., is a powerful tool for solving problems in classical mechanics since it has a very clear and compact method for encoding rotations. [DL07]

geometric compression: The compression of geometric structures, such as polygons. [TR98]

geometric constraint: A limitation on the possible physical arrangement or appearance of objects based on geometry. These types of constraint are used extensively in stereo vision (the epipolar constraint), motion analysis (the rigid motion constraint) and object recognition (focusing on specific classes of objects or relations between features). [Fau93:6.2.6]

geometric correction: In remote sensing, an algorithm or technique for correction of geometric distortion. [Jai89:8.16]

geometric deformable model: A deformable model in which the deformation of curves is based on the level set method and stops at object boundaries. A typical example is a geodesic active contour model. [HXP03]

geometric distance: In curve fitting and surface fitting, the shortest distance from a given point to a given surface. In many fitting problems, the geometric distance is expensive to compute but yields more accurate solutions. Compare algebraic distance. [HZ00:3.2.2]

geometric distortion: Deviations from the idealized image formation model (e.g., pinhole camera) of an imaging system. Examples include radial lens distortion in standard cameras. [JB05]

geometric feature: A general term describing a shape characteristic of some data that encompasses features such as edges, corners, geons etc. [WP:Feature_extraction]

geometric feature learning: Learning geometric features from examples of the feature. [WP:Geometric_feature_learning]

geometric feature proximity: A measure of the distance between geometric features, e.g., the distance between data and overlaid model features in hypothesize and verify. [HZLM01]

geometric hashing: A technique for matching models in which some geometric invariant features are mapped into a hash table that is used to perform the recognition. [BM02:4.5.4]

geometric heat flow: Evolution-based image segmentation approach using a heat flow analogy where the agglomeration motion is orthogonal to the edge normals. May also be used as a replacement for image smoothing and image enhancement since it is similar to anisotropic diffusion. [Sap06:2.3]

geometric invariant: A quantity describing some geometric configuration that remains unchanged under certain transformations (e.g., cross ratio and perspective projection). [WP:Geometric_invariant_theory]

geometric model: A model that describes the geometric shape of some object or scene. A model can be 2D (e.g., a polycurve) or 3D (e.g., a surface-based model). [WP:Geometric_modeling]

geometric model matching: Comparison of two geometric models or of a model and a set of image data shapes, for the purposes of object recognition. [RH95]

geometric morphometrics: Statistical tools for analyzing information about the relative geometry of organisms, specifically the changes in that geometry brought about by various processes. [ARS04]

geometric optics: A general term referring to the description of optics from a geometrical point of view. Includes concepts such as the simple pinhole camera model, magnification, lens etc. [Hec87:Ch. 3]

geometric reasoning: Reasoning with geometric shapes in order to address such tasks as robot motion planning, shape similarity, spatial position estimation etc. [MK90]

geometric representation: See geometric model. [WP:RGB_color_model#Geometric_representation]

geometric shape: A shape that takes a relatively simple geometric form (such as a square, ellipse, cube, sphere, generalized cylinder etc.) or that can be described as a combination of such geometric primitives. [WP: Geometric_primitive]

geometric transformation: A class of image-processing operations that transform the spatial relationships in an image. They are used for the correction of geometric distortions and general image manipulation. A geometric transformation requires the definition of a pixel coordinate transformation together with an interpolation scheme. The figure shows a rotation: [Umb98:3.5]

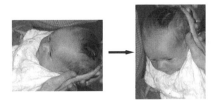

geon: GEometrical iON. A basic volumetric representation primitive proposed by Biederman and used in recognition by components. Some example geons are: [WP: Geon_(psychology)]

gesture analysis: Basic analysis of video data representing human gestures preceding the task of gesture recognition. [WP:Gesture_recognition]

gesture-based user interface: Various methods of communicating commands to electronic devices which are based on capturing and analyzing human motion, either facial or physical. It is critical that the analysis takes place at a very rapid rate in order to avoid lag between the command being issued and acted upon. [SPHK08]

gesture component space: Once a video sequence is split into atomic actions, the gestures which took place can be represented by a mixture model. To determine automatically how many typical groups exist, they can be represented in the gesture component space, where the axes are the principal components of the motion. [GX11:Ch. 5]

gesture recognition: The recognition of human gestures, generally for the purpose of human–computer interaction. See also hand sign recognition: [WP: Gesture]

gesture segmentation: The segmentation of a video sequence into a stream of atomic actions which can be mapped to a user-specified dictionary of pre-arranged templates. Gesture recognition can be performed on the segments to identify what they convey. [GX11:Ch. 5]

gesture tracking: Computing the gesture trajectory of a human (or animal) participant through the gesture component space. [GX11:Ch. 5]

ghost artifacts: Appearance of unwanted secondary (often weaker) signal artifacts superimposed on the main signal. In imaging this can be for a wide range of reasons including unintended optical, electrical, exposure or sensing effects. [Hen07:Ch. 11]

Gibbs point process: Models of how point-like objects (e.g., the particles in a gas) arrange themselves into a state of equilibrium. The simplest form is that of pairwise interaction since it is defined by a single parameter. [Hei94]

Gibbs sampling: A method for probabilistic inference based on transition probabilities (between states). [WP: Gibbs_sampling]

GIF: Graphics interchange format. A common image compression format based on the Lempel–Ziv–Welch algorithm. [Umb98:1.8]

GIS: See geographic information system. [WP:Geographic_information_system]

gist image descriptor: The spatial envelope model of a scene is based on four global properties of the image (naturalness, openness, roughness and expansion). Outputs from a set of image filters like Gabor filters (learned from image data) are combined to give an estimate of each of the four global properties. Collectively, the four values define a global descriptor for the image, suitable for image grouping and image indexing. [OT01]

glint: A specular reflection visible on a mirror-like surface: [WP:Glint]

Glint

global point signature: For a fixed point x, the global point signature $G(x)$ is a vector whose components are scaled eigenfunctions of the Laplace–Beltrami operator evaluated at x.

global positioning system (GPS): A system of satellites that allow the position of a *GPS receiver* to be determined in absolute, earth-referenced coordinates. Accuracy of standard civilian GPS is of the order of meters. Greater accuracy is obtainable using differential GPS. [WP: Global_Positioning_System]

global property: A property of a mathematical object that depends on all components of the object. For example, the average intensity of an image is a global property, as it depends on all the image pixels. [WP:Global_variable]

global structure extraction: Identification of high level structures or relationships in an image (e.g., symmetry detection). [OIA01]

global transform: A general term describing an operator that transforms an image into some other space. Sample global transforms include the discrete cosine transform, the

Fourier transform, the Haar transform, the Hadamard transform, the Hartley transform, histograms, the Hough transform, the Karhunen–Loéve transform, the Radon transform and the wavelet transform. [CTM+96]

gold standard: A term used to refer either to the ground truth or the result obtained using the current state-of-the-art (i.e., the best-performing) approach for a given task to which we are comparing.

golden template: An image of an unflawed object or scene that is used within template matching to identify any deviations from the ideal object or scene. [XG00]

gonioreflectometer: A light source and sensor arrangement used for collecting intensity data from many angles in order to generate a model of the bidirectional reflectance distribution function of a given surface or object. [Foo97]

gradient: Rate of change. Frequently associated with edge detection. See also gray scale gradient: [Nal93:3.1.2]

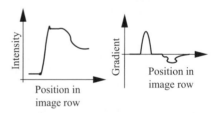

gradient-based flow estimation: Estimation of the optical flow based on gradient images. This computation can be done directly through the computation of a time derivative as long as the movement between frames is quite small. See also the aperture problem. [KTB87]

gradient constraint equation: Equation relating optical flow velocity in the image (u, v) to the image intensity function $I(x, y, t)$. The usual assumption in gradient-based approaches is that the intensity of an object point is constant over time and changes must be due entirely to the motion of the camera. Camera motion makes a point

113

(x, y, t) change position in the image over a time δt. Assuming constant intensity, the image point is the same at time t and time $t + \delta t$ thus:
$I(x, y, t) = I(d + \delta x, y + \delta y, t + \delta t)$,
thence from its Taylor series:
$I(x, y, t) = I(d + \delta x, y + \delta y, t + \delta t) = I(x, y, t) + \frac{\partial I}{\partial x}\delta x + \frac{\partial I}{\partial y}\delta y + \frac{\partial I}{\partial t}\delta t$
+ high-order terms. From this follows the gradient constraint equation:
$0 = \frac{\partial I}{\partial x}u + \frac{\partial I}{\partial y}v + \frac{\partial I}{\partial t}$. [Sze10:9.3]

gradient descent: A popular method of optimization. The central idea is to find a minimum of a function $f(\mathbf{x})$ by repeatedly moving in the direction of steepest descent (i.e., the gradient direction). If f has a minimum at $\mathbf{x_N}$ and we begin iterating at a point $\mathbf{x}_0$ then we search for a minimum of f in the direction $-\nabla f(\mathbf{x})$ which is the direction of steepest descent. For a suitable τ_i we iteratively compute $\mathbf{x}_{i+1} = \mathbf{x}_i - \tau_i \nabla f(\mathbf{x}_i)$ until convergence. [Kre83:pp. 871–872]

gradient edge detection: Edge detection based on image gradients. [BB82:3.3.1]

gradient feature: Semi-invariant features (often edges) computed after applying a gradient operator to an image. [Liu07]

gradient filter: A filter that is convolved with an image to create an image in which every point represents the gradient in the original image in an orientation defined by the filter. Normally two orthogonal filters are used; by combining them, a gradient vector can be determined for every point. Common filters include the Roberts cross gradient operator, the Prewitt gradient operator and the Sobel gradient operator. The Sobel horizontal gradient operator gives: [WP: Edge_detection]

 Gradient Filter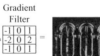

gradient image: See edge image. [WP: Image_gradient#Computer_vision]

gradient location and orientation histogram (GLOH) features: A 128-dimensional robust descriptor which is an extension of the SIFT descriptor that uses histograms with 17 location and 16 orientation bins in a log-polar configuration. The dimensionality is reduced via post-binning principal component analysis. [Sze10:4.1]

gradient magnitude thresholding: Thresholding of a gradient image in order to identify "strong" edge points: [KR82]

gradient matching stereo: An approach to stereo matching in which the image gradients (or features derived from the image gradients) are matched. [CS09:6.9]

gradient operator: An image-processing operator that produces a gradient image from a gray scale input image I. Depending on the usage of the term, the output could be the vectors ∇I of the x and y derivatives at each point or the magnitudes of these gradient vectors. The usual role of the gradient operator is to locate regions of strong gradients that signal the position of an edge. The figure shows a gray scale image and its intensity gradient magnitude image, where darker lines indicate stronger magnitudes:

The gradient was calculated using the Sobel gradient operator. [DH73:7.3]

gradient space: A representation of surface orientations in which each orientation is represented by a pair (p, q) where $p = \frac{\partial z}{\partial x}$ and $q = \frac{\partial z}{\partial y}$ (where the z axis is aligned with the optical axis of the viewing device): [Hor86:15.3]

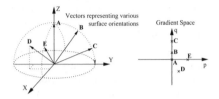

gradient vector: A vector describing the magnitude and direction of maximal change on an N-dimensional surface. [WP:Gradient]

gradient vector flow: In active contour models, a dense vector field derived by minimizing an energy function which comes from solving a pair of decoupled differential equations that diffuse the gradient vectors of an image. [XP98]

gradient vector flow snake (GVF): An extension of active contour models where the contours converge to boundary concavities and do not need to be initialized close to a boundary. [XP98]

graduated non-convexity: An algorithm for finding a global minimum in a function that has many sharp local minima (a non-convex function). This is achieved by approximating the function by a convex function with just one minimum (near the global minimum of the non-convex function) and then gradually improving the approximation. [Bla83]

grammar: A system of rules constraining the way in which primitives (such as words) can be combined. Used in computer vision to represent objects where the primitives are simple shapes, textures or features. [DH73:12.2.1]

grammatical representation: A representation that describes shapes using a

number of primitives that can be combined using a particular set of rules (the grammar). [RA06]

granulometric spectrum: The resultant distribution from a granulometry. [SD92]

granulometry: The study of the size characteristics of a set (e.g., the size of a set of regions). Most normally this is achieved by applying a series of morphological openings (with structured elements of increasing size and then studying the resultant size distributions. [WP:Granulometry_ (morphology)]

graph: A set of vertices V and a set of edges $E \subset V \times V$ linking pairs of vertices. Vertices u and v are *neighbors* if $(u, v) \in E$ or $(v, u) \in E$. See graph isomorphism and subgraph isomorphism. This is a graph with five vertices: [FP03:14.5.1]

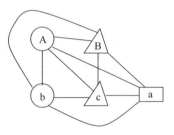

graph classification problem: A classification problem where each input object is a graph. [GHC02]

graph clustering: A clustering problem where each input object is a graph. Contrast with graph theoretic clustering. [RGS08]

graph cut: A partition of the vertices of a directed graph V into two disjoint sets S and T. The cost of the cut is the cost of all the edges that go from a vertex in S to a vertex in T. [CS09:6.11]

graph embedding: A mapping from a graph to a vector space. The extracted features could be used to define a graph kernel. [GVB11]

graph isomorphism: Two graphs are isomorphic if there exists a mapping (bijection) between their vertices that makes the edge sets identical. Determining whether two graphs are isomorphic is the "graph isomorphism problem", believed to be NP-complete. These small graphs are isomorphic with A:b, C:a and B:c: [Fau93:11.2.2]

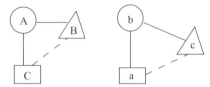

graph kernel: A kernel function (definition 3) that returns a scalar giving the similarity of two graphs. [VSKB10]

graph matching: A general term describing techniques for comparing two graph models. These techniques may attempt to find graph isomorphisms or subgraph isomorphisms, or may just try to establish similarity between graphs: [Fau93:11.2.2]

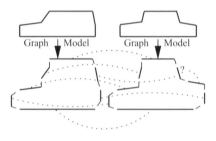

graph median: In graph theory, the vertex for which the sum of lengths of shortest paths to all other vertices is minimized. [MS79]

graph model: A model of data in terms of a graph. Typical uses in computer vision include object representation (see graph matching) and edge gradients (see graph searching). [WP: Graphical_model]

graph partitioning: The operation of splitting a graph into subgraphs satisfying some criteria. For example we might want to partition a graph of all polygonal edge segments in an image into subgraphs corresponding to objects in the scene. [WP: Graph_partition]

graph pruning: The simplification of a graph by the removal of vertices and edges.

graph representation: See graph model. [WP:Graph_(data_structure) #Representations]

graph searching: Looking for a specific node or path through a graph. Used for, among other things, border detection (e.g., in an edge gradient image) and object identification (e.g., a decision tree). [TSF95]

graph similarity: The degree to which two graph representations are similar. Typically (in computer vision) the representations are not exactly the same and hence a double subgraph isomorphism may need to be found to evaluate similarity. [WFKM97]

graph theoretic clustering: Clustering algorithms that use concepts from graph theory, in particular leveraging efficient graph-theoretic algorithms such as maximum flow. [WP: Cluster_analysis]

graphical model: See probabilistic graphical model.

grassfire algorithm: A technique for finding a region skeleton based on wave propagation. A virtual fire is lit on all region boundaries and the skeleton is defined by the intersection of the wave fronts: [LL92]

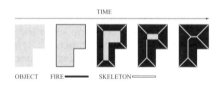

Grassmannian space: The set of k-dimensional linear subspaces in an n-dimensional vector space V, denoted as $Gr(n, k)$. [CHS95]

grating: See diffraction grating. [WP: Grating]

gray level . . .: See gray scale . . .

gray scale: A monochromatic representation of the value of a pixel. Typically this represents image brightness and ranges from 0 (black) to 255 (white): [Gal90:3.4]

0 255

gray scale co-occurrence: The occurrence of two particular gray levels some particular distance and orientation apart. Used in co-occurrence matrices. [Nev82:8.3.1]

gray scale correlation: The cross correlation of gray scale values in image windows or full images. [WKT01]

gray scale distribution model: A model of how gray scales are distributed in some image region. See also intensity histogram. [OPM02]

gray scale gradient: The rate of change of the gray levels in a gray scale image. See also edge, gradient image and first derivative filter. [SFWK02]

gray scale image: A monochrome image in which pixels typically represent brightness values ranging from 0 to 255. See also gray scale: [SQ04:4.1.1]

gray scale mathematical morphology: The application of a mathematical morphology operation to gray scale images. Each quantization level is treated as a distinct set where pixels are members of the set if they have a value greater than or equal to particular quantization levels. [SQ04:7.2]

gray scale moment: A moment that is based on image or region gray scales. See also binary moment. [PKK08]

gray scale morphology: See gray scale mathematical morphology.

gray scale similarity: See gray scale correlation.

gray scale texture moment: A moment that describes texture in a gray scale image (e.g., the Haralick texture operator describes image homogeneity). [CD94]

gray scale transformation: A general term describing a class of image-processing operations that apply to gray scale images and simply manipulate the gray scale of pixels. Example operations include contrast stretching and histogram equalization. [CK94]

gray value . . .: See gray scale . . .

greedy search: A search algorithm seeking to maximize a local criterion instead of a global one. Greedy algorithms sacrifice generality for speed. For instance, the stable configuration of a snake is typically found by an iterative energy minimization. The snake configuration at each step of the optimization can be found globally, by searching the space of all allowed configurations of all pixels simultaneously (a large space) or locally (greedy algorithm), by searching the space of all allowed configurations of each pixel individually (a much smaller space). [NA05:6.3.2]

grey . . .: See gray . . .

grid filter: An approach to noise reduction where a nonlinear function of features (pixels or averages of a number of pixels) from the local neighborhood are used. Grid filters require a training phase where noisy data and corresponding ideal data are presented. [VJ98]

ground following: See ground tracking.

ground plane: The horizontal plane that corresponds to the ground (the surface on which objects stand). This concept is only really useful when the ground is roughly flat. The ground plane is highlighted in the figure: [WP: Ground_plane]

ground tracking: A loosely defined term describing the robot navigation problem of sensing the ground plane and following some path. [WP: Ground_track]

ground truth: In performance analysis, the true value, or the most accurate value achievable, of the output of a specific instrument under analysis, e.g., a vision system measuring the diameter of circular holes. Ground truth values may be known theoretically, e.g., from formulae, or obtained through an instrument more accurate than the one being evaluated. [TV98:A.1]

group activity: An activity involving multiple individuals within a shared common space. [GX11:Ch. 7]

group association context: The use of contextual information in behavior analysis tasks that target the understanding of group activity derived from the association of several individuals within a group where some knowledge of individual behaviors is extracted via behavior classification. [GX11:Ch. 2]

grouping: 1) In human perception, the tendency to perceive certain patterns or clusters of stimuli as a coherent, distinct entity as opposed to a set of independent elements.
2) A whole class of segmentation algorithms based on the idea of grouping. Much of this work was inspired by the Gestalt school of psychology. See also segmentation, image segmentation, supervised classification and clustering. [FP03:Ch. 14]

grouping transform: An image analysis technique for grouping image features together (e.g., based on collinearity). [TV98:5.5]

H.263: <u>Video compression</u> standard that uses a very low-bitrate compressed format. As it was originally designed for video conferencing it supports several video frame sizes: 128×96, 176×144, 352×288, 704×576 and 1408×1152. [Gal91]

H.264: Also known as MPEG-4 Part 10 or AVC (Advanced Video Coding). A flexible popular standard for high-definition <u>video compression</u>. H.264/AVC contains many new features over <u>H.263</u> and offers a lower bitrate and more efficient compression and flexibility for application to a wide variety of network environments. It consists of two main layers: the video coding layer (VCL) which independently encodes the video and the network abstraction layer (NAL) which formats the video and provides header information allowing it to be transmitted. [Ric03]

Haar transform: A <u>wavelet transform</u> that is used in <u>image compression</u>. The basis functions are similar to those used by <u>first derivative</u> <u>edge detection</u> systems, resulting in images that are decomposed into horizontal, diagonal and vertical edges at different scales. [PS06:4.4]

Hadamard transform: An operation that can transform an image to its constituent Hadamard components. A fast version of the algorithms exist, which is similar to the <u>fast Fourier transform</u>, but all values in the basis functions are either $+1$ or -1. It requires significantly less computation and as such is often used for <u>image compression</u>. [Umb98:2.5.3]

Hahn moment: Given a digital image $f(x, y)$ of size $N \times N$, the $(m+n)$th order Hahn moment of the image is: $H_{m,n} = \sum_{x=0}^{N-1} \sum_{y=0}^{N-1} f(x, y) \tilde{h}_m^{(\mu,\nu)}(x, N) \tilde{h}_n^{(\mu,\nu)}(y, N)$ where $\tilde{h}_m^{(\mu,\nu)}(x, N)$ is the Hahn polynomial of order n. [ZSZ+05]

halftoning: See <u>dithering</u>. [WP: Halftone]

Hamming distance: The number of different bits in corresponding positions in two bit strings. For instance, the Hamming distance of 01110 and 01100 is 1, that of 10100 and 10001 is 2. A very important concept in digital communications. [CS09:6.3.2]

hand orientation: The direction of the hand. Axiomatically defined as the vector from the center point of the wrist to the base of the longest (second) finger.

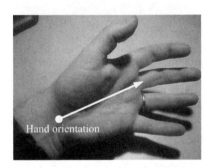

Hand orientation

hand-sign recognition: The recognition of hand gestures such as those used in sign language: [CSW95]

hand tracking: The tracking of a person's hand in a <u>video sequence</u>, often

Dictionary of Computer Vision and Image Processing, Second Edition.
R. B. Fisher, T. P. Breckon, K. Dawson-Howe, A. Fitzgibbon, C. Robertson, E. Trucco and C. K. I. Williams.

used in human–computer interaction. [RK94]

hand–eye calibration: The calibration of a manipulator (such as a robot arm) together with a visual system (such as a number of cameras). The main issue here is ensuring that both systems use the same frame of reference. See also camera calibration. [HD95]

hand–eye coordination: The use of visual feedback to direct the movement of a manipulator. See also hand-eye calibration. [HCM95]

handwriting verification: Verification that a style of handwriting corresponds to that of some particular individual. [WP:Handwriting_recognition]

handwritten character recognition: The automatic recognition of characters that have been written by hand: [WP:Handwriting_recognition]

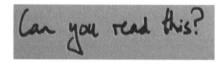

Hankel transform: A simplification of the Fourier transform for radially symmetric functions. [WP:Hankel_transform]

harmonic homology: A perspective (or projective) collineation of period two.

Harris corner detector: A corner detection system where a corner is detected if the eigenvalues of the matrix **M** are large and locally maximum ($f(i, j)$ is the intensity at point

(i,j)). $\mathbf{M} = \begin{bmatrix} \frac{\partial f}{\partial i}\frac{\partial f}{\partial i} & \frac{\partial f}{\partial i}\frac{\partial f}{\partial j} \\ \frac{\partial f}{\partial i}\frac{\partial f}{\partial j} & \frac{\partial f}{\partial j}\frac{\partial f}{\partial j} \end{bmatrix}$.

To avoid explicit computation of the eigenvalues, the local maxima of $det(\mathbf{M}) - 0.004 \times trace(\mathbf{M})$ can be used. This is also known as the Plessey corner finder. [WP:Harris_affine_region_detector#Harris_corner_measure]

Hartley transform: Similar transform to the Fourier transform, but the coefficients used are real (whereas those

used in the Fourier transform are complex). [Low91:13.4]

hat transform: See Laplacian of Gaussian operator (also known as Mexican hat operator) and top hat operator. [WP:Top-hat_transform]

Hausdorff distance: A measure of the distance between two sets of (image) points. For every point in both sets, determine the minimum distance to any point in the other set. The Hausdorff distance is the maximum of these minimum values. [Fau93:10.3.1]

HDR: See high dynamic range imaging.

HDTV: High Definition TeleVision. [WP:High-definition_television]

height image: See range image. [WP:Range_imaging]

Helmholtz reciprocity: An observation by Helmholtz about the bidirectional reflectance distribution function $f_r(\vec{i}, \vec{e})$ of a local surface patch, where $\vec{i}$ and $\vec{e}$ are the incoming and outgoing light rays respectively. The observation is that the reflectance is symmetric about the incoming and outgoing directions, i.e., $f_r(\vec{i}, \vec{e}) = f_r(\vec{e}, \vec{i})$. More generally, the principle states that a ray of light and its reverse have identical influences through an optical system which includes reflections, refractions and absorptions in a passive medium or at an interface. [FP03:4.2.2]

Helmholtz stereopsis: A surface reconstruction approach that attempts to exploit the symmetry of surface reflectance. Consider taking two images where the first is of the object illuminated by a point light source and the second swaps the light source and camera positions. Because of Helmholtz reciprocity, for corresponding pixels in the two images, the ratio of incident irradiance (onto the object) to emitted radiance (from the object) is the same. Depth and surface normals may be derived from the intensities of corresponding pixels independent of the bidirectional reflectance distribution function of the surface: [ZBK02]

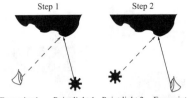

| Step 1 | Step 2 |

Eye point 1   Point light 1   Point light 2   Eye point 2

Hessian: The matrix of second derivatives of a multivalued scalar function. It can be used to design an orientation-dependent <u>second derivative</u> <u>edge</u> <u>detection</u> system: [FP03:3.1.2]

$$H = \begin{bmatrix} \frac{\partial^2 f(i,j)}{\partial i^2} & \frac{\partial^2 f(i,j)}{\partial i \partial j} \\ \frac{\partial^2 f(i,j)}{\partial j \partial i} & \frac{\partial^2 f(i,j)}{\partial j^2} \end{bmatrix}$$

heterarchical/mixed control: An approach to system control where control is shared amongst several systems. [DCM88]

heterogeneous sensor network: A collection of sensors, often low bandwidth and mobile, of varying types that aggregate data in an environment.

heuristic search: A process that employs commonsense rules (heuristics) to speed up searching. [BB82:4.4]

hexagonal image representation: An <u>image representation</u> where the <u>pixels</u> are hexagonal rather than rectangular. This representation might be used because it is similar to the human retina or because the distances to all adjacent pixels are equal, unlike with diagonally connected pixels in rectangular grids [WA89]

Hexagonal Sampling Grid

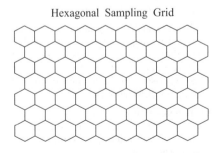

hidden Markov model (HMM): An HMM is a form of <u>state space model</u> where the hidden <u>state</u> is discrete.

There is a hidden <u>Markov chain</u> evolving according to a <u>state transition</u> <u>probability</u> distribution and observations giving partial information about the hidden state are made according to the <u>observation probability</u> distribution. The figure shows a <u>directed</u> <u>graphical model</u> representation of the HMM, where Z_i are the hidden state variables, X_i are the observation variables and **A** is the transition probabilities to the new state:

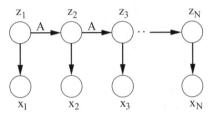

HMMs have been used extensively in vision tasks such as <u>activity analysis</u> and <u>handwritten</u> <u>character</u> <u>recognition</u>. [Bis06:13.2]

hidden state variable: A <u>state space</u> <u>model</u> consists of a state variable evolving over time, and observations related stochastically to the state. If the state variable is not directly observable it is called a hidden state variable. In a <u>hidden Markov model</u> the state variable is discrete; for the <u>Kalman filter</u>, it is a continuous-valued vector. [Bis06:13.1]

hierarchical: A general term referring to the approach of considering data at a low level of detail initially and then gradually increasing the level of detail. This approach often results in better performance. [WP:Hierarchy]

hierarchical clustering: An approach to <u>clustering</u> or <u>agglomerative</u> <u>clustering</u> in which each item is initially put in a separate cluster. The two most similar clusters are merged and this merging is repeated until some condition is satisfied (e.g., no clusters of less than a particular size remain). [DH73:6.10]

hierarchical coding: Coding of (image) data at multiple layers starting with the lowest level of detail and gradually increasing the resolution. See also hierarchical image compression. [CLP85]

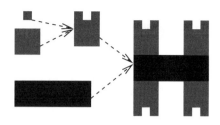

hierarchical hidden Markov model: A hierarchical extension of the hidden Markov model that models sequences with structure at many length or time scales. [Mur12:15.6.2]

hierarchical Hough transform: A technique for improving the efficiency of the standard Hough transform. Commonly used to describe any Hough-based technique that solves a sequence of problems beginning with a low-resolution Hough space and proceeding to high-resolution space, or using low-resolution images, or operating on subimages of the input image before combining the results. [QM89]

hierarchical image compression: Image compression using hierarchical coding. This leads to the concept of progressive image transmission. [Sha92]

hierarchical k-means: A divisive approach to hierarchical clustering. Initially k-means clustering is run on all the data with small k (e.g., $k = 2$) and each partition so created is divided again by k-means. This process is continued recursively until a stopping criterion is applied. The method is also known as tree-structured vector quantization. See also divisive clustering. [NS06]

hierarchical matching: Matching at increasingly greater levels of detail. This approach can be used when matching images or more abstract representations. [FS07]

hierarchical model: A model formed of submodels, each of which may have further smaller submodels. The model may contain multiple instances of the subcomponent models. The subcomponents may be placed relative to the model using a coordinate system transformation or may just be listed in a set structure. The figure shows a three-level hierarchical model with multiple usage of the subcomponents: [WP:Hierarchical_database_model]

hierarchical recognition: See hierarchical matching. [WP:Cognitive_neuroscience_of_visual_object_recognition#Hierarchical_Recognition_Processing]

hierarchical texture: A way of considering texture elements at multiple levels (e.g., basic texture elements may themselves be grouped together to form a texture element at another scale, and so on). [BB82:6.2]

hierarchical thresholding: A thresholding technique where an image is considered at different levels of detail in a pyramid data structure, and thresholds are identified at different levels in the pyramid starting at the highest level. [SHB08:5.1.4]

high dynamic range imaging (HDR/HDRI): Imaging method that allows the capture of a much wider span (i.e., dynamic range) of intensities across images that span multiple areas of contrast – e.g., bright sky and a relatively dark landscape. This technique can be achieved by blending multiple images at different exposure levels to create a scene or a specialist camera. [Sze10:10.2]

high-level vision: A general term referring to image analysis and understanding tasks (i.e., those tasks that address reasoning about what is seen, as opposed to basic processing of images). [BKKP05:5.10]

high-pass filter: A frequency domain filter that removes or suppresses all low-frequency components. [Umb98:2.5.4]

higher-order graph cut: An undirected graphical model (UGM) with clique sizes greater than two is known as a higher-order UGM. The graph cut algorithm can be used to carry out approximate inference in such a network. [RLKT10]

highlight: See specular reflection.

hinge loss function: The hinge loss for $x \in R$ is defined as $H(x) = \max(0, 1 - x)$. Used in training machine learning classifiers, typically support vector machines. [Bis06:Ch. 7]

histogram: A representation of the frequency distribution of some values. See intensity histogram: [Low91:5.2]

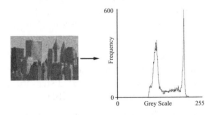

histogram analysis: A general term describing a group of techniques that abstract information from histograms (e.g., determining the anti-mode/trough in a bimodal histogram for use in thresholding). [Car87]

histogram dissimilarity measure: A dissimilarity metric between two histogram distributions. Converse to a similarity metric between the same distributions. [WZC05]

histogram equalization: An image enhancement operation that processes a single image and results in an image with a uniform distribution of intensity levels (i.e., whose intensity histogram is flat). When this technique is applied to a digital image, however, the resulting histogram will often have large values interspersed with zeros: [Low91:5.3]

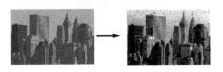

histogram modeling: A class of techniques, such as histogram equalization that modify the dynamic range and

contrast of an image by changing its intensity histogram into one with the desired properties. [DN98]

histogram modification: See histogram modeling.

histogram moment: A moment derived from a histogram. [WP: Algorithms_for_calculating_variance# Higher-order_statistics]

histogram of local appearance context (HLAC): Context-based shape descriptor that uses local appearance descriptors that are distinctive and resilient to noise. A histogram of these features is constructed to form the final descriptor. [SBH09]

histogram of oriented gradients (HOG) descriptor: A feature descriptor based on a histogram of local gradient orientation spatially aggregated over a set of blocks, each in turn sub-divided into cells, within the local image neighborhood. Not invariant to rotation. [DT05]

histogram of shape context (HOSC): A method of describing and comparing shapes that uses features measured in a relative coordinate system to allow for a degree of invariance. The coordinate system used is usually log-polar. [AT04]

histogram smoothing: The application of a smoothing filter (e.g., Gaussian smoothing) to a histogram. This is often required before histogram analysis operations can be applied: [ADA09]

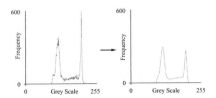

hit and miss (hit or miss) operator: A mathematical morphology operation where a new image is formed by using logical AND on corresponding bits for every pixel of an input image and a structuring element. This operator is most appropriate for binary images but may also be applied to gray scale images: [WP:Hit-or-miss_transform]

HK segmentation: See mean and Gaussian curvature shape classification. [WP:Gaussian_curvature]

HMM: See hidden Markov model.

holography: The process of creating a three dimensional image (a hologram) by recording the interference pattern produced by coherent laser light that has been passed through a diffraction grating. [WP:Holography]

homogeneous, homogeneity: See homogeneous coordinates and homogeneous texture.

homogeneous coordinates: Points described in projective space. For example an (x, y, z) point in Euclidean space would be described as $(\lambda x, \lambda y, \lambda z, \lambda)$ for any λ in homogeneous coordinates. Homogeneous quantities such as points are equal if they are scalar multiples of each other. For example a 2D point is represented as (x, y) in Cartesian coordinates and in homogeneous coordinates by the point $(x, y, 1)$ and any multiple thereof. [FP03:2.1.1]

homogeneous representation: A representation defined in projective space. [HZ00:1.2.1]

homogeneous texture: A two-dimensional (or higher) pattern, defined on a space $S \subset \mathbb{R}^2$ for which some functions (e.g., mean and standard deviation) applied to a window on S have values that are independent of the position of the window. [WP:Homogeneous_space]

homography: The relationship described by a homography transformation. [WP:Homography]

homography transformation: Any invertible linear transformation between projective spaces. It is commonly used for image transfer, which maps one planar image or region to another. The transformation can be estimated using four non-collinear point pairs. [WP:Homography]

homomorphic filtering: An image enhancement technique that simultaneously normalizes brightness and enhances contrast. It works by applying a high-pass filter to the original image in the frequency domain, hence reducing intensity variation (which changes slowly) and highlighting reflection detail (which changes rapidly). [Umb98:3.4.4]

homoscedastic noise: Noise which is independent of the variable, sample and signal with a normal distribution and a constant variance. [KBL04]

homotopic transformation: A continuous deformation that preserves the connectivity of object features (e.g., skeletonization). Two objects are homotopic if they can be made the same by some series of homotopic transformations. [SHB08:11.5.1]

Hopfield network: A form of neural network that is an undirected graphical model with pairwise potentials. Hopfield networks have been used as associative networks and to solve optimization problems. [Mac03:Ch. 42]

horizon line: The line defined by all vanishing points from the same plane. The most commonly used horizon line is that associated with the ground plane: [WP:Horizon#Geometrical_model]

Hough forest: An object detection method extending the Hough transform such that the part detections of an individual object to cast probabilistic votes for the location of the object centroid. The detection hypotheses (i.e., potential objects) then correspond to the maxima of the Hough image, which accumulates the votes from all parts. A class-specific random forest maps local image patch appearance to a probabilistic vote on the object centroid. [GYR+11]

Hough transform: A technique for transforming image features directly into the likelihood of occurrence of some shape. See Hough transform line finder and generalized Hough transform. [Low91:9.3]

Hough transform line finder: A version of the Hough transform based on the parametric equation of a line ($s = i \cos\theta + j \sin\theta$) in which a set of edge points $\{(i, j)\}$ is transformed into the likelihood of a line being present as represented in a (s, θ) space. The likelihood is quantified, in practice, by a histogram of the $\sin\theta, \cos\theta$ values observed in the images: [Low91:9.3.1]

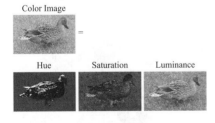

HSI: Hue–saturation–intensity color image format. [JKS95:10.4]

HSL: Hue–saturation–luminance color image format. [WP:HSL_and_HSV]

Color Image

Hue   Saturation   Luminance

HSV: Hue–saturation–value color image format. [FP03:6.3.2]

Hu moment: A set of seven rotation invariant, scale invariant and translation invariant

shape moments formed by combinations of central moments. [SB11:9.4]

hue: Describes color using the dominant wavelength of the light. Hue is a common component of color image formats. [FP03:6.3.2]

Hueckel edge detector: A parametric edge detector that models an edge using a parameterized model within a circular window (the parameters are edge contrast, edge orientation and distance background mean intensity). [Dav75]

Huffman encoding: An optimal, variable-length encoding of values (e.g., pixel values) based on the relative probability of each value. The code lengths may change dynamically if the relative probabilities of the data source change. This technique is commonly used in image compression. [Low91:15.3]

human–computer interaction: The study of the methods and practices of interaction between human users and computer systems. Often this study is undertaken in order to better design hardware and software interfaces or to improve workflow when using software.

human motion analysis: A general term describing the application of motion analysis to human subjects. Such analysis is used to track moving people, to recognize the pose of a person and to derive 3D properties. [WP: Motion_analysis#Human_motion_ analysis]

human motion tracking: Computing the location of human subjects in video sequences. There are two typical approaches: model-based and non-model-based, depending on whether predefined shape models are used. The representation used is often that of a stick figure. See model-based tracking and tracking.

human pose estimation: Image-based goniometric analysis of human joint poses. This is usually done following a skeleton-fitting from human motion tracking: [VMZ08]

Derived skeleton

HYPER: HYpothesis Predicted and Evaluated Recursively. A well-known vision system developed by Nicholas Ayache and Olivier Faugeras, in which geometric relations derived from polygonal models are used for recognition. [AF86]

hyperbolic surface region: A region of a 3D surface that is locally saddle-shaped. A point on a surface at which the Gaussian curvature is negative (so the signs of the principal curvatures are opposite): [EF97]

hyperfocal distance: The distance D at which a camera should be focused in order that the depth of field extends from $D/2$ to infinity. Equivalently, if a camera is focused at a point at distance D, points at $D/2$ and infinity are equally blurred. [JKS95:8.3]

hyperparameter: In a Bayesian statistical model, the prior distribution for the model parameters θ may depend on some parameters ϕ; these are known as hyperparameters, to distinguish them from the model parameters. [GCSR95:Ch. 5]

hyperplane: A geometrical construct which extends the idea of a plane in three dimensions to a general d-dimensional space. It is the set of points $\vec{x} = (x_1, x_2, \ldots, x_d)^\top$ satisfying the equation $a_1 x_1 + \ldots + a_d x_d = c$

where $\vec{a}$ is a fixed vector and c is a constant. [Nob69:p. 183]

hyperquadric: A class of volumetric representations that include superquadrics. Hyperquadric models can describe arbitrary convex polyhedra. [SQ04:9.11]

hyperspectral image: An image with a large number (perhaps hundreds) of spectral bands. An image with a lower number of spectral bands is referred to as multi-spectral image. [WP: Hyperspectral_imaging]

hyperspectral sensor: A sensor capable of collecting many (perhaps hundreds) of spectral bands simultaneously. Produces a hyperspectral image. [WP:Hyperspectral_imaging]

hypothesis testing: Testing of an assumption about a parameter which may or may not be true. This could be performed by examining the entire population but that is often impractical so a sample is tested. If this sample is consistent with the hypothesis then it is accepted, else it is rejected. See also RANSAC. [Bar12:12.6]

hypothesize and test: See hypothesize and verify.

hypothesize and verify: A common approach to object recognition in which possibilities (of object type and pose) are hypothesized and then evaluated against evidence from the images. This is done either until all possibilities are considered or until a hypothesis with a sufficiently high degree of fit is found: [JKS95:15.1]

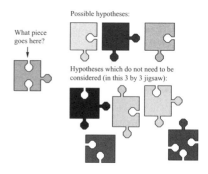

hysteresis tracking: See thresholding with hysteresis.

126

I

ICA: See independent component analysis. [WP:Independent_component_analysis]

iconic: Having the characteristics of an image. See iconic model. [SQ04:4.1.1]

iconic model: A representation having the characteristics of an image. For example the template used in template matching. [SQ04:4.1.1]

iconic recognition: Object recognition using an iconic model. [FH05]

ICP: See iterative closest point.

ideal line: A line described in the continuous domain as opposed to one in a digital image, which will suffer from rasterization. [HZ00:1.2.2]

ideal point: A point described in the continuous domain as opposed to one in a digital image, which will suffer from rasterization. May also be used to refer to a vanishing point. [HZ00:1.2.2]

IDECS: Image discrimination enhancement combination system. A well-known vision system developed by Haralick and Currier. [HC77]

identification: The process of associating some observations with a particular instance or class of object that is already known. [TV98:10.1]

identity verification: Confirmation of the identity of a person based on some biometrics (e.g., face authentication). This differs from the recognition of an unknown person in that only one model has to be compared with the information that is observed. [BAM99]

IGS: Interpretation guided segmentation. A vision technique for grouping image elements into regions based on semantic interpretations in addition to raw image values. Developed by Tenenbaum and Barrow. [TB77]

IHS: Intensity hue saturation color image format. [BB82:2.2.5]

IIR: See infinite impulse response filter. [WP:Infinite_impulse_response]

ill-posed problem: A mathematical problem that infringes at least one of the conditions in the definition of well-posed problem. Informally, these are that the solution must exist, be unique and depend continuously on the data. Ill-posed problems in computer vision have been approached using regularization theory. See regularization. [SQ04:6.2.1]

illuminance: The total amount of visible light incident upon a point on a surface. Measured in lux (lumens per meter squared), or footcandles (lumens per foot squared). Illuminance decreases as the distance between the viewer and the source increases. [JKS95:9.1.1]

illuminant direction: The direction from which illuminance originates. See also light source geometry. [TV98:9.3]

illumination: See illuminance.

illumination constancy: The phenomenon that allows humans to perceive the lightness (or brightness) of surfaces as approximately constant regardless of the illuminance. [HS94]

illumination estimation: Methods for computing the location and direction of light sources in an image using shading, shadow and specular reflections. [LLLS03]

illumination field calibration: Determination of the illuminance falling on a scene. Typically this is done by taking

Dictionary of Computer Vision and Image Processing, Second Edition.
R. B. Fisher, T. P. Breckon, K. Dawson-Howe, A. Fitzgibbon, C. Robertson, E. Trucco and C. K. I. Williams.
© 2014 John Wiley & Sons, Ltd. Published 2014 by John Wiley & Sons, Ltd.

an image of a white object of known brightness. [HS96]

illumination model: An expression of the components of light reflected from or refracted through a surface. There are three basic components to the standard illumination model: ambient light, diffuse illumination, and specular reflection. [FDFH96:Ch. 16]

illusory contour: A perceived border where there is no edge present in the image data. See also subjective contour. The figure shows the Kanizsa triangles: [FP03:14.2]

image: A function describing some quantity (such as brightness) in terms of spatial layout (see registration). Most frequently, computer vision is concerned with two-dimensional digital images. [SB11:1.1]

image addition: See pixel addition operator.

image alignment: The process of spatially matching (and aligning) one image, sometimes called a template image, with another image such that the transformation between them can be estimated. Also known as image registration. [SB11:Ch. 7]

image analysis: A general term covering all forms of analysis of image data. Generally image analysis operations result in a symbolic description of the image contents. [Jai89:1.5]

image annotation: The process of documenting the object contents or context of an image. See annotation.

image acquisition: See image capture.

image arithmetic: A general term covering image-processing operations

that are based on the application of an arithmetic or logical operator to two images. See also pixel addition operator, pixel subtraction operator, pixel multiplication operator, pixel division operator, image blending, AND operator, NAND operator, OR operator, XOR operator and XNOR operator. [SB11:3.2]

image based: A general term describing operations or representations that are based on images. [WP:Image_analysis]

image-based lighting: Image rendering technique which uses specialized hardware to capture a 3D wrap-around view of the lighting surrounding an object and then compute the lighting values for the scene based on the brightness of this view. [RWPD05]

image-based modeling: 3D modeling approach that takes a single image as input and represents the scene as a layered collection of depth images which it then attempts to compute, usually with user assistance. [OCDD01]

image-based rendering: Techniques used to render novel views directly from input images without knowing the full 3D geometry. See also view interpolation. [Sze10:13.1]

image blending: An image arithmetic operation similar to that using the pixel addition operator where a new image is formed by blending the values of corresponding pixels from two input images. Each input image is given a weight for the blending so that the total weight is 1.0: [SB11:3.2.1.1]

image capture: The acquisition of an image by a recording device, e.g., a camera. [TV98:2.3]

image classification: An image segmentation approach where all pixels in an image are placed into a finite number of sets or classes depending on classification criteria. An example use is that of the classification of land types in satellite imagery. [HSD73]

image coding: The mapping or algorithm required to encode or decode an image representation (such as a compressed image). [WP:Graphics_Interchange_Format#Image_coding]

image compression: A method of representing an image in order to reduce the amount of storage space that it occupies. Techniques can be lossless (which allows all image data to be recorded perfectly) or lossy (where some loss of quality is allowed, typically resulting in significantly better compression rates). [SB11:1.3.2]

image connectedness: See pixel connectivity.

image coordinates: See image plane coordinates and pixel coordinates.

image database indexing: The technique of associating an index (e.g., keywords) with images, which allows the images to be indexed efficiently within a database. [SQ04:13A.3]

image decomposition: A general term referring to the separation of an image into its constituent parts following an established set of basis functions (e.g., Fourier transform, wavelet transform, DCT or similar), a given set of color channels (e.g., RGB, HSV) or segmentation (including semantic scene segmentation). [Bov05:p. 973, p. 354]

image denoising: The process of removing corruption in an image (caused by noise). There are three broad categories of approach: those related to anisotropic diffusion or smoothing; those exploiting natural image statistics learned over a training set; sampling techniques that combine information from several image patches that are similar in appearance to the one under examination. The figure shows denoising by smoothing: [CYV00]

Noisy image   After denoising

image descriptor: A set of short vectors derived from an image, which are invariant to common transformations, providing a summary description that can be compared with other descriptors in a database to obtain matches according to some distance metric. Common examples of such descriptors are SIFT and SURF. [Sze10:4.1.2]

image difference: See pixel subtraction operator.

image digitization: The process of sampling and quantization of an analog image function to create a digital image. [Nal93:2.3.1]

image distortion: Any effect that alters an image from the ideal image. Most typically this term refers to geometric distortions, although it can also refer to other types of distortion such as image noise and effects of sampling and quantization: [WP: Distortion_(optics)]

Correct Image   Distorted Image

image encoding: The process of converting an image into a different representation. For example, see image compression. [WP:Image_compression]

image enhancement: A general term covering a number of image-processing operations that alter an image in order to make it easier for humans to perceive. Example operations include contrast stretching and histogram equalization. The figure shows a histogram equalization operation: [SB11:Ch. 4]

image epitome: A useful data-mining representation of an image which contains abbreviated statistical properties rather than the data itself. [JFK03]

image feature: A general term for an interesting image structure that could arise from a corresponding interesting scene structure. Features can be single points such as interest points, curve vertices, edges, lines, curves, surfaces etc. [TV98:4.1]

image feature extraction: A group of image-processing techniques concerned with the identification of particular image features. Examples include edge detection and corner detection. [TV98:4.1]

image flow: See optical flow.

image formation: A general term covering issues relating to the manner in which an image is formed. For example in the case of a digital camera this term would include the camera geometry as well as the process of sampling and quantization. [SB11:2.1]

image gallery: A collection of images used for statistical, texture or feature analysis or some other comparison.

image grid: A geometric map describing the image sampling in which every image point is represented by a vertex (or hole) in the map or grid. [FH04]

image indexing: See image database indexing.

image intensifier: A device for amplifying an image, so that the resultant sensed luminous flux is significantly higher. [WP:Image_intensifier]

image interleaving: Describes the way in which image pixels are organized, e.g., pixel interleaving (where the image data is ordered by pixel position) and band interleaving (where the image data is ordered by band and is then ordered by pixel position within each band). [WP:Interleaving]

image interpolation: A method for computing a value for a pixel in an output image based on non-integer coordinates in some input image. The computation is based on the values of nearby pixels in the input image. This type of operation is required for most geometric transformations and computations requiring subpixel interpolation.

Types of interpolation scheme include nearest-neighbor interpolation, bilinear surface interpolation, bicubic interpolation etc. The figure shows the result of interpolation in image enlargement: [Sch89:Ch. 2]

Enlarged image using bicubic interpolation

image interpretation: A general term for computer-vision processes that extract descriptions from images (as opposed to processes that produce output images for human viewing). There is often the assumption that the descriptions are very high-level, e.g., "the boy is walking to the store carrying a book" or "these cells are cancerous". A broader definition would also allow processes that extract information needed by a subsequent (usually non-image-processing) activity, e.g., the position of a bright spot in an image. [MZ89]

image invariant: An image feature or measurement image that is invariant to some properties. For example invariant color features are often used in image database indexing. [WP: Image_moment]

image irradiance equation: Usually expressed as $E(x, y) = R(p, q)$, this equality (up to a constant scale factor to account for illumination strength, surface color and optical efficiency) says that the observed brightness E at pixel (x, y) is equal to the reflectance R of the surface for surface normal $(p, q, -1)$. Usually there is a one-degree-of-freedom family of surface normals with the same reflectance value so the observed brightness only partially constrains local surface orientation and thus shape. [JKS95:9.3.1]

image magnification: The extent to which an image is expanded for viewing. If the image size is actually changed then image interpolation must be used. Normally quoted relative to the original size (e.g., ×2, ×10 etc.): [Jai89:7.4]

Magnified image (x4)

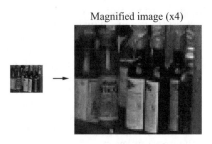

image matching: 1) The comparison of two images, often evaluated using cross correlation. See also template matching: [TV98:10.4.2]

2) Finding images in a database that correspond in some way to a given exemplar. [Sze10:9.2]

image memory: See frame store.

image modality: A general term for the sensing technique used to capture an image, e.g., visible light, infrared light or X-ray. [KH07]

image morphing: A gradual transformation from one image to another: [WP: Morphing]

image morphology: An approach to image processing that considers all operations in terms of set operations. See mathematical morphology operation. [WP:Mathematical_morphology]

image mosaic: A composition of several images, to provide a single larger image

covering a wider field of view. The figure shows a mosaic of three images: [Sch89:Ch. 2]

image motion estimation: Computation of optical flow for all pixels or features in an image. [WP: Motion_estimation]

image multiplication: See pixel multiplication operator.

image noise: Degradation of an image where pixels have values which are different from the ideal values. Often noise is modeled as having a Gaussian distribution with a zero mean, although it can take on different forms such as salt-and-pepper noise depending upon the cause of the noise (e.g., the environment or electrical interference). Noise is measured in terms of the signal-to-noise ratio: [SB11:2.3.3]

image normalization: Reducing or eliminating the effects of different illumination on the same or similar scenes. A typical approach is to subtract the mean of the image and divide by the standard deviation, which produces a zero-mean, unit variance image. Since images are not Gaussian random samples, this approach does not completely solve the problem. Further, light source placement can also cause variations in shading that are not corrected by this approach. The figure shows an original image (left)

131

and its normalization (right): [WP: Normalization_(image_processing)]

image of absolute conic: See absolute conic.

image orthicon tube: Electron emission tube used in early television sets where the number of electrons produced in the tube corresponded with the intensity of secondary emission of electrons on the screen itself. [Abr03]

image pair rectification: See image rectification.

image parsing: Methods used to find a semantically meaningful label for every pixel in a given image. [TCYZ05]

image plane: The mathematical plane behind the lens onto which an image is focused. In practice, the physical sensing surface aims to be placed here, but its position will vary slightly because of minor variations in sensor shape and placement. The term is also used to describe the geometry of the image recorded at this location: [JKS95:1.4]

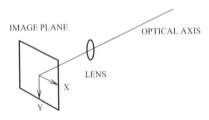
IMAGE PLANE
OPTICAL AXIS
LENS
X
Y

image plane coordinates: The position of points in the physical image sensing plane. They have physically meaningful values, such as centimeters, that can be converted to pixel coordinates, which are in pixels. The two meanings are sometimes used interchangeably. [JKS95:1.6]

image processing: A general term covering all forms of processing of captured image data. It can also mean processing that starts from an image and

results in an image, rather than ending with symbolic descriptions of the image contents or scene. [JKS95:1.2]

image-processing operator: A function that may be applied to an image in order to transform it in some way. See also image processing. [Dav90:2.2]

image pyramid: A hierarchical registration in which each level contains a smaller version of the image at the previous level. Often pixel values are obtained by a smoothing process. Usually the reduction is by a power of two (i.e., 2 or 4). The figure shows four levels of a pyramid in which each level is formed by averaging together two pixels from the previous layer:

The levels are enlarged to the original image size for inspection of the effect of the compression. [FP03:7.7]

image quality: A general term, usually referring to the extent to which the image data records the observed scene faithfully. The specific issues that are important to image quality are problem specific but may include low image noise, high image contrast, good image focus, low motion blur etc. [WP: Image_quality]

image querying: A shorthand term for image database indexing. This is often based on color, texture or shape indices. The database keys could be based on global or local measures. [WP:Content-based_image_retrieval#Query_techniques]

image reconstruction: A term used in image compression to describe the process of recreating a digital image from some compressed form. [HL94]

image rectification: A warping of a stereo pair of images such that conjugate epipolar lines (defined by the two cameras' epipoles and any 3D scene point) are collinear. Usually the lines are transformed to be parallel to the horizontal axis so that corresponding image features can be found on the same raster line. This reduces the computational complexity of the stereo correspondence problem. [FP03:11.1.1]

image registration: See registration.

image representation: A general term for how the image data is represented. Image data can be in one, two, three or more dimensions. Image data is often stored in arrays where the spatial layout of the array reflects the spatial layout of the data. The figure shows a small 10×10 pixel image patch with the gray scale values for the corresponding pixels: [Jai89:1.2]

```
123 123 123 123 123 123 123  96  96
123 123 112  96  96 123 123 123  96
123 123  96  96 112 123 137 123 123  96
123 123  96  96 123 214 234 178 123  96
123 100  72 109 178 230 230 137 123  96
125  78  51 142 218 178  96  76  96  96
 92 100  92  92  81  76  76  96 123 123
 81 109 129 129 100  81  92 123 123 123
 51 109 142 137 123 123 123 123 123 123
 33  76 123 123 137 137 123 123 123 123
```

image resolution: Usually used to record the number of pixels in the horizontal and vertical directions in an image but may also refer to the separation between pixels (e.g., 1 μm) or the angular separation between the lines of sight corresponding to adjacent pixels. [SB11:1.2]

image restoration: The process of removing some known (and modeled) distortion from an image, such as blur in an out-of-focus image. The process may not produce a perfect image, but may remove an undesired distortion (e.g., motion blur) at the cost of another ignorable distortion (e.g., phase distortion). [SB11:Ch. 6]

image retrieval: Search method for comparing images in a database with an exemplar (either an image or some text) and then presenting those images which most closely match the given criteria. [Sze10:Ch. 14]

image sampling: The process of measuring some pixel values from the physical image focused onto the image plane. The sampling could be monochrome, color or multi-spectral,

such as RGB. The sampling usually results in a rectangular array of pixels sampled at nearly equally spacing but other sampling could be used, such as a space-variant sensor. [Nal93:2.3.1]

image scaling: The operation of increasing or reducing the size of an image by some scale factor. This operation may require the use of some type of image interpolation method. See also image magnification. [WP:Image_scaling]

image segmentation: The grouping of image pixels into meaningful, usually connected, structures such as curves and regions. The term is applied to a variety of image modalities, such as intensity data or range data and properties, such as similar feature orientation, feature motion, surface shape or texture. [SB11:10.1]

image semantics: A general term referring to the meaning or understanding of image content. See semantic scene understanding [SWS+00]

image sequence: A series of images generally taken at regular intervals in time. Typically the camera or the objects in the scene (or all of them) will be moving: [TV98:8.1]

image sequence analysis: Techniques for merging, segmenting or understanding image content which utilize the temporal aspect of the image content (e.g., change detection). One particular area of usage is in compression algorithms such as MPEG-4 and behavior analysis.

image sequence fusion: The integration of information from the many images in an image sequence. Different types of fusion include 3D structure recovery, production of a mosaic of the scanned scene, tracking of a moving object, improved scene imaging because of average smoothing etc. [WP:Image_fusion]

image sequence matching: Computing the correspondence between pixels or image features in frames of the image sequence. With the correspondences, one can construct an image mosaic, carry out image stabilization (to remove jitter) or recover scene structure. [Moh98]

image sequence stabilization: Handheld video camera recordings contain some image motion because of jitter from the human operator. Image stabilization attempts to estimate the random portion of the camera motion jitter and translate the images in the sequence to reduce or remove the jitter. A similar application would be to remove systematic camera motions to produce a motionless image. See also feature stabilization and translation. [WP:Image_stabilization]

image sharpening operator: An image enhancement operator that increases the high spatial frequency component of the image, so as to make the edges of objects appear sharper or less blurred. See also edge enhancement. The figure shows a raw image (left) and an image sharpened with the unsharp operator (right): [SB11:4.6]

image size: The number of pixels in an image, e.g., 768 horizontally by 494 vertically. [WP:Wikipedia:What_is_a_featured_picture%3F/Image_size]

image smoothing: See noise reduction.

image stabilization: See image sequence stabilization [WP:Image_stabilization]

image stitching: Methods of combining multiple images taken with different orientations or geometry into a single panoramic image mosaic. The figure is composed from 12 images with

rotational and translational motion between them: [Sze10:9.3.3]

image storage devices: See frame store.

image subtraction operator: See pixel subtraction operator.

image tagging: Automatic or manual assignment of relevant keywords to images in a collection in order to aid retrieval. See annotation.

image texton: Proposed elementary units of texture perception which are somewhat analogous to the phonemes used in speech recognition. [MBSL99]

image transfer: 1) See novel view synthesis. 2) A general term describing the movement of an image from one device to another or from one representation to another. [WP:Picture_Transfer_Protocol]

image transform: An operation on an image that produces another image. The new image may have changed geometry from the original or may contain new, derived information. The usual purpose of applying such a transformation is to enhance or make explicit some desired information. [SB11:Chs 3, 5 & 7]

image understanding: A general term referring to the derivation of high-level (abstract) information from an image or series of images. This term is often used to refer to the emulation of human visual capabilities. [Jai89:9.15]

Image Understanding Environment (IUE): A C++-based collection of data types (classes) and standard computer vision algorithms. The motivation behind the development of the IUE was to reduce the independent re-invention of basic computer vision code in government-funded research into computer vision. [HR92]

image warping: A general term for transforming the positions of pixels in an image, usually while maintaining image topology (i.e., neighboring original pixels remain neighbors in the warped image). This results in an image with a new shape. This operation might be done, e.g., to correct some geometric distortion, align two images (see image rectification), or transform shapes into a more easily processed form (e.g., circles into straight lines). [SB11:7.10]

image watermarking: See digital image watermarking.

imaging geometry: A general term referring to the relative placement of sensors, structured light sources, point light sources etc. [BB82:2.2.2]

imaging spectroscopy: The acquisition and analysis of surface composition by using image data from multiple spectral channels. A typical sensor (AVIRIS) records 224 measurements at 10 nm increments from 400 nm to 2500 nm. The term might refer to the raw multidimensional signal or to the classification of that signal into surface types (e.g., vegetation or mineral types). [WP:Imaging_spectroscopy]

imaging surface: The surface within a camera on which the image is projected by the lens. This surface in a digital camera is composed of photosensitive elements that record the incident illumination. See also image plane. [PBP01]

implicit curve: A curve that is defined by an equation of the form $f(\vec{x}) = 0$. Then the curve is the set of points $S = \{\vec{x} | f(\vec{x}) = 0\}$. [FP03:15.3.1]

implicit surface: The representation of a surface as the set of points that makes a function have the value zero. For example, the sphere $x^2 + y^2 + z^2 = r^2$ of radius r at the origin could be represented by the function $f(x, y, z) = x^2 + y^2 + z^2 - r^2$. The set of points where $f(x, y, z) = 0$ is the implicit surface. [SQ04:4.1.2]

importance sampling: Consider the integral $\int f(x)p(x)dx$. This can be estimated using Monte Carlo methods by drawing samples from $p(x)$. However, if it is hard to sample from $p(x)$ we may sample from another distribution $q(x)$, and reweight each sample by a factor of $w_i = p(x^{(i)})/q(x^{(i)})$, known as an importance weight. Subsequently, the integral is approximated as $\frac{1}{N} \sum_{i=1}^{N} w_i f(x^{(i)})$, where the samples $x^{(1)}, \ldots, x^{(N)}$ are drawn from $q(x)$. [Bis06:11.1.4]

impossible object: An object that cannot physically exist: [Nal93:4.1.1]

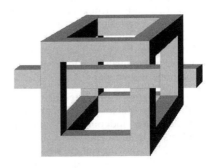

impulse noise: A form of image corruption where image pixels have their value replaced by the maximum value (e.g., 255). See also salt-and-pepper noise. The figure shows impulse noise on an image: [TV98:3.1.2]

incandescent lamp: A light source whose light arises from the glowing of a very hot structure, such as the tungsten filament in a light bulb. [WP: Incandescent_light_bulb]

incident light: A general term referring to the light that strikes or illuminates a surface. [WP:Incident_ light#Interaction_with_surfaces]

incident light measurement: Measuring the amount of light illuminating the subject rather than light reflected from the subject, thus ignoring the subject and background characteristics. [AT10]

incremental learning: Learning that is incremental in nature. See continuous learning. [WP:Population-based_incremental_learning]

independent component analysis (ICA): A multi-variate data analysis method that finds a linear transformation to make each component of the transformed data vectors independent of each other. Unlike principal component analysis, which considers only second-order properties (covariances) and transforms onto basis vectors that are orthogonal to each other, ICA considers properties of the whole distribution and transforms onto basis vectors that need not be orthogonal. [WP:Independent_component_analysis]

independent motion detection: Algorithmic approaches to the problem of detecting independently moving objects in a 3D scene when they are viewed by a moving camera which also causes all pixels to change. [SYAK99]

index of refraction: The absolute index of refraction in a material is the ratio of the speed of an electromagnetic wave in a vacuum to the speed in the material. More commonly used is the relative index of refraction of two media, which is the ratio of their absolute indices of refraction. This ratio is used in lens design and explains the bending of light rays as the light passes into a new material (Snell's law). [FP03:1.2.1]

indexing: The process of retrieving an element from a data structure using a key. A powerful concept imported into computer vision from programming. For example, the problem of establishing the identity of an object given an image and a set of candidate models is typically approached by locating some characterizing elements, or features, in the image and using the features' properties to index a database of models. See also model base indexing. [FP03:18.4.2]

industrial vision: A general term covering the application of machine-vision technology to industrial processes. Applications include product inspec-

tion, process feedback and part or tool alignment. A large range of lighting and sensing techniques are used. A common feature of industrial vision systems is fast processing rates (e.g., several times a second), which may require limiting the rate at which targets are analyzed or limiting the types of processing. [MPZ+03]

infinite impulse response filter (IIR): A filter that produces an output value (y_n) based on the current and past input values (x_i) together with past output values (y_j). $y_n = \sum_{i=0}^{p} a_i x_{n-i} + \sum_{j=1}^{q} b_j y_{n-j}$ where a_i and b_j are weights. [WP:Infinite_impulse_response]

inflection point: A point at which the second derivative of a curve changes its sign, corresponding to a change in concavity. See also curve inflection: [FP03:19.1.1]

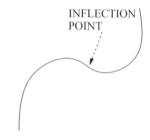

INFLECTION POINT

influence function: A function describing the effect of an individual observation on a statistical model. This allows us to evaluate whether the observation is having an undue influence on the model. [WP:Influence_function]

information fusion: Fusion of information from multiple sources. See sensor fusion. [WP:Information_integration]

infrared: See infrared light.

infrared imaging: Production of a image through use of an infrared sensor. [SB11:3.1]

infrared light: Electromagnetic energy with wavelengths approximately in the range 700 nm to 1 mm. Immediately shorter wavelengths are visible light and immediately longer wavelengths are microwave radio. Infrared light is often used in machine vision systems

136

because it is easily observed by most semiconductor image sensors yet is not visible to humans and because it is a measure of the heat emitted by the observed scene. [SB11:3.1]

infrared sensor: A sensor capable of observing or measuring infrared light. [SB11:3.1]

inlier: A sample that falls within an assumed probability distribution (e.g., within the 95th percentile). See also outlier. [WP:RANSAC]

inpainting: The process of replacing degraded, corrupted or missing parts of an image or video often by using statistics-based texture synthesis algorithms. [Wei03]

inspection: A general term for visually examining a target to detect defects. Common practical inspection examples include printed circuit boards for breaks or solder joint failures, paper production for holes or discolorations, and food for irregularities. [SQ04:17.4]

integer lifting: A method used to construct wavelet representations. [WP: Lifting_scheme]

integer wavelet transform: An integer version of the discrete wavelet transform. [CDSY98]

integral image: A data structure, I, (and its associated construction algorithm) for efficiently generating the sum of values in an image, i, over a given region of interest. Defined such that $I(x, y) = \sum_{x' \leq x, y' \leq y} i(x', y')$. Computed in a single pass over an image. Also known as the summed area table. [Sze10:3.2.2]

integral image compression: A three-dimensional integral image occupies a large amount of data. In order to present it with adequate resolution, integral image-compression algorithms (e.g., using MPEG) take advantage of the image's modality-specific characteristics. [YSJ04]

integral invariant: An integral (of some function) that is invariant under a set of transformations. For example, local integrals along a curve of curvature or arc length are invariant to rotation and

translation. Integral invariants potentially have greater stability to noise than, e.g., differential invariants such as curvature. [MHYS04]

integration time: The length of time that a light-sensitive sensor medium is exposed to the incident light (or other stimulus). Shorter times reduce the signal strength and possible motion blur (if the sensor or objects in the scene are moving). [NB04]

intensity: 1) The brightness of a light source.
2) Image data that records the brightness of the light that comes from the observed scene. [TV98:2.2.3]

intensity-based database indexing: This is a form of image database indexing that uses intensity descriptors such as histograms of pixel values (monochrome or color) or vectors of local derivative values. [SSTG03]

intensity cross correlation: Cross correlation using intensity data. [XJM94]

intensity data: Image data that represents the brightness of the measured light. There is not usually a linear mapping between the brightness of the measured light and the stored values. The term can also refer to the intensity of observed visible light. [SWP+83]

intensity gradient: The mathematical gradient operation ∇ applied to an intensity image I gives the intensity gradient ∇I at each image point. The intensity gradient direction shows the local image direction in which the maximum change in intensity occurs. The intensity gradient magnitude gives the magnitude of the local rate of change in image intensity:

At each of the two designated points, the length of the vector shows the magnitude of the change in intensity and the direction of the vector shows the direction of greatest change. [WP: Image_gradient]

intensity gradient direction: The local image direction in which the maximum change in intensity occurs. See also intensity gradient. [WP:Gradient# Interpretations]

intensity gradient magnitude: The magnitude of the local rate of change in image intensity. See also intensity gradient. The figure shows (left) a raw image and (right) its intensity gradient magnitude (the contrast has been enhanced for clarity). [WP:Gradient# Interpretations]

intensity histogram: A data structure that records the number of pixels of each intensity value. A typical gray scale image will have pixels with values in [0,255]. Subsequently, the histogram will have 256 entries recording the number of pixels that had value 0, the number having value 1 etc. The figure shows a dark object against a lighter background and its histogram: [SB11:3.4]

intensity image: An image that records the measured intensity data. [TV98:2.1]

intensity level slicing: An image-processing operation in which pixels with values other than the selected value (or range of values) are set to zero. If the image is viewed as a landscape, with height proportional to brightness, then the slicing operator takes a cross section through the height surface. The figure shows (left) an image and (right) its intensity level 80 (in black): [Jai89:7.2]

intensity matching: Finding corresponding points in a pair of images by matching the gray scale intensity patterns. The goal is to find image neighborhoods that have nearly identical pixel intensities. All image points, feature points or interest points could be considered for matching. An algorithm where intensity matching is used is correlation-based stereo matching. [Jia01]

intensity sensor: A sensor that measures intensity data. [BM02:1.9.1]

inter-camera appearance variance: The phenomenon that the appearance of an object in one camera may be very different from its appearance in another camera because of differences in illumination, pose, camera properties, geometry, occlusion or a host of other factors. [GX11:Ch. 13]

inter-camera gap: Generally, the unknown distance between two imaging devices when sampling a scene. In satellite imagery, this has a tendency to make image registration more difficult since the motion induces changes in contrast and brightness: [GX11:Ch. 13]

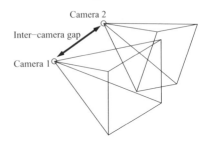

interest point: A general term for pixels that have some interesting property. Interest points are often used for making feature point correspondences between images. Subsequently, the points usually have some identifiable property. Further, because of the need to limit the combinatorial explosion that matching methods can produce, interest points are often expected to be infrequent in an image. Interest points are often points of high variation in pixel values. See also point feature. The figure shows interest points from the Harris corner detector (courtesy of Marc Pollefeys): [SB11:10.9]

interest point feature detector: An operator applied to an image to locate interest points. Well-known examples are the Moravec interest point operator and the Plessey corner finder. [SB11:10.9]

interference: When ordinary light interacts with matter that has dimensions similar to the wavelength of the light or coherent light interacts with itself. The most notable effect from a computer vision perspective is the production of interference fringes and the speckle of laser illumination. May alternatively refer to electrical interference which can affect an image when it is being transmitted on an electrical medium. [Hec87:Ch. 9]

interference fringe: When optical interference occurs, the most noticeable effect is the production of interference fringes where the light illuminates a surface. These are parallel, roughly equally spaced lighter and darker bands of brightness. One important consequence of these bands

is blurring of the edge positions. [Hec87:9.1]

interferometric SAR: An enhancement of synthetic aperture radar sensing to incorporate phase information from the reflected signal, increasing accuracy. [WP:Interferometric_synthetic_aperture_radar]

interior orientation: A photogrammetry term for the calibration of the intrinsic parameters of a camera, including its focal length, principal point, lens distortion etc. This allows transformation of measured image coordinates into camera coordinates. [JKS95:12.9]

interlaced scanning: A technique arising from television engineering, whereby alternate rows (rather than consecutive rows) of an image are scanned or transmitted. As a result, one television frame is transmitted by sending first the odd rows, forming the odd field, and then the even rows, forming the even field. [Gal90:4.1.2]

intermediate representation: A representation that is created as a stage in the derivation of a specific representation from an input representation. For example, in Marr's theory, the raw primal sketch, full primal sketch and 2.5D sketch were intermediate representations between input images and a 3D model. In the figure, a binary image of the noticeboard is an intermediate representation between the input image and the textual output. [NMP01]

Intermediate
Representation

internal energy (or force): A measure of the stability (such as smoothness) of an active shape model or deformable contour model which is part of the deformation energy. This measure is used to constrain the appearance of the model. [WP:Internal_energy]

internal parameter: See intrinsic parameter.

interpolation: A mathematical process whereby a value is inferred from other nearby values or from a mathematical function linking nearby values. For example, dense values along a curve can be linearly interpolated between two known curve points by fitting a line connecting the two curve points. Image, surface and volume values can be interpolated, as well as higher dimensional structures. Interpolating functions can be curved as well as linear. [BB82:A1.11]

interpretation tree search: A matching method used between members in two discrete sets. For each feature from the first set, it builds a depth-first search tree considering all possible matching features from the second set. After a match is found for one feature (by satisfying a set of consistency tests), then it tries to match the remaining features. The algorithm can cope when no match is possible for a given feature by allowing a given number of skipped features. The figure shows a partial interpretation tree that matches model features to data features: [TV98:10.2]

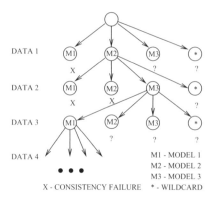

DATA 1 / DATA 2 / DATA 3 / DATA 4

M1 - MODEL 1
M2 - MODEL 2
M3 - MODEL 3
X - CONSISTENCY FAILURE   * - WILDCARD

inter-reflection: The reflection caused by light reflected off a surface and bouncing off another surface of the same object. See also mutual illumination. [WP:Diffuse_reflection# Interreflection]

interval tree: An efficient structure for searching in which every node in the tree is a parent to nodes in a particular interval of values. [WP:Interval_tree]

intrinsic parameter: Parameters, such as focal length, coefficients of radial lens distortion and the position of the principal point, that describe the mapping from image pixels to world rays in a camera. Determining the parameters of this mapping is the task of camera calibration. For a pinhole camera, world rays $\vec{r}$ are mapped to homogeneous image coordinates $\vec{x}$ by $\vec{x} = \mathbf{K}\vec{r}$ where $\mathbf{K}$ is the upper triangular 3×3 matrix

$$\mathbf{K} = \begin{pmatrix} \alpha_u f & s & u_0 \\ 0 & \alpha_v f & v_0 \\ 0 & 0 & 1 \end{pmatrix}$$

In this form, f represents the focal length, s is the skew angle between the image coordinate axes, (u_0, v_0) is the principal point and α_u and α_v are the aspect ratios (e.g., in pixels/mm) in the u and v image directions. [FP03:2.2]

intrinsic dimensionality: The number of dimensions (degrees of freedom) inherent in a data set, independent of the dimensionality of the space in which it is represented. For example, a curve in is intrinsically 1D although its points are represented in three dimensions. [WP:Intrinsic_dimension]

intrinsic image: A term describing one of a set of images registered with the input intensity image that describe properties intrinsic to the scene, instead of properties of the input image. Example intrinsic images include: distance to scene points, scene surface orientations, surface reflectance etc. The figure shows (left) an intensity image and (right) a depth image registered with it. [BB82:1.5]

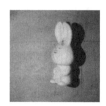

intruder detection: An application of machine vision, usually analyzing a

140

video sequence to detect the appearance of an unwanted person in a scene. [SQ04:17.5]

invariant: Something that does not change under specified operations (e.g., a translation-invariant moment). [WP:Invariant_(mathematics)]

invariant contour function: The contour function characterizes the shape of a planar figure based on the external boundary. Values invariant to position, scale or orientation can be computed from the contour functions. These invariants can be used for recognition of instances of the planar figure. [BCZ93]

invariant feature: Feature point that has properties that do not change despite differences in imaging circumstances such as illumination, camera geometry (i.e., spatial transformation) and scale. Used in object recognition, with a seminal example being the SIFT descriptor. [Low99]

invariant Legendre moments: An invariant extension to Legendre moments. [ZSH+10b]

invariant theory: A theoretical framework in algebra that covers invariant polynomials under various transformations in a closed linear group. [DC70]

inverse compositional algorithm: A fast and efficient image registration algorithm. Rather than updating the additive estimate of warp parameters $\Delta\mathbf{p}$, it iteratively solves for an inverse incremental warp $\mathbf{W}(\mathbf{x}; \Delta\mathbf{p})^{-1}$. [BM01]

inverse convolution: See deconvolution.

inverse Fourier transform: A transformation that allows a signal to be recreated from its Fourier coefficients. See Fourier transform. [Umb98:2.5.1]

inverse halftoning: Filtering or smoothing approaches that reconstruct a gray scale image from a given error diffused image. See also halftoning.

inverse imaging problem: The process of turning observed image model parameters back into image data. For example deconvolution, inverse

halftoning and decompression. See also inverse problems.

inverse light transport: The process of decomposing a rendered or real image into a sum of *bounce images*, where each one records the contribution of light that bounces a known number of times before reaching the camera. [SMK04]

inverse problem: Relating generated data to an underlying description of a problem. For example, computer graphics generates images from scenes of objects by modeling the image formation process. This is the regular, non-inverse problem case. By contrast, computer vision is concerned with the inverse problem, i.e., to go from the data (in this case, an image) to the underlying description. An inverse problem is often an ill-posed problem and may be tackled using regularization theory. [Pal99:1.2.3]

inverse rendering: A collection of techniques for reverse-engineering the geometry of real objects in a scene from images. These techniques include inverse light transport and inverse reflectance. Related to shape from shading. [MTHI03]

inverse square law: A physical law that says the illumination power received at distance d from a point light source is inversely proportional to the square of d, i.e., it is proportional to $\frac{1}{d^2}$. [WP: Inverse-square_law]

inverse tone mapping: A high dynamic range imaging technique that attempts to replicate the multiple-exposure approach by expanding the exposure range of a single image to span the range necessary for the creation of a high-dynamic range image. [BLDC06]

invert operator: A low-level image-processing operation where a new image is formed by replacing each pixel by an inverted value. For binary images, this is 1 if the input pixel is 0 and 0 if the input pixel is 1. For gray scale images, this depends on the maximum range of intensity values. If the range of intensity values is [0,255] then the inverse of a pixel with value x is $256 - x$. The result looks like a photographic negative: [Gal90:5.1.2]

IR: See infrared light.

iris recognition: A biometric imaging technique that uses the physiological structure of striations in the human iris to perform recognition. It is thought to be less accurate than biometrics based on retinal imaging although it is relatively easy to use. [Dau02]

irradiance: The amount of energy received at a point on a surface from the corresponding scene point. [JKS95:9.1]

irregular octree: Like an irregular quadtree except the splits are in three dimensions.

irregular quadtree: A quadtree decomposition is which each split need not be exactly in half.

isomap: *Iso*metric feature *map*ping. An algorithm for nonlinear dimensionality reduction where the data has manifold structure. Given n data points in high dimension, isomap returns n points in a lower dimensional space. It does this by approximating geodesic distances on the manifold by distances on a neighborhood graph determined from the data points and then applying classical multidimensional scaling to the resulting distance matrix. [Bis06:12.4.3]

isometry: A transformation that preserves distances. The transformation $T : x \mapsto u$ is an isometry if, for all pairs (x, y), $|x - y| = |T(x) - T(y)|$. [HZ00:1.4.1]

isophote curvature: An isophote is a curve of constant image intensity. The curvature is defined at any given pixel as $-\frac{L_{vv}}{L_w}$, where L_w is magnitude of the gradient perpendicular to the isophote

and L_{vv} is the curvature of the intensity surface along the isophote at that point. [VG08]

iso-surface: A surface in a 3D space where the value of some function is constant, i.e., $f(x, y, z) = C$ where C is a constant. [WP:Isosurface]

isotropic gradient operator: A gradient operator that computes the scalar magnitude of the gradient, i.e., a value that is independent of edge direction. [JKS95:5.1]

isotropic operator: An operator that produces the same output irrespective of the local orientation of the pixel neighborhood where the operator is applied. For example, a mean smoothing operator produces the same output value, even if the image data is rotated at the point where the operator is being applied. On the other hand, a directional derivative operator would produce different values if the image were rotated. This concept is particularly relevant to feature detection: some detectors are sensitive to the local orientation of the image pixel values and some are not (isotropic). [Gal90:6.4.1]

isotropic scaling: A uniform transformation that multiplies all values in a vector by the same scaling factor $\mathbf{x} = \alpha\mathbf{x}$ where α is the isotropic scaling factor.

iterated closest point: See iterative closest point.

iterative closest point (ICP): A shape alignment algorithm that works by iterating its two-stage process until some termination point:

1. Given an estimated transformation of the first shape onto the second, find the closest feature from the second shape for each feature of the first shape.

2. Given the new set of closest features, re-estimate the transformation that maps the first feature set onto the second.

Most variations of the algorithm need a good initial estimate of the alignment. [FP03:21.3.2]

IUE: See Image Understanding Environment.

142

Jacobian: The matrix of derivatives of a vector function. Typically if the function $\vec{f}(\vec{x})$ is written in component form as:

$$\vec{f}(\vec{x}) = \vec{f}(x_1, x_2, \ldots, x_p)$$

$$= \begin{pmatrix} f_1(x_1, x_2, \ldots, x_p) \\ f_2(x_1, x_2, \ldots, x_p) \\ \vdots \\ f_n(x_1, x_2, \ldots, x_p) \end{pmatrix}$$

then the Jacobian **J** is the $n \times p$ matrix

$$\mathbf{J} = \begin{pmatrix} \frac{\partial f_1}{\partial x_1} & \cdots & \frac{\partial f_1}{\partial x_p} \\ \vdots & & \vdots \\ \frac{\partial f_n}{\partial x_1} & \cdots & \frac{\partial f_n}{\partial x_p} \end{pmatrix}$$

[SQ04:2.2.1]

joint entropy registration: Registration of data using joint entropy (a measure of the degree of uncertainty) as a criterion. [WP:Mutual_information# Applications_of_mutual_information]

joint invariant: An invariant function $J : X_1 \times \ldots \times X_m \to \mathbb{R}$ for a Cartesian product of a group G such that $J(g \cdot x_1, \ldots, g \cdot x_m) = J(x_1, \ldots, x_m)$ for $\forall g \in G, x_i \in X_i$ [OT99:76–77]

joint probability distribution: Consider a vector-valued random variable $\vec{x} = (x_1, \ldots, x_d)$. For discrete random variables, the joint probability distribution $p(\vec{x})$ is the probability of the variables jointly taking on a certain configuration. For continuous random variables there is a corresponding probability density function $p(\vec{x})$, such as the multi-variate normal distribution. See also marginal distribution and conditional probability. [Bis06:1.2]

JPEG: A common format for compressed image representation designed by the Joint Photographic Experts Group (JPEG). [Umb98:1.8]

JPEG 2000: An image compression technique and algorithm based on JPEG where the DCT is replaced with two different wavelet decompositions, the "CDF 9/7" and "CDF 5/3" wavelet descriptors. The JPEG 2000 standard provides for both lossless compression and lossy compression. [AR05:Ch. 17]

junction label: A symbolic label for the pattern of edges meeting at a junction. This approach is mainly used in blocks world scenes where all objects are polyhedra, and thus all lines are straight and meet at only a limited number of configurations. See also line label. The figure shows a "Y" junction (i.e., the corner of a block seen front on) and and "arrow" junction (i.e., the corner of a block seen from the side): [Nal93:4.1.1]

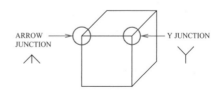

ARROW JUNCTION   Y JUNCTION

K

K2 algorithm: A heuristic algorithm that searches for the most probable belief-network structure given a database of cases by comparing various probability ratios and ranking the structures by their posterior probabilities. [CH91]

k-means: An iterative squared error clustering algorithm. Input is a set of points $\{\vec{x}_i\}_{i=1}^n$ and an initial guess at the locations $\vec{c}_1, \ldots, \vec{c}_k$ of k cluster centers. The algorithm alternates two steps: points are assigned to the cluster center closest to them, and then the cluster centers are recomputed as the mean of the associated points. Iterating yields an estimate of the k cluster centers that is likely to minimize $\sum_{\vec{x}} \min_{\vec{c}} |\vec{x} - \vec{c}|^2$. [FP03:14.4.2]

k-means clustering: See k-means.

k-medians (also k-medoids): A variant of k-means clustering in which multidimensional medians are computed instead of means. The definition of multidimensional median varies, but options for the median $\vec{m}$ of a set of points $\{\vec{x}^i\}_{i=1}^n$, i.e., $\{(x_1^i, \ldots, x_d^i)\}_{i=1}^n$, include the componentwise definition $\vec{m} = (\mathrm{median}\{x_1^i\}_{i=1}^n, \ldots, \mathrm{median}\{x_d^i\}_{i=1}^n)$ and the analog of the one-dimensional definition $\vec{m} = \mathrm{argmin}_{\vec{m} \in \mathbb{R}^d} \sum_{i=1}^n |\vec{m} - \vec{x}^i|$. [WP:K-medians_clustering]

k-nearest-neighbor algorithm: A nearest neighbor algorithm that uses the classifications of the nearest k neighbors when making a decision. [FP03:22.1.4]

Kalman filter: A recursive linear estimator of a varying state vector and associated covariance from observations, their associated covariances and a dynamic model of the state evolution. Improved estimates are calculated as new data is obtained. [FP03:17.3]

Karhunen–Loève transformation: The projection of a vector (or an image treated as a vector) onto an orthogonal space that has uncorrelated components constructed from the autocorrelation (scatter) matrix of a set of example vectors. An advantage is that the orthogonal components have a natural ordering (by the largest eigenvalues of the covariance of the original vector space) so that one can select the most significant variation in the dataset. The transformation can be used as a basis for image compression, for estimating linear models in high-dimensional datasets and for estimating the dominant modes of variation in a dataset etc. It is also known as the "principal component transformation" (see principal component analysis (PCA)). The following image shows a dataset before and after the KL transform was applied: [Jai89:5.11]

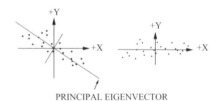

PRINCIPAL EIGENVECTOR

Kendall's shape space: A description system for semi-invariant geometric shapes where sets of point coordinates (configurations) are centered on the origin and scaled such that size is then defined as the sum of squared Euclidean distance from the point to the configuration centroid. [Ken89]

Dictionary of Computer Vision and Image Processing, Second Edition.
R. B. Fisher, T. P. Breckon, K. Dawson-Howe, A. Fitzgibbon, C. Robertson, E. Trucco and C. K. I. Williams.
© 2014 John Wiley & Sons, Ltd. Published 2014 by John Wiley & Sons, Ltd.

kernel: 1) A small matrix of numbers that is used by the image convolution operator. 2) The structuring element used in mathematical morphology operations. See also kernel function.

kernel canonical correlation analysis: An extension of canonical correlation analysis (CCA) which is equivalent to carrying out CCA in a high-dimensional feature space. The kernel trick means that the computations can be done on an $n \times n$ matrix (if there are n data points) rather than in the feature space. [SC04:6.5]

kernel Fisher discriminant analysis: A classification method using the kernel trick to lift Fisher linear discriminant analysis into feature space. This has the properties that: curved classification boundaries can be produced; the classification boundaries are defined locally by the classes rather than globally; and a high-dimensional feature space is avoided by using the kernel trick. [SC04:5.4]

kernel function: 1) A function in an integral transformation (e.g., the exponential term in the Fourier transform). 2) A function applied at every point in an image (see convolution operator). 3) A function $k(x, x')$ mapping two inputs x, x' to $\mathbb{R}$ so that the resulting Gram matrix is positive definite for any set inputs. The function in some sense quantifies the similarity of inputs x and x'. The kernel function can also be thought of as a dot-product in a feature space defined by a nonlinear mapping of x to $\phi(x)$. It is used, e.g., in kernel Fisher discriminant analysis and the support vector machine. An example kernel is the radial basis function kernel: $k(x, x') = exp(-\frac{1}{2\sigma^2} || x - x' ||^2)$. [SS02:p. 30]

kernel learning: For methods such as the support vector machine and Gaussian process regression which depend on a kernel function (definition 3), there may be some free parameters in the kernel which need to be set. Similarly, methods for making linear combinations of kernels (called multiple kernel learning) also require the setting of the relative weights of the different kernels. Kernel learning refers to the general process of setting these parameters. [Mur12:12.5]

kernel principal component analysis (KPCA): An extension of principal component analysis (PCA) that is equivalent to a nonlinear mapping of the data into a high-dimensional feature space in which the global axes of maximum variation are extracted. The kernel trick means that the computations can be done on an $n \times n$ matrix (for n data points) rather than in the feature space. KPCA can be used for feature extraction. [SS02:Ch. 14]

kernel regression: A non-parametric method for formulating regression problems. Given a dataset of input–output pairs $(\vec{x}_i, y_i)$ for $i = 1, \ldots, n$, the kernel regression estimate of the value of the function at input point $\vec{x}$ is given by $\sum_{i=1}^{n} y_i k(x, x_i)/ \sum_{i=1}^{n} k(x, x_i)$, where $k(\cdot, \cdot)$ denotes a kernel function. [Bis06:6.3]

kernel ridge regression: A generalization of linear regression which is equivalent to carrying out ridge regression in a high-dimensional feature space. The kernel trick means that the computations can be done on an $n \times n$ matrix (if there are n data points) rather than in the feature space. The resulting predictor has the form $f(\vec{x}) = \sum_{i=1}^{n} \alpha_i k(\vec{x}, \vec{x}_i)$, where $k(\cdot, \cdot)$ denotes a kernel function, and the coefficients $\{\alpha_i\}$ are determined by solving a linear system. See also Gaussian process regression. [SC04:2.2]

kernel trick: If an algorithm depends on the input data vector solely in terms of inner products between pairs of vectors, then it can be lifted into feature space by replacing occurrences of the inner products by the kernel function (definition 3). This is used, e.g., in kernel principal component analysis and kernel Fisher discriminant analysis. [SS02:p. 34]

key frame: Primarily a computer graphics animation technique, where key frames in a sequence are drawn by more experienced animators and intermediate interpolating frames are drawn by less experienced animators. In computer vision motion sequence analysis, key frames are the analogous video frames, typically displaying motion discontinuities between which the scene motion can be smoothly interpolated. [WP:Key_frame]

KHOROS: An image processing development environment with a large set of operators. The system comes with a pull-down interactive development workspace where operators can be instantiated and connected by click-and-drag operations. [KR94]

kinematic motion models: Mathematical descriptions of the mechanical movement of objects or collections of objects. Sometimes derived from motion capture or articulated object tracking. [Moe11:Ch. 10]

kinetic depth: A technique for estimating the depth at image feature points (usually edges) by exploiting a controlled sensor motion. This technique generally does not work at all points of the image because of insufficient image structure or sensor precision in smoothly varying regions, such as walls. See also shape from motion. A typical motion case is for the camera to rotate on a circular trajectory while fixating on a point in front of the camera: [WP:Depth_perception#Monocular_cues]

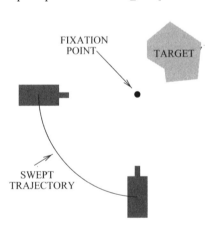

FIXATION POINT

TARGET

SWEPT TRAJECTORY

Kirsch compass edge detector: A first derivative edge detector that computes

the gradient in different directions according to which calculation mask is used. Edges have high gradient values, so thresholding the intensity gradient magnitude is one approach to edge detection. The following Kirsch mask detects edges at 45°: [Umb98:2.3.4]

$$\begin{bmatrix} -3 & 5 & 5 \\ -3 & 0 & 5 \\ -3 & -3 & -3 \end{bmatrix}$$

knowledge-based vision: A style of image interpretation that relies on multiple processing components capable of different image analysis processes, some of which may solve the same task in different ways. The components are linked by a reasoning algorithm that knows about the capabilities of the different components, when they might be usable or might fail. An additional common component is some form of task-dependent knowledge encoded in a knowledge representation that is used to help guide the reasoning algorithm. Also common is some uncertainty representation mechanism that records the confidence that the system has about the outcomes of its processing. For example, a knowledge-based vision system might be used for aerial analysis of road networks, containing specialized detection modules for straight roads, road junctions and forest roads as well as survey maps, terrain type classifiers, curve linking etc. [Nev82:10.2]

knowledge representation: A general term for methods of encoding knowledge in computers. In computer vision systems, this is usually knowledge about recognizable objects and visual-processing methods. A common knowledge representation scheme is the geometric model that records the 2D or 3D shapes of objects. Other commonly used vision knowledge representation schemes are graph models and frames. [BT88:Ch. 9]

Koenderink's surface shape classification: An alternative to the more common mean curvature and Gaussian curvature 3D surface shape classification labels. Koenderink's scheme decouples the two intrinsic shape parameters into one parameter (S) that represents the local surface shape (including cylindrical, hyperbolic, spherical and planar) and a second parameter (C) that encodes the magnitude of the curvedness of the shape. The figure illustrates the shape classes represented in Koenderink's classification scheme: [KvD79]

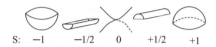

S: −1   −1/2   0   +1/2   +1

Kohonen network: A multi-variate data clustering and analysis method that produces a topological organization of the input data. The response of the whole network to a given data vector can be used as a lower-dimensional signature of the data vector. [WP:Counterpropagation_network]

Krawtchouk moments: Discrete orthogonal moments based on Krawtchouk polynomials $K_n(x : p, N) = \sum_{k=0}^{N} a_{k,n,p} x^k$. [YPO03]

kTC noise: A type of noise associated with field effect transistor (FET) image sensors. It is called "kTC" noise because the noise is proportional to $\sqrt{kTC}$ where T is the temperature, C is the capacitance of the image sensor and k is Boltzmann's constant. This noise arises during image capture at each pixel independently and is also independent of integration time. [WP:Johnson-Nyquist_noise# Thermal_noise_on_capacitors]

Kullback–Leibler divergence: A measure of the relative entropy or divergence between two probability densities $p_1(\vec{x})$ and $p_2(\vec{x})$, defined as $D(p_1 \| p_2) = \int p_1(\vec{x}) \log \dfrac{p_1(\vec{x})}{p_2(\vec{x})} d\vec{x}$. Note that it is not symmetric between the two arguments, and thus is not a distance. [CT91:Ch. 2]

kurtosis: A measure of the flatness of a probability distribution. If $m_4 = E[(X - \mu)^4]$ is the fourth central moment of the distribution of X relative to the mean μ and σ^2 is its variance, then kurtosis $= m^4/\sigma^4 - 3$. The -3 factor is chosen so that the Gaussian distribution has zero kurtosis. [PTVF92:14.1]

Kuwahara: An edge-preserving noise reduction filter. The filter uses four regions surrounding the pixel being smoothed. The smoothed value for that pixel is the mean value of the region with smallest variance. [BVV99]

147

L_1 **norm**: For a d-dimensional vector $\vec{x}$ $|\vec{x}|_1 = \sum_{i=1}^{d} |x_i|$. [GL89:p. 53]

L_2 **norm**: For a d-dimensional vector $\vec{x}$, $|\vec{x}|_2 = (\sum_{i=1}^{d} x_i^2)^{1/2}$. [GL89:p. 53]

L_∞ **image coding**: Image coding or compression techniques which directly address minimizing the L_∞ norm (maximum deviation norm) for reconstruction error, rather than the more common L_2 norm as used in JPEG.

label: A description associated with something for the purposes of identification (see region labeling). [BB82:12.4]

labeling problem: Given a set S of image structures (which may be pixels as well as more structured objects such as edges) and a set of labels L, the labeling problem is the question of how to assign a label $l \in L$ for each image structure $s \in S$. The process is usually dependent both on the image data and on neighboring labels. A typical remote-sensing application is to label image pixels by their land type, such as water, snow, sand, wheat field, forest etc. [BB82:12.4] In the figure, a range image (left) has its pixels labeled by the sign of their mean curvature (right: white is negative; light gray is zero; dark gray is positive; black is missing data):

 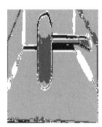

lacunarity: A scale-dependent measure of translational invariance based on the size distribution of holes within a set. High lacunarity indicates that the set is heterogeneous and low lacunarity indicates homogeneity. [PS06:3.3]

LADAR: LAser Detection And Ranging or Light Amplification for Detection and Ranging. See laser radar. [BB82:2.3.2]

Lagrange multiplier technique: A method of constrained optimization to find a solution to a numerical problem that includes one or more constraints. The classical form of the Lagrange multiplier technique finds the parameter vector $\vec{v}$ minimizing (or maximizing) the function $f(\vec{v}) = g(\vec{v}) + \mu h(\vec{v})$, where $g()$ is the function being minimized and $h()$ is a constraint function that has value zero when its argument satisfies the constraint. The Lagrange multiplier is μ. [Hor86:A.5]

Laguerre formula: A formula for computing the directed angle between two 3D lines based on the cross ratio of four points. Two points arise where the two image lines intersect the ideal line (i.e., the line through the vanishing points) and the other two points are the ideal line's absolute points (intersection of the ideal line and the absolute conic). [Fau93:2.4.8]

Lambert's law: The observed shading on ideal diffuse reflectors is independent of observer position and varies with the angle θ between the surface normal and the source direction: [JKS95:9.1.2]

LIGHT SOURCE
SURFACE NORMAL
CAMERA
θ

Dictionary of Computer Vision and Image Processing, Second Edition.
R. B. Fisher, T. P. Breckon, K. Dawson-Howe, A. Fitzgibbon, C. Robertson, E. Trucco and C. K. I. Williams.
© 2014 John Wiley & Sons, Ltd. Published 2014 by John Wiley & Sons, Ltd.

Lambertian surface: A surface whose reflectance obeys Lambert's law, more commonly known as a matte surface. These surfaces have equally bright appearance from all viewpoints. The shading of the surface thus depends only on the relative direction of the incident light. [FP03:4.3.3]

landmark detection: A general term for detecting an image feature that is commonly used for registration. The registration might be between a model and the image or it might be between two images. A landmark might be task specific, such as a component on an electronic circuit card or an anatomical feature (such as the tip of the nose), or it might be a more general image feature such as an interest point. [SB11:9.1]

LANDSAT: A series of satellites launched by the United States of America that are a common source of satellite images of the earth. LANDSAT 7 was launched in April 1999 and provides complete coverage of the earth every 16 days. [BB82:2.3.1]

Laplace–Beltrami operator: An operator f from differential geometry which describes the divergence of the gradient: $\Delta f = \operatorname{div} \operatorname{grad} f$. [Cha84]

Laplacian: Loosely, the Laplacian of a function is the sum of its second-order partial derivatives. For example the Laplacian of $f(x, y, z) : \mathbb{R}^3 \mapsto \mathbb{R}$ is $\nabla^2 f(x, y, z) = \frac{\partial^2 f}{\partial x^2} + \frac{\partial^2 f}{\partial y^2} + \frac{\partial^2 f}{\partial z^2}$. In computer vision, the Laplacian operator may be applied to an image, by convolution with the Laplacian kernel, one definition of which is given by the sum of second derivative kernels $[-1, 2, -1]$ and $[-1, 2, -1]^\top$, with zero padding to make the result 3×3: [JKS95:5.3.1]

$$\begin{pmatrix} 0 & -1 & 0 \\ -1 & 4 & -1 \\ 0 & -1 & 0 \end{pmatrix}$$

Laplacian eigenspace: A feature representation space where the eigenvectors corresponding to the smallest nonzero eigenvalues of the Laplacian matrix are used. [SC08]

Laplacian matrix: Matrix representation L of a graph G where:

$$\mathbf{L}_{i,j}(G) = \begin{cases} 1 & \text{if } i = j \text{ and } d_j \neq 0 \\ -\frac{1}{\sqrt{d_i d_j}} & \text{if } i \ \& \ j \text{ adjacent} \\ 0 & \text{otherwise} \end{cases}$$

where d is the vertex degree. [BCE00]

Laplacian of Gaussian operator: A low-level image operator that applies the second-derivative Laplacian operator (∇^2) after a Gaussian smoothing operation everywhere in an image. An isotropic operator, often used as part of a zero-crossing operator for edge detection because the locations where the value changes sign (positive to negative or vice versa) of the output image are located near the edges in the input image, and the detail of the detected edges can be controlled by use of the Gaussian smoothing scale parameter. The figure shows a mask that implements the Laplacian of Gaussian operator with smoothing parameter $\sigma = 1.4$: [JKS95:5.4]

0	1	1	2	2	2	1	1	0
1	2	4	5	5	5	4	2	1
1	4	5	3	0	3	5	4	1
2	5	3	-12	-24	-12	3	5	2
2	5	0	-24	-40	-24	0	5	2
2	5	3	-12	-24	-12	3	5	2
1	4	5	3	0	3	5	4	1
1	2	4	5	5	5	4	2	1
0	1	1	2	2	2	1	1	0

Laplacian pyramid: A compressed representation in which a pyramid of Laplacian images is created. At each level of the scheme, the current gray scale image has the Laplacian applied to it. The next level gray scale image is formed by Gaussian smoothing and subsampling. At the final level, the smoothed and subsampled image is kept. The original image can be approximately reconstructed level by level through expanding and smoothing the current level image and then adding the Laplacian. [FP03:9.2.1]

Laplacian smoothing: A mesh-smoothing algorithm where the current vertex is replaced by the mean value of the neighboring vertices. [HDZ05:8.1.3.2]

large field: 2D capture angles in a wide field of view image-capture system. [BSLB01:Ch. 5]

laser: Light Amplification by Stimulated Emission of Radiation. A very bright light source often used for machine-vision applications because of its properties: most light is at a single spectral frequency; the light is coherent, so various interference effects can be exploited; and the light beam can be processed so that divergence is slight. Two common applications are for structured light triangulation and range sensing. [Hec87:14.2]

laser illumination: A very bright light source useful because of its limited spectrum, bright power and coherence. See also laser. [Hec87:14.2]

laser radar (LADAR): A LIDAR range sensor that uses laser light. See also laser range sensor. [BB82:2.3.2]

laser range sensor: A range sensor that records the distance from the sensor to a target or target scene by detecting the image of a laser spot or stripe projected onto the scene. These sensors are commonly based on structured light triangulation, time of flight or phase difference technologies. [TV98:2.5.3]

laser speckle: A time-varying light pattern produced by interference of the reflection of light from a surface illuminated by a laser. [Hec87:14.2.2]

laser stripe triangulation: A structured light triangulation system that uses laser light. For example, a projected plane of light that would normally result in a straight line in the camera image is distorted by an object in the scene and the distortion is proportional to the height of the object.

The figure shows a typical triangulation geometry: [JKS95:11.4.1]

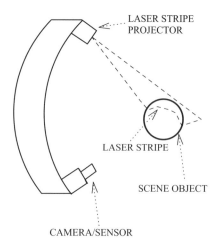

latent behavior: Unquantified or hidden geometric, statistical or relational properties exhibited by a system or entity. Generally referring to emerging or hidden behavior that is not readily measurable or quantifiable. See also latent variable model.

latent Dirichlet allocation (LDA): A latent variable model where each observation vector is generated from a combination of underlying sources or topics. This is achieved by drawing a latent probability vector from a Dirichlet distribution and generating observations from the combination of sources defined by these probabilities. In contrast, a mixture model forces each observation vector to come from only one of the sources. LDA is used for identifying topics in documents. See also topic model and probabilistic latent semantic analysis. [Mur12:24.3]

latent structure: Unquantified or hidden geometric, statistical or relational properties exhibited by a system.

latent variable model: A model of observed variables $\vec{x}$ in terms of some latent (or hidden) common "causes". A single discrete latent variable yields a mixture model. Models that use a continuous vector of latent variables include factor analysis, independent component analysis and latent Dirichlet allocation (LDA). [Bis06:Chs 9, 12]

lateral inhibition: A process in which a given feature weakens or eliminates nearby features. For example, in the Canny edge detector locally maximal intensity gradient magnitudes cause adjacent gradient values that lie across (rather than along) the edge to be set to zero. [Nev82:6.2]

lattice: A repeating set of points that may be used to describe an object if at least one of the dimensions is related to captured data. See also mesh model and surface mesh:

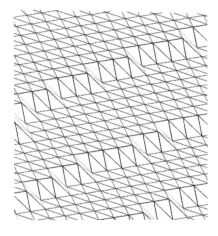

Laws' texture energy measure: A measure of the amount of image intensity variation at a pixel. The measure is based on five 1D finite difference masks convolved orthogonally to give 25 2D masks. The 25 masks are then convolved with the image. The outputs are smoothed nonlinearly and combined to give 14 contrast- and rotation-invariant measures. [PS06:4.6]

layered motion model: A statistical model that attempts to capture multiple objects and surfaces in full motion video by modeling each pixel as an additive mixture of Gaussian densities, each associated with an object. [AS94]

layered representation: A probabilistic model that operates at different levels of granularity and uses a multilayer hidden Markov model. [OHG02]

learning: 1) The acquisition of knowledge or skills. For a more specific definition in our context see machine learning. See also supervised learning and unsupervised learning. 2) The processes of parameter estimation and model selection. [Bis06:pp. 1–4]

learning from observation: See learning.

least mean square estimation: Also known as "least square estimation" or "mean square estimation". Let $\vec{v}$ be the parameter vector that we are searching for and $e_i(\vec{v})$ be the error meaasure associated with the ith of N data items. The error measure often used is the Euclidean distance, the algebraic distance or the Mahalanobis distance between the ith data item and a curve or surface being fitted, that is parameterized by $\vec{v}$. Then the mean square error is:

$$\frac{1}{N} \sum_{i=1}^{N} e_i(\vec{v})^2$$

The desired parameter vector $\vec{v}$ minimizes this sum. [WP:Least_squares]

least median of squares estimation: Let $\vec{v}$ be the parameter vector that we are searching for and $e_i(\vec{v})$ be the error associated with the ith of N data items. The error measure often used is Euclidean distance, the algebraic distance or the Mahalanobis distance between the ith data item and a curve or surface being fit that is parameterized by $\vec{v}$. Then the median square error is the middle value of the sorted set $\{e_i(\vec{v})^2\}$. The desired parameter vector $\vec{v}$ minimizes this median value. This estimator usually requires more computation for iterative and sorting algorithms but can be more robust to outliers than least mean square estimation. [JKS95:13.6.3]

least square curve fitting: A least mean square estimation process that fits a parametric model of a curve or a line to a collection of data points, usually 2D or 3D:

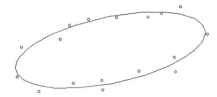

Fitting often uses the Euclidean distance, the algebraic distance or the Mahalanobis distance to evaluate the goodness of fit. [FP03:15.2–15.3]

least square estimation: See least mean square estimation. [WP:Least_squares]

least square surface fitting: A least mean square estimation process that fits a parametric model of a surface to a collection of data points, usually range data. Fitting often uses the Euclidean distance, the algebraic distance or the Mahalanobis distance to evaluate the goodness of fit. The range image (left) has planar and cylindrical surfaces fitted to the data (right): [JKS95:3.5]

least squares fitting: A general term for a least mean square estimation process that fits some parametric shape, such as a curve or surface, to a collection of data. Fitting often uses the Euclidean distance, the algebraic distance or the Mahalanobis distance to evaluate the goodness of fit. [BB82:A1.9]

leave-one-out test: A method for testing a solution in which one sample is left out of the training set and used instead for testing. This can be done for every sample. See also cross-validation. [FP03:22.1.5]

LED: Light Emitting semiconductor Diode. Often used as detectable point light source markers or controllable illumination. [Gal90:7.1]

left-handed coordinate system: A 3D coordinate system with the XYZ axes arranged as in the figure:

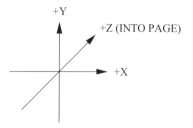

The alternative is a right-handed coordinate system. [WP:Cartesian_coordinate_system#Orientation_and_handedness]

Legendre moment: The Legendre moment of a piecewise continuous function $f(x, y)$ with order (m, n) is $\frac{1}{4}(2m + 1)(2n + 1) \int_{-1}^{+1} \int_{-1}^{+1} P_m(x)P_n(y)f(x, y)dxdy$ where $P_m(x)$ is the mth order Legendre polynomial. These moments can be used for characterizing image data and images can be reconstructed from the infinite set of moments. [TC88]

Lempel–Ziv–Welch (LZW): A form of file compression based on encoding commonly occurring byte sequences. This form of compression is used in the common GIF image file format. [Umb98:5.2.3]

lens: A physical optical device for focusing incident light onto an imaging surface, such as photographic film or an electronic sensor. Lenses can also be used to change magnification and to enhance or modify a field of view. [Hor86:2.3]

lens distortion: Unexpected variation in the light field passing through a lens. Examples are radial lens distortion or chromatic aberration and usually arise from how the lens differs from the ideal lens. [JKS95:12.9]

lens equation: The simplest case of a convex converging lens with focal length f perfectly focused on a target at distance D has distance d between the lens and the image plane as related by the lens equation $\frac{1}{f} = \frac{1}{D} + \frac{1}{d}$: [JKS95:8.1]

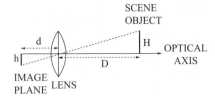

SCENE
OBJECT

IMAGE
PLANE LENS

OPTICAL
AXIS

lens flare/glare: An optical effect, usually unwanted, caused by stray light reflecting or refracting through an imaging system. It is generally caused by a relatively high intensity light source outwith the immediate imaging environment. [DeL01:5.5]

lens model: Mathematical treatment of the movement of light through the interfaces between substances of different refractive indices (commonly referred to as a lens). See also camera model and lens equation.

lens type: A general term for lens shapes and functions, such as convex or half-cylindrical, converging, magnifying etc. [Hor86:2.3]

level set: The set of data points $\vec{x}$ that satisfy a given equation of the form: $f(\vec{x}) = c$. Varying the value of c gives different sets of usually closely related points. A visual analogy is of a geographic surface and the ocean rising. If the function $f()$ is the sea level, then the level sets are the shore lines for different sea levels c. The figure shows an intensity image and the pixels at level (brightness) 80: [SQ04:8.6.1]

level set tree: A tree structure which is composed of the separate parts of the level sets of a function. They are useful to visualize estimates of mixed multivariate density functions, both their modes and their shape characteristics. [Kle04]

Levenberg–Marquardt optimization: A numerical multi-variate optimization method that switches smoothly between gradient descent when far from a (local) optimum and a second-order inverse Hessian (quadratic) method when nearer. [FP03:3.1.2]

Levenshtein edit distance: An information theoretical metric for determining the difference between two strings of character sequences. It is computed as the minimum number of edits required to turn one string into the other. Valid edit functions are deletion, insertion and substitution. [Chr12:Ch. 5]

license plate recognition: A computer vision application that aims to identify a vehicle's license plate from image data. Image data is often acquired from automatic cameras at places where vehicles slow down, such as bridges and toll barriers. [WP:Automatic_ number_plate_recognition]

LIDAR: LIght Detection And Ranging. A range sensor using (usually) laser light. It can be based on the time of flight of a pulse of laser light or the phase shift of a waveform. The measurement could be of a single point or an array of measurements if the light beam is swept across the scene or object. [BB82:2.3.2]

Lie group: A group that can be represented as a continuous and differentiable manifold of a space such that group operations are also continuous. An example of a Lie group is the orthogonal group $SO(3) = \{\mathbf{R} \in \mathcal{R}^{3 \times 3} : \mathbf{R}^\top \mathbf{R} = I, det(\mathbf{R}) = 1\}$ of rigid 3D rotations. [WP:Lie_group]

light: A general term for the electromagnetic radiation used in many computer-vision applications. The term could refer to the illumination in the scene or to the irradiance coming from the scene onto the sensor. Most computer vision applications use visible light, infrared light or ultraviolet light. [Jai89:3.2]

light field: An entire light environment consisting of light travelling in every direction at every point in space. [Sze10:13.3]

light source: A general term for the source of illumination in a scene, whether deliberate or accidental. The light source might be a point light source or an extended light source. [FP03:5.2]

light source detection: The process of detecting the position of or direction to the light sources in the scene, even if not observable. The light sources are usually assumed to be point light sources for this process. [BB04]

light source geometry: A general term referring to the light source placement and shape in a scene. [LR85]

light source placement: A general term for the positions of the light sources in a scene. It may also refer to the care that machine-vision applications engineers take when placing the light sources so as to minimize unwanted lighting effects (such as shadows and specular reflections) and to enhance the visibility of desired scene structures, e.g., by back lighting or oblique illumination. [Gum02]

light stripe ranging: See structured light triangulation.

light transport: In image-rendering techniques, the mathematical models of energy transfer between interfaces which alter whether surfaces of objects are visible. [Sze10:2.2.2]

lightfield: A function that encodes the radiance on an empty point in space as a function of the point's position and the direction of the illumination. A lightfield allows image-based rendering of new (unoccluded) scene views from arbitrary positions within the lightfield. [WP:Light_field]

lighting: A general term for the illumination in a scene, whether deliberate or accidental. [Gal90:2.1.1]

lighting capture: A method for recording the incident light, from all directions, at a point in space. Performed as part of high dynamic range imaging for imagery relighting. [RHD+10:9.3]

lightness: The estimated or perceived reflectance of a surface, when viewed in monochrome. [Nev82:6.1–6.2]

lightpen: A user-interface device that allows people to indicate places on a computer screen by touching the screen at the desired place with the pen. The computer can then draw items, select actions etc. It is effectively a type of mouse that acts on the display screen instead of on a mat. [WP:Light_pen]

likelihood function: In a statistical model M the connection between the parameters θ and the data D is through the likelihood function $L(\theta|M) = p(D|\theta, M)$. Notice that the likelihood is viewed as a function of the parameters θ and M with D fixed. [Bis06:1.2.3]

likelihood ratio: 1) The ratio of the likelihood functions of two different models for the same data. For example, in a Bayesian classifier for a binary classification problem, the ratio of posterior probabilities for the two classes would depend on the product of the likelihood ratio and the ratio of prior class probabilities.
2) In statistics, the likelihood ratio test is used to compare two statistical models for the same data based on the ratio of their likelihood scores. [Was04:10.6]

likelihood score: For a statistical model M with data D, the maximum value of the log likelihood function $L(\theta|M)$ with respect to θ, i.e., $\max_\theta \log L(\theta|M)$. [KF09:18.3.1]

limb extraction: A process of image interpretation that extracts the arms or legs of people or animals (e.g., for tracking) or extracts the barely visible edge of a curved surface as it curves away from an observer (derived from an astronomical term):

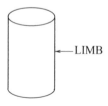

See also occluding contour. [TYO00]

limited angle tomography: In computed tomography (medical CT) it is rarely possible to collect data over the full angular range. In such cases data reconstruction from available information must be used, which can be achieved via a range of techniques. [DB98]

line: Usually refers to a straight ideal line that passes through two points, but may also refer to a general curve marking, e.g., on paper. [Sch89:App. 1]

line cotermination: When two lines have endpoints in exactly or nearly the same location: [Bie85]

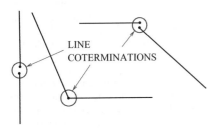

LINE COTERMINATIONS

line detection operator: A feature detection process that detects lines. Depending on the specific operator, locally linear line segments may be detected or straight lines might be globally detected. Note that this detects lines as contrasted with edges. [Nev82:7.3]

line-drawing analysis: 1) Analysis of hand-made or CAD drawings to extract a symbolic or shape description. For example, research has investigated extracting 3D building models from CAD drawings. Another application is the analysis of hand-drawn circuit sketches to form a circuit description. 2) Analysis of the line junctions in a polyhedral blocks world scene, in order to understand the 3D structure of the scene. [Nal93:Ch. 4]

line fitting: A curve-fitting problem where the objective is to estimate the parameters of a straight line that best interpolates given point data. [DH73:9.2]

line following: See line grouping.

line grouping: Generally refers to the process of creating a longer curve by grouping together shorter fragments found by a line detection operator. These might be short connecting locally detected line fragments or longer straight line segments separated by a gap. May also refer to the grouping of line segments on the basis of principles such as parallelism. See also edge tracking and perceptual organization and Gestalt.

line intersection: Where two or more lines intersect at a point. The lines cross or meet at a line junction: [Hor86:15.6]

LINE INTERSECTIONS

line junction: The point at which two or more lines meet. See junction labeling. [Nal93:4.1.1]

line label: In an ideal polyhedral blocks world scene, lines arise from only a limited set of physical situations such as convex or concave surface shape discontinuities (fold edges); occluding contours where a fold edge is seen against the background (blade edge); crack edges where two polyhedra have aligned edges; or shadow edges. Line labels identify the type of line as one of these types. Assigning labels is one step in scene understanding that helps deduce the 3D structure of the scene. See also junction label. The figure shows the usual line labels for convex (+), concave (−) and occluding (>) edges: [Hor86:15.6]

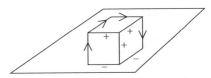

line linking: See line grouping.

line matching: The process of making a correspondence between the lines in two sets. One set might be a geometric model such as used in model-based recognition, model registration or alignment. Alternatively, the lines may have been extracted from different images, as when doing feature-based stereo or estimating the epipolar geometry between the two lines. [SZ97]

line moment: Similar to the traditional area moment but calculated only at points $(x(s), y(s))$ along the object contour. The pqth moment is: $\int x(s)^p y(s)^q ds$. The infinite set of line moments uniquely determine the contour. [WL93]

line moment invariant: A set of invariant values computable from the line moments. These may be invariant to translation, scaling and rotation. [LG95]

line of sight: A straight line from the observer or camera into the scene, usually to some target: [JKS95:1.4]

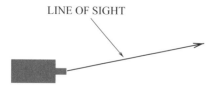

LINE OF SIGHT

line scan camera: A camera that uses a solid-state or semiconductor (e.g., CMOS) linear array sensor, in which all of the photosensitive elements are in a single 1D line. Typical line scan cameras have between 32 and 8192 elements. These sensors are used for a variety of machine-vision applications such as scanning, flow process control and position sensing. [BT88:Ch. 3]

line segmentation: See curve segmentation.

line spread function: Describes how an ideal infinitely thin line would be distorted after passing through an optical system. Normally, this can be computed by integrating the point spread functions of an infinite number of points along the line. [Hec87:11.3.5]

line thinning: See thinning.

linear: 1) Having a line-like form.
2) A mathematical description for a process in which the relationship between some input variables $\vec{x}$ and

some output variables $\vec{y}$ is given by $\vec{y} = A\vec{x}$ where A is a matrix. [Hor86:6.1]

linear array sensor: A solid-state or semiconductor (e.g., CMOS) sensor in which all of the photosensitive elements are in a single 1D line. Typical linear array sensors have between 32 and 8192 elements and are used in line scan cameras. [IJL87]

linear discriminant analysis: See linear discriminant function.

linear discriminant function: A basic classification process that determines which of two classes or cases a structure belongs to. Assume a feature vector $\vec{x}$ that is based on observations of a structure and is augmented by an extra term with value 1. The linear discriminant function uses the sign of the linear function $l = \vec{a} \cdot \vec{x} = \sum a_i x_i$, for a given coefficient vector $\vec{a}$. For example, to discriminate between unit side squares and unit diameter circles based on the area A, the feature vector is $\vec{x} = (A, 1)'$ and the coefficient vector $\vec{a} = (1, -0.89)'$. If $l > 0$, then the structure is a square, otherwise it is a circle. [SB11:11.6]

linear features: A general term for features that are locally or globally straight, such as lines or straight edges. [MN84]

linear filter: A filter whose output is a weighted sum of its inputs, i.e., all terms in the filter are either constants or variables. If $\{x_i\}$ are the inputs (which may be pixel values from a local neighborhood, from the same position in different images of the same scene etc.), then the linear filter output would be $\sum a_i x_i + a_0$, for some constants a_i. [FP03:Ch. 7]

linear regression: Estimation of the parameters of a linear relationship between two random variables X and Y given sets of samples $\vec{x}_i$ and $\vec{y}_i$. The objective is to estimate the matrix A and vector $\vec{a}$ that minimize the residual $r(\mathbf{A}, \vec{a}) = \sum_i \|\vec{y}_i - \mathbf{A}\vec{x}_i - \vec{a}\|^2$. In this form, the $\vec{x}_i$ are assumed to be noise-free quantities. When both variables are subject to error, orthogonal regression is preferred. [WP:Linear_regression]

156

linear transformation: A mathematical transformation of a set of values by addition and multiplication by constants. If the set of values is a vector $\vec{x}$, the general linear transformation produces another vector $\vec{y} = \mathbf{A}\vec{x}$, where $\vec{y}$ need not have the same dimension as $\vec{x}$ and $\mathbf{A}$ is a constant matrix (i.e., is not a function of $\vec{x}$). [SQ04:2.2.1]

linearly non-separable: For a classification problem, a dataset whose classes are not linearly separable is said to be linearly non-separable. [DH73:Ch. 5]

linearly separable: A binary classification problem is linearly separable if the two classes can be separated by a hyperplane. In the multiclass case, a problem is linearly separable if the decision boundaries can be represented by a linear classifier, i.e., a classifier where an input $\vec{x}$ is assigned to the class $i = 1, \ldots, c$ which maximizes $\vec{w}_i^\top \vec{x} + w_{0i}$. [DH73:Ch. 5]

lip shape analysis: An application of computer vision to understanding the position and shape of human lips as part of face analysis. The goal might be face recognition or expression understanding. [LBDX03]

lip tracking: An application of computer vision to following the position and shape of human lips in a video sequence. The goal might be for lip reading, augmentation of deaf sign analysis or focusing of resolution during image compression. [KDB96]

local: A *local property* of a mathematical object is one that is defined in terms only of a small neighborhood of the object, e.g., curvature. In image processing, a local operator operates on a small number of nearby pixels at a time. [Hor86:4.2]

local binary pattern: Given a local neighborhood about a point, use the value of the central pixel to threshold the neighborhood. This creates a local descriptor of the gray scale structure that is invariant to lightness and contrast transformations, that can be used to create local texture primitives. [PS06:4.7]

local contrast adjustment: A form of contrast enhancement that adjusts pixel intensities based on the values of nearby pixels instead of the values of all pixels in the image. The figure shows (left) an original image and (right) an image that has the eye area's brightness enhanced while maintaining the background's contrast: [KZQ05]

local curvature estimation: A part of surface or curve shape estimation that estimates the curvature at a given point based on the position of nearby parts of the curve or surface. For example, the curve $y = sin(x)$ has zero local curvature at the point $x = 0$ (i.e., the curve is locally uncurved or straight), although the curve has nonzero local curvature at other other points (e.g., at $\frac{\pi}{4}$). See also differential geometry. [WVVG01]

Local feature focus (LFF) method: A 2D part identification and pose estimation algorithm that can cope with large amounts of occlusion of the parts. The algorithm uses a mixture of property-based classifiers, graph models and geometric models. The key identification process is based around local configurations of image features that is more robust to occlusion. [BC82]

local invariant: See local point invariant.

local motion event: A spatio-temporal event within a video sequence describing the movement of an object locally within the viewed scene over some restricted period of time. See also spatio-temporal analysis. [SCZ11]

local operator: An image-processing operator that computes its output at each pixel from the values of the nearby pixels instead of using all or most of the pixels in the image. [JKS95:1.7.2]

local point invariant: A property of local shape or intensity that is invariant to translation, rotation, scaling, contrast or brightness changes etc. For example, a surface's Gaussian curvature is invariant to change in position. [Low99]

local surface shape: The shape of a surface in a "small" region around a point, often classified into one of a small number of surface shape classifications. Computed as a function of the surface curvatures. [KvD92]

local ternary patterns (LTP): A local texture descriptor which classifies all points in a region as being:
- approximately equal to the central point (where the absolute difference is less than some threshold);
- less than the central point by more than the threshold;
- greater than the central point by more than the threshold.

Local ternary patterns are an extension of local binary patterns. [TT07]

local variance contrast: The variance of the pixel values computed in a neighborhood about each pixel. Contrast is the difference between the larger and smaller values of this variance. Large values of this property occur in highly textured or varying areas. [FYF+01]

localization: Often referred to as "spatial localization". The identification of the position of a feature, object or target within an image, either in terms of coordinates or possibly a bounding box. Occasionally localization may mean temporal localization where the timing of an event, such as the abandonment of an object, is determined within a video sequence.

locally linear embedding (LLE): An algorithm for nonlinear dimensionality reduction, where the data has manifold structure. Given n data points in high dimension, LLE returns n points in a lower dimensional space, so that each point can be reconstructed as a linear combination of its neighbors. The LLE algorithm achieves this by solving a particular eigen-decomposition. [HTF08:14.9]

location-based retrieval: The retrieval of information based on the position of a mobile device. This term is most frequently associated with mobile phone services but can equally be relevant in augmented reality applications where information may be overlaid on images or videos in a particular location. [SAW94b]

log-likelihood: The log of the likelihood function.

log-normal distribution: If X is a random variable which follows a normal distribution (or Gaussian distribution), then $Y = e^X$ is said to follow a log-normal distribution; it has support in $(0, \infty)$. [MKB79:p. 43]

log-polar image: A representation in which the pixels are not in the standard Cartesian layout but instead have a space-varying layout. The image is parameterized by a polar coordinate θ and a radial coordinate r. However, unlike polar coordinates, the radial distance increases exponentially as r grows. The mapping from position (θ, r) to Cartesian coordinates is $(\beta^r cos(\theta), \beta^r sin(\theta))$, where β is some design parameter. Further, the amount of area of the image plane represented by each pixel grows exponentially with r, although the precise pixel size depends on factors such as the amount of pixel overlap. See also foveal image. The receptive fields of a log-polar image (courtesy of Herman Gomes) can be seen in the outer rings of the figure: [WZ00]

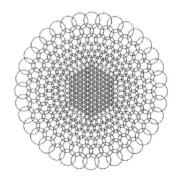

log-polar stereo: A form of stereo vision in which the input images come from log-polar sensors instead of the standard Cartesian layout. [GT00]

logarithmic transformation: See pixel logarithm operator.

logical object representation: An object representation based on some logical formalism such as predicate calculus. For example, a square can be defined as: $square(s) \iff polygon(s)$ & $number\_of\_sides(s, 4)$ & $\forall e_1 \; \forall e_2 (e_1 \neq e_2$ & $side\_of(s, e_1)$ & $side\_of(s, e_2)$ & $length(e_1) = length(e_2)$ & $(parallel(e_1, e_2)$ | $perpendicular(e_1, e_2)))$. [RM89]

logistic regression: A widely-used model for two-class classification. Let an input feature vector be denoted as $\vec{x}$. Subsequently, the logistic regression model predicts $p(C_1|\vec{x}) = \sigma(\vec{w}^\top \vec{x} + w_0)$, where σ denotes the logistic sigmoid function $\sigma(z) = (1 + e^{-z})^{-1}$, $\vec{w}$ is a vector of parameters, and w_0 is a bias (or offset) term. $p(C_2|\vec{x}) = 1 - p(C_1|\vec{x})$. The parameters can be fitted by maximum likelihood estimation and the optimization problem can be shown to be convex (i.e., no local optima). [Bis06:4.3.2]

long baseline stereo: See wide baseline stereo.

long motion sequence: A video sequence of more than just a few frames in which there is significant camera or scene motion. The essential idea is that the 3D scene structure can be inferred effectively by a stereo vision process. The matched image features can be tracked through the sequence, instead of having to solve the stereo correspondence problem. If a long sequence is not available, then analysis could use optical flow or short baseline stereo.

look-up table: Given a finite set of input values $\{x_i\}$ and a function on these values, $f(x)$, a look-up table records the values $\{(x_i, f(x_i))\}$ so that the value of the function $f()$ can be looked up directly rather than recomputed each time. Look-up tables can be used for color re-mapping or standard functions of integer pixel values (e.g., the logarithm of a pixel's value). [Hor86:10.14]

lossless compression: A category of image compression in which the original image can be exactly reconstructed from the compressed image. This contrasts with lossy compression. [SB11:1.3.2]

lossy compression: A category of image compression in which the original image cannot be exactly reconstructed from the compressed image. The goal is to lose insignificant image details (e.g., noise) while limiting perception of changes to the image appearance. Lossy algorithms generally produce greater compression than lossless compression. [SB11:1.3.2]

low-activity region: A region in a scene where little of interest occurs. For example in a surveillance application, little of interest occurs away from the ground plane (e.g., on the upper parts of buildings). [CK99]

low-angle illumination: A machine-vision technique, often used for industrial vision, where a light source (usually a point light source) is placed so that a ray of light from the source to the inspection point is almost perpendicular to the surface normal at that point. The situation can also arise naturally, e.g., from the sun position at dawn or dusk. One consequence of this low angle is that shallow surface shape defects and cracks cast strong shadows that may simplify the inspection process:

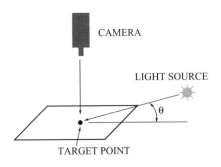

[Bil02:1.2.5]

low frequency: Usually referring to low spatial frequency in the context of computer vision. The low-frequency components of an image are the slowly changing intensity components of the image, such as large regions of bright and dark pixels. If low temporal frequency is the intended meaning, then low frequency refers to slowly changing patterns of brightness or darkness at the same pixel in a video sequence. This figure shows the low-frequency components of an image: [WP:Low_frequency]

low-level vision: A general and somewhat imprecisely defined term (the definition is contentious) for the initial stages of image analysis in a vision system. It can also be used for the initial stages of processing in biological vision systems. Roughly, low-level vision refers to the first few stages of processing applied to intensity images. Some authors use this term only for operations that result in other images. Edge detection is about where most authors would say that low-level vision ends and middle-level vision starts. [BB82:1.2]

low-pass filter: This term is imported from 1D signal-processing theory into image processing. The term "low" is a shorthand for "low frequency". In the context of a single image, that means low spatial frequency, i.e., intensity patterns that change over many pixels. A low-pass filter applied to an image thus leaves the low spatial frequency patterns, or large, slowly changing patterns, and removes the high spatial frequency components (sharp edges and noise). A low-pass filter is a kind of smoothing filter or noise reduction filter. Alternatively, filtering is applied to the changing values of a given pixel

over an image sequence. In this case the pixel values can be treated as a sampled time sequence and the original signal-processing definition of "low pass filter" is appropriate. Filtering this way removes rapid temporal changes. See also high-pass filter. The figure shows an image and its low-pass filtered version: [Gal90:6.2]

Lowe's curve segmentation method: An algorithm that tries to split a curve into a sequence of straight line segments. The algorithm has three main stages:
1. Recursive splitting of segments into two shorter, but more line-like, segments until all remaining segments are very short. This forms a tree of segments.
2. Merging segments in the tree in a bottom-up fashion according to a straightness measure.
3. Extracting the remaining unmerged segments from the tree as the segmentation result.
[Low87a]

Lucas–Kanade method: A differential method for the computation of optical flow in a video. It assumes that the flow is constant in a small area around the pixel under consideration and determines the flow based on a least square estimation for all pixels within that area. [LK81]

luma: The luminance component of light. Color can be divided into luma and chroma. [FP03:6.3.2]

lumigraph: A device, invented by Fischinger in the 1940s, that produces beams of colored light by a person pressing on a screen. More recently in computer vision, "lumigraph" refers to a representation used to store (a subset of) the plenoptic function (i.e., the flow of light in all positions and directions). [Sze10:13.3]

luminance: The measured intensity from a portion of a scene. [Jai89:3.2]

luminance efficiency: The sensor-specific function $V(\lambda)$ that determines how the observed light $I(x, y, \lambda)$ at sensor position (x, y) of wavelength λ contributes to the measured luminance $l(x, y) = \int I(\lambda)V(\lambda)d\lambda$ at that point. [Jai89:3.2]

luminosity coefficient: A component of the tristimulus theory of color perception. The luminosity coefficient is the amount of luminance contributed by a given primary color to the total perceived luminance. [Jai89:3.8]

luminous flux: The amount of light at all wavelengths that passes through a given region in space. Proportional to perceived brightness. [WP:Luminous_flux]

M

M-estimation: A robust generalization of least square estimation and maximum likelihood estimation. [FP03:15.5.1]

Mach band effect: An effect in the human visual system in which an observer perceives a variation in brightness at the edges of a region of constant brightness. This variation makes the region appear slightly darker when it is beside a brighter region and slightly brighter when it is beside a darker region. [Jai89:3.2]

machine learning: A set of methods for the automated analysis of structure in data. There two main strands of work:

- unsupervised learning or descriptive modeling, where the goal is to find interesting patterns or structure in the data;
- supervised learning or predictive modeling, where the goal is to predict the value of one or more variables given some others.

These goals are similar to those of data mining, but the focus is more on autonomous machine performance, rather than enabling humans to learn from the data. [Mur12:p. 1]

machine vision: A general term for processing image data by a computer; often synonymous with computer vision. There is a slight tendency to use "machine vision" for practical vision systems, such as industrial vision, and "computer vision" for more exploratory vision systems or for systems that aim at some of the competences of the human vision system. [JKS95:1.1]

macrotexture: The intensity pattern formed by spatially organized texture primitives on a surface, such as

a tiling. Contrast with microtexture. [JKS95:7.1]

magnetic resonance imaging (MRI): See nuclear magnetic resonance.

magnification: The process of enlargement (e.g., of an image). The amount of enlargement applied. [Jai89:7.4]

magnitude-retrieval problem: The reconstruction of a signal based on only the phase (not the magnitude) of the Fourier transform. [McD04]

Mahalanobis distance: The distance between two N-dimensional points scaled by the statistical variation in each component of the point. For example, if $\vec{x}$ and $\vec{y}$ are two points from the same distribution that has covariance matrix $\mathbf{C}$ then the Mahalanobis distance is given by

$$((\vec{x} - \vec{y})' \mathbf{C}^{-1} (\vec{x} - \vec{y}))^{\frac{1}{2}}$$

The Mahalanobis distance is the same as the Euclidean distance if the covariance matrix is the identity matrix. A common usage in computer vision systems is for comparing feature vectors whose elements are quantities having different ranges and amounts of variation, such as a 2-vector recording the properties of area and perimeter. [SB11:11.8]

mammogram analysis: Analyzing an X-ray of the human female breast (a mammogram), usually for the detection of potential signs of cancerous growths. [FB03]

man in the loop: The inclusion of a person within the control system of, e.g., an unmanned vehicle such as a drone aircraft. The man in the loop is required until these systems can be shown to be

Dictionary of Computer Vision and Image Processing, Second Edition.
R. B. Fisher, T. P. Breckon, K. Dawson-Howe, A. Fitzgibbon, C. Robertson, E. Trucco and C. K. I. Williams.
© 2014 John Wiley & Sons, Ltd. Published 2014 by John Wiley & Sons, Ltd.

reliable at performing tasks completely autonomously. [FDS90]

Manhattan distance: Also called the Manhattan metric. Motivated by the problem of only being able to walk along city blocks in dense urban environments, the distance between points (x_1, y_1) and (x_2, y_2) is $| x_1 - x_2 | + | y_1 - y_2 |$. [BB82:2.2.6]

Manhattan world: Scenes consisting of planar surfaces in three dominant orthogonal planes. Many real-world, manmade objects, such as the interior and exterior of most buildings, can be considered as Manhattan world scenes: [CW99]

manifold: A topological space that is locally Euclidean. Data analysis often involves dimensionality reduction, where a low-dimensional manifold is embedded in a higher-dimensional space. A linear manifold (or subspace) may be extracted using principal component analysis (PCA); for non-linear methods see dimensionality reduction. [Lov10:2.1]

many-to-many graph matching: A version of graph matching in which clusters of vertices from one graph are matched with clusters from another. This is particularly useful in vision applications where graphs cannot be perfectly matched using one-to-one matching.

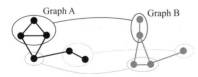

[DSD+04]

many view stereo: See multi-view stereo.

MAP: See maximum a posteriori probability.

map analysis: Analyzing an image of a map (e.g., obtained with a flat-bed scanner) in order to extract a symbolic description of the terrain described by the map. This is now largely obsolete, given digital map databases. [WP:Map_analysis]

map registration: The registration of a symbolic map to (usually) aerial or satellite image data. This may require identifying roads, buildings or land features. The figure shows a road model (black) overlaying an aerial image: [LM07]

marching cubes: An algorithm for determining a polygonal approximation to a surface from a voxel representation. Each vertex on the voxel is given a binary value depending on whether it is inside or outside the object and polygonal surfaces are defined for each group of eight vertices forming a virtual cube. The algorithm is very efficient as there are only 256 possible arrangements of each group of eight vertices. Given a function $f( )$ on the voxels, the algorithm estimates the position of the surface $f(\vec{x}) = c$ for some c. This requires estimating where the surface intersects each of the 12 edges of a voxel. Many implementations propagate from one voxel to its neighbors, hence the term "marching". [LC87]

marginal distribution: A probability distribution of a random variable X derived from the joint probability distribution of a number of random variables integrated over all variables except X. [WP:Marginal_distribution]

marginal likelihood: A Bayesian statistical model M has parameters θ. Given data D the marginal likelihood $p(D|M) = \int p(D|\theta, M)p(\theta|M)d\,\theta$ can be computed by integrating the likelihood function over the prior distribution. The marginal likelihood is used in Bayesian model selection. [Bis06:3.4]

marked point process: A random process of points, an instance of which will consist of a set of points generally in space (e.g., the locations of occurrences of particular features or events) or time (e.g., the times of occurrences of particular events). In a marked point process, parameters (the "marks") are associated with each point (in addition to the location or time information). [Cre93:8.7]

markerless motion capture: Capture of the way in which an object, person or animal moves through the analysis of video. Critically, the video is taken without physical markers attached to the subject. See also motion capture. [CMC+06]

Markov chain: A state system model in which the probability of the next state transition depends only on the current state. The figure shows transitions between four states including self transitions: [Bis06:11.2.1]

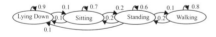

Markov chain Monte Carlo (MCMC): A statistical inference method useful for estimating the parameters of complex distributions. The method generates samples from the distribution by running the Markov chain that models the problem for a long time (hopefully to equilibrium) and

then uses the ensemble of samples to estimate the distribution. The states of the Markov chain are the possible configurations of the problem. [WP:Markov_chain_Monte_Carlo]

Markov decision process (MDP): A process in which an agent can sense a set of distinct states in the environment and has a set of actions which it can perform. If the agent is in state s_t at time t and takes action a_t, then it transitions into state s_{t+1}; $p(s_{t+1}|s_t, a_t)$ defines the transition probabilities for the MDP. The agent also receives a reward $r(s_t, s_{t+1}, a_t)$ associated with this transition. The Markov aspect of the MDP arises from the fact that the transition probability to the new state s_{t+1} depends only on the *current* state and action, not on earlier ones. The key problem for the agent is to find a policy (a possible stochastic mapping from states to actions) so as to maximize some cumulative function of the rewards. The MDP formalizes the problem of optimal control. [SB98:3.6]

Markov network: See Markov random field (MRF).

Markov process: A stochastic process in time whose past has no influence on the future if the present is specified. [Pap91:16.4]

Markov property: A property for which the conditional probability of a future state depends only on the present state rather than anything which preceded it. [Bis06:11.2.1]

Markov random field (MRF): An undirected graphical model. Compare with conditional random field (CRF). An application is as an image model in which the value at a pixel can be expressed as a linear weighted sum of the values of pixels in a finite neighborhood about the original pixel plus an additive random noise value. [Mur12:6.3]

Markovian assumption: The inherent assumption underlying Markov chains: the values in any state are affected only by the values in the previous state. [SHB08:p. 799]

Marr–Hildreth edge detector: A filter for edge detection based on multi-scale analysis of the zero crossing of the Laplacian of a Gaussian operator. [NA05:4.3.3]

Marr's theory: Shorthand for "Marr's theory of the human vision system". Some of the key stages in this integrated but incomplete theory are the raw primal sketch, the full primal sketch, the 2.5D sketch and 3D object recognition. [BT88:Ch. 11]

mask: An $m \times n$ array of numbers or symbolic labels, used as the smoothing mask in a convolution operator, the target in template matching, the kernel in a mathematical morphology operation etc. The figure shows a simple mask for computing an approximation to the Laplacian operator: [TV98:3.2]

0	1	0
1	-4	1
0	1	0

matched filter: An operator that produces a strong result in the output image when it processes a portion of the input image containing a pattern for which it is "matched". For example, the filter could be tuned for the letter "e" in a given font size and type style or a particular face viewed at the right scale. It is similar to template matching except the matched filter can be tuned for spatially separated patterns. This is a signal-processing term imported into image processing. [Jai89:9.12]

matching function: See similarity metric.

matching method: A general term for finding the correspondences between two structures (e.g., surface matching) or sets of features (see the stereo correspondence problem). [JKS95:15.5.2]

mathematical morphology operation: A class of mathematically defined image-processing operations, which can apply to both binary images and gray scale images, in which the result is based on the spatial pattern of the input data values rather than on the values themselves. For example, a morphological line-thinning algorithm (see thinning operator) would identify places in an image where a line description (i.e., the pattern to match) was represented by data more than 1 pixel wide. The thinning algorithm would choose one of the redundant pixels to be set to 0. This figure shows a small image patch before and after a thinning operation: [SQ04:Ch. 7]

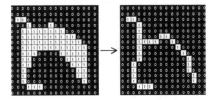

matrix: A mathematical structure of a given number of rows and columns with each entry usually containing a number. It can be used to represent a transformation between two coordinate systems, record the covariance of a set of vectors etc. A matrix for rotating a 2D vector by $\frac{\pi}{6}$ radians is: [Jai89:2.7]

$$\begin{bmatrix} cos\left(\frac{\pi}{6}\right) & sin\left(\frac{\pi}{6}\right) \\ -sin\left(\frac{\pi}{6}\right) & cos\left(\frac{\pi}{6}\right) \end{bmatrix}$$
$$= \begin{bmatrix} 0.866 & 0.500 \\ -0.500 & 0.866 \end{bmatrix}$$

matrix-array camera: A 2D solid-state chip sensor for imaging, such as those found in typical current video cameras, webcams and machine vision cameras. [Gal90:2.1.3]

matte extraction: The derivation of an alpha channel (i.e., transparency information) or binary mask for an image or video. Often the alpha channel, or matte, may be used to delineate an object of interest in a scene. [Sze10:10.4]

matte surface: A surface whose reflectance follows the Lambertian surface model. [BB82:3.5.1]

matting: The process of combining multiple images using a matte or mattes (binary masks) to indicate which parts of each image to use. [Sze10:3.1.3]

maximal clique: A clique for which no further nodes exist that are connected to all nodes. Maximal cliques may have different sizes – the issue is maximality, not size. Maximal cliques are used in association graph matching algorithms to represent maximally matched structures. The graph in the figure has two maximal cliques, BCDE and ABD: [BB82:11.3.3]

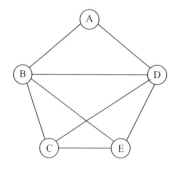

maximum *a posteriori* probability (MAP): The configuration of random variables in a statistical model that maximizes the posterior distribution. This term is often used in the context of parameter estimation, pose estimation or object recognition problems, in which case we wish to estimate the parameters, position or identity (respectively) that have highest posterior probability given the observed image data. However, this approach is, at best, an approximation to the full Bayesian statistical model treatment, which involves integration over the posterior distribution. [Mac03:p. 306]

maximum entropy: The probability density $p(x)$ that maximizes the entropy of the distribution subject to constraints of the form $\int r_i(x)p(x)dx = c_i$ for $i = 1, \ldots, m$. It can be shown that the solution has the form $p(x) = \exp(\lambda_0 +$

$\sum_{i=1}^{m} \lambda_i r_i(x))$ where the λs are chosen so that $p(x)$ satisfies the constraints and normalizes to 1. [CT91:11.1]

maximum entropy restoration: An image restoration technique based on maximum entropy. [PTVF92:18.7]

maximum flow: The route with maximum capacity (flow) from a source to a destination node in a network. [Gib85:4.2]

maximum margin: In a binary classification problem which is linearly separable, let the perpendicular distance from a separating hyperplane to the nearest +1 class point be d_+ and similarly d_- for nearest class −1 point. The margin is defined as $\min(d_+, d_-)$ and the support vector machine algorithm determines the hyperplane that gives rise to the maximum margin with $d_+ = d_-$. The figure shows the maximum margin line between two point sets: [SS02:7.3]

maximum margin Hough transform: An extension on the probabilistic Hough transform which learns weights for various features of objects in order to increase the likelihood of obtaining correct matches. [MM09]

MCMC: See Markov chain Monte Carlo.

MDL: See minimum description length.

mean: The mean μ of a random variable is the expectation value of X, i.e., $\mu = E[X]$. This is also commonly known as the statistical average. See also sample mean. [MKB79:2.2.2]

mean and Gaussian curvature shape classification: A classification of a local (i.e., very small) surface patch (often a single pixel from a range image) into one of a set of simple surface shape classes based on the signs of the mean curvature and Gaussian curvature. The standard set of shape classes is: {plane, concave cylinder, convex cylinder, concave ellipsoid, convex ellipsoid, saddle valley, saddle ridge, minimal}. Sometimes the classes saddle valley, saddle ridge and minimal are conflated into the single class "hyperbolic". This figure summarizes the classifications based on the curvature signs: [Rob01]

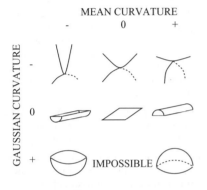

mean curvature: A mathematical characterization for a component of local surface shape at a point on a smooth surface. Each point can be uniquely described by a pair of principal curvatures. The mean curvature is the average of the principal curvatures. [JKS95:13.3.2]

mean field approximation: A method for approximate probabilistic inference in which a complex distribution is approximated by a simpler factorized one. [Bis06:10.1.1]

mean filter: See mean smoothing operator.

mean shift: An adaptive gradient ascent technique that operates by iteratively moving the center of a search window to the average of certain points within the window. [WP:Mean-shift]

mean shift filtering: A tracking technique that tracks the contents of a specified region from a frame of video. The contents of this region are represented by a weighted histogram and tracked

from frame to frame using gradient ascent and the Bhattacharyya coefficient. [CRM00]

mean smoothing operator: A noise reduction operator that can be applied to a gray scale image or to separate components of a multi-spectral image. The output value at each pixel is the average of the values of all pixels in a neighborhood of the input pixel. The size of the neighborhood determines how much smoothing (or noise reduction) is done, but also how much blur of fine detail occurs. The figure shows (left) an image with Gaussian noise with $\sigma = 13$ and (right) its mean smoothing: [JKS95:4.3]

mean value coordinates: The average coordinates of some planar surface. [Flo03]

measurement matrix: A matrix containing, e.g., the coordinates of features for an object, image or video. [Sze10:7.3]

measurement resolution: The degree to which two differing quantities can be distinguished by measurement. This may be the minimum spatial distance that two adjacent pixels represent (spatial resolution), the minimum time difference between visual observations (temporal resolution) etc. [WP: Resolution#Measurement_resolution]

medial: Pertaining to the midline. For example the medial line is the central axis in a shape. [WP:Medial_(disambiguation)]

medial axis skeletonization: See medial axis transform.

medial axis transform: An operation on a binary image that transforms regions into sets of pixels that are the centers of circles that are bitangent to the boundary and that fit entirely

167

within the region. The value of each point on the axis is the radius of the bitangent circle. This can be used to represent the region by a simpler axis-like structure and is most effective on elongated regions. The figure shows a region and its medial axis: [BB82:8.3.4]

medial line: A curve going through the middle of an elongated structure. See also medial axis transform. The figure shows a region and its medial line: [BB82:8.3.4]

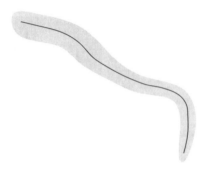

medial surface: The 3D generalization of the medial axis of a planar region. It is the locus of the centers of spheres that touch the surface of the volume at three or more points. [BB82:8.3.4]

median filter: See median smoothing.

median flow filtering: A noise reduction operation on vector data that generalizes the median smoothing on image data. The assumption is that the vectors in a spatial neighborhood about the current vector should be similar. Dissimilar vectors are rejected. The term "flow" arose through the filter's development in the context of image motion. [SSCW98]

median smoothing: An image noise reduction operator that replaces a pixel's value by the median (middle) of the sorted pixel values in its neighborhood. The figure shows an image with salt-and-pepper noise and the result of applying median smoothing: [JKS95:4.4]

medical image registration: A general term for the registration of two or more medical image types or an atlas registration with some image data. A typical registration would align X-ray CAT and NMR images. [WP:Image_registration#Applications]

membrane model: A surface-fitting model that minimizes a combination of the smoothness and the closeness of the fit surface to the original data. The surface class must have C^0 continuity and thus it differs from the smoother thin plate model that has C^1 continuity. [LMY92]

mesh compression: The simplification of the set of vertices, edges and faces of a 3D triangular mesh model. [KG00]

mesh model: A tessellation of an image or surface into polygonal patches, much used in computer-aided design (CAD). The vertices of the mesh are called nodes, or nodal points. A popular class of meshes is based on triangles, e.g., the Delaunay triangulation. Meshes can be uniform, i.e., all polygons are the same, or non-uniform. Uniform meshes can be represented by small sets of parameters. Surface meshes have been used for modeling freeform surfaces (e.g., faces and landscapes). See also surface fitting. This icosahedron is a mesh model of a nearly spherical object: [JKS95:13.5]

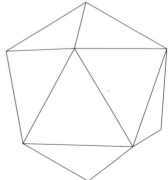

168

mesh subdivision: Methods for sub-dividing cells in a mesh model into progressively smaller cells. For example, see Delaunay triangulation. [WP:Mesh_subdivision]

message-passing process: A process where a computation is achieved by passing messages between different objects (or units). For example belief propagation can be used to carry out probabilistic inference in some probabilistic graphical models. [KF09:Ch. 10]

metameric colors: Colors that are defined by a limited number of channels each of which integrates a range of the spectrum. Hence the same metameric color can be caused by a variety of spectral distributions. [Hor86:2.5.1]

metric determinant: A measure of curvature. For surfaces, it is the square root of the determinant of the first fundamental form matrix of the surface. [JJK03]

metric property: A visual property that is a measurable quantity, such as a distance or area. This contrasts with logical properties, such as image connectedness. [HZ00:1.7]

metric reconstruction: Reconstruction of the 3D structure of a scene with correct spatial dimensions and angles. This contrasts with projective reconstruction. The figure shows the metrical and projective reconstructions of a cube:

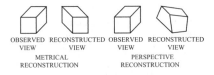

OBSERVED RECONSTRUCTED OBSERVED RECONSTRUCTED
VIEW   VIEW   VIEW   VIEW
METRICAL   PERSPECTIVE
RECONSTRUCTION   RECONSTRUCTION

The metrical projection looks "correct" from all views but the perspective projection may look "correct" only from the views in which the data was acquired. [WP:Camera_auto-calibration#Problem_statement]

metric stratum: The set of similarity transformations (i.e., rigid transformations with a scaling). They can be

recovered from image data without external information such as some known length. [Pol00]

metrical calibration: Calibration of intrinsic parameters and extrinsic parameters to enable metric reconstruction of a scene. [VH00]

Mexican hat operator: A convolution operator that implements either a Laplacian of Gaussian operator or difference-of-Gaussians operator (which produce very similar results). The mask that can be used to implement this convolution has a shape similar to a Mexican hat (a sombrero): [JKS95:5.4]

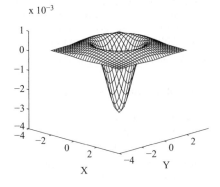

micro-mirror array: An array of tiny mirrors that can be used to provide control of both the geometric and radiometric characteristics of images produced by the system, by electronically altering their orientations. [NBB04]

micron: One millionth of a meter; a micrometer. [Hec87:2.2]

microscope: An optical device for observing small structures, such as organic cells, plant fibers or integrated circuits. [Hec87:5.7.5]

microtexture: See statistical texture.

mid-sagittal plane: The plane that separates the body (and brain) into left and right halves. In medical imaging (e.g., nuclear magnetic resonance), it usually refers to a view of the brain sliced down the middle between the two hemispheres. [WP:Sagittal_plane#Variations]

middle-level vision: A general term referring to the stages of visual data processing between low-level vision and high-level vision. There are many variations of the definition of this term but a usable rule of thumb is that middle-level vision starts with descriptions of the contents of an image and results in descriptions of the features of the scene. Consequently, binocular stereo would be a middle-level vision process because it acts on image edge fragments to produce 3D scene fragments. [Ker99]

millimeter-wave radiometric images: An image produced using submillimeter terahertz radiation (which is able to penetrate clothing). Most recently used within full body scanners at security checkpoints. [WP:Millimeter_wave_scanner]

MIMD: See multiple instruction multiple data.

minimal point: A point on a hyperbolic surface where the two principal curvatures are equal in magnitude but opposite in sign, i.e., $\kappa_1 = -\kappa_2$. [WP:Maxima_and_minima]

minimal spanning tree: Consider a graph G and a subset T of the arcs in G such that all nodes in G are still connected in T and there is exactly one path joining any two nodes. T is a spanning tree. If each arc has a weight (possibly constant), the minimal spanning tree is the tree with smallest total weight: [DH73:6.10.2.1]

GRAPH   MINIMAL SPANNING TREE

minimum bounding rectangle: The rectangle of smallest area that surrounds a set of image data. [WP:Minimum_bounding_rectangle]

minimum description length (MDL): A criterion for comparing descriptions usually based on the implicit assumption that the best description is the one that is shortest (i.e., takes the least bits to encode). The minimum description usually requires several components:

- the models observed (e.g., whether lines or circular arcs);
- the parameters of the models (e.g., the line endpoints);
- how the image data varies from the models (e.g., explicit deviations or noise model parameters);
- the remainder of the image that is not explained by the models. [FP03:16.3.4]

minimum distance classifier: Given an unknown sample with feature vector $\vec{x}$, select the class c with model vector $\vec{m}_c$ for which the distance $\| \vec{x} - \vec{m}_c \|$ is smallest. [SB11:11.8]

minimum spanning tree: See minimal spanning tree.

MIPS: millions of instructions per second. [WP:Instructions_per_second]

mirror: A surface with specular reflection for which incident light is reflected only at the same angle and in the same plane as the surface normal. [Hec87:5.4]

miss-one-out test: See leave-one-out test.

missing data: Data that is unavailable, hence requiring it to be estimated. For example, a moving person may become occluded resulting in missing position data for a number of frames. [FP03:16.6.1]

missing pixel: A pixel for which no value is available (e.g., if there was a problem with a sensing element in the image sensor). [FP03:16.6.1]

mixed pixel: A pixel whose measurement arises from more than one scene phenomenon. For example, a pixel that observes the edge between two regions has a gray scale level that lies between the gray levels of the two regions. [PMPP04]

mixed Poisson–Gaussian noise: Image noise which is composed of both signal-dependent Poisson noise and signal-independent Gaussian noise. [LBU11]

mixed reality: Image data that contains both original image data and overlaid computer graphics. See also augmented reality. This figure shows an example of mixed reality, where the butterfly is a graphical object added to the image of the small robot: [WP:Mixed_reality]

mixing proportion: In a mixture model, the probability π_i of selecting source i, with $\sum_i \pi_i = 1$. [Bis06:Ch. 9]

mixture model: A probabilistic representation in which more than one distribution is combined, modeling a situation where the data may arise from different sources or have different behaviors, each with different probability distributions. The overall distribution thus has the form $p(x) = \sum_i \pi_i p_i(x)$, where $p_i(x)$ denotes the density of source i and π_i is its mixing proportion. A mixture model may be fitted to data using the expectation maximization (EM) algorithm. [Bis06:Ch. 9]

maximum likelihood estimation: The value of the parameters of a statistical model that maximize the likelihood function. For example, the maximum likelihood estimate of the mean of a Gaussian distribution is the average of the observed samples drawn from that distribution. [Was04:9.3]

modal deformable model: A deformable model based on modal analysis (i.e., study of the shapes that an object can assume). [GKP+07]

mode filter: A noise reduction filter that, for each pixel, outputs the mode (most common) value in its local neighborhood. The figure shows (left) an image with salt-and-pepper noise and (right) the filtered version: [NA05:3.5.3]

model: An abstract representation of some object or class of objects. [WP:Model]

model acquisition: The process of learning a model, usually based on observed instances or examples of the structure being modeled. This may be simply learning the parameters of a distribution from examples. For example, one might learn the image texture properties that distinguish tumorous cells from normal cells. Alternatively, the structure of the object might be learned as well, such as constructing a model of a building from a video sequence. Another type of model acquisition involves learning the properties of an object, such as the properties and relations that define a square as compared to other geometric shapes. [FP03:21.3]

model-assisted search: An algorithm which searches for a match (e.g., face recognition) and uses a higher level model (e.g., a 3D model of the face) to assist the process.

model base: A database of models usually used as part of an identification process. [JKS95:15.1]

model base indexing: Selecting one or more candidate models from a model base of structures known by the system. This is usually to eliminate exhaustive testing with every member of the model base. [FP03:16.3]

model-based coding: A method of encoding the contents of an image (or video sequence) using a pre-defined or learned set of models. This could produce a more compact description (see model-based compression) or a symbolic description of the image data. For example, a Mondrian-style image could be encoded by the positions, sizes and colors of the colored rectangular regions. [AH95]

model-based compression: An application of model-based coding for the purpose of reducing the amount of memory required to describe an image while still allowing reconstruction of the original image. [Umb98:5.3.6]

model-based feature detection: Using a parametric model of a feature to locate instances of the feature in an image. For example, a parametric edge detector uses a parameterized model of a step edge that encodes edge direction and edge magnitude. [BNM98]

model-based object recognition: The identification of unknown objects through the use of known models. [FP03:Ch. 18]

model-based recognition: Identification of the structures in an image by using some internally represented model of the objects known to the computer system. The models are usually geometric models. The recognition process finds image features that match the model features with the right shape and position. The advantage of model-based recognition is that the model encodes the object shape thus allowing predictions of image data and less chance of coincidental features being falsely recognized. [TV98:10.1]

model-based segmentation: An image segmentation process that uses geometric models to partition the image into different regions. For example, aerial images could have the visible roads segmented using a GIS model of the road network. [FP03:Ch. 14]

model-based tracking: An image tracking process that uses models to locate the position of moving targets in an image sequence. For example, the estimated position, orientation and velocity of a modeled vehicle in one image allows a strong prediction of its location in the next image in the sequence. [FP03:Ch. 17]

model-based vision: A general term for using models of the objects expected to be seen in the image data to help

with image analysis. The model allows, among other things, prediction of additional model feature positions, verification that a set of features could be part of the model and understanding of the appearance of the model in the image data. [FP03:Ch. 18]

model building: See also model acquisition. The process of constructing a geometric model usually based on observed instances or examples of the structure being modeled, such as from a video sequence.

model exploitation: A directed exploration approach where both positive and negative knowledge are used to guide the search process.

model exploration: Undirected exploration of a model (as opposed to model exploitation).

model fitting: See model registration.

model inference: The process of parameter estimation in a model or of model selection over a number of models.

model invocation: See model base indexing.

model matching: The identification of a corresponding, typically known, model for some unknown data. For example, matching an unknown 2D or 3D shape extracted from an image with one from a database of known object models. See also object recognition. [TM87]

model order: The number of variables used to describe the model, e.g., the number of lagged variables used in an autoregressive model. [SVR08]

model order selection: A special case of model selection where there are a number of similar models of increasing complexity, e.g., polynomial regression with polynomials of different order or an autoregressive model with different lengths of history.

model parameter learning: See parameter estimation.

model parameter update: When carrying out model parameter learning, the performance of the model is typically optimized by an iterative algorithm, leading to updates of the model parameters on each iteration.

model reconstruction: See model acquisition.

model registration: A general term for aligning a geometric model to a set of image data. The process may require estimating the rotation, translation and scale that maps a model onto the image data. There may also be shape parameters, such as model length, that need to be estimated. The fitting may need to account for perspective distortion. The figure shows a 2D model registered on an intensity image of the same part: [Nev82:3.3]

model robustness: A statistical model whose fitting is not significantly influenced by outliers. See also robust statistics. [GCSR95:Ch. 12]

model selection: 1) The task of selecting one of a number of candidate models. The goal is to select the "best" model of the data; for a supervised learning task, best could be defined in terms of the predictive performance on test data. An important issue here is over-fitting – performance on the training set might not be a good indicator of performance on a test set. Typically models with more parameters have a greater danger of over-fitting, so methods such as the Akaike Information Criterion, Bayesian information criterion or minimum description length, which penalize the number of parameters can be used. Bayesian model comparison can be carried out on the basis of the marginal likelihood and prior probabilities for each model. Probably the most common way to select predictive models is via cross-validation. It is not always necessary to select one model; one might combine the predictions of

different models, see e.g., ensemble learning or Bayesian model averaging. [HTF08:Ch. 7].
2) See model base indexing. [FP03:16.3]

model structure: The organization of primitives such as surfaces or edge segments within a representation (model). [WP:Geometric_modeling]

model topology: A mathematical field considering properties of models which are invariant under continuous deformations of the objects being modeled, e.g., connectivity.

modulation transfer function (MTF): Informally, a measure of how well spatially varying patterns are observed by an optical system. More formally, in a 2D image, let $X(f_h, f_v)$ and $Y(f_h, f_v)$ be the Fourier transforms of the input $x(h, v)$ and output $y(h, v)$ images. Then, the MTF of a horizontal and vertical spatial frequency pair (f_h, f_v) is $|H(f_h, f_v)| / |H(0, 0)|$, where $H(f_h, f_v) = Y(f_h, f_v)/X(f_h, f_v)$. This is also the magnitude of the optical transfer function. [Jai89:2.6]

moiré fringe: An interference pattern that is observed when spatially sampling, at a given spatial frequency, a signal that has a slightly different spatial frequency. The result is a set of light and dark bands in the observed image. As well as causing image degradation, this effect can also be used in range sensors, where the fringe positions give an indication of surface depth. The figure shows typical observed fringe patterns: [Jai89:4.4]

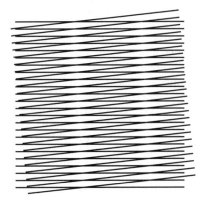

moiré interferometry: A technique for contouring surfaces that works by projecting a fringe pattern (e.g., of straight lines) and observing this pattern through another grating. This effect can be achieved in other ways as well. The technique is useful for measuring extremely small stress and distortion movements. [WP:Moire_pattern#Interferometric_approach]

moiré pattern: See moiré fringe.

moiré topography: A method for measuring the local shape of a surface by analyzing the spacing of moiré fringes on the target surface.

moment: A method for summarizing the distribution of pixel positions or values. Moments are a parameterized family of values. For example, if $I(x, y)$ is a binary image then $\Sigma_{x,y} I(x, y) x^p y^q$ computes its pqth moment m_{pq}. See also gray scale moment and moment of intensity. [Jai89:9.8]

moment characteristic: See moment invariant.

moment invariant: A function of image moment values that keeps the same value even if the image is transformed in some manner. For example, the value $\frac{1}{A^2}((\mu_{20})^2 + (\mu_{02})^2)$ is invariant where μ_{pq} are central moments of a binary image region and A is the area of the region. This value is a constant even if the image data has been subject to translation, rotation or scaling. [Jai89:9.8]

moment of intensity: An image moment value that takes account of the gray scales of the image pixels as well as their positions. For example, if $G(x, y)$ is a gray scale image, then $\Sigma_{x,y} G(x, y) x^p y^q$ computes its pqth moment of intensity g_{pq}. See also gray scale moment. [CC84]

Mondrian: A famous visual artist from the Netherlands, whose later paintings were composed of adjacent rectangular blocks of constant color (i.e., without shading). This style of image has been used for much color vision research and, in particular, color constancy because of its simplified image structure, without shading,

specularity, shadow or light source. [Hor86:9.2]

monochrome: Containing only shades of a single color, usually gray, going from pure black to pure white. [WP:Monochrome]

monocular: Using a single camera, sensor or eye. This contrasts with binocular and multi-ocular stereo where more than one sensor is used. Sometimes there is also the implication that the image data is acquired from a single viewpoint as a single camera taking images over time is mathematically equivalent to multiple cameras. [BB82:2.2.2]

monocular depth cue: Image evidence that indicates that one surface may be closer to the viewer than another. For example, motion parallax or occlusion relationships give evidence of relative depths. [WP: Depth_perception#Monocular_cues]

monocular visual space: The visual space behind the lens in an optical system. This space is commonly assumed to be without structure but scene depth can be recovered from the defocus blurring that occurs in this space. [Gro83]

monogenic wavelets: Wavelet functions in which complex valued functions are used rather than negative frequency components. [OM09]

monotonicity: A sequence of values or a function that is either continuously increasing (monotone increasing) or continuously decreasing (monotone decreasing). [WP:Monotonic_function]

Monte Carlo methods: Methods that use random samples to obtain approximate results. For example the integral $\int f(x) p(x) dx$ (the expectation value of the function $f(x)$ under the density $p(x)$) can be approximated using N samples $x^{(1)}, \ldots, x^{(N)}$ drawn from $p(x)$ as $\frac{1}{N} \sum_{i=1}^{N} f(x^{(i)})$. [Bis06:Ch. 11]

Moravec interest point operator: An operator that locates interest points at pixels where neighboring intensity values change greatly in at least one direction. These points can be used for stereo matching or feature point tracking. The operator computes the sum of the squares of pixel differences in a line vertically, horizontally and both diagonal directions in a 5 × 5 window about the given pixel. The minimum of these four values is selected and then all values that are not local maxima or are below a given threshold are suppressed. The figure shows the interest points found by the Moravec operator as white dots on the original image: [JKS95:14.3]

morphable models: A model which can be adapted to fit data (e.g., a morphable 3D face model which is altered to fit a previously unseen picture of an unknown face). [JP98]

morphing: The process of deforming from one image or shape to another in a seamless manner through a series of intermediate images, transforming shape and color: [Sze10:3.6.3]

morphological gradient: A gray scale mathematical morphology operation applied to gray scale images that results in an output image similar to the standard intensity gradient. The gradient is calculated by $\frac{1}{2}(D_G(A, B) - E_G(A, B))$ where $D_G()$ and $E_G()$ are the gray scale dilate and erode, respectively of image A by kernel B. [CS09:4.5.5]

morphological image processing: Processing of images using mathema-

tical morphology operations, such as the erode operator, the dilate operator etc. This approach considers images as point sets. [Sze10:3.3.2]

morphological segmentation: Using mathematical morphology operations applied to binary images to extract isolated regions of the desired shape. The desired shape is specified by the morphological kernel. The process could also be used to separate touching objects. [MB90]

morphological smoothing: A gray scale mathematical morphology operation applied to gray scale images that results in an output image similar to that produced by standard noise reduction. The smoothing is calculated by $C_G(O_G(A, B), B)$ where $C_G()$ and $O_G()$ are the gray scale close operation and open operation, respectively, of image A by kernel B. [SKP96]

morphological transformation: One of a large class of binary image and gray scale image transformations whose primary characteristic is that they react to the pattern of the pixel values rather than the values themselves. Examples include the dilate operator, the erode operator, skeletonization, the thinning operator etc. The figure shows (left) an image and (right) an application of the open operator, when using a disk-shaped structuring element 11 pixels in diameter: [Jai89:9.9]

 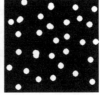

morphology: The shape of a structure. See also mathematical morphology operation. [Jai89:9.9]

morphometry: Techniques for the measurement of shape. [WP:Morphometrics]

mosaic: The construction of a larger image from a collection of partially overlapping images taken from different viewpoints. The reconstructed image could have different geometries, e.g., as if seen from a single perspective viewpoint or as if seen from an orthographic viewpoint. See also image mosaic. [Sch89:Ch. 2]

most probable explanation: Given a joint probability distribution over a set of random variables defined by a probabilistic graphical model, knowledge of the values of some set of variables e (the evidence) gives rise to the conditional distribution of the remaining variables x, i.e., $p(x|e)$. The most probable explanation x^* is the configuration of x that maximizes $p(x|e)$. See also maximum a posteriori probability. [Pea88:5.3]

mother wavelet: The prototype function (wavelet) used within a wavelet transformation, from which all other functions (wavelets) are derived. [PTVF92:13.10]

motion: In the context of computer vision, refers to analysis of an image sequence where the camera position or scene structure changes over time. [BB82:Ch. 7]

motion analysis: Analysis of an image sequence in order to extract useful information, such as the shape of the observed scene, the figure–ground separation, the egomotion estimation and estimates of a target's position and motion. [BB82:7.2–7.3]

motion blur: The blurring of an image that arises when either the camera or something in the scene moves while the image is being acquired. The figure shows the blurring that occurs when an object moves during image capture: [WP:Motion_blur]

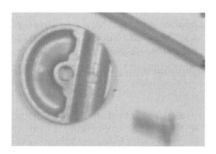

176

motion capture: The process of capturing the way in which an object, person or animal moves through analysis of video of the object, person or animal. The simplest way to achieve this is to attach markers to key points of the object, person or animal, although markerless motion capture is also possible. [WP:Motion_capture]

motion coding: 1) A component of video sequence compression in which efficient methods are used to represent movement of image regions between video frames.
2) A term for neural cells tuned to respond for direction and speeds of image motion. [WP:Motion_coding]

motion compensation: A technique used in the encoding of video where a picture is described with respect to some other (previous or future) picture together with motion information. This allows for high levels of video compression, as the frame-to-frame change is small in most videos. [WP:Motion_compensation]

motion deblurring: The removal of blurring effects of either camera or scene motion during image capture. See also image restoration. [SJA08]

motion descriptor: A descriptor of the motion of an object, point, region or feature in a video. [WP:Visual_descriptors]

motion detection: Analysis of an image sequence to determine if or when something in the observed scene moves. See also change detection. [JKS95:14.1]

motion direction profile: A summary of the directions of the motion vectors (e.g., optical flow) in a region or image.

motion discontinuity: When the smooth motion of the camera or something in the scene changes, such as the speed or direction of motion. Another form of motion discontinuity is between two groups of adjacent pixels that have different motions. [BYJF97]

motion estimation: Estimating the motion direction and speed of the camera or something in the scene. [Sch89:Ch. 5]

motion factorization: Given a set of tracked feature points through an image sequence, a measurement matrix can be constructed. This matrix can be factored into component matrices that represent the shape and 3D motion of the structure up to a 3D affine transformation (which is removable using knowledge of the intrinsic parameters). [TK92]

motion feature: Use of local motion information as a feature to describe object action. These features can be used, e.g., to recognize specific human activities. [GBS+07]

motion field: The projection of the relative motion vector for each scene point onto the image plane. In many circumstances this is closely related to the optical flow, but it may differ as image intensities can also change because of illumination changes. Similarly, motion of a uniformly shaded region is not observable locally because there is no change in image intensity data. [TV98:8.2]

motion history image (MHI): An image which shows the changing pixels from the current frame of a video together with aged versions of the previously changing pixels. The figure shows (left) a video and (right) the MHI made from it: [Dav01]

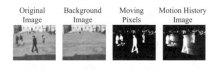

Original Image	Background Image	Moving Pixels	Motion History Image

motion history volume: A spatio-temporal volume that encodes moving pixels over some number of frames. [WRB06]

motion layer segmentation: The segmentation of an image into different regions where the motion is locally consistent. The layering effect is most noticeable when the observer is moving through a scene with objects at different depths (causing different

amounts of parallax) some of which might also be moving. [TV98:8.6]

motion model: A mathematical model of types of motion allowable for the target object or camera, such as linear motion along the optical axis with constant velocity. Another example might allow velocities and accelerations in any direction, with occasional discontinuities, such as for a bouncing ball. [BB82:Ch. 7]

motion moment: A moment computed from motion vectors rather than image intensities or pixel positions.

motion parallax: The apparent relative displacement of objects when viewed from different viewpoints, caused by movement of the camera. See also parallax. [WP:Parallax]

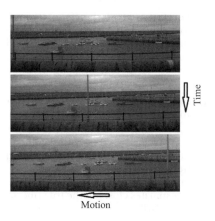

Motion

motion representation: See motion model.

motion segmentation: See motion layer segmentation.

motion sequence analysis: The class of computer vision algorithms that process sequences of images captured close together in space and time, typically by a moving camera. These analyses are often characterized by assumptions on temporal coherence that simplify computation. [BB82:7.3]

motion smoothness constraint: The assumption that nearby points in the image have similar motion directions and speeds or similar optical flow. This constraint is based on the fact that

177

adjacent pixels generally record data from the projection of adjacent surface patches from the scene. These scene components will have similar motion relative to the observer. This assumption can help reduce motion estimation errors or constrain the ambiguity in optical flow estimates arising from the aperture problem. [HL93]

motion tracking: Identification of the same target feature points through an image sequence. This could also refer to tracking complete objects as well as feature points, including estimating the trajectory or motion parameters of the target. [FP03:Ch. 17]

motion understanding: Analysis of the visual motion in an image to compute an understanding of the scene motion information. [Tso11]

movement analysis: A general term for analyzing an image sequence of a scene where objects are moving. It is often used for analysis of human motion, such as for people walking or using sign language. [BB82:7.2–7.3]

moving average smoothing: A form of noise reduction that occurs over time by averaging the most recent images together. It is based on the assumption that variations in time of the observed intensity at a pixel are random. Averaging the values will thus produce intensity estimates closer to the true (mean) value. [DH73:7.4]

moving light display: An image sequence of a darkened scene containing objects with attached point light sources. The light sources are observed as a set of moving bright spots. This sort of image sequence was used in the early research on structure from motion. [Joh73]

moving object detection: Analyzing an image sequence, usually with a stationary camera, to detect whether any objects in the scene move. [JKS95:14.1]

moving observer: A camera or other sensor that is moving. Moving observers have been extensively used in research on structure from motion. [Nal93:Ch. 8]

MPEG: Moving Picture Experts Group. A group developing standards for coding digital audio and video, as used in video CD, DVD and digital television. This term is often used to refer to media that is stored in the MPEG-1 format. [WP:Moving_Picture_Experts_Group]

MPEG-2: A standard formulated by the ISO Motion Pictures Expert Group (MPEG), a subset of ISO Recommendation 13818, meant for transmission of studio-quality audio and video. It covers four levels of video resolution. [WP:MPEG-2]

MPEG-4: A standard formulated by the ISO Motion Pictures Expert Group (MPEG), originally concerned with similar applications as H.263 (very low bit rate channels, up to 64 Kbps). Subsequently extended to encompass a large set of multimedia applications, including over the Internet. [WP:MPEG-4]

MPEG-7: A standard formulated by the ISO Motion Pictures Expert Group (MPEG). Unlike MPEG-2 and MPEG-4, which deal with compressing multimedia contents within specific applications, it specifies the structure and features of the compressed multimedia content produced by the different standards, e.g., to be used in search engines. [WP:MPEG-7]

MPEG-7 descriptor: Part of the MPEG-7 video encoding standard ISO/IEC 15938. The MPEG-7 descriptors describe low level video and audio features such as color, texture, motion or shape. [WP:MPEG-7]

MRF: See Markov random field.

MRI: Magnetic Resonance Imaging. See nuclear magnetic resonance. [FP03:18.6]

MSRE: Mean Squared Reconstruction Error. [Xu93]

MTF: See modulation transfer function.

multibaseline stereo: Use of more than two cameras for binocular stereo depth calculations resulting in multiple baselines between pairs of cameras. It is sometimes used to make the correspondence problem simpler to solve by reducing the length of the baseline between camera pairs thereby effectively providing a wide baseline between the more distant cameras. [Sze10:11.6]

multi-camera behavior correlation: The temporal and spatial correlation of activities or behaviors in multiple camera views. [LGX09]

multi-camera distributed behavior: The behavior of objects as viewed by multiple cameras. These behaviors must be correlated in the temporal as well as the spatial domain. [LGX09]

multi-camera system: Any system with multiple cameras providing observations.

multi-camera-system blind area: An area of a multi-camera system which is not observable, possibly caused by occlusion from objects within the scene as well as simply having no observing camera. [CKRH04]

multi-camera topology: The layout of cameras within an environment in a multi-camera system. Strictly, the topology can be expressed as a graph, where arcs indicate overlapping or linked views (e.g., by roads). Common use may also include geometric relations between cameras. Typically, this will include not just the positions of the cameras but also their orientations and fields of view. It is often shown in two dimensions, e.g., on a plan view. [EMB03]

multichannel kernel: A kernel or matrix of weights, one for each pixel, which is convolved with multiple channels rather than the normal single-channel convolution operator.

multidimensional edge detection: A variation on standard edge detection of gray scale images in which the input is a multi-spectral image (e.g., an RGB color image). The edge detection operator may detect edges and combine the edges in each dimension independently or may use all information at each pixel directly. The figure shows edges detected from the red, green and blue components of an RGB image: [MR81]

R

G

B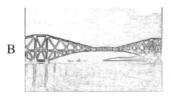

multidimensional histogram: A histogram with more than one dimension. For example consider measurements as vectors, e.g., from a multi-spectral image, with N dimensions in the vector. Then one could create a histogram represented by an array with dimension N. The N components in each vector are used to index into the array. Accumulating counts or other evidence values in the array makes it a histogram. [BB82:5.3.1]

multidimensional scaling (MDS): Scaling that starts with a (possibly incomplete) matrix of pairwise dissimilarities between observations and returns a set of points in low-dimensional space that reflects the dissimilarities. Classical scaling treats the dissimilarities as Euclidean distances and obtains the output configuration by solving a particular eigen-decomposition. [MKB79:Ch. 14]

multifilter bank: An abbreviation for "multiwavelet filter" bank. An array of wavelet filters with more than one scaling function which separates the input signal into multiple components. [LP11]

multifocal tensor: A geometric description of the linear relationship between four or more camera views. For two and three cameras, the tensors are called the bifocal tensor and the trifocal tensor, respectively. [TM99b]

multifocus images: Images fused from different images at different focus levels of a scene, creating images which are in focus for objects at very different depths: [HM98]

multigrid method: An efficient algorithm for solving systems of discretized differential (or other) equations. The term "multigrid" is used because the system is first solved at a coarse sampling level, which is then used to initialize a higher-resolution solution. [WP:Multigrid_method]

multi-image registration: A general term for the geometric alignment of two or more image datasets. Alignment allows pixels from the different source images to lie on top of each other or to be combined. See also sensor fusion. For example, two overlapping intensity images could be registered to help create a mosaic. Alternatively, the images could be from different types of sensor (see multimodal fusion). For example, nuclear magnetic resonance and computed axial tomography images of the same body part could be registered to provide richer information to a doctor. The figure shows (left) two unregistered range images and (right) the registered datasets: [FP03:21.3]

multilayer perceptron network (MLP): A form of neural network used for supervised learning problems. It maps input data $\vec{x}$ of dimension d to a space of outputs $\vec{y}$ of dimension d'. A multilayer perceptron network is a cascade of single-layer perceptron networks, with different weights

matrices at each layer. The layers of units which are neither input nor output units are known as hidden units; the number of hidden units in each layer is arbitrary. Typically, an MLP network is trained to predict the relationship between the $\vec{x}$s and $\vec{y}$s for a given collection of training examples by minimizing the error between the predicted and actual $\vec{y}$s on the training set. The derivatives of this error with respect to the weights in the network allow minimization using the back-propagation algorithm. [Bis06:5.1]

multilevel method: See multi-scale method.

multilinear constraint: A generic term for the geometric constraint on multiple views of a point. See epipolar constraint, trilinear constraint and quadrilinear constraint for two, three and four constraints respectively. [FP03:Ch. 10].

multilinear method: Multilinear algebra generalizes linear algebra to handle d-way arrays or tensors, as opposed to vectors (first-order tensors) and matrices (second-order tensors). Analogously to the singular value decomposition (SVD) for matrices, there is a d-mode SVD for tensors. An application in computer vision is to "tensor faces", where face images are analyzed for factors of variation including person identity, facial expression, viewpoint and illumination. [VT02]

multimodal analysis: A general term for image analysis using image data from more than one sensor type. There is often the assumption that the data is registered so that each pixel records data of two or more types from the same portion of the observed scene. [WP:Computer_Audition#Multimodal_analysis]

multimodal fusion: See sensor fusion. [WP:Multisensory Integration]

multimodal image alignment: The alignment of images acquired by sensors of different modalities, e.g., visible light and infrared light. Because different modalities generally have different

180

responses, alignment is generally performed by aligning common features rather than using intensity directly. [VW97]

multimodal neighborhood signature: A description of a feature point based on the image data in its neighborhood. The data comes from several registered sensors, such as X-ray and NMR. [MKK02]

multi-object behavior: The behavior (actions or movements) of multiple objects within a scene. [HTWM04]

multi-ocular stereo: A stereo triangulation process that uses more than one camera to infer 3D information. The terms "binocular stereo" and "trinocular stereo" are commonly used when there are only two or three cameras, respectively. [XL07]

multi-resolution method: See multi-scale method.

multi-scale description: See multi-scale method.

multi-scale integration: 1) Combining information extracted by using operators with different scales. 2) Combining information extracted from the registration of images with different scales. These two definitions could just be two ways of considering the same process if the difference in operator scale is only a matter of the amount of smoothing. An example of multi-scale integration occurs when combining edges extracted from images with different amounts of smoothing to produce more reliable edges. [SNS+98]

multi-scale method: A general term for a process that uses information obtained from more than one scale of image. The different scales might be obtained by reducing the image size or by Gaussian smoothing of the image. Both methods reduce the spatial frequency of the information. The main reasons for using multi-scale methods are:

- some structures have different natural scales (e.g., a thick bar could also be considered to be two back-to-back edges)

- coarse scale information is generally more reliable in the presence of image noise, but the spatial accuracy is better in finer scale information. Edge detection might use a coarse scale to reliably detect the edges and a finer scale to locate them more accurately. The figure shows an image with two scales of blurring: [Wit84]

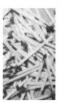

multi-scale representation: A representation having image features or descriptions that belong to two or more scales. An example might be zero crossings detected from intensity images that have received increasing amounts of Gaussian smoothing. A multi-scale model might represent an arm as a single generalized cylinder at a coarse scale, two generalized cylinders at an intermediate scale and with surface triangulation at a fine scale. The representation might have results from several discrete scales or from a more continuous range of scales, as in a scale space. The figure shows zero crossings found at two scales of Gaussian blurring: [WP:Scale_space#Related_multi-scale_representations]

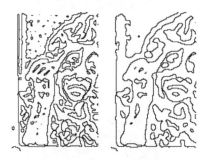

multi-sensor geometry: The relative placement of a set of sensors or multiple views from a single sensor but from different positions. One key consequence of the different placements is the ability to deduce the 3D structure

181

of the scene. The sensors need not be the same type but usually are, for convenience. [FP03:11.4]

multi-spectral analysis: Using the observed image brightness at different wavelengths to aid in the understanding of the observed pixels. A simple version uses RGB image data. Seven or more bands, including several infrared light wavelengths are often used for satellite remote sensing analysis. Recent hyperspectral sensors can give measurements at 100–200 different wavelengths. [SQ04:17.1]

multi-spectral image: An image containing data measured at more than one wavelength. The number of wavelengths may be as low as two (in some medical scanners) or three (e.g., RGB image data), or as high as seven or more bands, including several infrared light wavelengths (e.g., satellite remote sensing). Recent hyperspectral sensors can give measurements at 100–200 different wavelengths. The typical registration uses a vector to record the different spectral measurements at each pixel of an image array. The figure shows the red, green and blue components of an RGB image: [Umb98:1.7.4]

R

G

B

multi-spectral segmentation: Segmentation of a multi-spectral image. This can be addressed by segmenting the

image channels individually and then combining the results; alternatively the segmentation can be based on some combination of the information from the channels. [WP:Multispectral_segmentation]

multi-spectral thresholding: A segmentation technique for multi-spectral image data. A common approach is thresholding each spectral channel independently and then logically ANDing together the resulting images. An alternative is to cluster pixels in a multi-spectral space and choose thresholds that select desired clusters. The figure shows (left) a colored image, (middle) the image thresholded in the blue channel (0–100 accepted) and (right) the image ANDed with the thresholded green channel (0–100 accepted): [SHB08:5.1.3]

multi-tap camera: A camera that provides multiple outputs. [HCL07]

multi-thresholding: Thresholding using a number of thresholds giving a result that has a number of gray scales or colors. The figure shows an image with two thresholds (113 and 200): [KOA92]

multi-variate normal distribution: A Gaussian distribution for a variable that is a vector rather than a scalar. Let $\vec{x}$ be the vector variable with dimension N. Assume that this variable has mean value $\vec{\mu}_x$ and covariance matrix $\mathbf{C}$. Then the probability of observing the particular value $\vec{x}$ is given by: [SB11:11.11]

$$\frac{1}{(2\pi)^{\frac{N}{2}} \mid \mathbf{C} \mid^{\frac{1}{2}}}$$

$$\exp\left(-\frac{1}{2}(\vec{x} - \vec{\mu}_x)'\mathbf{C}^{-1}(\vec{x} - \vec{\mu}_x)\right)$$

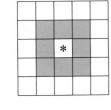

4D representation (3D-spatial + time)

age progression

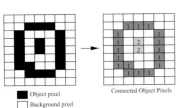

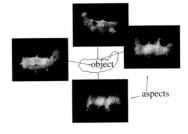

aspect graph

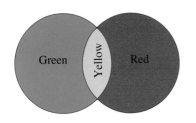

8 connectedness

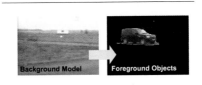

automated visual surveillance

Green   Yellow   Red

additive color

background subtraction

Dictionary of Computer Vision and Image Processing, Second Edition.
R. B. Fisher, T. P. Breckon, K. Dawson-Howe, A. Fitzgibbon, C. Robertson, E. Trucco and C. K. I. Williams.
© 2014 John Wiley & Sons, Ltd. Published 2014 by John Wiley & Sons, Ltd.

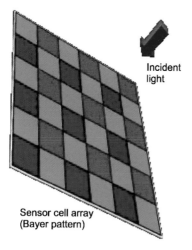

Incident
light

Sensor cell array
(Bayer pattern)

Bayer pattern

chroma keying

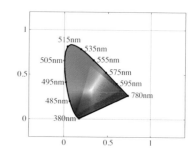

chromaticity diagram

Image 1   Image 2

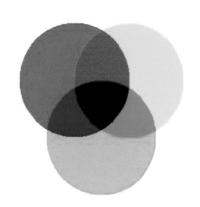

Dist. Trans.   Edges 2

CMYK

Best Match

color image segmentation

chamfer matching

Original · · · · · · Color remapped

color re-mapping

Original Image · · sigma = 1.0 · · · · Gaussian Smoothed Images sigma = 3.0

Gaussian pyramid

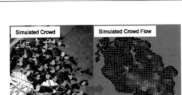

crowd flow analysis

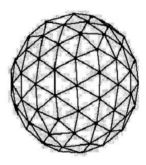

Gaussian smoothing

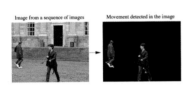

event detection

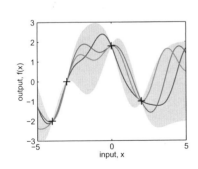

Gaussian sphere

gaze direction estimation

Gaussian process regression

Color Image

Hue   Saturation   Luminance

=

HSL

IMAGE
TEMPLATE

C

shape template

least square surface fitting

INPUT   SURF POINTS

SURF

pedestrian detection

pixel classification

texture boundary

range data segmentation

Zernike moment

multi-view geometry: See multi-sensor geometry.

multi-view image registration: See multi-image registration.

multi-view stereo: See multi-sensor geometry.

multiple instance learning: A variant on supervised learning. Rather than receiving a set of input–output pairs, the learner receives a set of *bags* of instances. Each bag contains many inputs, but only one label. The label is negative if all inputs in the bag are negative and positive otherwise. [Mur12:1.5.4]

multiple instruction multiple data (MIMD): A form of parallelism in which, at any given time, each processor might be executing a different instruction or program on a different dataset or pixel. This contrasts with single instruction multiple data parallelism where all processors execute the same instruction simultaneously although on different pixels. [Sch89:Ch. 8]

multiple kernel learning: Given a number of kernel functions that are suited to a problem, finding an optimal linear combination of these kernels. [BLJ04]

multiple light source detection: The location of multiple light sources within a scene. Much image analysis assumes a point light source for simplicity. [ZK02]

multiple motion segmentation: See motion segmentation.

multiple target tracking: A general term for tracking multiple objects simultaneously in an image sequence. Example applications include tracking football players or automobiles on a road. [HCP02]

multiple view interpolation: A technique for creating (or recognizing) new unobserved views of a scene from sample images captured from other viewpoints. [BE92]

multiplexed illumination: The use of multiple light sources separated by color or time to illuminate a scene so that images of the scene under each single light source can be obtained by demultiplexing. Images taken with multiple light sources are brighter (and hence higher quality) than those acquired using separate sources. [WGT+05]

multiplicative noise: A model for the corruption of a signal where the noise is proportional to the signal strength. $f(x, y) = g(x, y) + g(x, y).v(x, y)$ where $f(x, y)$ is the observed signal, $g(x, y)$ is the ideal (original) signal and $v(x, y)$ is the noise. [FSSH82]

multi-resolution image analysis: The processing of images at multiple resolutions simultaneously. This type of processing may be used, e.g., to consider objects at multiple scales or to identify features at particular scales (e.g., SIFT). See also Gaussian pyramid, Laplacian pyramid and wavelet transform. [Sze10:3.5.3, 3.5.4]

multi-sensor alignment: The alignment of images acquired by different sensors typically of different modalities, e.g., visible light and infrared light). See also multimodal image alignment. [IA98]

multi-sensory fusion: The combination of information from multiple different sensors. This problem can be very difficult as the information must be aligned and may be very different in form or content. See also sensor fusion. [WP:Image_fusion]

multi-view activity representation: A representation of activities across multiple views in a multi-camera system.

Munsell color notation system: A system for precisely specifying colors and their relationships, based on hue, value (brightness) and chroma (saturation). The *Munsell Book of Color* contains colored chips indexed by these three attributes. The color of any unknown surface can be identified by comparison with the colors in the book under specified lighting and viewing conditions. [GM03:5.3.6]

mutual illumination: When light reflecting from one surface illuminates another surface and vice versa.

The consequence of this is that light observed coming from a surface is a function of not only the light source spectrum and the reflectance of the target surface, but also the reflectance of the nearby surface (through the spectrum of the light reflecting from the nearby surface onto the first surface). The figure shows how mutual illumination can occur: [FZ89]

mutual information: The amount of information two random variables have in common. The mutual information $I(X; Y)$ is defined as $I(X; Y) = H(X) + H(Y) - H(X, Y) = H(X) - H(X|Y) = H(Y) - H(Y|X)$, where $H(\cdot)$ denotes entropy. Notice that $I(X; Y)$ is symmetric. [CT91:Ch. 2]

mutual interreflection: See mutual illumination.

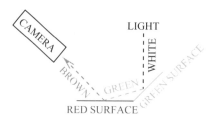

naïve Bayes classifier: A Bayesian classifier which uses an independence assumption to model the class-conditional distribution. If $\vec{x}$ denotes the d-dimensional feature vector and c the class label, then the naïve Bayes assumption is that $p(\vec{x}|c) = \prod_{i=1}^{d} p(x_i|c)$. [Bis06:p. 380]

NAND operator: An image arithmetic operation where a new image is formed by NANDing (logical AND followed by NOT) corresponding bits for every pixel of the two images. This operator is most appropriate for binary images but may also be applied to gray scale images. The figure shows the NAND operator applied to two binary images: [SB11:3.2.2]

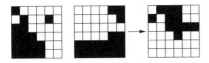

narrow baseline stereo: A form of stereo triangulation in which the sensor positions are close together. The baseline is the distance between the sensor positions. Narrow baseline stereo often occurs when the image data is from a video sequence taken by a moving camera. [TNM09]

natural image statistics: The statistics or statistical structure of images of the natural world. Often used in the computational modeling of biological vision systems. [SO01]

natural material recognition: The recognition of materials which occur naturally (as opposed to man-made materials). [LM01]

natural neighbor interpolation: A form of spatial interpolation employing a Voronoi segmented image to provide weighted values for the interpolation. [Cre93:pp. 374–376]

near infrared: Light wavelengths approximately in the range 750–5000 nm. [WP:Infrared]

near light source: A light source close to the illuminated object such that the rays of light are still effectively expanding from a point:

Far light source

Near light source

See also far light source.

near duplicate image/video retrieval: The identification of images or videos that are almost identical to a known image or video, perhaps after some transformations, such as compression, resizing or cropping. [SZH+07]

nearest neighbor: A classification, labeling or grouping principle in which a data item is associated with or takes the same label as the previously classified data item that is nearest to the first data item. The "nearness" might be based on spatial distance or a distance in a property space. In the figure, the unknown square is classified with the label of the nearest point, a circle: [JKS95:15.5.1]

Necker cube: A line drawing of a cube under orthographic projection, which can be interpreted in two ways: [Nal93:Ch. 4]

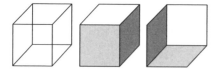

Necker reversal: An ambiguity in the recovery of 3D structure from multiple images. Under affine viewing conditions, the sequence of 2D images of a set of rotating 3D points is the same as the sequence produced by rotation in the opposite direction of a different set of points, so that two solutions to the structure and motion problem are possible. The different set of points is the reflection of the first set about any plane perpendicular to the optical axis of the camera. [HZ00:13.6]

needle map: An image representation used for displaying 2D and 3D vector fields, such as surface normals. Each pixel has a vector. Diagrams showing them use little lines with the magnitude and direction of the vector projected onto the image of a 3D vector. To avoid overcrowding the image, the pixels where the lines are drawn are a subset of the full image. The figure shows a needle map of the surface normals on the block sides: [Hor86:11.8]

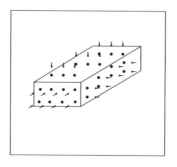

negate operator: See invert operator.

neighborhood: 1) The neighborhood of a vertex v in a graph is the set of vertices that are connected to v by an arc.

2) The neighborhood of a point (or pixel) x is a set of points "near" x. A common definition is the set of points within a certain distance of x, where the metric may be Manhattan distance or Euclidean distance. 3) The 4-connected neighborhood of a 2D location (x, y) is the set of image locations $\{(x + 1, y), (x - 1, y), (x, y + 1), (x, y - 1)\}$. The 8-connected neighborhood is the set of pixels $\{(x + i, y + j) | -1 \le i, j \le 1\}$. The 26-connected neighborhood of a 3D point (x, y, z) is defined analogously: [SQ04:4.5]

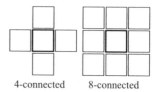

4-connected   8-connected

neural network: Artificial neural networks (ANNs) are composed of units (artificial neurons) connected into networks. The connections usually have adjustable strength, known as weights. The adjustment of the weights by learning algorithms (or training algorithms) allows neural networks to perform pattern recognition tasks such as supervised learning and unsupervised learning. ANNs can be thought of as simplified or abstracted models of biological networks, although a lot of work is solely concerned with the pattern recognition properties of these nonlinear models. ANNs can have different architectures, such as a feedforward layout from input to output via intermediate hidden layers (as used in the multilayer perceptron network and radial basis function network), or a recurrent architecture involving feedback (as used in the Hopfield network and the Kohonen network). [Bis06:Ch. 5]

neutral expression: A blank or nonemotional expression on a person's face. [WP:Facial_expression]

Newton optimization: To find a local minimum of function $f : \mathbb{R}^n \mapsto \mathbb{R}$ from starting position $\vec{x}_0$. Given the function's gradient ∇f and Hessian H evaluated at $\vec{x}_k$, the Newton update is $\vec{x}_{k+1} = \vec{x}_k - H^{-1} \nabla f$. If f is a quadratic form then a single Newton step will directly yield the global minimum. For general f, repeated Newton steps will generally converge to a local optimum. [FP03:3.1.2]

next view planning: When inspecting an object or obtaining a geometric model or appearance-based model, it may be necessary to observe the object from several places. Next view planning determines where to place the camera next (by moving either the object or the camera) based on what was observed (in the case of unknown objects) or a geometric model (in the case of known objects). [RSB04]

next view prediction: See next view planning.

NMR: See nuclear magnetic resonance.

node of graph: A symbolic representation of some entity or feature. It is connected to other nodes in a graph by arcs, that represent relationships between the different entities. [SQ04:12.1]

noise: A general term for the deviation of a signal away from its "true" value. In the case of images, this leads to pixel values (or other measurements) that are different from their expected values. The causes of noise can be random factors, such as thermal noise in the sensor, or minor scene events, such as dust or smoke. Noise can also represent systematic, but unmodeled, events such as short-term lighting variations or quantization. Noise might be reduced or removed using a noise reduction method. The figure shows images without and with salt-and-pepper noise: [TV98:3.1]

noise characteristics: See noise model.

noise model: A way to model the statistical properties of noise without having to model the causes of the noise. One general assumption about noise is that it has some underlying, but perhaps unknown, distribution. A Gaussian noise model is commonly used for random factors and a uniform distribution is often used for unmodeled scene effects. Noise could be modeled with a mixture model. The noise model typically has one or more parameters that control the magnitude of the noise. The noise model can also specify how the noise affects the signal, e.g. additive noise offsets the true value and multiplicative noise rescales the true value. The type of noise model can constrain the noise reduction method. [Jai89:8.2]

noise reduction: An image-processing method that tries to reduce the distortion of an image that has been caused by noise. For example, the images from a video sequence taken with a stationary camera and scene can be averaged together to reduce the effect of Gaussian noise because the average value of a signal corrupted with this type of noise converges to the true value. Noise-reduction methods often introduce other distortions, but these may be less significant to the application than the original noise. The figure shows (left) an image with salt-and-pepper noise and (right) its noise reduced by median smoothing: [TV98:3.2]

noise removal: See noise reduction.

noise source: A general term for phenomena that corrupt image data. It could be systematic unmodeled processes (e.g., 60 Hz electromagnetic noise) or random processes (e.g., electronic shot noise). The sources could be in the scene (e.g., chaff), in the medium (e.g., dust), in the lens (e.g., imperfections) or in the sensor (e.g., sensitivity variations). [WP:Noise]

noise suppression: See noise reduction.

noise-whitening filter: A noise-modifying filter that outputs images whose pixels have noise that is independent of other pixels' noise (spatial noise) or values of that pixel at other times (temporal noise). The resulting image's noise is white noise. [Jai89:6.2]

noiselets: Noise-like functions that are complementary to wavelets. They result in very poor or no compression for orthogonal wavelet compression functions. [WP:Noiselet]

non-accidentalness: A general principle that can be used to improve image interpretation based on the concept that when regularities appear in an image, they are most likely to result from regularities in the scene. For example, if two straight lines end near each other, then this could have arisen from a coincidental alignment of the line ends and the observer. However, it is much more probable that the two lines end at the same point in the observed scene. The figure shows line terminations and orientations that are unlikely to be coincidental: [OCEG04]

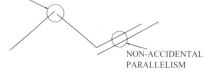

NON-ACCIDENTAL TERMINATION

NON-ACCIDENTAL PARALLELISM

non-affective gesture: Human gestures, such as sign language, which are not emotional. [WP:Gesture]

non-central camera: A camera which cannot be modeled by central projection. Such cameras have been developed for applications such as panoramic imaging. [MP04]

non-convexity: A description of a function, object, set or error-space which is not convex. This can lead local minima during optimization. [BV04:2.1.4, 3.1]

non-hierarchical control: A way of structuring the sequence of actions in an image interpretation system: there is no master process that orders the sequence of actions or operators applied. Instead, typically, each operator can observe the current results and decide if it is capable of executing and if it is desirable to do so. [SHB08:8.1.6]

non-Lambertian reflection, non-Lambertian surface: Light which is not reflected evenly in all directions from a surface is non-Lambertian. Many objects are non-Lambertian (e.g., those exhibiting specular reflections):

See also Lambertian surface. [Sze10:2.2.2]

nonlinear diffusion: A diffusion function which is dependent on image position. Nonlinear diffusion functions are based on partial differential equations and are used, e.g., in image processing for denoising images. [PGPO94]

nonlinear filter: A process where the outputs are a nonlinear function of the inputs. This covers a large range of algorithms. Examples of nonlinearity include:

- doubling the values of all input data does not double the values of the output results (e.g., a filter that reports the position at which a given value appears);
- applying an operator to the sum of two images gives different results from adding the results of the operator to the two original images (e.g., thresholding).

[Jai89:8.5]

non-local patches: Non-neighboring patches or image regions that can be used in image processing to address restoration, segmentation etc. [BCM05]

non-maximal suppression: A technique for suppressing multiple responses (e.g., high values of gradient magnitude) representing a single edge or other feature. The resulting edges should be a single pixel wide. [JKS95:5.6.1]

non-negative matrix factorization (NMF): Given a data matrix **X** containing non-negative entries, **X** is decomposed as the product **WH** of two lower rank non-negative matrices **W** and **H**. This can be interpreted as decomposing a data vector (a column of **X**) as a weighted combination of basis functions, where **H** contains the basis functions and the corresponding column of **W** gives the weights. Contrast with the singular value decomposition (SVD) of **X**, which does not impose non-negativity constraints. [HTF08:14.6]

non-overlapping field of view: Cameras which do not view any common area: [PD03]

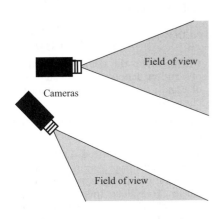

Field of view

Cameras

Field of view

non-parametric clustering: A data clustering process (such as the mean shift and support vector clustering methods) that uses peaks in the observed data distribution rather than

assuming an underlying probability distribution. [MMK04]

non-parametric method: A statistical model that allows the number of parameters to grow with the amount of data. This has the advantage of making fewer assumptions about the underlying distribution. The Parzen window and the k-nearest-neighbor algorithm are examples of non-parametric methods. [Mur12:1.2.11]

non-rigid model representation: A model representation where the shape of the model can change, perhaps under the control of a few parameters. These models are useful for representing objects whose shape can change, such as moving humans or biological specimens. The differences in shape may occur over time or between different instances. Changes in apparent shape because of perspective projection and observer viewpoint are not relevant here. By contrast, a rigid model would have the same actual shape irrespective of the viewpoint of the observer. [BY95]

non-rigid motion: A motion of an object in the scene in which the shape of the object also changes. Examples include the position of a walking person's limbs and the shape of a beating heart. Changes in apparent shape because of perspective projection and viewpoint are not relevant here. [KG92]

non-rigid registration: The problem of registering, or aligning, two shapes that can take on a variety of configurations (unlike rigid shapes). For instance, a walking person, a fish, and facial features like mouth and eyes are all non-rigid objects, the shape of which changes in time. This type of registration is frequently needed in medical imaging as many human body parts deform. Non-rigid registration is considerably more complex than rigid registration. See also alignment, registration and rigid registration. [CR03]

non-rigid structure from motion: The recovery of the structure of non-rigid

3D objects from a sequence of possibly uncalibrated 2D images where the non-rigid objects are moving. [THB08]

non-rigid tracking: A tracking process that is designed to track non-rigid objects. This means that it can cope with changes in actual object shape as well as apparent shape because of perspective projection and observer viewpoint. [CRM00]

non-symbolic representation: A model representation in which the appearance is described by a numerical or image-based description rather than a symbolic or mathematical description. For example, a non-symbolic model of a line would be a list of the coordinates of the points in the line or an image of the line. Compare with symbolic object representation. [FM98]

non-uniform illumination: Lighting which is uneven, resulting in different amounts of light falling on different parts of the scene. This type of illumination makes tasks like thresholding more difficult: [KY99]

nonverbal communication: Communication between people without words, e.g., through body language, facial expression or sign language. [WP:Nonverbal_communication]

normal curvature: A plane that contains the surface normal $\vec{n}$ at point $\vec{p}$ to a surface intersects that surface to form a planar curve Γ that passes through $\vec{p}$. The normal curvature is the curvature of Γ at $\vec{p}$. The intersecting plane can be at any specified orientation about the surface normal: [JKS95:13.3.2]

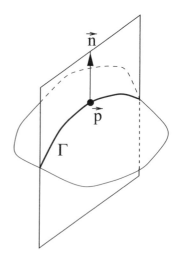

normal distribution: See Gaussian distribution.

normal flow: The component of optical flow in the direction of the intensity gradient. The orthogonal component is not locally observable because small motions orthogonally do not change the appearance of local neighborhoods. [CHHN98]

normalized compression distance (NCD): The normalized compression distance between any two objects x and y is given by

$$NCD(x, y) = \frac{C(xy) - \min(C(x), C(y))}{\max(C(x), C(y))},$$

where $C(x)$ is the compressed length of x and xy denotes the concatenation of x and y. It can be used as a basis for clustering. [CV05b]

normalized correlation: See correlation.

normalized discounted cumulative gain: In an image retrieval situation, the result of a query is a ranked list of images. To evaluate this result, assume that each image has been annotated with a relevance score. The discounted cumulative gain (DCG) measures quality of the result, penalizing highly relevant images which appear low down the ranked list. The normalization computes the ratio of the observed DCG to the best DCG that could be obtained. [MRS08:8.4]

NOT operator: See invert operator.

novel view synthesis: A process whereby a new view of an object is synthesized by combining information from several images of the object from different viewpoints. One method is by 3D reconstruction, e.g., from binocular stereo, and then rendering the reconstruction using computer graphics. However, the main approaches to novel view synthesis use epipolar geometry and the pixels of two or more images of the object to directly synthesize a new image without creating a 3D reconstruction. [AS97]

NP-complete: A concept in computational complexity covering a special set of problems. All of these problems currently can be solved, in the worst case, in time exponential $O(e^N)$ in the number or size N of their input data. For the subset of exponential problems called NP-complete, if an algorithm for one could be found that executes in polynomial time $O(N^p)$ for some p, then a related algorithm could be found for any other NP-complete algorithm. [SQ04:12.5]

NTSC: National Television System Committee. A television signal recording system used for encoding video data at approximately 60 video fields per second. Used in the USA, Japan and other countries. [Jai89:4.1]

nuclear magnetic resonance (NMR): An imaging technique based on magnetic properties of the atomic nuclei. Protons and neutrons within atomic nuclei generate a magnetic dipole that can respond to an external magnetic field. Several properties related to the relaxation of that magnetic dipole give rise to values that depend on the tissue type, thus allowing identification or at least visualization of the different soft tissue types. The measurement of the signal is a way of measuring the density of certain types of atoms, such as hydrogen in the case of biological NMR scanners. This technology is used for medical body scanning, where a detailed 3D volumetric image can be produced. Signal levels are highly correlated with different biological structures so one can easily observe different tissues and their positions. Also called magnetic resonance imaging (MRI). [FP03:18.6]

nuclear norm: A metric on the eigenvalues of a matrix, rather than on the entries. The norm of $m \times n$ matrix $\mathbf{A}$ with eigenvalues σ_i is defined as $||\,\mathbf{A}\,||_* = trace(\sqrt{\mathbf{A}^*\mathbf{A}}) = \sum_{i=1}^{min(m,n)} \sigma_i$. This norm is invariant to unitary transformations of $\mathbf{A}$, e.g., $||\,\mathbf{A}\,||_* = ||\,\mathbf{UAV}\,||_*$, where $\mathbf{U}$ and $\mathbf{V}$ are unitary matrices. The norm is often used in optimization or dimensionality reduction problems where there is a constraint on the rank of a matrix. [JS10]

number plate recognition: See license plate recognition.

NURBS: Non-uniform rational b-splines: a type of shape modeling primitive based on ratios of b-splines. Capable of accurately representing a wide range of geometric shapes including freeform surfaces. [WP:Non-uniform_rational_B-spline]

Nyquist frequency: The minimum sampling frequency for which the underlying true image (or signal) can be reconstructed from the samples. If sampling at a lower frequency, then aliasing will occur, creating apparent structure that does not exist in the original image. [SB11:2.3.2.1]

Nyquist sampling rate: See Nyquist frequency.

O

object: 1) A general term referring to a group of features in a scene that humans consider to compose a larger structure. In vision, it is generally thought of as that to which attention is directed. 2) A general system theory term, where the object is what is of interest (unlike the background). Resolution or scale may determine what is considered the object. [Low91:p. 236]

object-based representation: A representation that specifies the classes and poses of objects. This type of representation facilitates reasoning about the objects in a scene. [DM98]

object-centered representation: A model representation in which the position of the features and components of the model are described relative to the position of the object itself. This might be a relative description (the nose is 4 cm from the mouth) or might use a local coordinate system (e.g., the right eye is at position (0,25,10) where (0,0,0) is the nose.) This contrasts with, e.g., a viewer-centered representation. The figure shows a rectangular solid defined in its local coordinate system: [JKS95:15.3.2]

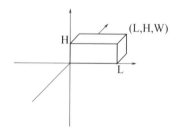

object class recognition (categorization): The identification of the class (or type) of an unknown object, as contrasted with identifying the specific type or even individual (e.g., identifying an unknown object as a chair rather than identifying it as a specific type of chair). [Sze10:14.4]

object contour: See occluding contour.

object detection: The discovery of objects within a scene or image. [Sze10:14.1]

object grouping: A general term meaning the clustering of all the image data associated with a distinct observed object. For example, when observing a person, the object grouping could cluster all of the pixels from the image of the person. [FP03:24.1]

object indexing: A method of organizing object models based on some (probably shape-based) primitive in order to allow similar models to be located efficiently. See also indexing and model base indexing. [RB95]

object localization: The process of determining the position of an object in a scene or image. [LBH08]

object plane: In the case of convex simple lenses, typically used in laboratory TV cameras, the object plane is the 3D scene plane where all points are exactly in focus on the image plane (assuming a perfect lens and the optical axis perpendicular to the image plane): [WP:Microscopy#Oblique_illumination]

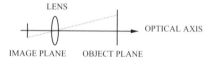

object recognition: A general term for identifying which of several (or many) possible objects is observed in an

Dictionary of Computer Vision and Image Processing, Second Edition.
R. B. Fisher, T. P. Breckon, K. Dawson-Howe, A. Fitzgibbon, C. Robertson, E. Trucco and C. K. I. Williams.
© 2014 John Wiley & Sons, Ltd. Published 2014 by John Wiley & Sons, Ltd.

image. The process may also include computing the object's image or scene position, or labeling the image pixels or image features that belong to the object. [FP03:21.4]

object representation: An encoding of an object into a form suitable for computer manipulation. The models could be, e.g., geometric models, graph models or appearance models. [JKS95:15.3]

object segmentation: The separation of objects within a scene or image. Typically addressed using either region-based segmentation or edge-based segmentation. Compare with image segmentation. [Sze10: Ch. 5]

object verification: A component of an object recognition process that attempts to verify a hypothesized object identity by examining evidence. Commonly, geometric models are used to verify that object features are observed in the correct image positions. [FP03:18.5]

objective function: 1) The cost function used in an optimization process. 2) A measure of the misfit between the data and the model. [SQ04:2.3]

oblique illumination: See low-angle illumination.

observation probability: In a state space model the underlying hidden state variable is not observed directly, but observations are made according to the observation (or emission) probability distribution $p(x_t|z_t)$, where z_t denotes the hidden state at time t and x_t denotes the corresponding observed variable. [Bis06:13.2]

observation variable: In a state space model there is an observation variable x_t at time t corresponding to the hidden state variable z_t. They are linked via the observation probability distribution. [Bis06:13.1]

observational space: In a state space model the hidden state variables reside in the state space, while the observation variables reside in the observational space. [Bis06:13.1]

observer: The individual (or camera) making observations. Most frequently this refers to the camera system from which images are being supplied. See also observer motion estimation. [WP:Observer]

observer motion estimation: When an observer is moving, image data of the scene provides optical flow or trackable scene feature points. These allow an estimate of how the observer is moving relative to the scene, which is useful for navigation control and position estimation. [Hor86:17.1]

obstacle detection: Using visual data to detect objects in front of the observer, usually for mobile robotics applications. [LAT02]

Occam's razor: An argument attributed to William of Occam (Ockham), an English nominalist philosopher of the early 14th century, stating that assumptions must not be needlessly multiplied when explaining something (*entia non sunt multiplicanda praeter necessitatem*). Often used simply to suggest that, other conditions being equal, the simplest solution must be preferred. Notice variant spelling *Ockham*. See also minimum description length. [WP:Occam's_razor]

occluding contour: The visible edge of a smooth curved surface as it bends away from an observer. The occluding contour defines a 3D space curve on the surface, such that a line of sight from the observer to a point on the space curve is perpendicular to the surface normal at that point. The 2D image of this curve may also be called the occluding contour. The contour can often be found by an edge detection process. In the figure, the left and right cylinder boundaries are occluding contours from our viewpoint: [FP03:19.2]

 OCCLUDING CONTOUR

occluding contour analysis: A general term that includes:
- occluding contour detection;
- inference of the shape of the 3D surface at the occluding contour;

- determination of the relative depth of the surfaces on both sides of the occluding contour. [FP03:19.2]

occluding contour detection: Determining which of the image edges arise from an occluding contour. [FP03:19.2]

occlusion: When an object lies between an observer and another object, the closer object occludes the more distant one in the acquired image. The occluded surface is the portion of the more distant object hidden by the closer object. In the figure, the cylinder occludes the more distant brick: [Dav90:7.7]

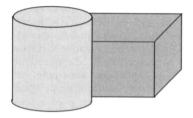

occlusion detection: The identification of features or objects within a scene which cause occlusion (visual overlapping) with other parts of the scene. The occlusion boundaries are highlighted in the image on the right: [ZK00]

occlusion recovery: The process of attempting to infer the shape and appearance of a surface hidden by occlusion. This recovery helps improve completeness when reconstructing scenes and objects for virtual reality. The figure shows two occluded pipes and an estimated recovery: [Dav90:7.7]

occlusion understanding: A general term for analyzing scene occlusions that may include occluding contour detection, determining the relative depths of the surfaces on both sides of an occluding contour and searching for tee junctions as a cue for occlusion, depth order etc. [Dav90:7.7]

occupancy grid: A map construction technique used mainly for autonomous vehicle navigation. The grid is a set of squares or cubes representing the scene, which are marked according to whether the observer believes the corresponding scene region is empty (hence navigable) or full. A probabilistic measure could also be used. Visual evidence from range sensors, binocular stereo sensors or acoustic sonar sensors are typically used to construct and update the grid as the observer moves. [WP:Occupancy_grid_mapping]

OCR: See optical character recognition.

octree: A volumetric representation in which 3D space is recursively divided into eight (hence "oct") smaller volumes by planes parallel to the XY, YZ, XZ coordinate system planes. A tree is formed by linking the eight subvolumes to each parent volume. Additional subdivision need not occur when a volume contains only object or empty space. This representation thus can be more efficient than a pure voxel representation. The figure ahows three levels of a pictorial representation of an octree, where one octant and the largest (leftmost) level is expanded to give the middle figure, and similarly an octant of the middle: [CH88]

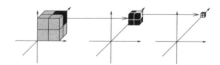

194

odd field: Standard interlaced scanning transmits all of the even scan lines in an image frame first and then all of the odd lines. The set of odd lines is the odd field. [Jai89:11.1]

off-axis imaging: Image formation based on light which arrives from directions other than along the optical axis. This may have benefits in reducing aberration effects but also means reduced brightness because of vignetting.

O'Gorman edge detector: A parametric edge detector in which a decomposition of the image and model by orthogonal Walsh function masks was used to compute the step edge parameters (contrast and orientation). One advantage of the parametric model is a goodness-of-model fit as well as the edge contrast that increases the reliability of the detected edges. [OG78]

omni-directional camera: A camera which can view all directions at once. Typically refers to a camera which can see in all directions on the ground plane (but not necessarily upwards or downwards). Often created by using a standard camera looking at a spherical mirror. [WP:Omnidirectional_camera]

omni-directional sensing: Literally, sensing all directions simultaneously. In practice, this means using mirrors and lenses to project most of the lines of sight at a point onto a single camera image. The space behind the mirrors and cameras is typically not visible. See also catadioptric optics. In this figure, a camera using a spherical mirror achieves a very wide field of view: [WP:Omnidirectional_camera]

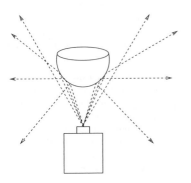

omni-directional stereo: Stereo vision based on two panoramic images. These images are normally created by rotating a stereo pair of cameras. [IYT92]

omni-directional vision: Any vision system using omni-directional cameras. [WGLS00]

online anomaly detection: An automated method for the location of interesting or unusual events typically within a continuous live data stream such as video. See also anomaly detection. [XG08]

online filtered inference: The inference of current state information (e.g., position) using techniques such as Kalman filtering or particle filtering, typically in a continuous (live) data stream. [Mur12:15.4.1]

online learning: A form of learning where the parameter updates are made each time a new training example is received. Contrast with batch learning. See also incremental learning. [HTF08:11.4]

online likelihood ratio test: A form of likelihood ratio test where the data arrives sequentially.

online model adaptation: Updating a model to deal with changing circumstances (e.g., altering a mean shift model to cope with scale changes of the object being tracked in a video). [SP02]

online processing: The processing of data when requested or when the data is acquired (as distinct from real-time or batch processing). See also real-time processing. [KH02]

online video screening: A model for detecting irregularities in a video stream, e.g., vehicles performing illegal actions. [HGX09]

one-class learning: Learning with the goal of taking as input a set of data points drawn from a probability distribution P and producing as output a "simple" subset S of the input space such that the probability that a test point drawn from P lies outside S is equal to some specified probability. One approach to this is through the one-class support vector machine. Another method would be to carry out probability density estimation and define S in terms of a probability contour. One-class learning can be used for outlier rejection and anomaly detection. [SS02:Ch. 8]

one-shot learning: Learning about a class based on only a few data points from that class. This can be possible by exploiting knowledge transfer from other classes that have already been learned. [FFP06]

one-versus-rest classification: In a multiclass classification problem with $K > 2$ classes, construct K one-versus-rest problems, each classifying one class against data from all the rest. A test point is classified by selecting the class with the largest strength of classifier output. This approach is commonly used for multiclass support vector machines. [HTF08:18.3.3]

opaque: When light cannot pass through a structure. This causes shadows and occlusion. [WP:Opacity_(optics)]

open operator: A mathematical morphology operation applied to a binary image. The operator is a sequence of N erode operators followed by N dilate operators, both using a specified structuring element. The operator is useful for separating touching objects and removing small regions. In the figure, the image on the right was created by opening the one on the left with an 11-pixel disk kernel: [SB11:8.15]

 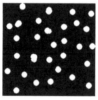

open set recognition: The recognition of an object where the set of possibilities is not closed, i.e., it is possible that the object is unknown to the system. See also closed set recognition. [FW05]

operator: A general term for a function that is applied to some data in order to

transform it in some way. For example see image-processing operator. [Gal90:Ch. 5]

opponent color: A color representation system, originally developed by Hering, in which an image is represented by three channels with contrasting colors: red–green, yellow–blue, and black–white. [BB82:2.2.5]

optical axis: The ray, perpendicular to the lens and through the optical center, around which the lens is symmetrical: [FP03:1.1.1]

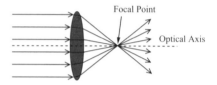

optical center: See focal point.

optical character recognition (OCR): A general term for extracting an alphabetic text description from an image of text. Common specialisms include bank numerals, handwritten digits, handwritten characters, cursive text, Chinese characters, Arabic characters etc. [JKS95:2.7]

optical coherence tomography: A method of acquiring a 3D image of the top 1-2 mm of an object, such as some biological tissue, using near-infrared interferometry. [WP:Optical_coherence_tomography]

optical flow: An instantaneous velocity measurement for the direction and speed of the image data across the visual field. This can be observed at every pixel, creating a field of velocity vectors. The set of apparent motions of the image pixel brightness values. [FP03:25.4]

optical flow boundary: A boundary between two regions where the optical flow is different in direction or magnitude. The regions can arise from objects moving in different directions or surfaces at different depths. See also optical flow field segmentation. In the figure, the dashed line is the boundary between optical flow moving left and optical flow moving right: [PGPO94]

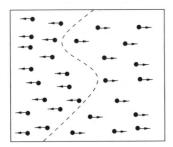

optical flow constraint equation: The equation $\frac{\partial I}{\partial t} + \nabla I \cdot \vec{u}_x = 0$ that links the observed change in image I's intensities over time $\frac{\partial I}{\partial t}$ at image position $\vec{x}$ to the spatial change in pixel intensities at that position ∇I and the velocity $\vec{u}_x$ of the image data at that pixel. The constraint does not completely determine the image motion, as this has two degrees of freedom. The equation provides only one constraint, thus leading to an aperture problem. [WP:Optical_flow#Estimation_of_the_optical_flow]

optical flow field: The field composed of the optical flow vector at each pixel in an image. [FP03:25.4]

optical flow field segmentation: The segmentation of an optical flow image into regions where the optical flow has a similar direction or magnitude. The regions can arise from objects moving in different directions or surfaces at different depths. See also optical flow boundary. [HPZC95]

optical flow region: A region where the optical flow has a similar direction or magnitude. Regions can arise from objects moving in different directions, or surfaces at different depths. See also optical flow boundary. [HS81]

optical flow smoothness constraint: The constraint that nearby pixels in an image usually have similar optical flow because they usually arise from projection of adjacent surface patches having similar motions relative to the observer. The constraint can be relaxed at the optical flow boundary. [Sny89]

optical image processing: An image-processing technique in which the processing occurs by use of lenses and coherent light instead of by a computer. The key principle is that a coherent light beam that passes through a transparency of the target image and is then focused produces the Fourier transform of the image at the focal point where frequency domain filtering can occur. The figure shows a typical processing arrangement: [PB01:Ch. 7]

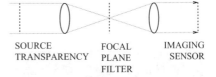

SOURCE TRANSPARENCY   FOCAL PLANE FILTER   IMAGING SENSOR

optical process: A process that uses light and lenses. [WP:Optics]

optical transfer function (OTF): Informally, the OTF is a measure of how well spatially varying patterns are observed by an optical system. More formally, in a 2D image, let $X(f_b, f_v)$ and $Y(f_b, f_v)$ be the Fourier transforms of the input $x(b, v)$ and output $y(b, v)$ images. Then, the OTF of a horizontal and vertical spatial frequency pair (f_b, f_v) is $H(f_b, f_v)/H(0, 0)$, where $H(f_b, f_v) = Y(f_b, f_v)/X(f_b, f_v)$. The optical transfer function is usually a complex number encoding both the reduction in signal strength at each spatial frequency and the phase shift. [SB11:5.11]

optics: A general term for the manipulation and transformation of light and images using lenses and mirrors. [JKS95:Ch. 8]

optimal basis encoding: A general technique for encoding image or other data by projecting onto some basis functions of a linear space and then using the projection coefficients instead of the original data. Optimal basis functions produce projection coefficients that allow the best discrimination between different classes of objects or members in a class (such as for face recognition). [LW00a]

optimization: A general term for finding the values of the parameters that maximize or minimize some quantity. [BB82:11.1.2]

optimization parameter estimation: See optimization.

OR operator: A pixelwise logical operator defined on binary variables. It takes as input two binary images, I_1 and I_2, and returns an image I_3 in which the value of each pixel is 0 if both I_1 and I_2 are 0, and 1 otherwise. In the figure, the image on the right shows the result of ORing the other two images (note that the white pixels have value 1): [SB11:3.2.2]

order statistics filter: A filter based on order statistics, a technique that sorts the pixels of a neighborhood by intensity value and assigns a rank (the position in the sorted sequence) to each. An order statistics filter replaces the central value of the filtering neighborhood with the value at a given rank in the sorted list. A popular example is the median filter. As this filter is less sensitive to outliers, it is often used in robust statistics processes. See also rank order filtering. [Umb98:3.3.1]

ordered texture: See macrotexture.

ordering: Sorting a collection of objects by a given property, e.g., intensity values, in an order statistics filter. [Umb98:3.3.1]

ordering constraint: A stereo vision constraint stating that two points which appear in a particular order in one image are likely to appear in the same order in the other stereo image. This constraint will fail if the points are from objects at different depths, should they exhibit parallax. [CM92]

orderless images: A form of image in which a probability distribution is associated with each point rather than an intensity or color. The probability distribution is computed from a local area around each point, ignoring the spatial structure. [KD99]

ordinal transformation: A one-to-one mapping of a set of values to another set of values such that the ordering relations are maintained. An example transformation replaces a value by its index in a sorted list of all values. For example, [36,20,19,42,58] is transformed to [3,2,1,4,5], which can be processed, e.g., by median filtering and then re-transformed back to the original domain.

Oren–Nayar model: A diffuse reflectance model for rough surfaces. [ON94]

orientation: The property of being directed towards or facing a particular region of space or a line; also, the pose or attitude of a body in space. For instance, the orientation of a vector (where the vector points to) is specified by its unit vector; the orientation of an ellipsoid is specified by its principal directions; the orientation of a wire-frame model is specified by its own reference frame with respect to a world reference frame. [WP:Orientation_(computer_vision)]

orientation error: The amount of error associated with an orientation value. [VG96]

orientation representation: See pose representation.

oriented projective geometry: A version of projective geometry where orientations may be associated with lines, e.g., the direction in which light is traveling. [WP:Oriented_projective_geometry]

oriented smoothness: A constraint which restricts changes in displacement vectors between two images in directions which have little gray scale variation. [Nag90]

oriented texture: A texture in which a preferential direction can be detected. For instance, the direction of the bricks in a regular brick wall. See also texture direction and texture orientation. [RS91]

orthogonal Fourier–Mellin moment invariants: Moment invariants based on Fourier-Mellin moments or rotational moments. [ZSH+10a]

orthogonal image transform: A well-known class of techniques for image compression. The key process is the projection of the image data onto a set of orthogonal basis functions. See, e.g., the discrete cosine transform, the Fourier transform and the Haar transform. This is a special case of the linear integral transform. [Cla85]

orthogonal regression: Also known as total least squares. Traditionally seen as the generalization of linear regression to the case where both x and y are measured quantities and subject to error. Given samples x_i and y_i, the objective is to find estimates of the "true" points $(\tilde{x}_i, \tilde{y}_i)$, and line parameters (a, b, c) such that $a\tilde{x}_i + b\tilde{y}_i + c = 0, \forall i$, and such that the error $\sum (x_i - \tilde{x}_i)^2 + (y_i - \tilde{y}_i)^2$ is minimized. This estimate is easily obtained as the line (plane etc., in higher dimensions) passing through the centroid of the data, in the direction of the eigenvector of the data scatter matrix that has the smallest eigenvalue. [WP:Total_least_squares]

orthographic: The characteristic property of orthographic (or perpendicular) projection onto the image plane. See orthographic projection. [FP03:2.3]

orthographic camera: A camera in which the image is formed according to an orthographic projection. [FP03:2.3]

orthographic projection: Rendering of a 3D scene as a 2D image by a set of rays orthogonal to the image plane. The size of the objects imaged does not depend on their distance from the viewer. As a consequence, parallel lines in the scene remain parallel in the image. The equations of orthographic projections are

$$x = X \quad y = Y$$

where x, y are the image coordinates of an image point in the camera reference frame (that is, in millimeters, not pixels) and X, Y, Z are the coordinates of the corresponding scene point: [FP03:2.3]

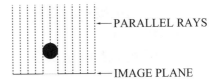

orthoimage: In photogrammetry, the warp of an aerial photograph to an approximation of the image that would have been taken had the camera pointed directly downwards. See also orthographic projection. [WP:Orthophoto]

orthonormal: A property of a set of basis functions or vectors. If $<, >$ is the inner product function and a and b are any two different members of the set, then we have $< a, a > = < b, b > = 1$ and $< a, b > = 0$. [WP:Orthonormal_basis]

OTF: See optical transfer function.

outlier: Exception points in a set of data that mostly conforms to some regular process or is well represented by a model. Classifying points as outliers depends both on the models used and the statistics of the data. This figure shows a line fit to some points and an outlying point: [CS09:3.4.6]

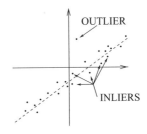

outlier detection: The identification of samples or points which lie outside the main distribution. [FP03:15.5]

outlier rejection: Identifying outliers and removing them from the current process. Identification is often a difficult process. [CS09:3.4.6]

out-of-focus blur: The fuzziness (blur) which appears in image as a result of the object which is viewed being out-side the depth of field of the camera: [KPP98]

over-fitting: A model is said to over-fit the training set if its performance on an independent test set drawn from the same data-generating distribution is worse than on the training set. [Mur12:1.2.6]

oversampling: The sampling density of a sampled continuous signal is greater than the Nyquist sampling rate. [WP:Oversampling]

over-segmented: The output of a segmentation algorithm in which the desired regions are represented by too many regions. In the figure, the image should be segmented into three regions but it was oversegmented into five regions: [SQ04:8.7]

paired boundaries: See <u>paired contours</u>.

paired contours: A pair of contours occurring together in images and joined by a spatial relationship, e.g., the contours generated by river banks in aerial images or the contours of a human limb:

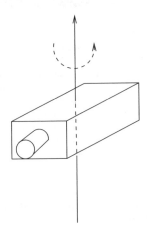

Co-occurrence can be exploited to make contour detection more robust. See also <u>feature extraction</u>. [HF94]

pair-wise correlation: See <u>correlation</u>.

pairwise geometric histogram (PGH): A line- or edge-based shape representation used for <u>object recognition</u>, especially 2D. <u>Histograms</u> are built by computing, for each line segment, the relative angle and perpendicular distance to all other segments. The representation is <u>invariant</u> to rotation and translation. A PGH can be compared using the <u>Bhattacharyya distance</u>. [AFRW98]

PAL camera: A camera conforming to the European phase alternation by line (PAL) standard. See also <u>NTSC</u>, <u>RS-170</u> and <u>CCIR camera</u>. [Jai89:4.1]

palette: The range of colors available. [NA05:2.2]

pan: Rotation of a camera about a single axis through the camera center and (approximately) parallel to the image vertical: [WP:Panning_(camera)]

pan–tilt–zoom (PTZ): A camera for which the direction (pan and tilt) in which it points and the <u>field of view</u> (zoom) can be controlled electronically. Very common in the <u>visual surveillance</u> domain. [WM96]

panchromatic: Sensitive to light of all visible wavelengths. [WP: Panchromatic_film]

panchromatic images: <u>Gray scale images</u> which are derived from all wavelengths of <u>visible light</u>. [GSCG04]

panoramic: Associated with a <u>wide field of view</u> often created or observed by a <u>panned</u> camera. [WP:Panoramic_ photography]

panoramic image mosaic: A class of techniques for collating a set of partially overlapping images into a single panoramic image. The figure shows a mosaic build from the frames of a hand-held camera sequence:

Dictionary of Computer Vision and Image Processing, Second Edition.
R. B. Fisher, T. P. Breckon, K. Dawson-Howe, A. Fitzgibbon, C. Robertson, E. Trucco and C. K. I. Williams.
© 2014 John Wiley & Sons, Ltd. Published 2014 by John Wiley & Sons, Ltd.

Typically, the mosaic yields both very high resolution and a large field of view, which cannot be simultaneously achieved by a physical camera. There are several ways to build a panoramic mosaic but, in general, there are three necessary steps: determine correspondences (see stereo correspondence problem) between adjacent images; use the correspondences to find a warping transformation between the two images (or between the current mosaic and a new image); blend the new image into the current mosaic. [SS97b]

panoramic image stereo: A stereo system working with a very large field of view, say 360° in azimuth and 120° in elevation. Disparity maps and depths are recovered for the whole field of view simultaneously. A normal stereo system would have to be moved and the results registered to achieve the same result. See also binocular stereo, multi-view stereo and omni-directional sensing. [PBP01]

Pantone matching system (PMS): A color matching system used by the printing industry to print spot colors. Colors are specified by Pantone name or number. PMS works well for spot colors but not for process colors, usually specified by the CMYK color model. [WP:Pantone]

Panum's fusional area: The region of space within which single vision is possible (that is, you do not perceive double images of objects) when the eyes fixate on a given point. [CS09:6.7.1.1]

parabolic point: A point on a smooth surface where the Gaussian curvature is positive. See also mean and Gaussian curvature shape classification. [Nal93:9.2.5]

parallax: The angle between the two straight lines that join a point (possibly

a moving one) to two viewpoints. In motion analysis, *motion parallax* occurs when two scene points that project to the same image point at one viewpoint later project to different points as the camera moves. The vector between the two new points is the parallax: [TV98:8.2.4]

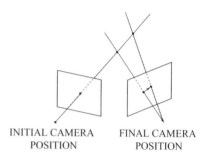

INITIAL CAMERA   FINAL CAMERA
POSITION   POSITION

parallel processing: An algorithm is executed in parallel, or through parallel processing, when it can be divided into a number of computations that are performed simultaneously on separate hardware. See also single instruction multiple data, multiple instruction multiple data, pipeline parallelism and task parallelism. [BB82:10.4.1]

parallel projection: A generalization of orthographic projection in which a scene is projected onto the image plane by a set of parallel rays not necessarily perpendicular to the image plane. This is a good approximation of perspective projection, up to a uniform scale factor, when the scene is small in comparison to its distance from the center of projection. Parallel projection is a subset of weak perspective viewing, where the weak perspective projection matrix is subject not only to orthogonality of the rows of the left 2×3 submatrix, but also to the constraint that the rows have equal norm. In orthographic projection, both rows have unit norm. [FP03:2.3.1]

parameter estimation: A class of techniques aimed at estimating the parameters of a given parametric model. For instance, assuming that a set of image points lie on an ellipse and considering the implicit ellipse model $ax^2 + bxy + cy^2 + dx + ey + f$, the parameter vector $[a, b, c, d, e, f]$ can be estimated, e.g., by least square surface fitting. [DH73:3.1]

parametric edge detector: An edge detection technique that seeks to match image data using a parametric model of edge points and thus detects edges when the image data fits the edge model well. See Hueckel edge detector. [Nal93:3.1.3]

parametric mesh: A type of surface-modeling primitive for 3D models in which the surface is defined by a mesh of points. A typical example is non-uniform rational b-splines (NURBS). [GK04]

parametric model: A mathematical model expressed as function of a set of parameters, e.g., the parametric equation of a curve or surface (as opposed to its implicit form), or a parametric edge model (see parametric edge detector). [Nal93:3.1.3]

parametric warps: Transformations that distort or correct images using a single global parametric function, e.g., a perspective transformation. [GM98]

paraperspective: An approximation of perspective projection, whereby a scene is divided into parts that are imaged separately by parallel projection with different parameters. [FP03:2.3.1–2.3.3]

Pareto optimal: For a nontrivial problem there is not a single solution that simultaneously optimizes each objective. A Pareto optimal point occurs if it is not possible to improve any of the objectives further without at the same time worsening another. The solution to this multi-objective problem is a possibly infinite set of Pareto points. [BV04:4.7]

part-based representation: A model that treats objects as a collection of parts. For example, a person can be considered to be composed of a head, a trunk, two arms and two legs. [Sze10:14.4.2]

part recognition: A class of techniques for recognizing assemblies or articulated objects from their subcomponents (parts), e.g., a human body from head, trunk, and limbs. Parts have been represented by 3D models, such as generalized cones and superquadrics. In industrial contexts, part recognition indicates the recognition of specific items (parts) in a production line, typically for classification and quality control. [CFH05]

part segmentation: A class of techniques for partitioning a set of data into components (parts) with an identity of their own, e.g., a human body into limbs, head and trunk. Part segmentation methods exist for both 2D and 3D data, that is, intensity images and range images, respectively. Various geometric models have been adopted for the parts, e.g., generalized cylinders, superellipses and superquadrics. See also articulated object segmentation. [BM02:6.2.2]

partial volume interpolation: A technique for performing interpolation of voxel values (e.g., MRI values) in which the interpolated values are not determined by averaging but rather by distributing existing local values. [HV03]

partially constrained pose: A situation whereby an object is subject to a number of constraints restricting the number of admissible orientations or positions, but not fixing one univocally. For instance, cars on a road are constrained to rotate around an axis perpendicular to the road. [WOFH93]

partially observable Markov decision (POMDP): A generalization of the Markov decision process where the agent cannot directly observe the underlying state, but where the observations made relate stochastically to that state. [TBF05:Ch. 15]

particle counting: An application of particle segmentation to counting the instances of small objects (particles), such as pebbles, cells or water droplets, in images or sequences: [WP:Particle_counter]

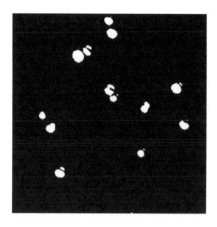

particle filter: A tracking strategy where the probability density of the model parameters is represented as a set of *particles*. A particle is a single sample of the model parameters, with an associated weight. The probability density represented by the particles is typically a set of delta functions or a set of Gaussians with means at the particle centers. At each tracking iteration, the current set of particles represents a prior on the model parameters, which is updated via a dynamical model and observation model to produce the new set representing the posterior distribution. See also condensation tracking. [WP:Particle_filter]

particle flow tracking: Determining the local flow by attempting to track individual local particles, e.g., smoke particles, in a flow. Groups of particles generally exhibit similar flow, although individual particles may not be particularly stable. [MEYD11]

particle segmentation: A class of techniques for detecting individual instances of small objects (particles), such as pebbles, cells or water droplets, in images or sequences. A typical problem is severe occlusion caused by overlapping particles. This problem has been approached successfully with the watershed transform. [KMMH07]

particle swarm optimization: An approach to optimization based on having a number of particles whose dynamics in the search space depend on rules originally inspired by the simulation of animal social behavior. Each particle has a pair of update functions as follows:

$$\vec{v}_{i,t+1} = \vec{v}_{i,t} + c_1.\text{rand}()(\underline{b}_{i,t} - \underline{p}_{i,t})$$
$$+ c_2.\text{rand}()(\underline{p}_{g,t} - \underline{p}_{i,t})$$
$$\underline{p}_{i,t+1} = \underline{p}_{i,t} + \vec{v}_{i,t}$$

where $\underline{p}_{i,t}$ is the position at time t of particle i; $\underline{v}_{i,t}$ is its velocity; $\underline{b}_i$ is its best recorded position; $\underline{p}_g$ is the position of the particle in the swarm achieving the best evaluation score; $f(\underline{p}_i)$ is the evaluation function mapping particle positions to values; and rand() is a randomly generated floating point number in the range [0, 1]. The pair of parameters c_1 and c_2 are weightings between the importance of local and global best values. [PKB07]

particle tracking: See condensation tracking.

Parzen window: 1) A non-parametric method for density estimation. Given a sample $\{\vec{x}_i\}$ with $i = 1, \ldots, n$ drawn from some underlying density, the Parzen window estimate is obtained as $\hat{p}(\vec{x}) = \frac{1}{n} \sum_i K(\vec{x}, \vec{x}_i)$ where K is a kernel function. The Gaussian distribution is one common choice for the kernel: [DH73:4.3]. [PTVF92:13.4] 2) A triangle-shaped weighting window used to limit leakage to spurious frequencies when computing the power spectrum of a signal:

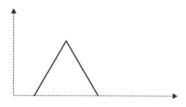

See also windowing and Fourier transform. [DH73:4.3]

passive sensing: A sensing process that does not emit any stimulus or where the sensor does not move. A normal stationary camera is a passive sensor. Compare with active sensing. [Nal93:1.1]

passive stereo algorithm: An algorithm that uses only the information obtainable by a stationary set of cameras and ambient illumination. This contrasts with the active vision paradigm in stereo, where the camera(s) might move or some projected stimulus might be used to help solve the stereo correspondence problem. [BM02:1.9.2]

patch classification: The problem of attributing a surface patch to a particular class in a shape catalog, typically computed from dense range data using curvature estimates or shading. See also curvature sign patch classification and mean and Gaussian curvature shape classification. [GVS03]

path coherence: A property used in tracking objects in an image sequence. The assumption is that the object motion is mostly smooth in the scene and thus the observed motion in a projected image of the scene is also smooth. [JKS95:14.6]

path finding: The problem of determining a path with given properties in a graph, e.g., the shortest path connecting two given nodes or two nodes with given properties. A path is defined as a linear subgraph. Path finding is a characteristic problem of state-space methods, inherited from symbolic artificial intelligence. See also graph searching. This term is also used in the context of dynamic programming search, e.g., applied to the stereo correspondence problem. [WP:Pathfinding]

pattern grammar: See shape grammar. [WP:Pattern_grammar]

pattern matching: See template matching.

pattern recognition: A large research area concerned with the recognition and classification of structures, relations or patterns in data. Classic techniques include syntactic pattern recognition, structural pattern recognition and statistical pattern recognition. [Sch89:Ch. 6]

PCA: See principal component analysis.

PDE: Partial differential equation.

PDM: See point distribution model. [WP:Point_distribution_model]

peak: A general term for when a signal value is greater than the neighboring signal values. An example of a signal peak measured in one dimension is when crossing a bright line lying on a dark surface along a scanline; if the pixel values 7, 45, 105, 54, 7 are observed, the peak is at 105. A two-dimensional example is when observing the image of a bright spot on a darker background. [SOS00:3.4.5]

Pearson's correlation coefficient: See correlation.

pedestrian detection: The automatic identification of people in a street scene: [Sze10:14.1.2]

pedestrian surveillance: See person surveillance.

pel: See pixel.

penalty term: In fitting models to data, it is often useful to carry out regularization, i.e., to add a smoothness or penalty term to the data fit term. If the data fit of a model M with parameters θ on dataset D is given by the negative log-likelihood $-\log p(D|\theta, M)$, then the penalized negative log likelihood takes the form $J(\theta) = -\log p(D|\theta, M) + \lambda \Phi(\theta)$, where $\Phi(\theta)$ is a penalty term on θ, and $\lambda > 0$ is a regularization constant. An example of a penalty term is a sum of squares $\Phi(\theta) = \sum_i \theta_i^2$ as used in ridge regression. For a Bayesian statistical model, the penalty term can be interpreted as the negative log of the prior distribution and the minimization of $J(\theta)$ is equivalent to finding the maximum a posteriori probability for θ. [HTF08:3.4]

pencil of lines: A bundle of lines passing through the same point:

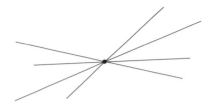

If $\vec{p}$ is a generic bundle line and $\vec{p}_0$ the point through which all lines pass, the bundle is

$$\vec{p} = \vec{p}_0 + \lambda \vec{v}$$

where λ is a real number and $\vec{v}$ is the direction of the individual line (both are parameters). [FP03:13.1.4]

penumbra: A region in which part of the light source is obscured and is thus in partial shadow. This is distinct from the umbra (the full shadow region).

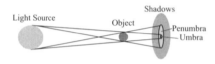

[WP:Umbra]

percentile method: A specialized technique used for selecting a threshold (see thresholding). The method assumes that the percentage of the scene that belongs to the desired object (e.g., a darker object against a lighter background) is known. The threshold that selects the correct percentage of pixels is used. [JKS95:3.2.1]

perception: The process of understanding the world through the analysis of sensory input (such as images). [DH73:1.1]

perceptron: A computational element $\phi(\vec{w} \cdot \vec{x} + b)$ that acts on a data vector $\vec{x}$, where $\vec{w}$ is a vector of weights, b is a scalar (called the bias) and $\phi(\cdot)$ is the activation function. Often $\phi(\cdot)$ is taken to be a step function. Perceptrons are often used for classifying data into one of two classes (i.e., $\phi(\vec{w} \cdot \vec{x} + b) \geq 0$ and $\phi(\vec{w} \cdot \vec{x} + b) < 0$). Perceptrons can be combined to make a multilayer perceptron network. See also classification, supervised classification and pattern recognition. [Bis06:4.1.7]

perceptron network: See multilayer perceptron network and single-layer perceptron network.

perceptual grouping: See perceptual organization.

perceptual organization: A theory based on Gestalt psychology, centered on the tenet that certain organizations (or interpretations) of visual stimuli are preferred over others by the human visual system. A famous example is that a drawing of a wire-frame cube is immediately interpreted as a 3D object, instead of a 2D collection of lines. This concept has been used in several low-level vision systems, typically to find groups of low-level features most probably generated by interesting objects. See also grouping and Lowe's curve segmentation method. The figure shows a more complex example, where the top ends of the features suggests a virtual horizontal line: [FP03:14.2]

performance characterization: A class of techniques aimed at assessing the performance of computer vision systems in terms of, e.g., accuracy, precision, robustness to noise, repeatability and reliability. [TV98:A.1]

perimeter: 1) In a binary image, the set of foreground pixels that touch the background.
2) The length of the path through those pixels. [JKS95:2.5.6]

periodic color filter arrays: An array or mosaic of color filters placed over individual sensing elements within a camera so as to allow pixels to sense different wavelengths of light and hence permit the creation of a color image. These color filters are normally arranged in a periodic fashion. See also Bayer pattern. [Sze10:pp. 85–86]

periodicity estimation: The problem of estimating the period of a phenomenon, e.g., determining a fixed pattern's size, given a texture created by its repetition. [LP96]

person surveillance: A class of techniques aimed at detecting, tracking, counting, and recognizing people or their behavior in CCTV videos, for security purposes. For example, systems have been reported for automated surveillance in car parks, banks, airports etc. A typical system must detect the presence of a person, track the person's movement over time, possibly identify the person using a database of known faces and classify the person's behavior according to a small class of pre-defined behaviors (e.g., normal or anomalous). See also anomalous behavior detection, face recognition and face tracking. [JJS04]

perspective: The rendering of a 3D scene as a 2D image according to perspective projection, the key characteristic of which is, intuitively, that the size of the imaged objects depend on their distance from the viewer. As a consequence, the image of a bundle of parallel lines is a bundle of lines converging into a point, the vanishing point. The geometry of perspective was formalized by the master painters of the Italian *Quattrocento* and Renaissance. [FP03:2.2]

perspective camera: A camera in which the image is formed according to perspective projection. The corresponding mathematical model is commonly known as the pinhole camera model. [FP03:2.2]

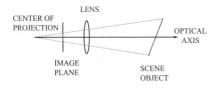

CENTER OF PROJECTION

LENS

OPTICAL AXIS

IMAGE PLANE

SCENE OBJECT

perspective distortion: A type of distortion in which lines that are parallel in the real world appear to converge in a perspective image. In the figure, notice how the train tracks appear to converge in the distance: [SB11:2.3.1]

perspective inversion: The problem of determining the position of a 3D point from its image, i.e., solving the perspective projection equations for 3D coordinates. See also absolute orientation. [FP03:2.2]

perspective projection: Imaging a scene with foreshortening. The projection equation of perspective is

$$x = f\frac{X}{Z} \quad y = f\frac{Y}{Z},$$

where x, y are the image coordinates of an image point in the camera reference frame (e.g., in millimeters, not pixels), f is the focal length and X, Y, Z are the coordinates of the corresponding scene point. [FP03:1.1.1]

perspective transformation: The transformation which a scene undergoes when viewed by a pinhole camera. [FP03:1.1.1]

PET: See positron emission tomography.

phase-based registration: An image registration technique that uses the local phase in the two images to determine the correct alignment. [GBN06]

phase congruency: The property whereby components of an image are maximally in phase at feature points, such as step edges or lines. Phase congruency is invariant to image brightness and contrast and has therefore been used as an absolute measure of the significance of feature points. See also image feature. [WP:Phase_congruency]

phase correlation: A motion estimation method that uses the translation-phase duality property of the Fourier transform (a shift in the spatial domain is equivalent to a phase shift in the frequency domain). When using log-polar coordinates and the rotation and scale properties of the Fourier transform, spatial rotation and scale can be estimated from the frequency shift, independent of spatial translation. See also planar motion estimation. [WP:Phase_correlation]

phase-matching stereo algorithm: An algorithm for solving the stereo correspondence problem by looking for similarity of the phase of the Fourier transform. [SMM04]

phase-retrieval problem: The problem of reconstructing a signal based on only the magnitude (not the phase) of the Fourier transform. [WP:Phase_retrieval]

phase spectrum: The Fourier transform of an image can be decomposed into its phase spectrum and its power spectrum. The phase spectrum is the relative phase offset of the given spatial frequency. [Hec87:11.2.1]

phase-unwrapping technique: The process of reconstructing the true phase shift from phase estimates "wrapped" into $[-\pi, \pi]$. The true phase shift values may not fall in this interval but may instead be mapped into the interval by addition or subtraction of multiples of 2π. The technique maximizes the smoothness of the phase image by adding or subtracting multiples of 2π at various image locations. See also Fourier transform. [JB94a]

phi–s curve (ϕ–s): A technique for representing planar contours. Each point in the contour is represented by the angle ϕ, formed by the line through P and the shape's center (e.g., the barycentrum or center of mass) with a fixed direction, and the distance s from the center to P:

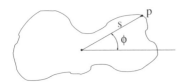

See also shape representation. [BB82:8.2.3]

Phong reflectance model: An empirical model of local illumination that models the way in which surfaces reflect light as a mixture of diffuse reflection and specular reflection. [Sze10:pp. 65-67]

photo consistency: See shape from photo consistency. [WP:Photo-consistency]

photodiode: The basic element, or pixel, of a CCD or other solid state sensor, converting light to an electric signal. [WP:Photodiode]

photogrammetry: A research area concerned with obtaining reliable and accurate measurements from noncontact imaging, e.g., a digital height map from a pair of overlapping satellite images. Consequently, accurate camera calibration is a primary concern. The techniques used overlap many typical of image processing and pattern recognition. [FP03:3.4]

photography: Taking pictures or videos with a camera or other device capable of recording an image. [WP:Photography]

photometric decalibration: The correction of intensities in an image so that the same surface (at the same orientation) will give the same response regardless of the position in which it appears in the image. [Dun70]

photometric invariant: A feature or characteristic of an image that is insensitive to changes in illumination. See also invariant. [GLU96]

photometric stereo: A technique recovering surface shape (more precisely, the surface normal at each surface point) using multiple images acquired from a single viewpoint but under different illumination conditions. These lead to different reflectance maps, which together constrain the surface normal at each point. [FP03:5.4]

photometry: A branch of optics concerned with the measurement of the amount or the spectrum of light. In computer vision, one frequently uses photometric models expressing the amount of light emerging from a surface, be it fictitious or the surface of a radiating source, or from an illuminated object. A well-known photometric model is Lambert's law. [WP:Photometry_(optics)]

photon noise: Noise generated by the statistical fluctuations associated with photon counting over a finite time interval in the CCD or other solid state sensor of a digital camera. Photon noise is not independent of the signal and is not additive. See also image noise and digital camera. [WP:Image_noise]

photopic response: The sensitivity-wavelength curve modeling the response of the human eye to normal lighting conditions. In such conditions, the cones are the photoreceptors on the retina that best respond to light. Their response curve peaks at 555 nm, indicating that the eye is maximally sensitive to green–yellow colors in normal lighting conditions. When light intensity is very low, the rods determine the eye's response, modeled by the *scotopic curve*, which peaks near to 510 nm. [Jai89:3.2]

photosensor spectral response: The characterization of a sensor's output as a function of the input light's spectral frequency. See also spectral response, Fourier transform, frequency spectrum and spectral frequency. [WP:Frequency_spectrum]

physics-based vision: An area of computer vision seeking to apply the laws or methods of physics (optics, surfaces, illumination etc.) to the analysis of images and videos. Examples include polarization-based methods, in which physical properties of the scene surfaces are estimated via estimates of the state of polarization of the incoming light and detailed radiometric models of image formation. [DKFH97]

pictorial pattern recognition: Object recognition or the recognition of patterns where the *a priori* known models are simply pictures of objects which have previously been observed: [Che69]

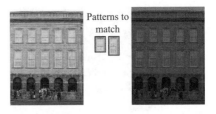
Patterns to match

picture element: A pixel. An indivisible image measurement. This is the smallest directly measured image feature. [SB11:Ch. 3]

picture tree: A recursive image and 2D shape representation in which a tree data structure is used. Each node in the tree represents a region that is then decomposed into subregions. These are represented by child nodes. The figure shows (left) a segmented image with four regions and (right) the corresponding picture tree: [JKS95:3.3.4]

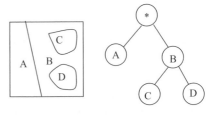

piecewise rigidity: The property of an object or scene that some of its parts, but not the object or scene as a whole, are rigid. Piecewise rigidity can be a convenient assumption, e.g., in motion analysis. [Koe86]

pincushion distortion: A form of radial lens distortion where image points are displaced away from the center of distortion by an amount that increases with the distance to the center. A straight line that would have been parallel to an image side is bowed towards the center of the image. This is the opposite of barrel distortion: [Hec87:6.3.1]

pinhole camera model: The mathematical model for an ideal perspective camera formed by an image plane and a point aperture through which all incoming rays must pass. For equations, see perspective projection. This is a good model for a simple convex lens camera, where all rays pass through the virtual pinhole at the focal point: [FP03:1.1]

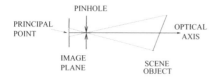

pink noise: Noise that is not white noise, i.e., when there is a correlation between the noise at two pixels or at two times. [WP:Pink_noise]

pipeline parallelism: Parallelism achieved with two or more, possibly dissimilar, computation devices. The non-parallel process comprises steps A and B and operates on a sequence of items x_i, $i > 0$, producing outputs y_i. The result of B depends on the result of A, so a sequential computer computes $a_i = A(x_i)$; $y_i = B(a_i)$; for each i. A parallel computer cannot compute a_i and y_i simultaneously as they are dependent, so the computation requires the following steps:

$$a_1 = A(x_1)$$
$$y_1 = B(a_1)$$
$$a_2 = A(x_2)$$
$$y_2 = B(a_2)$$
$$a_3 = A(x_3)$$
$$....$$
$$a_i = A(x_i)$$
$$y_i = B(a_i)....$$

Notice that we compute y_i just after y_{i-1}, so the computation can be arranged as:

$$a_1 = A(x_1)$$
$$a_2 = A(x_2) \qquad y_1 = B(a_1)$$
$$a_3 = A(x_3) \qquad y_2 = B(a_2)$$
$$....$$
$$a_{i+1} = A(x_{i+1}) \quad y_i = B(a_i)$$
$$....$$

Steps on the same line may be computed concurrently as they are independent. The output values y_i therefore arrive at a rate of one every cycle rather than one every two cycles without pipelining. The pipeline process can be visualized as: [AT01]

pit: 1) A general term for when a signal value is lower than the neighboring signal values, unlike signal peaks, which are higher than neighboring values. For example, a pit occurs when observing the image of a dark spot on a lighter background.
2) A local point-like concave shape defect in a surface. [CNH+03]

pitch: A 3D rotation representation (along with yaw and roll) often used for cameras or moving observers. The pitch component specifies a rotation about a horizontal axis to give an up–down change in orientation: [JKS95:12.2.1]

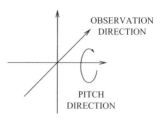

pixel: The intensity values of a digital image are specified at the locations of a discrete rectangular grid; each location is a pixel. A pixel is characterized by its coordinates (position in the image) and intensity value (see intensity and intensity image). Values can express physical quantities other than intensity for different kinds of images (e.g., depth image). In physical terms, a pixel is the photosensitive cell on the CCD or other solid state sensor of a digital camera. The CCD pixel has a precise size, specified by the manufacturer and determining the CCD's aspect ratio. See also intensity sensor and photosensor spectral response. [SB11:Ch. 3]

pixel addition operator: A low-level image-processing operator taking as input two gray scale images, I_1 and I_2, and returning an image I_3 in which the value of each pixel is $I_3 = I_1 + I_2$. The figure shows the sum of the two images on the left (divided by 2 to rescale to the original intensity level): [SB11:3.2.1]

pixel-based representation: Any representation where the data is in a 2D spatial array equivalent to an image. See also pixel.

pixel-change history: The values exhibited by a pixel over some past period in time. [XGP02]

pixel classification: The problem of assigning the pixels of an image to certain classes. This can use either supervised classification (with models of known classes) or unsupervised methods such as clustering (when no models are known). See also image segmentation. The figure shows (left) an image and (right) its pixels in four classes denoted by four shades of gray: [Nal93:3.3.1]

pixel connectivity: The pattern specifying which pixels are considered neighbors of a given one (X) for the purposes of computation. Common connectivity schemes are (left) 4 connectedness and (right) 8 connectedness: [SB11:4.2]

pixel coordinate transformation: The mathematical transformation linking two image reference frames, specifying how the coordinates of a pixel in one reference frame are obtained from the coordinate of that pixel in the other reference frame. One linear transformation can be specified by $i_1 = ai_2 + bj_2 + e$, $j_1 = ci_2 + dj_2 + f$ where the coordinates of $\vec{p}_2 = (i_2, j_2)$ are transformed into $\vec{p}_1 = (i_1, j_1)$. In matrix form, $\vec{p}_1 = \mathbf{A}\vec{p}_2 + \vec{t}$, with $\mathbf{A} = \begin{pmatrix} a & b \\ c & d \end{pmatrix}$ a rotation matrix and $\vec{t} = \begin{pmatrix} e \\ f \end{pmatrix}$ a translation vector. See also Euclidean transformation, affine transformation and homography transformation. [SK99]

pixel coordinates: The coordinates of a pixel in an image. Normally these are the row and column position. [JKS95:12.1]

pixel counting: A simple algorithm to determine the area of an image region by counting the numbers of pixels composing the region. See also region. [WP:Simulation_cockpit#Aircraft_Simpits]

pixel division operator: An operator taking as input two gray scale images, I_1 and I_2, and returning an image I_3 in which the value of each pixel is $I_3 = I_1/I_2$. [Dav90:Ch. 2]

pixel exponential operator: A low-level image-processing operator taking as input one gray scale image, I_1, and returning an image I_2 in which

211

the value of each pixel is $I_2 = cb^{I_1}$. This operator is used to change the dynamic range of an image. The value of the basis b depends on the desired degree of compression of the dynamic range and c is a scaling factor. See also logarithmic transformation and pixel logarithm operator. The figure shows (left) an image and (right) the image 1.005 raised to the pixel values: [BB82:Ch. 1]

pixel gray scale resolution: The number of different gray levels that can be represented in a pixel, depending on the number of bits associated with each pixel. For instance, an 8-bit pixel (or image) can represent $2^8 = 256$ different intensity values. See also intensity, intensity image and intensity sensor. [GAM01]

pixel interpolation: See image interpolation. [WP:Pixelation]

pixel jitter: A frame grabber must estimate the pixel sampling clock of a digital camera, i.e., the clock used to read out the pixel values, which is not included in the output signal of the camera. Pixel jitter is a form of image noise generated by time variations in the frame grabber's estimate of the camera's clock. [RWG+09]

pixel logarithm operator: An image-processing operator taking as input one gray scale image, I_1, and returning an image I_2 in which the value of each pixel is $I_2 = c \log_b(|I_1 + 1|)$. This operator is used to change the dynamic range of an image (see also contrast enhancement), such as for the enhancement of the magnitude of the Fourier transform. The base b of the logarithm function is often e, but

it does not actually matter because the relationship between logarithms of any two bases is only one of scaling. See also pixel exponential operator. The figure shows (left) an image and (right) the scaled logarithm of the pixel values of the image: [SB11:3.3.1]

pixel multiplication operator: An image-processing operator taking as input two gray scale images, I_1 and I_2, and returning an image I_3 in which the value of each pixel is $I_3 = I_1 * I_2$. The figure shows (left and middle) two images and (right) their product (scaled by 255 for contrast): [SB11:3.2.1.2]

pixel subsampling: The process of producing a smaller image from a given one by including only one pixel out of every N. Subsampling is rarely applied this literally, however, as severe aliasing is introduced; scale space filtering is applied instead. [AP08]

pixel subtraction operator: A low-level image-processing operator taking as input two gray scale images, I_1 and I_2, and returning an image I_3 in which the value of each pixel is $I_3 = I_1 - I_2$. This operator implements the simplest possible change detection algorithm. The figure shows (left and middle) two images and (right) the middle image subtracted from the left image (with 128 added): [SB11:3.2.1]

212

place recognition: The identification of the viewer's location. [Sze10:14.3.3]

planar facet model: See surface mesh.

planar mosaic: A panoramic image mosaic of a planar scene. The transformation linking different views of a planar scene is a homography. [CZ98]

planar motion estimation: A class of techniques aiming to estimate the motion parameters of bodies moving on a plane in space. See also motion estimation. [HZ00:18.8]

planar patch extraction: The problem of finding planar regions, or patches, most commonly in range images. Plane extraction can be useful, e.g., in 3D pose estimation, as several model-based matching techniques yield higher accuracy with planar than non-planar surfaces. [CZ01]

planar patches: See surface triangulation.

planar projective transformation: See homography.

planar rectification: A class of rectification algorithms projecting the original images onto a plane parallel to the baseline of the cameras. See also stereo and stereo vision. [RMC97]

planar scene: 1) When the depth of a scene is small with respect to its distance from the camera, the scene can be considered planar, and useful approximations can be adopted; e.g., the transformation between two views taken by a perspective camera is a homography. See also planar mosaic. 2) When all of the surfaces in a scene are planar, e.g., in a blocks-world scene. [BS03]

Planckian locus: The curve that an incandescent black body would follow in chromaticity space as it changes temperature. [WP:Planckian_locus]

plane: The locus of all points $\vec{x}$ such that the surface normal $\vec{n}$ of the plane and a point in the plane $\vec{p}$ satisfy the relation $(\vec{x} - \vec{p}) \cdot \vec{n} = 0$. In 3D space, e.g., a plane is defined by two vectors and a point lying on the plane, so that the plane's parametric equation is:

$$\vec{p} = a\vec{u} + b\vec{v} + \vec{p}_0,$$

where $\vec{p}$ is the generic plane point, $\vec{u}, \vec{v}$ are the two vectors and $\vec{p}_0$ is the point defining the plane. The implicit equation of a plane is $ax + by + cz + d = 0$, where $[x, y, z]$ are the coordinates of the generic plane point. In vector form, $\vec{p} \cdot \vec{n} = d$, where $\vec{p} = [x, y, z]$, $\vec{n} = [a, b, c]$ is a vector perpendicular to the plane, and $\frac{d}{\sqrt{\|\vec{n}\|}}$ is the distance of the plane from the origin. All of these definitions are equivalent. [JKS95:13.3.1]

plane conic: Any of the curves defined by the intersection of a plane with a 3D double cone: ellipse, hyperbola and parabola. Two intersecting lines and a single point represent degenerate conics, defined by special configurations of the cone and the plane. The implicit equation of a conic is $ax^2 + bxy + cy^2 + dx + ey + f = 0$. See also conic fitting. The figure shows an ellipse formed by intersection: [JKS95:6.6]

plane+parallax: A framework in which multiple cameras are arranged on a plane and in which parallax is used relative to a reference plane to estimate depth. [Sze10:p. 55]

plane projective transfer: An algorithm based on projective invariants that, given two images of a planar object, I_1 and I_2, and four feature correspondences, determines the position of any other point of I_1 in I_2. Interestingly, no knowledge of the scene or of the imaging system's parameters is necessary. [DZB92]

plane projective transformation: The linear transformation between the coordinates of two projective planes, also known as homography. See also projective geometry, projective plane and projective transformation. [FP03:18.4.1]

plane sweeping: An algorithm where a plane is virtually swept across a 3D volume, processing data as it is encountered. The 2D version of this approach is called line sweeping. [GFM+07]

plenoptic camera: A camera that records the flow of light at all positions and in all directions. [WP:Lightfield_camera]

plenoptic function representation: A parameterized function for describing everything that is visible from a given point in space. A fundamental representation in image-based rendering. [FP03:26.3]

plenoptic sampling: Sampling of the light field function (i.e., the plenoptic function). Often this term additionally refers to the sampling of the surface and texture information in the scene. [CTCS00]

Plessey corner finder: A well-known corner detector also known as the Harris corner detector, based on the local autocorrelation of first-order image derivatives. See also feature extraction. [WP:Corner_detection#The_Harris_.26_Stephens_.2F_Plessey_.2F_Shi.E2.80.93Tomasi_corner_detection_algorithm]

Plücker line coordinates: A representation of lines in projective 3D space. A line is represented by six numbers $(l_{12}, l_{13}, l_{14}, l_{23}, l_{24}, l_{34})$ that must satisfy the constraint that $l_{12}l_{34} + l_{13}l_{24} + l_{14}l_{23} = 0$. The numbers are the entries of the *Plücker matrix*, **L**, for the line. For any two points A, B on the line, **L** is given by $l_{ij} = A_i B_j - B_i A_j$. The pencil of planes containing the line are the nullspace of **L**. The six numbers may also be seen as a pair of 3-vectors, one

a point $\vec{a}$ on the line, one the direction $\vec{n}$ with $\vec{a} \cdot \vec{n} = 0$. [Fau93:2.5.1]

PMS: See Pantone matching system. [WP:Pantone]

PnP problem: The perspective n point problem; Estimating camera pose from n known 2D to 2D point correspondences. [Sze10:6.2.1]

point: A primitive concept of Euclidean geometry, representing an infinitely small entity. In computer vision, pixels are regarded as image points and one speaks of "points in the scene" as positions in the 3D space observed by the cameras. [WP:Point_(geometry)]

point-based rendering: Methods for drawing an image based on point primitives which are 3D points rather than polygonal patches. [BK03]

point cloud: A set (usually large) of points in 3D space. [WP:Point_cloud]

point distribution model (PDM): A shape representation for flexible 2D contours. It is a type of deformable template model and its parameters can be learned by supervised learning. It is suitable for 2D shapes that undergo general but correlated deformations or variations, such as component motion or shape variation. For instance, fronto-parallel images of leaves, fish or human hands, resistors on a board, people walking in surveillance videos etc. The shape variations of the contour in a series of examples are captured by principal component analysis. See also active shape model. [WP:Point_distribution_model]

point feature: An image feature that occupies a very small portion of an image, ideally one pixel, and is therefore local in nature. Examples are corners (see corner detection) or edge pixels. Notice that, although point features occupy only one pixel, they require a neighborhood to be defined; e.g., an edge pixel is characterized by a sharp variation of image values in a small neighborhood of the pixel. [CMS95]

point invariant: A property that can be measured at a point in an image and is <u>invariant</u> to some transformation. For instance, the ratio of a pixel's observed intensity to that of its brightest neighbor is invariant to changes in illumination and the magnitude of the <u>gradient</u> of intensity at a point is invariant to translation and rotation. (Both of these examples assume ideal images and observation.) [MS04]

point light source: A point-like <u>light source</u>, typically radiating energy radially, whose intensity decreases as $\frac{1}{r^2}$, where r is the distance to the source. [FP03:5.2.2]

point matching: A class of algorithms solving <u>feature matching</u> or the <u>stereo correspondence problem</u> for <u>point features</u>. [Zha94]

point of extreme curvature: A point where the <u>curvature</u> achieves an extremum, i.e., a maximum or a minimum. The figure shows one of each type of extremum: [WP:Vertex_(geometry)]

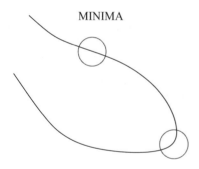

MINIMA

MAXIMA

point sampling: Selection of discrete points of data from a continuous signal. For example, a <u>digital camera</u> samples a continuous image function into a <u>digital image</u>. [WP:Sampling_(signal_processing)]

point similarity measure: A function measuring the similarity of image points (actually small neighborhoods to include sufficient information to characterize the image location), e.g., <u>cross correlation</u>, sum of absolute differences (SAD), or sum of squared differences (SSD). [JP73]

point source: A <u>point light source</u>. An ideal <u>illumination</u> source in which all light comes from a single spatial point. The alternative is an <u>extended light source</u>. The assumption of being a point source allows easier interpretation of <u>shading</u>, <u>shadows</u> etc. [FP03:5.2.2]

point spread function: The response of a 2D system or filter to an input Dirac impulse. The response is typically spread over a region surrounding the point of application of the impulse, hence the name. Analogous to the impulse response of a 1D system. See also <u>filter</u> and <u>linear filter</u>. [FP03:7.2.2]

Poisson distribution: A <u>discrete random variable</u> taking on the values $0, 1, 2, \ldots$ with probability mass function $p(x) = \frac{1}{x!}\lambda^x e^{-\lambda}$. λ is known as the rate parameter and $E[x] = \lambda$. [Was04:p. 27]

Poisson noise: Noise which has the form of a <u>Poisson distribution</u>, where the variance scales directly with the mean intensity. It can arise from CCD sensors.

| Original Image | Poisson Noise (enhanced) | Combined Image |

Poisson noise removal: The removal or attenuation of <u>Poisson noise</u>. [SHW93]

polar coordinates: A system of coordinates specifying the position of a point P in terms of the direction of the line through P and the origin, and the distance from P to the origin along that line. For example, the transformation between polar (r, θ) and Cartesian coordinates (x, y) in the plane is given by $x = r\cos\theta$ and $y = r\sin\theta$, or $r = \sqrt{x^2 + y^2}$ and $\theta = atan(\frac{y}{x})$. [BB82:A1.1.2]

polar harmonic transforms: Transformations that can be used to generate <u>rotation-invariant</u> features. [PXK10]

215

polar rectification: A rectification algorithm designed to cope with any camera geometry in the context of uncalibrated vision, re-parameterizing the images in polar coordinates around the epipoles. [PKG99]

polarization: The characterizing property of polarized light. [Hec87:Ch. 8]

polarized light: Unpolarized light results from the nondeterministic superposition of the x and y components of the electric field. Otherwise, light is said to be polarized and the tip of the electric field evolves on an ellipse (elliptically polarized light). Light is often partially polarized, that is, it can be regarded as the sum of completely polarized and completely unpolarized light. In computer vision, polarization analysis is an area of physics-based vision that has been used for metal–dielectric discrimination, surface reconstruction, fish classification, defect detection and structured light triangulation. [Hec87:Ch. 8]

polarizer: A device changing the state of polarization of light to a specific polarized state, e.g., producing linearly polarized light in a given plane. [Hec87:8.2]

Polya distribution: Another name for the negative binomial distribution. [WP:Negative_binomial_distribution]

polycurve: A simple curve C that is smooth everywhere but at a finite set of points and such that, given any point P on C, the tangent to C converges to a limit approaching P from each direction. Shape models in computer vision often describe boundary shapes using polycurve models consisting of a sequence of curved or straight

segments. See also polyline. The figure shows a polycurve with four circular arcs: [CF89]

polygon: A closed, piecewise linear, 2D contour. Squares and pentagons are examples of regular polygons, where all sides have equal length and all angles formed by contiguous sides are equal. This does not hold for a general polygon. [WP:Polygon]

polygon matching: A class of techniques for matching polygonal shapes. See polygon. [TVH05]

polygonal approximation: A polyline approximating a curve. The figure shows a circular arc (badly) approximated by a polyline: [BB82:8.2]

polyhedron: A 3D object with planar faces, a "3D polygon". A subset of $\mathbb{R}^3$ whose boundary is a subset of finitely many planes. The basic primitive of many 3D modeling schemes, as many hardware accelerators process polygons particularly quickly. A tetrahedron is the simplest polyhedron: [DH73:12.4]

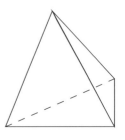

polyline: A piecewise linear contour. If closed, it becomes a polygon. See also polycurve, contour analysis and contour representation. [JKS95:6.4]

pose: The location and orientation of an object in a given reference frame, especially a world or camera reference frame. A classic problem of computer vision is pose estimation. [SQ04:4.2.2]

pose clustering: A class of algorithms solving the pose estimation problem using clustering techniques. See also clustering, pose and *k*-means clustering. [FP03:18.3]

pose consistency: An algorithm seeking to establish whether two shapes are equivalent. Given two sets of points G_1 and G_2, e.g., the algorithm finds a sufficient number of point correspondences to determine a transformation T between the two sets, then applies T to all other points of G_1. If the transformed points are close to points in G_2, consistency is satisfied. Also known as *viewpoint consistency*. See also feature point correspondence. [FP03:18.2]

pose determination: See pose estimation.

pose estimation: The problem of determining the orientation and translation of an object, especially a 3D one, from one or more images thereof. Often the term means finding the transformation that aligns a geometric model with the image data. Several techniques exist for this purpose. See also alignment, model registration, orientation representation and rotation representation. [WP:Pose_(computer_vision)#Pose_Estimation]

pose representation: The problem of representing the angular position, or pose, of an object (especially a 3D object) in a given reference frame. A common representation is the rotation matrix, which can be parameterized in different ways, e.g., Euler angles, pitch, yaw and roll angles, rotation angles around the coordinate axes, axis–angle curves and quaternions. See also orientation representation and rotation representation. [MGC96]

position: Location in space (either 2D or 3D). [WP:Position_(vector)]

position-dependent brightness correction: A technique seeking to counteract the brightness variation caused by a real imaging system, typically the fact that brightness decreases as one moves away from the optical axis in a lens system with finite aperture. This

effect may be noticeable only in the periphery of the image. See also lens. [SHB08:4.1.1]

position invariant: Any property that does not vary with position. For instance, the length of a 3D line segment is invariant to the line's position in 3D space, but the length of the line's projection on the image plane is not. See also invariant. [OAE95]

positron emission tomography (PET): A medical imaging method that can measure the concentration and movement of a positron-emitting isotope in living tissue. [Jai89:10.1]

postal code analysis: A set of image analysis techniques concerned with understanding written or printed postal codes. See handwritten character recognition and optical character recognition. [WP:Handwriting_recognition]

posterior distribution: A conditional probability distribution that describes the situation after some data or evidence has been observed. Contrast with the prior distribution. In a Bayesian statistical model, the posterior distribution $p(\theta|D, M)$ expresses the posterior uncertainty about the parameters θ in model M after the data D has been observed. See also *a posteriori* probability and Bayesian statistical model. [Bis06:1.2.3]

posterior probability: See posterior distribution.

posture analysis: A class of techniques aiming to estimate the posture of an articulated body, such as a human body (e.g., pointing, sitting, standing, crouching etc.). [WP:Motion_analysis# Applications]

potential field: A mathematical function that assigns some (usually scalar) value at every point in some space. In computer vision and robotics, this is usually a measure of some scalar property at each point of a 2D or 3D space or image, such as the distance from a structure. The representation is used in path planning, such that the potential at every point indicates, e.g., the ease or difficulty of getting to some destination. [DH73:5.11]

potential function: A real function with continuous partial second derivatives that satisfies Laplace's equation $\nabla^2 f = 0$; also known as a harmonic function. See also Laplacian. [Wei12:Harmonic Function]

power spectrum: In the context of computer vision, normally the amount of energy at each spatial frequency. The term could also refer to the amount of energy at each light frequency. Also called the "power spectrum density function" or "spectral density function". [Jai89:11.5]

precision: 1) The repeatability of the accuracy of a vision system (in general, of an instrument) over many measures carried out in the same conditions. Typically measured by the standard deviation of a target error measure. For instance, the precision of a vision system measuring linear size would be assessed by taking thousands of measurements of a perfectly known object and computing the standard deviation of the measurements. See also accuracy.
2) The number of significant bits in a floating point or double precision number that lie to the right of the decimal point. [WP:Accuracy_and_precision]

predictive compression method: A class of image compression algorithms using redundancy information, mostly correlation, to build an estimate of a pixel value from values of neighboring pixels. [WP:Linear_predictive_coding]

pre-processing: Operations on an image that, e.g., suppress some distortions or enhance some features. Examples include geometric transformations, edge detection, image restoration etc. There is no clear distinction between image pre-processing and image processing. [WP:Data_Pre-processing]

Prewitt gradient operator: An edge detection operator based on template matching. It applies a set of convolution masks, or kernels (see Prewitt kernel), implementing

matched filters for edges at various (generally eight) orientations. The magnitude (or strength) of the edge at a given pixel is the maximum of the responses to the masks. Some implementations use the sum of the absolute value of the responses from the horizontal and vertical masks. [JKS95:5.2.3]

Prewitt kernel: The horizontal and vertical masks used by the Prewitt gradient operator: [JKS95:5.2.3]

$$\begin{array}{|c|c|c|} \hline -1 & 0 & +1 \\ \hline -1 & 0 & +1 \\ \hline -1 & 0 & +1 \\ \hline \end{array} \qquad \begin{array}{|c|c|c|} \hline +1 & +1 & +1 \\ \hline 0 & 0 & 0 \\ \hline -1 & -1 & -1 \\ \hline \end{array}$$

Gx　　　　　　　　Gy

Prim's algorithm: An algorithm for finding the minimal spanning tree, in the sense of minimizing the weight of the edges, while still including every vertex. [Gib85:2.1.1]

primal sketch: A representation for early vision, introduced by Marr, focusing on low-level features, such as edges. The full primal sketch groups the information computed in the raw primal sketch (consisting largely of edge, bar, end and blob feature information extracted from the images), e.g., by forming subjective contours. See also Marr's theory, Marr–Hildreth edge detector and raw primal sketch. [Nev82:7.2]

primary color: A color coding scheme whereby a range of perceivable colors can be made by a weighted combination of primary colors. For example, color television and computer screens use light-emitting chemicals to produce the three primary colors (red, green and blue). The ability to use only three colors to generate all others arises from the tri-chromacy of the human eye, which has cones that respond to three different color spectral ranges. See also additive color and subtractive color. [Hec87:4.4]

principal component analysis (PCA): A statistical technique useful for reducing the dimensionality of data, at the basis of many computer vision techniques (e.g., point distribution models and eigenspace-based recognition). In essence, the deviation of a random vector, $\vec{x}$, from the population mean, μ, can be expressed as the product of $\mathbf{A}$, the matrix of eigenvectors of the covariance matrix of the population, and a vector y of projection weights:

$$\vec{y} = \mathbf{A}(\vec{x} - \vec{\mu})$$

so that

$$\vec{x} = \mathbf{A}^{-1}\vec{y} + \vec{\mu}$$

Usually only a subset of the components of $\vec{y}$ is sufficient to approximate $\vec{x}$. The elements of this subset correspond to the largest eigenvalues of the covariance matrix. See also Karhunen–Loève transformation. [FP03:22.3.1]

principal component basis space: In principal component analysis, the space generated by the basis formed by the eigenvectors, or eigendirections, of the covariance matrix. [WP:Principal_component_analysis]

principal component representation: See principal component analysis.

principal curvature: The maximum or minimum normal curvature at a surface point, achieved along a principal direction. The two principal curvatures and directions together completely specify the local surface shape. In the figure, the principal curvatures in the two directions at point X on the cylinder of radius r are 0 (along the axis) and $\frac{1}{r}$ (across the axis): [JKS95:13.3.2]

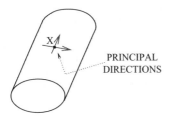

principal curvature sign class: See mean and Gaussian curvature shape classification.

principal direction: The direction in which the normal curvature achieves an extremum, that is, a principal curvature. The two principal curvatures and directions, together, specify completely the local surface shape. In the figure, the principal directions at point X on the cylinder are parallel to the axis and around the cylinder: [FP03:19.1.2]

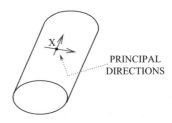

principal point: The point at which the optical axis of a pinhole camera model intersects the image plane: [JKS95:12.9]

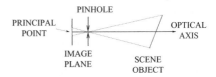

principal texture direction: An algorithm identifying the direction of a texture. A directional or oriented texture in a small image patch generates a peak in the Fourier transform. To determine the direction, the Fourier amplitude plot is regarded as a distribution of physical mass and the minimum-inertia axis is identified. [JS05]

prior distribution: A probability distribution that encodes an agent's beliefs about some uncertain quantity *before* some evidence or data is taken into account. For example in a Bayesian statistical model, the prior distribution $p(\theta|M)$ expresses the prior uncertainty about the parameters θ in model M. See also Bayesian statistical model. [Bis06:1.2.3]

prior domain knowledge: Information about the scenario or class of objects known in advance. See also *a priori probability*.

privileged viewpoint: A viewpoint where small motions cause image features to appear or disappear. This contrasts with a generic viewpoint. [Cow83]

probabilistic causal model: A representation used in artificial intelligence for causal models. The simplest causal model is a *causal graph*, in essence an acyclic graph in which nodes represent variables and directed arcs represent cause and effect. A probabilistic causal model is a causal graph with the probability distribution of each variable conditional to its causes. See also probabilistic graphical model. [PR87]

probabilistic data association: A form of data association for the tracking problem where all of the candidate observations for association to a track are combined in a single weighted sum. [FP03:17.4]

probabilistic distribution: See probability distribution.

probabilistic graphical model: A graphical model that defines a joint probability distribution over a set of random variables. The graphical structure encodes conditional independence relationships. There are two main types of probabilistic graphical model in common use, the directed graphical model (also known as a Bayesian network) and the undirected graphical model (also known as a Markov random field). [Bis06:Ch. 8]

probabilistic Hough transform: Computes an approximation to the Hough transform by using only a percentage of the image data. The goal is to reduce the computational cost of the standard Hough transform. A threshold effect has been observed: if the percentage sampled is above the threshold level then few false positives are detected. [WP:Randomized_Hough_Transform]

probabilistic inference: Given a joint probability distribution over a set of random variables and knowledge of the values of some set of variables e (the evidence), probabilistic inference is concerned with the conditional distribution of (a subset of) the remaining variables x, i.e., $p(x|e)$. If x has large cardinality then it will make sense to focus on summaries of $p(x|e)$; common choices are the posterior marginal distribution of each variable in the set x, or the maximum *a posteriori* probability configuration of $p(x|e)$. In a probabilistic graphical model, such summaries can often be computed via a message-passing process such as belief propagation. [Mur12:6.5]

probabilistic latent semantic analysis (PLSA): Usually described in relation to a set of documents and the words they contain. For computer vision, this could be translated to a set of images, each of which is described by a bag of features. PLSA models the distribution of words in a document in terms of the proportions of a smaller number of topics. PLSA is related to latent Dirichlet allocation but uses a point estimate over the proportions for each document rather than a Dirichlet prior. Simply applying principal component analysis to the words × documents matrix is known as latent semantic analysis; PLSA provides a better model for such data, taking into account constraints such as the non-negativity of word counts. See also topic model. [Mur12:24.2]

probabilistic model learning: The process of parameter estimation in a statistical model or model selection over a number of models. See also statistical learning. [Bis06:pp. 1–4]

probabilistic principal component analysis: A technique defining a probability model for principal component analysis (PCA). The original data is modeled as being generated by the reduced-dimensionality subspace typical of PCA plus Gaussian noise. The model can be extended to a mixture model, trained using the expectation maximization (EM) algorithm. Probabilistic PCA is a special case of factor analysis. [Bis06:12.2]

probabilistic relaxation: A method of data interpretation in which local inconsistencies act as inhibitors and local consistencies act as excitors. The hope is that the combination of these two influences constrains the probabilities. [CKP95]

probabilistic relaxation labeling: An extension of relaxation labeling in which each entity to be labeled, e.g., each image feature, is not simply assigned to a label, but to a set of probabilities, each giving the probability that the feature could be assigned a specific label. See also belief propagation. [BM02:2.9]

probability: A measure of the confidence one may have in the occurrence of an event, on a scale from 0 (impossible) to 1 (certain). The interpretation of probability is a subject of intense debate; we focus on two prominent theories. The *frequentist* interpretation defines probabilities as limiting proportions in an infinite ensemble of experiments. For instance, the probability of getting any number from a dice in a single throw is $\frac{1}{6}$. The *subjectivist* view regards probability as a subjective degree of belief, which need not involve random variables; e.g., one can hold a degree of belief in the statement "Shakespeare's plays were written by Francis Bacon". Degrees of belief can be mapped onto the rules of probability if they satisfy certain consistency rules known as the Cox axioms. [Mac03:2.2].

probability density: See probability density function.

probability density estimation: A class of techniques for estimating the density function or its parameters given a sample from a population. A related problem is testing whether a particular sample has been generated by a process characterized by a particular probability distribution. Two common tests are the *goodness-of-fit* test and the *Kolmogorov-Smirnov* test. The former is a parametric test best used with large samples; the latter gives good results with smaller samples, but is a non-parametric test and,

as such, does not produce estimates of the population parameters. See also non-parametric method. [Nal93:A2.2]

probability density function: For a continuous random variable X, the probability density function $p(x)$ is the derivative of the cumulative distribution function $F(x)$ so that $p(x) = dF(x)/dx$, and $F(x) = \int_{-\infty}^{x} p(x) \, dx$. If Δx is small, then $\text{Pr}(x \leq X \leq x + \Delta x) \simeq p(x)\Delta x$. This definition can be extended to vector-valued random variables. [Bis06:1.2.1]

probability distribution: A normalized statistical distribution described with probabilistic likelihoods for the occurrence of each possible outcome for a given variable over a number of trials. See also expectation value.

probe data: Data acquired by remote sensing or parameters (such as location) describing remote sensing.

probe image: 1) An image acquired by remote sensing, such as by an endoscope. Such images usually exhibit high levels of geometric distortion. 2) An image used to interrogate an image dataset. [SKI+00]

probe pattern: A pattern of projected light from a probe that can be used to assess depth from defocus.

probe set: A set of data used to search a dataset for a match. [PMRR00]

probe video: 1) A video taken using remote sensing. See probe image. 2) A video to be used for the retrieval of some object or video within a known dataset. [ZKC03]

procedural representation: A class of representations used in artificial intelligence to encode how to perform a task (procedural knowledge). A classic example is the production system. In contrast, *declarative representations* encode how an entity is structured. [Sch89:Ch. 7]

Procrustes analysis: A method for comparing two data sets through the minimization of squared errors, by translation, rotation and scaling. [WP:Procrustes_analysis]

Procrustes average: Procrustes analysis aligns a pair of shapes and defines a Procrustes distance between the two shapes. Given a set of shapes, one can find a reference shape that minimizes the Procrustes distance between each shape and the reference shape. This reference shape is the Procrustes average. [WP:Generalized_Procrustes_analysis]

production system: 1) An approach to computerized logical reasoning, whereby the logic is represented as a set of "production rules". A rule is of the form "LHS→RHS". This states that if the pattern or set of conditions encoded in the left-hand side (LHS) are true or hold, then do the actions specified in the right-hand side (RHS), which may simply be the assertion of some conclusion. A sample rule might be "If the number of detected edge fragments is less than 10, then decrease the threshold by 10%".
2) An industrial system that manufactures some product.
3) A system that is to be used, as compared to a demonstration system. [Sch89:Ch. 7]

profiles: A shape signature for image regions, specifying the number of pixels in each column (vertical profile) or row (horizontal profile). Used in pattern recognition. See also shape and shape representation. [SOS00:4.9.2]

progressive image transmission: A method of transmitting an image in which a low-resolution version is first transmitted, followed by details that allow progressively higher resolution versions to be recreated: [SGL92]

FIRST IMAGE   BETTER IMAGE   BEST IMAGE

progressive scan camera: A camera that transfers an entire image in the order of left-to-right, top-to-bottom,

without the alternate line interlaced scanning used in television standards. This is much more convenient for machine vision and other computer-based applications. [WP:Digital_video#Technical_overview]

projection: 1) The transformation of a geometric structure from one space to another, e.g., the projection of a 3D point onto the nearest point in a given plane. The projection may be specified by a linear function, i.e., for all points $\vec{p}$ in the initial structure, the points $\vec{p}'$ in the projected structure are given by $\vec{p}' = \mathbf{M}\vec{p}$ for some matrix $\mathbf{M}$. Alternatively, the projection need not be linear, e.g., $\vec{p}' = \vec{f}(\vec{p})$.
2) The specific case of projection of a scene that creates an image on a plane by use of, e.g., a perspective camera, according to the rules of perspective. [Nal93:2.1]

projection matrix: The matrix transforming the homogeneous projective coordinates of a 3D scene point $(x, y, z, 1)$ into the pixel coordinates $(u, v, 1)$ of the point's image in a pinhole camera. It can be factored as the product of the two matrices of the intrinsic parameters and extrinsic parameters. See also camera coordinates, image coordinates and scene coordinates. [FP03:2.2–2.3]

projective geometry: A field of geometry dealing with projective spaces and their properties. A projective geometry is one where only properties preserved by projective transformations are defined. Projective geometry provides a convenient and elegant theory to model the geometry of the common perspective camera. Most notably, the perspective projection equations become linear. [FP03:13.1]

projective invariant: A property, say I, that is not affected by a projective transformation. More specifically, assume an invariant, $I(\vec{P})$, of a geometric structure described by a parameter vector $\vec{P}$. When the structure is subject to a projective transformation ($\mathbf{M}$) this gives a structure with parameter vector $\vec{p}$, and $I(\vec{P}) =$

$I(\vec{p})$. The most fundamental projective invariant is the cross ratio. In some applications, invariants of weight w occur, which transform as $I(\vec{p}) = I(\vec{P})(\det \mathbf{M})^w$. [TV98:10.3.2]

projective plane: A plane, usually denoted by P^2, on which a projective geometry is defined. [TV98:A.4]

projective reconstruction: The problem of reconstructing the geometry of a scene from a set or sequence of images in a projective space. The transformation from projective to Euclidean coordinates is easy if the Euclidean coordinates of the five points in a projective basis are known. See also projective geometry and projective stereo vision. [WP:Fundamental_matrix_(computer_vision)#Projective_Reconstruction_Theorem]

projective space: A space of $(n+1)$-dimensional vectors, usually denoted by P^n, on which a projective geometry is defined. [FP03:13.1.1]

projective stereo vision: A class of stereo algorithms based on projective geometry. Key concepts expressed elegantly by the projective framework are epipolar geometry, fundamental matrix and projective reconstruction. [LZ99]

projective stratum: A layer in the stratification of 3D geometries. Moving from the simplest to the most complex, we have the projective, affine, metric and Euclidean strata. See also projective geometry and projective reconstruction. [Fau95]

projective transformation: Also known as "projectivity", from one projective plane to another. It can be represented by a non-singular 3×3 matrix acting on homogeneous coordinates. The transformation has eight degrees of freedom, as only the ratio of projective coordinates is significant. [FP03:2.1.2]

property-based matching: The process of comparing two entities (e.g., image features or patterns) using their properties, e.g., the moments of a region. See also classification, boundary property and metric property. [RC96]

property learning: A class of algorithms aiming at learning and characterizing attributes of spatio-temporal patterns. For example, learning the color and texture distributions that differentiate beween normal and cancerous cells. See also boundary property, metric property, unsupervised learning and supervised learning. [WP:Supervised_learning]

prototype: An object or model serving as a representative example for a class, capturing the defining characteristics of the class. [WP:Prototype]

proximity matrix: A matrix $\mathbf{M}$ occurring in cluster analysis. $\mathbf{M}(i, j)$ denotes the distance (e.g., the Hamming distance) between e.g., clusters i and j. [SL90]

pseudocolor: A way of assigning a color to pixels that is based on an interpretation of the data rather than the original scene color. The usual purpose of pseudocoloring is to label image pixels in a useful manner. For example, one common pseudocoloring assigns different colors according to the local surface shape class. A pseudocoloring scheme for aerial or satellite images of the earth assigns colors according to the land type, such as water, forest, wheat field etc. [JKS95:7.7]

PSF: See point spread function.

psychophysics: A field of study that considers the relationship between human (or other organism) perceptions and the physical stimuli which cause them. [Pal99:4.2]

PTZ: See pan–tilt–zoom.

purposive perception: Perception which is motivated directly by the purpose of the agent. For example a robot may need to search for a particular landmark to accomplish self-localization. [BC92]

purposive vision: An area of computer vision linking perception with purposive action; that is, modifying the position or parameters of an imaging system purposively, so that a visual task is facilitated or made possible. Examples include changing the lens parameters to obtain information about depth, as in depth from defocus, or moving around an object to achieve full shape information. [Alo90]

pyramid: A representation of an image including information at several spatial scales. The pyramid is constructed by the original image (maximum resolution) and a scale operator that reduces the content of the image (e.g., a Gaussian filter) by discarding details at coarser scales:

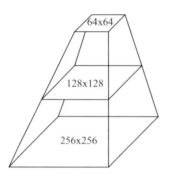

Applying the operator and subsampling the resulting image leads to the next (lower-resolution) level of the pyramid. See also scale space, image pyramid, Gaussian pyramid, Laplacian pyramid and pyramid transform. [JKS95:3.3.2]

pyramid architecture: A computer architecture supporting pyramid-based processing, typically occurring in the context of multi-scale processing. See also scale space, pyramid, image pyramid, Laplacian pyramid and Gaussian pyramid. [JKS95:3.3.2]

pyramid transform: An operator for building a pyramid from an image. See pyramid, image pyramid, Laplacian pyramid and Gaussian pyramid. [JKS95:3.3.2]

pyramid vector quantization: A fast method of implementing vector quantization based on a set of lattice points that fall on a hyperpyramid. [GG92:p. 465]

Q

QBIC: See query by image content. [WP:Content-based_image_retrieval# Other_query_methods]

quadratic form: A quadratic form is a homogeneous polynomial of degree two in a number of variables. Given a vector of d real variables $\vec{x} = (x_1, \ldots, x_d)^\top$, a $d \times d$ real matrix A defines a quadratic form in $\vec{x}$ as $Q(\vec{x}) = \vec{x}^\top A \vec{x}$. [Nob69:12.2]

quadratic variation: 1) Any function (here, expressing a variation of some variables) that can be modeled by a quadratic polynomial. 2) The specific measure of surface shape deformation $f_{xx}^2 + 2f_{xy}^2 + f_{yy}^2$ of a surface $f(x, y)$. This measure has been used to constrain the smoothness of reconstructed surfaces. [Hor86:8.2]

quadrature mirror filter: A class of filters occurring in wavelet and image compression filtering theory. The filter splits a signal into a high pass component and a low pass component, with the low pass component's transfer function a mirror image of that of the high pass component. [WP:Quadrature_mirror_filter]

quadric: A surface defined by a second-order polynomial. See also conic. [FP03:2.1.1]

quadric patch: A quadric surface defined over a finite region of the independent variables or parameters; e.g., in range image analysis, a part of a range surface that is well approximated by a quadric (e.g., an elliptical patch). [WP:Quadric]

quadric patch extraction: A class of algorithms aiming to identify the portions of a surface that are well approximated by quadric patches. Techniques are similar to those applied for conic fitting. See also surface fitting and least square surface fitting. [FFE97]

quadrifocal tensor: An algebraic constraint imposed on quadruples of corresponding points by the geometry of four simultaneous views, analogous to the epipolar constraint for the two-camera case and to the trifocal tensor for the three-camera case. See also stereo correspondence and epipolar geometry. [FP03:10.3]

quadrilinear constraint: The geometric constraint on four views of a point (i.e., the intersection of four epipolar lines). See also epipolar constraint and trilinear constraint. [FP03:10.3]

quadtree: A hierarchical structure representing 2D image regions, in which each node represents a region, and the whole image is the root of the tree. Each non-leaf node, representing a region R, has four children, that represent the four subregions into which R is divided:

Dictionary of Computer Vision and Image Processing, Second Edition.
R. B. Fisher, T. P. Breckon, K. Dawson-Howe, A. Fitzgibbon, C. Robertson, E. Trucco and C. K. I. Williams.
© 2014 John Wiley & Sons, Ltd. Published 2014 by John Wiley & Sons, Ltd.

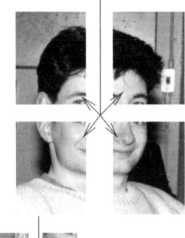

Suggested in the framework of computational theories of human vision. [Nal93:10]

quantization: See spatial quantization.

quantization error: The approximation error created by the quantization of a continuous variable, typically using a regularly spaced scale of values. The figure shows a continuous function (dashed) and its quantized version (solid line) using six values only:

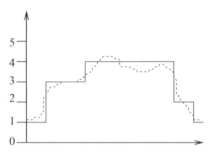

The quantization error is the vertical distance between the two curves. For instance, the intensity values in a digital image can only take on a certain number of discrete values (often 256). See also sampling theorem and Nyquist sampling rate. [SQ04:4.2.1]

quantization noise: See quantization error.

quasi-affine reconstruction: A projective reconstruction with an additional constraint that the plane at infinity is not split. This is an intermediate level between projective reconstruction and affine reconstruction. [Nis01]

quasi-invariant: An approximation of an invariant. For instance, quasi-invariant parameterizations of image curves have been built by approximating the invariant arc length with lower spatial derivatives. [WP:Quasi-invariant_measure]

Hierarchical subdivision continues until the remaining regions have constant properties. Quadtrees can be used to create a compressed image structure. The 3D extension of a quadtree is the octree. [SQ04:5.9.1]

qualitative vision: A paradigm based on the idea that many perceptual tasks could be better accomplished by computing only qualitative descriptions of objects and scenes from images, as opposed to quantitative information, such as accurate measurements.

quaternion: A forerunner of the modern vector concept, invented by Hamilton, used in vision to represent rotations. Any 3D-rotation matrix, $\mathbf{R}$, can be parameterized by a vector of four numbers, $\vec{q} = (q_0, q_1, q_2, q_3)$ where $\sum_{k=0}^{3} q_k^2 = 1$, that uniquely define the rotation. A rotation has two representations, $\vec{q}$ and $-\vec{q}$. See rotation matrix for alternative representations of rotations. [FP03:21.3.1]

query by image content (QBIC): A class of techniques for selecting members from a database of images by using examples of the desired image content (as opposed to textual search). Examples of contents include color, shape, and texture. See also image database indexing. [WP:Content-based_image_retrieval#Other_query_methods]

R

R–S curve: A contour representation giving the distance, r, of each point of the contour from an origin, chosen arbitrarily, as a function of the arc length, s. Allows rotation-invariant comparison of contour. See also contour, shape representation: [SHLW89]

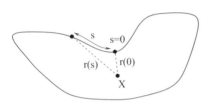

radar: An active sensor detecting the presence of distant objects. A narrow beam of very high-frequency radio pulses is transmitted and reflected by a target back to the transmitter. The direction of the reflected beam and the time of flight of the pulse determine the target's position. See also time-of-flight range sensor. [TV98:2.5.2]

radial basis function (RBF): A function whose value depends only on the radial distance of the input $\vec{x}$ from some center $\vec{c}$, i.e., $\phi(\vec{x}) = \phi(\|\vec{x} - \vec{c}\|)$. Typically Euclidean distance is used, and a very common choice for the radial function is $\phi(r) = e^{-\beta r^2}$ (for some positive constant β). [Bis06:6.3]

radial basis function network: A neural network composed of radial basis function units. It is used for supervised learning problems and maps input data $\vec{x}$ to a space of outputs $\vec{y}$. The standard RBF network architecture has a hidden layer of RBF units connected to the input $\vec{x}$; the number of units in this layer is arbitrary. The outputs of these hidden units are then connected to the output layer by a matrix of parameters (weights), optionally with an additional nonlinearity. One common way of specifying the centers in the RBF network is to randomly select a subset of the data points. [Bis06:6.3]

radial lens distortion: A type of geometric distortion introduced by a real lens. The effect is to shift the position of each image point, p, away from its true position along the line through the image center and p. See also lens, lens distortion, barrel distortion, tangential distortion, pincushion distortion and distortion coefficient. This figure shows the typical deformations of a square (exaggerated): [FP03:3.3]

radiance: The amount of light (radiating energy) leaving a surface. The light can be generated by the surface itself, as in a light source, or reflected by it. The surface can be real (e.g., a wall) or imaginary (e.g., an infinite plane). See also irradiance and radiometry. [FP03:4.1.3]

radiance map: A map of radiance for a scene. Sometimes used to refer to a high dynamic range image. [FP03:4.1.3]

radiant flux: The radiant energy per time unit; that is, the amount of energy transmitted or absorbed per time unit. See also radiance, irradiance and radiometry. [Hec87:3.3.1]

Dictionary of Computer Vision and Image Processing, Second Edition.
R. B. Fisher, T. P. Breckon, K. Dawson-Howe, A. Fitzgibbon, C. Robertson, E. Trucco and C. K. I. Williams.
© 2014 John Wiley & Sons, Ltd. Published 2014 by John Wiley & Sons, Ltd.

radiant intensity: See radiant flux.

radiation: 1) Any form of emission in the electromagnetic spectrum. 2) Emissions given off by radioactive materials, which could include electromagnetic emissions (i.e., gamma ray photons). [WP:Radiation]

radiometric calibration: A process seeking to estimate radiance from pixel values. The rationale for radiometric calibration is that the light entering a real camera (the radiance) is, in general, altered by the camera itself. A simple calibration model is $E(i, j) = g(i, j)I + o(i, j)$, where, for each pixel (i, j), E is the radiance to estimate, I is the measured intensity, and g and o are a pixel-specific gain and offset to be calibrated. Ground truth values for E can be measured using a *photometer* (see photometry). [WP:Radiometric_calibration]

radiometric response function: A function that defines how recorded irradiance values are transformed into intensity values within an imaging device. [LZ05]

radiometry: The measurement of optical radiation, i.e., electromagnetic radiation between 3×10^{11} and 3×10^{16} Hz (wavelengths between 0.01 and 1000μm). This includes ultraviolet, visible and infrared radiation. Common units encountered are $\frac{watts}{m^2}$ and $\frac{photons}{sec-steradian}$. Compare with photometry, which is the measurement of visible light. [FP03:4.1]

radius vector function: A contour or boundary representation based about a point $\vec{c}$ in the center of the figure (usually the center of gravity or a physically meaningful point). The representation then records the distance $r(\theta)$ from $\vec{c}$

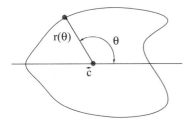

to points on the boundary, as a function of θ, which is the angle between the direction and some reference direction. The representation has problems when the vector at angle θ intersects the boundary more than once: [Kin03]

Radon transform: A transformation mapping an image into a parameter space highlighting the presence of lines. It can be regarded as an extension of the Hough transform. One definition is

$$g(\rho, \theta) =$$

$$\iint I(x, y)\delta(\rho - x\cos\theta - y\sin\theta)dxdy$$

where $I(x, y)$ is the image (gray values) and $\rho = x\cos\theta + y\sin\theta$ is a parametric line in the image. Lines are identified by peaks in the ρ, θ space. See also Hough transform line finder. [Jai89:10.2]

RAG: See region adjacency graph.

random access camera: A camera characterized by the possibility of accessing any image location directly, unlike a sequential scan camera, in which image values are transmitted in a standard order. [GAHK91]

random dot stereogram: A stereo pair formed by one random dot image (that is, a binary image in which each pixel is assigned to black or white at random) and a second image that is derived from the first. The figure shows an example in which a central square is shifted horizontally:

Looking cross-eyed at close distance, you should perceive a strong 3D effect. See also stereo and stereo vision. [Nal93:7.1]

random forest: An example of ensemble learning where a classifier is made up of many decision trees.

Diversity between the decision trees is obtained by training on random subsets of the training set or by the random selection of features. The overall classification result for a given example is obtained by bagging over the set of learned decision trees. [HTF08:Ch. 15]

random process: See stochastic process.

random sample consensus: See RANSAC.

random variable: A scalar or a vector variable that takes on a random value. The set of possible values may be describable by a standard distribution, such as Gaussian distribution, Gaussian mixture model, uniform distribution or Poisson distribution. [Nal93:A2.2]

randomized Hough transform: A variation of the standard Hough transform designed to produce higher accuracy with less computational effort. The line-finding variant of the algorithm selects pairs of image edge points randomly and increments the accumulator cell corresponding to the line through these two points. The selection process is repeated a fixed number of times. [WP:Randomized_Hough_Transform]

range compression: Reducing the dynamic range of an image to enhance the appearance of the image. This is often needed for images resulting from the magnitude of the Fourier transform which might have pixels with both large and very low values. Without range compression, it is hard to see the structure in the pixels with low values. In the figure, you can see (left) the magnitude of a 2D Fourier transform with a single bright spot in the middle and (right) the logarithm of that image, revealing more details: [Jai89:7.2]

range data: A representation of the spatial distribution of a set of 3D points. The data is often acquired by stereo vision or by a range sensor. In computer vision, range data are often represented as a *cloud of points*, i.e., a set of triplets representing the X, Y, Z coordinate of each point, or as range images, also known as *moiré* patches. The figure shows a range image of an industrial part, where brighter pixels are closer: [TV98:2.5]

range data fusion: The merging of multiple sets of range data, especially for the purpose of extending the portion of an object's surface described by the range data, or increasing the accuracy of measurements by exploiting the redundancy of multiple measures available for each point of the surface area. See also information fusion, fusion, sensor fusion. [Haa94]

range data integration: See range data fusion.

range data registration: See registration.

range data segmentation: A class of techniques partitioning range data into a set of regions. For instance, HK segmentation produces a set of surface patches. In the figure, the plane, cylinder and spherical patches on the right have been extracted from the range image on the left. See also surface segmentation: [Nev82:9.3]

range edge: See surface shape discontinuity.

range flow: A class of algorithms for the measurement of motion in time-varying range data, made possible by the evolution of fast range sensors. See also optical flow. [YBBR93]

range image: A representation of range data as an image. The pixel coordinates are related to the spatial position of each point on the range surface and the pixel value represents the distance of the surface point from the sensor (or from an arbitrary, fixed background). The figure shows a range image of a face, in which darker pixels are closer: [JKS95:11.4]

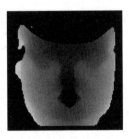

range image edge detector: An edge detector working on range images. Typically, edges occur where depths or surface normal directions (fold edges) change rapidly. See also edge detection and range images. In the figure, the depth and fold edges on the right have been extracted from the range image on the left: [JB99]

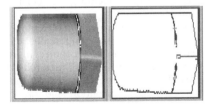

range sensor: Any sensor acquiring range data. The most popular range sensors in computer vision are based on optical and acoustic technologies. A laser range sensor often uses structured light triangulation. A time-of-flight range sensor measures the round-trip time of an acoustic or optical pulse. See also depth estimation. The figure shows a triangulation range sensor: [TV98:2.5.2]

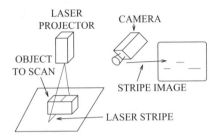

rank-based gradient estimation: Estimation of the gradient value (rate of change) in the presence of noise through the use of an ordered list of local data points.

rank order filtering: A class of filters the output of which depends on an ordering (ranking) of the pixels within the region of support. The classic example is the median filter which selects the middle value of the set of input values. More generally, the filter selects the kth largest value in the input set. [SB11:4.4.3] [AFP91]

RankBoost: A pairwise method for addressing the ranking problem using the boosting method. [FISS03]

ranking function: Any function that solves the ranking problem. [SC04:8.1]

ranking problem: The problem of determining the order (or rank) of a number of items. [SC04:8.1]

rank support vector machine (SVM): A pairwise method for addressing the ranking problem using a support vector machine. See also support vector ranking. [SC04:8.1]

RANSAC: Acronym from *random sample consensus*, a robust estimator seeking to counter the effect of outliers in data used, e.g., in a least square estimation problem. In essence, RANSAC considers a number of data subsets of the minimum size necessary to solve the problem (e.g., a parametric surface fit), then looks for statistical agreement of the results. See also least median of squares estimation, M-estimation and outlier rejection. [FP03:15.5.2]

raster scan: A "raster" is the region of a monitor, e.g., a cathode ray tube (CRT) or a liquid crystal display (LCD), capable of rendering images. In a CRT, the raster is a sequence of horizontal lines that are scanned rapidly with an electron beam from left to right and top to bottom, largely in the same way as a TV picture tube is scanned. In an LCD, the raster (usually called a "grid") covers the whole device area and image elements are displayed individually. [Low91:4.2]

rate distortion: A statistical method useful in analog-to-digital conversion. It determines the minimum number of bits required to encode data while tolerating a given level of distortion or the amount of distortion created by using a given number of bits. [Jai89:2.13]

rate-distortion function: The number of bits per sample (the rate R_d) to encode an analog image (or other signal) value given the allowable distortion D (or mean square of the error). Also needed is the variance σ^2 of the input value (assuming it is a Gaussian random variable). Then $R_d = max(0, \frac{1}{2}log_2(\frac{\sigma^2}{D}))$. [Jai89:2.13]

rate invariant action recognition: The recognition of actions regardless of the speed at which they are performed. See action recognition. [VSRC09]

raw primal sketch: The first representation built in the perception process according to Marr's theory of vision, heavily based on detection of local edge features. It represents the location, orientation, contrast and scale of center–surround, edge, bar and truncated bar features. See also primal sketch. [MH80]

RBC: See recognition by components.

real-time processing: Any computation performed within the time limits imposed by a given process. For example, in visual servoing a tracking system feeds positional data to a control algorithm generating control signals; if the control signals are generated too slowly, the whole system may become unstable. Different processes can impose very different constraints for real-time processing. When processing video-stream data, "real time" means complete processing of one frame of data in the time before the next frame is acquired (possibly with several frames lag time, as in pipeline parallelism). [WP:Real-time_computing]

receiver operating curve (ROC): A diagram showing the performance of a classifier. It plots the number or percentage of true positives against the number or percentage of false positives as one varies some parameter of the classifier. See also performance characterization, test set and classification. [FP03:22.2.1]

receptive field: 1) The retinal area generating the response to a photostimulus. The main cells responsible for visual perception in the retina are the *rods* and the *cones*, active in high- and low-intensity situations respectively. 2) The region of visual space giving rise to photopic response. 3) The region of an image that is input to the calculation of each output value. (See region of support.) [FP03:1.3]

recognition: See identification.

recognition by components (RBC): 1) A theory of human image understanding devised by Biederman. The foundation is a set of 3D shape primitives called geons, reminiscent of Marr's generalized cones. Different combinations of geons yield a large variety of 3D shapes, including articulated objects. 2) The recognition of a complex object by recognizing subcomponents and combining them to recognize more complex objects. See also hierarchical matching, shape representation, model-based recognition and object recognition. [WP:Recognition-by-components_theory]

recognition by parts: See recognition by components. [WP:Object_recognition_(computer_vision)]

recognition by structural decomposition: See recognition by components.

reconstruction: The problem of computing the shape of a 3D object or surface from one or more intensity sensors or range images. Typical techniques include model acquisition and the many shape from X methods reported (see shape from contour and following entries). [TV98:7.4]

reconstruction error: Inaccuracies in a model when compared to reality, caused by inaccurate sensing or compression. See lossy compression. [WP:3D_reconstruction_from_multiple_images#Algebraic_vs_geometric_error]

rectification: A technique warping two images into some form of geometric alignment, e.g., so that the vertical pixel coordinates of corresponding points are equal. See also stereo image rectification. The figure shows a stereo pair (top) and its rectified version (bottom), highlighting some of the scanlines where corresponding image features lie: [JKS95:12.5]

recursive region growing: A class of recursive algorithms for region growing. An initial pixel is chosen and its neighboring pixels are explored (the neighbors are determined by an adjacency rule, e.g., 8-adjacency). If any pixel meets the criteria for addition to the region, the growing procedure is called recursively on that pixel. The process continues until all connected image pixels have been examined. See also adjacency, image connectedness, neighborhood and recursive splitting. [SQ04:8.3.1]

recursive splitting: A class of recursive algorithms for region segmentation (dividing an image into a region set). The region set is initialized to the whole image. A homogeneity criterion is then applied; if not satisfied, the image is split according to a given scheme (e.g., into four sub-images, as in a quadtree), leading to a new region set. The procedure is applied recursively to all regions in the new region set, until all remaining regions are homogeneous. See also region segmentation, region-based segmentation and recursive region growing. [Nev82:8.1.1]

reference frame transformation: See coordinate system transformation. [WP:Rotating_reference_frame]

reference image: An image of a known scene or of a scene at a particular time used for comparison with a current image. See, e.g., change detection. [SSB06]

reference plane: An arbitrary plane to which all other planes may be compared. [RC02]

reference views: In iconic recognition, the views chosen as most representative for a 3D object. See also eigenspace-based recognition and characteristic view. [WS00]

reference white: A sample image value which corresponds to a known white object. The knowledge of such a value facilitates white balance correction. [WP:White_point]

reflectance: The ratio of reflected to incident flux; in other words, the ratio of reflected to incident (light) power. See also bidirectional reflectance distribution function. [JKS95:9.1.2]

reflectance estimation: A class of techniques for estimating the bidirectional reflectance distribution function (BDRF). Used notably within the techniques for shape from shading and image-based rendering, which seek to render arbitrary images of scenes from video material – all information about geometry and photometry (e.g., the BDRF) is derived from video. See also physics-based vision. [FP03:4.2.2]

reflectance map: The reflectance map expresses the reflectance of a material in terms of a viewer-centered represen-tation of local surface orientation. The most commonly used is the Lambertian reflectance map, based on Lambert's law. See also shape from shading, photometric stereo. [JKS95:9.3]

reflectance model: A model that represents how light is reflected by a material. See also Lambertian surface, Oren–Nayar model and Phong reflectance model. [Sze10:2.2.2]

reflectance ratio: A photometric invariant used for segmentation and recognition. It is based on the obser-vation that the illumination on both sides of a reflectance or color edge is nearly the same. So, although we cannot factor out the reflectance and illumination from only the observed lightness, the ratio of the lightnesses on either side of the edge equals the ratio of the reflectances, independent of illumination. The ratio is thus invariant to illumination and local surface geometry for a significant class of reflectance maps. See also invariant and physics-based vision. [NB93]

reflection: 1) A mathematical transfor-mation where the output image is the input image flipped about a given trans-formation line in the image plane. See reflection operator.
2) An optics phenomenon whereby all light incident on a surface is deflected away, without absorption, diffusion or scattering. An ideal mirror is the per-fect reflecting surface. Given a single ray of light incident on a reflecting surface, the angle of incidence equals the angle of reflection, as shown in the figure. See also specular reflection. [WP:Reflection_(physics)]

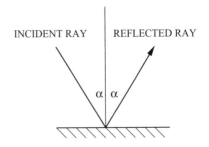

reflection operator: A linear transfor-mation that intuitively changes each vector or point of a given space to its mirror image:

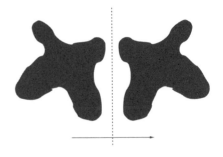

The transformation corresponding matrix, **H**, has the property $\mathbf{HH} = \mathbf{I}$, i.e., $\mathbf{H}^{-1} = \mathbf{H}$: a reflection matrix is its own inverse. See also rotation. [SP89]

refraction: An optical phenomenon whereby a ray of light is deflected while passing through different optical media, e.g., from air to water:

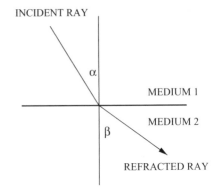

The amount of deflection is governed by the difference between the refraction indices of the two media, according to Snell's law:

$$\frac{n_1}{sin(\alpha_1)} = \frac{n_2}{sin(\alpha_2)}$$

where n_1 and n_2 are the refraction indices of the two media and α_1 and α_2 are the respective refraction angles. [Hec87:4.1]

region: A connected part of an image, usually homogeneous with respect to a given criterion. [BB82:5.1]

region adjacency graph (RAG): A graph expressing the adjacency relations among image regions, e.g., generated by a segmentation algorithm. See also region segmentation and region-based segmentation. In the figure, the adjacency relations of the regions on the left are encoded in the RAG on the right: [JKS95:3.3.4]

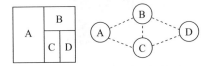

region-based active contours: An active contour model where (one of) the energy functions is based on local region energies. [CV01]

region-based segmentation: A class of segmentation techniques producing a number of image regions, typically on the basis of a given homogeneity criterion. For instance, intensity image regions can be homogeneous by color (see color image segmentation) or texture properties (see texture field segmentation); range image regions can be homogeneous by shape or curvature properties (see HK segmentation). [JKS95:3.2]

region boundary extraction: The problem of computing the boundary of a region, e.g., the contour of a region in an intensity image after color image segmentation. [PY09]

region decomposition: A class of algorithms aiming to partition an image or region thereof into regions.

See also region-based segmentation. [JKS95:3.2]

region descriptor: 1) One or more properties of a region, such as compactness or moments. 2) The data structure containing all data pertaining to a region. For instance, its position in the image (e.g., the coordinates of the center of mass), its contour (e.g., a list of 2D coordinates), some indicator of its shape (e.g., compactness or perimeter squared over area) and the value of its homogeneity index. [NA05:7.3]

region detection: A vast class of algorithms seeking to partition an image into regions with particular properties. See region identification, region labeling, region matching and region-based segmentation. [SOS00:4.3.2]

region filling: A class of algorithms assigning a given value to all the pixels in the interior of a closed object contour identifying a region. For instance, one may want to fill the interior of a closed contour in a binary image with zeros or ones. See also morphology, mathematical morphology operation and binary mathematical morphology. [SOS00:4.3.2]

region growing: A class of algorithms that construct a connected region by incrementally expanding the region, usually at the boundary. New data consistent with the region are merged into the region. The region is often redescribed after each new set of data is added to it. Many region-growing algorithms have the following form:

1. Describe the region based on its current pixels (e.g., fit a linear model to the intensity distribution).
2. Find all pixels adjacent to the current region.
3. Add an adjacent pixel to the region if the region description also describes this pixel (e.g., it has a similar intensity).
4. Repeat from Step 1 as long as new pixels continue to be added.

A similar algorithm exists for region growing with 3D points, giving a surface fitting. The data points could come from a regular grid (pixel or voxel) or from an unstructured list. In the latter case, it is harder to determine adjacency. [JKS95:3.5]

region identification: A class of algorithms seeking to identify regions with special properties, e.g., human figures in a surveillance video or road vehicles in an aerial sequence. Region identification covers a very wide area of techniques spanning many applications, including remote sensing, visual surveillance, surveillance, and agricultural and forestry surveying. See also target recognition, automatic target recognition (ATR), binary object recognition, object recognition and pattern recognition. [OM98]

region invariant: 1) A property of a region that does not change after some transformation is applied to the region, such as translation, rotation or perspective projection.
2) A property or function which is invariant over a region. [SH95]

region labeling: A class of algorithms that are used to assign a label or meaning to each image region in a given image segmentation to achieve an appropriate image interpretation. Representative techniques are relaxation labeling, probabilistic relaxation labeling, and interpretation trees (see interpretation tree search). See also labeling problem. [TA02]

region matching: 1) Establishing the correspondences between matching members of two sets of regions.
2) Determining the degree of similarity between two regions, i.e., solving the feature matching problem for regions. See, e.g., template matching, color matching and color histogram matching. [LWW00]

region merging: A class of algorithms that fuse two image regions into one if a given homogeneity criterion is satisfied. See also region, region-based segmentation and region splitting. [Sch89:Ch. 6]

region neighborhood graph: See region adjacency graph.

region of interest: A subregion of an image where processing is to occur. Regions of interest may be used to reduce the amount of computation that is required or to focus processing so that image data outside the region do not distract from or distort results. As an example, when tracking a target through an image sequence, most algorithms for locating the target in the next video frame only consider image data from a region of interest surrounding the predicted target position. The figure shows a boxed region of interest: [WP:Region_of_interest]

region of support: The subregion of an image that is used in a particular computation. For example, edge detection usually only uses a subregion of pixels neighboring the pixel under consideration for being an edge. [KMJ05:5.4.1–5.4.2]

region propagation: The problem of tracking moving image regions. [RC99]

region representation: A class of methods to represent the defining characteristics of an image region. For encoding the shapes, see axial representation, convex hull, graph model, quadtree, run-length coding and skeletonization. For encoding a region by its properties, see moments, curvature scale space, Fourier shape descriptor, wavelet descriptor and shape representation. [JKS95:3.3]

region segmentation: See region-based segmentation.

region snake: A snake representing the boundary of some region. The operation of computing the snake may be

236

used as a region segmentation technique. [CRB99]

region splitting: A class of algorithms dividing an image, or a region thereof, into parts (subregions) if a given homogeneity criterion is not satisfied over the region. See also region, region-based segmentation and region merging. [Sch89:Ch. 6]

regional activity: An activity that takes place in a localized region (as opposed to a global activity). [LXG09]

registration: A class of techniques aiming to align, superimpose, or match two objects of the same kind (e.g., images, curves or models); more specifically, they compute a geometric transformation superimposing one object on the other. For instance, image registration determines the region common to two images, thereby finding the planar transformation (rotation and translation) that brings them into alignment; similarly, curve registration determines the transformation aligning a similar (or the same) part of two curves. The figure shows the registration (on the right) of the solid (left) and dashed (middle) curves:

The transformation need not be rigid; non-rigid registration is common in medical imaging, e.g., in digital subtraction angiography. Notice also that most often there is no exact solution, as the two objects are not exactly the same, and the best approximate solution must be found by least squares or more complex methods. See also Euclidean transformation, medical image registration, model registration and multi-image registration. [FP03:21.3]

regression: A regression problem is a supervised learning problem where the response variable is one or more continuous variables. In linear regression, a linear relationship between the input and response variables is assumed. Nonlinear models can also be considered, e.g., support vector regression and Gaussian process regression. See also curve fitting and surface fitting. [Bis06:p. 3]

regression testing: Regression testing verifies that changes to the implementation of a system have not caused a loss of functionality, or *regression* to the state where that functionality did not exist. [WP:Regression_testing]

regularization: A class of mathematical techniques to solve an ill-posed problem. In essence, to determine a single solution, one introduces the constraint that the solution must be smooth, in the intuitive sense that similar inputs must correspond to similar outputs. The problem is then cast as a variational problem, in which the variational integral depends both on the data and on the smoothness constraint. For instance, a regularization approach to the problem of estimating a function f from a set of values $y_1, y_2, \ldots, y_n$ at the data point $\vec{x}_1, \ldots, \vec{x}_n$, leads to the minimization of the functional

$$H(f) = \sum_{i=1}^{N} (f(\vec{x}_i) - y_i)^2 + \lambda \Phi(f)$$

where $\Phi(f)$ is the *smoothness functional* and λ is a positive parameter called the *regularization number*. [JKS95:13.7]

relational graph: A graph in which the arcs express relations between the properties of image entities (e.g., regions or other features) that are the nodes in the graph. For regions, commonly used properties are adjacency, inclusion, connectedness and relative area size. See also region adjacency graph (RAG) and shape representation. In the figure, the adjacency relations of the regions (left) are encoded in the RAG (right): [DH73:12.2.2]

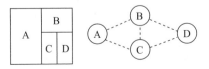

relational matching: A class of matching algorithms based on relational descriptors. See also relational graph. [BB82:11.2]

relational model: See relational graph.

relational shape description: A class of shape representation techniques based on relations between the properties of image entities (e.g., regions or other features). For regions commonly used properties are adjacency, inclusion, connectedness and relative area size. See also relational graph and region adjacency graph. [Sha80]

relative depth: The difference in depth (distance from some observer) values for two points. In certain situations, it may not be possible to compute actual or absolute depth but it may be possible to compute relative depth. [Pra80]

relative motion: The motion of an object with respect to some other, possibly also moving, frame of reference (typically the observer's). [Reg86]

relative orientation: The problem of computing the orientation of an object with respect to another coordinate system, such as that of the sensor. More specifically, the rotation matrix aligning the reference frames attached to the object and second object. See also pose and pose estimation. [JKS95:12.4]

relaxation: A technique for assigning values from a continuous or discrete set to the nodes of a network or graph by propagating the effects of local constraints. The network can be an image grid, in which case the pixels are nodes, or features such as edges or regions. At each iteration, each node interacts with its neighbors, altering its value according to the local constraints. As the number of iterations increases, the effect of local constraints are propagated to more parts of the network. Convergence is achieved when no more changes occur or changes become insignificant. See also discrete relaxation, relaxation labeling and probabilistic relaxation labeling. [SQ04:6.1]

relaxation labeling: A relaxation technique for assigning a label from a discrete set to each node of a network or graph. A classic example in artificial intelligence is the Waltz line labeling algorithm (see also line-drawing analysis). [JKS95:14.3]

relaxation matching: A relaxation labeling technique for model matching, the purpose of which is to label (match) each model primitive with a scene primitive. Starting from an initial labeling, the algorithm iteratively harmonizes neighboring labels using a coherence measure for the set of matches. See also discrete relaxation, relaxation labeling and probabilistic relaxation labeling. [LS88]

relaxation segmentation: A class of segmentation techniques based on relaxation. See also image segmentation. [BT88:Ch. 5]

relevance feedback: Feedback (e.g., from a user) on whether results returned (e.g., from a search or image retrieval) are relevant. This feedback information can be used to improve further searches. [MRS08:Ch. 9]

relevance learning: Some methods such as the k-nearest-neighbor algorithm depend on measuring the similarity of instances in terms of a distance metric in the input feature space. In relevance learning, this metric may be varied (e.g., by re-weighting different dimensions) to improve performance. [XNJR03]

relevance vector machine (RVM): A Bayesian sparse kernel method for regression and classification problems. The prediction function $f(x) = \sum_{i=1}^{n} w_i k(x, x_i)$ is represented by a linear combination of kernel functions, where $i = 1, \ldots, n$ indexes the data points. As in support vector regression (and in contrast to Gaussian process regression and kernel ridge regression), the RVM solution for the w coefficients is sparse, i.e., many of them are zero. [Bis06:7.2]

relighting: A technique for altering an image so that it appears to have been taken under different lighting conditions. [WGT+05]

remote sensing: The acquisition, analysis and understanding of imagery, mainly of the earth's surface, acquired by airplanes or satellites. Used frequently in agriculture, forestry, meteorological and military applications. See also multi-spectral analysis, multi-spectral image and geographic information system. [Sch89:Ch. 6]

representation: A description or model specifying the properties defining an object or class of objects. A classic example is shape representation – a group of techniques for describing the geometric shape of 2D and 3D objects. See also Koenderink's surface shape classification. Representations can be symbolic or non-symbolic (see symbolic object representation and non-symbolic representation), a distinction inherited from artificial intelligence. [WP:Representation_ (mathematics)]

resection: The computation of the position of a camera given the images of some known 3D points. Also known as camera calibration or pose estimation. [HZ00:21.1]

residual: In a regression problem, the difference between the observed response and the corresponding prediction. [Mur12:16.3]

resolution: The number of pixels per unit area, length, visual angle etc. [Low91:p. 236]

restoration: Given a noisy sample of some true data, the goal of restoration is to recover the best possible estimate of the original true data. [TV98:3.1.1]

reticle: The network of fine wires or receptors placed in the focal plane of an optical instrument for measuring the size or position of the objects under observation. [WP:Reticle]

retina: The photosensitive surface at the back of the eye. The retina is a highly complex manifold structure that turns incident light into nerve impulses that are carried to the visual pathways of the brain. [FP03:1.3]

retinal image: The image which is formed on the retina of the eye. [Nal93:1.2.2]

retinex: An image enhancement algorithm based on *retinex theory*, aiming to compute an illuminant-independent quantity called lightness at each image pixel. The key observation is that normal illumination on a surface changes slowly, leading to slow changes in the observed brightness of a surface. This contrasts with strong changes in brightness at reflectance and fold edges. The retinex algorithm removes the slowly varying components by exploiting the fact that the observed brightness $B = L \times I$ is the product of the surface lightness (or reflectance) L and the illumination I. By taking the logarithm of B at each pixel, the product of L and I become a sum of logarithms. Slow changes can be detected by differentiation and then removed by thresholding. Reintegration of the result produces the lightness image (up to an arbitrary scale factor). [Hor86:9.3]

retro-illumination: The reflection of unfocused light off a surface in order to observe the back lighting of a different structure (e.g., the lens in the human eye). [KO80]

retroreflection: The reflection of light back towards its source with the minimum possible scattering. [WP:Retroreflector]

reverse engineering: In the field of computer vision, the problem of generating a model of a 3D object from a set of views, e.g., a VRML or a triangulated model. The model can be purely geometric (describing just the object's shape) or can combine shape and textural properties. Techniques exist for reverse engineering from both range images and intensity images. See also geometric model and model acquisition. [TV98:4.6]

RGB: A format for color images, encoding the red, green, and blue components of each pixel in separate channels. See also YUV and color image. [FP03: 6.3.1]

ribbon: A shape representation for pipe-like planar objects whose contours are approximately parallel, e.g., roads in aerial imagery. See also generalized cones and shape representation. [FP03:24.2.2–24.2.3]

Ricci flow: A type of nonlinear diffusion equation on a Riemannian manifold used in shape analysis. [WSG10]

ridge: A particular type of discontinuity of the intensity function, giving rise to thick edges and lines. The figure shows a characteristic dark-to-light-to-dark intensity ridge profile along a scan line:

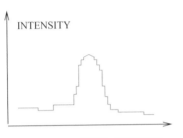

PIXEL POSITION

See also step edge, roof edge and edge detection. [WP:Ridge_detection]

ridge detection: A class of algorithms, especially edge and line detectors, for detecting ridges in images. [WP:Ridge_detection]

ridge regression: A method for the regularization of linear regression and related methods, where a penalty term is added. The penalty term consists of the sum of squares of the regression coefficients, thus penalizing large coefficients. [HTF08:3.4]

Riemannian manifold: A differentiable manifold that is endowed with a metric tensor which may vary smoothly from point to point. [Lov10:5.1]

right-handed coordinate system: A 3D coordinate system with the XYZ axes arranged as shown:

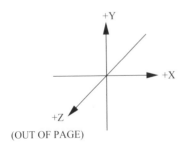

(OUT OF PAGE)

The alternative is a left-handed coordinate system. [FP03:2.1.1]

rigid body segmentation: The problem of automatic partitioning of the image of an articulated object or deformable model into a number of rigid subcomponents. See also part segmentation and recognition by components (RBC). [WM97]

rigid motion estimation: A class of techniques aiming to estimate the 3D motion of a rigid body or scene in space from a sequence of images by assuming that there are no changes in shape. Rigidity simplifies the problem significantly so that changes in appearance arise solely from changes in relative position and projection. Techniques exist for using known 3D models; for estimating the motion of a general cloud of 3D points or from image feature points; and for estimating motion from optical flow. See also motion estimation and egomotion. [Hor86:17.2]

rigid registration: Registration where neither the model nor the data is allowed to deform. This reduces registration to estimating the Euclidean transformation that brings the model into alignment with the data. See also non-rigid registration. [RPMA01]

rigidity constraint: The assumption that a scene or object under analysis is rigid, implying that all 3D points remain in the same relative positions in space. This constraint can significantly simplify many algorithms, e.g., shape reconstruction (see shape and the following "shape from" entries) and motion estimation. [JKS95:14.7]

ring artifact: An artifact in which rings (circular patterns) appear in computed axial tomography (CT) images. [Rav98]

road structure analysis: A class of techniques used to derive information about roads from images. These can be close-up images (e.g., images of the tarmac as acquired from a moving vehicle, used to map defects automatically over extended distances) or remotely sensed images (e.g., to analyze the geographical structure of road networks). [SCW95]

Roberts cross gradient operator: An operator used for edge detection, computing an estimate of perpendicular components of the image gradient at each pixel. The image is convolved with the two Roberts kernels, yielding two components, G_x and G_y, for each pixel. The gradient magnitude $\sqrt{G_x^2 + G_y^2}$ and orientation $\arctan \frac{G_y}{G_x}$ can then be estimated as for any 2D vector. See also edge detection, entries for specific edge detectors (Canny, Deriche, Hueckel, Kirsch compass, Marr–Hildreth, O'Gorman and Robinson), Sobel gradient operator and Sobel kernel. [JKS95:5.2.1]

Roberts kernel: A pair of kernels, or masks, used to estimate perpendicular components of the image gradient within the Roberts cross gradient operator:

0	1
−1	0

1	0
0	−1

The masks respond maximally to edges oriented to $\pm 45\,°$ from the vertical axis of the image. [JKS95:5.2.1]

Robinson edge detector: An operator for edge detection, computing an estimate of the directional first derivatives of the image in eight directions. The image is convolved with the eight kernels, three of which are shown here:

1	1	1
1	−2	1
−1	−1	−1

1	1	1
−1	−2	1
−1	−1	1

−1	1	1
−1	−2	1
−1	1	1

Two of these, typically those responding maximally to differences along the coordinate axes, can be taken as estimates of the two components of the gradient, G_x and G_y. The gradient magnitude $\sqrt{G_x^2 + G_y^2}$ and orientation $\arctan \frac{G_y}{G_x}$ can then be estimated as for any 2D vector. See also edge detection, Roberts cross gradient operator, Sobel gradient operator, Sobel kernel and entries for specific edge detectors (Canny, Deriche, Hueckel, Kirsch compass, Marr–Hildreth and O'Gorman). [Umb98:2.3.5]

robot behavior: The actions of a robotic device. [HV99]

robot vision: Any automated vision system used to provide a robotic device with visual information or feedback. Robot vision is somewhat different from traditional computer vision in that it can be part of a closed-loop system where the vision system guides the robot motion which in turn is observed by the vision system allowing the robot motion to be adapted or corrected. [HS92] [Hor86]

robust: A general term referring to a technique which is insensitive to noise or other perturbations. [FP03:15.5]

robust estimator: A statistical estimator that, unlike normal least square estimation, is not distracted by even a significant percentage of outliers in the data. Popular robust estimators include RANSAC, least median of squares and M-estimation. See also outlier rejection. [FP03:15.5]

robust regression: A form of regression that does not use outlier values in computing the fitting parameters. For example, normal regression methods use all data points to carry out a least squares straight line fit; this can give distorted results if even one point is far away from the "true" line. Robust processes either eliminate these outlying points or reduce their contribution to the results. The figure shows a rejected outlying point: [JKS95:6.8.3]

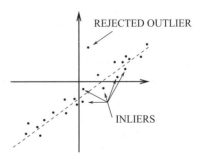

robust statistics: A general term describing statistical methods that are not significantly influenced by outliers. [WP:Robust_statistics]

robust technique: See robust estimator.

ROC: See receiver operating curve and performance analysis for vision.

Rodrigues rotation formula: An efficient algorithm for rotating a vector by some angle in 3D space around a specified axis. [Sze10:p. 42]

rod (in eye): Photoreceptor cells in the human eye which are very sensitive to all wavelengths of visible light (i.e., they sense the luminance level). Rods are complemented by cones within the retina. [FP03:1.3]

roll: A 3D rotation representation component (along with pitch and yaw) often used for cameras or moving observers. The roll component specifies a rotation about the optical axis or line of sight. The figure shows the roll rotation direction: [JKS95:12.2.1]

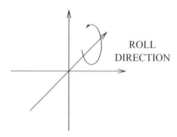

ROLL DIRECTION

rolling shutter camera: A camera in which the time at which a pixel collects photons varies from pixel to pixel. This may occur for mechanical or electronic reasons. It allows continued acquisition of photons from most other pixels while a given pixel is being sampled. This contrasts with a camera where all pixels capture photons and are read out simultaneously. [WP:Rolling_shutter]

roof edge: 1) An image edge where the values increase continuously to a maximum and then decrease continuously, such as the brightness values on a Lambertian surface cylinder when lit by a point light source or

the orientation discontinuity (the fold edge) in a range image. 2) A scene edge where an orientation discontinuity occurs. The figure shows a horizontal roof edge in a range image: [JKS95:Ch. 5]

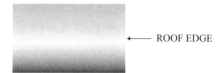

ROOF EDGE

rotating mask: A mask which is considered in a number of orientations relative to some pixel. See, e.g., the masks used in the Robinson edge detector. Most commonly used as a type of average smoothing: the most homogeneous mask is used to compute the smoothed value for every pixel. In the figure, the major boundaries have not been smoothed although image detail has been reduced: [DVD+93]

rotation: A circular motion of a set of points or an object around a given point (2D) or line (3D, called the axis of rotation). [JKS95:12.2.1-12.2.2]

rotation estimation: The estimation rotation from raw or processed image, video or range data, typically from two sets of corresponding points (or lines or planes) taken from rotated versions of a pattern. The problem usually appears in one of three forms:

- estimating the 3D rotation from 3D data (three points are needed);
- estimating the 3D rotation from 2D data (three points are needed but lead to multiple solutions);
- estimating the 2D rotation from 2D data (two points are needed).

A second issue to consider is the effect of noise: typically more than the minimum number of points are needed to counteract the effects of noise, which leads to least square algorithms. [OK98]

rotation invariant: A property that keeps the same value even if any of the data values, the camera, the image or the scene from which the data comes is rotated. One needs to distinguish between 2D (i.e., in the image) and 3D (i.e., in the scene) rotation invariance. For example, the angle between two image lines is invariant to image rotation, but not to rotation of the lines in the scene. [WP:Rotational_invariance]

rotation matrix: A linear operator rotating a vector in a given space. The inverse of a rotation matrix equals its transpose. A rotation matrix has only three degrees of freedom in 3D and one in 2D. In 3D space, there are three eigenvalues: 1, $\cos\theta + i\sin\theta$, $\cos\theta - i\sin\theta$, where i is the imaginary unit. A rotation matrix in 3D has nine entries but only three degrees of freedom, as it must satisfy six orthogonality constraints. It can be parameterized in various ways, usually through Euler angles, yaw–pitch–roll, rotation angles around the coordinate axes and axis–angle curve representations. See also orientation estimation, rotation representation and quaternions. [FP03:2.1.2]

rotation operator: A linear operator expressed by a rotation matrix. [JKS95:12.2.1]

rotation representation: A formalism describing rotations and their algebra. The most frequent is definitely the rotation matrix, but quaternions, Euler angles, yaw–pitch–roll, rotation angles around the coordinate axes and axis–angle curve representations have also been used. [Hor86:18.10]

rotational symmetry: The property of a set of points or an object to remain unchanged after a given rotation. For instance, a cube has several rotational symmetries, with respect to any $90°$ rotation around any axis passing through the centers of opposite faces. See also rotation and rotation matrix. [WP:Rotational_symmetry]

rotoscoping: A technique for creating an animation from a live action sequence in which features (such as an outline of body position) are copied frame by frame from the live action sequence: [WP:Rotoscoping]

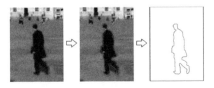

RS-170: The standard black-and-white video format in the United States. The Electronic Industry Association (EIA) is the standards body that originally defined the 525-line, 30-frame-per-second, TV standard for North America, Japan and a few other parts of the world. The EIA standard, also defined under US standard RS-170A, defines only the monochrome picture component but is mainly used with the NTSC color encoding standard. A version exists for PAL cameras. [Gal90:4.1.3]

rubber sheet model: See membrane model. [WP:Gravitational_well#The_rubber-sheet_model]

rule-based classification: A method of object recognition, drawn from artificial intelligence, in which logical rules are used to infer object type. [WP:Concept_learning#Rule-based_theories_of_concept_learning]

run code: See run-length coding.

run-length coding: A lossless compression technique used to reduce the size of a repeating string of characters, called a "run", also applicable to images. The algorithm encodes a run of symbols into two bytes, a count and a symbol. For instance, the six-byte string "xxxxxx" would become "6x" and would occupy only two bytes. It can compress any type of information content, but the content itself affects, obviously, the compression ratio. Compression ratios are not high compared to other methods, but the algorithm is easy to implement and quick to execute. Run-length coding is supported by bitmap file formats such as TIFF, BMP and PCX. See also image compression, video compression and JPEG. [Jai89:11.2, 11.9]

run-length compression: See run-length coding.

saccade: A movement of the eye or camera, changing the direction of fixation sharply. [WP:Saccade]

salience: The extent to which something (e.g., a visual feature) stands out relative to other nearby features (from the Latin *salire* meaning to leap). [Itt01]

saliency map: A representation encoding the saliency of given image elements, typically features or groups thereof. See also salient feature, Gestalt, perceptual grouping and perceptual organization. [WP:Salience_(neuroscience)]

salient behavior: Behavior of a person or system which is distinct from normal behavior.

salient feature: A feature associated with a high value of a saliency measure, quantifying feature suggestiveness for perception. For instance, inflection points have been indicated as salient features for representing contours. Saliency is a concept that originated from Gestalt psychology. See also perceptual grouping and perceptual organization. [KK98]

salient pixel group: A group of pixels that exhibits a distinct pattern relative to neighboring pixels. [XG06]

salient point: Typically, a feature which is distinct relative to those around it. [SL03]

salient regions: Image regions that are interesting relative to their local image context. They should be stable to global transformations (including scale, illumination and perspective distortions) and image noise. They can be used for object representation, correspondence matching, tracking etc. [KZB04]

salt-and-pepper noise: A type of impulsive noise. Let $x, y \in [0, 1]$ be two uniform random variables, I the true image value at a given pixel and I_n the corrupted (noisy) version of I. We can define the effect of salt-and-pepper noise as $I_n = i_{min} + y(i_{max} - i_{min})$ iff $x \geq l$, where l is a parameter controlling how much of the image is corrupted and i_{min}, i_{max} are the range of the noise. See also image noise and Gaussian noise. The figure was corrupted with 1% noise: [TV98:3.1.2]

sample covariance: For a d-dimensional data set represented as a set of n column vectors $\vec{x}_i$ for $i = 1, \ldots, n$ with sample mean $\vec{m}$, the sample covariance is the $d \times d$ matrix $S = \frac{1}{n} \sum_{i=1}^{n} (\vec{x}_i - \vec{m})(\vec{x}_i - \vec{m})^\top$. See also covariance matrix. [MKB79:1.4.1]

sample mean: For a d-dimensional data set represented as a set of n column vectors $\vec{x}_i$ for $i = 1, \ldots, n$, the sample mean is $\vec{m} = \frac{1}{n} \sum_{i=1}^{n} \vec{x}_i$. See also mean. [MKB79:1.4.1]

sampling: The transformation of a continuous signal into a discrete one by recording its values at discrete instants or locations. Most digital images are

Dictionary of Computer Vision and Image Processing, Second Edition.
R. B. Fisher, T. P. Breckon, K. Dawson-Howe, A. Fitzgibbon, C. Robertson, E. Trucco and C. K. I. Williams.
© 2014 John Wiley & Sons, Ltd. Published 2014 by John Wiley & Sons, Ltd.

sampled in space, time and intensity, as intensity values are defined only on a regular spatial grid and can only take integer values. The figure shows a continuous signal and its samples: [FP03:7.4.1]

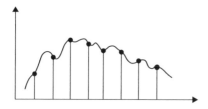

sampling bias: If samples are collected from a <u>random variable</u> according to the true distribution then any statistic computed from the sample should not deviate systematically from the population expectation. If the sample does not represent the true distribution there is said to be "sampling bias". [WP:Bias_(statistics)]

sampling density: The density of a sampling grid, that is, the number of samples collected per unit interval. See also <u>sampling</u>. [BB82:2.2.6]

sampling theorem: If an image is sampled at a rate higher than its <u>Nyquist frequency</u> then an analog image could be reconstructed from the sampled image whose mean square error with the original image converges to zero as the number of samples goes to infinity. [Jai89:4.2]

Sampson approximation: An approximation to the <u>geometric distance</u> in the fitting of implicit curves or <u>implicit surfaces</u> that are defined by a parameterized function of the form $f(\vec{a}; \vec{x}) = 0$ for $\vec{x}$ on the surface $S(\vec{a})$ defined by parameter vector $\vec{a}$. Fitting the surface to the set of points $\{\vec{x}_1, \ldots, \vec{x}_n\}$ consists in minimizing a function of the form $e(\vec{a}) = \sum_{i=1}^{n} d(\vec{x}_i, S(\vec{a}))$. Simple solutions are often available if the distance function $d(\vec{x}, S(\vec{a}))$ is the <u>algebraic distance</u> $d(\vec{x}, S(\vec{a})) = f(\vec{a}; \vec{x})^2$. Under certain common assumptions, the optimal solution arises when d is the more complicated <u>geometric</u>

<u>distance</u> $d(\vec{x}, S(\vec{a})) = \min_{\vec{y} \in S} \|\vec{x} - \vec{y}\|^2$. The Sampson approximation defines

$$d(\vec{x}, S(\vec{a})) = \frac{f(\vec{a}; \vec{x})^2}{\|\nabla f(\vec{a}; \vec{x})\|^2}$$

which is a first-order approximation to the geometric distance. If an efficient algorithm for minimizing weighted algebraic distance is available, then the *Sampson iterations* are a further approximation, where the kth iterate $\vec{a}_k$ is the solution to

$$\vec{a}_k = \operatorname*{argmin}_{\vec{a}} \sum_{i=1}^{n} w_i f(\vec{a}; \vec{x}_i)^2$$

with weights computed using the previous estimate so $w_i = 1/\|\nabla f(\vec{a}_{k-1}; \vec{x}_i)\|^2$. [HZ00:3.2.6, 11.4]

SAR: see <u>synthetic aperture radar</u>. [WP:Synthetic_aperture_radar]

SAT: See <u>symmetric axis transform</u>.

satellite image: An image of a section of the earth acquired using a <u>camera</u> mounted on an orbiting satellite. [WP:Satellite_imagery]

saturation: Reaching the upper limit of a dynamic range. For instance, intensity saturation occurs for an 8-bit monochromatic image when intensities greater than 255 are recorded: any such value is encoded as 255, the largest possible value in the range. [WP:Colorfulness]

Savitzky–Golay filtering: A class of filters achieving <u>least squares fitting</u> of a polynomial to a moving window of a signal. Used for fitting and data smoothing. See also <u>linear filter</u> and <u>curve fitting</u>. [WP:SavitzkyGolay filter for smoothing and differentiation]

scalability: A general property of computer algorithms that means that the performance of the algorithm does not degrade significantly as the number of inputs increases. For example, an image-processing algorithm is scalable if its computation time remains nearly constant or grows only with the image size rather than as the square of the image size. It may also refer to actions on image databases where one would like nearly constant speeds irrespective of the size of the database. [WP:Scalability]

scalar: A one-dimensional entity; a real number. [WP:Scalar_(mathematics)]

scale: 1) The ratio between the size of an object, image or feature and that of a reference or model.
2) The property that some image features are apparent only when viewed at a given size, such as a line being enlarged so much that it appears as a pair of parallel edge features.
3) A measure of the degree to which fine features have been removed from or reduced in an image. One can analyze images at multiple spatial scales, whereby only features in certain size ranges appear at each scale (see scale space and pyramid). [Nal93:3.1.2]

scale invariant: A property that keeps the same value even if the data, the image or the scene from which the data comes is shrunk or enlarged. The ratio $\frac{perimeter^2}{area}$ is invariant to image scaling. [WP:Scale_invariance]

scale operator: An operator, e.g., Gaussian smoothing, that suppresses details (high-frequency contents) in an image. Details at small scales are discarded. The resulting content can be represented in a smaller image. See also scale space, image pyramid, Gaussian pyramid, Laplacian pyramid and pyramid transform. [OP97]

scale reduction: The result of the application of a scale operator. [CH01]

scale selection: 1) When making some measurement (e.g., edge strength) that varies as the image or smoothing scale varies, there may be scale settings that are significant, e.g., when the measurement achieves a local maxima or minima for some scale or when the measurement is stable over wide ranges of scale. The goal of scale selection is to identify these scales. Another well-known use is in the SIFT operator, where the feature points are selected based, in part, upon the local minima of the Laplacian.
2) Selecting the size of operator that is tuned to a particular size of target. For example, an eye location needs to be tuned to the approximate likely size of eyes in the image. [Lin09]

scale space: A theory for early vision developed to account properly for the multi-scale nature of images. The rationale is that, in the absence of *a priori* information on the optimal spatial scale at which a specific problem should be treated (e.g., edge detection), images should be analyzed at all possible scales, the coarser ones representing simplifications of the finer ones. The finest scale is the input image itself. See scale-space representation for details. [CS09:Ch. 5]

scale space filtering: The filtering operation that transforms one resolution level into another in a scale space, e.g., Gaussian filtering. [Sch89:Ch. 7]

scale space matching: A class of matching techniques that compare shape at various scales. See also scale space and image matching. [CS09:5.2.3]

scale-space representation: A representation of an image and more generally of a signal, making explicit the information contained at multiple spatial scales and establishing a causal relationship between adjacent scale levels. The scale level is identified by a scalar parameter called the "scale parameter". A crucial requirement is that coarser levels, obtained by successive applications of a scale operator, should constitute simplifications of previous (finer) levels, i.e., it should introduce no spurious details. A popular scale-space representation is the Gaussian scale space, in which the next coarser image is obtained by convolving the current image with a Gaussian kernel. The variance of this kernel is the scale parameter. See also image pyramid and Gaussian smoothing. [CS09:5.3]

scaling: 1) The process of zooming or shrinking an image.
2) Enlarging or shrinking a model to fit a set of data.
3) The process of transforming a set of values so that they lie inside a standard range (e.g., $[-1,1]$), often to improve numerical stability. [Nal93:6.2.1]

scaling factor: A numerical value commonly used to resize a set of values. For example, one could divide a dataset by the difference between the largest and smallest values, resulting in values in $[0,1]$. It may be useful to also subtract the mean first. This operation is typically done for two reasons: to ensure that all data from different properties have approximately the same magnitude and to ensure that all values are not too large or too small. Both aspects tend to improve the numerical performance of an algorithm. [Bis06:p. 425]

scanline: A single (horizontal) line of an image. Originally this term was used for cameras in which the image is acquired line by line by a sensing element that generally scans each pixel on a line and then moves onto the next line. [WP:Scan_line]

scanline slice: The cross section of a structure along an image scanline. The figure shows the scanline slice of a convex polygon in a binary image: [SM97]

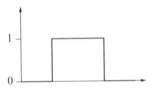

scanline stereo matching: The stereo matching problem with rectified images, whereby corresponding points lie on scanlines with the same index. See also rectification and stereo correspondence problem. [OK85]

scanning electron microscope (SEM): A scientific microscope introduced in 1942. It uses a beam of highly energetic electrons to examine objects on a very fine scale. The imaging process is essentially the same as for a light microscope apart from the type of radiation used. Magnification is much higher than what can be achieved with light. The images are rendered in gray shades. This technique is particularly useful for investigating microscopic details of surfaces. [Hor86:11.1.3]

scatter matrix: For a set of d-dimensional points represented as column vectors $\{\vec{x}_1, \ldots, \vec{x}_n\}$, with mean $\vec{\mu} = \frac{1}{n}\sum_{i=1}^{n} \vec{x}_i$, the scatter matrix is the $d \times d$ matrix

$$\mathbf{S} = \sum_{i=1}^{n}(\vec{x}_i - \vec{\mu})(\vec{x}_i - \vec{\mu})^\top$$

It is n times the sample covariance matrix. [DH73:4.10]

scattergram: See scatterplot.

scatterplot: A data display technique in which each data item is plotted as a single point in an appropriate coordinate system that might help a person to better understand the data. For example, if a set of estimated surface normals is plotted in a 3D scatterplot, then planar surfaces should produce tight clusters of points. The figure shows a set of data points plotted according to their values of features 1 and 2: [DH73:1.2]

scene: The part of 3D space captured by an imaging sensor, and every visible object therein. [Sch89:Ch. 1]

scene analysis: The process of examining an image or video, for the purpose of inferring information about the scene, such as the shape of the visible surfaces, the identity of objects and their spatial or dynamic relationships. See also shape from contour and the following "shape from" entries, object recognition and symbolic object representation. [Sch89:6,7]

scene classification: Deciding the genre of a particular image or frame from a video. For example, a system might categorize images as being captured from one of {office scene, outdoor urban scene, domestic scene, outdoor natural scene}. [BZM06]

scene constraint: Any constraint imposed on the image data by the nature of the scene, e.g., rigid motion, the orthogonality of walls and floors etc. [HZ00:9.4.1–9.4.2]

scene coordinates: A 3D coordinate system that describes the position of scene objects relative to a given coordinate system origin. Alternative coordinate systems are camera coordinates, viewer-centered coordinates and object-centered coordinates. [JKS95:1.4.2]

scene decomposition: Segmentation of an image into semantically meaningful regions. For example, an interior office image might be segmented into regions such as {desk, chair, table, cabinet}. See also semantic image segmentation. [GFK09]

scene labeling: The problem of identifying scene elements from image data and associating them with labels representing their nature and roles. See also labeling problem, region labeling, relaxation labeling, image interpretation and scene understanding. [BB82:12.4]

scene layout: The position of the main elements in a scene. This knowledge can be used to help with scene decomposition or scene labeling. For example, an outdoor scene layout could consist of sky above, then green fields, then a gray road, with a vehicle on the road.

scene modeling: Constructing a geometric model, graph model or other type of model that describes the contents and positioning of structures in a scene. [vdHDT+07]

scene recognition: See scene classification.

scene reconstruction: The problem of estimating the 3D geometry of a scene, e.g., the shape of visible surfaces or contours, from image data. See also reconstruction, shape from contour and the following "shape from" entries, architectural model reconstruction, volumetric reconstruction, surface reconstruction and slice-based reconstruction. [WP:Computer_vision #Scene_reconstruction]

scene understanding: The problem of constructing a semantic interpretation of a scene from image data, that is, how to describe the scene in terms of object identities and relationships among objects. See also image interpretation, object recognition, symbolic object representation, semantic net, graph model and relational graph. [LSF09]

scene vector: A representation used in video analysis to describe what is happening in the current frame. Each position k in the scene vector $(s_t^1, \ldots, s_t^k, \ldots, s_t^K)$ corresponds to a different event class (e.g., a person walking) and the value s_t^k is the number of detected instances of class k at time t. [GX11:7.2]

SCERPO: Spatial correspondence, evidential reasoning and perceptual organization. A well-known vision system developed by David Lowe that demonstrated recognition of complex polyhedral objects (e.g., razors) in a complex scene. [Low85]

screw motion: A 3D transformation comprising a rotation about an axis $\vec{a}$ and translation along $\vec{a}$. The general Euclidean transformation $\vec{x} \mapsto \mathbf{R}\vec{x} + \vec{t}$ is a screw transformation if $\mathbf{R}\vec{t} = \vec{t}$. [Nal93:8.2.1]

search tree: A data structure that records the choices that could be made in a problem-solving activity, while searching through a space of alternative choices for the next action or decision. The tree could be explicitly created or could be implicit in the sequence of actions. For example, a tree that records alternative model-to-data feature matching is a specialized search tree used for interpretation tree searches. If each non-leaf node has two children, we have a binary search tree. See also decision tree and tree classifier. [DH73:12.4.1]

SECAM: *Sequential Couleur avec Mémoire* is the television broadcast standard in France, the Middle East and most of Eastern Europe. SECAM broadcasts 819 lines per second. It is one of three main television standards throughout the world, the other two being PAL (see PAL camera) and NTSC. [Jai89:4.1]

second-derivative operator: A linear filter estimating the second derivative from an image at a given point and in a given direction. Numerically, a simple approximation of the second derivative of a 1D function f is the central (finite) difference, derived from the Taylor approximation of f:

$$f_i'' = \frac{f_{i+1} - 2f_i + f_{i-1}}{b^2} + O(b)$$

where b is the sampling step (assumed constant) and $O(b)$ indicates that the truncation error vanishes as b. A similar but more complicated approximation exists for estimating the second derivative in a given direction in an image. See also first derivative filter. [JKS95:5.3]

second fundamental form: See surface curvature.

seed region: The initial region used in a region-growing process, such as surface fitting in range data or intensity region finding in an intensity image. The figure shows a patch on a surface that is a potential seed region for growing the full cylindrical patch: [JKS95:3.5]

segmentation: The problem of dividing a data set into parts according to a given set of rules. The assumption is that the different segments correspond to different structures in the original input domain observed in the image. See image segmentation, color image segmentation, curve segmentation, motion segmentation, part segmentation, range data segmentation and texture segmentation. [FP03:14–14.1.2]

self-calibration: The problem of estimating the calibration parameters using only information extracted from a sequence or set of images (typically feature point correspondences in subsequent frames of a sequence or in several simultaneous views), as opposed to traditional calibration in photogrammetry, which adopts specially built calibration objects. Self-calibration is intimately related to the basic concepts of multi-view geometry. See also camera calibration, autocalibration, stratification and projective geometry. [FP03:13.6]

self-localization: The problem of estimating the sensor's position within an environment from image or video data. The problem can be cast as geometric model matching if models of sufficiently complex objects are available, i.e., containing enough points to allow a full solution of the pose estimation problem. In some situations it is possible to identify a sufficient number of landmark points (see landmark detection). If no information at all is available about the scene, one can still apply tracking or optical flow techniques to get corresponding points over time, or stereo correspondences in multiple simultaneous frames. See also motion estimation, egomotion and stereo correspondence problem. [Ols00]

self-occlusion: Occlusion in which part of an object is occluded by another part of the same object. In the figure, the left leg of the person is occluding their right leg: [DF99]

self-similarity matrix: Given a set of objects $\{o_1, o_2, \dots o_n\}$ described by a set of property vectors $\{\vec{p}_1, \vec{p}_2, \dots \vec{p}_n\}$

then one can define a self-similarity matrix [$\mathbf{M}_{ij}$] where each entry $\mathbf{M}_{ij}$ is defined by some user selected similarity function $sim(\bar{p}_i, \bar{p}_j)$ between objects o_i and o_j. The Euclidean distance between the vectors $\bar{p}_i$ and $\bar{p}_j$ is one of many possible similarity metrics. Given the matrix, one can do different things, such as clustering similar objects together. See spectral clustering. [MKB79:13.4]

SEM: See scanning electron microscope.

semantic gap: The difference between two different representations of an object. For example, one could describe a square as a set of four equal-length lines at right angles or using a specific collection of pixels in a binary image. While both describe a square, it would require a lot of computation to demonstrate that the two descriptions are largely equivalent. [WP:Semantic_gap]

semantic image annotation and retrieval: Image retrieval from a database based on symbolic descriptors, e.g., keywords that describe the image, which have been inferred from descriptions of the image data. For example, instead of describing the figure in terms of, e.g., color histograms, one can use the histograms and other information to infer the presence of a car, people, bicycles etc.:

The descriptors could have a probability reflecting the certainty that the description actually holds for the image. [CV05a]

semantic image segmentation: A form of image segmentation, usually into regions that are simultaneously extracted and labeled with their object category or identity. This approach exploits visual context as well as specific object visual appearance properties and relationships and is in contrast to segmentation algorithms that only use image properties. For example, segmenting and identifying a road sign is easier in the context of an outdoor road scene than in a cluttered indoor room. [SWRC06]

semantic net: A graph representation in which nodes represent the objects of a given domain and arcs represent the properties and relations between objects. See also symbolic object representation, graph model and relational graph. The figure shows an arch and its semantic net representation: [BB82:10.2]

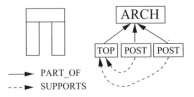

semantic primitive: A meaningful "thing", such as an object in a scene or image or an instantaneous action in a video (e.g. a jumping action). By contrast, a collection of pixels probably would not be considered a semantic primitive, unless they formed a recurring pattern. A more abstract semantic primitive might be a cluster of similar feature vectors, in which case the semantic primitive is the cluster, which may not correspond to an entity recognizable by a human. [KTF02]

semantic region: 1) A region in an image that corresponds to some semantic primitive, e.g. a nameable pattern or object.
2) An image region that participates in multiple behaviors. [WG08]

semantic region growing: A region merging scheme incorporating *a priori* knowledge about adjacent regions, e.g., in aerial imagery of countryside areas, the fact that roads are usually surrounded by fields. Constraint propagation can then be applied to achieve a globally optimal region segmentation. See also constraint satisfaction, relaxation labeling, region segmentation, region-based segmentation and recursive region growing. [BB82:5.5]

semantic scene segmentation: See semantic image segmentation.

semantic scene understanding: A concept related to semantic image segmentation but could be slightly wider to allow multiple images or video, with the similar goals of isolating the distinct objects in the image data and recognizing their type. An associated goal could be to recognize and label everything in the data. See also image segmentation and object recognition.

semantic texton forest: A forest is an ensemble (set) of decision trees, where the leaf nodes contain a distribution of potential labels for the input structure under consideration. The decision result comes from averaging the partial results of each tree in the ensemble. A variant of the forest is the random forest which uses different randomly generated tests at each splitting node in each tree. The texton extension is to use a function of the values of one or a pair of pixels in an image patch. One common application of the semantic texton forest is to do semantic image segmentation. [SJC08]

semantic video indexing: Video indexing based on conceptual units such as words, image patches or video clips illustrating the desired video content. Contrast with using collections of numerical properties such as color histograms. [NH01]

semantic video search: See semantic video indexing.

semi-supervised learning: In supervised learning the dataset contains a number of input–output pairs. In semi-supervised learning, the learner is given more examples for which only the input is available (these

examples are unlabeled). The goal is to produce improved performance on the unlabeled examples by exploiting information in the labeled examples. [Mur12:1.5.3]

sensitivity: A binary classifier $c(x)$ returns + or − labels for an example x. Comparing these predictions to the actual label gives rise to a true positive (TP), true negative (TN), false positive (FP) or false negative (FN). The sensitivity is defined as the true positive rate, i.e., $TP/(TP + FN)$, or the percentage of true examples that are correctly labeled. The term is mainly used in medical contexts. See also specificity. [HTF08:9.2]

sensor: A general word for a mechanism that records information from the "outside world", generally for processing by a computer. The sensor might obtain raw measurements, e.g., a video camera, or partially processed information, e.g., depth from a stereo triangulation process. [BM02:1.9]

sensor fusion: A vast class of techniques aiming to combine the different information contained in data from different sensors, in order to achieve a richer or more accurate description of a scene or action. Among the many paradigms for fusing sensory information are the Kalman filter, Bayesian statistical models, fuzzy logic, Dempster–Shafer evidential reasoning, production systems and neural networks. [WP:Sensor_fusion]

sensor modeling: The process of characterizing the capabilities of a sensor, such as its optical, spatial and temporal frequency response.

sensor motion compensation: A class of techniques aiming to suppress the motion of a sensor (or its effects) in a video sequence or in data extracted from the sequence. A typical example is image sequence stabilization, in which a target moving across the image in the original sequence appears stationary in the output sequence. Another example is keeping a robot stationary in front of a target using only visual data (known as "station keeping"). Suppression of jitter in hand-held video recorders is now commercially available. Basic ingredients are tracking and motion estimation. See also egomotion. [SGB+00]

sensor motion estimation: See egomotion.

sensor network: A collection of sensors connected through a communication channel, which may communicate raw data or processed results. The data could be low level, such as temperature, brightness or raw video, or higher-level objects or events, such as recognized objects (e.g., car number plates) or the counts of people passing. The sensors could communicate individually to a base station or forward results to neighboring sensors, which ultimately reach a base station. [WP:Wireless_sensor_network]

sensor path planning: See sensor planning.

sensor placement determination: See camera calibration and sensor planning.

sensor planning: A class of techniques aimed at determining the optimal sensing strategies for a reconfigurable sensor system, normally given a task and a geometric model of the target object (which may be partially acquired in previous views). For example, given a geometric feature on an object for which a CAD-like model is known and the task of verifying the feature's size, a sensor-planning system would determine the best position and orientation of, say, a single camera and associated illumination for estimating the size of each feature. The two basic approaches have been *generate-and-test*, in which sensor configurations are generated and then evaluated with respect to the task constraints, and *synthetic methods*, in which task constraints are characterized analytically and the resulting equations solved to yield the optimal sensor configuration. See also active vision and purposive vision. [TAT95]

sensor position estimation: See pose estimation. [WP:Pose_(computer_vision)#Pose_Estimation]

sensor response: The output of a sensor, or a characterization of some key output quantities, given a set of inputs. Typically expressed in the frequency domain, as a function linking the magnitude and phase of the Fourier transform of the output signal with the known frequency of the input. See also phase spectrum, power spectrum and spectral response. [TH94]

sensor sensitivity: In general, the weakest input signal that a sensor can detect. It can be inferred from the sensor response curve. For the common CCD sensor of video cameras, sensitivity depends on various parameters, mainly the *fill factor* (the percentage of the sensor's area actually sensitive to light) and the *well capacity* (the amount of charge that a photosensitive element can hold). The larger the values of the above parameters, the more sensitive the camera. See also sensor spectral sensitivity. [FHD06]

sensor spectral sensitivity: A characterization of a sensor's response in frequency. The figure shows the spectral sensitivity of a typical CCD sensor (actually its spectral response, from which the spectral sensitivity can be inferred):

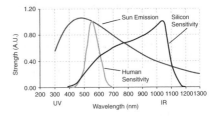

Notice that the high sensitivity of silicon in the infrared means that IR-blocking filters should be considered for fine measurements, depending on camera intensities. We also notice that a CCD camera makes a very good sensor for the near-infrared range (750–3000 nm). [WP:Spectral_sensitivity]

separability: A term used in classification problems referring to whether the data is capable of being split into distinct subclasses by some automatic decision process. If

253

property values of two classes overlap, then the classes are not separable. The figure shows a *linearly* separable circle class and inseparable × and box classes:

FEATURE 2

[WP:Linear_separability]

separable filter: A 2D (in image processing) filter that can be expressed as the product of two filters, each of which acts independently on rows and columns. The classic example is the linear Gaussian filter (see Gaussian convolution). Separability implies a significant reduction in computational complexity, typically reducing processing costs from $O(N^2)$ to $O(2N)$, where N is the filter size. See also linear filter and separable template. [Nar81]

separable template: A template or structuring element in a filter, e.g., a morphological filter (see morphology), that can be decomposed into a sequence of smaller templates, similar to separable kernels for linear filters. The main advantage is a reduction in the computational complexity of the associated filter. See also separable filter. [Gad91]

set theoretic modeling: See constructive solid geometry.

shading: The pattern formed by the graded areas of an intensity image, suggesting light and dark. Variations in the lightness of surfaces in the scene may be caused by variations in illumination, surface orientation and surface reflectance. See also illumination and shadow. [Hor86:10.10]

shading correction: A class of techniques for changing undesirable shading effects, e.g., strongly uneven brightness distribution caused by nonuniform illumination. All techniques assume a shading model, i.e., a photometric model of image formation, formalizing the dependency of the measured image brightness on camera parameters (typically gain and offset), illumination and reflectance. See also shadow and photometry. [TB04]

shading from shape: A technique recovering the reflectance of isolated objects given a single image and a geometric model, but not exactly the inverse of the classic shape from shading problem. See also photometric stereo. [VV90]

shadow: Part of a scene that direct illumination does not reach because of self-occlusion (attached shadow or self-shadow) or occlusion caused by other objects (cast shadow):

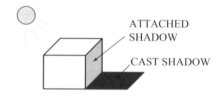

This region appears darker than its surroundings. See also shape from shading, shading from shape and photometric stereo. [FP03:5.3.1]

shadow detection: The problem of identifying image regions corresponding to shadows in the scene, using photometric properties. Useful for true color estimation and region analysis. See also color, color image segmentation, color matching, photometry and region segmentation. [HHD99]

shadow type labeling: A problem similar to shadow detection, but requiring classification of different types of shadow. [CAK07]

shadow understanding: Estimating various properties of a 3D scene, e.g., building height, based on the appearance or size of shadows. See also shadow type labeling. [GDH11]

shape: Informally, the form of an image or scene object. Typically described in computer vision through geometric representations (see shape representation), e.g., modeling image contours with polynomials or b-splines, or range data patches with quadric surfaces. More formal definitions are:

1. (adj) The quality of an object that is invariant to changes of the coordinate system in which it is expressed. If the coordinate system is a Euclidean space, this corresponds to the conventional idea of shape. In an affine coordinate system, the change of coordinates may be affine, so that, e.g., an ellipse and a circle have the same *shape*.

2. (n) A family of point sets, any pair being related by a coordinate system transformation.

3. (n) A specific set of n-dimensional points, e.g., the set of squares. For example, a curve in $\mathbb{R}^2$ defined parametrically as $\vec{c}(t) = (x(t), y(t))$ comprises the point set or *shape* $\{\vec{c}(t) \mid -\infty < t < \infty\}$. The volume inside the unit sphere in 3D is the shape $\{\vec{x} \mid \|\vec{x}\| < 1, \vec{x} \in \mathbb{R}^3\}$. [ZRH03:2.3]

shape class: One in a set of classes representing different types of shape in a given classification, e.g., "locally convex" or "hyperbolic" in mean and Gaussian curvature shape classification of a range image. [TV98:4.4.1]

shape context: A descriptor for 2D image shapes, based on the distribution of vectors between pairs of points. The distribution uses a 2D histogram whose bins have a log-polar spatial quantization. Taking each point $\vec{p}$ on the shape in turn, the histogram records the number of other points $\vec{q}$ also in the shape, whose relative position vector $(\vec{q} - \vec{p})$ lies in each bin. The histogram is a 2D shape descriptor that can be compared, e.g., by using a dot product. [BMP02]

shape decomposition: See segmentation and hierarchical modeling.

shape descriptor: One of a family of numerical descriptors that

characterize the shape of an object. For example, when describing a closed region, one might use area, moment invariants, shape context, Fourier shape descriptors etc., all of which characterize some aspect of the shape of the region. Other descriptors are possible for curves, volumes, symbols, trademarks etc. [BB82:Ch. 8]

shape from contour: A class of algorithms for estimating the shape of a 3D object from the contour it generates in an image. A well-known technique, shape from silhouette, consists of extracting the object's silhouette from a number of views and intersecting the 3D cones generated by the silhouettes' contours and the centers of projections. The intersection volume is known as the visual hull. Work also exists on understanding shape from the differential properties of apparent contours. [Koe84]

shape from defocus: A class of algorithms for estimating scene depth at each image pixel, and therefore surface shape, from multiple images acquired at different, controlled focus settings. A closed-form model of the relation between depth and image focus is assumed, containing a number of parameters (e.g., the optics parameters) that must be calibrated. Depth is estimated using this model once image readings (pixel values) are available. Notice that the camera uses a large aperture, so that the points in the scene are in focus over the smallest possible depth interval. See also shape from focus. [Kro87]

shape from focus: A class of algorithms for estimating scene depth at each image pixel, and therefore surface shape, by varying the focus setting of a camera until the image achieves optimal focus (minimum blur) in a neighborhood of the pixel under examination. Obviously, pixels corresponding to different depths would achieve optimal focus for different settings. A model of the relation between depth and image focus is assumed, containing a number of parameters (e.g., the optics parameters) that must be calibrated. Notice that the camera uses a large aperture, so that the smallest possible depth interval generates in-focus image points. See also shape from defocus. [Kre83]

shape from interreflection: Standard shape from shading or photometric stereo algorithms assume that the surfaces are illuminated by a single point source. When surfaces are nearby, they are also illuminated by interreflections from other surfaces, which leads to errors in the recovered shape. By modeling how the interreflections occur, algorithms can iteratively remove the effect of the interreflections, and thus lead to better estimates of the true shape. [NIK90]

shape from line drawings: A class of symbolic algorithms inferring 3D properties of scene objects (as opposed to exact shape measurements, as in other "shape from" methods) from line drawings. First, assumptions are made about the type of line drawings admissible, e.g., polyhedral objects only, no surface markings or shadows, maximum three lines forming an image junction. Then, a dictionary of line junctions is formed, assigning a symbolic label to every possible appearance of the line junctions in space under the given assumptions. The figure shows part of a simple dictionary of junctions and a labeled shape:

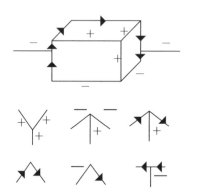

where + means planes intersecting in a convex shape, − means a concave shape, and the arrows a discontinuity (occlusion) between surfaces. Each image junction is then assigned the set of all possible labels that its shape admits locally (e.g., all possible two-line junction labels for a two-line junction). Finally, a constraint satisfaction algorithm is used to prune labels inconsistent with the context. See also Waltz line labeling and relaxation labeling. [CSD+09]

shape from monocular depth cues: A class of algorithms estimating shape from information related to depth detected in a single image, i.e., from monocular cues. See shape from contour, shape from line drawings, shape from perspective, shape from shading, shape from specularity, shape from structured light and shape from texture. [HJ93]

shape from motion: A vast class of algorithms for estimating 3D shape (structure), and often depth, from the motion information contained in an image sequence. Methods exist that rely on tracking sparse sets of image features (e.g., the Tomasi–Kanade factorization) as well as dense motion fields, i.e., optical flow, seeking to reconstruct dense surfaces. See also motion factorization. [JKS95:11.3]

shape from multiple sensors: A class of algorithms recovering shape from information collected from a number of sensors of the same type (see multi-view stereo) or of different types (see sensor fusion). [ME88]

shape from optical flow: See optical flow.

shape from orthogonal views: See shape from contour.

shape from perspective: A class of techniques estimating depth for various features from perspective cues, e.g., the fact that a translation along the optical axis of a perspective camera changes the size of the imaged objects. See also pinhole camera model. [SQ04:9A.2.1]

shape from photo consistency: A technique based on space carving for recovering shape from multiple views (photos). The basic constraint is that the underlying shape must be "photo-consistent" with all the input photos,

256

i.e., roughly speaking, it must give rise to compatible intensity values in all cameras. [KS00]

shape from photometric stereo: See photometric stereo.

shape from polarization: A technique recovering local shape from the polarization properties of a surface under observation. The basic idea is to illuminate a surface with known polarized light, estimate the polarization state of the reflected light, then use this estimate in a closed-form model linking the surface normals with the measured polarization parameters. In practice, polarization estimates can be noisy. This method can be useful wherever intensity images do not provide information, e.g., featureless specular surfaces. See also polarization-based methods. [Wol92]

shape from scatter trace: A method of shape recovery from transparent or translucent objects by combining multiple observations of a point with a moving light source (or a moving camera, or both). The set of measurements at each pixel is its scatter trace. [MK07]

shape from shading: The problem of estimating shape, here in the sense of a field of normals from which a surface can be recovered up to a scale factor, from the shading pattern (light and shadows) of an image. The key idea is that, assuming a reflectance map for the scene (typically a Lambertian surface), an image irradiance equation can be written linking the surface normals to the illuminant direction and the image intensity. The constraint can be used to recover the normals assuming local surface smoothness. [JKS95:9.4]

shape from shadows: A technique for recovering geometry from a number of images of an outdoor scene acquired at different times, i.e., with the sun at different angles. Geometric information can be recovered under various assumptions and knowledge of the sun's position. Also called "shape from darkness". See also shape from shading and photometric stereo. [CL89]

shape from silhouette: See shape from contour.

shape from specularity: A class of algorithms for estimating local shape from surface specularities. A specularity constrains the surface normal – the incident and reflection angles must coincide. The detection of specularities in images is, in itself, a non-trivial problem. [HB88]

shape from structured light: See structured light triangulation.

shape from texture: The problem of estimating shape, here in the sense of a field of normals from which a surface can be recovered up to a scale factor, from the image texture. The deformation of a planar texture recorded in an image (the texture gradient) depends on the shape of the surface to which the texture is applied. Techniques exist for shape estimation from statistical texture and regular texture patterns. [FP03:9.4–9.5]

shape from X: A generic term for a method that generates 3D shape or position estimates from one of a variety of possible techniques, such as shape from multiple sensors, shape from shading, shape from focus etc. [TV98:9.1]

shape from zoom: The problem of computing shape (in the sense of the distance of each scene point from the sensor) from two or more images acquired at different zoom settings, achieved through a zoom lens. The basic idea is to differentiate the projection equations with respect to the focal length, f, achieving an expression linking the variations of f and pixel displacement with depth. [MO90]

shape grammar: A grammar specifying a class of shapes, whose rules specify patterns for combining more primitive shapes. Rules are composed of two parts: a description of a specific shape and how to replace or transform it. Used also in design, CAD and architecture. See also production system and expert system. [BB82:6.3.2]

shape index: A measure, usually indicated by S, of the type of shape of a surface patch in terms of its principal curvature. Formally,

$$S = -\frac{2}{\pi} \arctan \frac{\kappa_M + \kappa_m}{\kappa_M - \kappa_m}$$

where κ_m and κ_M are the principal curvatures. S is undetermined for planar patches. A related parameter, R, measures the amount of *curvedness* of the patch:

$$\sqrt{(\kappa_M^2 + \kappa_m^2)/2}$$

All curvature-based shape classes map to the unit circle in the R–S plane, with planar patches at the origin. See also mean and Gaussian curvature shape classification and shape representation. [KvD92]

shape magnitude class: Part of a local surface curvature representation scheme in which each point has a surface class and a magnitude of curvature (shape magnitude). This representation is an alternative to the more common shape classification based on either the two principal curvatures or the mean and Gaussian curvature. [KvD92]

shape matching: Matching could be at a high level, in which one is comparing semantic descriptions in terms of the different parts of the shapes (e.g., matching a mountain bicycle to a racing bicycle), or at a low level, where one establishes point-to-point correspondence between the shapes (e.g., when matching faces). [BMP02]

shape modeling: Constructing some sort of compact representation of a shape, through, e.g., geometric modeling for exact models or point distribution models for modeling a family of shapes. Usually the model is a somewhat simplified or abstracted representation of the real object.

shape moment: A moment as applied to a 2D region or 3D volume.

shape prior: A piece of domain knowledge that helps constrain the space of all possible shapes, e.g., as used during shape recognition. Examples could be property based, such as a prior that tries to maximize the smoothness of a boundary, or probabilistic, such as a distribution of possible shapes (shape parameters). [GCK91]

shape recognition: Recognizing either the class of a shape, e.g., that it is a star shape or is "volcano-shaped", or the specific shape it has, e.g., a particular trademark's shape. [MZS03]

shape recovery: Reconstructing the 3D shape of an object from image data. There are many methods for this. See shape from X.

shape representation: A large class of techniques seeking to capture the salient properties of shapes, both 2D and 3D, for analysis and comparison purposes. Many representations have been proposed in the literature, including skeletons for 2D and 3D shapes (see medial axis skeletonization and distance transform), curvature-based representations (e.g., the curvature primal sketch, the curvature scale space and the extended Gaussian image), generalized cones for articulated objects, invariants, and flexible object models (e.g., snakes, deformable superquadrics and deformable template models). [ZRH03:2.3]

shape template: A geometric pattern used for matching with the image data, e.g., by correlation matching. The shape could be rigid or parameterized. The template is usually swept over a region of the image (or subjected to Fourier matched-filter object recognition). In the figure, the template is the letter "C" which is matched against the text image: [ZDDD07]

TEMPLATE

C

IMAGE

shape texture: The texture of a surface from the point of view of the variation in the shape, as contrasted to the variation in the reflectance patterns on the surface. See also surface roughness characterization. [WY08]

shapeme histogram: A shapeme is a distinctive cluster of shape features on the boundary of a 2D shape or surface of a 3D shape, giving a 2D shape descriptor or 3D shape descriptor. The shapeme histogram records a count of the instances of the different shapemes on the object. Object recognition is based on matching histograms. The figure shows (left) an L-shape with three shapemes consisting of a convex corner, a concave corner and a straight section and (right) its the shapeme histogram: [SSMK06]

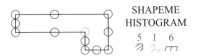

SHAPEME HISTOGRAM

sharp–unsharp masking: A form of image enhancement that makes the edges of image structures crisper. The operator can either add a weighted amount of a gradient or high-pass filter of the image or subtract a weighted amount of a smoothing filter or low-pass filter of the image. The figure shows (left) an image and (right) an unsharp masked version of it: [Umb98:4.3]

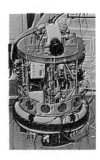

shear transformation: An affine image transformation changing one coordinate only. The corresponding transformation matrix, S, is equal to the identity apart from $s_{12} = s_x$, which changes

the first image coordinate. Shear on the second image coordinate is obtained similarly by $s_{21} = s_y$. The figure shows the result of a shear transformation: [SQ04:9.1]

shock graph: A graph description of the medial axis of a 2D planar shape. The four node types are based on the radius function along the axis (1=monotonic, 2=local minimum radius, 3=constant, 4=local maximum radius). The graph can be organized into a tree for efficient object recognition by graph matching. The figure shows a simple shape with its overlaid medial axis and corresponding shock graph: [SSDZ99]

shock tree: A 2D shape representation technique based on the singularities (see singularity event) of the radius function along the medial axis (MA). The MA is represented by a tree with the same structure, and is divided into continuous segments of uniform behavior (local maximum, local minimum, constant, monotonic). See also medial axis skeletonization and distance transform. [SSDZ99]

short baseline stereo: See narrow baseline stereo.

shot noise: See impulse noise and salt-and-pepper noise.

shutter: A device allowing the light into a camera for enough time to form an image on a photosensitive film or chip. Shutters can be mechanical, as in traditional photographic cameras, or electronic, as in a digital camera. In the former case, a window-like mechanism is opened to allow the light to be recorded by a photosensitive film. In the latter case, a CCD or other type of sensor is triggered electronically to record the amount of incident light at each pixel. [WP:Shutter_(photography)]

shutter control: The device controlling the length of time that the shutter is open. [WP:Exposure_(photography) #Exposure_control]

side-looking radar: A radar projecting a fan-shaped beam illuminating a strip of the scene at the side of the instrument, typically used for mapping a large area. The map is produced as the instrument is carried along by a vehicle sweeping the surface to the side. See also acoustic sonar. [Leb79]

SIFT: A feature point descriptor that aims to give a distinctive signature for the pattern of intensity values in a 16×16 neighborhood around the feature point. The descriptor is computed from eight cell histograms of the gradient magnitudes and directions from 4×4 blocks within the 16×16 pixel neighborhood. The histograms are concatenated to form a 128 vector. [Low04]

signal coding system: A system for encoding a signal into another, typically for compression or security purposes. See image compression and digital watermarking. [CSE00]

signal processing: The collection of mathematical and computational tools for the analysis of typically 1D (but also 2D, 3D etc.) signals such as audio recordings or other intensity against time or position measurements. Digital signal processing is the subset of signal processing which pertains to signals that are represented as streams of binary digits. [WP:Signal_processing]

signal-to-noise ratio (SNR): A measure of the relative strengths of the interesting and uninteresting (noise) parts of a signal. In signal processing, SNR is usually expressed in decibels as the ratio of the power of signal and noise, i.e., $10 \log_{10} \frac{P_s}{P_n}$. With statistical noise, the SNR can be defined as 10 times the log of the ratio of the standard deviations of signal and noise. [Jai89:3.6]

signature curve: Consider a smooth planar curve such as the boundary of a region found by region segmentation, and parameterize that curve by arc length s. Let $\kappa(s)$ be the curvature of the curve and $\kappa_s(s)$ be its derivative with respect to arc length. Then $(\kappa(s), \kappa_s(s))$ gives the Euclidean signature curve. Extensions exist for an affine signature curve using the affine curvature and affine arc length. A signature curve can be a useful shape descriptor for object recognition of planar shapes. [SL05]

signature identification: A class of techniques for verifying a written signature. Also known as "dynamic signature verification". An area of biometrics. See also handwriting verification, handwritten character recognition, fingerprint identification and face identification. [WP:Handwriting_recognition]

signature verification: The problem of authenticating a signature automatically with image-processing techniques; in practice, deciding whether a signature matches a specimen sufficiently well. See also handwriting verification and handwritten character recognition. [WP:Handwriting_recognition]

silhouette: See object contour.

SIMD: See single instruction multiple data.

similarity: The property that makes two entities (images, models, objects, features, shape, intensity values etc.) or sets thereof similar, that is, how they resemble each other. A similarity transformation creates perfectly similar structures and a similarity metric quantifies the degree of similarity of two possibly non-identical structures. Examples of similar structures are two polygons identical except for a change in size; two image neighborhoods whose intensity values are identical except for scaling by a multiplicative factor. The concept of similarity lies at the heart of several classic vision problems, including the stereo correspondence problem, image matching and geometric model matching. [JKS95:14.3]

similarity metric: A metric quantifying the similarity of two entities. For instance, cross correlation is a common similarity metric for image regions. For similarity metrics on specific objects encountered in vision, see feature similarity, graph similarity and gray scale similarity. See also point similarity measure and matching method. [DH73:6.7]

similarity transformation: A transformation that changes an object into a similar-looking one; formally, a conformal mapping preserving the ratio of distances (the magnification ratio). The transformation matrix, $\mathbf{T}$, can be written as $\mathbf{T} = \mathbf{B}^{-1}\mathbf{A}\mathbf{B}$, where $\mathbf{A}$ and $\mathbf{B}$ are similar matrices, that is, representing the same transformation after a change of basis. Examples include rotation, translation, expansion and contraction (scaling). [SQ04:9.1]

simple lens: A lens composed by a single piece of refracting material, shaped in such a way as to achieve the desired lens behavior. For example, a convex focusing lens. [Hor86:2.3]

simulated annealing: Simulated annealing is a generic heuristic method for the optimization of an objective function $E(x)$. We consider minimization of $E(x)$, corresponding to the physics origin of the problem, where a minimum energy configuration is desired. Under the Boltzmann distribution, the probability of configuration x is given by $p(x) \propto \exp(-E(x)/T)$, where T is the temperature (and Boltzmann's constant has been set to 1). At very high temperatures the probability distribution over the states is uniform, but at $T = 0$ the state(s) with the minimum value of the objective have all of the probability mass. The algorithm works by proposing a change x' to the current state and accepting this change depending on $(E(x') - E(x))/T$ with greater propensity to accept downhill changes. (The algorithm gives a nonzero probability of accepting "uphill" moves, which helps

it avoid the local minima of greedy search.) This process is run while gradually decreasing (or "annealing") the temperature to zero. [PTVF92:10.9]

single-camera system: A vision system that uses only one camera. Contrast with a multi-camera system.

single instruction multiple data (SIMD): A computer architecture allowing the same instruction to be simultaneously executed on multiple processors and thus different portions of the data set (e.g., different pixels or image neighborhoods). Useful for a variety of low-level image processing operations. See also MIMD, pipeline parallelism, data parallelism and parallel processing. [Sch89:Ch. 8]

single-layer perceptron network: A form of neural network used for supervised learning problems. It maps input data $\vec{x}$ of dimension d to a space of outputs $\vec{y}$ of dimension d'. A single-layer perceptron network is characterized by a $d' \times d$ matrix of weights (parameters) $\mathbf{W}$ and a transfer function σ so that $f(\vec{x}) = \sigma(\mathbf{W}\vec{x})$ where σ is applied element-wise to vector arguments. Each output unit is a perceptron, with σ being its activation function; the logistic sigmoid function $\sigma(z) = (1 + e^{-z})^{-1}$ is a common choice. See also multilayer perceptron network. [Bis06:5.1]

single-lens reflex camera: A camera that uses a mirror system to allow the photographer to see what image will be captured. These cameras are popular for quality photography because of the ability to interchange lenses and filters. [WP:Single-lens_reflex_camera]

single photon emission computed tomography (SPECT): A medical imaging technique that involves the rotation of a photon detector array around the body in order to detect photons emitted by the decay of previously injected radionuclides. This technique is particularly useful for creating a volumetric image showing metabolic activity. Resolution is lower than PET but imaging is cheaper and some SPECT radiopharmaceuticals may be used where PET nuclides cannot. [WP:Single-photon emission computed tomography]

singular value decomposition (SVD): A factorization of any $m \times n$ matrix **A** into $\mathbf{A} = \mathbf{UDV}^T$. The columns of the $m \times m$ matrix **U** are mutually orthogonal unit vectors, as are the columns of the $n \times n$ matrix **V**. The $m \times n$ matrix **D** is diagonal, and its nonzero elements, the *singular values* σ_i, satisfy $\sigma_1 \geq \sigma_2 \geq \ldots \geq \sigma_n \geq 0$. The SVD has extremely useful properties. For example:

- **A** is nonsingular if and only if all its singular values are nonzero and the number of nonzero singular values gives the rank of **A**;
- the columns of **U** corresponding to the nonzero singular values span the range of **A**; the columns of **V** corresponding to the nonzero singular values span the null space of **A**;
- the squares of the nonzero singular values are the nonzero eigenvalues of both $\mathbf{AA}^T$ and $\mathbf{A}^T\mathbf{A}$, the columns of **U** are eigenvectors of $\mathbf{AA}^T$ and the columns of **V** of $\mathbf{A}^T\mathbf{A}$.

Moreover, the pseudoinverse of a matrix, occurring in the solution of rectangular linear systems, can be easily computed from the SVD definition. [FP03:12.3.2]

singularity event: A point in the domain of the map of a geometric curve or surface where the first derivatives vanish. [WP:Singular_point_of_a_curve]

sinusoidal projection: A family of linear image transforms, C, the rows of which are the eigenvalues of a special symmetric tridiagonal matrix. This includes the discrete cosine transform (DCT). [Jai89:5.12]

situation graph tree: A behavior representation for describing activities, including the alternative sequences that actions can take, used for video-based behavior classification. A graph is formed where nodes are based on schemas that contain logical predicates for recognizing a state and for the actions expected when in that state. The arcs are probabilistic transitions between the schemas. The states can be expanded hierarchically, creating a tree of subgraphs. [GVRV04]

situational awareness: A general psychological term referring to the ability to perceive the important factors in an environment in such a manner as to be able to make predictions about how the environment will change. In the context of image analysis, it generally refers to coupling scene understanding with event understanding. [WP:Situation_awareness]

skeleton: A curve, or tree-like set of curves, capturing the basic structure of an object. The figure shows a linear skeleton for a puppet-like 2D shape:

The curves forming the skeleton are typically central to the shape. Several algorithms exist for computing skeletons, e.g., the medial axis transform (see medial axis skeletonization) and the distance transform, for which the grassfire algorithm can be applied. [Jai89:9.9]

skeleton by influence zones (SKIZ): Commonly known as the Voronoi diagram. [SQ04:7.3.2]

skeleton model: An articulated model consisting of rigid links connected by joints, typically used for modeling humans, robots, animals, etc., where the rigid links represent the limbs. [SBS02]

skeletonization: A class of techniques that try to reduce a 2D (or 3D) binary image to a "skeleton" form in which every remaining pixel is a skeleton pixel, but the essential shape of the input image is captured. Definitions of the skeleton include the set of centers of circles bitangent to the object boundary and smoothed local symmetries. [Sch89:Ch. 6]

sketch-based image retrieval: A type of image retrieval in which the database index is based on a user's sketch of the desired target. For example, it may be a sketch of a face, a mechanical part or a trademark. Part of what makes this retrieval difficult is the fact that the sketch will not be a faithful copy of the desired target, yet the expectation is that the shape of the sketch is relatively accurate. Typically, the retrieval will be based on the shape properties of the sketch rather than on the color and texture statistics, as in many other image-retrieval applications. [GR95]

skew: An error introduced in the imaging geometry by a non-orthogonal pixel grid, in which rows and columns of pixels do not form an angle of exactly 90°. This is usually considered only in high-accuracy photogrammetry applications. [JKS95:12.10.2]

skew correction: A transformation compensating for the skew error. [JKS95:12.10.2]

skew symmetry: A *skew symmetric contour* is a planar contour such that every straight line oriented at an angle ϕ with respect to a particular axis, called the "skew symmetry axis" of the contour, intersects the contour at two points equidistant from the axis: [BB82:9.5.4]

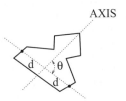

skin color analysis: A set of techniques for color analysis applied to images containing skin, e.g., for retrieving images from a database

(see color-based image retrieval). See also color, color image, color image segmentation, color matching and colorimetry. [TOS+03]

skin color model: A statistical model of the appearance of human skin in images. Typical models might be based on histograms of observed pixel colors or Gaussian mixture models. The core underlying observation is that, when corrected for lightness, almost all human skin has a similar color, which is distinct from many of the other observed colors in scenes. Complications include variations in scene lighting and shadows. Skin color models are commonly used in applications such as face detection or online pornography screening. [JR99]

SKIZ: See skeleton by influence zones.

SLAM: Simultaneous localization and mapping. A vision algorithm used particularly by the mobile robotics community. It allows the incremental construction and update of a geometric model by a robot as it explores an unknown environment. Given the constructed partial model, the robot can determine its location (self-localization) relative to the model. [TBF05:Ch. 10]

slant: The angle between a surface normal in the scene and the viewing direction:

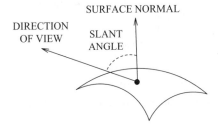

See also tilt and shape from texture. [FP03:9.4.1]

slant normalization: A class of algorithms used in handwritten character recognition, transforming slanted cursive characters into vertical ones. See handwritten character recognition and optical character recognition. [EGSS99]

slice-based reconstruction: The reconstruction of a 3D object from a number of planar slices, or sections taken across the object. The slice plane is typically advanced at regular spatial intervals to sweep the working volume. See also tomography, computed axial tomography, single photon emission computed tomography and nuclear magnetic resonance. [SSPP07]

sliding window: A common component of an image-processing (and signal-processing) algorithm whereby the calculation is based on a neighborhood or window of data about the current point. After the calculation is done at the given point, the calculation typically moves to an adjacent point and the neighborhood (window) moves (slides) to that adjacent point: [SOS00:7.1.3]

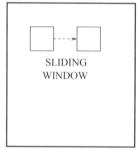

IMAGE

slope density function: This is the histogram of the tangential orientations (slopes) of a curve or region boundary. It can be used to represent the curve shape in a manner invariant to translation and rotation (up to a shift of the density function). [BB82:8.4.5]

small motion model: A class of mathematical models representing very small (ideally, infinitesimal) camera-scene motion between frames. Used typically in shape from motion. See also optical flow. [LAT02]

smart camera: A hardware device incorporating a camera and an on-board computer in a single, small container, thus achieving a programmable vision system within the size of a normal video camera. [TV98:2.3.1]

smooth motion curve: The curve defined by a motion that can be expressed by smooth (that is, differentiable: derivatives of all orders exist) parametric functions of the image coordinates. Notice that "smooth" is often used in an intuitive sense, not in the strict mathematical sense above (clearly, an exacting constraint), as in image smoothing. See also motion and motion analysis. [AF02]

smooth surface: A common-sense term for a surface with all orders of derivatives defined at each point in the surface (a C^∞ surface). In practice, C^2 continuity, meaning that at least two derivatives exist at all points, is considered smooth. [Wei12:Smooth Function]

smoothed local symmetries: A class of skeletonization algorithms, associated with Asada and Brady. Given a 2D curve that bounds a closed region in the plane, the skeleton as computed by smoothed local symmetries is the locus of chord midpoints of bitangent circles. Compare the symmetric axis transform. The figure shows two skeleton points as defined by smoothed local symmetries: [BA84]

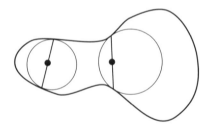

smoothing: Generally, any modification of a signal intended to remove the effects of noise. Often used to mean the attenuation of high spatial frequency components of a signal. As many models of noise have a flat power spectral density (PSD), while natural images have a PSD that decays toward zero at high spatial frequencies, suppressing the high frequencies increases the overall signal-to-noise ratio of the image. See also discontinuity preserving regularization, anisotropic diffusion, power spectrum and adaptive smoothing. [FP03:7.1.1]

smoothing filter: Smoothing is often achieved by using the convolution operator with a smoothing filter to reduce noise or high spatial frequency detail. Such filters include discrete approximations to the symmetric probability densities such as the Gaussian distribution, binomial distribution and uniform distribution. For example, in 1D, the discrete signal $x_1 \ldots x_n$ is convolved with the kernel $[\frac{1}{6} \frac{4}{6} \frac{1}{6}]$ to produce the smoothed signal $y_1 \ldots y_{n+2}$ in which $y_i = \frac{1}{6}x_{i-1} + \frac{4}{6}x_i + \frac{1}{6}x_{i+1}$. [FP03:7.1.1]

smoothness constraint: An additional constraint used in data interpretation problems. The general principle is that results derived from nearby data must themselves have similar values. Traditional examples of where the smoothness constraint can be applied are in shape from shading and optical flow. The underlying observation that supports this computational constraint is that the observed real-world surfaces and motions are smooth almost everywhere. [JKS95:9.4]

snake: The combination of a deformable model and an algorithm for fitting that model to image data. In one common embodiment, the model is a parameterized 2D curve, e.g., a b-spline parameterized by its control points. Image data, which might be a gradient image or 2D points, induces forces on points on the snake that are translated to forces on the control points or parameters. An iterative algorithm adjusts the control points according to these forces and recomputes the forces. Stopping criteria, step lengths, and other issues of optimization are all issues that must be dealt with in an effective snake. [TV98:5.4]

SNR: See signal-to-noise ratio.

Sobel edge detector: A method of edge detection based on Sobel kernels. The edge magnitude of image E is the square root of the sum of squares of the convolution of the image with horizontal and vertical Sobel kernels,

given by $E = \sqrt{(K_x * I)^2 + (K_y * I)^2}$. The figure shows (left) an image and (right) the Sobel operator applied to it: [JKS95:5.2.2]

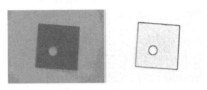

Sobel gradient operator: See Sobel kernel.

Sobel kernel: A gradient estimation kernel used for edge detection. The horizontal kernel is the convolution of a smoothing filter, $s = [1, 2, 1]$ in the horizontal direction and a gradient operator $d = [-1, 0, 1]$ in the vertical direction. The kernel

$$K_y = s * d^\top = \begin{pmatrix} -1 & -2 & -1 \\ 0 & 0 & 0 \\ 1 & 2 & 1 \end{pmatrix}.$$

highlights horizontal edges. The vertical kernel K_x is the transpose of K_y. [JKS95:5.2.2]

soft mathematical morphology: An extension of gray scale mathematical morphology in which the min and max operations are replaced by other rank operations e.g., replacing each pixel in an image by the 90th percentile value in a 5×5 window centered at the pixel. Weighted ranks may be computed. See also fuzzy morphology. [GAT98]

soft morphology: See soft mathematical morphology.

soft vertex: A point on a polyline whose connecting line segments are almost collinear. Soft vertices may arise from segmentation of a smooth curve into line segments. They are called "soft" because they may be removed if the segments of the polyline are replaced by curve segments. [JKS95:6.6]

solid angle: A property of a 3D object: the amount of the unit sphere's surface that the object's projection onto the unit sphere occupies. The unit sphere's surface area is 4π, so the maximum value of a solid angle is 4π steradians: [FP03:4.1.2]

SOLID ANGLE

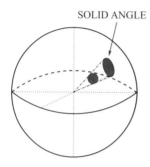

source: An emitter of energy that illuminates the vision system's sensors. [WP:Light_source#Light_sources]

source geometry: See light source geometry.

source image: The image on which an image processing or an image analysis operation is based: [PGB03]

Source Image   Target Image

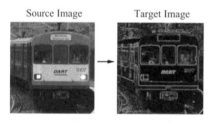

source placement: See light source placement.

space carving: A method for creating a 3D volumetric representation from 2D images. Starting from a voxel representation in which a 3D cube is marked "occupied", voxels are removed if they fail to provide photo-consistency in the set of 2D images in which they appear. The order in which the voxels are processed is a key aspect of space carving, as it allows otherwise intractable visibility computations to be avoided. [KS00]

space curve: A curve that may follow a path in 3D space (i.e., it is not restricted to lying in a plane). [WP:Space_curve#Topology]

space–time cuboid: A block of time-varying image data concatenated to form a 3D (or higher) solid. The term "cuboid" refers to a generally small subset of the full dataset. For example, given a space-time interest point from a video sequence, one could construct a space-time cuboid by concatenating an $N \times N$ neighborhood of data from each of the T previous and succeeding frames, plus the current frame, to form an $N \times N \times (2T + 1)$ block of data. This data might then be analyzed to create a unique descriptor for similar space-time patterns: [BPSK11]

MULTIPLE   3D DATA
2D FRAMES   VOLUME
        "SPACE–TIME CUBOID"

space–time descriptor: A descriptor of image behavior that incorporates both spatial and temporal elements. For example, it could be based on properties of a space-time cuboid positioned at a space-time interest point, or the cumulative motion history image. These descriptors are used particularly for behavior analysis and behavior classification. [BGX09]

space–time interest point: An interest point which is distinctive because of both the spatial and temporal properties of the pixels in its neighborhood. These points can be used for action recognition or feature point tracking. [BGX09]

space-variant processing: Distributing the image processing power unevenly (in the geometric sense) around the image, e.g., with a log-polar image or when the processing is concentrated at the fovea or at a region of interest [MvSG90]

space-variant sensor: A sensor in which the pixels are not uniformly sampling the projected image data. For example, a log-polar image sensor

266

has rings of pixels of exponentially increasing size as one moves radially from the central point: [WP: Space_Variant_Imaging#Foveated_sensors]

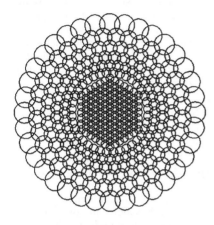

sparse coding: A method for describing some data by using a few instances of a large set of descriptors (or the firing of a few of many neurons). For example, a set of Gabor filters of different sizes, scales and orientations could be the descriptor set. Then a particular image patch could be described in terms of the nonzero coefficients of a few Gabor filters, selected so as to reconstruct the patch well. See also sparse representation. [Mur12:11.8]

sparse data: 1) Data containing many zero entries.
2) Data in which there are few examples of a specific configuration, so that the estimation of probabilities related to this configuration becomes unreliable. [Mur12:3.5.4]

sparse graphical model: A graphical model in which each random variable depends on only a small number of other variables. [HTF08:Ch. 17]

sparse representation: Given a large vocabulary of N possible image descriptors or image features, one can describe an object or image by a binary vector of length N that indicates which of the features apply to the object. Since only a few will typically apply, the description is sparse. The representation can be extended to

include encoding the presence of relations. See also sparse coding. [AR02]

sparsity problem: A general machine learning problem where there is insufficient data to accurately or completely estimate a model. This could be a statistical model where the probabilities are inaccurate for sparse events, or a graphical model where there are missing links between nodes. See also sparse data. [Mur12:3.5.4]

spatial angle: The area on a unit sphere that is bounded by a cone with its apex in the center of the sphere:

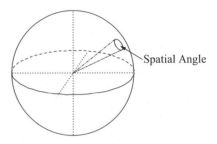

Measured in steradians. This is frequently used when analyzing luminance. [WP:Solid_angle]

spatial averaging: The pixels in the output image are weighted averages of their neighboring pixels in the input image. Mean smoothing and Gaussian smoothing are examples of spatial averaging. [Jai89:7.4]

spatial domain smoothing: An implementation of smoothing in which each pixel is replaced by a value that is directly computed from other pixels in the image. In contrast, smoothing with a frequency domain filter first processes all pixels to create a linear transformation of the image, such as a Fourier transform and expresses the smoothing operation in terms of the transformed image. [Sch89:Ch. 4]

spatial frequency: The rate of repetition of intensities *across* an image. In a 2D image, the space to which "spatial" refers is the image's X–Y plane. The figure has significant repetition at a spatial frequency of $\frac{1}{10}$ pixel^{-1} in the horizontal direction:

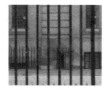

The 2D Fourier transform represents spatial frequency contributions in all directions, at all frequencies. A discrete approximation is efficiently computed using the fast Fourier transform (FFT). [Hec87:7.7]

spatial hashing: See spatial indexing. [WP:Spatial_index]

spatial indexing: 1) Conversion of a shape to a number, so that it may be quickly compared to other shapes. Intimately linked with the computation of invariants to spatial transformations and imaging distortions of the shape. For example, a shape represented as a collection of 2D boundary points might be indexed by its compactness. 2) The design of efficient data structures for search and storage of geometric quantities. For example closest-point queries are made more efficient by the computation of spatial indices such as the Voronoi diagram, distance transform, k-D trees or binary space partitioning (BSP) trees. [WP:Spatial_index]

spatial light modulator: A programmable optical filter (often based on liquid crystal technology) used to control the amount of light that passes through the filter. Can be found in data projectors. Another application is in optical image processing, where the filter is placed in the Fourier transform plane to allow frequency domain filtering. [WP:Spatial_light_modulator]

spatial matched filter: See matched filter.

spatial normal fields: Adjacent points on a surface have spatially adjacent surface normals, resulting in a field of surface normals. These fields might arise from shape from shading algorithms. [Bal11]

spatial occupancy: A form of object or scene representation in which a 3D space is divided into a grid of voxels. Voxels containing a part of the object are marked as being occupied and other voxels are marked as free space. This representation is particularly useful for tasks where properties of the object are less important than simply the presence and position of the object, as in robot navigation. [JKS95:15.3.2]

spatial proximity: The distance between two structures in real space (as contrasted with proximity in a feature or property space). [JKS95:3.1]

spatial pyramid matching: A form of pyramid matching, in which the hierarchical subdivision is spatial, e.g., by recursively subdividing by a factor of two in each direction. The advantage over pyramid matching is that it takes account of the spatial distribution of the different features. At each level and spatial subdivision, a form of bag-of-words matching takes place, and then the matching results are combined hierarchically with weights related to the size of the spatial region. [LSP06]

spatial quantization: The conversion of a signal defined on an infinite domain to a finite set of limited-precision samples. For example, the function $f(x, y)$: $\mathbb{R}^2 \mapsto \mathbb{R}$ might be quantized to the image g, of width w and height h defined as $g(i, j)$: $\{1..w\} \times \{1..h\} \mapsto \mathbb{R}$. The value of a particular sample $g(i, j)$ is determined by the point-spread function $p(x, y)$, and is given by $g(i, j) = \int p(x - i, y - j) f(x, y) \mathrm{d}x \mathrm{d}y$. [Umb98:2.2.4]

spatial reasoning: Inference from geometric rather than symbolic or linguistic information. See also geometric reasoning. [Fra92]

spatial relation: An association of two or more spatial entities, expressing the way in which such entities are connected or related. Examples include perpendicularity or parallelism of lines or planes, and inclusion of one image region in another. [BKKP05:5.8]

spatial resolution: The smallest separation between distinct signal features that can be measured by a sensor. For a CCD camera, this is dictated by the distance between adjacent pixel centers. It is often specified as the angle between the 3D rays corresponding to adjacent pixels. The inverse of the highest spatial frequency that a sensor can represent without aliasing. [JKS95:8.2]

spatial statistics: The statistical analysis of patterns that occur in space. In the case of image analysis, the statistics could refer, for example, to the image properties or to the distribution of image features or objects. [Cre93]

spatio-temporal analysis: The analysis of moving images by processing that operates on the 3D volume formed by the stack of 2D images in a sequence. Examples include kinetic occlusion, the epipolar plane image (EPI) and spatio-temporal autoregressive models (STAR). [WSK84]

spatio-temporal relationship match: Given a set of feature points in spatio-temporal space, found e.g., by the FAST interest point detector, one can describe the spatial relation (e.g., "near") and temporal relation (e.g., "before") between a pair of points. These together form a rich description of activities, particularly involving multiple agents. Matching instances of these complex descriptions allows behavior classification. [RA09]

spatio-temporal space: A representation for a portion or all of a video sequence, usually 3D, in which the 2D video frames are stacked on top of each other to form a 3D volume:

MULTIPLE   3D DATA
2D FRAMES   VOLUME
"SPACE–TIME CUBOID"

This can be generalized to 4D, e.g., by combining 3D datasets (e.g., MRI) captured over time. One can also treat the spatio-temporal space as continuous, e.g., when analyzing differential geometry.

special case motion: A subproblem of the general structure from motion problem, where the camera motion is known to be constrained *a priori*. Examples include planar motion estimation, turntable motion (single-axis rotation), and pure translation. In each case, the constrained motion simplifies the general problem, yielding one or more of: closed-form solutions, greater efficiency, increased accuracy. Similar benefits can be obtained from approximations such as the affine camera and weak perspective. [Saw94a]

specificity: A binary classifier $c(x)$ returns $+$ or $-$ labels for an example x. Comparing these predictions to the actual label gives rise to a true positive (TP), true negative (TN), false positive (FP) or false negative (FN). The specificity is defined as the true negative rate, i.e., $TN/(TN + FP)$, or the percentage of those labeled as negative are true negatives. The term is mainly used in medical contexts. See also sensitivity. [HTF08:9.2]

speckle: A pattern of light and dark spots superimposed on the image of a scene that is illuminated by coherent light, such as from a laser. Rough surfaces in the scene change the path lengths and thus the interference effects of different rays, so a fixed scene, laser and imager configuration results in a fixed speckle pattern on the imaging surface: [Jai89:8.13]

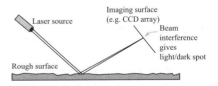

speckle reduction: Restoration of images corrupted with speckle noise, such as laser or ultrasound images. [Jai89:8.13]

SPECT: See single-photon emission computed tomography

spectral analysis: 1) Analysis performed in the spatial, temporal or electromagnetic frequency domains. 2) Generally, any analysis that involves the examination of eigenvalues. This is a nebulous concept, and consequently the number of "spectral techniques" is large. Often equivalent to principal component analysis. [WP:Spectral_theory]

spectral clustering: A form of graph theoretic clustering. The similarities between pairs of data points are recorded in a square similarity matrix. Spectral graph partitioning is then run to obtain a clustering. [HTF08: 14.5.3]

spectral decomposition method: See spectral analysis. [WP:Eigendecomposition_of_a_matrix]

spectral density function: See power spectrum.

spectral distribution: The spatial power spectrum or electromagnetic spectrum distribution. [JMW+64]

spectral factorization: A method for designing linear filters based on difference equations that have a given spectral density function when applied to white noise. [Jai89:6.3]

spectral filtering: Modifying the light before it enters the sensor by using a filter tuned to different spectral frequencies. A common use is with laser sensing, in which the filter is chosen to pass only light at the laser's frequency. Another usage is to eliminate ambient infrared light in order to increase the sharpness of an image (as most silicon-based sensors are also sensitive to infrared light). [Buc87]

spectral frequency: Electromagnetic spectrum or spatial frequency. [Hec87:7.7]

spectral graph partitioning: A graph partitioning obtained using eigenanalysis of a matrix associated with the graph. Shi and Malik have used it for image segmentation. [SM00]

spectral graph theory: The study of the properties of graphs revealed by an eigenanalysis of associated matrices, e.g., the adjacency matrix or graph Laplacian. [Chu97]

spectral reflectance: See reflectance.

spectral response: The response R of an imaging sensor illuminated by monochromatic light of wavelength λ is the product of the input light intensity I and the spectral response at that wavelength $s(\lambda)$, so $R = Is(\lambda)$. [OGFN05]

spectrum: A range of values such as the electromagnetic spectrum. [WP:Spectrum]

specular reflection: Mirror-like reflection or highlight. Formed when a light source at 3D location L, surface point P, surface normal N at that point and camera center C are all coplanar, and the angles LPN and NPC are equal: [FP03:4.3.4–4.3.5]

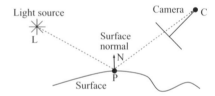

specularity: See specular reflection.

sphere: 1) A surface in any dimension defined by $\vec{x}$ such that $\|\vec{x} - \vec{c}\| = r$ for a center $\vec{c}$ and radius r. 2) The volume of space bounded by the above, or $\vec{x}$ such that $\|\vec{x} - \vec{c}\| \leq r$. [WP:Sphere]

spherical: Having the shape of, characteristics of or associations with a sphere. [WP:Sphere]

spherical aberration: A form of optical distortion that arises from the use of spherical lenses, rather than aspherical lenses tuned to the index of refraction of the glass. The result of the aberration is that parallel incoming light rays do not focus at a point; instead rays hitting the lens at different distances from the optical axis focus at different distances: [FP03:p. 11]

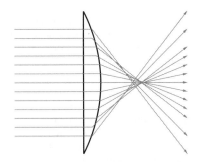

spherical harmonic: A function defined on the unit sphere, of the form

$$Y_l^m(\theta, \phi) = \eta_{lm} P_l^m(cos\theta)e^{im\phi},$$

where η_{lm} is a normalizing factor, and P_l^m is a Legendre polynomial. Any real function defined on the sphere $f(\theta, \phi)$ has an expansion in terms of the spherical harmonics of the form

$$f(\theta, \phi) = \sum_{l=0}^{\infty} \sum_{m=-l}^{l} \alpha_l^m Y_l^m(\theta, \phi)$$

That is analogous to the Fourier expansion of a function defined on the plane, with the α_l^m analogous to the Fourier coefficients. Polar plots of the first ten spherical harmonics, for $m = 0 \ldots 2, l = 0 \ldots m$ show $r = 1 + Y_l^m(\theta, \phi)$ in polar coordinates: [BB82:9.2.3]

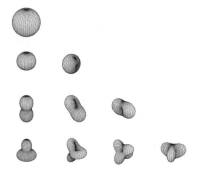

spherical mirror: Sometimes used in catadioptric cameras. A mirror whose shape is a portion of a sphere. [WP:Spherical_mirror#Mirror_shape]

spherical spin image: A generalization of the spin image to apply to freeform surfaces of 3D objects. It produces a local surface shape description that can be used for image database indexing and object recognition. [RSM01]

sphericity ratio: A measure in [0, 1] of how close a volume is to a perfect sphere (1.0). If A and V are the surface area and volume of the shape respectively, then its sphericity is:

$$\frac{1}{A}\pi^{\frac{1}{3}}(6V)^{\frac{2}{3}}$$

[WP:Sphericity]

spin image: A local surface representation of Johnson and Hebert. At selected points $\vec{p}$ with surface normal $\vec{n}$, all other surface points $\vec{x}$ can be represented on a 2D basis as $(\alpha, \beta) = (\sqrt{|| \vec{x} - \vec{p} ||^2 - (\vec{n} \cdot (\vec{x} - \vec{p}))^2}, \vec{n} \cdot (\vec{x} - \vec{p}))$. The spin image is the histogram of all the (α, β) values for the surface. Each selected point $\vec{p}$ leads to a different spin image. Matching points compares their spin images by correlation. Key advantages of the representation are that it is independent of pose and it avoids ambiguities of representation that can occur with nearly flat surfaces. [FP03:21.4.2] [JH99]

splash: An invariant representation of the region about a 3D point. It gives a local shape representation useful for position-invariant object recognition. [SM92]

spline: 1) A curve $\vec{c}(t)$ defined as a weighted sum of control points: $\vec{c}(t) = \sum_{i=0}^{n} w_i(t)\vec{p}_i$, where the control points are $\vec{p}_{1 \ldots n}$ and one weighting (or "blending") function w_i is defined for each control point. The curve may interpolate the control points or approximate them. The construction of the spline offers guarantees of continuity and smoothness. With *uniform* splines the weighting functions for each point are translated copies of each other, so $w_i(t) = w_0(t - i)$. The form of w_0 determines the type of spline: for b-splines and Bezier curves, $w_0(t)$ is a polynomial (typically cubic) in t. *Nonuniform* splines reparameterize the t axis, $\vec{c}(t) = \vec{c}(u(t))$ where $u(t)$ maps the integers $k = 0..n$ to knot points $t_{0..n}$ with linear interpolation for non-integer values of t. *Rational*

splines with n-D control points are perspective projections of normal splines with $(n + 1)$-D control points.
2) *Tensor-product* splines define a 3D surface $\vec{x}(u, v)$ as a product of splines in u and v. [JKS95:6.7]

spline smoothing: Smoothing of a discretely sampled signal $x(t)$ by replacing the value at t_i by the value predicted at that point by a spline $\hat{x}(t)$ fitted to neighboring values. [Jai89:8.7]

split and merge: A two-stage procedure for segmentation or clustering. The data is divided into subsets, with the initial division being a single set containing all the data. In the *split* stage, subsets are repeatedly subdivided depending on the extent to which they fail to satisfy a coherence criterion (e.g., similarity of pixel colors). In the *merge* stage, pairs of adjacent sets are found that, when merged, again satisfy a coherence criterion. Even if the coherence criteria are the same for both stages, the merge stage may still find subsets to merge. [Nal93:3.3.2]

SPOT: *Systeme Probatoire de l'Observation de la Terre*. A series of satellites launched by France that are a common source of satellite images of the earth. SPOT-5 was launched in May 2002 and provides complete coverage of the earth every 26 days. [WP:SPOT (satellite)]

spot detection: An image-processing operation for finding small bright or dark locations against contrasting backgrounds. The issues are the size of spot and the amount of contrast. [RT71]

spur: A short segment attached to a more significant line or edge:

SPURS

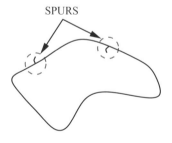

Spurs often arise when linear structures are tracked through noisy data, such as in edge detection. [SOS00: 5.2]

squared error clustering: A class of clustering algorithms that attempt to find cluster centers $\vec{c}_1 \ldots \vec{c}_n$ that minimize the squared error $\sum_{\vec{x} \in \mathcal{X}} \min_{i \in \{1 \ldots n\}} (\vec{x} - \vec{c}_i)^2$ where $\mathcal{X}$ is the set of points to be clustered. See also: k-means [Mir 99]

stadimetry: The computation of distance to an object of known size based on its apparent size in the camera's field of view. [WP:Stadimeter]

standard illuminant: A published standard spectrum (usually internationally agreed by the CIE) for a given situation, e.g., an incandescent lamp, which allows color researchers and manufacturers to use an agreed color spectral distribution for an illuminant. [WP:Standard_illuminant]

state inference: Given a system that could be in more than one state (e.g., a person walking, running or standing), state inference is the process of deciding which of the states the system is in. The algorithm could be rule-based, probabilistic or based on fuzzy reasoning etc.

state space model: A state space model is a probabilistic model with a hidden state variable evolving dynamically in time. Observations are made according to an observation probability distribution, giving partial information about the hidden state. Canonical examples of state space models are the hidden Markov model (HMM) with discrete state and the Kalman filter with continuous state. [Bis06: 13.1]

state transition probability: In a Markov process in discrete time, the state transition probability distribution specifies $p(z_{t+1}|z_t)$ where z_t denotes the state at time t. [Bis06:13.2]

state vector: In a Kalman filter, the hidden state variable is a continuous-valued vector variable known as the state vector. [Bis06:13.3]

stationary camera: A camera whose optical center does not move. The camera may pan, tilt and rotate about its optical center, but it may not translate. Images taken by a stationary camera are always related by a planar homography. Also known as a "rotating" or "non-translating" camera. The term may also refer to a camera that does not move at all. [JKKW06]

statistical behavior model: A statistical form of a behavior model, such as a hidden Markov model. An advantage of the statistical form is that one can keep an estimate of the probability of a hypothesized behavior.

statistical classifier: A function mapping from a space of input data to a set of labels. Input data are points $\vec{x} \in \mathbb{R}^n$ and labels are scalars. The classifier $c(\vec{x}) = l$ assigns the label l to point $\vec{x}$. The classifier is typically a parameterized function, such as a neural network (with weights as parameters) or a support vector machine. The classifier parameters could be set by optimizing performance on a training set of known $(\vec{x}, l)$ pairs or by a self-organizing learning algorithm. [Jai89:9.14]

statistical distribution: A description of the relative number of times each possible outcome will occur for a given variable over a number of trials. For example, for a fair dice, each value will occur an equivalence of $\frac{1}{6}$ times. See also probability distribution.

statistical fusion: A general term for estimating a value A (and possibly its distribution) from a set of other values $\{B_i\}$ and their distributions $\{D_i\}$. A simple example is: given two estimates of a value V_1 and V_2, with associated probabilities p_1 and p_2, then a fused estimate is $(p_1 V_1 + p_2 V_2)/(p_1 + p_2)$. The Kalman filter is a more sophisticated algorithm for statistical fusion. [Gus10]

statistical independence: The random variables X and Y are said to be independent if their joint probability distribution $p(X, Y)$ factorizes as $p(X)p(Y)$. See also conditional independence. [Bis06: p. 17]

statistical insufficiency problem: The problem of having insufficient training examples to be able to estimate a sound statistical model for some phenomenon. This occurs particularly in unusual behavior detection, where there are many examples of common normal behaviors, but there may be only a few or no examples of the many different abnormal behaviors. See also sparse data. [GX11: p. 252]

statistical learning: The process of using data and a statistical model to make inferences about the distribution that generated the data. Supervised learning and unsupervised learning are the major categories. [Was04:Ch. 6]

statistical model: A statistical model for a dataset is a set of probability distributions. A parametric model has a finite number of parameters; a non-parametric model cannot be parameterized by a finite number of parameters. Examples of parametric models include the Gaussian distribution and linear regression with a probabilistic error model. [Was04:Ch. 6]

statistical moment: There are a number of statistical moments that provide information regarding the distribution and shape of statistical data (i.e., a probability distribution). Common ones are the infinite family $\int p(x)x^n$ for positive integers $n > 0$ and a probability distribution $p(x)$. For $n = 1$ we obtain the mean of the distribution. Moments are a special case of expectation values. Another family are histogram moments. [Was04: p. 49]

statistical pattern recognition: Pattern recognition that depends on classification rules learned from examples rather than constructed by designers. Compare structural pattern recognition. [Sch89:Ch. 6]

statistical shape model: A parameterized shape model where the parameters are assumed to be random variables drawn from a known probability distribution. The distribution is learned from training examples. Examples include point distribution models. See also active shape model. [WP:Point_distribution_model]

statistical shape prior: Shape priors are useful for constraining the estimation of shapes from noisy or under-constraining image data, e.g., to stabilize the estimation or to ensure that the recovered shape comes from a given family of shapes. The statistical aspect adds a bias towards the recovered shape having higher probability under the prior distribution. Examples include the active shape model and the point distribution model. [Cre06]

statistical texture: A texture whose description is in terms of the statistics of image neighborhoods. General examples are co-occurrence statistics of pairs of neighboring pixels, Fourier texture descriptors, autocorrelation and autoregressive models. A specific example is the statistics of the distribution of entries in 5×5 neighborhoods. These statistics may be learned from a set of training images or automatically discovered via clustering. [Nev82:8.3.1]

steerable filter: A filter applied to a 2D image, whose response is dependent on a scalar "orientation" parameter θ, but for which the response at any arbitrary value of θ may be computed as a function of a small number of basis responses, thus saving computation. For example, the directional derivative at orientation θ may be computed in terms of the x and y derivatives I_x and I_y as

$$\frac{dI}{d\vec{n}_\theta} = \begin{pmatrix} \cos\theta\, I_x \\ \sin\theta\, I_y \end{pmatrix}$$

For non-steerable filters, such as the Gabor filter, the response must be computed at each orientation, leading to higher computational complexity. [SF96]

steganography: Concealing of information in non-suspect "carrier" data. For example, encoding information in the low-order bits of a digital image. [WP:Steganography]

step edge: 1) A discontinuity in image intensity (compare with fold edge). 2) An idealized model of a step-change in intensity. The figure shows a plot of intensity I against X position with a step edge discontinuity in intensity I at a: [JKS95:Ch. 5]

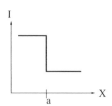

steradian: The unit of solid angles. [FP03:4.1.2]

stereo: General term for a class of problems in which multiple images of the same scene are used to recover a 3D property such as surface shape, orientation or curvature. In binocular stereo, two images are taken from different viewpoints allowing the computation of 3D structure. In trifocal, trinocular stereo and multi-view stereo, three or more images are available. In photometric stereo, the viewpoint is the same, but lighting conditions are varied in order to compute surface orientation. [WP:Stereoscopy]

stereo camera calibration: The computation of intrinsic parameters and extrinsic parameters for a pair of cameras. Important extrinsic variables are relative orientation: the rotation and translation relating the two cameras. Calibration can be achieved in several ways: conventional camera calibration of each camera independently; computation of the essential matrix or fundamental matrix relating the pair, from which relative orientation may be computed along with one or two intrinsic parameters; for a rigid stereo rig, moving the rig and capturing multiple image pairs. [TV98:7.1.3]

stereo convergence: The angle α between the optical axes of two sensors in a stereo configuration: [Stu99]

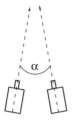

stereo correspondence problem: The key to recovering depth from stereo is to identify 2D image points that are projections of the same 3D scene point. Pairs of such image points are called "correspondences". The correspondence problem is to determine which pairs of image points are correspondences. Unfortunately, matching features or image neighborhoods is usually ambiguous, leading to massive amounts of computation and many alternative solutions. To reduce the space of matches, corresponding points are usually required to satisfy some constraints, such as having similar orientation and contrast, local smoothness or uniqueness of match. A powerful constraint is the epipolar constraint: from a single view, an image point is constrained to lie on a 3D ray, whose projection onto the second image is an epipolar curve. For pinhole cameras, the curve is an epipolar line. This greatly reduces the space of potential matches. [JKS95:11.2]

stereo fusion: The ability of the human vision system, when presented with a pair of stereo images, one to each eye independently, to form a consistent 3D interpretation of the scene, essentially solving the stereo correspondence problem. The fact that humans can perform fusion even on random dot stereograms means that high-level recognition is not required to solve all stereo correspondence problems. [BB82:3.4.2]

stereo image rectification: For a pair of images taken by pinhole cameras, points in stereo correspondence lie on corresponding epipolar lines. Stereo image rectification resamples the 2D images to create two new images, with the same number of rows, so that points on corresponding epipolar lines lie on corresponding rows. This reduces computation for some stereo algorithms, although certain relative orientations (e.g., translation along the optical axis) make rectification difficult to achieve. [JKS95:12.5]

stereo matching: See stereo correspondence problem.

stereo triangulation: Determining the 3D position of a point given its 2D positions in each of two images taken by cameras in known positions. In the noise-free case, each 2D point defines a 3D ray by back projection and the 3D point is at the intersection of the two rays. With noisy data, the optimal triangulation is computed by finding the 3D point that maximizes the probability that the two imaged points are noisy projections thereof. Also used for the analogous problem in multiple views. [WP:Range_imaging#Stereo_triangulation]

stereo vision: The ability to determine three-dimensional structure using two eyes. See also stereo. [TV98:7.1]

stimulus: 1) Any object or event that a computer vision system may detect. 2) The perceived radiant energy itself. [WP:Stimulus]

stochastic gradient descent: An optimization algorithm for minimizing a convex cost function. [WP:Stochastic_gradient_descent]

stochastic completion field: A strategy for algorithmic discovery of illusory contours. [WJ95]

stochastic process: A family of random variables $X(t)$, where t runs over an index set. This set could be taken as the real line (for a continuous-time process), over the integers (for a discrete-time process) or could index space, e.g., $\mathbb{R}^d$ (for a random field). [GS92:8.1]

stratification: A class of solutions to self-calibration in which a projective reconstruction is first converted to an affine reconstruction (by computing the plane at infinity) and then to a Euclidean reconstruction. [HZ00:18.5]

streaming video: Video presented as a sequence of images or frames. An algorithm processing such video cannot easily select a particular frame. [WP:Streaming_media]

stripe ranging: See structured light triangulation.

strobe duration: The time for which a strobed light is illuminated. [Gal90:2.1.1]

strobed light: A light that is illuminated for a very short period, generally at high intensity. [Gal90:2.1.1]

strong learner: A learner that gives an error that is (with high probability) arbitrarily close to zero. Contrast with weak learner. Boosting is a method to combine many weak learners to produce a strong learner. [FS97]

structural description: A representation that contains explicit information about object parts and the relationships between them. See also part-based representation and geometric model. [Pal99:8.2.4]

structural pattern recognition: Pattern recognition where classification is achieved using high-level rules or patterns, often specified by a human designer. See also syntactic pattern recognition. [WP:Syntactic_pattern_recognition]

structural texture: A texture that is formed by the regular repetition of a primitive structure, e.g., an image of bricks or windows. [Jai89:9.11]

structure and motion recovery: The simultaneous computation of 3D scene structure and 3D camera positions from a sequence of images of a scene. Common strategies depend on tracking of 2D image entities (e.g., interest points or edges) through multiple views and thus obtaining constraints on the 3D entities (e.g., points and lines) and camera motion. Constraints are embodied in entities such as the fundamental matrix and trifocal tensor, which may be estimated from

image data alone and then allow computation of the 3D camera positions. Recovery is up to certain equivalence classes of scenes, where any member of the class may generate the observed data, such as projective reconstruction or affine reconstruction. [MM95]

structure factorization: See motion factorization.

structure from motion: Recovery of the 3D shape of a set of scene points from their motion. For a more modern treatment, see structure and motion recovery. [JKS95:14.7]

structure from optical flow: Recovery of camera motion by computing optical flow constrained by the infinitesimal motion fundamental matrix. The small motion approximation replaces the rotation matrix $\mathbf{R}$ by $\mathbf{I} - [\vec{\omega}]_\times$ where $\vec{\omega}$ is the axis of rotation, the unique vector such that $\mathbf{R}\vec{\omega} = \vec{\omega}$. [Adi85]

structure learning: 1) Learning geometric models.
2) Learning the nodes and arcs of graphical models, as in a Bayesian network, a Hidden Markov model or a more general graph, e.g., a directed acyclic graph. [KF09:Ch. 18]

structure matching: See recognition by components.

structure tensor: Typically a 2D or 3D matrix that characterizes the dominant gradient directions at a point by a weighted combination of the gradient values within a given window. Larger window sizes increase stability but reduce sensitivity to small structures. The eigenvalues of the structure tensor encode the extent to which there are different gradient directions within the window. The structure tensor is important to interest point feature detectors, the Harris corner detector and also for characterizing texture and other applications. [WP:Structure_tensor]

structured light: A class of techniques where carefully engineered illumination is employed to simplify computation of scene properties. Common examples include structured light triangulation and moiré fringe sensing. [JKS95:11.4.1]

structured light source calibration: The special case of calibration in a structured light system where the position of the light source is determined. [BMS98]

structured light triangulation: Recovery of 3D structure by computing the intersection of a ray (or plane or other light shape) of light with the ray determined by the image of the illuminated scene surface: [JKS95:11.4.1]

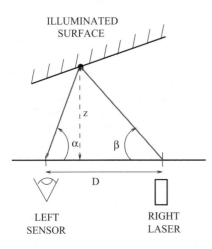

ILLUMINATED
SURFACE

LEFT
SENSOR

RIGHT
LASER

structured model: See hierarchical model.

structured SVM: The basic support vector machine (SVM) is a binary classifier. It can be generalized to have a structured output space, e.g., a set of interdependent labels in a chain or on a grid. See also conditional random field for a similar goal using probabilistic modeling. [Mur12:1.2.14, 17.5]

structuring element: The basic neighborhood structure of morphological image processing. The structuring element is an image, typically small, that defines a shape pattern. Morphological operations on a source image combine the structuring element with the source image in various ways. [JKS95:2.6]

subband coding: A means of coding a discrete signal for transmission.

The signal is passed through a set of bandpass filters and each channel is quantized separately. The sampling rate of the individual channels is set such that, before quantization, the sum of the number of per-channel samples is the same as the number of samples of the original system. By varying the quantization for different bands, the number of samples may be reduced with small losses in signal quality. [WP:Subband_coding]

subcategory recognition: Once an object category, such as "animal", has been recognized then subcategories such as "horse" or "dog" can be recognized. The hierarchy can be extended, e.g., from "dog" to "terrier" and then to "Skye terrier". [TA08]

subcomponent: An object part used in a hierarchical model. [Fis87]

subcomponent decomposition: Representation of a complete object part by a collection of smaller objects in a hierarchical model. [PR88]

subgraph isomorphism: Equivalence of a pair of subgraphs of two given graphs. Given graphs A and B, the subgraph isomorphism problem is to enumerate all pairs of subgraphs (a, b) where: $a \subset A$; $b \subset B$; a is isomorphic to b; and some given predicate $p(a, b)$ is true. Appropriate modifications of the problem allow the solution of many graph problems including determining shortest paths and finding maximal cliques. A given graph has a number of subgraphs exponential in the number of vertices and the general problem is NP-complete. The figure shows a subgraph isomorphism with the matching graph being A:b–C:a–B:c: [JKS95: 15.6.3]

subjective contour: An edge perceived by humans in an image because of

277

Gestalt completion, particularly when no image evidence is present. In the figure (Kanizsa's triangle), the triangle that appears to float above the black discs is bounded partially by a subjective contour: [Nev82:7.4]

subpixel edge detection: Estimation of the location of an image edge by subpixel interpolation of the gradient operator response, to give a position more accurately than an integer pixel value. [JKS95:5.7]

subpixel interpolation: A class of techniques that essentially interpolate the position of local maxima in images to positions at a resolution smaller than integer pixel coordinates. Examples include subpixel edge detection and interest point detection. A rule of thumb is that 0.1 pixel accuracy is often possible. If the input is an image $z(x, y)$ containing the response of some kernel to a source image, a typical approach might be as follows:
(a) Identify a local maximum where $z(x, y) \geq z(a, b)$ where $(a, b) \in$ neighborhood(x, y).
(b) Fit the quadratic surface $z = ai^2 + bij + cj^2 + di + ej + f$ to the set of samples $(i, j, z(x + i, y + j))$ in a neighborhood about (x, y).
(c) Compute the position of the local maximum of the quadratic surface:

$$\begin{pmatrix} i \\ j \end{pmatrix} = -\begin{pmatrix} 2a & b \\ b & 2c \end{pmatrix}^{-1} \begin{pmatrix} d \\ e \end{pmatrix}$$

(d) If $-\frac{1}{2} < \{i, j\} < \frac{1}{2}$ then report a maximum at subpixel location $(x + i, y + j)$.
Similar strategies apply when computing the subpixel location of edges. [JKS95:5.7]

subsampling: Reducing the size of an image by producing a new image whose pixel values are more widely sampling the original image (e.g., every third pixel). Interpolation can produce more accurate samples. To avoid aliasing, any spatial frequency higher than the Nyquist frequency of the coarse grid should be removed by low-pass filtering the image. Also known as "downsampling". [SOS00:3.6]

subspace: A subset of a vector space that is closed under addition and scalar multiplication. In data analysis, subspace structure may be detected, e.g., by principal component analysis. [Nob69: 14.2]

subspace analysis: The description of a dataset in terms of one of more subspaces. A probabilistic formulation is a mixture model of probabilistic principal component analysis components.

subspace learning: A subspace method where the subspace is learned from a number of observations. [DLTB03]

subspace method: A general term describing methods that convert a vector space into a lower-dimensional subspace, e.g., projecting a set of N-dimensional vectors onto their first two principal components to produce a 2D subspace. See principal component basis space. [Ho98]

subsurface scattering: When light is reflected not only from the surface of an object, but also partially from the interior of the surface through a sequence of reflections before exiting the surface. This is an important factor in the appearance of surfaces such as human skin. [WP:Subsurface_scattering]

subtractive color: The way in which color appears because of the attenuation or absorption of frequencies of light by materials (e.g., we perceive that something is red it is because it is attenuating or absorbing all wavelengths other than those corresponding to red). See also additive color. [WP:Subtractive_color]

superellipse: A class of 2D curves, including ellipses and Lamé curves as special cases. The general form of the superellipse is

$$\left(\frac{x}{a}\right)^{\alpha} + \left(\frac{y}{b}\right)^{\beta} = 1$$

although several alternative forms exist. Fitting superellipses to data is difficult because of the strongly non-linear dependence of the shape on the parameters α and β. The figure shows a convex superellipse with $\alpha = \beta = 3$ and a concave one with $\alpha = \beta = \frac{1}{2}$: [WP:Super_ellipse]

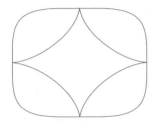

supergrid: A representation that is larger than the original image and represents explicitly both the image points and the crack edges between them: [JKS95:3.3.4]

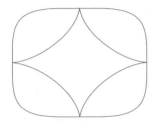

superparamagnetic clustering: A method for data clustering that takes account of the density of nearby points, rather than simply the distance to nearby points, as in other clustering algorithms. The algorithm is influenced by the Potts spin model of magnetic behavior, in which data points are assigned a spin that influences and is influenced by neighboring points and their spins. [BSD96]

superpixel: 1) A segmented group of pixels that are similar.
2) A pixel in a high-resolution image. An anti-aliasing computer graphics technique produces lower resolution image data by a weighted sum of the superpixels. [FVS09]

superquadric: A 3D generalization of the superellipse, the solution set of

$$\left(\frac{x}{a}\right)^{\alpha} + \left(\frac{y}{b}\right)^{\beta} + \left(\frac{z}{c}\right)^{\gamma} = 1$$

As with superellipses, fitting to 3D data is non-trivial, although some success has been achieved. The figure shows superquadrics, both with $\gamma = 2$; the convex superquadric has $\alpha = \beta = 3$ and the concave one has $\alpha = \beta = \frac{1}{2}$: [SQ04:9.11]

superresolution: Generation of a high-resolution image from a collection of low-resolution images of the same object taken from different viewpoints. The key to successful superresolution is in the accurate estimation of the registration between viewpoints. [WP:Super_resolution]

supervised classification: See classification.

supervised learning: The task in supervised learning is to predict a response variable or output y given an input x based on a set of training examples. The output may be a class label, (a classification problem), a continuous-valued variable (a regression problem), or a more general object. Compare with unsupervised learning. [Bis06: Ch. 1]

support vector machine: A statistical classifier assigning labels l to points $\vec{x}$ in $\mathbb{R}^n$. The support vector machine has two defining characteristics. Firstly, the classifier places the decision surface that separates points $\vec{x}_i$ and $\vec{x}_j$, which have different labels $l_i \neq l_j$, in such a way as to maximize the margin between them. Roughly speaking, the decision surface is as far as possible from any $\vec{x}$. Secondly, the classifier operates not on the raw feature vectors $\vec{x}$, but on high dimensional projections $\vec{f}(\vec{x}) : \mathbb{R}^n \mapsto \mathbb{R}^N, N > n$. However, because the classifier only ever requires dot products such as $\vec{f}(\vec{x}) \cdot \vec{f}(\vec{y})$, we never form $\vec{f}$ explicitly, but specify instead the kernel function $K(\vec{x}, \vec{y}) = \vec{f}(\vec{x}) \cdot \vec{f}(\vec{y})$. Wherever the dot product between high-dimensional vectors is required, the kernel function is used instead. [SQ04:14A.2]

support vector ranking: A modification of the support vector machine (SVM) to tackle the ranking problem. [SC04:8.1]

support vector regression: A range of techniques for function estimation that uses a subset of the data to determine a function to model the data. See also support vector machine and hinge loss function. [WP:Support_vector_machine#Regression]

SURF: Speeded up robust features: An image feature detector and descriptor. The detector achieves improved speed by replacing the scale-space Gaussian smoothing by ± 1 weighted masks based on Haar wavelets (see Haar transform). The descriptor associated with the detected points is based on a 4×4 set of square subregions, each of which is described by four values, again computed using the Haar wavelets. The result is an operator that is similar to, but is several times faster and more stable than, the SIFT operator. The figure shows some SURF points overlaying the original image: [BET08]

INPUT   SURF POINTS

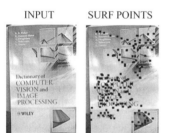

surface: In general parlance, a 2D shape that is located in three dimensions.

Mathematically, it is a 2D subset of $\mathbb{R}^3$ that is almost everywhere locally topologically equivalent to the open unit ball in $\mathbb{R}^2$. This means that a cloud of points is not a surface, but the surface may have cusps or boundaries. A parameterization of the surface is a function from $\mathbb{R}^2$ to $\mathbb{R}^3$ that defines the 3D surface point $\vec{x}(u, v)$ as a function of 2D parameters (u, v). Restricting (u, v) to subsets of $\mathbb{R}^2$ yields a subset of the surface. The surface is the set S of points on it, defined over a domain D [WP:Surface]:

$$S = \{\vec{x}(u, v) | (u, v) \in D \subset \mathbb{R}^2\}$$

surface area: Given a parametric surface $S = \{\vec{x}(u, v) | (u, v) \in D \subset \mathbb{R}^2\}$, with unit tangent vectors $\vec{x}_u(u, v)$ and $\vec{x}_v(u, v)$, the area of the surface is [TV98:A.5]

$$\int_S |\vec{x}_u(u, v) \times \vec{x}_v(u, v)| du dv$$

surface boundary representation: A method of defining surface models in computer graphics. It defines a 3D object as a collection of surfaces with boundaries. The model topology states which surfaces are connected and which boundaries are shared between patches. The figure shows three faces:

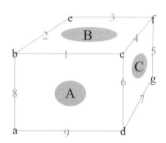

A B-rep model of this image comprises: faces A, B, C along with the parameters of their 3D surfaces; edges 1–9 with 3D curve descriptions; vertices a–g; and the connectivities of these entities, e.g., face B is bounded by curves 1–4 and curve 1 is bounded by vertices b and c. [JKS95:15.3.2]

surface class: Koenderink's classification of local surface shape into classes based on two functions of the principal curvatures: the *shape index* $S = -\frac{2}{\pi}\tan^{-1}\frac{\kappa_M+\kappa_m}{\kappa_M-\kappa_m}$ and the *curvedness* $C = \sqrt{\frac{1}{2}(\kappa_M^2 + \kappa_m^2)}$ where $\kappa_M > \kappa_m$ are the principal curvatures. The surface classes are planar ($C = 0$), hyperboloid ($|S| < \frac{3}{8}$) or ellipsoid ($|S| > \frac{5}{8}$) and cylinder ($\frac{3}{8} < |S| < \frac{5}{8}$), subdivided into concave ($S < 0$) and convex ($S > 0$). Alternative classification systems exist based on the mean curvature and Gaussian curvature, or the principal curvature. The former distinguishes more classes of hyperboloid surfaces. [KvD79]

surface completion: The process of filling in the holes in a scanned surface, which may have arisen because of defects in the sensing process or the inability of the sensor to see the given portion of the surface, e.g., because of occlusion. Algorithms that fill in the holes typically exploit local continuities around the hole and use image and shape data from elsewhere in the image or scene. [BF05]

surface continuity: Mathematically defined at a single point parameterized by (u, v) on the surface $\{\vec{x}(u, v)|(u, v) \in D \subset \mathbb{R}^2\}$. The surface is continuous *at that point* if infinitesimal motions in any direction away from (u, v) can never cause a sudden change in the value of $\vec{x}$. The surface is "everywhere continuous" (or just "continuous") if it is continuous at all points in D. [ML05]

surface curvature: A measure of the shape of a 3D surface (the characteristics of the surface that are constant if the surface is rotated or translated in 3D space). The shape is specified by the surface's principal curvatures at each point. To compute the principal curvatures, we need the first and second fundamental forms. In the differential geometry of surfaces, the first fundamental form encapsulates the arc length of curves in a surface. If the surface is defined in *parametric* form by a smooth function $\vec{x}(u, v)$, the surface's tangent vectors at (u, v) are given by the partial derivatives $\vec{x}_u(u, v)$ and $\vec{x}_v(u, v)$. From these, we

define the dot products $E(u, v) = \vec{x}_u \cdot \vec{x}_u$, $F(u, v) = \vec{x}_u \cdot \vec{x}_v$, $G(u, v) = \vec{x}_v \cdot \vec{x}_v$. Then arc length along a curve in the surface is given by the first fundamental form $ds^2 = E\,du^2 + 2F\,du\,dv + G\,dv^2$. The matrix of the first fundamental form is the 2×2 matrix

$$\mathbf{I} = \begin{pmatrix} E & F \\ F & G \end{pmatrix}$$

The second fundamental form encapsulates the curvature information. The second partial derivatives are $\vec{x}_{uu}(u, v)$ etc. The surface normal at (u, v) is the unit vector $\vec{n}(u, v)$ along $\vec{x}_u \times \vec{x}_v$. Then the matrix of the second fundamental form at (u, v) is the 2×2 matrix

$$\mathbf{II} = \begin{pmatrix} \vec{x}_{uu} \cdot \vec{n} & \vec{x}_{uv} \cdot \vec{n} \\ \vec{x}_{vu} \cdot \vec{n} & \vec{x}_{vv} \cdot \vec{n} \end{pmatrix}.$$

If $\vec{d} = (du, dv)^\top$ is a direction in the tangent space (so its 3D direction is $\vec{t}(\vec{d}) = du\vec{x}_u + dv\vec{x}_v$), then the normal curvature in the direction $\vec{d}$ is given by $\kappa(\vec{d}) = \frac{\vec{d}^\top \mathbf{II} \vec{d}}{\vec{d}^\top \mathbf{I} \vec{d}}$. The minima and maxima of κ as $\vec{d}$ varies at a point (u, v) are the principal curvatures at the point, given by the generalized eigenvalues of $\mathbf{II}\vec{z} = \kappa \mathbf{I}\vec{z}$, i.e., the solutions to the quadratic equation in κ given by $\det(\mathbf{II} - \kappa\mathbf{I}) = 0$. [FP03:19.1.2]

surface description: A description of a surface, which can include color, reflectance or shape texture, local differential geometry or global properties, such as its elongatedness or shape class (e.g., spherical).

surface discontinuity: A point at which the surface, or its normal vector, is not continuous. These are often fold edges, where the surface normal has a large change in direction. See also surface continuity. [SS92]

surface fitting: A family of parametric surfaces $\vec{x}_\theta(u, v)$ is parameterized by a vector of parameters θ. For example, the family of 3D spheres is parameterized by four parameters: three for the center and one for the radius. Given a set of n sampled data points $\{\vec{p}_1, .., \vec{p}_n\}$, the task of surface fitting is to find the parameters θ of the surface that best fits the given data. Common interpretations of "best fit" include finding the surface for which the sum of Euclidean distances from the points to the surface is smallest or that maximize the probability that the data points could be noisy samples from the surface. General techniques include least squares fitting or nonlinear optimization over the surface parameters. [JKS95:13.7]

surface interpolation: Generating a continuous surface from sparse data such as 3D points. For example, given a set of n sampled data points $S = \{\vec{p}_1, .., \vec{p}_n\}$, one might wish to generate other points in $\mathbb{R}^3$ that lie on a smooth surface that passes through all the points in S. Techniques include radial basis functions, splines and natural neighbor interpolation. [JKS95:13.6]

surface light field: A function, defined at every point $\vec{x}$ on a surface, that assigns an RGB color $\vec{c}(\vec{x}, \vec{d})$ to every ray $\vec{d}$ exiting from that point. The concept is mainly used for computer graphics as it allows more realistic rendering of surfaces with specularity. [WAA+00]

surface matching: Identifying corresponding points on two 3D surfaces, often as a precursor to surface registration. [ZH99]

surface mesh: A surface boundary representation in which the faces are typically planar and the edges are straight lines. Such representations are often associated with efficient data structures (e.g., winged edge and quad edge) that allow fast computation of various geometric and topological properties. Hardware acceleration of polygon rendering is a feature of many computers. [JKS95:13.5.1]

surface model: A geometric model of a surface, often for the purpose of rendering or object recognition. There are many types of surface model, e.g., triangulated models or freeform surfaces. [BB82:Sec. 9.2]

surface normal: The direction perpendicular to a surface. For a parametric surface $\vec{x}(u, v)$, the normal is the unit vector parallel to $\frac{\partial \vec{x}}{\partial u} \times \frac{\partial \vec{x}}{\partial v}$. For an

implicit surface $F(\vec{x}) = 0$, the normal is the unit vector parallel to $\nabla F = [\frac{\partial F}{\partial x}, \frac{\partial F}{\partial y}, \frac{\partial F}{\partial z}]$. The figure shows the surface normal as defined by the small neighborhood at point X: [TV98:A.5]

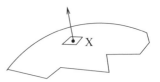

surface orientation: The convention that decides whether the surface normal or its negation points outside the space bounded by the surface. [JKS95:9.2]

surface patch: A surface whose domain is finite. [JKS95:13.5.2]

surface reconstruction: The process of constructing a 3D surface model from a set of related data, such as a set of 3D points, a set of cross-sections from scanner data (e.g., MRI) or a set of filled voxels. [HDD+92]

surface reflectance: A description of the manner in which a surface interacts with light. See reflectance. [JKS95:9.1.2]

surface roughness: The measure of the shape texture of a surface, i.e., the variation of the surface away from an aligned ideal smooth surface. The texture affects the appearance of the surface because of the way in which light is reflected, by the various possibilities for the reflected light. Image analysis applications might attempt surface roughness characterization as part of a manufacturing inspection process. [WP:Surface_roughness]

surface roughness characterization: An inspection application where estimates of the roughness of a surface are made, e.g., when inspecting spray-painted surfaces. [Mye62]

surface segmentation: Division of a surface into simpler patches. Given a surface defined over a domain D, determine a partition $D = \{D_{1..n}\}$ on which some goodness criteria are well satisfied. For example, it might be required that the maximal distance of a point of each D_i from the best-fit quadric surface is below a threshold. See also range data segmentation. [SQ04:8.6]

surface shape classification: The use of curvature information of a surface to classify each point on the surface as locally ellipsoidal, hyperbolic, cylindrical or planar. See also surface class. For example, given a parametric surface $\vec{x}(u, v)$, the classification function $c(u, v)$ is a mapping from the domain of (u, v) to a set of discrete class labels. [FJ88]

surface shape discontinuity: A discontinuity in the value of a surface shape classification over a surface, e.g. a discontinuity in the classification function $c(u, v)$. The figure shows a discontinuity at the fold edge at point X: [Wit81]

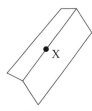

surface tracking: Identification of the same surface through the frames of a video sequence. [GU89]

surface triangulation: See surface mesh.

surflet: An oriented surface point $(\vec{p}, \vec{n})$ consisting of a surface point $\vec{p}$ plus its surface normal $\vec{n}$. A pair of surflets gives a local descriptor that is translation invariant and rotation invariant; an aggregation of these into a histogram creates a compact descriptor of a 3D object. [WHH03]

surveillance: An application area of vision concerned with the monitoring of activities in a scene. Typically this will involve at least background modeling and human motion analysis. [WP:Surveillance]

SUSAN corner finder: A popular interest point detector developed by Smith and Brady. Combines the smoothing and central difference stages of a derivative-based operator into a single center-surround comparison. [WP:Corner_detection#The_SUSAN_corner_detector]

SVD: See singular value decomposition.

SVM: See support vector machine.

Swendsen–Wang Algorithm: An algorithm for random simulation by Markov chain Monte Carlo methods in a discrete Markov random field (MRF). [SW87]

swept object representation: A volumetric representation scheme in which 3D objects are formed by sweeping a 2D cross section along an axis or trajectory. A brick can be formed by sweeping a rectangle. Some schemes, such as the geon or generalized cylinder representation, allow changes to the size of the cross section and curved trajectories. The figure shows a cone defined by sweeping a circle along a straight axis with a linearly decreasing radius: [JKS95:15.3.2]

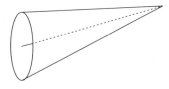

symbolic: Inference or computation expressed in terms of a set of *symbols* rather than a signal. Where a digital signal is a discrete representation of a continuous function, symbols are inherently discrete. For example, an image (signal) is converted to a list of the names of people who appear in it (symbols). [WP:Symbolic_computation]

symbolic object representation: Representation of an object by lists of symbolic terms such as "plane", "quadric", "corner", or "face" etc., rather than the points or pixels of the shape itself. The representation may include the shape and position of the objects. [JKS95:15.6.3]

symmetric axis transform (SAT): A transformation that locates all points on the skeleton of a region by identifying those points that are the locus of centers of bitangent circles. See also medial axis skeletonization. The figure shows the medial axis derived from a binary segmentation of a moving subject: [Nal93:9.2.2]

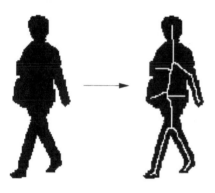

symmetry: A shape that remains invariant under at least one non-identity transformation from some pre-specified transformation group. For example, the set of points comprising an ellipse is the same after the ellipse is subjected to the Euclidean transformation of rotation by 180° about its center. The image of the outline of a surface of revolution under perspective projection is invariant under a certain homography, so the silhouette exhibits a projective symmetry. Affine symmetry is sometimes known as skew symmetry and symmetry induced by reflection about a line is called "bilateral symmetry". [SQ04:9.3]

symmetry detection: A class of algorithms that search for symmetry in imaged curves, surfaces and point sets. [SS97a]

symmetry group: For a given object, the group of all isometries (transformations) that leave the object identical to the original. For example, a square with its center of mass at the origin has both rotational symmetry (four isometries) and reflection (five isometries) that mean the symmetry group contains $4 \cdot 5 = 20$ members. [Wey52]

symmetry line: The axis of a bilateral symmetry. In the figure, the solid line rectangle has two dashed lines of symmetry: [WP:Reflection symmetry]

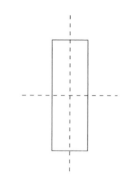

symmetry plane: The axis of a bilateral symmetry in 3D. In the figure, the dashed lines show three symmetry planes of a cube: [HMS98]

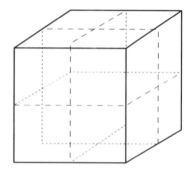

sync pulse: Abbreviation of "synchronization pulse". Any electrical signal that allows two or more electronic devices to share a common time frame. Commonly used to synchronize the capture instants of two cameras in a stereo image capture system. [Gal90:4.1.1]

syntactic pattern recognition: Object identification by converting an image of the object into a sequence or array of symbols and using grammar-parsing techniques to match the sequence of symbols to grammar rules in a database. [Sch89:Ch. 6]

syntactic texture description: Description of texture in terms of grammars of local shapes or image patches and transformation rules. Good for modeling synthetic artificial textures. [SHB08:14.2]

synthetic aperture radar (SAR): An imaging device that transmits long-wavelength (in comparison to visible light) radio waves from airborne or space platforms and builds a 2D image of the intensities of the returned reflections. Clouds are transparent at these (centimeter) wavelengths and the active transmission means that images may be taken at night. The images are captured as a sequence of low-resolution ("small aperture") 1D slices as the platform translates across the target area, with a final high-resolution ("synthetic aperture") image recoverable via a Fourier transform after all slices have been captured. The time-of-flight of the returned signal determines the distance from the transmitter and therefore, assuming a planar (or known geometry) surface, the pixel location in the cross-path direction. [WP:Synthetic_aperture_radar]

systolic array: A class of parallel computer in which processors are arranged in a directed graph. The processors synchronously receive data from one set of neighbors (e.g., North and West in a rectangular array), perform a computation, and transmit the computed quantity to another set of neighbors (e.g., South and East). [Sch89:Ch. 8]

tabu search: A heuristic search technique that seeks to avoid cycles by forbidding or penalizing moves taking the search to previously visited solution spaces (hence "tabu"). [WP:Tabu_search]

tangent angle function: Given a curve $(x(t), y(t))$, the function $\theta(t) = \tan^{-1}\frac{y(t)}{x(t)}$. [TC94]

tangent plane: The plane passing through a point on a surface that is perpendicular to the surface normal. [FP03:19.1.2]

tangent space: In differential geometry, the vector space formed by the set of all tangent vectors at a point on a differentiable manifold. This is a generalization of the notion of the tangent plane to a surface. [Lov10:3.3]

tangential distortion (lens): A particular lens aberration created, among others, by lens decentering, usually modeled only in high-accuracy calibration systems. [LL96]

target image: The image resulting from an image-processing operation: [EF01]

Source Image   Target Image

target recognition: See automatic target recognition. [WP:Automatic_target_recognition]

target tracking: The following of a given object over time, possibly through repeated detections of the object or by a single detection followed by feature tracking. Traditional applications are military, but the term might now include other objects, e.g., people or vehicle tracking. There might be single or multiple simultaneous targets. [FP03:Ch. 17]

task parallelism: Parallel processing achieved by the concurrent execution of relatively large subsets of a computer program. A large subset might be defined as one whose run time is of the order of tens of milliseconds. The parallel tasks need not be identical, e.g., from a binary image, one task may compute a moment while another computes the perimeter. [WP:Task_parallelism]

tattoo retrieval: An application of image retrieval in which the patterns are tattoos. The intent is to help with identifying people in legal situations. [JLRG09]

Tchebichef/Chebyshev moments: A set of moments based on the orthogonal Tchebichef/Chebyshev polynomials, defined on a set of discrete points which makes them suitable for digital images. The moments can be used to define properties of shapes suitable for object recognition, or for image compression, noise reduction etc. [FSZ09:6.2.5]

tee junction: An intersection between line segments (possibly representing edges) where a straight line meets and terminates somewhere along another line segment. See also blocks world. A tee junction can give useful depth-ordering cues. In this figure, we can hypothesize that surface C lies in front of the surfaces A and B, given the tee junction at p: [Nal93:4.1.1]

Dictionary of Computer Vision and Image Processing, Second Edition.
R. B. Fisher, T. P. Breckon, K. Dawson-Howe, A. Fitzgibbon, C. Robertson, E. Trucco and C. K. I. Williams.
© 2014 John Wiley & Sons, Ltd. Published 2014 by John Wiley & Sons, Ltd.

telecentric optics: A lens system arranged such that moving the image plane along the optical axis does not change the magnification or image position of imaged world points. One embodiment is to place an aperture in front of the lens so that when an object is imaged off the focal plane of the lens, the center of the (blurred) object is the ray through the center of the aperture, rather than the center of the lens. Placing the aperture at the lens's front focal plane will ensure these rays are parallel after the lens: [WP:Telecentric_lens]

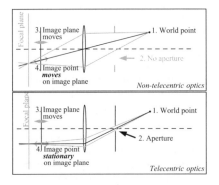

telepresence: Interaction with objects at a location remote from the user via vision or robotic devices. Examples include slaving of remote cameras to the motion of a head-mounted display worn by the user, transmission of audio from the remote location, use of local controls to operate remote machinery and haptic (i.e., touch) feedback from the remote to the local environment. [WP:Telepresence]

template-based representation: A form of model or object representation in which the representation is composed of some form of image-based modeling, such as an image of the shape, the edges that bound the desired shape or a process for generating the template, such as a

principal component representation. [BB82:3.2.1]

template image: An image used as part of a template-based representation for template matching, detection or template tracking of an object. [BB82:3.2.1]

template matching: A strategy for location of an object in an image. The *template*, a 2D image of the object, is compared with all windows of the same size as the template in the image to be searched. Windows where the difference with the template (as computed by, e.g., normalized correlation or a sum of squared differences (SSD)) is within a threshold are reported as instances of the object. This is interesting as a brute-force matching strategy. To obtain invariance to scale, rotation or other transformations, the template must be subjected explicitly to the transformations. [FP03:25.3.2]

template tracking: A method of target tracking in video that uses small amounts of local image data as the templates to be tracked. The templates could be based on neighborhoods; image features taken from previous frames (e.g., SIFT features); or ideal models (e.g., based on drawings). The core idea is to search for and match the template (e.g., via correlation) with image data in a new image to find the best correspondence. The figure shows a template match using correlation between a template (on the left) and patches (on the right): [JD02]

BOOK AS TEMPLATE   BOOK TRACKED IN NEW IMAGE

TRACKED IN MORE DISTORTED IMAGE

temporal alignment: The process of making time-to-time correspondences between two time-based signals. Examples are the frames in video sequences, objects or motions extracted from the video, properties measured from data in the video, or other signals like speech. A key problem is that signals may not advance at the same rate and there may be local variations in rates (e.g., synchronizing two people running cross country). Dynamic time-warping is a common technique used for temporal alignment. [CI02]

temporal averaging: Any procedure for noise reduction in which a signal that is known to be static over time is sampled at different times and the results averaged. [LGZ+94]

temporal correlation: The similarity of two time-varying signals and the process of assessing the similarity. For example, the pattern of leg motion in a runner over one gait cycle is very similar to the pattern of other cycles and other runners; the dropping of a drinking glass is followed by the glass breaking when it hits the floor; the image noise at a pixel is often related to the noise measured from the next image frame. The similarity of consecutive video frames can be exploited to improve video compression. [BAP06]

temporal event analysis: 1) An analysis that considers the temporal correlation of two events. For example, it may assess how often the event of a person looking at a store window display leads to the event of that person buying something in the shop.
2) An analysis that assesses the match of some observed data to a temporal model of the data, e.g., the probability that a sequence of observations is explained by a given hidden Markov model. [ZI01]

temporal model: A model that encodes how some phenomenon changes over time. The model could be explicit (e.g., a cosine signal), probabilistic (e.g., a hidden Markov model) or statistical (e.g. a temporal Gaussian process model). [BS00a]

temporal offset: 1) The amount of time shift needed for temporal alignment of two time-based sequences or signals, e.g., how many seconds or frames between the start of two gait cycles.
2) The time between two events, e.g., the start and end of a meal. [MSMP08]

temporal process: A process or signal that changes over time. See also time series and time-varying random process.

temporal reasoning: The process of analyzing the temporal relationships between signals or events. For example, one might attempt to determine if an event seen in one video stream is a good predictor of an event seen in another video stream. See temporal event analysis. [WP:Spatial-temporal_reasoning]

temporal representation: A model representation that encodes the dynamics of how an object's shape or position can vary over time. [SCH08]

temporal resolution: The frequency of observations with respect to time (e.g., one per second) as opposed to the spatial resolution. [Kul71]

temporal segmentation: The segmentation of a time signal into discrete continuous subsets. For example, a sequence might identify when a given action start and stops (e.g., a person standing up) or a situation changes (as in video cut analysis) or a repetitive signal may be split into complete cycles. [WA94]

temporal stereo: 1) Stereo achieved through movement of one camera rather than using two separate cameras.
2) Integration of multiple stereo views of a dynamic scene to produce a better estimate of each view. [NA02]

temporal synchronization: See temporal alignment.

temporal topology: A way of expressing the temporal relationships between signals, events and activities independent of actual times. For example, one can say that event A happened before event B, without specifying how long before. An analogous situation is in the relation of a geometric model to a graph model, in which the geometric model specifies where each feature is, but the graph model may only specify adjacency between features. [NRCC08]

temporal tracking: See tracking.

tensor product surface: A parametric model of a curved surface commonly used in computer modeling and graphics applications, The surface shape is defined by the product of two polynomial (usually cubic) curves in the independent surface coordinates. [JKS95:13.5.3]

terrain analysis: Analysis and interpretation of data representing the shape of the planet's surface. Typical data structures are digital elevation maps or triangulated irregular networks (TINs). [WG00:1.1]

tessellated viewsphere: A division of the viewsphere into distinct subsets of (approximately) equal area. Often used as a data structure for representing functions of the form $f(\vec{n})$ where $\vec{n}$ is a unit normal vector in $\mathbb{R}^3$. Typically constructed by subdivision of the viewsphere into a polygon mesh such as an icosahedron: [HY93]

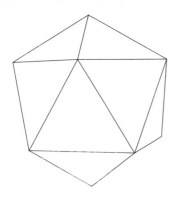

test set: The set used to verify a classifier or other algorithm. The test set contains only examples not included in the training set. [WP:Test_set]

tetrahedral spatial decomposition: A method of decomposing 3D space into packed tetrahedrons instead of

the more commonly used rectangular voxel decomposition. A tetrahedral decomposition allows a recursive subdivision of a tetrahedron into eight smaller tetrahedra. The figure illustrates the decomposition with one of the eight smaller volumes shaded: [KL96]

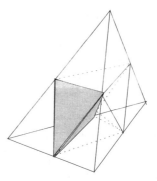

texel: See texture element.

texon: See texture element.

text analysis: In the context of image analysis, this term refers to the detection and decoding of characters and words in image and video data. [WP:Optical_character_recognition]

textel: See texture element.

texton: Julesz's 1981 definition of the units in which texture might be perceived. In the texton-based view, a texture is a regular assembly of textons. [Jul81]

texton boost: An approach to RGB pixel classification to label images in terms of textons: distinct clusters of textures (found by clustering multi-scale image derivatives), spatial layout and image context. Layout is based on rectangular regions over which texton type should be constant. Pairs of (texton,layout regions) become weak classifiers of pixels and a strong classifier is learned through a boosting method. Context exploits the relative spatial placement of the layout regions. Texton boosting can be used simultaneously for region segmentation and labeling. [SWRC09]

289

texture: The phenomenon by which uniformity is perceived in regular (etymologically, "woven") patterns of (possibly irregular) elements. In computer vision, texture usually refers to patterns in the appearance or reflectance on a surface. The texture may be regular, i.e., it may satisfy some texture grammar, or it may be statistical texture, i.e., the distribution of pixel values may vary over the image. Texture can also refer to variations in the local shape on a surface, e.g., its degree of roughness. See also shape texture. [NA05:8.2]

texture-based image retrieval: Content-based image retrieval that uses texture as its classification criterion. [WP:Content-based_image_retrieval]

texture boundary: The boundary between adjacent regions in texture segmentation. Also, the boundary perceived by humans between two regions of different textures. The figure shows the boundary between three regions of different color and shape texture: [KE89]

texture classification: Assignment of an image (or a window of an image) to one of a set of texture classes, which are typically defined by presentation by a human of training set images representing each class. The basis of texture segmentation. [NA05:8.4]

texture descriptor: A vector-valued function computed on an image subwindow that is designed to produce similar outputs when applied to different subwindows of the same texture. The size of the image subwindow controls the scale of the detector. If the response at a pixel position (x, y)

is computed as the maximum over several scales, an additional scale output $s(x, y)$ is available. See also texture primitive. [NA05:8.3]

texture direction: The texture gradient or a $90°$ rotation thereof. [BB82:6.5]

texture element (texel): A small geometric pattern that is repeated frequently on some surface resulting in a texture. [BB82:6.2]

texture energy measure: A single-valued texture descriptor with strong response in textured regions. A texture descriptor may be formed by combining the results of several texture energy measures into a vector. [JRL97]

texture enhancement: A procedure analogous to edge-preserving smoothing in which texture boundaries rather than edges are to be preserved. [Wei95]

texture field grouping: See texture segmentation.

texture field segmentation: See texture segmentation.

texture gradient: The gradient of a single scalar output $\nabla s(x, y)$ of a texture descriptor. A common example is the scale output, for homogeneous texture, whose texture gradient can be used to compute the foreshortening direction. [BB82:6.5]

texture grammar: Grammar used to describe textures as instances of simpler patterns with a given spatial relationship (including other textures defined previously in this way). A sentence from this grammar would be a syntactic texture description. [BB82:6.3.1]

texture mapping: In computer graphics, rendering a polygonal surface where the surface color at each output screen pixel is obtained by interpolating values from an image. The source image pixel location is computed using correspondences between the polygon's vertex coordinates and texture coordinates on the texture map. [WP:Texture_mapping]

texture matching: Matching of regions based on texture descriptions. [SZ01]

texture model: The theoretical basis for a class of texture descriptor. For example, autocorrelation of linear filter responses, statistical texture descriptions or syntactic texture descriptions. [PS00]

texture modeling: A family of techniques for generating surface color texture and shape texture, such as texture mapping or bump mapping. Special classes, such as hair or skin, can be modeled and the texture can vary over time. The models can be used to generate texture for computer graphics, for a texture descriptor, as a property used for region segmentation etc. [Elb05]

texture motion: The blurring that is produced when a textured surface moves relative to the camera. This is mainly of interest in computer graphics, for the generation of realistic blurred textures when seen by a moving observer.

texture orientation: See texture gradient.

texture primitive: A basic unit of texture (e.g., a small pattern that is repeated) as used in syntactic texture descriptions. [LWY99]

texture recognition: See texture classification.

texture region extraction: See texture field segmentation.

texture representation: See texture model.

texture segmentation: Segmentation of an image into patches of coherent texture. The figure shows a region segmented into three regions based on color and shape texture: [FP03:Ch. 9]

texture synthesis: The generation of synthetic images of textured scenes. More particularly, the generation of images that appear perceptually to share the texture of a set of training examples of a texture. [FP03:Ch. 9]

Theil–Sen estimator: A robust estimator for curve fitting. A family of curves is parameterized by parameters $a_{1..p}$, and is to be fit to data $\vec{x}_{1..n}$. If q is the smallest number of points that uniquely define $a_{1..p}$, then the Theil–Sen estimate of the optimal parameters $\hat{a}_{1..p}$ are the parameters that have the median error measure of all the q-point estimates. For example, for line fitting, the number of parameters (slope and intercept) is $p = 2$ and the number of points required to give a fit is also $q = 2$. Thus the Theil–Sen estimate of the slope gives the median error of the $\binom{n}{q}$ two-point slope estimates. The Theil–Sen estimator is not statistically efficient, nor does it have a particularly high breakdown point, in contrast to such estimators as RANSAC and least median of squares. [AML95]

thermal imaging: Acquiring image data in the infrared light range (approximately 750 nanometers to 300 micrometers wavelength). There are advantages to the use of infrared:

- It allows passive sensing, even in the dark.

- It allows measurement of the temperature of objects, which can be used for a variety of diagnostic purposes, such as health or energy loss monitoring.

[WP:Thermography]

thermal noise: In CCD cameras, additional electrons released by thermal vibration in the substrate that are counted with those released by incident photons. Thus, the gray scale values are corrupted by an additive Poisson noise process. [WP:Johnson–Nyquist noise]

thickening operator: Thickening is a mathematical morphology operation that is used to grow selected regions of foreground pixels in binary images, somewhat like the dilate operator or

close operator. It has several applications, including determining the approximate convex hull of a shape and the skeleton by influence zone. Thickening is normally only applied to binary images and it produces a binary image as output. The figure shows thickening six times in the horizontal direction: [Jai89:9.9]

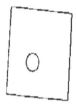

thin plate model: A model of surface smoothness used in the variational approach. The internal energy (or bending energy) of a thin plate represented as a parametric surface $(x, y, f(x, y))$ is given by $f_{xx}^2 + 2f_{xy}^2 + f_{yy}^2$. [FP03:26.1.1]

thinning operator: Thinning is a mathematical morphology operation that is used to remove selected foreground pixels from binary images, somewhat like the erode operator or the open operator. It can be used for several applications, but is particularly useful for skeletonization and to tidy up the output of edge detection by reducing all lines to one-pixel thickness. Thinning is normally only applied to binary images and produces a binary image as output. The figure shows the thinning of a region: [JKS95:2.5.11]

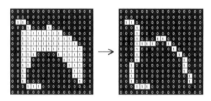

three-CCD camera: An imaging camera that uses three separate CCD sensors to capture the red, green and blue components of an image, in contrast to a single-CCD sensor that uses three different filters on the single CCD chip (e.g., using the Bayer pattern). The

advantage of using three sensors is better color quality and spatial resolution. [Sze10:pp. 85-86]

three-view geometry: See trinocular stereo.

threshold selection: The automatic choice of threshold values for conversion of a scalar signal (such as a gray scale image) to a binary image. Often proceeds by analysis of the histogram of the sample values (e.g., Otsu's 1979 method). Different assumptions about the underlying distributions yield different strategies. [JKS95:3.2.1]

thresholding: Quantization into two values. For example, conversion of a scalar signal (such as a gray scale image) to a binary image. The figure shows an input image and its threshold output: [JKS95:2.1, 3.2.1]

thresholding with hysteresis: Thresholding of a time-varying scalar signal where the threshold value is a function of previous signal and threshold values. For example a thermostatic control based on temperature receives a signal $s(t)$ and generates an output signal $b(t)$ of the form

$$b(t) = \begin{cases} s(t) > \tau_{cold} & \text{if } b(t-1) = 0 \\ s(t) < \tau_{hot} & \text{if } b(t-1) = 1 \end{cases}$$

where the value at time t depends on the previous decision $b(t-1)$. In computer vision, often associated with the edge following stage of the Canny edge detector. [NA05:4.2.5]

tie point: A pair of matched points in two different images (or in an image and a map etc). Given enough tie points, one can estimate geometric relations between the images, such as rectification or image alignment geometric transformations, or the fundamental matrix. [LRKH06:4.2.5.1]

TIFF: Tagged image file format. [Umb98:1.8]

tilt: The *tilt direction* of a 3D surface patch as observed in a 2D image is parallel to the projection of the 3D surface normal into the image. If the 3D surface is represented as a depth map $z(x, y)$ in image coordinates, then the tilt direction at (x, y) is the unit vector parallel to $(\frac{\partial z}{\partial x}, \frac{\partial z}{\partial y})$. The *tilt angle* may be defined as $\tan^{-1}(\frac{\partial z}{\partial y} / \frac{\partial z}{\partial x})$. [FP03:9.4.1]

time delay index: An integer index of the lag between two functions: if $g(t) = f(t - n\Delta_t)$ then the n is the time delay index, Δ_t is the sample time and $n\Delta_t$ is the total delay or lag of g behind f.

time derivative: A technique for computing how an image sequence changes over time. Typically used as part of shape from motion. [KWM94]

time-of-flight range sensor: A sensor that computes distance to target points by emitting electromagnetic (or other) radiation and measuring the time between emitting the pulse and observing the reflection of the pulse. [BM02:1.9.2]

time series: One or more variables observed sequentially in time. [Cha89:p. 1]

time to collision: See time to contact.

time to contact: From a sequence of images $I(t)$, computation of the value of t at which, assuming constant motion, an image object will intersect the plane parallel to the image plane that contains the camera center. It can be computed even in the absence of metric information about the imaging system, i.e., in an uncalibrated vision setting. [CB92]

time to impact: See time to contact.

time-varying random process: A stochastic process in which the index variable is time.

time-varying shape: A shape that varies over time or in an image sequence. Examples include the shape of a person as they walk, a person growing and the beating of a heart. A variety of deformable models can be used to model the shape, such as the active shape model. [SBS02]

tolerance band algorithm: An algorithm for incremental segmentation of a curve into straight-line elements. Assume that the current straight line segment defines two parallel boundaries of a tolerance zone at a preselected distance from the line segment. When a new curve point leaves the tolerance zone, the current line segment is ended and a new segment is started. [JKS95:6.4.2]

TOLERANCE   EXIT
ZONE   POINT

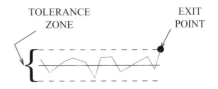

tolerance interval: An interval within which a stated proportion of some population will lie. [WP:Tolerance_interval]

Tomasi–Kanade factorization: A maximum-likelihood solution to structure and motion recovery in the situation where points in a static scene are observed by affine cameras and the observed (x, y) positions are corrupted by Gaussian noise. The method depends on the observation that if m points are observed over n views, the $2n \times m$ measurement matrix containing all the observations (after certain transformations have been performed) is of rank 3. The closest rank-3 approximation of the matrix is reliably obtained via singular value decomposition, after which the 3D points and camera positions are easily extracted, up to an affine ambiguity. [TK92]

tomography: A technique for the reconstruction of a 3D volumetric dataset based on a number of 2D slices. The most common examples occur in medical imaging (e.g., nuclear magnetic resonance and positron emission tomography). [WP:Tomography]

tongue print: A form of personal biometric that is supposed to be unique to individuals, much like fingerprints. [ZLYS07]

top-down: A reasoning approach that searches for evidence for high-level hypotheses in the data. For example, a hypothesize-and-test algorithm might have a strategy for making good guesses as to the position of circles in an image and then compare the hypothesized circles to edges in the image, choosing those that have good support. Another example is a human body recognizer that employs body part (e.g., heads, legs and torso) recognizers that directly use image data or recognize even smaller subparts. [BB82:10.4.2]

top-down model inference: A form of reasoning where the analysis proceeds from the whole object to the subcomponents. High-level information generates predictions of structure at lower levels and these predictions are then tested. For example, one could construct a statistical classifier that assessed the likelihood that a region contained a person, before refining that region with a subclassifier that assessed subregions for the likelihood of containing a head, and then further, using a subclassifier that looked for an eye. Failure of the lower levels of inference might lead to failure at the top level. This contrasts with the bottom-up approach. [BB82:10.4, pp. 343]

top-hat operator: A mathematical morphology operation used to remove structures from images. The top-hat filtering of image I by structuring element S is the difference $I -$ open(I, S), where open(I, S) is the morphological open operator of I by S. [ZLP06]

topic model: Usually described in relation to a set of documents and the words they contain. For computer vision, this could be translated to a set of images, each of which is described by a bag of features. The idea is to model the distribution of words in a document in terms of the proportions of a smaller number of topics. See also latent Dirichlet allocation (LDA) and probabilistic latent semantic analysis (PLSA). [Mur12:24.3]

topographic map: 1) A representation that shows both geometric shape and identified features, such as man-made structures in a land map. Heights are typically represented using elevation contours. This sort of map can also be used to represent the results of image analysis.
2) In the nervous system, a layout of neurons where neural response properties vary systematically with the spatial position of the neuron within the neural area. [WP:Topographic_map]

topological property: Properties that are not linked to the metric property on the space, in other words, are invariant to general geometric transformations (e.g., rotation, scaling and translation). Examples of topological properties are adjacency, connectedness, number of regions or components etc. [Wei12:Topology]

topological representation: Any representation that encodes connectedness of elements. For example, in a surface boundary representation comprising faces, edges and vertices, the *topology* of the representation is the list of face–edge and edge–vertex connections, which is independent of the *geometry* (spatial positions and sizes) of the representation. In this case, the fundamental relation is "bounded by", so a face is bounded by one or more edges and an edge is bounded by zero or more vertices. [CWSI87]

topology: 1) Properties of point sets (such as surfaces) that are unchanged by continuous reparameterizations (homeomorphisms) of space.
2) The connectedness of objects in discrete geometry (see topological representation). One speaks of the topology of a network, meaning the set of connections within the network or, equivalently, the set of neighborhood relationships that describe the network. [Sch89:Ch. 6]

topology inference: 1) Construction of the graph of relations between image structures, such as the overlap between different images of the same portion of a scene.

2) Construction of the graph of relations between nodes in a probabilistic graphical model.

3) Inference of the connectivity of a communications network.

What these definitions have in common is the inference of a graph or network from data. [SHK98]

torsion: A concept in the differential geometry of curves formally representing the intuitive notion of the local twisting of a 3D curve as you move along the curve. The torsion $\tau(t)$ of a 3D space curve $\vec{c}(t)$ is the scalar

$$-\vec{n}(t) \cdot \frac{\mathrm{d}}{\mathrm{d}t} \vec{b}(t) = \frac{\left[\dot{\vec{c}}(t), \ddot{\vec{c}}(t), \dddot{\vec{c}}(t) \right]}{\| \ddot{\vec{c}}(t) \|^2}$$

where $\vec{n}(t)$ is the curve normal and $\vec{b}(t)$ the curve binormal. The notation $[\vec{x}, \vec{y}, \vec{z}]$ denotes the scalar triple product $\vec{x} \cdot (\vec{y} \times \vec{z})$. [FP03:19.1.1]

torsion scale space (TSS): A description of a space curve based on movement along the curve of the zero-crossing points of the torsion function of the curve as the smoothing scale increases. The smoothing is accomplished by Gaussian smoothing of the space curve with increasing scale. A visual representation of the TSS is typically organized as a 2D plot of the scale at which zero crossings appear as a function of the arc length. [MB03:3.4]

torus: 1) The volume swept by moving a sphere along a circle in 3D.

2) The surface of such a volume. [WP:Torus]

total least squares: See orthogonal regression.

total variation: A class of *regularizer* in the variational approach. The total variation regularizer of function $f(\vec{x}) : \mathbb{R}^n \mapsto \mathbb{R}$ is of the form $R(f) = \int_\Omega |\nabla f(\vec{x})| d\vec{x}$ where Ω is (a subset of) the domain of f. [WP:Total_variation]

total variation regularization: A type of regularization where the penalty term is of total variation form. [WP:Total_variation_denoising]

tracking: A means of estimating the parameters (e.g., feature point positions, target object positions, human joint angles) of a dynamic system that evolve over time and for which there are *measurements* (e.g., photographs) obtained at successive time instants. The task of tracking is to maintain an estimate of the probability distribution over the model parameters, given the measurements, as well as *a priori* models of how the parameters change over time. Common algorithms for tracking include the Kalman filter and particle filters. Tracking may be viewed as a class of algorithms that operate on sequences of inputs, using assumptions about the coherence of successive inputs to improve performance of the algorithm. Often the task of the algorithm may be cast as estimation of a state vector – a set of parameters, such as the joint angles of a human body – at successive time instants t. The state vector $\vec{x}(t)$ is to be estimated using a set of sensors that yield observations $\vec{z}(t)$, such as the 2D positions of bright spots attached to a human. In the absence of temporal coherence assumptions, $\vec{x}$ must be estimated at each time step solely using the information in $\vec{z}(t)$. With coherence assumptions, the system uses the set of all observations so far $\{\vec{z}(\tau), \tau < t\}$ to compute the estimate at time t. In practice, the estimate of the state is represented as a probability density over all possible values, and the current estimate uses only the previous state estimate $\vec{x}(t-1)$ and the current measurements $\vec{z}(t)$ to estimate $\vec{x}(t)$. [FP03:Ch. 17]

traffic analysis: Analysis of video data of automobile traffic, e.g., to identify number plates, detect accidents or congestion, compute throughput etc. [KWH+94]

traffic sign recognition: An algorithm for the recognition or classification of road traffic information signs, such as "stop" signs, from single images or video. Detection of the sign is usually a fundamental initial step. This capability is needed by autonomous vehicles. [WP:Traffic_sign_recognition]

training set: The set of labeled examples used to learn the parameters of a classifier. In order to build an effective classifier, the training set should be representative of the examples that will be encountered in the eventual domain of application. [WP:Training_set]

trajectory: The path that a moving point makes over time. It could also be the path that a whole object takes if less precision of usage is desired. [WP:Trajectory]

trajectory-based representation: A description of an object, vehicle or behavior based on the trajectory or path of the observed object. The path may be described in either the image or the scene space. A typical application is the detection of potential car crime activities in a car-parking lot by watching for atypical patterns of people walking. [BKS07]

trajectory estimation: Determination of the 3D trajectory of an object observed in a set of 2D images. [LSG07]

trajectory transition descriptor: A descriptor of a trajectory and its state transitions in the form of a directed graph. The graph is transformed into a translation-invariant and scale-invariant form, with the resulting displacements between consecutive frames quantized into bins, which form the nodes of a graph. Consecutive bin positions along the trajectory become the arcs in the graph. Finally the arcs acquire a label according to the number of times the arc is traversed. The graph can be encoded as a transition matrix, from which a vector descriptor is obtained that encodes the trajectory. [GX11:p. 153]

transformation: A mapping of data in one space (such as an image) into another space. All image-processing operations are transformations. [WP:Transformation_(function)]

transformation matrix: A matrix (e.g., M) used in a linear space to transform a vector (e.g., $\vec{x}$) by multiplication (e.g., $M\vec{x}$). Transformation matrices can be used for geometric transformations (e.g., rotation) of position vectors, color transformations of (e.g., RGB) color vectors, projections from 3D into 2D etc. [Sze10:2.1]

translation: A transformation of Euclidean space that can be represented in the form $\vec{x} \mapsto T(\vec{x}) \equiv \vec{x} \mapsto \vec{x} + \vec{t}$. In projective space, a transformation that leaves the plane at infinity pointwise invariant. [BB82:A1.7.4]

translation invariant: A property that keeps the same value even if the data, the scene or the image from which the data comes is translated. The distance between two points is translation invariant. [RP98]

translucency: The transmission of light through a diffusing interface such as frosted glass. Light entering a translucent material has multiple possible exit directions. [WP:Translucence]

transmittance: The ratio of the ("outgoing") power transmitted by a transparent object to the incident ("incoming") power. [WP:Transmittance]

transparency: The property of a surface to be traversed by radiation (e.g., by visible light), so that objects on the other side can be seen. A non-transparent surface is opaque. [WP:Transparency_and_translucency]

transparent layer: An image display technique whereby an image is made partially transparent before it is overlaid on another image, thus allowing image data from both to be seen. A similar effect is occasionally seen in real scenes, e.g., when one can see reflections on a window as well as the scene through the window.

tree classifier: A classifier that applies a sequence of tests to input points $\vec{x}$ in order to determine the label l of the class to which it belongs. See also decision tree. [SL91]

tree search method: A class of algorithms to optimize a function defined on tuples of values taken from a finite set. The tree describes the set of all such tuples and the order in which tuples are explored is defined by the particular search algorithm, such as depth-first, breadth-first, A^* and best-first searches. Applications include the interpretation tree search. [WP:Tree traversal]

triangulated model: See surface mesh.

triangular norms: Also known as T-norms. A family of binary operators for combining $[0,1]$ certainty values in a form of AND or logical conjunction suitable for uncertainty reasoning. There are several possible T-norms with different combining functions, including the classical logical AND. [WP:T-norm]

triangulation: See Delaunay triangulation, surface triangulation, stereo triangulation and structured light triangulation.

trichromacy: Having three independent color receptor channels, as in RGB for cameras and long, medium and short (LMS) wavelength receptors for the primate retina. [FP03:6.2.2]

trifocal tensor: The geometric entity that relates the images of 3D points observed in three perspective 2D views. Algebraically represented as a $3 \times 3 \times 3$ array of values T_i^{jk}. If a single 3D point projects to x, x', x'' in the first, second, and third views respectively, it must obey the nine equations (using Einstein summation notation over α, β, i, j, k)

$$x^i(x'^j \epsilon_{j\alpha r})(x''^k \epsilon_{k\beta s}) T_i^{\alpha\beta} = 0_{rs}$$

for r and s varying from 1 to 3; ϵ is the epsilon tensor for which

$$\epsilon_{ijk} = \begin{cases} 1 & ijk \text{ an even} \\ & \text{permutation of } 123 \\ 0 & \text{two of } i, j, k \text{ equal} \\ -1 & ijk \text{ an odd} \\ & \text{permutation of } 123 \end{cases}$$

As this equation is linear in the elements of T, it can be used to estimate them given enough 2D point correspondences x, x', x''. As not all $3 \times 3 \times 3$ arrays represent realizable camera configurations, estimation must also incorporate several nonlinear constraints on the tensor elements. [FP03:10.2]

trilinear constraint: The geometric constraint on three views of a point (i.e., the intersection of three epipolar lines). This is similar to the epipolar constraint which is applied in the two-view scenario. [FP03:10.2.1-10.2.3]

trilinear tensor: Another name for the trifocal tensor. [FP03:10.2]

trilinearity: An equation in a set of three variables in which holding two of the variables fixed yields a linear equation in the remaining one. For example $xyz = 0$ is trilinear in x, y and z, while $x^2 = y$ is not, as holding y fixed yields a quadratic in x. [HZ00:14.2.1]

trimap: An image segmentation, often manually, into three regions of foreground, background and unknown. The trimap can be used as a shape prior to guide segmentation or labeling. [RRRS08]

trinocular stereo: A multi-view stereo process that uses three cameras. [Fau93:6.9]

tristimulus theory of color perception: The human visual system has three types of cone, with three different spectral response curves, so that the perception of any incident light is represented as three intensities, roughly corresponding to long (maximum about 558-580 nm), medium (531-545 nm) and short (410-450 nm) wavelengths. [WP:CIE_1931_color_space#Tristimulus_values]

tristimulus values: The relative amounts of the three primary colors that need to be combined to match a given color. [Jai89:3.8]

true negative: A binary classifier $c(x)$ returns + or - for an example x. A *true negative* occurs when the classifier returns - for an example that is in reality -. Compare with false negative. [Mur12:8.3.4]

true positive: A binary classifier $c(x)$ returns + or - for an example x. A *true positive* occurs when the classifier returns + for an example that is in reality +. Compare with false positive. [Mur12:8.3.4]

truncated median filter: An approximation to mode filtering when image neighborhoods are small. The filter uses an image sharpening operator on blurred image edges as well as noise reduction methods. The algorithm truncates the local distribution on the mean side of the median and then recomputes the median of the new distribution. The algorithm can iterate and, under normal circumstances, converges approximately to the mode even if the observed distribution has very few samples with no obvious peak. [Dav90:3.4]

tube camera: See tube sensor.

tube sensor: A vacuum tube with a photoconductive window that converts light to a video signal. Once the only type of light sensor, the tube camera is now largely superseded by the CCD but it remains useful for some high dynamic range imaging. The image orthicon tube (or "immy") is remembered in the name of the US Academy of Television, Arts and Sciences Emmy awards. [Gal90:2.1.3]

twist: A 3D rotation representation component that specifies a rotation about the vector defined by the azimuth and elevation. The figure shows the pitch rotation direction: [SHKM92]

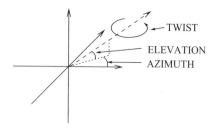

twisted cubic: The curve $(1, t, t^2, t^3)$ in projective 3-space, or any projective transformation thereof. The general form is thus

$$\begin{pmatrix} x_1 \\ x_2 \\ x_3 \\ x_4 \end{pmatrix} = \begin{pmatrix} a_{11} & a_{12} & a_{13} & a_{14} \\ a_{21} & a_{22} & a_{23} & a_{24} \\ a_{31} & a_{32} & a_{33} & a_{34} \\ a_{41} & a_{42} & a_{43} & a_{44} \end{pmatrix} \begin{pmatrix} 1 \\ t \\ t^2 \\ t^3 \end{pmatrix}$$

The projection of a twisted cubic into a 2D image is a rational cubic spline. [HZ00:2.3]

two-view geometry: See binocular stereo.

type I error: A true hypothesis that has been rejected. [Nal93:3.1.1]

type II error: A false hypothesis that has been accepted. [Nal93:3.1.1]

ultrasonic imaging: Creation of images by the transmission and recording of reflected ultrasonic pulses. A phased array of transmitters emits a set of pulses, and then records the returning pulse intensities. By varying the relative timings of the pulses, the returned intensities can be made to correspond to locations in space, allowing measurements to be taken from within ultrasonic-transparent materials (including the human body, excluding air and bone). [FP03:18.6.1]

ultrasound sequence registration: Registration of overlapping ultrasound images. [FP03:18.6]

ultraviolet (UV): Description of electromagnetic radiation with wavelengths between about 300–420 nm (near ultraviolet) and 40–300 nm (far ultraviolet). The short wavelengths make it useful for fine-scale examination of surfaces. Ordinary glass is opaque to UV radiation; quartz glass is transparent. Often used to excite fluorescent materials. [Hec87:3.6.5]

umbilic: A point on a surface where the curvature is the same in every direction. Every point on a sphere is an umbilic point. [JKS95:13.3.2]

umbra: The completely dark area of a shadow caused by a particular light source (i.e., where no light falls from the light source): [FP03:5.3.2]

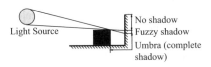

No shadow
Fuzzy shadow
Umbra (complete shadow)
Light Source

uncalibrated approach: See uncalibrated vision.

uncalibrated camera: This term is typically encountered in applications involving projective geometry where there is no camera calibration. The typical calibration parameters are the extrinsic parameters (e.g., position and orientation) and the intrinsic parameters (e.g., focal length, scene-to-sensor scaling and lens distortion). The assumption is that one can recover the desired information, e.g., scene geometry, without having to explicitly calibrate the camera. For example, it might be possible to effectively infer the calibration by exploiting constraints implicit in the data. [BCB97]

uncalibrated stereo: Stereo reconstruction performed without precalibration of the cameras. Particularly, given a pair of images taken by unknown cameras, the fundamental matrix is computed from point correspondences, after which the images may be subject to stereo image rectification and conventional calibrated stereo may proceed. The results of uncalibrated stereo are 3D points in a projective coordinate system, rather than the Euclidean coordinate system that a calibrated setup admits. [Fau92]

uncalibrated vision: The class of vision techniques that require no quantitative information about the camera used in capturing the images on which they operate. These techniques can be applied to archive footage. In particular, they can be applied to geometric problems, such as stereo reconstruction, that traditionally required that the images be from a camera system upon which calibration measurements had been made. In some uncalibrated approaches (such as uncalibrated stereo), the traditional

Dictionary of Computer Vision and Image Processing, Second Edition.
R. B. Fisher, T. P. Breckon, K. Dawson-Howe, A. Fitzgibbon, C. Robertson, E. Trucco and C. K. I. Williams.
© 2014 John Wiley & Sons, Ltd. Published 2014 by John Wiley & Sons, Ltd.

calibration step is replaced by procedures that can use image features directly; in others (such as time-to-contact computations), the calibration parameters can be factored out. In general, uncalibrated systems have degrees of freedom that cannot be measured, such as overall scale or projective ambiguity. [Har92]

uncertainty: Having limited knowledge, so that it is not possible to specify exactly the current state or a future outcome. Probability theory provides one framework for reasoning under uncertainty. [KF09:p. 2]

uncertainty representation: A strategy for representation of the probability density of a variable as used in a vision algorithm. In a similar manner, an interval can be used to represent a range of possible values. [Nal93:8.3]

under-fitting: Assume a set of models for a data set with increasing model complexity, e.g., arising from polynomial regression, where the order of the polynomial determines the complexity, or from a multilayer perceptron network that has an increasing number of hidden units. As the model complexity varies from low to high, the model will initially under-fit the data generator, in that it does not have sufficient flexibility to model the structure in the data. After passing through a point of optimum complexity, the model will then start over-fitting the data. [Mur12:1.2.6]

under-segmented: Given an image where a desired segmentation result is known, the algorithm under-segments if regions output by the algorithm are generally the union of many desired regions. This image should be segmented into three regions but it was under-segmented into two regions: [SQ04:8.7]

undirected graph: A graph in which the arcs go in both directions (in contrast to a directed graph). Adjacency is a property that can be used in an undirected graph: adj(A,B) means region A is adjacent to region B and implies adj(B,A), i.e., region B is adjacent to region A. [Wei12:Undirected Graph]

Undirected graph   Directed graph

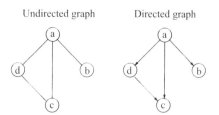

undirected graphical model (UGM): Defines a joint probability distribution over a set of random variables (denoted $\vec{x}$). The graphical structure is an undirected graph. The joint distribution is defined by a product of positive factors, one for each maximal clique in the graph, as $p(\vec{x}) = \frac{1}{Z} \prod_c \psi_c(\vec{x}_c)$. Here $\psi_c(\vec{x}_c)$ denotes the clique function for clique c, and Z is the partition function or normalization constant required to make $p(\vec{x})$ sum to 1. In the figure, the maximal cliques are $(1, 2)$, $(2, 3, 5)$, $(3, 4)$, $(4, 6)$ and $(5, 6)$:

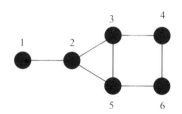

Because the potentials $\psi_c(\vec{x}_c)$ are strictly positive, it is convenient to express them as exponentials, i.e., $\psi_c(\vec{x}_c) = \exp(-E_c(\vec{x}_c))$. With this representation we obtain $p(\vec{x}) = \frac{1}{Z} \exp(-\sum_c E_c(\vec{x}_c))$, which is known as the Boltzmann distribution. A UGM can also be called a Markov random field (MRF); the Markov term here relates to the fact that the conditional distribution of variable x_i, given the other variables, depends only on its neighbors in the graph. One common use of a UGM in computer vision is with a grid graphical structure corresponding to nearest neighbor interactions between pixels, with a variable at each node (e.g., a binary variable indicating a foreground or background label). The pairwise interactions typically encode the regularity that nearby sites will have the same label. See also conditional random field (CRF). [Mur12:6.3]

uniform distribution: A probability distribution in which a variable can take any value in the given range with equal probability. [WP:Uniform_distribution_(continuous)]

uniform illumination: An idealized configuration in which the arrangement of lighting within a scene is such that each point receives the same amount of light energy. In computer vision, sometimes uniform illumination has a different meaning: that each point in an image of the scene (or a part thereof such as the background) has similar imaged intensity. [LO83]

uniform noise: Additive corruption of a sampled signal. If the signal's samples are s_i then the corrupted signal is $\hat{s}_i = s_i + n_i$ where the n_i are uniformly randomly drawn from a specified range $[\alpha, \beta]$. [SS77]

unimodal: A function or distribution with a single peak. [Wei12:Unimodal]

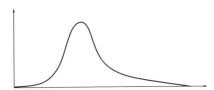

uniqueness stereo constraint: When performing stereo matching or stereo reconstruction, matching can be simplified by assuming that a point in one image corresponds to only one point in other images. This is generally true, except at object boundaries and other places where pixels are not completely opaque. [Fau93:6.2.2]

unit ball: An n-dimensional sphere of radius 1. [Nal93:2.2]

unit quaternion: A four-vector $\vec{q} \in \mathbb{R}^4$. Quaternions of unit length can be used to parameterize 3D rotation matrices. Given a quaternion with components (q_0, q_1, q_2, q_3) the corresponding rotation matrix $\mathbf{R}$ (letting $S = q_0^2 - q_1^2 - q_2^2 - q_3^2$) is:

$$\begin{bmatrix} S + 2q_1^2 & 2q_1q_2 + 2q_0q_3 & 2q_3q_1 - -2q_0q_2 \\ 2q_1q_2 - -2q_0q_3 & S + 2q_2^2 & 2q_2q_3 + 2q_0q_1 \\ 2q_3q_1 + 2q_0q_2 & 2q_2q_3 - -2q_0q_1 & S + 2q_3^2 \end{bmatrix}$$

The identity rotation is given by the quaternion $(1, 0, 0, 0)$. The rotation axis is the unit vector parallel to (q_1, q_2, q_3). [WP:Quaternion]

unit vector: A vector of length 1. [WP:Unit_vector]

unitary transform: A reversible transformation (e.g., the discrete Fourier transform). $\mathbf{U}$ is a unitary matrix where $\mathbf{U}^*\mathbf{U} = \mathbf{I}$, $\mathbf{U}^*$ is the adjoint matrix and $\mathbf{I}$ is the identity matrix. [Jai89:2.7, 5.2]

universal image quality index (UIQI): A model for quantifying image distortion based on loss of correlation, luminance distortion and contrast distortion, which correlates better with human perception of distortion than traditional sum-of-squared-error methods. [WB02a]

unrectified: When a stereo camera pair has not been subject to stereo image rectification. [JKS95:12.5]

unsharp operator: An image enhancement operator that sharpens edges by adding a version of an image put through a high-pass filter to itself. The high-pass filter is implemented by subtracting a smoothed version of the image yielding

$$I_{unsharp} = I + \alpha(I - I_{smooth})$$

The figure shows an input image and its unsharped output: [Sch89:Ch. 4]

unsupervised behavior modeling: A form of unsupervised learning used for learning behavior models based on examples, without human intervention. For example, one could build models based on clustering trajectory-based representations. [XG08]

unsupervised clustering: An unsupervised learning method that outputs a clustering. [HTF08:14.3]

unsupervised feature selection: Feature selection for an unsupervised learning problem, where there is no response or target variable. For example one may eliminate features that are highly correlated or dependent with the retained subset or select a subset of features so as to maximize an index of clustering performance. [MMP02]

unsupervised learning: Finding interesting patterns or structure in the data without teaching or a supervisory signal to guide the search process. Clustering, latent variable models and dimensionality reduction are examples of unsupervised learning. Contrast with supervised learning. [Bis06:Ch. 1]

unusual behavior detection: The discovery of unusual behavior, usually by analysis of video data. Examples of unusual behaviors include traffic traveling in the wrong direction, people fighting, people in inappropriate locations (e.g., in secure areas of prisons) etc. Models of normal behavior can be created using supervised classification, semi-supervised learning or unsupervised behavior modeling methods. See also anomaly detection. [XG08]

updating eigenspace: Algorithms for the incremental updating of eigenspace representations. These algorithms facilitate approaches such as active learning. [CMW+97]

upsampling: Increasing the sampling rate of a signal by creating more samples. For example, doubling the size of an image requires a 2:1 upsampling. Upsampling may require interpolating the existing samples. [Sze10:3.5.1]

USB camera: A camera conforming to the universal serial bus (USB) standard. [WP:Webcam]

validation: Testing whether or not some hypothesis is true. See also hypothesize and verify. [WP:Validation]

validation set: Compares the performance of different models which have been trained on a training set, in order to carry out model selection. The selected model is then used to make predictions on the test set. If model selection is carried out on the test set, this is likely to produce a downward-biased estimate of the true generalization error. See also cross-validation. [HTF08:7.2]

valley: A dark elongated object in a gray scale image, so called because it corresponds to a valley in the image viewed as a 3D surface or elevation map of intensity versus image position. [GP93]

valley detection: An image processing operator that enhances linear features rather than light-to-dark edges. See also bar detector. [LLSV99]

value quantization: When a continuous number is encoded as a finite number of integer values. A common example of this occurs when a voltage or current is encoded as integers in the range 0-255. [Kam89]

vanishing line: The 2D line that is the image of the intersection of a 3D plane with the plane at infinity. The horizon line in an image is the intersection of the ground plane with the plane at infinity, just as a pair of railway lines meeting in a vanishing point is the intersection of two parallel lines and the plane at infinity. The figure shows the vanishing line for the ground plane with a road and railroad: [HZ00:7.6]

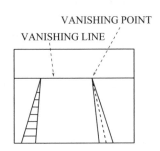

vanishing point: The image of the point at infinity where two parallel 3D lines meet. A pair of parallel 3D lines are represented as $\vec{a} + \lambda\vec{n}$ and $\vec{b} + \lambda\vec{n}$. The vanishing point is the image of the 3D direction $\begin{pmatrix} \vec{n} \\ 0 \end{pmatrix}$. The figure shows the vanishing points for a road and railroad: [TV98:6.2.3]

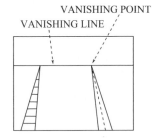

variable focus: 1) A camera system with a lens that allows zoom to be changed under user or program control. 2) An image sequence in which focal length varies through the sequence. [KH04]

variance: The variance, denoted σ^2, of a random variable X is the expectation value of the square of the deviation of the variable from the mean. If μ is the mean, then $\sigma^2 = E[(X - \mu)^2]$. [Bis06:1.2.2]

variational analysis: An extension to the calculus of variations to problems in optimization theory. [RW05]

variational approach: Signal processing expressed as a problem of variational calculus. The input signal is a function $I(t)$ on the interval $t \in [-1, 1]$. The processed signal is a function P defined on the same interval that minimizes an *energy functional* $E(P)$ of the form

$$E(P) = \int_{-1}^{1} f(P(t), \dot{P}(t), I(t))\mathrm{d}t.$$

The calculus of variations shows that the minimizing P is the solution to the associated Euler–Lagrange equation

$$\frac{\partial f}{\partial P} = \frac{\mathrm{d}}{\mathrm{d}t}\frac{\partial f}{\partial \dot{P}}$$

In computer vision, the functional is often of the form

$$E = \int \text{truth}(P, I) + \lambda \times \text{beauty}(P)$$

where the "truth" term measures fidelity to the data and the "beauty" term is a *regularizer*. These can be seen in a specific example: smoothing. In the conventional approach, smoothing might be considered the result of an *algorithm*, e.g., convolve the image with a Gaussian kernel. In the variational approach, the smoothed signal P is the signal that best trades off smoothness, measured as the square of the second derivative $\int(\dot{P}(t))^2\mathrm{d}t$, and fidelity to the data, measured as the squared difference between the input and the output $\int(P(t) - I(t))^2\mathrm{d}t$, with the balance chosen by a parameter λ:

$$E(P) = \int (P(t) - I(t))^2 + \lambda(\dot{P}(t))^2 \mathrm{d}t$$

[TBAB98]

variational calculus: Synonym for calculus of variations, a field of mathematics which deals with optimizing (maximizing or minimizing) functionals. [Fox88]

variational mean field method: A form of variational model in which the target probability distribution is factored into a product of terms which are assumed to be independent. This allows optimization of one term while keeping the other marginal terms fixed at their "mean field" value. [Bis06:10.1]

variational method: See variational approach.

variational model: A family of problem-solving methods that involve formulating the problem numerically as set of constraints on the solution which are integrated over the whole problem space. Numerical minimization methods are used to find a solution. Examples include estimating optical flow, the fundamental matrix and image segmentation. [MS94]

variational problem: See variational approach.

vector field: A multivalued function $\vec{f}$: $\mathbb{R}^n \mapsto \mathbb{R}^m$. The figure shows the 2D-to-2D function $\vec{f}(x, y) = (y, \sin \pi x)$:

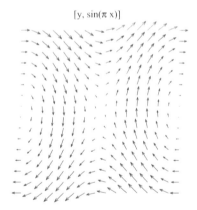

[y, sin(π x)]

An RGB image $I(x, y) = (r(x, y), g(x, y), b(x, y))$ is an example of a 2D-to-3D vector field. [WP:Vector_field]

vector quantization: Representation of a set of vectors by associating each possible vector with one of a small set of "codebook" vectors. For example, each pixel in an RGB image has 256^3 possible values, but one might expect that a particular image uses only a small subset of these values. If a 256-element colormap is computed, and each RGB value is represented by the nearest RGB vector in the colormap, the RGB space has been *quantized* into 256 elements. Clustering of the data is often used to identify the best subsets for each element. [GG92:Ch.]

vehicle detection: An example of the object-recognition problem where the task is to find vehicles in video imagery. [SBM06]

vehicle license (number) plate analysis: A visual system locates the license plate in a video image and then recognizes the characters. [HC04]

vehicle tracking: An example of the tracking problem applied to images of vehicles. [FP03:17.5.1]

velocity: Rate of change of position. Generally, for a curve $\vec{x}(t) \in \mathbb{R}^n$ the velocity is the n-vector $\frac{\partial \vec{x}(t)}{\partial t}$ [BB82:3.6.1]

velocity field: The image velocity of each point in an image. See also optical flow field. [Sch89:Ch. 5]

velocity moment: A moment that integrates information about region velocity as well as position and shape distribution. Let $m_{pq}^{[i]}$ be the pqth central moment of a binary region in the ith image. Then the Cartesian velocity moments are defined as $v_{pqrs} = \sum_i (\bar{x}_i - \bar{x}_{i-1})^r (\bar{y}_i - \bar{y}_{i-1})^s m_{pq}^{[i]}$, where $(\bar{x}_i, \bar{y}_i)$ is the center of mass in the ith image. [SN01b]

velocity smoothness constraint: Changes in the magnitude or direction of an image's velocity field occur smoothly. [Hil84]

vergence: 1) The angle between the optical axes in a stereo system, when the two cameras fixate on the same scene point.
2) The difference between the pan angle settings of two cameras. [FP03:11.2]

vergence maintenance: The action of a control loop that ensures that the optical centers of two cameras – whose positions are under program control – are looking at the same scene point. [OP89]

verification: In the context of object recognition, a class of algorithms aim-

ing to test the validity of various hypotheses (models) explaining the data. Back projection is such a technique, typically used with geometric models. See also object verification. [JKS95:15.1]

vertex: A point at the end of a line (edge) segment. Often vertices are common to two or more line segments. [Low91:10.2]

video: 1) Generic term for a set of images taken at successive instants with small time intervals between them.
2) The analog signal emitted by a video camera. Each frame of video corresponds to about 40 ms of electrical signal that encodes the start of each scan line, the image of each video scan line, and synchronization information.
3) A video recording. [Umb98:1.4]

video analysis: A general term for extracting information from a video, which includes extracting measurements related to the objects (such as sports players) being observed in the video, video clip categorization, cut detection, video key frame detection etc. [WP:Video_content_analysis]

video annotation: The association of symbolic objects, such as text descriptions or index terms, with frames of video. [FML04]

video camera: A camera that records a sequence of images over time. [FP03:Ch. 1]

video clip categorization: Determining which category the content of a video belongs to, such as sports video, action video, outdoor scenery etc. [BCC08]

video coding: The conversion of video to a digital bitstream. The source may be analog or digital. Generally, coding also compresses or reduces the bitrate of the video data. [WP:Data_compression#Video]

video compression: Video coding with the specific aim of reducing the number of bits required to represent a video sequence. Examples include MPEG, H.263 and DIVX. [WP:Data_compression#Video]

video content analysis: A collection of approaches to extracting different types of information from videos, such as the main characters, sports behavior quantization, types of scene, types of technique used, appearance of logos etc. [WP:Video_content_analysis]

video corpus: A collection or body (Latin *corpus*) of videos or video clips, typically to be analyzed, e.g., to see the frequency of some occurrence. The videos may be subject to video annotation. [AQ08]

video deinterlacing: Traditional broadcast video transmitted each frame as two video fields, consisting of the odd lines of the frame and then the even lines. Deinterlacing is the process of combining the two fields back to a single image, which can then be the subject of progressive image transmission. One difficulty that can arise is if the two fields were captured at slightly different times, thus creating pixel jitter on moving objects. [Sze10:8.4.3]

video descriptor: 1) A set of properties that summarize the content of a video, such as a color histogram, statistics on the number of scenes or the amount of motion observed etc.
2) A specialized code for the format of the video, e.g., 720p which stands for a 1280 × 720, 60 Hz progressive scan video stream. [WP:Extended_display_identification_data]

video deshearing: Shearing can occur in an image or video when the camera

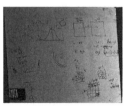

BEFORE

AFTER

(or scene) moves while progressively capturing a video. The result is "tilted" structure in the image and perpendicular scene structures are no longer observed as perpendicular. Deshearing removes this shear. The figure shows an image before and after deshearing: [Sze10:8.2]

video error concealment: Compressed video is typically transmitted in blocks, which can be affected by the loss of a block. The loss of data will affect the reconstruction of the video frame, which can lead to blank sections in a video frame. Error concealment attempts to reconstruct the missing data, e.g., by using data from the previous or succeeding frame. As the repairs are only estimated, this can lead to blocking artifacts or glitch artifacts. Video error concealment attempts both to replace the missing data and correct any introduced artifacts. [WP:Packet_loss_concealment]

video indexing: Video annotation with the aim of allowing queries of the form "At what frame did event *x* occur?" or "Does object *x* appear?". [SZ94]

video key frame: 1) In video compression, a frame which is stored completely, and which is then used as the basis for incremental compression. New key frames are needed when there is a large change in the viewpoint, a significant scene change, etc.
2) In video analysis, key frames are detected under the same criteria as for compression; they can be used for understanding the action or for video summarization.
3) In computer animation, key frames define the start and end of a smooth transformation which can be interpolated. [FP03:p. 311]

video mining: A general term used for extracting information from a video, which could include detection of suspicious objects (e.g., abandoned objects) or inspection of manufactured objects. A more advanced use is to discover patterns in a video or collection of videos, such as analysis of traffic patterns to enhance safety, statistical analysis of sports performances, identifying the cast of a video, quantifying customer behavior in a store etc. [RDD03]

video mosaic: 1) A collection of video key frames which creates a video summarization of the action in the video.
2) A collage of videos (or still images) used to create a video in the same way that individual images can be combined to create a static image mosaic, usually for artistic or entertainment effect. [WP:Photographic_mosaic]

video quality assessment: When video data is transformed from one encoding to another or video compression is applied, there is the possibility that the quality is reduced. Quality assessment measures the amount of degradation; it may have both a subjective and an objective component. [Win05]

video rate system: A real-time processing system that operates at the frame rate of the ambient video standard. Typically 25 or 30 frames per second, 50 or 60 fields per second. [KYO+96]

video restoration: Application of image restoration to video, often making use of the temporal coherence of video, or correcting for video-specific degradations. [ZYZH10]

video retrieval: The selection of a video from a database of videos. Retrieval could be based on associated keywords, text or metadata, or by similar video content (general interest, sports, or even a specific team or player). [EKO+04]

video screening: 1) a public presentation of a video.
2) Reviewing the content of a video, e.g., for the detection of offensive material.

video search: 1) Discovering and collecting links to videos across the web.
2) Locating videos inside a database of videos (See video retrieval).
3) Looking for specific content within a video. [WP:Video_search_engine]

video segmentation: Application of segmentation to video, with the requirement that the segmentation exhibit the temporal coherence of the original footage and to split the video sequence into different groups of consecutive frames, e.g., when there is a change of scene. [BW98]

video semantic content analysis: Analysis that gives a description of the content of a video in terms of actors, objects, relationships or activities, in contrast to more numerical quantities such as amount of movement, number of frames or color histograms. [BLJS07]

video sequence: See video. [WP:Video]

video sequence synchronization: The frame-by-frame registration of two (or more) video sequences, or of matching components of the content observed in them. Applications include visual surveillance from two viewpoints and wide baseline stereo. If the sequences have a different sample rate then dynamic time warping can be used. [TG04]

video stabilization: A set of methods compensating for the observed jitter blur in a video caused by minor motions of the camera, particularly if it is handheld. The primary methods are to slightly move the lens, the imaging chip or the digitized image to reduce motion. [Sze10:8.2.1]

video stream: The sequence of individual images captured by a video camera. The stream may be raw or compressed images.

video structure parsing: Exploiting the known *a priori* structure and properties of a video to classify segmented shots. The *a priori* structure is found in video streams with a distinct sequential or hierarchical structure, where major scenes can be predicted and detected, e.g., television news or weather reports. [LTZ96]

video summarization: This produces a short image-based summary of the important events of a video, e.g., by extracting the video key frames without repetition while maintaining their order. An example of this is a short video of sporting match highlights. [CF02]

video texture: A potentially infinitely variable video constructed by randomly concatenating segments of a real video at frames where the connection is not noticeable. This is used by computer graphics to generate dynamic non-repeating image motion. [SSSE00]

video thumbnail: A small image (thumbnail) that gives an impression of the content of a video. There are many software packages to do this. See Google's Videos page for examples.

video transmission format: A description of the precise form of the analog video signal coding conventions in terms of duration of components such as number of lines, number of pixels, front porch, sync and blanking. [WP:Moving_image_formats#Transmission]

vidicon: A type of tube camera, successor of the image orthicon tube. [Sch89:Ch. 8]

view-based object recognition: Recognition of 3D objects using multiple 2D images of the objects rather than a 3D model. [BSB+96]

view combination: A class of techniques combining prototype views linearly to form appearance models. See also eigenspace-based recognition, prototype, representation. [Ull98]

view-dependent reconstruction: The process of creating a new image or video from an arbitrary viewpoint, given two or more original images or videos, usually using a combination of projective geometry and stereo fusion techniques. A typical application allows a viewer to change viewpoint while watching or replaying a sporting event. [CTMS03]

view integration: Creation of a composite image (or video) by mosaicing several overlapping images (or video streams).

view interpolation: A family of techniques for synthesizing a new view of an object or scene based on two or more previously captured views.

Techniques for doing this include simple interpolation using feature point correspondence between images and projective transfer using the trifocal tensor. [CW93]

view-invariant action recognition: Many action recognition techniques are based on models created from data from a given viewpoint, which limits their use to video seen only from the same viewpoint. Viewpoint-invariant techniques construct models that can be used to recognize actions independent of the viewpoint. [GM11]

view selection: 1) See viewpoint selection.
2) Some object recognition or action recognition algorithms store multiple models of the object or action from different viewpoints. They must then select the view best suited for the current recognition task. [HZK08]

view volume: The infinite volume of 3D space bounded by the camera's center of projection and the edges of the viewable area on the image plane. The volume might also be bounded near and far by other planes because of focusing and depth of field constraints. This figure illustrates the view volume: [JKS95:8.4]

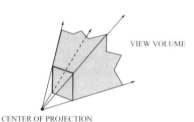

VIEW VOLUME

CENTER OF PROJECTION

viewer-centered representation: A representation of the 3D world that an observer (e.g., a robot or a human) maintains. The global coordinate system is maintained on the observer, and the representation of the world changes as the observer moves. Compare with object-centered representation. [TV98:10.6.2]

viewfield: See field of view.

viewing space: The set of all possible locations from which an object or

308

scene could be viewed. Typically these locations are grouped to give a set of typical or characteristic views of the object. If orthographic projection is used, then the full 3D space of views can be simplified to a viewsphere. [Bli82]

viewpoint: The position and orientation of the camera when an image was captured. The viewpoint may be expressed in absolute coordinates or relative to some arbitrary coordinate system, in which case the relative position of the camera and the scene (or other cameras) is the relevant quantity. [WP:Camera_angle#Angles_and_their_effects]

viewpoint consistency constraint: Lowe's term for the concept that a 3D model matched to a set of 2D line segments must admit at least one 3D camera position that projects the 3D model to those lines. Essentially, the 3D and 2D data must allow pose estimation. [Low87b]

viewpoint-dependent representations: See viewer-centered representation.

viewpoint invariance: A property that has the same value or a process that performs at the same level independent of the viewpoint from which the data was taken, e.g., projective invariants or face recognition using 3D models. [WCL+08]

viewpoint planning: Deciding where an active vision system will look next, in order to maximize the likelihood of achieving some preset goal. A common example is computing the location of a range sensor in several successive positions in order to gain a complete 3D model of a target object. After n pictures have been captured, the viewpoint planning problem is to choose the position of picture $n + 1$ in order to maximize the amount of new data acquired, while ensuring that the new position will allow the new data to be registered to the n existing images. [MC97]

viewpoint selection: When rendering a view or acquiring a 3D model,

it is important to choose a view that is highly informative, which is the goal of viewpoint selection. It is also important to choose a good set of source views for image-based rendering. [VFSH01]

viewsphere: The set of camera positions from which an object can be observed. If the camera is orthographic, the viewsphere is parameterized by the 2D set of points on the 3D unit sphere. At the camera position corresponding to a particular point on the viewsphere, all images of the object caused by camera rotation are related by a 2D-to-2D image transformation, i.e., no parallax effects occur. See aspect graph. The figure shows the placement of a camera on the viewsphere: [NG99]

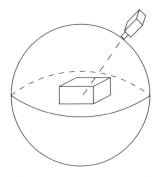

vignetting: Darkening of the corners of an image relative to the image center, which is related to the degree to which the points are off the optical axis. [Low91:3.11]

virtual bronchoscopy: Creation of virtual views of the pulmonary system based on, e.g., magnetic resonance imaging as a replacement for endoscope imaging. [WP:Bronchoscopy]

virtual endoscopy: Simulation of a traditional endoscopy procedure using a virtual reality representation of physiological data such as that obtained by an X-ray CAT-scan or magnetic resonance imaging. [Vin96]

virtual reality: The use of computer graphics and other interaction tools to confer on a user the sensation of being in, and interacting with, an alternative environment. This includes simulation of visual, aural and haptic cues. The visual environment may be displayed by rendering a 3D model of the world into a head-mounted display whose viewpoint is tracked in 3D so that the user's head movements generate images corresponding to their viewpoint. Alternatively, the user may be placed in a computer-augmented virtual environment (CAVE), where as much as possible of the user's field of view can be manipulated by the controlling computer. [WP:Virtual_reality]

virtual view: Visualization of a model from a particular viewpoint. [MTG97]

viscous model: A deformable model based on the concept of a viscous fluid (i.e., a fluid with a relatively high resistance to flow). [WP:Viscosity]

viseme: A model of the visual appearance of the face and mouth movements that occur when uttering a phoneme. [WP:Viseme]

visibility: Whether or not a particular feature is visible from a camera position. [WP:Visibility_(geometry)]

visibility class: The set of points where exactly the same portion of an object or scene is visible. For example, when viewing the corner of a cube, an observer can move about in about one-eighth of the full viewing space before entering a new visibility class. [AMS09]

visibility locus: All camera positions from which a particular feature is visible. [Goa87]

visible light: Description of electromagnetic radiation with wavelengths between about 400 nm (blue) and 700 nm (red), corresponding to the range in which the rods and cones of the human eye are sensitive. [WP:Visible_spectrum]

VISIONS: The early scene understanding system of Hanson and Riseman. [HR78]

visual appearance: The observed appearance of an object, which depends on a number of factors, such as the surface structure, orientation and reflectance of the object, the illumination, the spectral sensor sensitivity, the light reflected from the scene and the depth ordering of other objects in the scene. [WP:Visual_appearance]

visual attention: The process by which low-level feature detection directs high-level scene analysis and object recognition strategies. In humans, the results of the process are evident in the pattern of fixations and saccades in normal observation of the world. [WP:Attention]

visual behavior: 1) An observed action, or the visually observable portion of an action, such as opening a door. 2) The behavior shown when sensing, such as reorienting a camera. 3) The biological processes and activities that enable visual sensing. [IGM82]

visual codeword: See codebook and bag of features.

visual context: The knowledge of the visual environment encountered while doing some task that helps with the performance of the task. For example, when looking for a street sign in a new city, experience of this particular context (situation) tells one to look at the corners of buildings, signs on posts at corners, or signs hanging from wires in the intersection. Contrast with a context-independent visual search algorithm that would look everywhere. [CJ98]

visual cortex: A part of the brain dedicated to the processing of visual information. [WP:Visual_cortex]

visual cue: An aspect of the information extracted from visual data that helps the observer better understand the scene. For example, an occluding contour helps us understand the depth order of objects and shading gives a clue to the shape of the surface (see shape from shading). [Jac02]

visual event: When some aspect of visual behavior changes, such as entering a new location, an agent performing a different action or an interaction between two agents. [KSH05]

visual hull: A space-carving method for approximating shape from multiple images. The method finds the silhouette contours of a given object in each image. The region of space defined by each camera and the associated image contour imposes a constraint on the shape of the target object. The visual hull is the intersection of all such constraints. As more views are taken, the approximation becomes better. See the shaded areas: [FP03:26.4]

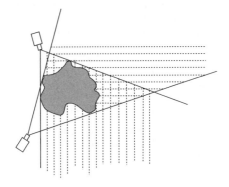

visual illusion: The perception of a scene, object or motion not corresponding to the world actually causing the image or sequence. Illusions are caused, in general, by the combination of special arrangements of the visual stimuli, viewing conditions and responses of the human vision system. Well-known examples include the Ames room (in which two people are seen as having very different heights in a seemingly normal room) and the Ponzo illusion (in which two equal segments seem to be different lengths when interpreted as 3D projections):

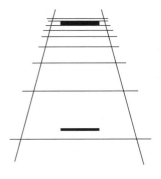

The well-known ambiguous figure–background drawings of Gestalt psychology, such as the chalice–faces pattern, are a related subject. [CS09:3.2]

visual industrial inspection: The use of computer vision techniques in order to effect quality control or to control processes in an industrial setting. [WP:Visual_inspection]

visual inspection: A general term for analyzing a visual image to inspect some item, such as might be used for quality control on a production line. [WP:Visual_inspection]

visual learning: The problem of learning visual models from sets of images (examples). In general, knowledge that can be used to carry out vision tasks. An area of the vast field of automated learning. Important applications employing visual learning include face recognition and image database indexing. See also unsupervised learning and supervised learning.

visual localization: The problem of estimating the location of a target in space given one or more images of it. Solutions differ according to several factors including the number of input images (one in model-based pose estimation; multiple discrete images in stereo vision; or a video sequence in motion analysis), the *a priori* knowledge assumed (i.e., whether camera calibration, a full perspective or simplified projection model, and a geometric model of the target are available). [DM02]

visual navigation: The problem of navigating (steering) a vehicle through an environment using visual data, typically video sequences. It is possible, under diverse assumptions, to determine the distance from obstacles, the time-to-contact, and the shape and identity of the objects in view. Both video and range sensors have been used, including acoustic sensors (see acoustic sonar). See also visual servoing and visual localization. [MS95]

visual rhythm: 1) A visual summary of a complete video, e.g., by displaying keyframes and shot transitions in a single display.

2) A repeating visual pattern, such as an observed row of windows. [KLY+01]

visual routine: Ullman's 1984 term for a subcomponent of a visual system that performs a specific task, analogous to a behavior in robotics. [WP:Visual_routine]

visual salience: A (numerical) assessment of the degree to which pixels or areas of a scene attract visual attention. The principle of Gestalt organization. [WP:Salience_(neuroscience)]

visual search: The task of searching an image for a particular prespecified object. Often used as an experimental tool in psychophysics. [WP:Visual_search]

visual servoing: Using observed motions in the image as feedback for guiding a robot. For example, moving the robot to visually align the robot's end effector with the desired target. Typically, the system has little or no *a priori* knowledge of the camera locations, their relation to the robot, or the robot kinematics. These parameters are learned as the robot moves. Visual servoing allows the calibration to change during robot operation. Such systems can adapt well to anomalous conditions, such as an arm bending under a load or motor slippage, or where calibration may not provide sufficient precision to allow the desired actions to be reliably produced purely from the modeled robot kinematics and dynamics. Because only image measurements are available, the inverse kinematic problem may be harder than in conventional servoing. [WP:Visual_Servoing]

visual surveillance: The use of video cameras to observe situations usually involving people or vehicles. Applications using visual surveillance include secure area monitoring, crowd flow analysis, consumer behavior summarizing, etc. [WP:Surveillance]

visual tracking: Links points or objects from one video frame to the next during analysis of a video stream. A normal prerequisite is to have detected the item to be tracked in advance, but this can happen simultaneously, e.g., during mean-shift tracking. Tracking is often part of visual surveillance or behavior analysis. [FP03:Ch. 17]

Viterbi algorithm: A dynamic programming algorithm used to determine the most probable explanation for the hidden state sequence in a hidden Markov model (HMM) given the observed data. [Bis06:13.2.5]

vocabulary tree: An organization of an image database into a hierarchical tree structure where the search for matching images compares the description of the index image to the descriptors at each branch of the tree. The tree is constructed from the database by hierarchical *k*-means clustering. [NS06]

volume: 1) A region of 3D space. A subset of $\mathbb{R}^3$. A (possibly infinite) 3D point set.

2) The space bounded by a closed surface. [Nal93:9.2]

volume detection: The detection of volume-shaped entities in 3D data sets, such as might be produced by a nuclear magnetic resonance scanner. [Bot87]

volume matching: Identification of correspondence between objects or subsets of objects using a volumetric representation. [BS97]

volume skeletons: The skeletons of 3D point sets, by extension of the definitions for 2D curves or regions. [SdB03]

volumetric image: A voxmap or 3D array of points where each entry typically represents some measure of material density or other property in 3D space. Common examples include computed axial tomography and nuclear magnetic resonance data. [MM02]

volumetric reconstruction: Any of several techniques that derive a volumetric representation from image data. Examples include X-ray CAT, space carving and visual hull computation. [BM02:3.7.3]

volumetric representation: A data structure by means of which a subset of 3D space is represented digitally. Examples include voxmap, octree and the space bounded by surface representations. [Nal93:9.2]

volumetric scattering: A physical illumination and sensing effect where the sensing energy is redistributed by materials in the medium through which the radiation (e.g., light) travels, such as by dust, fog etc. Also known as volume scattering. [Max94]

von Kries hypothesis: A hypothesis that the primate color constancy process scales each color channel multiplicatively and independently. This can be implemented by multiplication with a diagonal matrix. [CGZ07]

Voronoi cell: See Voronoi diagram.

Voronoi diagram: Given n points $\vec{x}_{1..n}$, the Voronoi diagram of the point set is a partition of space into n regions or cells $R_{1..n}$. Every point p in cell R_i is closer to point $\vec{x}_i$ than to any other $\vec{x}$. The hyperplanes separating the Voronoi regions are the perpendicular bisectors of the edges in the Delaunay triangulation of the point set. In the figure, the Voronoi diagram of the four points are the four cells surrounding them: [SQ04:7.3.2]

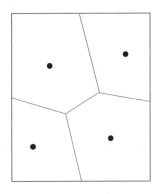

voxel: A region of 3D space, named from "volume element" by analogy with "pixel". Usually a voxel is an axis-aligned rectangular solid or cube. A component of the voxmap representation for a 3D volume. A voxel, like a pixel, may have associated attributes such as color, occupancy or density of some measurement. [FP03:21.3.3]

voxel carving: See space carving.

voxel coloring: A method for object or scene model recovery from multiple images. The core idea is to intersect observation rays from different viewpoints into a volumetric space and exploit the viewpoint consistency constraint, i.e., that true intersections should have the same color (the color of the surface in the voxel where the rays intersect). See also space carving. [SD97]

voxmap: A volumetric representation that describes a 3D volume by dividing space into a regular grid of voxels, arranged as a 3D array $v(i, j, k)$. For a Boolean voxmap, cell (i, j, k) intersects the volume iff $v(i, j, k) = 1$. The advantages of the representation are that it can represent an arbitrarily complex topology and is fast to look up. The major disadvantage is the large use of memory, addressed by the octree representation. [MPT05]

VRML: Virtual Reality Markup Language. A means of defining 3D geometric models intended for Internet delivery. [WP:VRML]

Wachspress coordinates: A generalization of Barycentric coordinates to represent points in the interior of a polygon as a weighted function of the polygon's vertex positions. The generalization allows polygons with an arbitrary number of vertices (instead of the three in Barycentric coordinates). Wachspress coordinates are useful for representing and manipulating articulated objects and deformable shapes. [Wac75].

walkthrough: A classification of the infinite number of paths between two points into one of nine equivalence classes of the eight relative directions between the points plus the ninth having no movement. In the figure, point B is in equivalence class 2 relative to A: [BV98]

Walsh function: The Walsh functions of order n are a particular set of square waves $W(n, k) : [0, 2^n) \mapsto \{-1, 1\}$ for k from 1 to 2^n. They are orthogonal and the product of Walsh functions is a Walsh function. The square waves transition only at integer lattice points so each function can be specified by the vector of values it takes on the points $\{\frac{1}{2}, 1\frac{1}{2}, \ldots, 2^n-\frac{1}{2}\}$. The collection of these values for a given order n is the Hadamard transform matrix $\mathbf{H}_{2^n}$

of order 2^n. The two functions of order 1 are the rows of

$$H_2 = \begin{bmatrix} 1 & 1 \\ 1 & -1 \end{bmatrix}$$

and the four of order 2 are

$$\mathbf{H}_4 = \begin{bmatrix} \mathbf{H}_2 & \mathbf{H}_2 \\ \mathbf{H}_2 & -\mathbf{H}_2 \end{bmatrix}$$

$$= \begin{bmatrix} 1 & 1 & 1 & 1 \\ 1 & -1 & 1 & -1 \\ 1 & 1 & -1 & -1 \\ 1 & -1 & -1 & 1 \end{bmatrix}$$

In general, the functions of order $n + 1$ are generated by the relation

$$\mathbf{H}_{2^{n+1}} = \begin{bmatrix} \mathbf{H}_{2^n} & \mathbf{H}_{2^n} \\ \mathbf{H}_{2^n} & -\mathbf{H}_{2^n} \end{bmatrix}$$

and this recurrence is the basis of the fast Walsh transform. The figure shows the four Walsh functions of order 2: [Umb98:2.5.3]

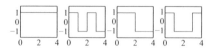

Walsh transform: Expression of a 2^n element vector v in terms of a basis of order n Walsh functions; the multiplication by the corresponding Hadamard matrix. The Walsh transform has applications in image coding, logic design and the study of genetic algorithms. [Umb98:2.5.3]

Waltz line labeling: A scheme for the interpretation of line images of polyhedra in the blocks world. Each image line is labeled to indicate what class of

Dictionary of Computer Vision and Image Processing, Second Edition.
R. B. Fisher, T. P. Breckon, K. Dawson-Howe, A. Fitzgibbon, C. Robertson, E. Trucco and C. K. I. Williams.
© 2014 John Wiley & Sons, Ltd. Published 2014 by John Wiley & Sons, Ltd.

scene edge gave rise to it: concave, convex, occluding, crack or shadow. By including the constraints supplied by junction labeling in a constraint satisfaction problem, Waltz demonstrated that collections of lines whose labels were locally ambiguous could be globally disambiguated. The figure shows a simple example of Waltz line labeling with concave edges ($-$), convex edges ($+$) and occluding edges ($>$): [BB82:9.5.3]

warping: Transformation of an image by reparameterization of the 2D plane. Given an image $I(\vec{x})$ and a 2D-to-2D mapping $w : \vec{x} \mapsto \vec{x}'$, the warped image $W(\vec{x})$ is $I(w(\vec{x}))$. Warping functions w are often designed so that certain control points $\vec{p}_{1..n}$ in the source image are mapped to specified locations $\vec{p}'_{1..n}$ in the destination image. See also image morphing. The figure shows an original image, $I(\vec{x})$; a warping function represented by arrows joining points $\vec{x}$ to $w^{-1}(\vec{x})$; and the warped image $W(\vec{x})$: [SB11:7.10]

watermark: See digital watermarking. [WP:Watermark]

watershed segmentation: Image segmentation by means of the watershed transform. A typical implementation proceeds thus:
- Detect edges.
- Compute the distance transform D of the edges.
- Compute watershed regions in $-D$.

The figure shows a) the original image; b) Canny edges; c) the distance transform; d) region boundaries of the watershed transform of (c); e) mean color in the watershed regions;

f) regions overlaid on the image: [SB11:10.10]

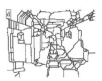

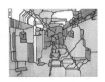

watershed transform: A tool for morphological image segmentation. The watershed transform views the image as an elevation map, with each local minimum in the map given a unique integer label. The watershed *transform* of the image assigns to each *non-minimum* pixel, p, the label of the minimum to which a drop of water would fall if placed at p. Points on "ridges" or watersheds of the elevation map that could fall into one of two minima are called watershed points and the set of pixels surrounding each minimum that share its label are called watershed regions. Efficient algorithms exist for the computation of the watershed transform. The figure shows an image with minima superimposed; the same image viewed as a 3D elevation map; and the watershed transform of the image, where different minima have different colored regions and watershed pixels are shown in white; a particular watershed is indicated by arrows: [SB11:10.10]

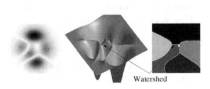

Watershed

315

wavelength: The distance between successive peaks of the wave. Denoted λ, it is the wave's speed divided by the frequency. Electromagnetic waves, particularly visible light, are important in computer vision, with wavelengths of the order of 400–700 nm. [Hec87:2.2]

wavelet: A function $\phi(x)$ that has certain properties that mean it can be used to derive a set of basis function representations in terms of which other functions can be approximated. Comparing to the Fourier transform basis functions, note that they can be viewed as a set of scalings and translations of $f(x) = sin(\pi x)$, e.g., $cos(3\pi x) = sin(3\pi x + \frac{\pi}{2}) = f(\frac{6x+1}{2})$. Similarly, a wavelet basis is made from a mother wavelet $\phi(x)$ by translating and scaling: each basis function $\phi_{jk}(x)$ is of the form $\phi_{jk}(x) = const \cdot \phi(2^{-j}x - k)$. The conditions on ϕ ensure that different basis functions (i.e., with different j and k) are orthonormal. There are several popular choices (e.g., by Haar and Daubechies) for ϕ, that trade off various desirable properties, such as compactness in space and time, and the ability to approximate certain classes of functions. The figure shows the mother Haar transform wavelet and some of the derived wavelets $\phi_{j,k}$: [Mal89]

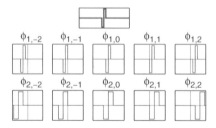

wavelet descriptor: Description of a shape in terms of the coefficients of a wavelet decomposition of the original signal, in a manner similar to Fourier shape descriptors for 2D curves. See also wavelet transform. [FP03:22.5.2]

wavelet transform: Representation of a signal in terms of a basis of wavelets. Similar to the Fourier transform, but as the wavelet basis is a two-parameter family of functions ϕ_{jk}, the wavelet transform of a d-D signal is a $(d+1)$-D function. However, the number of distinct values needed to represent transform of a discrete signal of length n is just $O(n)$. The wavelet transform has similar applications to the Fourier transform, but the wavelet basis offers advantages when representing natural signals such as images. [Umb98:2.5.5]

wavelet tree: In text indexing, a structure that may be used to compress data and text. It works by converting a string into a balanced binary tree of bit vectors where 0 replaces half of the symbols and 1 replaces the other half. The tree is filtered and re-encoded so that the resulting ambiguity lessens and this sequence is repeated until no ambiguity is left. [FGM06]

weak calibration: The process of estimating the epipolar geometry, e.g., the fundamental matrix, from a set of feature point correspondences matched between a pair of images captured from uncalibrated perspective cameras. [PGM96]

weak learner: A learner that is guaranteed (with high probability) to perform better than chance but with performance poorly aggregated against the ground truth for a given problem. Contrast with strong learner. Boosting is a method to combine many weak learners to produce a strong learner. [Bis06:14.3]

weak perspective: An approximation of viewing geometry between the pinhole camera or full perspective camera and the orthographic imaging model. The projection of a homogeneous 3D point $\vec{X} = (X, Y, Z, 1)^\top$ is given by the formula

$$\begin{pmatrix} x \\ y \end{pmatrix} = \begin{pmatrix} p_{11} & p_{12} & p_{13} & p_{14} \\ p_{21} & p_{22} & p_{23} & p_{24} \end{pmatrix} \vec{X}$$

for the affine camera but with the additional constraint that the vectors (p_{11}, p_{12}, p_{13}) and (p_{21}, p_{22}, p_{23}) are scaled rows of a rotation matrix, i.e.,

$$p_{11}p_{21} + p_{12}p_{22} + p_{13}p_{23} = 0$$

[TV98:2.2.4]

weakly calibrated stereo: Any two-view stereo algorithm for which the only calibration information needed is the fundamental matrix between the cameras is said to be *weakly calibrated*. In the general, multi-view case, the camera calibration is known up to a projective ambiguity. Weakly calibrated systems cannot determine Euclidean properties such as absolute scale but return results that are projectively equivalent to the Euclidean reconstructions. [FP03:10.1.5]

weakly supervised learning: A general distinction in machine learning is between supervised learning and unsupervised learning. However, the supervisory information provided may be weak relative to the task at hand. For example in learning to carry out object localization, one may be given only the information that an image does or does not contain an instance of the specified object, but not its location. Another example of weak supervision is multiple instance learning. [Mur12:1.5.4]

wearable camera: A video camera that can be carried on a person's body or head for the purpose of analyzing, recording or transmitting what that person sees. It can be used for military purposes or as part of an augmented reality system wherein a data projector annotates the observed environment with useful information. [WP:Wearable_computer]

Weber's Law: If a difference can be perceived between two stimuli of values I and $I + \delta I$ then it should be possible to perceive a difference between two stimuli with different values J and $J + \delta J$ where $\frac{\delta I}{I} \leq \frac{\delta J}{J}$. [Jai89:3.2]

weighted least squares: A least mean square estimation process in which the data elements also have a weight associated. The weights might specify the confidence or quality of the data item. The use of weights can help make the estimation more robust. [WP:Weighted_least_squares#Weighted_least_squares]

weighted walkthrough: A discrete measure of the relative position of two regions. The measure is a histogram of the walkthrough relative positions of every pair of points selected from the two regions. [BBV03]

weld seam tracking: Using visual feedback to control a robotic welding device, so it maintains the weld along the desired seam. [BLA02]

white balance: A system of color correction to deal with differing light conditions, in order for white objects to appear white. [WP:Color_balance]

white noise: A noise process in which the noise power at all frequencies is equal (as compared to pink noise). When considering spatially distributed noise, white noise means that there is distortion at every spatial frequency (i.e., large distortions as well as small). [WP:White_noise]

whitening filter: See noise-whitening filter.

wide angle lens: A lens with a field of view greater than about 45°. Wide angle lenses allow more information to be collected in a single image, but often suffer a loss of resolution, particularly at the periphery of the image. Wide angle lenses are also more likely to require correction for nonlinear lens distortion. [WP:Wide_angle_lens]

wide-area scene analysis (WASA): Video-based surveillance over an area larger than a single camera's view, using a network of cameras. [SCK+11]

wide baseline stereo: The stereo correspondence problem when the two images for which correspondence is to be determined are significantly different because the cameras are separated by a long baseline. In particular, a 2D window around a point in one image is expected to look significantly different in the second image because of foreshortening, occlusion, and lighting effects. [MCUP04]

wide field of view: Where the optics is designed to capture light rays forming large angles (60° or more) with the optical axis. See also wide angle lens, panoramic image mosaic, panoramic image stereo and plenoptic function representation. [ZZX04]

width function: Given a 2D shape (closed subset of the plane) $S \subset \mathbb{R}^2$, the width function $w(\theta)$ is the width of the shape as a function of orientation. Specifically, the projection $P(\theta) := \{x \cos \theta + y \sin \theta \mid (x, y) \in S\}$, and $w(\theta) := \max P(\theta) - \min P(\theta)$. [BN78]

Wiener filter: A regularized inverse convolution filter. Given a signal g that is known to be the convolution of an unknown signal f and a known corrupting signal k, it is desired to undo the effect of k and recover f. If (F, G, K) are the respective Fourier transforms of (f, g, k), then $G = F \cdot K$, so the inverse filter can recover $F = G \div K$. In practice, however, G is corrupted by noise, so that when an element of K is less than the average noise level, the noise is amplified. Wiener's filter combats this tendency by adding an estimate of the noise to the divisor. Because the divisor is complex, a real formulation is as follows:

$$F = \frac{G}{K} = \frac{GK^*}{KK^*} = \frac{GK^*}{|K|^2}$$

Adding the frequency domain filter noise estimate N, we obtain the Wiener reconstruction of F given G and K:

$$F = \frac{GK^*}{|K|^2 + N}$$

[Jai89:8.3]

window: See region of interest.

window scanning: Separating an image into systematic, adjacent and possibly overlapping regions of interest in order to perform some form of operation. Commonly used for object detection and localization.

windowing: Looking at a small portion of a signal or image through a "window". For example, given the vector $\vec{x} = \{x_1, \ldots, x_{100}\}$, one might look at the window of 11 values centered around 50, $\{x_{45..55}\}$. Often used in order to restrict some computation such as the Fourier transform to a small part of the image. In general, windowing is described by a *windowing function*,

which is multiplied by the signal to give the windowed signal. For example, a signal $f(\vec{x}) : \mathbb{R}^n \mapsto \mathbb{R}$ and windowing function $w(\sigma; \vec{x})$ are given, where σ controls the scale or width of w. Then the windowed signal is

$$f_w(\vec{x}) = f(\vec{x})w(\sigma; \vec{x} - \vec{c})$$

where $\vec{c}$ is the center of the window. The figure shows the Bartlett $(1 - \frac{|\vec{x}|}{\sigma})$, Hanning $(\frac{1}{2} + \frac{1}{2} \cos \frac{\pi|\vec{x}|}{\sigma})$, and Gaussian $(\exp(-\frac{|\vec{x}|^2}{\sigma^2}))$ windowing functions in 2D: [SOS00:7.1.3]

winged edge representation: A graph representation for polyhedra in which the nodes represent vertices, edges and faces. Faces point to bounding edge nodes, which point to vertices, which point back to connecting edges, which point to adjacent faces. The term "winged edge" comes from the fact that edges have four links that connect to the previous and successor edges around each of the two faces that contain the given edge: [JKS95:13.5.1]

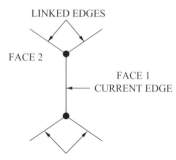

winner-takes-all: A strategy in which only the best candidate (e.g., algorithm or solution) is chosen and any other is abandoned. Commonly found in the neural network and learning literature. [WP:Winner-take-all]

wire frame representation: A representation of 3D geometry in terms of vertices and edges linking the vertices.

It does not include descriptions of the surface between the edges and, in particular, does not include information for hidden line removal. The figure shows a wire frame model of a cube: [BT88:Ch. 8]

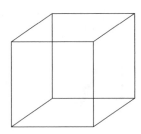

within-class scatter matrix: In a classification problem, the scatter matrix for class C_i is defined as $\mathbf{S}_i = \sum_{\vec{x} \in C_i} (\vec{x} - \vec{m}_i)(\vec{x} - \vec{m}_i)^\top$ where $\vec{m}_i$ is the mean of class i. The within-class scatter matrix is obtained by summing the individual scatter matrices, and is used in the computation of the Fisher linear discriminant (FLD). See also between-class scatter matrix. [Bis06:4.1]

world coordinates: A coordinate system useful for placing objects in a scene. Usually this is a 3D coordinate system with some arbitrarily placed origin (e.g., at a corner of a room). This contrasts with object-centered representations, viewer-centered representations or camera coordinates. [JKS95:1.4.2]

Wyner–Ziv video coding: A type of lossy video encoding that has low computational complexity at the encoder (e.g., a low-power wireless mobile device) and higher computational complexity at the decoder. The WZ method uses side information, such as an estimate of the camera motion. [WP: Distributed_source_coding#Wyner. E2.80.93Ziv_bound]

319

X

X-ray: Electromagnetic radiation of shorter wavelengths than ultraviolet light, i.e., less than about 4–40 nm. Very short X-rays are called gamma rays. Useful for medical imaging, because of their power to penetrate most materials, and for other areas, such as lithography. [Hec87:3.6.6]

X-ray CAT/CT: Computed axial tomography or computer-assisted tomography. A technique for dense 3D imaging of the interior of a material, particularly the human body. Characterized by use of an X-ray source and an imaging system that rotate around the object being scanned. [Nev82:10.3.4]

XNOR operator: A combination of two binary images, A and B, where each pixel (i, j) in A XNOR B is 0 if exactly one of $A(i, j)$ and $B(i, j)$ is 1. The output is the complement of the XOR operator. In the figure, the image on the right is the XNOR of the two images on the left: [SB11:3.2.2]

XOR operator: A combination of two binary images, A and B, where each pixel (i, j) in A XOR B is 1 if exactly one of $A(i, j)$ and $B(i, j)$ is 1. The output is the complement of the XNOR operator. In the figure, the image on the right is the XOR of the two images on the left: [SB11:3.2.2]

Dictionary of Computer Vision and Image Processing, Second Edition.
R. B. Fisher, T. P. Breckon, K. Dawson-Howe, A. Fitzgibbon, C. Robertson, E. Trucco and C. K. I. Williams.
© 2014 John Wiley & Sons, Ltd. Published 2014 by John Wiley & Sons, Ltd.

YARF: Yet Another Road Follower. An autonomous driving system from Carnegie Mellon University. [KT95]

yaw: A 3D rotation representation component (along with pitch and roll) often used for cameras or moving observers. The yaw component specifies a rotation about a vertical axis to give a side-to-side change in orientation. The figure shows the yaw rotation direction: [JKS95:12.2.1]

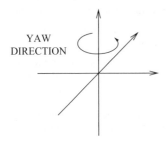

YAW DIRECTION

YCrCb: See YUV where $U = Cr$ and $V = Cb$.

YIQ: Color space used in NTSC television. Separates luminance (Y) and two color signals: in-phase (roughly orange/blue) and quadrature (roughly purple/green). Conversion to YIQ from RGB is by $[Y, I, Q]' = \mathbf{M}[R, G, B]'$ where: [BB82:2.2.5]

$$\mathbf{M} = \begin{bmatrix} 0.299 & 0.596 & 0.212 \\ 0.587 & -0.275 & -0.523 \\ 0.114 & -0.321 & 0.311 \end{bmatrix}$$

YUV: A color representation system in which each point is represented by luminance (Y) and two chrominance channels (U, which is red minus Y, and V which is blue minus Y). [WP:YUV]

Dictionary of Computer Vision and Image Processing, Second Edition.
R. B. Fisher, T. P. Breckon, K. Dawson-Howe, A. Fitzgibbon, C. Robertson, E. Trucco and C. K. I. Williams.
© 2014 John Wiley & Sons, Ltd. Published 2014 by John Wiley & Sons, Ltd.

Z

Zernike moment: A rotationally invariant moment formed from the dot product of an image with one of the Zernike polynomials. The Zernike polynomial

$$U_n^m(\rho, \phi) = R_n^m(\rho)e^{im\phi}$$

is defined in polar coordinates (ρ, ϕ) on the plane, only within the unit disk. When projecting an image, data outside the unit disk are generally ignored. The real and imaginary parts are called the *even* and *odd* polynomials respectively. The *radial* function $R_n^m(t)$ is given by

$$\sum_{l=0}^{(n-m)/2} (-1)^l \frac{t^{n-2l}(n-l)!}{l!\left(\frac{n+m}{2}-l\right)!\left(\frac{n-m}{2}-l\right)!}$$

The Zernike polynomials have a history in optics, as basis functions for modeling nonlinear lens distortion. In the figure, the Column 1 shows the real and imaginary parts of $e^{im\phi}$ for $m = 1$. Columns 2–4 show the real and imaginary parts of Zernike polynomials U_1^1, U_3^1, and U_2^2: [Jai89:9.8]

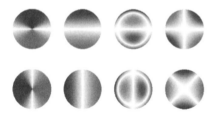

zero-crossing operator: A class of feature detector that detects zero crossings in the second derivative (rather than maxima in the first derivative). An advantage of finding zero crossings rather than maxima is that the edges always form closed curves, so that regions are clearly delineated. A disadvantage is that noise is enhanced, so the image must be carefully smoothed before the second derivative is computed. A common kernel that combines smoothing and second derivative computation is the Laplacian of Gaussian. [FP03: 8.3.1]

zero crossing of the Laplacian of a Gaussian: See zero-crossing operator.

zip code analysis: See postal code analysis.

zoom: 1) A change the effective focal length of a camera in order to increase magnification of the center of the field of view.
2) Refers to the current focal-length setting of a zoom lens. [Jai89:7.4]

zoom lens: A lens that allows the effective focal length (or "zoom") to be varied after manufacture. Zoom lenses may be manipulated manually or electrically. [WP:Zoom_lens]

Zucker–Hummel operator: A convolution kernel for surface detection in volumetric images. There is one $3 \times 3 \times 3$ kernel for each of the three derivatives. For example, if $v(x, y, z)$ is the volume image, $\frac{\partial v}{\partial z}$ is computed as the convolution of the kernel $D_z(i, j, k) = S(i, j)c(k)$, where $i, j, k \in \{1, 2, 3\}$, $c = [-1, 0, 1]$

$$S = \begin{bmatrix} a & b & a \\ b & 1 & b \\ a & b & a \end{bmatrix}$$

Dictionary of Computer Vision and Image Processing, Second Edition.
R. B. Fisher, T. P. Breckon, K. Dawson-Howe, A. Fitzgibbon, C. Robertson, E. Trucco and C. K. I. Williams.
© 2014 John Wiley & Sons, Ltd. Published 2014 by John Wiley & Sons, Ltd.

$a = 1/\sqrt{3}$ and $b = 1/\sqrt{2}$. The kernels for $\frac{\partial v}{\partial x}$ and $\frac{\partial v}{\partial y}$ are permutations of D_z given by $D_x(i, j, k) = D_z(j, k, i)$ and $D_y(i, j, k) = D_z(k, i, j)$. [BB82:3.3.3]

Zuniga–Haralick operator: A corner detection operator that is based on the coefficients of a cubic polynomial approximating the local neighborhood. [ZH83]

References

Many entries in the dictionary end with a citation in the form [A:B]. The A component usually refers to one of the items in the following list of references and the B component to a chapter, section or page in reference A. For example, [CS09:1.2] refers to section 1.2 in the book by Cyganek and Siebert. Where we have been unable to cite a book, we have tried to include a reference to a well-cited research paper or Wikipedia. A WP reference is not included in the following list, rather it is a reference to a page on Wikipedia. The B component is the name of the relevant Wikipedia page. For example, [WP:Sonar] refers to http://en.wikipedia.org/wiki/Sonar.

[AAO05] Án, M. C., Alfonseca, M., and Ortega, A. Common pitfalls using normalized compression distance: what to watch out for in a compressor. *Communications in Information and Systems 5*, 4 (2005), pp. 367–384.

[AAR04] Agarwal, S., Awan, A., and Roth, D. Learning to detect objects in images via a sparse, part-based representation. *IEEE Trans. on Pattern Analysis and Machine Intelligence 26*, 11 (2004), pp. 1475–1490.

[AB01] Alexander, D. C., and Buxton, B. F. Statistical modeling of colour data. *Int. Journal of Computer Vision 44*, 2 (2001), pp. 97–109.

[ABD+91] Anderson, S., Bruce, W. H., Denyer, P. B., *et al.* A single chip sensor and image processor for fingerprint verification. In *Proc. the IEEE Custom Integrated Circuits Conference* (1991), IEEE, pp. 12–1.

[ABF06] Andrade, E. L., Blunsden, S., and Fisher, R. B. Hidden Markov models for optical flow analysis in crowds. In *Int. Conf. on Pattern Recognition* (2006), pp. 460–463.

[Abr03] Abramson, A. *The history of television, 1942 to 2000.* McFarland, 2003.

[AC09] Aghajan, H., and Cavallaro, A. *Multi-camera Networks: Principles and Applications.* Academic Press, 2009.

[ADA09] Arici, T., Dikbas, S., and Altunbasak, Y. A histogram modification framework and its application for image contrast enhancement. *IEEE Trans. on Image Processing 18*, 9 (2009), pp. 1921–1935.

[Adi85] Adiv, G. Determining three-dimensional motion and structure from optical flow generated by several moving objects. *IEEE Trans. on Pattern Analysis and Machine Intelligence 4* (1985), pp. 384–401.

[AF02] Arikan, O., and Forsyth, D. A. Interactive motion generation from examples. *ACM Trans. Graphics (TOG) 21*, 3 (2002), pp. 483–490.

[AF05] Abraham, S., and Förstner, W. Fish-eye-stereo calibration and epipolar rectification. *ISPRS J. Photogrammetry and Remote Sensing 59*, 5 (2005), pp. 278–288.

[AF86] Ayache, N., and Faugeras, O. D. HYPER: A new approach for the recognition and positioning of two-dimensional objects. *IEEE Trans. on Pattern Analysis and Machine Intelligence 1* (1986), pp. 44–54.

[AFF85] Ansaldi, S., Floriani, L. D., and Falcidieno, B. Geometric modeling of solid objects by using a face adjacency graph representation. In *Proc. Annual Conference on Computer Graphics and Interactive Techniques* (1985), pp. 131–139.

[AFP91] Algazi, V. R., Ford, G. E., and Potharlanka, R. Directional interpolation of images based on visual properties and rank order filtering. *Int. Conf. on Acoustics, Speech, and Signal Processing* (1991), pp. 3005–3008.

Dictionary of Computer Vision and Image Processing, Second Edition.
R. B. Fisher, T. P. Breckon, K. Dawson-Howe, A. Fitzgibbon, C. Robertson, E. Trucco and C. K. I. Williams.
© 2014 John Wiley & Sons, Ltd. Published 2014 by John Wiley & Sons, Ltd.

[AFRW98] Ashbrook, A., Fisher, R., Robertson, C., and Werghi, N. Finding surface correspondence for object recognition and registration using pairwise geometric histograms. In *Proc. Euro. Conf. Computer Vision* (1998), pp. 674-686.

[AGTL09] Aja-Fernández, S., de Luis García, R., Tao, D., and Li, X., Eds. *Tensors in Image Processing and Computer Vision*. Springer, 2009.

[AH95] Aizawa, K., and Huang, T. S. Model-based image coding advanced video coding techniques for very low bit-rate applications. In *Proc. the IEEE* (1995), vol. 83, pp. 259-271.

[Alo90] Aloimonos, J. Purposive and qualitative active vision. In *Proc. IEEE Int. Conf. on Pattern Recognition* (1990), vol. 1, pp. 346-360.

[AML95] Akritas, M. G., Murphy, S. A., and Lavalley, M. P. The Theil-Sen estimator with doubly censored data and applications to astronomy. *Journal of the American Statistical Association 90*, 429 (1995), pp. 170-177.

[AMS09] Aydin, T. O., Myszkowski, K., and Seidel, H.-P. Predicting display visibility under dynamically changing lighting conditions. *Computer Graphics Forum 28*, 2 (2009), pp. 173-182.

[AP08] Alzoubi, H., and Pan, W. D. Fast and accurate global motion estimation algorithm using pixel subsampling. *Information Sciences 178*, 17 (2008), pp. 3415-3425.

[AQ08] Ayache, S., and Quenot, G. Video corpus annotation using active learning. In *Proc. Eur. Conf. on Advances in Information Retrieval, Springer-Verlag LNCS 4956* (2008), pp. 187-198.

[AR02] Agarwal, S., and Roth, D. Learning a sparse representation for object detection. In *Proc. European Conf. on Computer Vision* (2002).

[AR05] Acharya, T., and Roy, A. K. *Image Processing*. John Wiley & Sons, 2005.

[ARS04] Adams, D., Rohlf, F. J., and Slice, D. Geometric morphometrics: Ten years of progress following the revolution. *Italian Journal of Zoology 71*, 1 (2004), pp. 5-16.

[AS94] Ayer, S., and Sawhney, H. S. Layered representation of motion video using robust maximum-likelihood estimation of mixture models and minimum description length encoding. In *Proc. Int. Conf. Computer Vision* (1994), pp. 777-784.

[Bas95] Basu, A. Active calibration of cameras: theory and implementation. *IEEE Trans. on Systems, Man and Cybernetics 25*, 2 (1995), pp. 256-265.

[AS97] Avidan, S., and Shashua, A. Novel view synthesis in tensor space. In *Proc. IEEE Computer Society Conference on Computer Vision and Pattern Recognition* (1997), pp. 1034-1040.

[AT01] Arita, D., and Taniguchi, R. RPV-II: A stream-based real-time parallel vision system and its application to real-time volume reconstruction. *Computer Vision Systems* (2001), pp. 174-189.

[AT04] Agarwal, A., and Triggs, B. 3D human pose from silhouettes by relevance vector regression. In *Proc. Computer Vision and Pattern Recognition* (2004).

[AT10] Allen, E., and Triantaphillidou, S. *The Manual of Photography and Digital Imaging*. Focal Press, 2010.

[AWJ90] Amini, A. A., Weymouth, T. E., and Jain, R. C. Using dynamic programming for solving variational problems in vision. *IEEE Trans. on Pattern Analysis and Machine Intelligence 12*, 9 (1990), pp. 855-867.

[BA02] Burnham, K., and Anderson, D. *Model Selection and Multi-Model Inference*. Springer, 2002.

[BA84] Brady, M., and Asada, H. Smoothed local symmetries and their implementation. *The Int. J. Robotics Research 3*, 3 (1984), pp. 36-61.

[Bal11] Balzer, J. A Gauss–Newton method for the integration of spatial normal fields in shape space. *J. Math. Imaging Vis. 44*, 1 (2011), pp. 65-79.

[BAM99] Ben-Yacoub, S., Abdeljaoued, Y., and Mayoraz, E. Fusion of face and speech data for person identity verification. *IEEE Trans. on Neural Networks 10*, 5 (1999), pp. 1065-1074.

[BAP06] Brites, C., Ascenso, J., and Pereira, F. Studying temporal correlation noise modeling for pixel based Wyner-Ziv video coding. In *Proc. IEEE Int. Conf. on Image Processing* (2006), pp. 273-276.

[Bar12] Barber, D. *Bayesian Reasoning and Machine Learning*. Cambridge University Press, Cambridge, 2012.

[Bau00] Baumberg, A. Reliable feature matching across widely separated views. In *Proc. IEEE Conference on Computer Vision and Pattern Recognition* (2000), vol. 1, pp. 774–781.

[BB04] Bouganis, C.-S., and Brookes, M. Multiple light source detection. *IEEE Trans. on Pattern Analysis and Machine Intelligence 26*, 4 (2004), pp. 509–514.

[BB82] Ballard, D., and Brown, C. *Computer Vision*. Prentice Hall, 1982.

[BBM87] Bolles, R. C., Baker, H. H., and Marimont, D. H. Epipolar-plane image analysis: An approach to determining structure from motion. *Int. J. Computer Vision 1*, 1 (1987), pp. 7–55.

[BBV03] Berretti, S., Bimbo, A. D., and Vicario, E. Weighted walkthroughs between extended entities for retrieval by spatial arrangement. *IEEE Trans. on Multimedia 5*, 1 (2003), pp. 52–70.

[BC82] Bolles, R. C., and Cain, R. A. Recognizing and locating partially visible objects, the local-feature-focus method. *Int. J of Robotics Research 1* (1982), pp. 57–82.

[BC92] Bajcsy, R., and Campos, M. Active and exploratory perception. *CVGIP: Image Understanding 56*, 1 (1992), pp. 31–40.

[BCB97] Brooks, M. J., Chojnacki, W., and Baumela, L. Determining the egomotion of an uncalibrated camera from instantaneous optical flow. *Jour. Optical Society of America A 14*, 10 (1997), 2670.

[BCC08] Brezeale, D., and Cook, D. J. Automatic video classification: A survey of the literature. *IEEE Trans. on Systems, Man, and Cybernetics, Part C: Applications and Reviews 38*, 3 (2008), pp. 416–430.

[BCD97] Bradburn, S., Cathey, W. T., and Dowski, E. R. Realizations of focus invariance in optical–digital systems with wave-front coding. *Applied Optics 36*, 35 (1997), pp. 9157–9166.

[BCE00] Bendito, E., Carmona, A., and Encinas, A. M. Shortest paths in distance-regular graphs. *Europ. J. Combinatorics 21* (2000), pp. 153–166.

[BCGJ98] Basri, R., Costa, L., Geiger, D., and Jacobs, D. Determining the similarity of deformable shapes. *Vision Research 38*, 15 (1998), pp. 2365–2385.

[BCM05] Buades, A., Coll, B., and Morel, J. M. A non local algorithm for image denoising. In *Proc. Computer Vision and Pattern Recognition* (2005), vol. 2, pp. 60–65.

[BCM94] Basak, J., Chanda, B., and Majumder, D. D. On edge and line linking with connectionist models. *IEEE Trans. on Systems, Man and Cybernetics 24*, 3 (1994), pp. 413–428.

[BCZ93] Blake, A., Curwen, R., and Zisserman, A. Affine-invariant contour tracking with automatic control of spatiotemporal scale. In *Proc. Int. Conf. Computer Vision* (1993), pp. 66–75.

[BD07] Bidyuk, B., and Dechter, R. Cutset sampling for Bayesian networks. *J Artificial Intelligence Research 28*, 1 (2007), pp. 1–48.

[BE92] Bülthoff, H. H., and Edelman, S. Psychophysical support for a two-dimensional view interpolation theory of object recognition. In *Proc. the National Academy of Sciences* (1992), vol. 89, pp. 60–64.

[BET08] Bay, H., Ess, A., Tuytelaars, T., and Gool, L. V. SURF: Speeded up robust features. *Computer Vision and Image Understanding 110*, 3 (2008), pp. 346–359.

[BF05] Breckon, T. P., and Fisher, R. B. Non-parametric 3D surface completion. In *Proc. 3-D Digital Imaging and Modeling* (2005), pp. 573–580.

[BF93] Bouthemy, P., and François, E. Motion segmentation and qualitative dynamic scene analysis from an image sequence. *Int. J. Computer Vision 10*, 2 (1993), pp. 157–182.

[BFY98] Black, M. J., Fleet, D. J., and Yacoob, Y. A framework for modeling appearance change in image sequences. In *IEEE Int. Conf. on Computer Vision* (1998).

[BGX09] Bregonzio, M., Gong, S.-G., and Xiang, T. Recognising action as clouds of space–time interest points. In *Proc. Int. Conf. Computer Vision and Pattern Recognition* (2009), pp. 1948–1955.

[BHK+89] Bares, J., Hebert, M., Kanade, T., Krotkov, E., Mitchell, T., Simmons, R., and Whittaker, W. AMBLER: An autonomous rover for planetary exploration. *Computer 22*, 6 (1989), pp. 18-26.

[BHR12] Breckon, T. P., Han, J. W., and Richardson, J. Consistency in multi-modal automated target detection using temporally filtered reporting. In *Proc. SPIE Security and Defence: Electro-Optical Remote Sensing* (2012), vol. 8542A.

[BHU00] Brigger, P., Hoeg, J., and Unser, M. B-spline snakes: a flexible tool for parametric contour detection. *IEEE Trans. on Image Processing 9*, 9 (2000), pp. 1484-1496.

[BI05] Boiman, O., and Irani, M. Detecting irregularities in images and in video. In *Proc. Int. Conf. Computer Vision* (2005), pp. 462-469.

[Bie85] Biederman, I. Human image understanding: Recent research and a theory. *Computer vision, graphics, and image processing 32*, 1 (1985), pp. 29-73.

[Bie87] Biederman, I. Recognition-by-components: a theory of human image understanding. *Psychological Review 94*, 2 (1987), 115.

[Bil02] Billingsley, J. B. *Low-angle Radar Land Clutter: Measurements and empirical models*. Inst of Engineering & Technology, 2002.

[Bis06] Bishop, C. M. *Pattern Recognition and Machine Learning*. Springer-Verlag, 2006.

[BJ71] Box, G. E. P., and Jenkins, G. M. *Time Series Analysis: Forecasting and Control*. John Wiley & Sons, 1971.

[BJ98] Black, M. J., and Jepson, A. D. EigenTracking: Robust matching and tracking of articulated objects using a view-based representation. *Int. Journal of Computer Vision 26*, 1 (1998), pp. 63-84.

[BK03] Botsch, M., and Kobbelt, L. High-quality point-based rendering on modern GPUs. In *Proc. Computer Graphics and Applications* (2003), pp. 335-343.

[BKKP05] Bezdek, J. C., Keller, J., Krisnapuram, R., and Pal, N. *Fuzzy Models and Algorithms for Pattern Recognition and Image Processing*. Springer-Verlag, 2005.

[BKS07] Bashir, F. I., Khokhar, A. A., and Schonfeld, D. Object trajectory-based activity classification and recognition using hidden Markov models. *IEEE Trans. on Image Process 16*, 7 (2007), pp. 1912-1919.

[BKY99] Belhumeur, P. N., Kriegman, D. J., and Yuille, A. L. The bas-relief ambiguity. *Int. J. Computer Vision 35*, 1 (1999), pp. 33-44.

[BLA02] Bae, K.-Y., Lee, T.-H., and Ahn, K.-C. An optical sensing system for seam tracking and weld pool control in gas metal arc welding of steel pipe. *Journal of Materials Processing Technology 120*, 1 (2002), pp. 458-465.

[Bla83] Blake, A. The least-disturbance principle and weak constraints. *Pattern Recognition Letters 1*, 5 (1983), pp. 393-399.

[BLDC06] Banterle, F., Ledda, P., Debattista, K., and Chalmers, A. Inverse tone mapping. pp. 349-356.

[Bli82] Blinn, J. F. A generalization of algebraic surface drawing. *ACM Trans. Graphics (TOG) 1*, 3 (1982), pp. 235-256.

[BLJ04] Bach, F. R., Lanckriet, G. R. G., and Jordan, M. I. Multiple kernel learning, conic duality, and the SMO algorithm. In *Proc. Int. Conf. on Machine Learning* (2004), pp. 6-13.

[BLJS07] Bai, L., Lao, S., Jones, G. J. F., and Smeaton, A. F. Video semantic content analysis based on ontology. In *Proc. Int. Machine Vision and Image Processing Conf.* (2007).

[BLL07] Bai, X., Latecki, L. J., and Liu, W.-Y. Skeleton pruning by contour partitioning with discrete curve evolution. *IEEE Trans. on Pattern Analysis and Machine Intelligence 29*, 3 (2007), pp. 449-462.

[BLM90] Biemond, J., Lagendijk, R. L., and Mersereau, R. M. Iterative methods for image deblurring. In *Proc. the IEEE 78* (1990), vol. 5, pp. 856-883.

[Blu67] Blum, H. A transformation for extracting new descriptors of shape. In *Models for Perception of Speech and Visual Form*, W. Wathen-Dunn, Ed. MIT Press, Cambridge, MA, 1967.

[BM01] Baker, S., and Matthews, I. Equivalence and efficiency of image alignment algorithms. In *Proc. Conf. on Computer Vision and Pattern Recognition* (2001), pp. 1090-1097.

[BM02] Bennamoun, M., and Mamic, G. J. *Object Recognition: Fundamentals and Case Studies*. Springer-Verlag, 2002.

[BM76] Burke, H. K., and Michon, G. J. Charge injection imaging: operating techniques and performances characteristics. *IEEE Journal of Solid-State Circuits 11*, 1 (1976), pp. 121-128.

[BMP02] Belongie, S., Malik, J., and Puzicha, J. Shape matching and object recognition using shape contexts. *IEEE Trans. on Pattern Analysis and Machine Intelligence 24*, 4 (2002), pp. 509-522.

[BMS98] Batlle, J., Mouaddib, E., and Salvi, J. Recent progress in coded structured light as a technique to solve the correspondence problem: a survey. *Pattern recognition 31*, 7 (1998), pp. 963-982.

[BN78] Blum, H., and Nagel, R. N. Shape description using weighted symmetric axis features. *Pattern Recognition 10*, 3 (1978), pp. 167-180.

[BN89] Beghdadi, A., and Negrate, A. L. Contrast enhancement technique based on local detection of edges. *Computer Vision, Graphics, and Image Processing 46*, 2 (1989), pp. 162-174.

[BNM98] Baker, S., Nayar, S. K., and Murase, H. Parametric feature detection. *Int. J. Computer Vision 27*, 1 (1998), pp. 27-50.

[Bor88] Borgefors, G. Hierarchical chamfer matching: A parametric edge matching algorithm. *IEEE Trans. on Pattern Analysis and Machine Intelligence 10*, 6 (1988), pp. 849-865.

[Bot87] Bottomley, P. A. Spatial localization in NMR spectroscopy in vivo. *Annals of the New York Academy of Sciences 508*, 1 (1987), pp. 333-348.

[Bov05] Bovik, A. C. *Handbook of Image and Video Processing*. Academic Press, 2005.

[BP98] Bowyer, K., and Phillips, P. J. *Empirical Evaluation Techniques in Computer Vision*. IEEE Computer Society Press, 1998.

[BPNG99] Bloom, P., Peterson, M. A., Nadel, L., and Garrett, M. F. *Language and Space*. MIT Press, 1999.

[BPSK11] Brkic, K., Pinz, A., Segvic, S., and Kalafatic, Z. Histogram-based description of local space-time appearance. In *Proc. Scandinavian Conf. on Image Analysis* (2011), pp. 206-217.

[BR03] Buss, S. R. *3D Computer Graphics: A mathematical introduction with OpenGL*. Cambridge University Press, 2003.

[Bre07] Breckon, T. P. *Applications of Computer Vision*, Course Notes. Cranfield University (2007).

[BS00a] Bowden, R., and Sarhadi, M. Building temporal models for gesture recognition. In *Proc. Brit. Machine Vis. Conf* (2000), pp. 32-41.

[BS00b] Brejl, M., and Sonka, M. Object localization and border detection criteria design in edge-based image segmentation: Automated learning from examples. *IEEE Trans. on Medical Imaging 19*, 10 (2000), pp. 973-985.

[BS03] Bartoli, A., and Sturm, P. Constrained structure and motion from multiple uncalibrated views of a piecewise planar scene. *Int. J. Computer Vision 52*, 1 (2003), pp. 45-64.

[BS97] Barequet, G., and Sharir, M. Partial surface and volume matching in three dimensions. *IEEE Trans. on Pattern Analysis and Machine Intelligence 19*, 9 (1997), pp. 929-948.

[BS99] Bernardino, A., and Santos-Victor, J. Binocular tracking: integrating perception and control. *IEEE Trans. on Robotics and Automation 15*, 6 (1999), pp. 1080-1094.

[BSB+96] Blanz, V., Schölkopf, B., Bülthoff, H., Burges, C., Vapnik, V., and Vetter, T. Comparison of view-based object recognition algorithms using realistic 3D models. *Artificial Neural Networks-ICANN 1112* (1996), pp. 251-256.

[BSD96] Blatt, M., S, W., and Domany, E. Superparamagnetic clustering of data. *Phys. Rev. Lett 76* (1996), pp. 3251-3254.

[BSLB01] Bushberg, J. T., Seibert, J. A., Leidholdt, E. M., and Boone, J. M. *The Essential Physics of Medical Imaging*. Lippincott Williams & Wilkins, 2001.

[BT03] Bhanu, B., and Tan, X. Fingerprint indexing based on novel features of minutiae triplets. *IEEE Trans. on Pattern Analysis and Machine Intelligence 25*, 5 (2003), pp. 616–622.

[BT88] Boyle, R. D., and Thomas, R. C. *Computer Vision: A First Course*. Blackwell, 1988.

[BU08] Borenstein, E., and Ullman, S. Combined top-down / bottom-up segmentation. *IEEE Trans. on Pattern Analysis and Machine Intelligence 30*, 12 (2008), pp. 2109–2125.

[Buc87] Buckley, K. Spatial/spectral filtering with linearly constrained minimum variance beamformers. *IEEE Trans. on Acoustics, Speech and Signal Processing 35*, 3 (1987), pp. 249–266.

[BV04] Boyd, S., and Vandenberghe, L. *Convex Optimization*. Cambridge University Press, Cambridge, 2004.

[BV98] Bimbo, A. D., and Vicario, E. Using weighted spatial relationships in retrieval by visual contents. In *Proc. IEEE Workshop on Content-Based Access of Image and Video Libraries* (1998), pp. 35–39.

[BVV99] Bakker, P., Vliet, L. J. V., and Verbeek, P. W. Edge preserving orientation adaptive filtering. In *Proc. IEEE Computer Society Conference on Computer Vision and Pattern Recognition* (1999), vol. 1.

[BW98] Boreczky, J. S., and Wilcox, L. D. A hidden Markov model framework for video segmentation using audio and image features. In *Proc. IEEE Int. Conf. on Acoustics, Speech and Signal Processing* (1998), vol. 6, pp. 3741–3744.

[BWB+05] Buelow, T., Wiemker, R., Blaffert, T., *et al.* Automatic extraction of the pulmonary artery tree from multi-slice CT data. *Medical Imaging 2005: Physiology, Function, and Structure from Medical Images* (2005).

[BWKW98] Backhaus, W. G. K., Werner, G. K., Kliegl, R., and Werner, J. S. *Color Vision: Perspectives from Different Disciplines*. de Gruyter, 1998.

[BY95] Black, M. J., and Yacoob, Y. Tracking and recognizing rigid and non-rigid facial motions using local parametric models of image motion. In *Proc. Int. Conf. Computer Vision* (1995), pp. 374–381.

[BYJF97] Black, M. J., Yacoob, Y., Jepson, A. D., and Fleet, D. J. Learning parameterized models of image motion. In *Proc. IEEE Computer Society Conference on Computer Vision and Pattern Recognition* (1997), pp. 561–567.

[BZ98] Bin, Z., and Zhu, L. Diffraction property of an axicon in oblique illumination. *Applied Optics 37*, 13 (1998), pp. 2563–2568.

[BZM06] Bosch, A., Zisserman, A., and Munoz, X. Scene classification via pLSA. In *Proc. Eur. Conf. on Computer Vision, Springer LNCS* (2006), vol. 3954, pp. 517–530.

[BZW+95] Banta, J. E., Zhen, Y., Whang, X. Z., Zhang, G., *et al. Best-next-view algorithm for three-dimensional scene reconstruction using range images.* 1995.

[CAK07] Chandraker, M., Agarwal, S., and Kriegman, D. Shadowcuts: Photometric stereo with shadows. In *Proc. CVPR'07 IEEE Conference on Computer Vision and Pattern Recognition* (2007), pp. 1–8.

[Cal05] Calway, A. Recursive estimation of 3D motion and surface structure from local affine flow parameters. *IEEE Trans. on Pattern Analysis and Machine Intelligence 27*, 4 (2005), pp. 562–574.

[Car01] Carlson, A. *Why Everyone Needs a Front Porch*. iUniverse, 2001.

[Car87] Carlotto, M. J. Histogram analysis using a scale-space approach. *IEEE Trans. on Pattern Analysis and Machine Intelligence 1* (1987), pp. 121–129.

[CB92] Cipolla, R., and Blake, A. Surface orientation and time to contact from image divergence and deformation. In *Proc. Euro. Conf. Computer Vision* (Berlin/Heidelberg, 1992), Springer, pp. 187–202.

[CC84] Consortini, A., and Conforti, G. Detector saturation effect on higher-order moments of intensity fluctuations in atmospheric laser propagation measurement. *Jour. Optical Society of America A 1*, 11 (1984), pp. 1075–1077.

[CCL04] Chang, F., Chen, C.-J., and Lu, C.-J. A linear-time component-labeling algorithm using contour tracing technique. *Computer Vision and Image Understanding 93*, 2 (2004), pp. 206-220.

[CD94] Chen, Y., and Dougherty, E. R. Gray-scale morphological granulometric texture classification. *Optical Engineering 33*, 8 (1994), pp. 2713-2722.

[CDD94] Chen, Q.-S., Defrise, M., and Deconinck, F. Symmetric phase-only matched filtering of Fourier–Mellin transforms for image registration and recognition. *IEEE Trans. on Pattern Analysis and Machine Intelligence 16*, 12 (1994), pp. 1156-1168.

[CDSY98] Calderbank, A. R., Daubechies, I., Sweldens, W., and Yeo, B.-L. Wavelet transforms that map integers to integers. *Applied and computational harmonic analysis 5*, 3 (1998), pp. 332-369.

[Cel90] Celenk, M. A color clustering technique for image segmentation. *Computer Vision, Graphics, and Image Processing 52*, 2 (1990), pp. 145-170.

[CF02] Cooper, M., and Foote, J. Summarizing video using non-negative similarity matrix factorization. In *Proc. IEEE Multimedia Signal Processing Workshop* (2002).

[CF09] Cai, C., and Ferrari, S. Information-driven sensor path planning by approximate cell decomposition. *IEEE Trans. on Systems, Man, and Cybernetics, Part B: Cybernetics 39*, 3 (2009), pp. 672-689.

[CF89] Choo, C. Y., and Freeman, H. Computation of features of 2-D polycurve-encoded boundaries. In *Proc. IEEE Int. Conf. on Systems, Man and Cybernetics* (1989), pp. 1041-1047.

[CF90] Campbell III, A. T., and Fussell, D. S. Adaptive mesh generation for global diffuse illumination. *ACM SIGGRAPH Computer Graphics 24*, 4 (1990), pp. 155-164.

[CFH05] Crandall, D., Felzenszwalb, P., and Huttenlocher, D. Spatial priors for part-based recognition using statistical models. *IEEE Computer Society Conference on Computer Vision and Pattern Recognition 1* (2005), pp. 10-17.

[CG84] Chassery, J. M., and Garbay, C. An iterative segmentation method based on a contextual color and shape criterion. *IEEE Trans. on Pattern Analysis and Machine Intelligence 6* (1984), pp. 794-800.

[CGLL84] Cohen, D. K., Gee, W. H., Ludeke, M., and Lewkowicz, J. Automatic focus control: the astigmatic lens approach. *Applied Optics 23*, 4 (1984), pp. 565-570.

[CGZ07] Chong, H. Y., Gortler, S. J., and Zickler, T. The von Kries hypothesis and a basis for color constancy. In *Proc. IEEE Int. Conf. on Computer Vision* (2007).

[CH01] Corke, P. I., and Hutchinson, S. A. A new partitioned approach to image-based visual servo control. *IEEE Trans. on Robotics and Automation 17*, 4 (2001), pp. 507-515.

[CH88] Chen, H. H., and Huang, T. S. A survey of construction and manipulation of octrees. *Computer Vision, Graphics and Image Processing 43* (1988), pp. 409-431.

[CH91] Cooper, G. F., and Herskovits, E. A Bayesian method for the induction of probabilistic networks from data. Technical report, KSL-pp. 91-02, Knowledge Systems Laboratory. Medical Computer Science. Stanford University School of Medicine, Stanford, 1991.

[Cha84] Chavel, I. *Eigenvalues in Riemannian Geometry*, 2nd ed., vol. 115 of *Pure and Applied Mathematics*. Academic Press, 1984.

[Cha89] Chatfield, C. *The Analysis of Time Series: An introduction*, 4th ed. Chapman and Hall, London, 1989.

[Che69] Cheng, G. C. Pictorial pattern recognition. *Pattern Recognition 1*, 3 (1969), pp. 187-188.

[Che90] Chen, H. H. Pose determination from line-to-plane correspondences: Existence condition and closed-form solutions. In *Proc. Int. Conf. Computer Vision* (1990), pp. 274-278.

[CHHN98] Coombs, D., Herman, M., Hong, T.-H., and Nashman, M. Real-time obstacle avoidance using central flow divergence, and peripheral flow. *IEEE Trans. on Robotics and Automation 14*, 1 (1998), pp. 49-59.

[Chr12] Christen, P. *Data Matching*. Springer, 2012.

[CHS95] Conway, J. H., Hardin, R. H., and Sloane, N. J. A. Packing lines, planes, etc.: Packings in Grassmannian spaces. *Experimental Mathematics 5*, 2 (1995), pp. 139-159.

[Chu97] Chung, F. R. K. *Spectral Graph Theory*. American Mathematical Society, 1997.

[CI02] Caspi, Y., and Irani, M. Spatio-temporal alignment of sequences. *IEEE Trans. Pat. Anal. Mach. Intel 24*, 11 (2002), pp. 1409-1424.

[CJ98] Chun, M. M., and Jiang, Y. Contextual cueing: implicit learning and memory of visual context guides spatial attention. *Cognitive Psychology 36*, 1 (1998), pp. 28-71.

[CK94] Chen, J.-L., and Kundu, A. Rotation and gray scale transform invariant texture identification using wavelet decomposition and hidden Markov model. *IEEE Trans. on Pattern Analysis and Machine Intelligence 16*, 2 (1994), pp. 208-214.

[CK99] Cote, G., and Kossentini, F. Optimal intra coding of blocks for robust video communication over the internet. *EURASIP Journal for Visual Communication, Special Issue on Real-time Video over the Internet* (1999), pp. 25-34.

[CKP95] Christmas, W. J., Kittler, J., and Petrou, M. Structural matching in computer vision using probabilistic relaxation. *IEEE Trans. on Pattern Analysis and Machine Intelligence 17*, 8 (1995), pp. 749-764.

[CKRH04] Chilgunde, A., Kumar, P., Ranganath, S., and Huang, W. M. Multi-camera target tracking in blind regions of cameras with non-overlapping fields of view. In *Proc. Brit Mach. Vision Conf* (2004), pp. 397-406.

[CKS97] Caselles, V., Kimmel, R., and Sapiro, G. Geodesic active contours. *Int. J. Computer Vision 22*, 1 (1997), pp. 61-79.

[CL04] Chen, S. Y., and Li, Y. F. Automatic sensor placement for model-based robot vision. *IEEE Trans. on Systems, Man, and Cybernetics, Part B: Cybernetics 34*, 1 (2004), pp. 393-408.

[CL89] Cavanagh, P., and Leclerc, Y. G. Shape from shadows. *Journal of Experimental Psychology: Human Perception and Performance 15*, 1 (1989), 3.

[Cla85] Clarke, R. J. Transform coding of images. *Astrophysics 1* (1985).

[CLFS07] Chen, T., Lensch, H. P. A., Fuchs, C., and Seidel, H. Polarization and phase-shifting for 3D scanning of translucent objects. In *Proc. Comp. Vis. and Patt. Recog* (2007), pp. 1-8.

[CLMC92] Catte, F., Lions, P.-L., Morel, J.-M., and Coll, T. Image selective smoothing and edge detection by nonlinear diffusion. *SIAM Journal on Numerical Analysis 29*, 1 (1992), pp. 182-193.

[CLP85] Cohen, Y., Landy, M. S., and Pavel, M. Hierarchical coding of binary images. *IEEE Trans. on Pattern Analysis and Machine Intelligence 3* (1985), pp. 284-298.

[CM04] Chanda, B., and Majumder, D. D. *Digital Image Processing and Analysis*. PHI Learning Pvt, 2004.

[CM92] Cochran, S. D., and Medioni, G. 3D surface description from binocular stereo. *IEEE Trans. Pattern Analysis Machine Intelligence 14*, 10 (1992), pp. 981-994.

[CMC+06] Corazza, S., Mandermann, L., Chaudhari, A. M., Demattio, T., Cobelli, C., and Andriacchi, T. P. A markerless motion capture system to study musculoskeletal biomechanics: Visual hull and simulated annealing approach. *Annals of Biomedical Engineering 34*, 6 (2006), pp. 1019-1029.

[CMS95] Christensen, J., Marks, J., and Shieber, S. An empirical study of algorithms for point-feature label placement. *ACM Trans. Graphics (TOG) 14*, 3 (1995), pp. 203-232.

[CMW+97] Chandrasekaran, S., Manjunath, B. S., Wang, Y.-F., Winkeler, J., and Zhang, H. An eigenspace update algorithm for image analysis. *Graphical Models and Image Processing 59*, 5 (1997), pp. 321-332.

[CN06] Christensen, H. I., and Nagel, H.-H., Eds. *Cognitive Vision Systems: Sampling the Spectrum of Approaches*, vol. LNCS 3948. Springer-Verlag, 2006.

[CNH+03] Codaro, E. N., Nakazato, R. Z., Horovistiz, A. L., Ribeiro, L. M. F., Ribeiro, R. B., and de O. Hein, L. R. An image analysis study of pit formation on Ti-6Al-4V. *Materials Science and Engineering: A 341 1* (2003), pp. 202-210.

[Cow83] Cowie, R. I. D. The viewer's place in theories of vision. In *Proc. International Joint Conference on Artificial Intelligence* (1983), pp. 952–958.

[CR02] Cohen, W. W., and Richman, J. Learning to match and cluster large high-dimensional data sets for data integration. In *Proc. ACM SIGKDD Int. Conf. on Knowledge Discovery and Data Mining* (2002), ACM, pp. 475–480.

[CR03] Chui, H., and Rangarajan, A. A new point matching algorithm for non-rigid registration. *Computer Vision and Image Understanding 89*, 2 (2003), pp. 114–141.

[CRB99] Chesnaud, C., Réfrégier, P., and Boulet, V. Statistical region snake-based segmentation adapted to different physical noise models. *IEEE Trans. on Pattern Analysis and Machine Intelligence 21*, 11 (1999), pp. 1145–1157.

[Cre06] Cremers, D. Dynamical statistical shape priors for level set-based tracking. *IEEE Trans. on Pattern Analysis and Machine Intelligence 28*, 8 (2006), pp. 1262–1273.

[Cre93] Cressie, N. A. C. *Statistics for Spatial Data*. John Wiley & Sons, New York, 1993.

[CRH93] Cox, I. J., Rehg, J. M., and Hingorani, S. A Bayesian multiple-hypothesis approach to edge grouping and contour segmentation. *Int. J. Computer Vision 11*, 1 (1993), pp. 5–24.

[Cri11] Criminisi, A. Decision forests: A unified framework for classification, regression, density estimation, manifold learning and semi-supervised learning. *Foundations and Trends in Computer Graphics and Vision 7*, 2-3 (2011), pp. 81–227.

[Cri85] Crimmins, T. R. Geometric filter for speckle reduction. *Applied Optics 24*, 10 (1985), pp. 1438–1443.

[CRM00] Comaniciu, D., Ramesh, V., and Meer, P. Real-time tracking of non-rigid objects using mean shift. In *Proc. IEEE Conference on Computer Vision and Pattern Recognition* (2000), vol. 2, pp. 142–149.

[CS09] Cyganek, B., and Siebert, J. P. *An Introduction to 3D Computer Vision Techniques and Algorithms*. John Wiley & Sons, 2009.

[CS92] Chen, X., and Schmitt, F. Intrinsic surface properties from surface triangulation. In *Proc. Euro. Conf. Computer Vision* (1992), pp. 739–743.

[CSBT03] Criminisi, A., Shotton, J., Blake, A., and Torr, P. H. S. Gaze manipulation for one-to-one teleconferencing. In *Ninth IEEE Int. Conf. Computer Vision* (2003), pp. 191–198.

[CSD+09] Cole, F., Sanik, K., DeCarlo, D., Finkelstein, A., Funkhouser, T., Rusinkiewicz, S., and Singh, M. How well do line drawings depict shape? *ACM Trans. Graphics (TOG) 28*, 3 (2009).

[CSE00] Christopoulos, C., Skodras, A., and Ebrahimi, T. The JPEG2000 still image coding system: an overview. *IEEE Trans. on Consumer Electronics 46*, 4 (2000), pp. 1103–1127.

[CSW95] Cui, Y., Swets, D. L., and Weng, J. J. Learning-based hand sign recognition using SHOSLIF-M. In *Proc. IEEE Int. Conf. on Computer Vision* (1995), pp. 631–636.

[CT91] Cover, T. M., and Thomas, J. A. *Elements of Information Theory*. John Wiley & Sons, 1991.

[CT98] Cutler, R., and Turk, M. View-based interpretation of real-time optical flow for gesture recognition. In *Proc. IEEE Int. Conf. on Automatic Face and Gesture Recognition* (1998), pp. 416–421.

[CTCS00] Chai, J., Tong, X., Chan, S., and Shum, H. Plenoptic sampling. In *Proc. SIGGRAPH* (2000), pp. 307–318.

[CTM+96] Cuisenaire, O., Thiran, J.-P., Macq, B., Michel, C., Volder, A. D., and Marques, F. Automatic registration of 3D MR images with a computerized brain atlas. *IEEE Trans. on Medical Imaging 2710* (1996), pp. 438–448.

[CTMS03] Carranza, J., Theobalt, C., Magnor, M. A., and Seidel, H.-P. Free-viewpoint video of human actors. In *Proc. ACM SIGGRAPH* (2003), pp. 569–577.

[CV01] Chan, T., and Vese, L. Active contours without edges. *IEEE Trans. on Image Processing 10*, 2 (2001), pp. 266–277.

[CV05a] Carneiro, G., and Vasconcelos, N. A database centric view of semantic image annotation and retrieval. In *Proc. Annual Int. ACM SIGIR Conference on Research and Development in Information Retrieval* (2005).

[CV05b] Cilibrasi, R., and Vitanyi, P. M. B. Clustering by compression. *IEEE Trans. on Information Theory 51*, 4 (2005), pp. 1523-1545.

[CW93] Chen, S. E., and Williams, L. View interpolation for image synthesis. In *Proc. SIGGRAPH Conf. on Computer Graphics and Interactive Techniques* (1993).

[CW99] Coughlan, J. M., and Yuille, A. L. Manhattan world: Compass direction from a single image by Bayesian inference. In *Proc. Int. Conf. Computer Vision* (1999), pp. 941-947.

[CWSI87] Chin, R. T., Wan, H.-K., Stover, D. L., and Iverson, R. D. A one-pass thinning algorithm and its parallel implementation. *Computer Vision, Graphics, and Image Processing 40*, 1 (1987), pp. 30-40.

[CY92] Chang, L.-W., and Yu, S.-S. A new implementation of generalized order statistic filter by threshold decomposition. *IEEE Trans. on Signal Processing 40*, 12 (1992), pp. 3062-3066.

[CYV00] Chang, S. G., Yu, B., and Vetterli, M. Adaptive wavelet thresholding for image denoising and compression. *IEEE Trans. on Image Processing 9*, 9 (2000), pp. 1532-1546.

[CZ01] Cobzas, D., and Zhang, H. Planar patch extraction with noisy depth data. In *Proc. Int. Conf. on 3-D Digital Imaging and Modeling* (2001), IEEE, pp. 240-245.

[CZ98] Capel, D., and Zisserman, A. Automated mosaicing with super-resolution zoom. In *Proc. IEEE Computer Society Conference on Computer Vision and Pattern Recognition* (1998), pp. 885-891.

[DA92] Debrunner, C., and Ahuja, N. Motion and structure factorization and segmentation of long multiple motion image sequences. In *Proc. Euro. Conf. Computer Vision* (1992), pp. 217-221.

[Dau02] Daugman, J. How iris recognition works. *IEEE Trans. on Circuits and Systems for Video Technology 14* (2002), pp. 21-30.

[Dav01] Davis, J. Hierarchical motion history images for recognizing human motion. In *Proc. Detection and Recognition of Events in Video* (2001), pp. 39-46.

[Dav12] Davidson, A. *Video content re-targeting for vehicle driver brake-testing simulator*. Master's thesis, School of Engineering, Cranfield University, 2012.

[Dav75] Davis, L. S. A survey of edge detection techniques. *Computer Graphics and Image Processing 4*, 3 (1975), pp. 248-270.

[Dav90] Davies, E. R. *Machine Vision*. Academic Press, 1990.

[DB98] Delaney, A. H., and Bresler, Y. Globally convergent edge-preserving regularized reconstruction: An application to limited-angle tomography. *IEEE Trans. on Image Processing 7*, 2 (1998), pp. 204-221.

[DC70] Dieudonn, J. A., and Carrell, J. B. Invariant theory, old and new. *Advances in Mathematics 4* (1970), pp. 1-80.

[DCM88] Duffie, N. A., Chitturi, R., and Mou, J.-I. Fault-tolerant heterarchical control of heterogeneous manufacturing system entities. *Journal of Manufacturing Systems 7*, 4 (1988), pp. 315-328.

[DeL01] DeLoura, M. *Game Programming Gems 2, No. 184*. Cengage Learning, 2001.

[Der87] Deriche, R. Using Canny's criteria to derive a recursively implemented optimal edge detector. *Int. J. Computer Vision 1*, 2 (1987), pp. 167-187.

[DF99] Delamarre, Q., and Faugeras, O. 3D articulated models and multi-view tracking with silhouettes. In *Proc. IEEE Int. Conf. on Computer Vision* (1999), vol. 2, pp. 716-721.

[DH73] Duda, R. O., and Hart, P. E. *Pattern Classification and Scene Analysis*. Wiley Interscience, 1973.

[DKFH97] Davis, M. H., Khotanzad, A., Flamig, D. P., and Harms, S. E. A physics-based coordinate transformation for 3-D image matching. *IEEE Trans. on Medical Imaging 16*, 3 (1997), pp. 317-328.

[DL07] Doran, C., and Lasenby, A. *Geometric Algebra for Physicists*. Cambridge University Press, Cambridge, 2007.

[DLL03] Doermann, D., Liang, J., and Li, H. Progress in camera-based document image analysis. In *Proc. IEEE International Conference on Document Analysis and Recognition* (2003), pp. 606–616.

[DLSZ91] Duncan, J. S., Lee, F. A., Smeulders, A. W. M., and Zaret, B. L. A bending energy model for measurement of cardiac shape deformity. *IEEE Trans. on Medical Imaging 10*, 3 (1991), pp. 307–320.

[DLTB03] De La Torre, F., and Black, M. J. A framework for robust subspace learning. *Int. J. Computer Vision 54*, 1 (2003), pp. 117–142.

[DM02] Davison, A. J., and Murray, D. W. Simultaneous localization and map-building using active vision. *IEEE Trans. on Pattern Analysis and Machine Intelligence 24*, 7 (2002), pp. 865–880.

[DM77] Dennis Jr, J. E., and More, J. J. Quasi-Newton methods, motivation and theory. *SIAM review 19*, 1 (1977), pp. 46–89.

[DM96] DeCarlo, D., and Metaxas, D. The integration of optical flow and deformable models with applications to human face shape and motion estimation. In *Proc. IEEE Computer Society Conference on Computer Vision and Pattern Recognition* (1996), pp. 231–238.

[DM98] Deng, Y., and Manjunath, B. S. NeTra-V: Toward an object-based video representation. *IEEE Trans. Circuits and Systems for Video Technology 8*, 5 (1998), pp. 616–627.

[DMK03] Dhillon, I. S., Mallela, S., and Kumar, R. A divisive information theoretic feature clustering algorithm for text classification. *Journal of Machine Learning Research 3* (2003), pp. 1265–1287.

[DMS99] Deng, Y., Manjunath, B. S., and Shin, H. Color image segmentation. In *IEEE Computer Society Conference on Computer Vision and Pattern Recognition* (1999), vol. 2, IEEE.

[DN98] Dana, K. J., and Nayar, S. K. Histogram model for 3D textures. In *Proc. IEEE Computer Society Conference on Computer Vision and Pattern Recognition* (1998), pp. 618–624.

[DN99] Dana, K. J., and Nayar, S. K. Correlation model for 3D texture. In *Proc. IEEE Int. Conf. on Computer Vision* (1999), pp. 1061–1066.

[Dod07] Dodge, R. An experimental study of visual fixation. *Psychological Monographs: General and Applied 8*, 4 (1907).

[Doy00] Doya, K. Reinforcement learning in continuous time and space. *Neural computation 12*, 1 (2000), pp. 219–245.

[DSD+04] Demirci, M. F., Shokoufandeh, A., Dickinson, S., Keselman, Y., and Bretzner, L. Many-to-many feature matching using spherical coding of directed graphs. In *Proc. European Conf. on Computer Vision* (2004), pp. 332–335.

[DT05] Dalal, N., and Triggs, B. Histograms of oriented gradients for human detection. In *Proc. Comp. Vis. and Patt. Recog* (2005), pp. 886–893.

[DTS06] Dalal, N., Triggs, B., and Schmid, C. Human detection using oriented histograms of flow and appearance. In *Proc. Euro. Conf. Computer Vision* (2006), pp. 428–441.

[Dun70] Dunne, J. A. Mariner 1969 television image processing. *Pattern Recognition 2*, 4 (1970), pp. 261–268.

[DV05] Do, M. N., and Vetterli, M. The contourlet transform: an efficient directional multi-resolution image representation. *IEEE Trans. on Image Processing 14*, 12 (2005), pp. 2091–2106.

[DV95] Degtiarev, E. V., and Vorontsov, M. A. Spatial filtering in nonlinear two-dimensional feedback systems: phase-distortion suppression. *Jour. Optical Society of America B 12*, 7 (1995), pp. 1238–1248.

[DVD+93] Duplain, G., Verly, P. G., Dobrowolski, J. A., *et al.* Graded-reflectance mirrors for beam quality control in laser resonators. *Applied Optics 32*, 7 (1993), pp. 1145–1153.

[DZB92] Demey, S., Zisserman, A., and Beardsley, P. Affine and projective structure from motion. In *Proc. British Machine Vision Conference (BMVC)* (1992), pp. 49–58.

[EF01] Efros, A. A., and Freeman, W. T. Image quilting for texture synthesis and transfer. In *Proc. Annual Conference on Computer Graphics and Interactive Techniques* (2001), ACM, pp. 341-346.

[EF78] Ekman, P., and Friesen, W. *Facial Action Coding System: A Technique for the Measurement of Facial Movement*. Consulting Psychologists Press, Palo Alto, 1978.

[EF97] Elber, G., and Fish, R. 5-axis freeform surface milling using piecewise ruled surface approximation. *Trans. of the American Society of Mechanical Engineers - Journal of Manufacturing Science and Engineering 119* (1997), pp. 383-387.

[EGP85] Eric, W., Grimson, L., and Pavlidis, T. Discontinuity detection for visual surface reconstruction. *Computer Vision, Graphics, and Image Processing 30*, 3 (1985), pp. 316-330.

[EGSS99] El-Yacoubi, A., Gilloux, M., Sabourin, R., and Suen, C. Y. An HMM-based approach for off-line unconstrained handwritten word modeling and recognition. *IEEE Trans. on Pattern Analysis and Machine Intelligence 21*, 8 (1999), pp. 752-760.

[EKO+04] Enser, P., Kompatsiaris, Y., O'Connor, N. E., Smeaton, A. F., and Smeulders, A. W. M., Eds. *Image and Video Retrieval, 3115*. Springer LNCS, 2004.

[EKSX96] Ester, M., Kriegel, H. P., Sander, J., and Xu, X. A density-based algorithm for discovering clusters in large spatial databases with noise. In *Proc. Int. Conf. on Knowledge Discovery and Data Mining* (1996), pp. 226-231.

[Ela10] Elad, M. *Sparse and redundant representations: from theory to applications in signal and image processing*. Springer, 2010.

[Elb05] Elber, G. Geometric texture modeling. *IEEE Computer Graphics and Applications 25*, 4 (2005).

[EMB03] Ellis, T. J., Makris, D., and Black, J. K. Learning a multi-camera topology. In *Proc. Joint IEEE International Workshop on Visual Surveillance and Performance Evaluation of Tracking and Surveillance* (2003), pp. 165-171.

[EW11] Elboher, E., and Werman, M. Cosine integral images for fast spatial and range filtering. In *Proc. Int. Conf. Computer Vision* (2011), pp. 89-92.

[Fau92] Faugeras, O. What can be seen in three dimensions with an uncalibrated stereo rig? In *Proc. Euro. Conf. Computer Vision* pp. 563-578.

[Fau93] Faugeras, O. *Three-Dimensional Computer Vision: A geometric viewpoint*. MIT Press, Cambridge, Massachusetts, 1993.

[Fau95] Faugeras, O. Stratification of three-dimensional vision: projective, affine, and metric representations. *Jour. Optical Society of America A 12*, 3 (1995), pp. 465-484.

[FB03] Ferreira, C. B. R., and Borges, D. L. Analysis of mammogram classification using a wavelet transform decomposition. *Pattern Recognition Letters 24*, 7 (2003), pp. 973-982.

[FBH+01] Fang, X., Bao, H., Heng, P. A., *et al*. Continuous field based free-form surface modeling and morphing. *Computers and Graphics 25*, 2 (2001), pp. 235-243.

[FBM10] Flitton, G. T., Breckon, T. P., and Megherbi, N. Object recognition using 3D SIFT in complex CT volumes. In *Proc. British Machine Vision Conference* (2010), pp. 1-12.

[FD93] Funt, B. V., and Drew, M. S. Color space analysis of mutual illumination. *IEEE Trans. on Pattern Analysis and Machine Intelligence 15*, 12 (1993), pp. 1319-1326.

[FDFH96] Foley, J. D., Dam, A. V., Feiner, S. K., and Hughes, J. F. *Computer Graphics: Principles and Practice*. Addison-Wesley, 1996.

[FDS90] Fischer, P., Daniel, R., and Siva, K. V. Specification and design of input devices for teleoperation. In *Proc. IEEE Robotics and Automation* (1990), vol. 1, pp. 540-545.

[FFE97] Fisher, R. B., Fitzgibbon, A. W., and Eggert, D. Extracting surface patches from complete range descriptions. In *Int. Conf. on Recent Advances in 3-D Digital Imaging and Modeling* (1997), pp. 148-154.

[FFP06] Fei-Fei, L., Fergus, R., and Perona, P. One-shot learning of object categories. *IEEE Trans. on Pattern Analysis and Machine Intelligence 28*, 4 (2006), pp. 594–611.

[FGM06] Ferragina, P., Giancarlo, R., and Manzini, G. The myriad virtues of wavelet trees. In *Proc. Int. Colloquium on Automata and Languages* (2006), pp. 561–572.

[FGP96] Frosini, A., Gori, M., and Priami, P. A neural network-based model for paper currency recognition and verification. *IEEE Trans. on Neural Networks 7*, 6 (1996), pp. 1482–1490.

[FH04] Felzenszwalb, P. F., and Huttenlocher, D. P. Efficient graph-based image segmentation. *Int. J. Computer Vision 59*, 2 (2004), pp. 167–181.

[FH05] Felzenszwalb, P. F., and Huttenlocher, D. P. Pictorial structures for object recognition. *Int. J. Computer Vision 61*, 1 (2005), pp. 55–79.

[FHD06] Finlayson, G., Hordley, S., and Drew, M. Removing shadows from images. In *Proc. Euro. Conf. Computer Vision* (2002), vol. 2353, pp. 129–132.

[FHM+93] Faugeras, O., Hotz, B., Mathieu, H., *et al.* Real time correlation-based stereo: Algorithm, implementations and applications, 1993.

[Fis87] Fisher, R. SMS: a suggestive modelling system for object recognition. *Image and Vision Computing 5*, 2 (1987), pp. 98–104.

[FISS03] Freund, Y., Iyer, R., Schapire, R. E., and Singer, Y. An efficient boosting algorithm for combining preferences. *J. Mach Learn. Res 4* (2003), pp. 933–969.

[FJ88] Flynn, P. J., and Jain, A. K. Surface classification: Hypothesis testing and parameter estimation. In *Proc. Computer Society Conference on Computer Vision and Pattern Recognition* (1988), pp. 261–267.

[Flo03] Floater, M. S. Mean value coordinates. *Comp Aided Geom Design 20* (2003), pp. 19–27.

[FM98] Fisher, R., and MacKirdy, A. Integrating iconic and structured matching. In *Proc. Euro. Conf. Computer Vision* (1998), pp. 687–698.

[FML04] Feng, S. L., Manmatha, R., and Lavrenko, V. Multiple Bernoulli relevance models for image and video annotation. In *Proc. IEEE Computer Society Conference on Computer Vision and Pattern Recognition* (2004), vol. 2, pp. II-1002 – II-1009.

[FMN+91] Fishman, E. K., Magid, D., Ney, D. R., *et al.* Three-dimensional imaging. *Radiology 181*, 2 (1991), pp. 321–337.

[Foo97] Foo, S. C. A gonioreflectometer for measuring the bidirectional reflectance of materials for use in illumination computations. Master's thesis, Cornell University, 1997.

[Fox88] Fox, C. *An Introduction to the Calculus of Variations*. Dover, New York, 1988.

[FP03] Forsyth, D., and Ponce, J. *Computer Vision: A modern approach*. Prentice Hall, 2003.

[FPF99] Fitzgibbon, A., Pilu, M., and Fisher, R. B. Direct least square fitting of ellipses. *IEEE Trans. on Pattern Analysis and Machine Intelligence 21*, 5 (1999), pp. 476–480.

[FPZ03] Fergus, R., Perona, P., and Zisserman, A. Object class recognition by unsupervised scale-invariant learning. In *Proc. Computer Vision and Pattern Recognition* (2003), vol. 2, pp. 264–271.

[FPZ05] Fergus, R., Perona, P., and Zisserman, A. A sparse object category model for efficient learning and exhaustive recognition. In *Proc. IEEE Computer Society Conference on Computer Vision and Pattern Recognition* (2005), vol. 1, pp. 380–387.

[Fra92] Frank, A. U. Qualitative Spatial Reasoning About Distances and Directions in Geographic Space. *Journal of Visual Languages and Computing 3*, (1992), pp. 342–371.

[FS07] Felzenszwalb, P. F., and Schwartz, J. D. Hierarchical matching of deformable shapes. In *Proc. IEEE Conference on Computer Vision and Pattern Recognition* (2007), pp. 1–8.

[FS97] Freund, Y., and Schapire, R. E. A decision-theoretic generalization of on-line learning and an application to boosting. *Journal of Computer and System Sciences 55*, 1 (1997), pp. 119–139.

[FSS06] Fensholt, R., Sandholt, I., and Stisen, S. Evaluating MODIS, MERIS, and VEGE-TATION vegetation indices using in situ measurements in a semiarid environment. *IEEE Trans. on Geoscience and Remote Sensing 44*, 7 (2006), pp. 1774-1786.

[FSSH82] Frost, V. S., Stiles, J. A., Shanmugan, K. S., and Holtzman, J. C. A model for radar images and its application to adaptive digital filtering of multiplicative noise. *IEEE Trans. on Pattern Analysis and Machine Intelligence 2* (1982), pp. 157-166.

[FSZ09] Flusser, J., Suk, T., and Zitová, B. *Moments and Moment Invariants in Pattern Recognition*. John Wiley & Sons, 2009.

[FtHRKV92] Florack, L. M. J., ter Haar Romeny, B. M., Koenderink, J. J., and Viergever, M. A. Scale and the differential structure of images. *Image and Vision Computing 10*, 6 (1992), pp. 376-388.

[Fuk90] Fukunaga, K. *Introduction to Statistical Pattern Recognition*. Academic Press, 1990.

[FVS09] Fulkerson, B., Vedaldi, A., and Soatto, S. Class segmentation and object localization with superpixel neighborhoods. *IEEE Int. Conf. Computer Vision* (2009), pp. 670-677.

[FW05] Fayin, L., and Wechsler, H. Open set face recognition using transduction. *IEEE Trans. on Pattern Analysis and Machine Intelligence 27*, 11 (2005), pp. 1686-1697.

[FYF+01] Fan, J., Yu, J., Fujita, G., *et al.* Spatiotemporal segmentation for compact video representation. *Signal processing: Image communication 16*, 6 (2001), pp. 553-566.

[FZ89] Forsyth, D., and Zisserman, A. Mutual illumination. In *Proc. IEEE Computer Society Conference on Computer Vision and Pattern Recognition* (1989), pp. 466-473.

[Gad91] Gader, P. D. Separable decompositions and approximations of greyscale morphological templates. *CVGIP: Image Understanding 53*, 3 (1991), pp. 288-296.

[GAHK91] Gallagher, N. C., Allebach, J. P., Haugen, P., and Kranz, D. Random access camera. In *Proc. Asilomar Conference on Signals, Systems and Computers* (1991), pp. 1047-1051.

[Gal90] Galbiati, L. J. *Machine Vision and Digital Image Processing Fundamentals*. Prentice Hall, 1990.

[Gal91] Gall, D. L. MPEG: A video compression standard for multimedia applications. *Communications of the ACM 34*, 4 (1991), pp. 46-58.

[GAM01] Gunturk, B. K., Altunbasak, Y., and Mersereau, R. Gray-scale resolution enhancement. *IEEE Workshop on Multimedia Signal Processing* (2001), pp. 155-160.

[GAT98] Gasteratos, A., Andreadis, I., and Tsalides, P. Fuzzy soft mathematical morphology. In *IEE Proc. Vision, Image and Signal Processing* (1998), vol. 145, pp. 41-49.

[GBN06] Grau, V., Becher, H., and Noble, J. Phase-based registration of multi-view real-time three-dimensional echocardiographic sequences. In *Proc. Medical Image Computing and Computer-Assisted Intervention* (2006), pp. 612-619.

[GBS+07] Gorelick, L., Blank, M., Shechtman, E., *et al.* Actions as space-time shapes. *IEEE Trans. on Pattern Analysis and Machine Intelligence 29*, 12 (2007), pp. 2247-2253.

[GC93] Galvez, J. M., and Canton, M. Normalization and shape recognition of three-dimensional objects by 3D moments. *Pattern Recognition 26*, 5 (1993), pp. 667-681.

[GCK91] Grenander, U., Chow, Y., and Keenan, D. M. *Hands: A Pattern Theoretic Study of Biological Shapes*. Springer-Verlag, 1991.

[GCSR95] Gelman, A., Carlin, J. B., Stern, H. S., and Rubin, D. B. *Bayesian Data Analysis*. Chapman and Hall, London, 1995.

[GDH11] Guo, R., Dai, Q., and Hoiem, D. Single-image shadow detection and removal using paired regions. *IEEE Conference on Computer Vision and Pattern Recognition* (2011), pp. 2033-2040.

[GFK09] Gould, S., Fulton, R., and Koller, D. Decomposing a scene into geometric and semantically consistent regions. In *Proc. IEEE Int. Conf. on Computer Vision* (2009), pp. 1-8.

[GFM+07] Gallup, D., Frahm, J., Mordohai, P., *et al.* Real-time plane-sweeping stereo with multiple sweeping directions. In *Proc. Computer Vision and Pattern Recognition* (2007), pp. 1-8.

[GG07] Guennebaud, G., and Gross, M. Algebraic point set surfaces. *ACM Trans. Graphics 26*, 3 (2007).

[GG92] Gersho, A., and Gray, R. *Vector Quantization and Signal Compression*. Kluwer, 1992.

[GGWG12] Gevers, T., Gijsenij, A., van de Weijer, J., and Geusebroek, J. M. *Color in computer vision: Fundamentals and applications*. John Wiley & Sons, 2012.

[GHC+00] Gong, G., He, Y., Concha, L., Lebel, C., Gross, D. W., Evans, A. C., and Beaulieu, C. Mapping anatomical connectivity patterns of human cerebral cortex using in vivo diffusion tensor imaging tractography. *Cerebral Cortex 19*, 3 (2000), pp. 524-536.

[GHC02] Gonzalez, J., Holder, L. B., and Cook, D. J. Graph-based relational concept learning. In *Proc. the International Machine Learning Conference* (2002).

[Gib85] Gibbons, A. *Algorithmic Graph Theory*. Cambridge University Press, Cambridge, 1985.

[Gib86] Gibson, J. J. *The Ecological Approach to Visual Perception*. Houghton Mifflin, 1986.

[Gib98] Gibson, C. G. *Elementary Geometry of Algebraic Curves: An Undergraduate Introduction*. Cambridge University Press, 1998.

[GJ79] Garey, M. R., and Johnson, D. S. *Computers and Intractability: A Guide to the Theory of NP-Completeness*, W. H. Freeman, 1979.

[GK04] Guskov, I., and Khodakovsky, A. Wavelet compression of parametrically coherent mesh sequences. In *Proc. ACM SIGGRAPH/Eurographics Symposium on Computer Animation* (2004), Eurographics Association, pp. 183-192.

[GKP+07] Glocker, B., Komodakis, N., Paragios, N., *et al.* Inter and intra-modal deformable registration: Continuous deformations meet efficient optimal linear programming. *Information Processing in Medical Imaging* (2007), pp. 408-420.

[GL86] Gower, J. C., and Legendre, P. Metric and Euclidean properties of dissimilarity coefficients. *Journal of Classification 3*, 1 (1986), pp. 5-48.

[GL89] Golub, G. H., and Loan, C. F. V. *Matrix Computations*, second ed. Johns Hopkins University Press, 1989.

[GLU96] Gool, V., Luc, T. M., and Ungureanu, D. Affine/photometric invariants for planar intensity patterns. In *Proc. Euro. Conf. Computer Vision* (1996), pp. 642-651.

[GM03] Green, P., and MacDonald, L., Eds. *Colour Engineering*. John Wiley & Sons, 2003.

[GM11] Gong, D., and Medioni, G. Dynamic manifold warping for view invariant action recognition. In *Proc. IEEE Int. Conf. on Computer Vision* (2011).

[GM98] Glasbey, C. A., and Mardia, K. V. A review of image warping methods. *J. Applied Statistics 25* (1998), pp. 155-171.

[GMA83] Gil, B., Mitiche, A., and Aggarwal, J. K. Experiments in combining intensity and range edge maps. *Computer Vision, Graphics, and Image Processing 21*, 3 (1983), pp. 395-411.

[Goa87] Goad, C. Special purpose automatic programming for 3D model-based vision. *Readings in Computer Vision* (1987), pp. 371-381.

[Gol10] Goldstein, E. B. *Sensation and Perception*. Wadsworth Publishing Company, 2010.

[Goy01] Goyal, V. K. Multiple description coding: Compression meets the network. *IEEE Signal Processing Magazine 18*, 5 (2001), pp. 74-93.

[GP93] Gauch, J. M., and Pizer, S. M. Multiresolution analysis of ridges and valleys in grey-scale images. *IEEE Trans. on Pattern Analysis and Machine Intelligence 15*, 6 (1993), pp. 635-646.

[GPSG01] Geisler, W. S., Perry, J. S., Super, B. J., and Gallogly, D. P. Edge co-occurrence in natural images predicts contour grouping performance. *Vision Research 41*, 6 (2001), pp. 711-724.

[GR95] Gudivada, V. N., and Raghavan, V. V. Content based image retrieval systems. *Computer 28*, 9 (1995), pp. 18-22.

[Gri85] Grimson, W. E. L. Computational experiments with a feature based stereo algorithm. *IEEE Trans. on Pattern Analysis and Machine Intelligence 1* (1985), pp. 17-34.

[Gro83] Grossberg, S. The quantized geometry of visual space: The coherent computation of depth, form, and lightness. *Behavioral and Brain Sciences 6*, 4 (1983), pp. 625-657.

[Gro94] Gros, P. How to use the cross ratio to compute projective invariants from two images. *Applications of Invariance in Computer Vision* (1994), pp. 107-126.

[GS05] Gill, M., and Spriggs, A. *Assessing the impact of CCTV.* UK Home Office Research, Development and Statistics Directorate, 2005.

[GS92] Grimmett, G. R., and Stirzaker, D. R. *Probability and Random Processes*, 2nd ed. Clarendon Press, Oxford, 1992.

[GSCG04] Gonzalez-Audicana, M., Saleta, J., Catalan, R., and Garcia, R. Fusion of multispectral and panchromatic images using improved IHS and PCA mergers based on wavelet decomposition. *IEEE Trans. on Geoscience and Remote Sensing 42*, 6 (2004), pp. 1291-1299.

[GT00] Grosso, E., and Tistarelli, M. Log-polar stereo for anthropomorphic robots. In *Proc. Euro. Conf. Computer Vision* 2000, pp. 299-313.

[GT95] Grosso, E., and Tistarelli, M. Active/dynamic stereo vision. *IEEE Trans. on Pattern Analysis and Machine Intelligence 17*, 9 (1995), pp. 868-879.

[GU89] Gordon, D., and Udupa, J. K. Fast surface tracking in three-dimensional binary images. *Computer Vision, Graphics, and Image Processing 45*, 2 (1989), pp. 196-214.

[Gum02] Gumhold, S. Maximum entropy light source placement. In *Proc. Visualization* (2002), pp. 275-282.

[Gus10] Gustafsson, F. *Statistical Sensor Fusion, Studentlitteratur.* 2010.

[GVB11] Gibert, J., Valveny, E., and Bunke, H. Graph embedding in vector spaces, GbR tutorial, 2011.

[GVRV04] Gonzalez, J., Varona, J., Roca, F. X., and Villanueva, J. J. Situation graph trees for human behavior modeling. In *Proc. Catalan Conf. for Artificial Intelligence, Barcelona, Spain* (2004).

[GVS03] Guillamet, D., Vitria, J., and Schiele, B. Introducing a weighted non-negative matrix factorization for image classification. *Pattern Recognition Letters 24*, 14 (2003), pp. 2447-2454.

[GW91] Grossberg, S., and Wyse, L. A neural network architecture for figure-ground separation of connected scenic figures. *Neural Networks 4*, 6 (1991), pp. 723-742.

[GX11] Gong, S., and Xiang, T. *Visual Analysis of Behaviour: From Pixels to Semantics.* Springer-Verlag, 2011.

[GYR+11] Gall, J., Yao, A., Razavi, N., et al. Hough forests for object detection, tracking, and action recognition. *IEEE Trans. on Pattern Analysis and Machine Intelligence 33*, 11 (2011), pp. 2188-2202.

[GZSM07] Geng, X., Zhou, Z. H., and Smith-Miles, K. Automatic age estimation based on facial aging patterns. *IEEE Trans. on Pattern Analysis and Machine Intelligence 29*, 12 (2007), pp. 2234-2240.

[HA87] Hammond, J. H., and Austin, J. *The Camera Lucida in Art and Science.* Adam Hilger, Bristol, 1987.

[Haa94] Haala, N. Detection of buildings by fusion of range and image data. *Spatial Information from Digital Photogrammetry and Computer Vision:* In *Proc. ISPRS Commission III Symposium* (1994), pp. 341-346.

[Har84] Haralick, R. M. Digital step edges from zero crossing of second directional derivatives. *IEEE Trans. on Pattern Analysis and Machine Intelligence 1* (1984), pp. 58-68.

[Har92] Hartley, R. Estimation of relative camera positions for uncalibrated cameras. In *Proc. Euro. Conf. Computer* (1992), pp. 579-587.

[Har94] Hartley, R. Euclidean reconstruction from uncalibrated views. *Applications of Invariance in Computer Vision* (1994), pp. 235-256.

[Has78] Hastenes, M. Conjugate direction methods in optimization. In *Optimization Techniques Part 1*, J. Stoer, Ed., vol. 6 of *Lecture Notes in Control and Information Sciences*. 1978, pp. 8-27.

[HB88] Healey, G., and Binford, T. O. Local shape from specularity. *Computer Vision, Graphics, and Image Processing 42*, 1 (1988), pp. 62-86.

[HB93] Heitz, F., and Bouthemy, P. Multimodal estimation of discontinuous optical flow using Markov random fields. *IEEE Trans. on Pattern Analysis and Machine Intelligence 15*, 12 (1993), pp. 1217-1232.

[HBS09] Han, D., Bo, L., and Sminchisescu, C. Selection and context for action recognition. In *Proc. Int. Conf. Computer Vision* (2009), pp. 1933-1940.

[HC00] Huang, F. J., and Chen, T. Tracking of multiple faces for human-computer interfaces and virtual environments. *IEEE Int. Conf. on Multimedia and Expo 3* (2000), pp. 1563-1566.

[HC04] Hongliang, B., and Changping, L. A hybrid license plate extraction method based on edge statistics and morphology. In *Proc. Int. Conf. on Pattern Recognition* (2004), vol. 2, pp. 831-834.

[HC77] Haralick, R. M., and Currier, P. Image discrimination enhancement combination system (IDECS). *Computer Graphics and Image Processing 6*, 4 (1977), pp. 371-381.

[HC96] Huang, Z., and Cohen, F. S. Affine-invariant B-spline moments for curve matching. *IEEE Trans. on Image Processing 5*, 10 (1996), pp. 1473-1480.

[HCL07] Hori, T., Cheng, C. B. P., and Lin, H. J. Multi-tap camera, US patent # 7,236,199, 2007.

[HCM95] Hager, G. D., Chang, W.-C., and Morse, A. S. Robot hand-eye coordination based on stereo vision. *IEEE Control Systems 15*, 1 (1995), pp. 30-39.

[HCP02] Hue, C., Cadre, J.-P. L., and Pérez, P. Sequential Monte Carlo methods for multiple target tracking and data fusion. *IEEE Trans. on Signal Processing 50*, 2 (2002), pp. 309-325.

[HD95] Horaud, R., and Dornaika, F. Hand-eye calibration. *Int. J. Robotics Research 14*, 3 (1995), pp. 195-210.

[HDD+92] Hoppe, H., Derose, T., Duchamp, T., *et al.* Surface reconstruction from unorganized points. In *Proc. Computer Graphics and Interactive Techniques (ACM SIGGRAPH)* (1992), pp. 71-78.

[HDZ05] Hansen, G. A., Douglass, R. W., and Zardecki, A. *Mesh Enhancement: Selected elliptic methods, foundations and applications*. Imperial College Press, 2005.

[Hec87] Hecht, E. *Optics*. Addison-Wesley, 1987.

[Hei94] Heikkinen, J. *Estimation of Gibbs Point Processes by Monte Carlo Methods*. PhD thesis, Licentiate Thesis, University of Jyvaskyla, Finland, 1994.

[Hen03] Henderson, J. M. Human gaze control during real-world scene perception. *Trends in Cognitive Sciences 7*, 11 (2003), pp. 498-504.

[Hen07] Hendrick, E. R. *Breast MRI: fundamentals and technical aspects*. Springer, 2007.

[Hen97] Henkel, R. *Fast stereovision by coherence detection*. Springer, Berlin/Heidelberg, 1997, pp. 297-304.

[HF94] Han, C.-C., and Fan, K.-C. Skeleton generation of engineering drawings via contour matching. *Pattern Recognition 27*, 2 (1994), pp. 261-275.

[HF98] Halir, R., and Flusser, J. Numerically stable direct least squares fitting of ellipses. In *Proc. Int. Conf. in Central Europe on Computer Graphics, Visualization and Interactive Digital Media* (1998).

[HFR06] Hilton, A., Fua, P., and Ronfard, R. Modeling people: Vision-based understanding of a person's shape, appearance, movement, and behavior. *Computer Vision and Image Understanding 104*, pp. 2-3 (2006), pp. 87-89.

[HGX09] Hospedales, T., Gong, S., and Xiang, T. A Markov clustering topic model for mining behaviour in video. In *Proc. Int. Conf. Computer Vision* (2009), pp. 1165-1172.

[HH89] Hansen, C., and Henderson, T. C. CAGD-based computer vision. *IEEE Trans. on Pattern Analysis and Machine Intelligence 11*, 11 (1989), pp. 1181-1193.

[HHD99] Horprasert, T., Harwood, D., and Davis, L. S. A statistical approach for real-time robust background subtraction and shadow detection. In *Proc. IEEE Int. Conf. Computer Vision* (1999), pp. 256-261.

[HHR01] Hu, S., Hoffman, E. A., and Reinhardt, J. M. Automatic lung segmentation for accurate quantitation of volumetric X-ray CT images. *IEEE Trans. on Medical Imaging 20*, 6 (2001), pp. 490-498.

[Hil84] Hildreth, E. C. The computation of the velocity field. In *Proc. the Royal Society of London Series B. Biological Sciences* (1984), vol. 221, pp. 189-220.

[HJ01] Hsu, R.-L., and Jain, A. K. Face modeling for recognition. In *Proc. Int. Conf. on Image Processing* (2001), vol. 2, pp. 693-696.

[HJ87] Hoffman, R., and Jain, A. K. Segmentation and classification of range images. *IEEE Trans. on Pattern Analysis and Machine Intelligence 5* (1987), pp. 608-620.

[HJ93] Humphrey, G. K., and Jolicoeur, P. An examination of the effects of axis fore-shortening, monocular depth cues, and visual field on object identification. *The Quarterly Journal of Experimental Psychology 46*, 1 (1993), pp. 137-159.

[HJL+89] Haralick, R. M., Joo, H., Lee, C., *et al.* Pose estimation from corresponding point data. *IEEE Trans. on Systems, Man and Cybernetics 19*, 6 (1989), pp. 1426-1446.

[HL93] Hwang, S. H., and Lee, S. U. A hierarchical optical flow estimation algorithm based on the interlevel motion smoothness constraint. *Pattern Recognition 26*, 6 (1993), pp. 939-952.

[HL94] Hudson, H. M., and Larkin, R. S. Accelerated image reconstruction using ordered subsets of projection data. *IEEE Trans. on Medical Imaging 13*, 4 (1994), pp. 601-609.

[HM98] Hiura, S., and Matsuyama, T. Depth measurement by the multi-focus camera. In *Proc. Computer Vision and Pattern Recognition* (1998), pp. 953-959.

[HMS98] Hattori, K., Matsumori, S., and Sato, Y. Estimating pose of human face based on symmetry plane using range and intensity images. In *Proc. Int. Conf. on Pattern Recognition* (1998), pp. 1183-1187.

[HN00] Huertas, A., and Nevatia, R. Detecting changes in aerial views of man-made structures. *Image and Vision Computing 18*, 8 (2000), pp. 583-596.

[HNH+87] Helmcke, F., Nanda, N. C., Hsiung, M. C., Soto, B., Adey, C. K., Goyal, R. G., and Gatewood, R. P. Color Doppler assessment of mitral regurgitation with orthogonal planes. *Circulation 75*, 1 (1987), pp. 175-183.

[Ho98] Ho, T. K. The random subspace method for constructing decision forests. *IEEE Trans. on Pattern Analysis and Machine Intelligence 20*, 8 (1998), pp. 832-844.

[Hor86] Horn, B. K. P. *Robot Vision*. MIT Press, Cambridge, Massachusetts, 1986.

[HP98] Herman, B., and Ploem, J. S. *Fluorescence Microscopy*. Springer, 1998.

[HPZC95] Huang, Y., Palaniappan, K., Zhuang, X., and Cavanaugh, J. E. Optic flow field segmentation and motion estimation using a robust genetic partitioning algorithm. *IEEE Trans. on Pattern Analysis and Machine Intelligence 17*, 12 (1995), pp. 1177-1190.

[HR78] Hanson, A. R., and Riseman, E. M. VISIONS: A computer system for interpreting scenes. *Computer Vision Systems* (1978).

[HR92] Haralick, R. M., and Ramesh, V. Image understanding environment. In *SPIE/Symposium on Electronic Imaging: Science and Technology* (1992), International Society for Optics and Photonics., pp. 159-167.

[HS81] Horn, B. K. P., and Schunck, B. G. Determining optical flow. *Artificial Intelligence 17*, 1 (1981), pp. 185-203.

[HS92] Haralick, R. M., and Shapiro, L. G. *Computer and Robot Vision*. Addison-Wesley Longman Publishing, 1992.

[HS94] Healey, G., and Slater, D. Global color constancy: recognition of objects by use of illumination-invariant properties of color distributions. *Jour. Optical Society of America A 11*, 11 (1994), pp. 3003-3010.

[HS96] Heikkila, J., and Silven, O. Calibration procedure for short focal length off-the-shelf CCD cameras. In *Proc. Int. Conf. on Pattern Recognition* (1996), vol. 1, pp. 166-170.

[HS98] Harris, J. W., and Stocker, H. *Handbook of Mathematics and Computational Science*. Springer, 1998.

[HSD73] Haralick, R. M., Shanmugam, K., and Dinstein, I. H. Textural features for image classification. *IEEE Trans. on Systems, Man and Cybernetics 6* (1973), pp. 610–621.

[HSE+95] Hafner, J., Sawhney, H. S., Equitz, W., *et al.* Efficient color histogram indexing for quadratic form distance functions. *IEEE Trans. on Pattern Analysis and Machine Intelligence 17*, 7 (1995), pp. 729–736.

[HSL+98] Huang, N. E., Shen, Z., Long, S. R., Wu, M. L., Shih, H. H., Zheng, Q., Yen, N. C., Tung, C. C., and Liu, H. H. The empirical mode decomposition and Hilbert spectrum for nonlinear and non-stationary time series analysis. In *Proc. Roy. Soc London A* (1998), vol. 454, pp. 903–995.

[HSS+08] Hofmann, M., Steinke, F., Scheel, V., Charpiat, G., Farquhar, J., Aschoff, P., Brady, M., Schölkopf, B., and Pichler, B. J. MRI-based attenuation correction for PET/MRI: A novel approach combining pattern recognition and atlas registration. *J. Nuclear Medicine 49*, 11 (2008), pp. 1875–1883.

[HTC92] Hill, A., Taylor, C., and Cootes, T. Object recognition by flexible template matching using genetic algorithms. In *Proc. Euro. Conf. Computer Vision* (1992), Springer, Berlin/Heidelberg, pp. 852–856.

[HTF08] Hastie, T. J., Tibshirani, R. J., and Friedman, J. *The Elements of Statistical Learning*. Springer-Verlag, 2008.

[HTM99] Hayman, E., Thorhallson, T., and Murray, D. W. Zoom-invariant tracking using points and lines in affine views: An application of the affine multifocal tensors. In *Proc. IEEE Int. Conf. on Computer Vision* (1999), pp. 269–277.

[HTWM04] Hu, W., Tan, T., Wang, L., and Maybank, S. A survey on visual surveillance of object motion and behaviors. *IEEE Trans. on Systems, Man, and Cybernetics, Part C: Applications and Reviews 34*, 3 (2004), pp. 334–352.

[Hum77] Hummel, R. Image enhancement by histogram transformation. *Computer Graphics and Image Processing 6*, 2 (1977), pp. 184–195.

[Hun04] Hunt, R. W. G. *The Reproduction of Colour*. John Wiley & Sons, 2004.

[Hun73] Hunt, B. R. The application of constrained least squares estimation to image restoration by digital computer. *IEEE Trans. on Computers 100*, 9 (1973), pp. 805–812.

[Hur10] Hurkman, A. V. *The Color Correction Handbook: Professional Techniques for Video and Cinema*. Peachpit Press, 2010.

[HV03] Hua-Mei, C., and Varshney, P. K. Mutual information-based CT-MR brain image registration using generalized partial volume joint histogram estimation. *IEEE Trans. on Medical Imaging 22*, 9 (2003), pp. 1111–1119.

[HV99] Han, K., and Veloso, M. Automated robot behavior recognition applied to robotic soccer. In *Proc. IJCAI Workshop on Team Behavior and Plan-Recognition* (1999), pp. 249–256.

[HXP03] Han, X., Xu, C., and Prince, J. L. A topology preserving level set method for geometric deformable models. *IEEE Trans. on Pattern Analysis and Machine Intelligence 25*, 6 (2003), pp. 755–768.

[HY93] Hwang, S. C., and Yang, H. S. Efficient view sphere tessellation method based on halfedge data structure and quadtree. *Computers and Graphics 17*, 5 (1993), pp. 575–581.

[HZ00] Hartley, R., and Zisserman, A. *Multiple View Geometry*. Cambridge University Press, Cambridge, 2000.

[HZK08] Hornung, A., Zeng, B., and Kobbelt, L. Image selection for improved multi-view stereo. In *Proc. IEEE Int. Conf. on Computer Vision and Pattern Recognition* (2008), pp. 1–8.

[HZLM01] Hoff III, K. E., Zaferakis, A., Lin, M., and Manocha, D. Fast and simple 2D geometric proximity queries using graphics hardware. In *Proc. Symposium on Interactive 3D Graphics* (2001), pp. 145–148.

[IA98] Irani, M., and Anandan, P. Robust multi-sensor image alignment. In *Proc. Int. Conf. on Computer Vision* (1998), pp. 959–966.

[IAP+08] Ion, A., Artner, N. M., Peyre, G., *et al.* Matching 2D and 3D articulated shapes using eccentricity. In *Proc. Computer Vision and Pattern Recognition Workshops* (2008), pp. 1-8.

[IB95] Intille, S. S., and Bobick, A. F. Closed-world tracking. In *Proc. Int. Conf. Computer Vision* (1995), pp. 672-678.

[IB96] Isard, M., and Blake, A. Contour tracking by stochastic propagation of conditional density. In *Proc. Euro. Conf. Computer Vision* (1996), pp. 343-356.

[IB98] Isard, M., and Blake, A. Condensation: conditional density propagation for visual tracking. *Int. J. Computer Vision 29*, 1 (1998), pp. 5-28.

[IGM82] Ingle, D. J., Goodale, M. A., and Mansfield, R. J. W., Eds. *Analysis of Visual Behavior*. MIT Press, 1982.

[IJL87] Irons, J. R., Johnson, B. L., and Linebaugh, G. H. Multiple-angle observations of reflectance anisotropy from an airborne linear array sensor. *IEEE Trans. on Geoscience and Remote Sensing 3* (1987), pp. 372-383.

[INN07] Igarashi, T., Nishino, K., and Nayar, S. K. The appearance of human skin: A survey. *Foundations and Trends in Computer Graphics and Vision 3*, 1 (2007).

[ISO02] ISO/IEC. Information technology – Multimedia content description interface – Part 8: Extraction and use of MPEG-7 descriptions TR 15938-8:2002. Tech. rep., 2002.

[ISO04] ISO/IEC. Photography and graphic technology – Extended colour encodings for digital image storage, manipulation and interchange – Part 1: Architecture and requirements, TR pp. 22028-1:2004. Tech. rep., 2004.

[Itt01] Itti, L., and Koch, C. Computational modelling of visual attention. *Nature reviews neuroscience 2*, 3 (2001), pp. 194-203.

[IYT92] Ishiguro, H., Yamamoto, M., and Tsuji, S. Omni-directional stereo. *IEEE Trans. Pattern Analysis and Machine Intelligence 14*, 2 (1992), pp. 257-262.

[Jac02] Jacobs, R. A. What determines visual cue reliability? *Trends in Cognitive Sciences 6*, 1 (2002), pp. 345-350.

[Jai89] Jain, A. *Fundamentals of Digital Image Processing*. Prentice Hall, 1989.

[JB05] Jezzard, P., and Balaban, R. S. Correction for geometric distortion in echo planar images from B0 field variations. *Magnetic Resonance in Medicine 34*, 1 (2005), pp. 65-73.

[JB94] Jiang, X., and Bunke, H. Fast segmentation of range images into planar regions by scan line grouping. *Machine Vision and Applications 7*, 2 (1994), pp. 115-122.

[JB94a] Judge, T. R., and Bryanston-Cross, P. J. A review of phase unwrapping techniques in fringe analysis. *Optics and Lasers in Engineering 21*, 4 (1994), pp. 199-239.

[JB99] Jiang, X., and Bunke, H. Edge detection in range images based on scan line approximation. *Computer Vision and Image Understanding 73*, 2 (1999), pp. 183-199.

[JD02] Jurie, F., and Dhome, M. Hyperplane approximation for template matching. *IEEE Trans. Pat. Anal. Mach. Intel 24*, 7 (2002), pp. 996-1000.

[JF99] Johnson, G. M., and Fairchild, M. D. Full-spectral color calculations in realistic image synthesis. *Computer Graphics and Applications 19*, 4 (1999), pp. 47-53.

[JFK03] Jojic, N., Frey, B. J., and Kannan, A. Epitomic analysis of appearance and shape. In *Proc. Int. Conf. Computer Vision* (2003), pp. 34-41.

[JH98] Jain, A., and Healey, G. A multiscale representation including opponent color features for texture recognition. *IEEE Trans. on Image Processing 7*, 1 (1998), pp. 124-128.

[JH99] Johnson, A. E., and Hebert, M. Using spin images for efficient object recognition in cluttered 3D scenes. *IEEE Trans. on Pattern Analysis and Machine Intelligence 21*, 5 (1999), pp. 433-449.

[Jia01] Jianchao, Y. Image registration based on both feature and intensity matching. In *Proc. (ICASSP'01) 2001 IEEE Int. Conf. on Acoustics, Speech, and Signal Processing* (2001), vol. 3, pp. 1693-1696.

[JJK03] Janke, W., Johnston, D. A., and Kenna, R. Information geometry of the spherical model. *Physical Review E 67*, 4 (2003), 046106.

[JJS04] Junejo, I. N., Javed, O., and Shah, M. Multi feature path modeling for video surveillance. In *Proc. Int. Conf. on Pattern Recognition ICPR 2004* (2004), vol. 2, IEEE, pp. 716–719.

[JK05] Johanyak, Z. C., and Kovacs, S. Distance based similarity measures of fuzzy sets. In *Proc. Symp. on Applied Machine Intelligence and Informatics* (2005).

[JKKW06] Jain, A., Kopell, D., Kakligian, K., and Wang, Y.-F. Using stationary-dynamic camera assemblies for wide-area video surveillance and selective attention. *2006 IEEE Computer Society Conference on Computer Vision and Pattern Recognition 1* (2006), pp. 537–544.

[JKS95] Jain, R., Kasturi, R., and Schunck, B. *Machine Vision*. McGraw Hill, 1995.

[JLRG09] Jain, A. K., Lee, J. E., Rong, J., and Gregg, N. Content-based image retrieval: An application to tattoo images. *IEEE Int. Conf. on Image Processing (ICIP)* (2009), pp. 2745–2748.

[JM92] Jolion, J. M., and Montanvert, A. The adaptive pyramid: A framework for 2D image analysis. *CVGIP: Image Understanding 55*, 3 (1992), pp. 339–348.

[JMW+64] Judd, D. B., MacAdam, D. L., Wyszecki, G., Budde, H. W., Condit, H. R., Henderson, S. T., and Simonds, J. L. Spectral distribution of typical daylight as a function of correlated color temperature. *Jour. Optical Society of America 54*, 8 (1964), pp. 1031–1040.

[Joh73] Johansson, G. Visual perception of biological motion and a model for its analysis. *Attention, Perception, & Psychophysics 14*, 2 (1973), pp. 201–211.

[Jon11] Jones, D. K., Ed. *Diffusion MRI: Theory, methods, and applications*. Oxford University Press, 2011.

[JP73] Jarvis, R. A., and Patrick, E. A. Clustering using a similarity measure based on shared near neighbors. *IEEE Trans. on Computers 100*, 11 (1973), pp. 1025–1034.

[JP98] Jones, M., and Poggio, T. Multidimensional morphable models. In *Proc. Computer Vision* (1998), pp. 683–688.

[JR99] Jones, M. J., and Rehg, J. M. Statistical color models with application to skin detection. *Int. J. of Computer Vision 46*, 1 (1999), pp. 274–280.

[JRL97] Jain, A. K., Ratha, N. K., and Lakshmanan, S. Object detection using Gabor filters. *Pattern Recognition 30*, 2 (1997), pp. 295–309.

[JRW97] Jobson, D. J., ur Rahman, Z., and Woodell, G. A. Properties and performance of a center/surround retinex. *IEEE Trans. on Image Processing 6*, 3 (1997), pp. 451–462.

[JS05] Jafari-Khouzani, K., and Soltanian-Zadeh, H. Radon transform orientation estimation for rotation invariant texture analysis. *IEEE Trans. on Pattern Analysis and Machine Intelligence 27*, 6 (2005), pp. 1004–1008.

[JS10] Jaggi, M., and Sulovský, M. A simple algorithm for nuclear norm regularized problems. In *Proc. Int. Conf. on Machine Learning* (2010), pp. 471–478.

[JT03] Jia, J., and Tang, C.-K. Image repairing: Robust image synthesis by adaptive ND tensor voting. In *Computer Society Conference on Computer Vision and Pattern Recognition* (2003), vol. 1, pp. I–643.

[Jul81] Julesz, B. Textons, the elements of texture perception, and their interactions. *Nature 290* (1981), pp. 91–97.

[JV05] Jian, B., and Vemuri, B. C. A robust algorithm for point set registration using mixture of Gaussians. In *Proc. Int. Conf. Computer Vision* (2005), pp. 1246–1251.

[JY00] Jiang, X., and Yau, W.-Y. Fingerprint minutiae matching based on the local and global structures. In *Proc. Int. Conf. on Pattern Recognition* (2000), vol. 2, pp. 1038–1041.

[JYW05] Jin, M., Yang, Y., and Wernick, M. N. Reconstruction of cardiac-gated dynamic spect images. In *Proc. Int. Conf. Image Processing* (2005), pp. III–752.

[JZD98] Jain, A. K., Zhong, Y., and Dubuisson-Jolly, M.-P. Deformable template models: A review. *Signal Processing 71*, 2 (1998), pp. 109–129.

[Kam89] Kamgar-Parsi, B. Evaluation of quantization error in computer vision. *IEEE Trans. on Pattern Analysis and Machine Intelligence 11*, 9 (1989), pp. 929–940.

[Kan97] Kang, S. B. *A Structure from Motion Approach using Constrained Deformable Models and Appearance Prediction*. Digital, Cambridge Research Laboratory, 1997.

[KBL04] Kvalheim, O. M., Brakstad, F., and Liang, Y. Preprocessing of analytical profiles in the presence of homoscedastic or heteroscedastic noise. *Analytical Chemistry 66*, 1 (2004), pp. 43–51.

[KCT00] Kanade, T., Cohn, J. F., and Tian, Y. Comprehensive database for facial expression analysis. In *Proc. IEEE International Conference on Automatic Face and Gesture Recognition* (2000), pp. 46–53.

[KD99] Koenderink, J., and Doorn, A. V. The structure of locally orderless images. *Int. J. of Computer Vision 31*, 2 (1999), pp. 159–168.

[KDB96] Kaucic, R., Dalton, B., and Blake, A. Real-time lip tracking for audio-visual speech recognition applications. In *Proc. Euro. Conf. Computer Vision* (1996), pp. 376–387.

[KE89] Kashyap, R. L., and Eom, K.-B. Texture boundary detection based on the long correlation model. *IEEE Trans. on Pattern Analysis and Machine Intelligence 11*, 1 (1989), pp. 58–67.

[Ken89] Kendall, D. G. A survey of the statistical theory of shape. *Statistical Science 4*, 2 (1989), pp. 87–120.

[Ker99] Kersten, D. *High-Level Vision as Statistical Inference*. 1999, p. 353.

[KF09] Koller, D., and Friedman, N. *Probabilistic Graphical Models*. MIT Press, Cambridge, Massachusetts, 2009.

[KG00] Karni, Z., and Gotsman, C. Spectral compression of mesh geometry. *SIGGRAPH* (2000), pp. 279–286.

[KG92] Kambhamettu, C., and Goldgof, D. B. Point correspondence recovery in non-rigid motion. In *Proc. IEEE Computer Society Conference on Computer Vision and Pattern Recognition CVPR* (1992), pp. 222–227.

[KH02] Kim, C., and Hwang, J.-N. Object-based video abstraction for video surveillance systems. *IEEE Trans. on Circuits and Systems for Video Technology 12*, 12 (2002), pp. 1128–1138.

[KH03] Kumar, S., and Hebert, M. Discriminative random fields: A discriminative framework for contextual interaction in classification. In *Proc. Int. Conf. Computer Vision* (2003), pp. 1150–1157.

[KH04] Kuiper, S., and Hendriks, B. H. W. Variable-focus liquid lens for miniature cameras. *Applied Physics Letters 85*, 7 (2004), pp. 1128–1130.

[KH07] Kalpathy-Cramer, J., and Hersh, W. Automatic image modality based classification and annotation to improve medical image retrieval. *Studies in Health Technology and Informatics 129*, 2 (2007), 1334.

[KH90] Khotanzad, A., and Hong, Y. H. Invariant image recognition by Zernike moments. *IEEE Trans. on Pattern Analysis and Machine Intelligence 12*, 5 (1990), pp. 489–497.

[KI93] Kang, S. B., and Ikeuchi, K. The complex EGI: A new representation for 3-D pose determination. *IEEE Trans. on Pattern Analysis and Machine Intelligence 15*, 7 (1993), pp. 707–721.

[Kim03] Kim, C. Content-based image copy detection. *Signal Processing: Image Communication 18*, 3 (2003), pp. 169–184.

[Kim97] Kim, Y.-T. Contrast enhancement using brightness preserving bi-histogram equalization. *IEEE Trans. on Consumer Electronics 43*, 1 (1997), pp. 1–8.

[Kin03] Kindratenko, V. V. On using functions to describe the shape. *Journal of Mathematical Imaging and Vision 18*, 3 (2003), pp. 225–245.

[KK01] Kreyenkamp, O., and Klemm, R. Doppler compensation in forward-looking STAP radar. *IEE Proc. Radar, Sonar and Navigation 148*, 5 (2001), pp. 253–258.

[KK98] Kim, Y.-S., and Kim, W.-Y. Content-based trademark retrieval system using a visually salient feature. *Image and Vision Computing 16*, 12 (1998), pp. 931–939.

[KKK03] Khang, B.-G., Koenderink, J. J., and Kappers, A. M. L. Perception of surface reflectance of 3-D geometrical shapes: Influence of the lighting mode. *Perception 11* (2003), pp. 1311–1324.

[KL09] Kwon, J., and Lee, K. M. Tracking of a non-rigid object via patch-based dynamic appearance modeling and adaptive basin hopping Monte Carlo sampling. In *Proc. IEEE Conference on Computer Vision and Pattern Recognition* (2009), pp. 1208–1215.

[KL96] Kenwright, D. N., and Lane, D. A. Interactive time-dependent particle tracing using tetrahedral decomposition. *IEEE Trans. on Visualization and Computer Graphics 2*, 2 (1996), pp. 120-129.

[KLCL05] Kim, J. C., Lee, K. M., Choi, B. T., and Lee, S. U. A dense stereo matching using two-pass dynamic programming with generalized ground control points. *IEEE Computer Society Conference on Computer Vision and Pattern Recognition 2* (2005), pp. 1075-1082.

[Kle04] Klemelä, J. Visualization of multivariate density estimates with level set trees. *J Computational and Graphical Statistics 13*, 33 (2004), pp. 599-620.

[KLP94] Katzir, N., Lindenbaum, M., and Porat, M. Curve segmentation under partial occlusion. *IEEE Trans. on Pattern Analysis and Machine Intelligence 16*, 5 (1994), pp. 513-519.

[KLT05] Katz, S., Leifman, G., and Tal, A. Mesh segmentation using feature point and core extraction. *The Visual Computer 21*, 8 (2005), pp. 649-658.

[KLY+01] Kim, H., Lee, J., Yang, J.-H., et al. Visual rhythm and shot verification. *Multimedia Tools and Applications 15*, 3 (2001), pp. 227-245.

[KMJ05] Kumar, B. V. K. V., Mahalanobis, A., and Juday, R. D. *Correlation Pattern Recognition*. Cambridge University Press, Cambridge, 2005.

[KMK95] Krupnik, H., Malah, D., and Karnin, E. Fractal representation of images via the discrete wavelet transform. In *Proc. Convention of Electrical and Electronics Engineers in Israel* (1995), pp. 2.2.2/pp. 1-2.2.2/5.

[KMMH07] Koh, T. K., Miles, N., Morgan, S., and Hayes-Gill, B. Image segmentation of overlapping particles in automatic size analysis using multi-flash imaging. *WACV'07. IEEE Workshop on Applications of Computer Vision* (2007), 47.

[KN00] Kerre, E. E., and Nachtegael, M., Eds. *Fuzzy Techniques in Image Processing*, vol. 52. Physica-Verlag HD, 2000.

[KO80] Kawara, T., and Obazawa, H. A new method for retroillumination photography of cataractous lens opacities. *American J of Ophthalmology 90*, 2 (1980), pp. 186-9.

[KOA92] Kurita, T., Otsu, N., and Abdelmalek, N. Maximum likelihood thresholding based on population mixture models. *Pattern Recognition 25*, 10 (1992), pp. 1231-1240.

[Koe84] Koenderink, J. J. What does the occluding contour tell us about solid shape? *Perception 13* (1984), pp. 321-330.

[Koe86] Koenderink, J. J. Optic flow. *Vision Research 26*, 1 (1986), pp. 161-179.

[Kos95] Koschan, A. A comparative study on color edge detection. In *Proc. Asian Conference on Computer Vision* (1995), vol. 3, pp. 574-578.

[KPP98] Kim, S. K., Park, S. R., and Paik, J. K. Simultaneous out-of-focus blur estimation and restoration for digital auto-focusing system. *IEEE Trans. on Consumer Electronics 44*, 3 (1998), pp. 1071-1075.

[KPSP97] Kim, J. K., Park, J. M., Song, K. S., and Park, H. W. Adaptive mammographic image enhancement using first derivative and local statistics. *IEEE Trans. on Medical Imaging 16*, 5 (1997), pp. 495-502.

[KPW+10] Knopp, J., Prasad, M., Willems, G., et al. Hough transform and 3D SURF for robust three dimensional classification. In *Proc. European Conf. Computer Vision* (2010), pp. 589-602.

[KR82] Kitchen, L., and Rosenfeld, A. Gray-level corner detection. *Pattern Recognition Letters 1*, 2 (1982), pp. 95-102.

[KR88] Koenderink, J. J., and Richards, W. Two-dimensional curve operators. *Journal of the Optical Society of America 5*, 7 (1988), pp. 1136-1141.

[KR94] Konstantinides, K., and Rasure, J. R. The Khoros software development environment for image and signal processing. *IEEE Trans. on Image Processing 3*, 3 (1994), pp. 243-252.

[Kre83] Kreyzig, E. *Advanced Engineering Mathematics*, 5th ed. John Wiley & Sons, 1983.

[Kro87] Krotkov, E. Focusing. *Int. J of Computer Vision 1* (1987), pp. 223-237.

[KS00] Kutulakos, K. N., and Seitz, S. M. A theory of shape by space carving. *Int. J. Computer Vision 38*, 3 (2000), pp. 199-218.

[KS88] Kramer, S. C., and Sorenson, H. W. Bayesian parameter estimation. *IEEE Trans. on Automatic Control 33*, 2 (1988), pp. 217-222.

[KSH04] Ke, Y., Sukthankar, R., and Huston, L. *Efficient Near-duplicate Detection and Sub-image Retrieval*, Proc. ACM Int. Conf. on Multimedia, 2004.

[KSH05] Ke, Y., Sukthankar, R., and Hebert, M. Efficient visual event detection using volumetric features. In *Proc. Int. Conf. Computer Vision* (2005), vol. 1, pp. 166-173.

[KSSS86] Kalvin, A., Schonberg, E., Schwarz, J. T., and Sharir, M. Two-dimensional, model-based, boundary matching using footprints. *Int. J. Robotics Research 5*, 4 (1986), pp. 38-55.

[KT95] Kluge, K., and Thorpe, C. The YARF system for vision-based road following. *Mathematical and Computer Modelling 22* (1995), pp. 213-233.

[KTB87] Kearney, J. K., Thompson, W. B., and Boley, D. L. Optical flow estimation: An error analysis of gradient-based methods with local optimization. *IEEE Trans. on Pattern Analysis and Machine Intelligence 2* (1987), pp. 229-244.

[KTF02] Kojima, A., Tamura, T., and Fukunaga, K. Natural language description of human activities from video images based on concept hierarchy of actions. *Int. J. of Computer Vision 50*, 2 (2002), pp. 171-184.

[Kul71] Kulikowski, J. J. Some stimulus parameters affecting spatial and temporal resolution of human vision. *Vision Research 11*, 1 (1971), pp. 83-93.

[KvD79] Koenderink, J. J., and van Doorn, A. J. The internal representation of solid shape with respect to vision. *Biological Cybernetics 32*, 4 (1979), pp. 211-216.

[KvD92] Koenderink, J. J., and van Doorn, A. J. Surface shape and curvature scales. *Image and Vision Computing 10*, 8 (1992), pp. 557-564.

[KWH+94] Koller, D., Weber, J., Huang, T., Malik, J., Ogasawara, G., Rao, B., and Russell, S. Towards robust automatic traffic scene analysis in real-time. In *Proc. IAPR Int. Conf. Computer Vision & Image Processing* (1994), vol. 1, pp. 126-131.

[KWM94] Koller, D., Weber, J., and Malik, J. Robust multiple car tracking with occlusion reasoning. In *Proc. Euro. Conf. Computer Vision* (1994), pp. 189-196.

[KY99] Kondo, T., and Yan, H. Automatic human face detection and recognition under non-uniform illumination. *Pattern Recognition 32* (1999), pp. 1707-1718.

[KYO+96] Kanade, T., Yoshida, A., Oda, K., *et al.* A stereo machine for video-rate dense depth mapping and its new applications. In *Proc. CVPR'96 IEEE Computer Society Conference on Computer Vision and Pattern Recognition* (1996), pp. 196-202.

[KZB04] Kadir, T., Zisserman, A., and Brady, M. An affine invariant salient region detector. *Proc. Euro. Conf. on Computer Vision* (2004), pp. 228-241.

[KZM05] Kenney, C. S., Zuliani, M., and Manjunath, B. S. An axiomatic approach to corner detection. In *Proc. Computer Vision and Pattern Recognition* (2005), pp. 191-197.

[KZQ05] Kaiqi, H., Zhenyang, W., and Qiao, W. Image enhancement based on the statistics of visual representation. *Image and Vision Computing 23*, 1 (2005), pp. 51-57.

[Lan12] Langford, M. *Advanced Photography*. CRC Press, 2012.

[LAT02] Labayrade, R., Aubert, D., and Tarel, J.-P. Real time obstacle detection in stereovision on non flat road geometry through. In *Proc. Intelligent Vehicle Symposium* (2002), vol. 2, pp. 646-651.

[LB07] Li, X., and Breckon, T. P. Combining motion segmentation and feature based tracking for object classification and anomaly detection. In *Proc. European Conference on Visual Media Production* (2007), pp. I-6.

[LB87] Leavers, V. F., and Boyce, J. F. The Radon transform and its application to shape parametrization in machine vision. *Image and Vision Computing 5*, 2 (1987), pp. 161-166.

[LBD+89] LeCun, Y., Boser, B., Denker, J. S., Henderson, D., Howard, R. E., Hubbard, W., and Jackel, L. D. Backpropagation applied to handwritten zip code recognition. *Neural Computation 1*, 4 (1989), pp. 541-551.

347

[LBDX03] Lee, D. J., Bates, D., Dromey, C., and Xu, X. A vision system performing lip shape analysis for speech pathology research. In *Proc. IECON'03. The 29th Annual Conference of the IEEE Industrial Electronics Society* (2003), vol. 2, pp. 1086-1091.

[LBH08] Lampert, C. H., Blaschko, M. B., and Hofmann, T. Beyond sliding windows: Object localization by efficient subwindow search. In *Proc. Computer Vision and Pattern Recognition* (2008), pp. 1-8.

[LBU11] Luisier, F., Blu, T., and Unser, M. Image denoising in mixed Poisson–Gaussian noise. *IEEE Trans. Image Processing 20*, 3 (2011), pp. 696-708.

[LC87] Lorensen, W., and Cline, H. Marching cubes: a high resolution 3D surface construction algorithm. *Computer Graphics 21* (1987), pp. 163-169.

[LCST06] Liao, M. H.-Y., Chen, D.-Y., Sua, C.-W., and Tyan, H.-R. Real-time event detection and its application to surveillance systems. In *Proc. the International Symposium on Circuits and Systems ISCAS* (2006), p. 4.

[Leb79] Leberl, F. Accuracy analysis of stereo side-looking radar. *Photogrammetric Engineering and Remote Sensing 45* (1979), pp. 1083-1096.

[Lee64] Lees, G. A new method for determining the angularity of particles. *Sedimentology 3*, 1 (1964), pp. 2-21.

[Lee76] Lee, D. N. A theory of visual control of braking based on information about time-to-collision. *Perception 5*, 4 (1976), pp. 437-459.

[LG95] Lambert, G., and Gao, H. Line moments and invariants for real time processing of vectorized contour data. In *Image Analysis and Processing*, C. Braccini, L. DeFloriani, and G. Vernazza, Eds., vol. 974 of *Lecture Notes in Computer Science*. Springer, Berlin/Heidelberg, 1995, pp. 347-352.

[LGX09] Li, J., Gong, S., and Xiang, T. Discovering multi-camera behaviour correlations for on-the-fly global activity prediction and anomaly detection. In *Proc. Int. Workshop on Visual Surveillance* (Kyoto, 2009).

[LGZ+94] Li, W., Gussenhoven, E. J., Zhong, Y., Pieterman, H., van Urk, H., and Bom, K. Temporal averaging for quantification of lumen dimensions in intravascular ultrasound images. *Ultrasound in Medicine & Biology 20*, 2 (1994), pp. 117-122.

[LH06] Leykin, A., and Hammoud, R. Robust multi-pedestrian tracking in thermal-visible surveillance videos. *CVPRW'06. Conference on Computer Vision and Pattern Recognition Workshop* (2006), pp. 136-136.

[LHKG10] Liu, Y., Hel-Or, H., Kaplan, C. S., and Gool, L. V. Computational symmetry in computer vision and computer graphics. *Foundations and Trends in Computer Graphics and Vision 5*, 1-2 (2010), pp. 1-195.

[Lin09] Lindeberg, T. *Scale-space*. John Wiley & Sons, 2009, pp. 2495-2504.

[Liu07] Liu, X. Gradient feature selection for online boosting. In *Proc. Int. Conf. on Computer Vision* (2007).

[LJ11] Li, S. Z., and Jain, A. K. *Handbook of Face Recognition*. 2011, Springer.

[LJL+03] List, P., Joch, A., Lainema, J., et al. Adaptive deblocking filter. *IEEE Trans. on Circuits and Systems for Video Technology 13*, 7 (2003), pp. 614-619.

[LK81] Lucas, B. D., and Kanade, T. An iterative image registration technique with an application to stereo vision. *Int. Joint Conf. on Artificial Intelligence* (1981), pp. 674-679.

[LL92] Leymarie, F., and Levine, M. D. Simulating the grassfire transform using an active contour model. *IEEE Trans. on Pattern Analysis and Machine Intelligence 14*, 1 (1992), pp. 56-75.

[LL93] Leymarie, F., and Levine, M. D. Tracking deformable objects in the plane using an active contour model. *IEEE Trans. on Pattern Analysis and Machine Intelligence 15*, 6 (1993), pp. 617-634.

[LL96] Li, M., and Lavest, J.-M. Some aspects of zoom lens camera calibration. *IEEE Trans. on Pattern Analysis and Machine Intelligence 18*, 11 (1996), pp. 1105-1110.

[LLLS03] Li, Y., Lin, S., Lu, H., and Shum, H. Y. Multiple-cue illumination estimation in textured scenes. In *Proc. Computer Vision* (2003), pp. 1366-1373.

[LLSV99] Lopez, A. M., Lumbreras, F., Serrat, J., and Villanueva, J. J. Evaluation of methods for ridge and valley detection. *IEEE Trans. on Pattern Analysis and Machine Intelligence 21*, 4 (1999), pp. 327-335.

[LM01] Leung, T., and Malik, J. Representing and recognizing the visual appearance of materials using three-dimensional textons. *Int. J. of Computer Vision 43*, 1 (2001), pp. 29–44.

[LM07] Lin, Y., and Medioni, G. Map-enhanced UAV image sequence registration and synchronization of multiple image sequences. In *Proc. IEEE Conference on Computer Vision and Pattern Recognition* (2007), pp. 1–7.

[LMY92] Lee, T., Mumford, D., and Yuille, A. Texture segmentation by minimizing vector-valued energy functionals: The coupled-membrane model. In *Proc. Euro. Conf. Computer Vision* (Berlin/Heidelberg, 1992), Springer, pp. 165–173.

[LN98] Lin, C., and Nevatia, R. Building detection and description from a single intensity image. *Computer Vision and Image Understanding 72*, 2 (1998), pp. 101–121.

[LO83] Lehmberg, R. H., and Obenschain, S. P. Use of induced spatial incoherence for uniform illumination of laser fusion targets. *Optics Communications 46*, 1 (1983), pp. 27–31.

[Lov10] Lovett, S. *Differential Geometry of Manifolds*. Peters, 2010.

[Low04] Lowe, D. G. Distinctive image features from scale-invariant keypoints. *Int. J. of Computer Vision 60*, 2 (2004), pp. 91–110.

[Low85] Lowe, D. G. Visual recognition from spatial correspondence and perceptual organization. In *Proc. IJCAI* (1985), pp. 953–959.

[Low87a] Lowe, D. G. Three-dimensional object recognition from single two-dimensional images. *Artificial Intelligence 31*, 3 (1987), pp. 355–395.

[Low87b] Lowe, D. G. The viewpoint consistency constraint. *Int. J. of Computer Vision 1*, 1 (1987), pp. 57–72.

[Low89] Lowe, D. G. Organization of smooth image curves at multiple scales. *Int. J. Computer Vision 3*, 2 (1989), pp. 119–130.

[Low91] Low, A. *Introductory Computer Vision and Image Processing*. McGraw-Hill, 1991.

[Low99] Lowe, D. G. Object recognition from local scale-invariant features. In *Proc. IEEE Int. Conf. on Computer Vision* (1999), vol. 2, pp. 1150–1157.

[LP11] Li, B., and Peng, L. Balanced multifilter banks for multiple description coding. *IEEE Trans. on Image Processing 20*, 3 (2011), pp. 866–872.

[LP90] Liow, Y.-T., and Pavlidis, T. Use of shadows for extracting buildings in aerial images. *Computer Vision, Graphics, and Image Processing 49*, 2 (1990), pp. 242–277.

[LP96] Liu, F., and Picard, R. W. Periodicity, directionality, and randomness: Wold features for image modeling and retrieval. *IEEE Trans. on Pattern Analysis and Machine Intelligence 18*, 7 (1996), pp. 722–733.

[LQ05] Lhuillier, M., and Quan, L. A quasi-dense approach to surface reconstruction from uncalibrated images. *IEEE Trans. on Pattern Analysis and Machine Intelligence 27*, 3 (2005), pp. 418–433.

[LR85] Lee, C.-H., and Rosenfeld, A. Improved methods of estimating shape from shading using the light source coordinate system. *Artificial Intelligence 26*, 2 (1985), pp. 125–143.

[LRF93] Li, H., Roivainen, P., and Forchheimer, R. 3D motion estimation in model-based facial image coding. *IEEE Trans. on Pattern Analysis and Machine Intelligence 15*, 6 (1993), pp. 545–555.

[LRKH06] Luhmann, T., Robson, S., Kyle, S., and Harley, I. *Close Range Photogrammetry*. Whittles, 2006.

[LRR06] Lerner, R., Rivlin, E., and Rotstein, H. P. Pose and motion recovery from feature correspondences and a digital terrain map. *IEEE Trans. on Pattern Analysis and Machine Intelligence 28*, 9 (2006), pp. 1404–1417.

[LS88] Lam, L., and Suen, C. Y. Structural classification and relaxation matching of totally unconstrained handwritten zip-code numbers. *Pattern Recognition 21*, 1 (1988), pp. 19–31.

[LS90] Liu, H.-C., and Srinath, M. D. Partial shape classification using contour matching in distance transformation. *IEEE Trans. on Pattern Analysis and Machine Intelligence 12*, 11 (1990), pp. 1072–1079.

[LSF09] Li, L.-J., Socher, R., and Fei-Fei, L. Towards total scene understanding: Classification, annotation and segmentation in an automatic framework. In *IEEE Conference on Computer Vision and Pattern Recognition* (2009), pp. 2036–2043.

[LSG07] Leibe, B., Schindler, K., and Gool, L. V. Coupled detection and trajectory estimation for multi-object tracking. *IEEE 11th Int. Conf. Computer Vision* (2007), pp. 1–8.

[LSP05] Lazebnik, S., Schmid, C., and Ponce, J. A sparse texture representation using local affine regions. *IEEE Trans. on Pattern Analysis and Machine Intelligence* 27, 8 (2005), pp. 1265–1278.

[LSP06] Lazebnik, S., Schmid, C., and Ponce, J. Beyond bags of features: Spatial pyramid matching for recognizing natural scene categories. In *Proc. IEEE Conf. on Computer Vision and Pattern Recognition* (2006), pp. 2169–2178.

[LSW88] Lamdan, Y., Schwartz, J. T., and Wolfson, H. J. Object recognition by affine invariant matching. *Computer Society Conference on Computer Vision and Pattern Recognition* (1988), pp. 335–344.

[LTZ96] Low, C. Y., Tian, Q., and Zhang, H. An automatic news video parsing, browsing system indexing and browsing system. In *Proc. ACM Int. Conf. on Multimedia, Boston* (1996), pp. 425–426.

[LW00a] Liu, C., and Wechsler, H. Evolutionary pursuit and its application to face recognition. *IEEE Trans. on Pattern Analysis and Machine Intelligence 22*, 6 (2000), pp. 570–582.

[LW00b] Liu, C., and Wechsler, H. Robust coding schemes for indexing and retrieval from large face databases. *IEEE Trans. on Image Processing 9*, 1 (2000), pp. 132–137.

[LWL00] Liu, S., Wang, Q., and Liu, G. A versatile method of discrete convolution and FFT (DC-FFT) for contact analyses. *Wear 243*, 1 (2000), pp. 101–111.

[LWW00] Li, J., Wang, J. Z., and Wiederhold, G. IRM: integrated region matching for image retrieval. In *Proc. ACM international conference on Multimedia* (2000), ACM, pp. 147–156.

[LWW83] Lohmann, A. W., Weigelt, G., and Wirnitzer, B. Speckle masking in astronomy: triple correlation theory and applications. *Applied Optics 22*, 24 (1983), pp. 4028–4037.

[LWY99] Lin, H.-C., Wang, L.-L., and Yang, S.-N. Regular-texture image retrieval based on texture-primitive extraction. *Image and Vision Computing 17*, 1 (1999), pp. 51–63.

[LXAG09] Li, C., Xu, C., Anderson, A., and Gore, J. MRI tissue classification and bias field estimation based on coherent local intensity clustering: A unified energy minimization framework. *Information Processing in Medical Imaging* (2009), pp. 288–299.

[LXG09] Loy, C., Xiang, T., and Gong, S. Multi-camera activity correlation analysis. In *Proc. Computer Vision and Pattern Recognition* (2009), pp. 1988–1995.

[LZ03] Li, P., Zhang, T., and Pece, A. E. C. Visual contour tracking based on particle filters. *Image and Vision Computing 21*, 1 (2003), pp. 111–123.

[LZ05] Lin, S., and Zhang, L. Determining the radiometric response function from a single gray scale image. *Proc. Computer Vision and Pattern Recognition 2* (2005), pp. 66–73.

[LZ99] Loop, C., and Zhang, Z. Computing rectifying homographies for stereo vision. *IEEE Computer Society Conference on Computer Vision and Pattern Recognition 1* (1999).

[Mac03] MacKay, D. J. C. *Information Theory, Inference, and Learning Algorithms.* Cambridge University Press, Cambridge, 2003.

[Mac92] MacKay, D. J. C. Bayesian interpolation. *Neural Computation 4*, 3 (1992), pp. 415–447.

[Mal89] Mallat, S. G. A theory for multiresolution signal decomposition: The wavelet representation. *IEEE Trans. on Pattern Analysis and Machine Intelligence 11* (1989), pp. 674–693.

[Mar03] Martínez, J. M. MPEG-7 overview. Tech. rep., ISO/IEC JTC 1-SC29-WG11, 2003.

[Mar82] Marr, D. *Vision*. Freeman, 1982.

[Max94] Max, N. Efficient light propagation for multiple anisotropic volume scattering. In *Proc. Eurographics Workshop on Rendering* (1994).

[May05] Maybank, S. J. The Fisher-Rao metric for projective transformations of the line. *Int. J. of Computer Vision 63*, 3 (2005), pp. 191–206.

[MB03] Mokhtarian, F., and Bober, M. *Curvature Scale Space Representation: Theory, Applications and MPEG-7 Standardization*, vol. 25 of *Computational Imaging and Vision Series*. Springer-Verlag, 2003.

[MB73] Muller-Krumbhaar, H., and Binder, K. Dynamic properties of the Monte Carlo method in statistical mechanics. *Journal of Statistical Physics 8*, 1 (1973), pp. 1–24.

[MB90] Meyer, F., and Beucher, S. Morphological segmentation. *J. Visual Communication and Image Representation 1*, 1 (1990), pp. 21–46.

[MB99] Mortensen, E. N., and Barrett, W. A. Toboggan-based intelligent scissors with a four-parameter edge model. In *Proc. Computer Society Conference on Computer Vision and Pattern Recognition* (1999), vol. 2.

[MBG+00] Milickovic, N., Baltas, D., Giannouli, S., *et al.* CT imaging based digitally reconstructed radiographs and their application in brachytherapy. *Phys. Med. Biol. 45*, (2000), pp. 2787–2800.

[MBLS01] Malik, J., Belongie, S., Leung, T., and Shi, J. Contour and texture analysis for image segmentation. *Int. J. Computer Vision 43*, 1 (2001), pp. 7–27.

[MBSL99] Malik, J., Belongie, S., Shi, J., and Leung, T. Textons, contours and regions: Cue integration in image segmentation. In *IEEE Int. Conf. on Computer Vision* (1999), pp. 918–925.

[MC11] Maggio, E., and Cavallaro, A. *Video Tracking: Theory and practice*. John Wiley & Sons, 2011.

[MC96] Morimoto, C., and Chellappa, R. Fast electronic digital image stabilization. In *Proc. Int. Conf. on Pattern Recognition* (1996), vol. 3, pp. 284–288.

[MC97] Madsen, C. B., and Christensen, H. I. A viewpoint planning strategy for determining true angles on polyhedral objects by camera alignment. *IEEE Trans. on Pattern Analysis and Machine Intelligence 19*, 2 (1997), pp. 158–163.

[MCB+01] Medioni, G., Cohen, I., Brémond, F., *et al.* Event detection and analysis from video streams. *IEEE Trans. on Pattern Analysis and Machine Intelligence 23*, 8 (2001), pp. 873–889.

[McD04] McDonald, J. N. Phase retrieval and magnitude retrieval of entire functions. *Journal of Fourier Analysis and Applications 10*, 3 (2004), pp. 259–267.

[MCUP04] Matas, J., Chum, O., Urban, M., and Pajdla, T. Robust wide-baseline stereo from maximally stable extremal regions. *Image and Vision Computing 22*, 10 (2004), pp. 761–767.

[MDN97] Meyer, D., Denzler, J., and Niemann, H. Model based extraction of articulated objects in image sequences for gait analysis. In *Int. Conf. on Image Processing* (1997), vol. 3, pp. 78–81.

[MDWW04] Ma, Y., Ding, X., Wang, Z., and Wang, N. Robust precise eye location under probabilistic framework. In *Proc. IEEE Int. Conf. on Automatic Face and Gesture Recognition* (2004), pp. 339–344.

[ME88] Matthies, L., and Elfes, A. Integration of sonar and stereo range data using a grid-based representation. In *Proc. IEEE Int. Conf. on Robotics and Automation* (1988), pp. 727–733.

[MEYD11] Matov, A., Edvall, M. M., Yang, G., and Danuser, G. Optimal-flow minimum-cost correspondence assignment in particle flow tracking. *Computer Vision and Image Understanding 115*, 4 (2011), pp. 531–540.

[MGC96] McKenna, S., Gong, S., and Collins, J. J. Face tracking and pose representation. *British Machine Vision Conference 2* (1996), pp. 755–764.

[MGD98] Montesinos, P., Gouet, V., and Deriche, R. Differential invariants for color images. In *Proc. the IEEE Fourteenth Int. Conf. on Pattern Recognition* (1998), vol. 1, pp. 838–840.

[MH80]   Marr, D., and Hildreth, E. Theory of edge detection. In *Proc. the Royal Society of London Series B. Biological Sciences* (1980), vol. 207, pp. 187-217.

[MHYS04]   Manay, S., Hong, B.-W., Yezzi, A., and Soatto, S. Integral invariant signatures. In *Proc. Euro. Conf. Computer Vision* (2004), pp. 87-99.

[Mir99]   Mirkin, B. Concept learning and feature selection based on square-error clustering. *Machine Learning 35*, 1 (1999), pp. 25-39.

[Mit97]   Mitchell, T. M. *Machine Learning*. McGraw-Hill, New York, 1997.

[MK00]   Mora, C. F., and Kwan, A. K. H. Sphericity, shape factor, and convexity measurement of coarse aggregate for concrete using digital image processing. *Cement and Concrete Research 30*, 3 (2000), pp. 351-358.

[MK07]   Morris, N. J. W., and Kutulakos, K. N. Reconstructing the surface of inhomogeneous transparent scenes by scatter-trace photography. In *Proc. IEEE Int. Conf. on Computer Vision* (2007).

[MK90]   Marefat, M., and Kashyap, R. L. Geometric reasoning for recognition of three-dimensional object features. *IEEE Trans. on Pattern Analysis and Machine Intelligence 12*, 10 (1990), pp. 949-965.

[MKB79]   Mardia, K. V., Kent, J. T., and Bibby, J. M. *Multivariate Analysis*. Academic Press, London, 1979.

[MKK02]   Matas, J., Koubaroulis, D., and Kittler, J. The multimodal neighborhood signature for modeling object color appearance and applications in object recognition and image retrieval. *Computer Vision and Image Understanding 88*, 1 (2002), pp. 1-23.

[ML05]   Murray, D., and Little, J. J. Patchlets: Representing stereo vision data with surface elements. *WACV/MOTIONS'05 Volume 1. Seventh IEEE Workshops on Application of Computer Vision 1* (2005), pp. 192-199.

[MLF07]   Moreno-Noguer, F., Lepetit, V., and Fua, P. Accurate non-iterative O(n) solution to the PnP problem. In *Proc. Int. Conf. Computer Vision* (2007), pp. 1-8.

[MM02]   Masutani, Y., and MacMahon, H. Computerized detection of pulmonary embolism in spiral CT angiography based on volumetric image analysis. *IEEE Trans. on Medical Imaging 21*, 12 (2002), pp. 1517-1523.

[MM09]   Maji, S., and Malik, J. Object detection using a max-margin Hough transform. In *Proc. CVPR* (2009).

[MM95]   McLauchlan, P. F., and Murray, D. W. A unifying framework for structure and motion recovery from image sequences. In *Proc. Int. Conf. Computer Vision* (1995), pp. 314-320.

[MMG99]   Mindru, F., Moons, T., and Gool, L. V. Recognizing color patterns irrespective of viewpoint and illumination. In *IEEE Computer Society Conference on Computer Vision and Pattern Recognition* (1999), vol. 1, IEEE.

[MMJP09]   Maltoni, D., Maio, D., Jain, A. K., and Prabhakar, S. *Handbook of Fingerprint Recognition*. Springer, 2009.

[MMK04]   Martinez, A. M., Mittrapiyanuruk, P., and Kak, A. C. On combining graph-partitioning with non-parametric clustering for image segmentation. *Computer Vision and Image Understanding 95*, 1 (2004), pp. 72-85.

[MMN06]   Migliore, D. A., Matteucci, M., and Naccari, M. A revaluation of frame difference in fast and robust motion detection. In *Int. Workshop on Video Surveillance and Sensor Networks* (2006), pp. 215-218.

[MMP02]   Mitra, P., Murthy, C. A., and Pal, S. K. Unsupervised feature selection using feature similarity. *IEEE Trans. Pattern Analysis and Machine Intelligence 24*, 4 (2002), pp. 301-312.

[MN84]   Medioni, G., and Nevatia, R. Matching images using linear features. *IEEE Trans. on Pattern Analysis and Machine Intelligence 6* (1984), pp. 675-685.

[MNTT12]   Matsuyama, T., Nobuhara, S., Takai, T., and Tung, T. *3D Video and Its Applications*. Springer, 2012.

[MO90]   Ma, J., and Olsen, S. I. Depth from zooming. *J. Optical Society of America A 7* (1990), pp. 1883-1890.

[Moe11]   Moeslund, T. B. *Visual Analysis of Humans*. Springer, 2011.

[Moh98]   Mohan, R. Video sequence matching. In *Proc. IEEE Int. Conf. on Acoustics, Speech and Signal Processing* (1998), vol. 6, pp. 3697-3700.

[Mon86] Montanvert, A. Medial line: graph representation and shape description. In *Proc. Int. Conf. on Pattern Recognition* (Paris, France, 1986), Paris, pp. 430–432.

[Mor88] Moravec, H. P. Sensor fusion in certainty grids for mobile robots. *AI Magazine 9*, 2 (1988), 61.

[Mor95] Moreton, H. P. Simplified curve and surface interrogation via mathematical packages and graphics libraries and hardware. *Computer-Aided Design 27*, 7 (1995), pp. 523–543.

[MP04] Micusik, B., and Pajdla, T. Autocalibration & 3D reconstruction with non-central catadioptric cameras. In *Proc. Computer Vision and Pattern Recognition* (2004), vol. 1, pp. I-pp. 58-I-65.

[MP79] Marr, D., and Poggio, T. A computational theory of human stereo vision. In *Proc. the Royal Society of London, Series B. Biological Sciences* (1979), vol. 204, pp. 301–328.

[MPT05] McNeely, W. A., Puterbaugh, K. D., and Troy, J. J. Six degree-of-freedom haptic rendering using voxel sampling. In *ACM SIGGRAPH 2005 Courses*. ACM, 2005, p. 42.

[MPZ+03] Malamas, E. N., Petrakis, E. G. M., Zervakis, M., et al. A survey on industrial vision systems, applications and tools. *Image and Vision Computing 21*, 2 (2003), pp. 171–188.

[MR81] Morgenthaler, D. G., and Rosenfeld, A. Multidimensional edge detection by hypersurface fitting. *IEEE Trans. on Pattern Analysis and Machine Intelligence 4* (1981), pp. 482–486.

[MR98] Morris, D. D., and Rehg, J. M. Singularity analysis for articulated object tracking. In *Proc. the IEEE Conference on Computer Vision and Pattern Recognition* (1998).

[MRS08] Manning, C. D., Raghavan, P., and Schütze, H. *Introduction to Information Retrieval*. Cambridge University Press, Cambridge, 2008.

[MS03] Melgani, F., and Serpico, S. B. A Markov random field approach to spatio-temporal contextual image classification. *IEEE Trans. on Geoscience and Remote Sensing 41*, 11 (2003), pp. 2478–2487.

[MS04] Mikolajczyk, K., and Schmid, C. Scale & affine invariant interest point detectors. *Int. J. Computer Vision 60*, 1 (2004), pp. 63–86.

[MS79] Mulder, H. M., and Schrijver, A. Median graphs and Helly hypergraphs. *Discrete Mathematics 15*, 1 (1979), pp. 41–50.

[MS94] Morel, J.-M., and Solimini, S. *Variational Models for Image Segmentation: With seven image processing experiments*. Birkhauser, 1994.

[MS95] Maciel, P. W. C., and Shirley, P. Visual navigation of large environments using textured clusters. In *Proc. Symposium on Interactive 3D Graphics* (1995), ACM, p. 95ff.

[MSMP08] Meyer, B., Stich, T., Magnor, M., and Pollefeys, M. *Subframe Temporal Alignment of Non-Stationary Cameras*. Proc. British Machine Vision Conf, 2008.

[MSS92] Meyers, D., Skinner, S., and Sloan, K. Surfaces from contours. *ACM Trans. Graphics (TOG) 11*, 3 (1992), pp. 228–258.

[MTG97] Moezzi, S., Tai, L.-C., and Gerard, P. Virtual view generation for 3D digital video. *IEEE, Multimedia 4*, 1 (1997), pp. 18–26.

[MTHI03] Miyazaki, D., Tan, R. T., Hara, K., and Ikeuchi, K. Polarization-based inverse rendering from a single view. In *Proc. Int. Conf. Computer Vision* (2003), pp. 982–987.

[Mur12] Murphy, K. P. *Machine Learning: A probabilistic perspective*. MIT Press, Cambridge, Massachusetts, 2012.

[MvSG90] Mallot, H. A., von Seelen, W., and Giannakopoulos, F. Neural mapping and space-variant image processing. *Neural Networks 3*, 3 (1990), pp. 245–263.

[MYA95] Madigan, D., York, J., and Allard, D. Bayesian graphical models for discrete data. *International Statistical Review/Revue Internationale de Statistique* (1995), pp. 215–232.

[Mye62] Myers, N. O. Characterization of surface roughness. *Wear 5*, 3 (1962), pp. 182–189.

[MZ00] Matsumoto, Y., and Zelinsky, A. An algorithm for real-time stereo vision implementation of head pose and gaze direction measurement. In *Proc. IEEE Int. Conf. on Automatic Face and Gesture Recognition* (2000), pp. 499-504.

[MZ82] Mizumoto, M., and Zimmermann, H.-J. Comparison of fuzzy reasoning methods. *Fuzzy Sets and Systems 8*, 3 (1982), pp. 253-283.

[MZ89] Modestino, J. W., and Zhang, J. A Markov random field model-based approach to image interpretation. In *Proc. IEEE Computer Society Conference on Computer Vision and Pattern Recognition* (1989), pp. 458-465.

[MZS03] Mikolajczyk, K., Zisserman, A., and Schmid, C. Shape recognition with edge-based features. In *Proc. British Machine Vision Conf.* (2003), vol. 2, pp. 779-788.

[NA02] Neumann, J., and Aloimonos, Y. Spatio-temporal stereo using multi-resolution subdivision surfaces. *Int. J. Computer Vision 47*, 1 (2002), pp. 181-193.

[NA05] Nixon, M., and Aguado, A. *Feature Extraction & Image Processing*. Elsevier Newnes, 2005.

[Nag00] Nagy, G. Twenty years of document image analysis in PAMI. *IEEE Trans. on Pattern Analysis and Machine Intelligence 22*, 1 (2000), pp. 38-62.

[Nag90] Nagel, H. Extending the oriented smoothness constraint into the temporal domain and the estimation of derivatives of optical flow. In *Proc. Euro. Conf. Computer Vision* (1990), pp. 139-148.

[Nal93] Nalwa, V. S. *A Guided Tour of Computer Vision*. Addison-Wesley, 1993.

[Nar81] Narendra, P. M. A separable median filter for image noise smoothing. *IEEE Trans. on Pattern Analysis and Machine Intelligence 1* (1981), pp. 20-29.

[Nay06] Nayar, S. K. Computational cameras: Redefining the image. *Computer 39*, 8 (2006), pp. 30-38.

[NB04] Nayar, S. K., and Ben-Ezra, M. Motion-based motion deblurring. *IEEE Trans. on Pattern Analysis and Machine Intelligence 26*, 6 (2004), pp. 689-698.

[NB93] Nayar, S. K., and Bolle, R. M. Reflectance ratio: A photometric invariant for object recognition. In *Proc. Int. Conf. Computer Vision* (1993), pp. 280-285.

[NBB04] Nayar, S. K., Branzoi, V., and Boult, T. E. Programmable imaging using a digital micromirror array. In *Proc. Int. Conf. Computer Vision and Pattern Recognition* (2004), pp. 436-443.

[NCLS06] Ng, T. T., Chang, S. F., Lin, C. Y., and Sun, Q. Passive-blind image forensics. *Multimedia Security Technologies for Digital Rights* (2006), pp. 383-412.

[ND10] Newcombe, R. A., and Davison, A. J. Live dense reconstruction with a single moving camera. In *Conference on Computer Vision and Pattern Recognition (CVPR)* (2010), pp. 1498-1505.

[Nev82] Nevatia, R. *Machine Perception*. Prentice Hall, 1982.

[NG99] Ng, J., and Gong, S. Multi-view face detection and pose estimation using a composite support vector machine across the view sphere. In *Proc. International Workshop on Recognition, Analysis, and Tracking of Faces and Gestures in Real-Time Systems* (1999), pp. 14-21.

[NH01] Naphade, M. R., and Huang, T. S. A probabilistic framework for semantic video indexing, filtering, and retrieval. *IEEE Trans. on Multimedia 3*, 1 (2001), pp. 141-151.

[NIK90] Nayar, S. K., Ikeuchi, K., and Kanade, T. Shape from interreflections. In *Proc. Int. Conf. on Computer Vision* (1990), pp. 2-11.

[Nis01] Nister, D. Calibration with robust use of cheirality by quasi-affine reconstruction of the set of camera projection centres. In *Proc. Int. Conf. Computer Vision* (2001), vol. 2, pp. 116-123.

[NK97] Neugebauer, P. J., and Klein, K. Adaptive triangulation of objects reconstructed from multiple range images. *IEEE Visualization 97, Late Breaking Hot Topics* (1997), pp. 20-24.

[NM90] Nitzberg, M., and Mumford, D. B. The 2.1-D sketch. In *Proc. Int. Conf. on Computer Vision* (1990), pp. 138-144.

[NMP01] Nedevschi, S., Marita, T., and Puiu, D. Intermediate representation in model based recognition using straight line and ellipsoidal arc primitives. *Proc. Int. Conf. on Image Analysis and Processing* (2001), pp. 156-161.

[NMRZ00] Newman, R., Matsumoto, Y., Rougeaux, S., and Zelinsky, A. Real-time stereo tracking for head pose and gaze estimation. In *Proc. IEEE Int. Conf. on Automatic Face and Gesture Recognition* (2000), pp. 122-128.

[NN02] Narasimhan, S. G., and Nayar, S. K. Vision and the atmosphere. *Int. J. Computer Vision 48*, 3 (2002), pp. 233-254.

[NN99] Nayar, S. K., and Narasimhan, S. G. Vision in bad weather. In *Proc. IEEE Int. Conf. on Computer Vision* (1999), vol. 2, pp. 820-827.

[Nob69] Noble, B. *Applied Linear Algebra*. Prentice Hall, 1969.

[NP87] Nalwa, V. S., and Pauchon, E. Edgel aggregation and edge description. *Computer Vision, Graphics, and Image Processing 40*, 1 (1987), pp. 79-94.

[NRCC08] Nam, Y., Ryu, J., Choi, Y.-J., and Cho, W.-D. Learning spatio-temporal topology of a multi-camera network by tracking multiple people. *Int. J. of Signal Processing 4*, 4 (2008), 254.

[NS06] Nister, D., and Stewenius, H. Scalable recognition with a vocabulary tree. In *Proc. Computer Vision and Pattern Recognition* (2006), pp. 2161-2168.

[NSNI92] Nomura, Y., Sagara, M., Naruse, H., and Ide, A. Simple calibration algorithm for high-distortion lens camera. *IEEE Trans. on Pattern Analysis and Machine Intelligence 14*, 11 (1992), pp. 1095-1099.

[NWF08] Niebles, J. C., Wang, H., and Fei-Fei, L. Unsupervised learning of human action categories using spatial-temporal words. *Int. J. of Computer Vision 79*, 3 (2008), pp. 299-318.

[OAE95] Olshausen, B. A., Anderson, C. H., and Essen, D. C. A multiscale dynamic routing circuit for forming size-and position-invariant object representations. *J. Computational Neuroscience 2*, 1 (1995), pp. 45-62.

[OCDD01] Oh, B. M., Chen, M., Dorsey, J., and Durand, F. Image-based modeling and photo editing. In *Proc. Computer Graphics and Interactive Techniques* (2001), pp. 433-442.

[OCEG04] Ozden, K. E., Cornelis, K., Eycken, L. V., and Gool, L. V. Reconstructing 3D independent motions using non-accidentalness. In *Proc. IEEE Computer Society Conference on Computer Vision and Pattern Recognition* (2004), vol. 1, pp. I-819.

[OG78] O'Gorman, F. Edge detection using Walsh functions. *Artificial Intelligence 10*, 2 (1978), pp. 215-223.

[OGFN05] Otazu, X., Gonzalez-Audicana, M., Fors, O., and Nunez, J. Introduction of sensor spectral response into image fusion methods: Application to wavelet-based methods. *IEEE Trans. on Geoscience and Remote Sensing 43*, 10 (2005), pp. 2376-2385.

[OHG02] Oliver, N., Horvitz, E., and Garg, A. Layered representations for human activity recognition. In *Proc. Int. Conf. on Multimodal Interfaces* (2002), pp. 3-8.

[OI06] Ohnishi, N., and Imiya, A. Dominant plane detection from optical flow for robot navigation. *Pattern Recognition Letters 27*, 9 (2006), pp. 1009-1021.

[OIA01] Omachi, S., Inoue, M., and Aso, H. Structure extraction from decorated characters using multiscale images. *IEEE Trans. on Pattern Analysis and Machine Intelligence 23*, 3 (2001), pp. 315-322.

[OK85] Ohta, Y., and Kanade, T. Stereo by intra-and inter-scanline search using dynamic programming. *IEEE Trans. on Pattern Analysis and Machine Intelligence 2* (1985), pp. 139-154.

[OK93] Okutomi, M., and Kanade, T. A multiple-baseline stereo. *IEEE Trans. on Pattern Analysis and Machine Intelligence 15*, 4 (1993), pp. 353-363.

[OK98] Ohta, N., and Kanatani, K. Optimal estimation of three-dimensional rotation and reliability evaluation. In *Proc. Euro. Conf. Computer Vision* (1998), pp. 175-187.

[Oko82] Okoshi, T. Heterodyne and coherent optical fiber communications: recent progress. *IEEE Trans. on Microwave Theory and Techniques 30*, 8 (1982), pp. 1138-1149.

[Oli93] Oliensis, J. Local reproducible smoothing without shrinkage. *IEEE Trans. on Pattern Analysis and Machine Intelligence 15*, 3 (1993), pp. 307-312.

[Ols00] Olson, C. F. Probabilistic self-localization for mobile robots. *IEEE Trans. on Robotics and Automation 16*, 1 (2000), pp. 55-66.

[OM09] Olhede, S. C., and Metikas, G. The monogenic wavelet transform. *IEEE Trans. Signal Processing 57*, 9 (2009), pp. 3426-3441.

[OM84] O'Callaghan, J. F., and Mark, D. M. The extraction of drainage networks from digital elevation data. *Computer Vision, Graphics, and Image Processing 28*, 3 (1984), pp. 323-344.

[OM98] Osberger, W., and Maeder, A. J. Automatic identification of perceptually important regions in an image. In *Proc. Int. Conf. on Pattern Recognition* (1998), vol. 1, pp. 701-704.

[ON94] Oren, M., and Nayar, S. K. Generalization of Lambert's reflectance model. In *ACM 21st Annual Conf. on Computer Graphics and Interactive Techniques (SIGGRAPH)* (1994), pp. 239-246.

[OP89] Olson, T. J., and Potter, R. D. Real time vergence control. In *Proc. IEEE Computer Society Conference on Computer Vision and Pattern Recognition* (1989), pp. 404-409.

[OP97] O'Ruanaidh, J. J. K., and Pun, T. Rotation, scale and translation invariant digital image watermarking. In *Proc. Int. Conf. on Image Processing* (1997), vol. 1, pp. 536-539.

[OPM02] Ojala, T., Pietikainen, M., and Maenpaa, T. Multiresolution gray-scale and rotation invariant texture classification with local binary patterns. *IEEE Trans. on Pattern Analysis and Machine Intelligence 24*, 7 (2002), pp. 971-987.

[OT01] Olivia, A., and Torralba, A. Modeling the shape of the scene: a holistic representation of the spatial envelope. *Int. J. Computer Vision 42*, 3 (2001), pp. 145-175.

[OT99] Olver, P. J. *Classical Invariant Theory*. No. 44 in London Mathematical Society Student Texts. Cambridge University Press, Cambridge, 1999.

[Oys99] Oyster, C. W. *The Human Eye: Structure and Function*. Sinauer Associates, 1999.

[PA06] Park, S., and Aggarwal, J. K. Simultaneous tracking of multiple body parts of interacting persons. *Computer Vision and Image Understanding 102*, 1 (2006), pp. 1-21.

[Pal99] Palmer, S. E. *Vision Science: Photons to Phenomenology*. MIT Press, Cambridge, Massachusetts, 1999.

[Pap91] Papoulis, A. *Probability, Random Variables, and Stochastic Processes*, 3rd ed. McGraw-Hill, New York, 1991.

[Par02] Paragios, N. A variational approach for the segmentation of the left ventricle in cardiac image analysis. *Int. J. Computer Vision 50*, 3 (2002), pp. 345-362.

[Par82] Parker, D. L. Optimal short scan convolution reconstruction for fan beam CT. *Medical Physics 9*, 2 (1982).

[Paw06] Pawley, J. *Handbook of Biological Confocal Microscopy*, vol. 236. Springer, 2006.

[PB01] Poon, T. C., and Banerjee, P. P. *Contemporary Optical Image Processing with MATLAB*. Elsevier, Science, 2001.

[PBP01] Peleg, S., Ben-Ezra, M., and Pritch, Y. Omnistereo: Panoramic stereo imaging. *IEEE Trans. on Pattern Analysis and Machine Intelligence 23*, 3 (2001), pp. 279-290.

[PCM89] Ponce, J., Chelberg, D., and Mann, W. B. Invariant properties of straight homogeneous generalized cylinders and their contours. *IEEE Trans. on Pattern Analysis and Machine Intelligence 11*, 9 (1989), pp. 951-966.

[PD02] Paragios, N., and Deriche, R. Geodesic active regions and level set methods for supervised texture segmentation. *Int. J. Computer Vision 46*, 3 (2002), pp. 223-247.

[PD03] Porikli, F., and Divakaran, A. Multi-camera calibration object tracking and query generation. In *Proc. Multimedia and Expo* (2003), vol. 1, pp. 653-656.

[Pea88] Pearl, J. *Probabilistic Reasoning in Intelligent Systems: Networks of plausible inference*. Morgan Kaufmann, San Mateo, CA, 1988.

[Pen84] Pentland, A. P. Fractal-based description of natural scenes. *IEEE Trans. on Pattern Analysis and Machine Intelligence 6* (1984), pp. 661-674.

[Pet95] Peters II, R. A. A new algorithm for image noise reduction using mathematical morphology. *IEEE Trans. on Image Processing 4*, 5 (1995), pp. 1554-568.

[PGB03] Perez, P., Gangnet, M., and Blake, A. Poisson image editing. *ACM Trans. Graphics (TOG) 22*, 3 (2003), pp. 313-318.

[PGM96] Ponce, J., and Genc, Y. Epipolar geometry and linear subspace methods: A new approach to weak calibration. *Int. J. of Computer Vision 28* (1996), pp. 776-781.

[PGPO94] Proesmans, M., Gool, L. V., Pauwels, E., and Oosterlinck, A. Determination of optical flow and its discontinuities using non-linear diffusion. In *Proc. Euro. Conf. Computer Vision* (1994), pp. 294-304.

[PH03] Pottmann, H., and Hofer, M. Geometry of the squared distance function to curves and surfaces. *Visualization and Mathematics III* (2003), pp. 221-242.

[PKB07] Poli, R., Kennedy, J., and Blackwell, T. Particle swarm optimization: an overview. *Swarm Intelligence 1*, 1 (2007), pp. 33-57.

[PKG99] Pollefeys, M., Koch, R., and Gool, L. V. A simple and efficient rectification method for general motion. In *Proc. IEEE Int. Conf. on Computer Vision* (1999), pp. 496-501.

[PKK08] Papakostas, G. A., Karakasis, E. G., and Koulouriotis, D. E. Efficient and accurate computation of geometric moments on gray-scale images. *Pattern Recognition 41*, 6 (2008), pp. 1895-1904.

[PKVG00] Pollefeys, M., Koch, R., Vergauwen, M., and Gool, L. V. Automated reconstruction of 3D scenes from sequences of images. *ISPRS Journal of Photogrammetry and Remote Sensing 55*, 4 (2000), pp. 251-267.

[PL01] Pears, N., and Liang, B. Ground plane segmentation for mobile robot visual navigation. In *Proc. IEEE/RSJ Int. Conf. on Intelligent Robots and Systems* (2001), vol. 3, pp. 1513-1518.

[PM90] Perona, P., and Malik, J. Scale-space and edge detection using anisotropic diffusion. *IEEE Trans. on Pattern Analysis and Machine Intelligence 12* (1990), pp. 629-639.

[PM96] Pegard, C., and Mouaddib, E.-M. A mobile robot using a panoramic view. In *IEEE Int. Conf. on Robotics and Automation* (1996), vol. 1, pp. 89-94.

[PMF85] Pollard, S. B., Mayhew, J. E., and Frisby, J. P. PMF: a stereo correspondence algorithm using a disparity gradient limit. *Perception* (1985).

[PMPP04] Plaza, A., Martinez, P., Perez, R., and Plaza, J. A new approach to mixed pixel classification of hyperspectral imagery based on extended morphological profiles. *Pattern Recognition 37*, 6 (2004), pp. 1097-1116.

[PMRR00] Phillips, P., Moon, H., Rizvi, S., and Rauss, P. The FERET evaluation methodology for face-recognition algorithms. *IEEE Trans. Pattern Analysis and Machine Intelligence 22*, 10 (2000), pp. 1090-1104.

[Pol00] Pollefeys, M. Obtaining 3D models with a hand-held camera/3D modeling from images. In *Proc. Euro. Conf. Computer Vision, Course/Tutorial notes, presented at SIGGRAPH 2002/2001/DIM 2001/2003* (2000).

[Pom89] Pomerleau, D. A. ALVINN: An autonomous land vehicle in a neural network. Technical report, AIP-77, Carnegie Mellon University, 1989.

[PP03] Pitrelli, J. F., and Perrone, M. P. Confidence-scoring post-processing for off-line handwritten-character recognition verification. In *Proc. Int. Conf. on Document Analysis and Recognition* (2003), IEEE, pp. 278-282.

[PR87] Peng, Y., and Reggia, J. A. A probabilistic causal model for diagnostic problem solving, Part I: Integrating symbolic causal inference with numeric probabilistic inference. *IEEE Trans. on Systems, Man and Cybernetics 17*, 2 (1987), pp. 146-162.

[PR88] Phillips, T. H., and Rosenfeld, A. Decomposition of 3D objects into compact subobjects by analysis of cross-sections. *Image and Vision Computing 6*, 1 (1988), pp. 33-51.

[Pra80] Prazdny, K. Egomotion and relative depth map from optical flow. *Biological Cybernetics 36*, 2 (1980), pp. 87-102.

[Pri12] Prince, S. J. D. *Computer Vision: Models, learning, and inference*. Cambridge University Press, Cambridge, 2012.

[PRS+95] Piper, J., Rutovitz, D., Sudar, D., Kallioniemi, A., Kallioniemi, O. P., Waldman, F. M., Gray, J. W., and Pinkel, D. Computer image analysis of comparative genomic hybridization. *Cytometry 19*, 1 (1995), pp. 10-26.

[PS00] Portilla, J., and Simoncelli, E. P. A parametric texture model based on joint statistics of complex wavelet coefficients. *Int. J. Computer Vision 40*, 1 (2000), pp. 49-70.

[PS06] Petrou, M., and Sevilla, P. G. *Image Processing: Dealing with Texture*. John Wiley & Sons, 2006.

[PS95] Pu, C. C., and Shih, F. Y. Threshold decomposition of gray-scale soft morphology into binary soft morphology. *Graphical Models and Image Processing 57*, 6 (1995), pp. 522-526.

[PSG01] Powell, M. W., Sarkar, S., and Goldgof, D. A simple strategy for calibrating the geometry of light sources. *IEEE Trans. on Pattern Analysis and Machine Intelligence 23*, 9 (2001), pp. 1022-1027.

[PTVF92] Press, W. H., Teukolsky, S. A., Vetterling, W. T., and Flannery, B. P. *Numerical Recipes in C*, second ed. Cambridge University Press, Cambridge, 1992.

[PVJ01] Picard, R. W., Vyzas, E., and Healey, J. Toward machine emotional intelligence: analysis of affective physiological state. *IEEE Trans. on Pattern Analysis and Machine Intelligence 23*, 10 (2001), pp. 1175-1191.

[PWS08] Pan, G., Wu, Z., and Sun, L. *Liveness Detection for Face Recognition*. 2008, pp. 109-124.

[PXK10] Pew-Thian, Y., Xudong, J., and Kot, A. Two-dimensional polar harmonic transforms for invariant image representation. *IEEE Trans. on Pattern Analysis and Machine Intelligence 32*, 7 (2010), pp. 1259-1270.

[PY01] Park, H., and Yoo, J. Structuring element decomposition for efficient implementation of morphological filters. In *Vision, Image and Signal Processing* (2001), vol. 148, IET, pp. 31-35.

[PY09] Poullis, C., and You, S. Automatic reconstruction of cities from remote sensor data. *CVPR 2009. IEEE Conference on Computer Vision and Pattern Recognition* (2009), pp. 2775-2782.

[QM89] Quan, L., and Mohr, R. Determining perspective structures using hierarchical Hough transform. *Pattern Recognition Letters 9*, 4 (1989), pp. 279-286.

[Qua93] Quan, L. Affine stereo calibration for relative affine shape reconstruction. In *Proc. British Machine Vision Conference* (1993), pp. 659-668.

[RA06] Ryoo, M. S., and Aggarwal, J. K. Recognition of composite human activities through context-free grammar based representation. In *Proc. IEEE Computer Society Conference on Computer Vision and Pattern Recognition* (2006), vol. 2, pp. 1709-1718.

[RA09] Ryoo, M. S., and Aggarwal, J. K. Spatio-temporal relationship match: Video structure comparison for recognition of complex human activities. In *Proc. IEEE Int. Conf. on Computer Vision* (2009), pp. 1593-1600.

[Rav98] Raven, C. Numerical removal of ring artifacts in microtomography or as the consequence of other computational or optical properties. *Review of Scientific Instruments 69*, 8 (1998), pp. 2978-2980.

[RB95] Rao, R. P. N., and Ballard, D. H. Object indexing using an iconic sparse distributed memory. In *Proc. Inf. Conf. on Computer Vision* (1995), pp. 24-31.

[RBB09] Rusu, R. B., Blodow, N., and Beetz, M. Fast point feature histograms (FPFH) for 3D registration. In *IEEE Int. Conf. on Robotics and Automation* (2009), pp. 3212-3217.

[RBV06] Romdhani, S., Blanz, V., and Vetter, T. Face identification by fitting a 3D morphable model using linear shape and texture error functions. In *Proc. Euro. Conf. Computer Vision* (2006), pp. 3-19.

[RC02] Rother, C., and Carlsson, S. Linear multi view reconstruction and camera recovery using a reference plane. *Int. J. of Computer Vision 49* (2002), pp. 117-141.

[RC96] Reddy, B. S., and Chatterji, B. N. An FFT-based technique for translation, rotation, and scale-invariant image registration. *IEEE Trans. on Image Processing 5*, 8 (1996), pp. 1266–1271.

[RC99] Rekeczky, C., and Chua, L. O. Computing with front propagation: Active contour and skeleton models in continuous-time CNN. *The Journal of VLSI Signal Processing 23*, 2 (1999), pp. 373–402.

[RCJ95] Ratha, N. K., Chen, S., and Jain, A. K. Adaptive flow orientation-based feature extraction in fingerprint images. *Pattern Recognition 28*, 11 (1995), pp. 1657–1672.

[RD06] Rosten, E., and Drummond, T. Machine learning for high-speed corner detection. In *Proc. Euro. Conf. on Computer Vision* (2006), pp. 430–443.

[RDD03] Rosenfeld, A., Doermann, D., and DeMenthon, D., Eds. *Video Mining*. Kluwer Academic, 2003.

[RDR94] Rivlin, E., Dickinson, S. J., and Rosenfeld, A. Recognition by functional parts. In *Proc. IEEE Computer Society Conference on Computer Vision and Pattern Recognition (CVPR'94)* (1994), pp. 267–274.

[Reg86] Regan, D. Visual processing of four kinds of relative motion. *Vision Research 26*, 1 (1986), pp. 127–145.

[RG08] Ratha, N. K., and Govindaraju, V. *Advances in Biometrics: Sensors, algorithms and systems*. Springer, 2008.

[RGS08] Reforgiato, D., Gutierrez, R., and Shasha, D. GraphClust: A method for clustering database of graphs. *J. Information & Knowledge Management 7*, 4 (2008), pp. 231–241.

[RH95] Rigoutsos, I., and Hummel, R. A Bayesian approach to model matching with geometric hashing. *Computer Vision and Image Understanding 62*, 1 (1995), pp. 11–26.

[RHBL07] Ranzato, M. A., Huang, F. J., Boureau, Y. L., and LeCun, Y. Unsupervised learning of invariant feature hierarchies with applications to object recognition. In *IEEE Conference on Computer Vision and Pattern Recognition* (2007), pp. 1–8.

[RHD+10] Reinhard, E., Heidrich, W., Debevec, P., Pattanaik, S., Ward, G., and Myszkowski, K. *High dynamic range imaging: acquisition, display, and image-based lighting*. Morgan Kaufmann, 2010.

[Ric03] Richardson, I. E. G. *H.264 and MPEG-4 Video Compression: Video Coding for Next Generation Multimedia*. John Wiley & Sons, 2003.

[RK82] Rosenfeld, A., and Kak, A. C. *Digital Picture Processing*. Academic Press, 1982.

[RK94] Rehg, J., and Kanade, T. Visual tracking of high DOF articulated structures: An application to human hand tracking. In *Proc. Euro. Conf. Computer Vision* (1994), pp. 35–46.

[RK95] Rehg, J. M., and Kanade, T. Model-based tracking of self-occluding articulated objects. In *Proc. Int. Conf. Computer Vision* (1995).

[RK96] Rahardja, K., and Kosaka, A. Vision-based bin-picking: recognition and localization of multiple complex objects using simple visual cues. In *IEEE/RSJ Int. Conf. on Intelligent Robots and Systems* (1996), pp. 1448–1457.

[RKCJ96] Ratha, N. K., Karu, K., Chen, S., and Jain, A. K. A real-time matching system for large fingerprint databases. *IEEE Trans. on Pattern Analysis and Machine Intelligence 18*, 8 (1996), pp. 799–813.

[RLKT10] Russell, C., Ladicky, L., Kohli, P., and Torr, P. H. S. Exact and approximate inference in associative hierarchical random fields using graph-cuts. In *Proc. Conf. on Uncertainty in Artificial Intelligence* (2010).

[RM89] Reiter, R., and Mackworth, A. K. A logical framework for depiction and image interpretation. *Artificial Intelligence 41*, 2 (1989), pp. 125–155.

[RM91] Rom, H., and Medioni, G. *Hierarchical decomposition and axial representation of shape*. Geometric Methods in Computer Vision, 1991.

[RMC97] Roy, S., Meunier, J., and Cox, I. J. Cylindrical rectification to minimize epipolar distortion. In *Proc. IEEE Computer Society Conference on Computer Vision and Pattern Recognition* (1997), pp. 393–399.

[Rob01] Roberts, A. Curvature attributes and their application to 3D interpreted horizons. *First Break 19*, 2 (2001), pp. 85-100.

[Ros09] Rosen, J. *Encyclopedia of Physics*. Infobase Publishing, 2009.

[RP98] O'Ruanaidh, J. J. K., and Pun, T. Rotation, scale and translation invariant spread spectrum digital image watermarking. *Signal processing 66*, 3 (1998), pp. 303-317.

[RPLK08] Roy, P. P., Pal, U., Llados, J., and Kimura, F. Convex hull based approach for multi-oriented character recognition from graphical documents. In *19th Int. Conf. on Pattern Recognition* (2008), pp. 1-4.

[RPMA01] Roche, A., Pennec, X., Malandain, G., and Ayache, N. Rigid registration of 3-D ultrasound with MR images: a new approach combining intensity and gradient information. *IEEE Trans. on Medical Imaging 20*, 10 (2001), pp. 1038-1049.

[RRRS08] Rhemann, C., Rother, C., Rav-Acha, A., and Sharp, T. High resolution matting via interactive trimap segmentation. In *Proc. IEEE Conf. Computer Vision and Pattern Recognition* (2008), pp. 1-8.

[RS91] Rao, A. R., and Schunck, B. G. Computing oriented texture fields. *CVGIP: Graphical Models and Image Processing 53*, 2 (1991), pp. 157-185.

[RSB04] Roy, D., Sumantra, S. C., and Banerjee, S. Active recognition through next view planning: a survey. *Pattern Recognition 37*, 3 (2004), pp. 429-446.

[RSM01] Ruiz-Correa, S., Shapiro, L. G., and Melia, M. A new signature-based method for efficient 3-D object recognition. In *Proc. IEEE Conf. on Computer Vision and Pattern Recognition* (2001), pp. I-pp. 769-I-776.

[RT71] Rosenfeld, A., and Thurston, M. Edge and curve detection for visual scene analysis. *IEEE Trans. on Computers 20*, 5 (1971), pp. 562-569.

[RT99] Ruzon, M. A., and Tomasi, C. Color edge detection with the compass operator. In *IEEE Computer Society Conference on Computer Vision and Pattern Recognition* (1999), vol. 2.

[RW05] Rockafellar, R. T., and Wets, R. J. B. *Variational Analysis*. Springer-Verlag, 2005.

[RW06] Rasmussen, C. E., and Williams, C. K. I. *Gaussian Processes for Machine Learning*. MIT Press, Cambridge, Massachusetts, 2006.

[RWG+09] Richardson, J., Walker, R., Grant, L., Stoppa, D., Borghetti, F., Charbon, E., Gersbach, M., and Henderson, R. K. A 32x32 50ps resolution 10 bit time to digital converter array in 130nm CMOS for time correlated imaging. In *Proc. Custom Integrated Circuits Conference CICC'09* (2009), pp. 77-80.

[RWPD05] Reinhard, E., Ward, G., Pattanaik, S., and Debevec, P. *High Dynamic Range Imaging: Acquisition, Display, and Image-Based Lighting*. Morgan Kaufmann, 2005.

[RYS95] Ramesh, N., Yoo, J. H., and Sethi, I. K. Thresholding based on histogram approximation. *IEEE Proc. on Vision, Image and Signal Processing 142*, 5 (1995), pp. 271-279.

[SAG95] Sawhney, H. S., Ayer, S., and Gorkani, M. Model-based 2D and 3D dominant motion estimation for mosaicing and video representation. In *Proc. Int. Conf. Computer Vision* (1995), pp. 583-590.

[San88] Sanger, T. D. Stereo disparity computation using Gabor filters. *Biological Cybernetics 59*, 6 (1988), pp. 405-418.

[Sap06] Sapiro, G. *Geometric Partial Differential Equations and Image Analysis*. Cambridge University Press, 2006.

[Saw94a] Sawhney, H. S. 3D geometry from planar parallax. In *Proc. IEEE Computer Society Conference on Computer Vision and Pattern Recognition (CVPR'94)* (1994), pp. 929-934.

[SAW94b] Schilit, B. N., Adams, N., and Want, R. Context-aware computing applications. In *Proc. Workshop on Mobile Computing Systems and Applications* (1994), pp. 85-90.

[SB11] Solomon, C., and Breckon, T. *Fundamentals of Digital Image Processing*. Wiley-Blackwell, 2011.

[SB91] Sullivan, G. J., and Baker, R. L. Motion compensation for video compression using control grid interpolation. In *Int. Conf. on Acoustics Speech, and Signal Processing* (1991), pp. 2713-2716.

[SB94] Stark, L., and Bowyer, K. Function-based generic recognition for multiple object categories. *CVGIP: Image Understanding 59*, 1 (1994), pp. 1-21.

[SB98] Sutton, R. S., and Barto, A. G. *Reinforcement Learning.* MIT Press, Cambridge, Massachusetts, 1998.

[SBH09] Suman, S., Bennamoun, M., and Huynh, D. Context-based appearance descriptor for 3D human pose estimation from monocular images. *Digital Image Computing: Techniques and Applications* (2009), pp. 484-491.

[SBK05] Selesnick, I. W., Baraniuk, R. G., and Kingsbury, N. G. The dual-tree complex wavelet transform. *IEEE Signal Processing Magazine 22*, 6 (2005), pp. 123-151.

[SBM06] Sun, Z., Bebis, G., and Miller, R. On-road vehicle detection: A review. *IEEE Trans. on Pattern Analysis and Machine Intelligence 28*, 5 (2006), pp. 694-711.

[SBS02] Sidenbladh, H., Black, M. J., and Sigal, L. Implicit probabilistic models of human motion for synthesis and tracking. In *European Conf. on Computer Vision, Springer-Verlag LNCS 2353* (2002), vol. I, pp. 784-800.

[SC04] Shawe-Taylor, J., and Cristianini, N. *Kernel Methods for Pattern Analysis.* Cambridge University Press, Cambridge, 2004.

[SC08] Sundaresan, A., and Chellappa, R. Model-driven segmentation of articulating humans in Laplacian eigenspace. *IEEE Trans. on Pattern Analysis and Machine Intelligence 30*, 10 (2008), pp. 1771-1785.

[SCD02] Starck, J., Candes, E. J., and Donoho, D. L. The curvelet transform for image denoising. *IEEE Trans. on Image Processing 11*, 6 (2002), pp. 670-684.

[SCH08] Sridhar, M., Cohn, A. G., and Hogg, D. C. Learning functional object-categories from a relational spatio-temporal representation. In *Proceeding of the 2008 Conference on ECAI* (2008), pp. 606-610.

[Sch89] Schalkoff, R. J. *Digital Image Processing and Computer Vision.* John Wiley & Sons, 1989.

[Sch99] Schmid, C. A structured probabilistic model for recognition. *IEEE Computer Society Conference on Computer Vision and Pattern Recognition 2* (1999).

[SCK+11] Song, B., Chong, D., Kamal, A. T., *et al.* Distributed camera networks. *IEEE Signal Processing Magazine 28*, 3 (2011), pp. 20-31.

[SCW95] Soh, J., Chun, B. T., and Wang, M. Analysis of road image sequences for vehicle counting. In *Proc. IEEE Int. Conf. on Systems, Man and Cybernetics, 1995. Intelligent Systems for the 21st Century* (1995), vol. 1, pp. 679-683.

[SCZ11] Shabani, A.-H., Clausi, D., and Zelek, J. S. Improved spatio-temporal salient feature detection for action recognition. In *Proc. BMVC* (2011), pp. 100.pp. 1-100.12.

[SD02] Shen, D., and Davatzikos, C. HAMMER: Hierarchical attribute matching mechanism for elastic registration. *Med. Imaging 21* (2002), pp. 1421-1439.

[SD03] Schoepflin, T. N., and Dailey, D. J. Dynamic camera calibration of roadside traffic management cameras for vehicle speed estimation. *IEEE Trans. on Intelligent Transportation Systems 4*, 2 (2003), pp. 90-98.

[SD92] Sand, F., and Dougherty, E. R. Asymptotic normality of the morphological pattern-spectrum moments and orthogonal granulometric generators. *Journal of Visual Communication and Image Representation 3*, 2 (1992), pp. 203-214.

[SD97] Seitz, S. M., and Dyer, C. R. Photorealistic scene reconstruction by voxel coloring. *Int. J. of Computer Vision 35*, 2 (1997), pp. 151-173.

[SdB03] Svensson, S., and di Baja, G. S. Simplifying curve skeletons in volume images. *Computer Vision and Image Understanding 90*, 3 (2003), pp. 242-257.

[Sel07] Selbrede, M. G. US patent # 7,218,437, 2007.

[SF96] Simoncelli, E. P., and Farid, H. Steerable wedge filters for local orientation analysis. *IEEE Trans. on Image Processing 5*, 9 (1996), pp. 1377-1382.

[SFWK02] Shi, M., Fujisawa, Y., Wakabayashi, T., and Kimura, F. Handwritten numeral recognition using gradient and curvature of gray scale image. *Pattern Recognition 35*, 10 (2002), pp. 2051-2059.

[SGB+00] Schweikard, A., Glosser, G., Bodduluri, M., *et al.* Robotic motion compensation for respiratory movement during radiosurgery. *Computer Aided Surgery 5*, 4 (2000), pp. 263-277.

[SGL92] Sridharan, S., Ginige, A., and Lowe, D. Progressive image transmission. *Int. Conf. on Image Processing and its Applications* (1992), pp. 115-118.

[SH95] Slater, D., and Healey, G. Combining color and geometric information for the illumination invariant recognition of 3-D objects. In *Proc. Int. Conf. Computer Vision* (1995), pp. 563-568.

[Sha06] Sharma, K. K. *Optics: Principles and Applications*. Academic Press, 2006.

[Sha80] Shapiro, L. G. A structural model of shape. *IEEE Trans. on Pattern Analysis and Machine Intelligence 2* (1980), pp. 111-126.

[Sha92] Shapiro, J. M. An embedded wavelet hierarchical image coder. In *Proc. IEEE Int. Conf. on Acoustics, Speech, and Signal Processing (ICASSP-92)* (1992), vol. 4, pp. 657-660.

[SHB08] Sonka, M., Hlavac, V., and Boyle, R. *Image Processing, Analysis, and Machine Vision*. Thompson, 2008.

[SHK03] Sun, S., Haynor, D. R., and Kim, Y. Semiautomatic video object segmentation using Vsnakes. *IEEE Trans. on Circuits and Systems for Video Technology 13*, 1 (2003), pp. 75-82.

[SHK98] Sawhney, H. S., Hsu, S., and Kumar, R. Robust video mosaicing through topology inference and local to global alignment. In *Proc. European Conf. on Computer Vision* (1998), pp. 103-119.

[SHKM92] Sammut, C., Hurst, S., Kedzier, D., and Michie, D. Learning to fly. In *Proc. Int. Conf. on Machine Learning* (1992), pp. 385-393.

[SHLW89] Sinclair, B., Hannam, A. G., Lowe, A. A., and Wood, W. W. Complex contour organization for surface reconstruction. *Computers & Graphics 13*, 3 (1989), pp. 311-319.

[Sho07] Shores, T. S. *Applied Linear Algebra and Matrix Analysis*. Springer, 2007.

[SHW93] Snyder, D. L., Hammoud, A. M., and White, R. L. Image recovery from data acquired with a charge-coupled-device camera. *J. Opt. Soc. Amer. A 10*, 5 (1993), pp. 1014-1023.

[SI05] Shechtman, E., and Irani, M. Space-time behavior based correlation. *Proc. Computer Vision and Pattern Recognition* (2005), pp. 405-412.

[SI98] Scarloff, S., and Isidoro, J. Active blobs. In *Proc. Int. Conf. Computer Vision* (1998), pp. 1146-1153.

[SJA08] Shan, Q., Jia, J., and Agarwala, A. High-quality motion deblurring from a single image. *ACM Trans. Graphics (SIGGRAPH) 27*, 3 (2008).

[SJC08] Shotton, J., Johnson, M., and Cipolla, R. Semantic texton forests for image categorization and segmentation. In *Proc. Computer Vision and Pattern Recognition* (2008), pp. 1-8.

[SK05] Sbalzarini, I. F., and Koumoutsakos, P. Feature point tracking and trajectory analysis for video imaging in cell biology. *Journal of Structural Biology 151*, 2 (2005), pp. 182-195.

[SK99] Sawhney, H. S., and Kumar, R. True multi-image alignment and its application to mosaicing and lens distortion correction. *IEEE Trans. on Pattern Analysis and Machine Intelligence 21*, 3 (1999), pp. 235-243.

[SKB+01] Sauer, F., Khamene, A., Bascle, B., et al. Augmented reality visualization of ultrasound images: System description, calibration, and features. In *Proc. IEEE and ACM International Symposium on Augmented Reality* (2001), pp. 30-39.

[SKG+98] Sawhney, H. S., Kumar, R., Gendel, G., Bergen, J., Dixon, D., and Paragano, V. VideoBrush: Experiences with consumer video mosaicing. In *Fourth IEEE Workshop on Applications of Computer Vision* (1998), pp. 56-62.

[SKI+00] Sivak Jr, M., Kobayashi, K., Izatt, J., Rollins, A., Ung-runyawee, R., Chak, A., Wong, R., Isenberg, G., and Willis, J. High-resolution endoscopic imaging of the GI tract using optical coherence tomography. *Gastrointestinal Endoscopy 51*, 4 (2000), pp. 474-479.

[SKM98] Sochen, N., Kimmel, R., and Malladi, R. A general framework for low level vision. *IEEE Trans. on Image Processing 7*, 3 (1998), pp. 310-318.

[SKP96] Song, K. Y., Kittler, J., and Petrou, M. Defect detection in random colour textures. *Image and Vision Computing 14*, 9 (1996), pp. 667-683.

[SL03] Sebe, N., and Lew, M. Comparing salient point detectors. *Pattern Recognition Letters 24*, 1-3 (2003), pp. 89-96.

[SL05] Shakiban, C., and Lloyd, R. Classification of signature curves using latent semantic analysis. *Computer Algebra and Geometric Algebra with Applications, Springer LNCS 3519* (2005), pp. 135-152.

[SL90] Scott, G. L., and Longuet-Higgins, H. C. Feature grouping by relocalisation of eigenvectors of the proximity matrix. In *Proc. British Machine Vision Conference* (1990), pp. 103-108.

[SL91] Safavian, S. R., and Landgrebe, D. A survey of decision tree classifier methodology. *IEEE Trans. on Systems, Man and Cybernetics 21*, 3 (1991), pp. 660-674.

[SM00] Shi, J., and Malik, J. Normalized cuts and image segmentation. *IEEE Trans. on Pattern Analysis and Machine Intelligence 22*, 8 (2000), pp. 888-905.

[SM12] Sencar, H. T., and Memon, N., Eds. *Digital Image Forensics.* Springer, 2012.

[SM92] Stein, F., and Medioni, G. Structural indexing: Efficient 3-D object recognition. *IEEE Trans. Pattern Anal. Machine Intell 14*, 2 (1992), pp. 125-145.

[SM97] Silva, C. T., and Mitchell, J. S. B. The lazy sweep ray casting algorithm for rendering irregular grids. *IEEE Trans. on Visualization and Computer Graphics 3*, 2 (1997), pp. 142-157.

[SMC05] Schilders, W. H. A., ter Maten, E. J. W., and Ciarlet, P. G. *Numerical Methods in Electromagnetics: Special Volume.* Elsevier, 2005.

[SMK04] Seitz, S. M., Matsushita, Y., and Kutulakos, K. N. A theory of inverse light transport. In *Proc. Int. Conf. Computer Vision* (2004), pp. 1440-1447.

[SMM04] Stefano, L. D., Marchionni, M., and Mattoccia, S. A fast area-based stereo matching algorithm. *Image and Vision Computing 22*, 12 (2004), pp. 983-1005.

[SN01a] Schechner, Y. Y., and Nayar, S. K. Generalized mosaicing. In *Proc. Int. Conf. Computer Vision* (2001), pp. 17-24.

[SN01b] Shutler, J. D., and Nixon, M. S. Zernike velocity moments for description and recognition of moving shapes. In *Proc. British Machine Vision Conference.* 2001, p. 11.

[SNS+98] Sato, Y., Nakajima, S., Shiraga, N., Atsumi, H., Yoshida, S., Koller, T., Gerig, G., and Kikinis, R. Three-dimensional multi-scale line filter for segmentation and visualization of curvilinear structures in medical images. *Medical Image Analysis 2*, 2 (1998), pp. 143-168.

[Sny89] Snyder, M. A. On the mathematical foundations of smoothness constraints for the determination of optical flow and for surface reconstruction. In *Proc. Workshop on Visual Motion* (1989), pp. 107-115.

[SO01] Simoncelli, E. P., and Olshausen, B. A. Natural image statistics and neural representation. *Annual Review of Neuroscience 24* (2001), pp. 1193-1216.

[SOS00] Seul, M., O'Gorman, L., and Sammon, M. J. *Practical Algorithms for Image Analysis.* Cambridge University Press, Cambridge, 2000.

[SP02] Sung, W. B., and Pachowicz, P. W. Online model modification for adaptive texture recognition in image sequences. *IEEE Trans. on Systems, Man and Cybernetics, Part A: Systems and Humans 32*, 6 (2002), pp. 625-639.

[SP89] Sillion, F., and Puech, C. A general two-pass method integrating specular and diffuse reflection. *ACM SIGGRAPH Computer Graphics 23*, 3 (1989), pp. 335-344.

[SPHK08] Soutschek, S., Penne, J., Hornegger, J., and Kornhuber, J. 3D gesture-based scene navigation in medical imaging applications using time-of-flight cameras. In *Proc. Computer Vision and Pattern Recognition Workshops* (2008), pp. 1-6.

[SQ04] Snyder, W. E., and Qi, H. *Machine Vision.* Cambridge, 2004.

[SRM93] Saint-Marc, P., Rom, H., and Medioni, G. B-spline contour representation and symmetry detection. *IEEE Trans. on Pattern Analysis and Machine Intelligence 15*, 11 (1993), pp. 1191-1197.

[SRT11] Sturm, P., Ramalingam, S., and Tardif, J. P. *Camera Models and Fundamental Concepts used in Geometric Computer Vision.* Now, 2011.

[SS02] Schölkopf, B., and Smola, A. *Learning with Kernels*. MIT Press, Cambridge, Massachusetts, 2002.

[SS77] Sripad, A., and Snyder, D. A necessary and sufficient condition for quantization errors to be uniform and white. *IEEE Trans. on Acoustics, Speech and Signal Processing 25*, 5 (1977), pp. 442–448.

[SS92] Sinha, S. S., and Schunck, B. G. A two-stage algorithm for discontinuity-preserving surface reconstruction. *IEEE Trans. on Pattern Analysis and Machine Intelligence 14*, 1 (1992), pp. 36–55.

[SS94] Subbarao, M., and Surya, G. Depth from defocus: a spatial domain approach. *Int. J. Computer Vision 13*, 3 (1994), pp. 271–294.

[SS97a] Sun, C., and Sherrah, J. 3D symmetry detection using the extended Gaussian image. *IEEE Trans. on Pattern Analysis and Machine Intelligence 19*, 2 (1997), pp. 164–168.

[SS97b] Szeliski, R., and Shum, H.-Y. Creating full view panoramic image mosaics and environment maps. In *Proc. Annual Conference on Computer Graphics and Interactive Techniques* (1997), ACM Press/Addison-Wesley.

[SSB06] Sheikh, H. R., Sabir, M. F., and Bovik, A. C. A statistical evaluation of recent full reference image quality assessment algorithms. *IEEE Trans. on Image Processing 15*, 11 (2006), pp. 3440–3451.

[SSC08] Stankovic, V., Stankovic, L., and Cheng, S. Compressive video sampling. In *Proc. Euro. Signal Processing Conf* (2008), pp. 2–6.

[SSCW98] Smith, P., Sinclair, D., Cipolla, R., and Wood, K. Effective corner matching. In *Proc. British Machine Vision Conference* (1998), pp. 545–556.

[SSD94] Stevenson, R. L., Schmitz, B. E., and Delp, E. J. Discontinuity preserving regularization of inverse visual problems. *IEEE Trans. on Systems, Man and Cybernetics 24*, 3 (1994), pp. 455–469.

[SSDZ99] Siddiqi, K., Shokoufandeh, A., Dickinson, S. J., and Zucker, S. W. Shock graphs and shape matching. *Int. J. Computer Vision 35*, 1 (1999), pp. 13–32.

[SSM06] Sidhu, R., Sanders, D. S., and McAlindon, M. E. Gastrointestinal capsule endoscopy: from tertiary centers to primary care. *British Medical Journal 332*, 7540 (2006), pp. 528–531.

[SSMK06] Shan, Y., Sawhney, H. S., Matei, B., and Kumar, R. Shapeme histogram projection and matching for partial object recognition. *IEEE Trans. on Pattern Analysis and Machine Intelligence 28*, 4 (2006), pp. 568–577.

[SSPP07] Solimene, R., Soldovieri, F., Prisco, G., and Pierri, R. Three-dimensional microwave tomography by a 2-D slice-based reconstruction algorithm. *Geoscience and Remote Sensing Letters 4*, 4 (2007), pp. 556–560.

[SSSE00] Schoedl, A., Szeliski, R., Salesin, D. H., and Essa, I. Video textures. In *Proc. ACM SIGGRAPH Conf* (2000), pp. 489–498.

[SSTG03] Shao, H., Svoboda, T., Tuytelaars, T., and Gool, L. V. HPAT indexing for fast object/scene recognition based on local appearance. In *Proceedings of the 2nd International Conference on Image and video retrieval* (Berlin, Heidelberg, 2003), Springer-Verlag, pp. 71–80.

[ST99] Sun, M., and Takayama, K. Conservative smoothing on an adaptive quadrilateral grid. *Journal of Computational Physics 150*, 1 (1999), pp. 143–180.

[Stu97] Sturm, P. Critical motion sequences for monocular self-calibration and uncalibrated Euclidean reconstruction. *Computer Society Conference on Computer Vision and Pattern Recognition* (1997), pp. 1100–1105.

[Stu99] Sturm, P. Critical motion sequences for the self-calibration of cameras and stereo systems with variable focal length. In *Proc. British Machine Vision Conference (BMVC'99)* (1999), pp. 63–72.

[Sub88] Subbarao, M. Parallel depth recovery by changing camera parameters. In *2nd Int. Conf. Computer Vision* (1988), pp. 149–155.

[SVR08] Schilders, W. H. A., van der Vorst, H. A., and Rommes, J. *Model Order Reduction: Theory Research Aspects and Applications*. Springer, 2008.

[SW87] Swendsen, R. H., and Wang, J. Nonuniversal critical dynamics in Monte Carlo simulations. *Phys Rev. Lett 58*, 2 (1987), pp. 86–88.

[SWP+83] Sutton, M. A., Wolters, W. J., Peters, W. H., Ranson, W. F., and McNeill, S. R. Determination of displacements using an improved digital correlation method. *Image and Vision Computing 1*, 3 (1983), pp. 133-139.

[SWRC06] Shotton, J., Winn, J., Rother, C., and Criminisi, A. TextonBoost: Joint appearance shape and context modeling for multi-class object recognition and segmentation. In *Proc. European Conf. on Computer Vision* (2006), pp. 1-15.

[SWRC09] Shotton, J., Winn, J., Rother, C., and Criminisi, A. TextonBoost for image understanding: Multi-class object recognition and segmentation by jointly modeling texture, layout, and context. *Int. J. of Computer Vision 81*, 1 (2009), pp. 2-23.

[SWS+00] Smeulders, A. W. M., Worring, M., Santini, S., Gupta, A., and Jain, R. Content-based image retrieval at the end of the early years. *IEEE Trans. on Pattern Analysis and Machine Intelligence 22* (2000), pp. 1349-1380.

[SYAK99] Sawhney, H. S., Yanlin, G., Asmuth, J., and Kumar, R. Independent motion detection in 3D scenes. In *Proc. Int. Conf. Computer Vision* (1999), pp. 612-619.

[SZ01] Schaffalitzky, F., and Zisserman, A. Viewpoint invariant texture matching and wide baseline stereo. In *Proc. IEEE Int. Conf. Computer Vision* (2001), vol. 2, pp. 636-643.

[SZ94] Smoliar, S. W., and Zhang, H. Content based video indexing and retrieval. *Multimedia 1*, 2 (1994), pp. 62-72.

[SZ97] Schmid, C., and Zisserman, A. Automatic line matching across views. In *Proc. IEEE Computer Society Conference on Computer Vision and Pattern Recognition* (1997), pp. 666-671.

[Sze10] Szeliski, R. *Computer Vision: Algorithms and applications*. Springer-Verlag, 2010.

[SZH+07] Shen, H. T., Zhou, X., Huang, Z., Shao, J., and Zhao, X. UQLIPS: A real-time near-duplicate video clip detection system. In *Proc. VLDB* (2007), pp. 1374-1377.

[SZH+10] Shen, T., Zhang, S., Huang, J., Huang, X., and Metaxas, D. Integrating Shape and Texture in 3D Deformable Models: From Metamorphs to Active Volume Models, in Multi Modality State-of-the-Art Medical Image Segmentation and Registration Methodologies, Springer, 2010.

[SZL+05] Sun, Q. S., Zheng, S. G., Liu, Y., Heng, P. A., and Xia, D. S. A new method of feature fusion and its application in image recognition. *Pattern Recognition 38*, 12 (2005), pp. 2437-2448.

[TA02] Tsaig, Y., and Averbuch, A. Automatic segmentation of moving objects in video sequences: a region labeling approach. *IEEE Trans. on Circuits and Systems for Video Technology 12*, 7 (2002), pp. 597-612.

[TA08] Todorovic, S., and Ahuja, N. Learning subcategory relevances for category recognition. In *Proc. Int. Conf. on Computer Vision and Pattern Recognition* (2008).

[TAT95] Tarabanis, K. A., Allen, P. K., and Tsai, R. Y. A survey of sensor planning in computer vision. *IEEE Trans. on Robotics and Automation 11*, 1 (1995), pp. 86-104.

[TB04] Tsoi, Y.-C., and Brown, M. S. Geometric and shading correction for images of printed materials: a unified approach using boundary. In *Proc. IEEE Computer Society Conference on Computer Vision and Pattern Recognition* (2004), vol. 1, pp. I-240.

[TB77] Tenenbaum, J. M., and Barrow, H. G. Experiments in interpretation-guided segmentation. *Artificial Intelligence 8*, 3 (1977), pp. 241-274.

[TBAB98] Teboul, S., Blanc-Feraud, L., Aubert, G., and Barlaud, M. Variational approach for edge-preserving regularization using coupled PDEs. *IEEE Trans. on Image Processing 7*, 3 (1998), pp. 387-397.

[TBF05] Thrun, S., Burgard, W., and Fox, D. *Probabilistic Robotics*. MIT Press, Cambridge, Massachusetts, 2005.

[TC88] Teh, C.-H., and Chin, R. T. On image analysis by the methods of moments. *IEEE Trans. on Pattern Analysis and Machine Intelligence 10*, 4 (1988), pp. 496-513.

[TC94] Tsai, D.-M., and Chen, M.-F. Curve fitting approach for tangent angle and curvature measurements. *Pattern Recognition 27*, 5 (1994), pp. 699-711.

[TCYZ05] Tu, Z., Chen, X., Yuille, A. L., and Zhu, S.-C. Image parsing: Unifying segmentation, detection, and recognition. *Int. J. of Computer Vision 63*, 2 (2005), pp. 113–140.

[TFCS11] Thompson, W. B., Fleming, R. W., Creem-Regehr, S. H., and Stefanucci, J. K. *Visual Perception for Computer Graphics.* CRC Press, 2011.

[TG00] Tuytelaars, T., and Gool, L. V. Wide baseline stereo matching based on local, affinely invariant regions. In *Proc. the British Machine Vision Conference* (2000), pp. 42–56.

[TG04] Tuytelaars, T., and Gool, L. V. Synchronizing video sequences. In *Proc. Computer Vision and Pattern Recognition (CVPR)* (2004), pp. I–pp. 768–I–762.

[TGPM98] Tuytelaars, T., Gool, L. V., Proesmans, M., and Moons, T. The cascaded Hough transform as an aid in aerial image interpretation. In *Proc. Int. Conf. Computer Vision* (1998), pp. 67–72.

[TH81] Tsai, R., and Huang, T. Estimating three-dimensional motion parameters of a rigid planar patch. *IEEE Trans on Acoustics, Speech and Signal Processing 29*, 6 (1981), pp. 1147–1152.

[TH94] Teo, P. C., and Heeger, D. J. Perceptual image distortion. In *Proc. IEEE Int. Conf. on Image Processing* (1994), vol. 2, pp. 982–986.

[TH99] Tsai, D.-M., and Hsieh, C.-Y. Automated surface inspection for directional textures. *Image and Vision Computing 18*, 1 (1999), pp. 49–62.

[THB08] Torresani, L., Hertzmann, A., and Bregler, C. Non-rigid structure-from-motion: Estimating shape and motion with hierarchical priors. *IEEE Trans. on Pattern Analysis and Machine Intelligence 30*, 5 (2008), pp. 878–892.

[TK92] Tomasi, C., and Kanade, T. Shape and motion from image streams under orthography: a factorization method. *Int. J. Computer Vision 9*, 2 (1992), pp. 137–154.

[TKC05] Tian, Y.-L., Kanade, T., and Cohn, J. F. *Facial Expression Analysis.* 2005, pp. 247–275.

[TM08] Tuytelaars, T., and Mikolajczyk, K. Local invariant feature detectors: a survey. *Foundations and Trends in Computer Graphics and Vision 3*, 3 (2008), pp. 177–280.

[TM87] Thompson, D., and Mundy, J. Three-dimensional model matching from an unconstrained viewpoint. In *Proc. Robotics and Automation* (1987), pp. 208–220.

[TM90] Terzopoulos, D., and Metaxas, D. Dynamic 3D models with local and global deformations: Deformable superquadrics. *Third Int. Conf. Computer Vision* (1990), pp. 606–615.

[TM99a] Tang, C.-K., and Medioni, G. Robust estimation of curvature information from noisy 3D data for shape description. In *Proc. IEEE Int. Conf. on Computer Vision* (1999), vol. 1, IEEE, pp. 426–433.

[TM99b] Thorballsson, T., and Murray, D. The tensors of three affine views. In *Proc. Computer Vision and Pattern Recognition* (1999), vol. 1, pp. 450–456.

[TMB85] Thompson, W. B., Mutch, K. M., and Berzins, V. A. Dynamic occlusion analysis in optical flow fields. *IEEE Trans. on Pattern Analysis and Machine Intelligence 4* (1985), pp. 374–383.

[TNM09] Tung, T., Nobuhara, S., and Matsuyama, T. Complete multi-view reconstruction of dynamic scenes from probabilistic fusion of narrow and wide baseline stereo. In *Proc. IEEE Int. Conf. Computer Vision* (2009), pp. 1709–1716.

[TO02] Torralba, A., and Oliva, A. Depth estimation from image structure. *IEEE Trans. on Pattern Analysis and Machine Intelligence 24*, 9 (2002), pp. 1226–1238.

[TOS+03] Tsumura, N., Ojima, N., Sato, K., Shiraishi, M., Shimizu, H., Nabeshima, H., Akazaki, S., Hori, K., and Miyake, Y. Image-based skin color and texture analysis/synthesis by extracting hemoglobin and melanin information in the skin. *ACM Trans. Graphics (TOG) 22*, 3 (2003), pp. 770–779.

[Tos11] Toselli, A. H. *Multimodal Interactive Pattern Recognition and Applications.* Springer, 2011.

[TR98] Taubin, G., and Rossignac, J. Geometric compression through topological surgery. *ACM Trans. Graphics (TOG) 17*, 2 (1998), pp. 84-115.

[TS93] Tistarelli, M., and Sandini, G. On the advantages of polar and log-polar mapping for direct estimation of time-to-impact from optical flow. *IEEE Trans. on Pattern Analysis and Machine Intelligence 15*, 4 (1993), pp. 401-410.

[TSF95] Thedens, D. R., Skorton, D. J., and Fleagle, S. R. Methods of graph searching for border detection in image sequences with applications to cardiac magnetic resonance imaging. *IEEE Trans. on Medical Imaging 14*, 1 (1995), pp. 42-55.

[TSK01] Tao, H., Sawhney, H. S., and Kumar, R. A global matching framework for stereo computation. In *Proc. IEEE Int. Conf. on Computer Vision* (2001), vol. 1, pp. 532-539.

[Tso11] Tsotsos, J. K. Motion understanding: Task-directed attention and representations that link perception with action. *Int. J. of Computer Vision 45*, 3 (2011), pp. 265-280.

[TT07] Tan, X., and Triggs, B. Enhanced local texture feature sets for face recognition under difficult lighting conditions. *Analysis and Modelling of Faces and Gestures, LNCS 4778* (2007), pp. 168-182.

[TV07] Tron, R., and Vidal, R. A benchmark for the comparison of 3D motion segmentation algorithms. In *Proc. Computer Vision and Pattern Recognition* (2007), pp. 1-8.

[TV98] Trucco, E., and Verri, A. *Introductory Techniques for 3-D Computer Vision.* Prentice Hall, 1998.

[TVH05] Tanase, M., Veltkamp, R., and Haverkort, H. Multiple polyline to polygon matching. *Algorithms and Computation* (2005), pp. 60-70.

[TY89] Tsumiyama, K. S. Y., and Yamamoto, K. Active net: active net model for region extraction. *IPSJ SIG notes 89*, 96 (1989), pp. 1-8.

[Tyl96] Tyler, C. W. *Human Symmetry Perception.* Psychology Press, 1996.

[TYO00] Tamaki, T., Yamamura, T., and Ohnishi, N. Extraction of human limb regions and parameter estimation based on curl of optical flow. In *Proc. Asian Conference on Computer Vision (ACCV2000)* (2000), pp. 1008-1013.

[TYW01] Tsai, A., Yezzi Jr, A., and Willsky, A. S. Curve evolution implementation of the Mumford–Shah functional for image segmentation, denoising, interpolation, and magnification. *IEEE Trans. on Image Processing 10*, 8 (2001), pp. 1169-1186.

[Ull98] Ullman, S. Three-dimensional object recognition based on the combination of views. *Cognition 67*, 1 (1998), pp. 21-44.

[Umb98] Umbaugh, S. E. *Computer Vision and Image Processing.* Prentice Hall, 1998.

[UN00] Ulrich, I., and Nourbakhsh, I. Appearance-based place recognition for topological localization. In *Proc. Robotics and Automation* (2000), vol. 2, pp. 1023-1029.

[vdHDT+07] van de Hengel, A., Dick, A., Thormählen, T., Ward, B, and Torr, P. H. S. VideoTrace: Rapid interactive scene modelling from video. *ACM Trans. Graphics 26*, 3 (2007), pp. 86.1-86.5.

[VFC05] Vogiatzis, G., Favaro, P., and Cipolla, R. Using frontier points to recover shape, reflectance and illumination. In *Proc. Int. Conf. on Computer Vision* (2005), pp. 228-235.

[VFJZ01] Vailaya, A., Figueiredo, M. A. T., Jain, A. K., and Zhang, H. Image classification for content-based indexing. *IEEE Trans. on Image Processing 10*, 1 (2001).

[VFSH01] Vazquez, P.-P., Feixas, M., Sbert, M., and Heidrich, W. Viewpoint selection using viewpoint entropy. In *Proc. Conf. on Vision Modeling and Visualization* (2001), pp. 273-280.

[VG08] Valenti, R., and Gevers, T. Accurate eye center location and tracking using isophote curvature. *Proc. IEEE Conference on Computer Vision and Pattern Recognition* (2008), pp. 1-8.

[VG96] Vizcaya, P. R., and Gerhardt, L. A. A nonlinear orientation model for global description of fingerprints. *Pattern Recognition 29*, 7 (1996), pp. 1221-1231.

[VH00] Veit, K., and Häusler, G. Metrical calibration of a phase measuring triangulation sensor. *Vision, Modeling, and Visualization* (2000), pp. 33-38.

[Vic92] Vickers, J. N. Gaze control in putting. *Perception 21*, 1 (1992), pp. 117-132.

[Vin96] Vining, D. J. Virtual endoscopy: is it reality? *Radiology 200*, 1 (1996), pp. 30–31.

[VJ98] Veldhuizen, T. L., and Jernigan, M. E. Grid filters for local nonlinear image restoration. In *Proc. IEEE International Conference on Acoustics, Speech and Signal Processing* (1998), vol. 5, pp. 2885–2888.

[VMZ08] Ferrari, V., Marin-Jimenez, M., and Zisserman, A. Progressive search space reduction for human pose estimation. In *Proc. Computer Vision and Pattern Recognition* (2008), pp. 1–8.

[VSK05] Vedula, S., Sundar, S. B., and Kanade, T. Image-based spatio-temporal modeling and view interpolation of dynamic events. *ACM Trans. Graphics (TOG) 24*, 2 (2005), pp. 240–261.

[VSKB10] Vishwanathan, S. V. N., Schraudolph, N. N., Kondor, R., and Borgwardt, K. M. Graph kernels. *Journal of Machine Learning Research 11* (2010), pp. 1201–1242.

[VSRC09] Veeraraghavan, A., Srivastava, A., Roy-Chowdhury, A. K., and Chellappa, R. Rate-invariant recognition of humans and their activities. *IEEE Trans. Image Processing 18*, 6 (2009), pp. 1326–1339.

[VT02] Vasilescu, M. A. O., and Terzopoulos, D. Multilinear analysis of image ensembles: TensorFaces. In *Proc. European Conf. Computer Vision* (2002), pp. 447–460.

[VV90] Verbeek, P. W., and Verwer, B. J. H. Shading from shape, the eikonal equation solved by grey-weighted distance transform. *Pattern Recognition Letters 11*, 10 (1990), pp. 681–690.

[VW97] Viola, P., and Wells III, W. M. Alignment by maximization of mutual information. *Int. J. of Computer Vision 24*, 2 (1997), pp. 137–154.

[VWJL04] Vaish, V., Wilburn, B., Joshi, N., and Levoy, M. Using plane + parallax for calibrating dense camera arrays. In *Proc. Computer Vision and Pattern Recognition* (2004), vol. 1, pp. 2–9.

[VYCL03] Vemuri, B. C., Ye, J., Chen, Y., and Leonard, C. M. Image registration via level-set motion: applications to atlas-based segmentation. *Medical Image Analysis 7*, 1 (2003), pp. 1–20.

[WA89] Watson, A. B., and Ahumada Jr, A. J. A hexagonal orthogonal-oriented pyramid as a model of image representation in visual cortex. *IEEE Trans. on Biomedical Engineering 36*, 1 (1989), pp. 97–106.

[WA94] Wang, J. Y. A., and Adelson, E. H. Spatio-temporal segmentation of video data. In *Proc. SPIE* (1994), vol. 2182, pp. 120–131.

[WAA+00] Wood, D., Azuma, D., Aldinger, W., Curless, B., Duchamp, T., Salesin, D., and Stuetzle, W. Surface light fields for 3D photography. In *Proc. SIGGRAPH* (2000).

[Wac75] Wachspress, E. *A Rational Finite Element Basis*. Academic Press, 1975.

[WAF+98] Waxman, A. M., Aguilar, M., Fay, D. A., *et al.* Solid-state color night vision: fusion of low-light visible and thermal infrared imagery. *Lincoln Laboratory Journal 11*, 1 (1998), pp. 41–60.

[Wak82] Wakayama, T. A core-line tracing algorithm based on maximal square moving. *IEEE Trans. on Pattern Analysis and Machine Intelligence 1* (1982), pp. 68–74.

[Was04] Wasserman, L. A. *All of Statistics*. Springer-Verlag, 2004.

[WB02a] Wang, Z., and Bovik, A. C. A universal image quality index. *IEEE Signal Processing Letters 9*, 3 (2002), pp. 81–84.

[WB02b] Wang, Y., and Yuan, B. Fast method for face location and tracking by distributed behaviour-based agents. In *Proc. IEEE Vision, Image and Signal Processing* (2002), vol. 149, pp. 173–178.

[WB94] Wani, M. A., and Batchelor, B. G. Edge-region-based segmentation of range images. *IEEE Trans. on Pattern Analysis and Machine Intelligence 16*, 3 (1994), pp. 314–319.

[WCL+08] Wu, C., Clipp, B., Li, X., Frahm, J. F., and Pollefeys, M. 3D model matching with viewpoint invariant patches (VIPs). In *Proc. Int. Conf. Computer Vision and Pattern Recognition* (2008), pp. 1–8.

[Wec06] Wechsler, H. *Reliable Face Recognition Methods: System Design, Implementation and Evaluation*. Springer, 2006.

[Wei03] Wei, L. Y. Texture synthesis from multiple sources. In *Proc. SIGGRAPH Applications and Sketches* (2003), pp. 1632-1642.

[Wei12] Weisstein, E. W. MathWorld - a Wolfram web resource, March 2012.

[Wei88] Weiss, I. Projective invariants of shapes. In *Computer Society Conference on Computer Vision and Pattern Recognition* (1988), pp. 291-297.

[Wei95] Weickert, J. Multiscale texture enhancement. *Computer Analysis of Images and Patterns* (1995), pp. 230-237.

[Wey52] Weyl, H. *Symmetry*. Princeton University Press, 1952.

[WF90] Wang, R., and Freeman, H. Object recognition based on characteristic view classes. In *Proc. Int. Conf. on Pattern Recognition* (1990), vol. 1, pp. 8-12.

[WFKM97] Wiskott, L., Fellous, J.-M., Kuiger, N., and von der Malsburg, C. Face recognition by elastic bunch graph matching. *IEEE Trans. on Pattern Analysis and Machine Intelligence 19*, 7 (1997), pp. 775-779.

[WG00] Wilson, J. P., and Gallant, J. C., Eds. *Terrain Analysis: Principles and Applications*. John Wiley & Sons, 2000.

[WG08] Wang, X., Ma, K. T., Ng, G. W., and Grimson, E. Trajectory analysis and semantic region modeling using a nonparametric Bayesian model. In *Proc. IEEE Conf. on Computer Vision and Pattern Recognition* (2008).

[WGG99] Wyvill, B., Guy, A., and Galin, E. Extending the CSG tree: Warping, blending and Boolean operations in an implicit surface modeling system. *Computer Graphics Forum 18*, 2 (1999), pp. 149-158.

[WGLS00] Winters, N., Gaspar, J., Lacey, G., and Santos-Victor, J. Omni-directional vision for robot navigation. In *Proc. IEEE Workshop on Omnidirectional Vision* (2000), pp. 21-28.

[WGT+05] Wenger, A., Gardner, A., Tchou, C., *et al.* Performance relighting and reflectance transformation with time-multiplexed illumination. *ACM Trans. Graphics (TOG) 24*, 3 (2005), pp. 756-764.

[WH97] Wilson, R. C., and Hancock, E. R. Structural matching by discrete relaxation. *IEEE Trans. on Pattern Analysis and Machine Intelligence 19*, 6 (1997), pp. 634-648.

[Whe73] Wheeler, M. F. A priori L_2 error estimates for galerkin approximations to parabolic partial differential equations. *SIAM Journal on Numerical Analysis 10*, 4 (1973), pp. 723-759.

[WHH03] Wahl, E., Hillenbrand, U., and Hirzinger, G. Surflet-pair-relation histograms: a statistical 3D-shape representation for rapid classification. In *Proc. Int. Conf. on 3-D Digital Imaging and Modeling* (2003), pp. 474-481.

[WHR99] Wartell, Z., Hodges, L. F., and Ribarsky, W. Balancing fusion, image depth and distortion in stereoscopic head-tracked displays. In *Proc. Conf. Computer Graphics and Interactive Techniques (SIGGRAPH)* (1999), pp. 351-358.

[Win05] Winkler, S. *Digital Video Quality*. John Wiley & Sons, 2005.

[Wit81] Witkin, A. P. Recovering surface shape and orientation from texture. *Artificial Intelligence 17*, 1 (1981), pp. 17-45.

[Wit84] Witkin, A. Scale-space filtering: A new approach to multi-scale description. In *IEEE International Conference ICASSP'84 on Acoustics, Speech, and Signal Processing* (1984), vol. 9, pp. 150-153.

[WJ95] Williams, L. R., and Jacobs, D. W. Stochastic completion fields: a neural model of illusory contour shape and salience. In *Proc. Int. Conf. Computer Vision* (1995), pp. 408-415.

[WKT01] Wakahara, T., Kimura, Y., and Tomono, A. Affine-invariant recognition of gray-scale characters using global affine transformation correlation. *IEEE Trans. on Pattern Analysis and Machine Intelligence 23*, 4 (2001), pp. 384-395.

[WL93] Wen, W., and Lozzi, A. Recognition and inspection of manufactured parts using line moments of their boundaries. *Pattern recognition 26*, 10 (1993), pp. 1461-1471.

[WLCC08] Wu, S. H., Lin, K. P., Chen, C. M., and Chen, M. S. Asymmetric support vector machines: low false-positive learning under the user tolerance. In *Proc. Int. Conf. on Knowledge Discovery and Data Mining* (2008), pp. 749-757.

[WM00] Wada, T., and Matsuyama, T. Multiobject behavior recognition by event driven selective attention method. *IEEE Trans. on Pattern Analysis and Machine Intelligence 22*, 8 (2000), pp. 873–887.

[WM96] Wada, T., and Matsuyama, T. Appearance sphere: Background model for pan-tilt-zoom camera. *Proc. on Pattern Recognition 1* (1996), pp. 718–722.

[WM97] Weber, J., and Malik, J. Rigid body segmentation and shape description from dense optical flow under weak perspective. *IEEE Trans. on Pattern Analysis and Machine Intelligence 19*, 2 (1997), pp. 139–143.

[WOFH93] Waite, M., Orr, M., Fisher, R., and Hallam, J. Statistical partial constraints for 3D model matching and pose estimation problems. In *Proc. BMVC93 British Machine Vision Association Conference* (1993), Surrey, pp. 105–114.

[Wol90] Wolfson, H. J. On curve matching. *IEEE Trans. on Pattern Analysis and Machine Intelligence 12*, 5 (1990), pp. 483–489.

[Wol92] Wolff, L. B. *Shape from Polarization Images*. Jones and Bartlett Publishers, Inc, 1992, pp. 193–199.

[WR11] Wu, J., and Rehg, J. M. CENTRIST: A visual descriptor for scene categorization. *IEEE Trans. on Pattern Analysis and Machine Intelligence 33*, 8 (2011), pp. 1489–1501.

[WRB06] Weinland, D., Ronfard, R., and Boyer, E. Free viewpoint action recognition using motion history volumes. *Computer Vision and Image Understanding 104*, 2-3 (2006), pp. 249–257.

[WS00] Wexler, Y., and Shashua, A. On the synthesis of dynamic scenes from reference views. In *Proc. IEEE Conference on Computer Vision and Pattern Recognition* (2000), vol. 1, pp. 576–581.

[WSG10] Wei, Z., Samaras, D., and Gu, D. Ricci flow for 3D shape analysis. *IEEE Trans. Pattern Analysis and Machine Intelligence 32*, 4 (2010), pp. 662–677.

[WSK84] Wax, M., Shan, T.-J., and Kailath, T. Spatio-temporal spectral analysis by eigenstructure methods. *EEE Trans. Acoustics, Speech and Signal Processing 32*, 4 (1984), pp. 817–827.

[WVVG01] Van De Weijer, J., Vliet, L. J. V., Verbeek, P. W., and van Ginkel, R. Curvature estimation in oriented patterns using curvilinear models applied to gradient vector fields. *IEEE Trans. on Pattern Analysis and Machine Intelligence 23*, 9 (2001), pp. 1035–1042.

[WY08] Wang, J., and Yagi, Y. Integrating color and shape-texture features for adaptive real-time object tracking. *IEEE Trans. on Image Processing 17*, 2 (2008), pp. 235–240.

[WZ00] Wolberg, G., and Zokai, S. Robust image registration using log-polar transform. In *Proc. Int. Conf. on Image Processing* (2000), vol. 1, pp. 493–496.

[WZ02] Werner, T., and Zisserman, A. New techiques for automated architectural reconstruction from photographs. In *European Conference on Computer Vision II* (2002), pp. 541–555.

[WZC05] Wang, J., Zha, H., and Cipolla, R. Combining interest points and edges for content-based image retrieval. In *Proc. Int. Conf. Image Processing* (2005), pp. III–1256.

[XG00] Xie, P., and Guan, S.-U. A golden-template self-generating method for patterned wafer inspection. *Machine Vision and Applications 12*, 3 (2000), pp. 149–156.

[XG06] Xiang, T., and Gong, S. Beyond tracking: Modelling activity and understanding behaviour. *Int. J. of Computer Vision 67*, 1 (2006), pp. 21–51.

[XG08] Xiang, T., and Gong, S. Video behaviour profiling for anomaly detection. *IEEE Trans. Pattern Analysis and Machine Intelligence 30*, 5 (2008), pp. 893–908.

[XGP02] Xiang, T., Gong, S., and Parkinson, D. Autonomous visual events detection and classification without explicit object centred segmentation and tracking. In *Proc. British Machine Vision Conference* (2002), pp. 233–242.

[XJM94] Xu, P., Jayaram, G., and Marks, L. D. Cross-correlation method for intensity measurement of transmission electron diffraction patterns. *Ultramicroscopy 53*, 1 (1994), pp. 15–18.

[XL07] Xiao, Y., and Lim, K. B. A prism-based single-lens stereovision system: From trinocular to multi-ocular. *Image and Vision Computing 25*, 11 (2007), pp. 1725–1736.

[XNJR03] Xing, E., Ng, A., Jordan, M., and Russell, S. Distance metric learning with application to clustering with side-information. *Advances in Neural Information Processing Systems 15* (2003), pp. 521–528.

[XOK90] Xu, L., Oja, E., and Kultanen, P. A new curve detection method: Randomized Hough transform (RHT). *Pattern Recognition Letters 11*, 5 (1990), pp. 331–338.

[XP98] Xu, C., and Prince, J. L. Snakes, shapes, and gradient vector flow. *IEEE Trans. on Image Processing 7*, 3 (1998), pp. 359–369.

[Xu93] Xu, L. Least mean square error reconstruction principle for self-organizing neural-nets. *Neural Networks 6*, 5 (1993), pp. 627–648.

[Yak76] Yakimovsky, Y. Boundary and object detection in real world images. *Journal of the ACM (JACM) 23*, 4 (1976), pp. 599–618.

[YBBR93] Yamamoto, M., Boulanger, P., Beraldin, J.-A., and Rioux, M. Direct estimation of range flow on deformable shape from a video rate range camera. *IEEE Trans. on Pattern Analysis and Machine Intelligence 15*, 1 (1993), pp. 82–89.

[YGK95] Yang, Y., Galatsanos, N. P., and Katsaggelos, A. K. Projection-based spatially adaptive reconstruction of block-transform compressed images. *IEEE Trans. on Image Processing 4*, 7 (1995), pp. 896–908.

[YJ84] You, Z., and Jain, A. K. Performance evaluation of shape matching via chord length distribution. *Computer Vision, Graphics, and Image Processing 28*, 2 (1984), pp. 185–198.

[YK06] Yoon, K. J., and Kweon, I. Adaptive support-weight approach for correspondence search. *IEEE Trans. on Pattern Analysis and Machine Intelligence 28*, 4 (2006), pp. 650–656.

[YMH09] Yang, M., Ming, Y. W., and Hua, G. Context-aware visual tracking. *IEEE Trans. on Pattern Analysis and Machine Intelligence 31*, 7 (2009), pp. 1195–1209.

[YP06] Yan, J., and Pollefeys, M. A general framework for motion segmentation: independent, articulated, rigid, non-rigid, degenerate and non-degenerate. In *European Conference on Computer Vision IV* (2006), pp. 94–106.

[YP11] Yang, J., and Peng, G. Subpixel edge location based on Gaussian–Hermite moments. *Journal of Information CRGHM Computational Science 8*, 14 (2011), pp. 3131–3140.

[YP84] Yuille, A. L., and Poggio, T. *A Generalized Ordering Constraint for Stereo Correspondence*. 1984, MIT AI Lab memo 777.

[YPO03] Yap, P.-T., Paramesran, R., and Ong, S.-H. Image analysis by Krawtchouk moments. *IEEE Trans. on Image Processing 12*, 11 (2003), pp. 1367–1377.

[YSJ04] Yeom, S., Stern, A., and Javidi, B. Compression of 3D color integral images. *Optics Express 12*, 8 (2004), pp. 1632–1642.

[ZA08] Zhang, B., and Allebach, J. P. Adaptive bilateral filter for sharpness enhancement and noise removal. *IEEE Trans. on Image Processing 17*, 5 (2008), pp. 664–678.

[Zar71] Zariski, O. *Algebraic Surfaces*. Springer-Verlag, 1971.

[ZBK02] Zickler, T. E., Belhumeur, P. N., and Kriegman, D. J. Helmholtz stereopsis: Exploiting reciprocity for surface reconstruction. *Int. J. Computer Vision 49*, 2 (2002), pp. 215–227.

[ZBR+01] Zweig, G., Bilmes, J., Richardson, T., *et al.* Structurally discriminative graphical models for automatic speech recognition: Results from the 2001 Johns Hopkins summer workshop. In *Proc. the Int. Conf. on Acoustics, Speech, and Signal Processing* (2001), pp. I-93.

[ZDDD07] Zhe, L., Davis, L. S., Doermann, D., and DeMenthon, D. Hierarchical part-template matching for human detection and segmentation. In *Proc. Int. Conf. on Computer Vision IEEE* (2007).

[ZDFL95] Zhang, Z., Deriche, R., Faugeras, O., and Luong, Q.-T. A robust technique for matching two uncalibrated images through the recovery of the unknown epipolar geometry. *Artificial Intelligence 78*, 1 (1995), pp. 87–119.

[ZGT99] Zappalá, A., Gee, A., and Taylor, M. Document mosaicing. *Image and Vision Computing 17*, 8 (1999), pp. 589–595.

[ZH02] Zeng, P., and Hirata, T. On-loom fabric inspection using multi-scale differentiation filtering. In *Proc. Industry Applications Conference, 37th IAS Annual Meeting* (2002), vol. 1, pp. 320–326.

[ZH83] Zuniga, O. A., and Haralick, R. M. Corner detection using the facet model. In *Proc. the IEEE Conference on Computer Vision and Pattern Recognition* (1983), pp. 30–37.

[ZH99] Zhang, D., and Hebert, M. Harmonic maps and their applications in surface matching. *IEEE Computer Society Conference on Computer Vision and Pattern Recognition II* (1999), p. 524.

[Zha94] Zhang, Z. Iterative point matching for registration of free-form curves and surfaces. *Int. J. Computer Vision 13*, 2 (1994), pp. 119–152.

[ZI01] Zelnik-Manor, L., and Irani, M. Event-based analysis of video. In *Proc. IEEE Int. Conf. on Computer Vision and Pattern Recognition* (2001), pp. 123–130.

[ZJ05] Zhang, Y., and Ji, Q. Active and dynamic information fusion for facial expression understanding from image sequences. *IEEE Trans. on Pattern Analysis and Machine Intelligence 27*, 5 (2005), pp. 699–714.

[ZJD00] Zhong, Y., Jain, A. K., and Dubuisson-Jolly, M.-P. Object tracking using deformable templates. *IEEE Trans. on Pattern Analysis and Machine Intelligence 22*, 5 (2000), pp. 544–549.

[ZK00] Zitnick, C. L., and Kanade, T. A cooperative algorithm for stereo matching and occlusion detection. *IEEE Trans. on Pattern Analysis and Machine Intelligence 22*, 7 (2000), pp. 675–684.

[ZK02] Zhou, W., and Kambhamettu, C. Estimation of illuminant direction and intensity of multiple light sources. In *Proc. Euro. Conf. Computer Vision* (2002), pp. 206–220.

[ZKC03] Zhou, S., Krueger, V., and Chellappa, R. Probabilistic recognition of human faces from video. *Computer Vision and Image Understanding 91*, 1-2 (2003), pp. 214–245.

[ZLP06] Zeng, M., Li, J., and Peng, Z. The design of top-hat morphological filter and application to infrared target detection. *Infrared Physics & Technology 48*, 1 (2006), pp. 67–76.

[ZLYS07] Zhang, D., Liu, Z., Yan, J.-Q., and Shi, P.-F. Tongue-print: A novel biometrics pattern. *Advances in Biometrics, Springer LNCS 4642* (2007), pp. 1174–1183.

[ZRH03] Zhou, X. S., Rui, Y., and Huang, T. S. *Exploration of Visual Data.* Kluwer Academic, 2003.

[ZS93] Ziv, Z., and Springer, E. More applications of coaxial illumination in fingerprint detecting and photography. *Journal of Forensic Identification 43*, 4 (1993), pp. 362–367.

[ZSH+10a] Zhang, H., Shu, H. Z., Haigron, P., Li, B. S., and Luo, L. Construction of a complete set of orthogonal Fourier–Mellin moment invariants for pattern recognition applications. *Image and Vision Computing 28*, 1 (2010), pp. 38–44.

[ZSH+10b] Zhang, H., Shu, H., Han, G. N., Coatrieux, G., Luo, L. M., and Coatrieux, J. L. Blurred image recognition by Legendre moment invariants. *IEEE Trans. on Image Processing 19*, 3 (2010), pp. 596–611.

[ZSZ+05] Zhou, J., Shu, H., Zhu, H., Toumoulin, C., and Luo, L. Image analysis by discrete orthogonal Hahn moments. In *Proc. Image Analysis and Recognition* (2005), pp. 524–531.

[ZYZH10] Zhang, H., Yang, J., Zhang, Y., and Huang, T. Non-local kernel regression for image and video restoration. In *Proc. ECCV* (2010), pp. 566–579.

[ZZX04] Zhang, C., Zhao, B., and Xiangli, B. Wide-field-of-view polarization interference imaging spectrometer. *Applied Optics 43*, 33 (2004), pp. 6090–6094.